The Secret Team

The Secret Team

THE CIA AND ITS ALLIES IN CONTROL OF THE UNITED STATES AND THE WORLD

L. Fletcher Prouty

Skyhorse Publishing

Skyhorse Publishing books may be purchased in bulk at special discounts for sales promotion, corporate gifts, fund raising, or educational purposes. Special editions can also be created to specifications. For details, contact Special Sales Department, Skyhorse Publishing, 555 Eighth Avenue, Suite 903, New York, NY 10018 or info@skyhorsepublishing.com.

www.skyhorsepublishing.com

Library of Congress Cataloging-in-Publication Data

Prouty, L. Fletcher (Leroy Fletcher), 1917–
    The secret team : the CIA and its allies in control of the United States and the world / L. Fletcher Prouty.
       p. cm.
    Includes bibliographical references and index.
    ISBN 978-1-60239-229-8 (alk. paper)
    1. United States. Central Intelligence Agency.
    2. Intelligence service—United States. 3. Espionage, American. I. Title.

JK468.I6P76 2008
327.1273—dc22
                                    2007046044

10 9 8 7 6 5 4

Printed in Canada

CONTENTS

ACKNOWLEDGMENTS ix

Author's Note xi

Preface 1972 xvii

Preface to the Second Edition xxix

Preface: "THE SECRET TEAM II" 1997 xxxiii

PART I THE SECRET TEAM

Chapter 1 The "Secret Team"—the Real Power Structure 1

Chapter 2 The Nature of Secret Team Activity:
A Cuban Case Study 27

PART II THE CIA: HOW IT RUNS

Chapter 3 An Overview of the CIA 65

Section I. Intelligence versus Secret Operations 65

Section II. Origins of the Agency and the Seeds
of Secret Operations 77

Section III. A Simple Coup d'État to a Global Mechanism 90

Chapter 4 From the Word of the Law to the Interpretation:
President Kennedy Attempts to Put the CIA
Under Control 111

Chapter 5 "Defense" as a National Military Philosophy,
the Natural Prey of the Intelligence Community 143

Chapter 6 "It Shall Be the Duty of the Agency: to Advise,
to Coordinate, to Correlate and Evaluate
and Disseminate and to Perform Services
of Common Concern . . ." 165

Chapter 7   From the Pines of Maine to the Birches
               of Russia: The Nature of Clandestine
               Operations   187

Chapter 8   CIA: "The Cover Story" Intelligence Agency
               and the Real-Life Clandestine Operator   211

Chapter 9   The Coincidence of Crises   237

Chapter 10   The Dulles-Jackson-Correa Report in Action   263

       PART III THE CIA: HOW IT IS ORGANIZED

Chapter 11   The Dulles Era Begins   287

Chapter 12   Personnel: The Chameleon Game   313

Chapter 13   Communications: The Web of the World   331

Chapter 14   Transportation: Anywhere in the World—Now   347

Chapter 15   Logistics by Miracle   359

        PART IV THE CIA: SOME EXAMPLES
              THROUGHOUT THE WORLD

Chapter 16   Cold War: The Pyrrhic Gambit   373

Chapter 17   Mission Astray, Soviet Gamesmanship   391

Chapter 18   Defense, Containment, and Anti-Communism   403

Chapter 19   The New Doctrine: Special Forces and the
               Penetration of the Mutual Security Program   425

Chapter 20   Khrushchev's Challenge: The U-2 Dilemma   445

Chapter 21   Time of Covert Action: U-2 to
               Kennedy Inaugural   457

Chapter 22   Camelot: From the Bay of Pigs to Dallas,
             Texas   469

Chapter 23   Five Presidents: "Nightmares We Inherited"   499

APPENDICES

I. Definition of Special Operations   511

II. Powers and Duties of the CIA   513

III. Training Under the Mutual Security Program   531

ACKNOWLEDGMENTS

... to Len Osanic and all at Bandit Productions for bringing all my work back to life.

... to Patrick Fourmy, Dave Ratcliffe and Tom Davis, old friends who have insisted I revise and re-write this old "classic."

... to Bill Mullan, Charlie Czapar, Bill Peters, and Dave Fleming, who worked with me in the Pentagon during the fifties, for those fascinating years with "Team B" in Headquarters, U.S. Air Force.

... to Charles Peters of *The Washington Monthly* for publishing the first "Secret Team" article, and Derek Shearer for breathing the whole concept into life.

... to General Graves B. (the big "E") Erskine and General Victor H. ("Brute") Krulak, both of the U.S. Marine Corps, my immediate "bosses" and good friends, in the Office of the Secretary of Defense and in the Office of the Joint Chiefs of Staff, for close personal relationships that shaped the course of these events.

... and to the hundreds of men with whom I shared these experiences and who must remain nameless and silent because that is the "code" of their chosen profession.

AUTHOR'S NOTE: 1997

After I had given the manuscript of the original draft of this book to my editor at Prentice-Hall, in 1972, and had received the galley proof of the first edition back from him, he called me to suggest that I keep it in a safe place at all times. He told me that his home had been broken into the night before, and he suspected it was an attempt to steal his copy of that galley proof. He said, "They didn't get it. It was under the seat of the Volkswagen."

A few days later a nationwide release by the well-known Washington columnist, Jack Anderson, appeared across the country, "Book Bares CIA's Dirty Tricks." In that column, Anderson reported that the CIA had contacted a well-known bookstore in Washington and asked one of the employees to see if he could get a copy of the galley from me, and agreed to pay him $500, if he did. I agreed to meet him at my home that evening.

I suspected his call, but invited him anyway. In the meantime I set up a tape recorder in the umbrella stand near my front door and arranged for it to turn on when I switched on the overhead light on the front porch. With that arrangement, I recorded the whole visit including his final burst, "They promised me $500.00, if I got that galley proof." I took that tape to Anderson, and it was the basis of his March 6, 1973 column. The underground attack didn't quit there.

After excellent early sales of *The Secret Team* during which Prentice-Hall printed three editions of the book, and it had received more than 100 favorable reviews, I was invited to meet Ian Ballantine, the founder of Ballantine Books. He told me that he liked the book and would publish 100,000 copies in paperback as soon as he could complete the deal with Prentice-Hall. Soon there were 100,000 paperbacks in bookstores all around the country.

Then one day a business associate in Seattle called to tell me that the bookstore next to his office building had had a window full of books the day before, and none the day of his call. They claimed they had never had the book. I called other associates around the country. I got the same story from all over the country. The paperback had vanished. At the same time I learned that Mr. Ballantine had sold his company. I traveled to New York to visit the new "Ballantine Books" president. He professed to know nothing about me, and my book. That was the end of that surge of publication. For some unknown reason Prentice-Hall was out of my book also. It became an extinct species.

Coincidental to that, I received a letter from a Member of Parliament in Canberra, Australia, who wrote that he had been in England recently visiting in the home of a friend who was a Member of the British Parliament. While there, he discovered *The Secret Team* on a coffee table and during odd hours had begun to read it.

Upon return to Canberra he sent his clerk to get him a copy of the book. Not finding it in the stores, the clerk had gone to the Customs Office where he learned that 3,500 copies of *The Secret Team* had arrived, and on that same date had been purchased by a Colonel from the Royal Australian Army. The book was dead everywhere.

The campaign to kill the book was nationwide and world-wide. It was removed from the Library of Congress and from College libraries as letters I received attested all too frequently.

That was twenty years ago. Today I have been asked to rewrite the book and bring it up to date. Those who have the book speak highly of it, and those who do not have it have been asking for it. With that incentive, I have begun from page one to bring it up to date and to provide information that I have learned since my first manuscript.

In the beginning, this book was based upon my unusual experience in the Pentagon during 1955–1964 and the concept of the book itself was the outgrowth of a series of luncheon conversations, 1969–1970, with my friends Bob Myers, Publisher of the *New*

Republic, Charlie Peters, founder of *The Washington Monthly*, and Ben Schemmer, editor and publisher of the *Armed Forces Journal*, and Derek Shearer. They were all experienced in the ways and games played in Washington, and they tagged my stories those of a "Secret Team." This idea grew and was polished during many subsequent luncheons.

After my retirement from the Air Force in 1964, I moved from an office in the Joint Chiefs of Staff area of the Pentagon to become Manager of the Branch Bank on the Concourse of that great building. This was an interesting move for many reasons, not the least of which was that it kept me in business and social contact with many of the men I had met and worked with during my nine years of Air Force duties in that building. It kept me up-to-date with the old "fun-and-games" gang.

After graduating from the Graduate School of Banking, University of Wisconsin, I transferred to a bank in Washington where in the course of business I met Ben Schemmer. He needed a loan that would enable him to acquire the old *Armed Forces Journal*. During that business process I met two of Ben's friends, Bob Myers and Charlie Peters. We spent many most enjoyable business luncheons together. This is where "The Secret Team" emerged from a pattern of ideas to a manuscript.

As they heard my stories about my work with the CIA, and especially about the role of the military in support of the world-wide, clandestine operations of the CIA, they urged me to write about those fascinating nine years of a 23-year military career. During the Spring of 1970 I put an article together that we agreed to call "The Secret Team," and Charlie Peters published it in the May 1970 issue of *The Washington Monthly*.

Before I had seen the published article myself, two editors of major publishers in New York called me and asked for appointments. I met with both, and agreed to accept the offer to write a book of the same name, and same concept of *The Secret Team* from Bram Cavin, Senior Editor with Prentice-Hall.

After all but finishing the manuscript, with my inexperienced typing of some 440 pages, I sat down to a Sunday breakfast on

June 13, 1971 and saw the headlines of the *New York Times* with its publication of the "purloined" *Pentagon Papers*.[1] One of the first excerpts from those papers was a TOP SECRET document that I had worked on in late 1963. Then I found more of the same. With that, I knew that I could vastly improve what I had been writing by making use of that hoard of classified material that "Daniel Ellsberg had left on the doorstep of the *Times*," and other papers. Up until that time I had deliberately avoided the use of some of my old records and copies of highly classified documents. The publication of the *Pentagon Papers* changed all that. They were now in the public domain. I decided to call my editor and tell him what we had with the "Pentagon Papers" and to ask for more time to re-write my manuscript. He agreed without hesitation. From that time on I began my "Doctorate" course in, a) book publishing and, b) book annihilation.

As we see, by some time in 1975 *The Secret Team* was extinct; but unlike the dinosaur and others, it did not even leave its footprints in the sands of time. There may be some forty to fifty thousand copies on private book shelves. A letter from a professor informed me that his department had ordered more than forty of the books to be kept on the shelves of his university library for assignment purposes. At the start of the new school year his students reported that the books were not on the shelves and the registry cards were not in the master file. The librarians informed them that the book did not exist.

With that letter in mind, I dropped into the Library of Congress to see if *The Secret Team* was on the shelves where I had seen it earlier. It was not, and it was not even in that library's master file. It is now an official non-book.

---

1. Any reader of the "Pentagon Papers" should be warned that although they were commissioned on June 17, 1967, by the Secretary of Defense as "the history of United States involvement in Vietnam from World War II [Sept 2, 1945] to the present" [1968], they are unreliable, inaccurate and marred by serious omissions. They are a contrived history, at best, even though they were written by a selected Task Force under Pentagon leadership.

I was a writer whose book had been cancelled by a major publisher and a major paperback publisher under the persuasive hand of the CIA. Now, after more than twenty years the flames of censorship still sweep across the land. Despite that, here we go again with a new revised edition of *The Secret Team*.

PREFACE 1972

From President to Ambassador, Cabinet Officer to Commanding General, and from Senator to executive assistant—all these men have their sources of information and guidance. Most of this information and guidance is the result of carefully laid schemes and ploys of pressure groups. In this influential coterie one of the most interesting and effective roles is that played by the behind the scenes, faceless, nameless, ubiquitous briefing officer.

He is the man who sees the President, the Secretary, the Chairman of the Joint Chiefs of Staff almost daily, and who carries with him the most skillfully detailed information. He is trained by years of experience in the precise way to present that information to assure its effectiveness. He comes away day after day knowing more and more about the man he has been briefing and about what it is that the truly influential pressure groups at the center of power and authority are really trying to tell these key decision makers. In Washington, where such decisions shape and shake the world, the role of the regular briefing officer is critical.

Leaders of government and of the great power centers regularly leak information of all kinds to columnists, television and radio commentators, and to other media masters with the hope that the material will surface and thus influence the President, the Secretary, the Congress, and the public. Those other inside pressure groups with their own briefing officers have direct access to the top men; they do not have to rely upon the media, although they make great use of it. They are safe and assured in the knowledge that they can get to the decision maker directly. They need no middleman other than the briefing officer. Such departments as Defense, State, and the CIA use this technique most effectively.

For nine consecutive, long years during those crucial days from 1955 through January 1, 1964, I was one of those briefing officers. I had the unique assignment of being the "Focal Point" officer for contacts between the CIA and the Department of Defense on matters pertaining to the military support of the Special Operations[2] of that Agency. In that capacity I worked with Allen Dulles and John Foster Dulles, several Secretaries of Defense, and Chairmen of the Joint Chiefs of Staff, as well as many others in key governmental places. My work took me to more than sixty countries and to CIA offices and covert activities all over the world—from such hot spots as Saigon and to such remote places as the South Pole. Yes, there have been secret operations in Antarctica.

It was my job not only to brief these men, but to brief them from the point of view of the CIA so that I might win approval of the projects presented and of the accompanying requests for support from the military in terms of money, manpower, facilities, and materials. I was, during this time, perhaps the best informed "Focal Point" officer among the few who operated in this very special area. The role of the briefing officer is quiet, effective, and most influential; and, in the CIA, specialized in the high art of top level indoctrination.

It cannot be expected that a John Kennedy, Lyndon Johnson, a Richard Nixon, or a following President will have experienced and learned all the things that may arise to confront him during his busy official life in the White House. It cannot be expected that a Robert McNamara or a Melvin Laird, a Dean Rusk or a William Rogers, etc. comes fully equipped to high office, aware of all matters pertaining to what they will encounter in their relationship with the Congo or Cuba, Vietnam or Pakistan, and China or Russia and the emerging new nations. These men learn about these places and the many things

---

2. Special Operations is a name given in most cases, but not always, to any clandestine, covert, undercover, or secret operations by the government or by someone, U.S. citizen or a foreign national ... even in special cases a stateless professional, or U.S. or foreign activity or organization. It is usually secret and highly classified. It is to be differentiated from Secret intelligence and in a very parochial sense from Secret or Special Intelligence Operations.

that face them from day to day from an endless and unceasing procession of briefing officers.

Henry Kissinger was a briefing officer. General John Vogt was one of the best. Desmond Fitzgerald, Tracy Barnes, Ed Lansdale, and "Brute" Krulak, in their own specialties, were top-flight briefing officers on subjects that until the publication of the "Pentagon Papers," few people had ever seen in print or had ever even contemplated.

(You can imagine my surprise when I read the June 13, 1971, issue of the Sunday *New York Times* and saw there among the "Pentagon Papers" a number of basic information papers that had been in my own files in the Joint Chiefs of Staff area of the Pentagon. Most of the papers of that period had been source documents from which I had prepared dozens—even hundreds—of briefings, for all kinds of projects, to be given to top Pentagon officers. Not only had many of those papers been in my files, but I had either written many of them myself or had written certain of the source documents used by the men who did.)

The briefing officer, with the staff officer, writes the basic papers. He researches the papers. He has been selected because he has the required knowledge and experience. He has been to the countries and to the places involved. He may know the principals in the case well. He is supposed to be the best man available for that special job. In my own case, I had been on many special assignments dating back to the Cairo and Tehran conferences of late 1943 that first brought together the "Big Four" of the Allied nations of WW II: Franklin D. Roosevelt, Winston Churchill, Chiang Kai-shek and Joseph Stalin.

The briefing officer reads all of the messages, regardless of classification. He talks to a number of other highly qualified men. He may even have staff specialists spread out all over the world upon whom he may call at any time for information. Working in support of the "Focal Point" office, which I headed, there were hundreds of experts and agents concealed in military commands throughout the world who were part of a network I had been directed to establish in 1955–1956 as a stipulation of National Security Council directive 5412, March 1954.

In government official writing, the man who really writes the paper—or more properly, the men whose original work and words are put together to become the final paper—are rarely, if ever, the men whose names appear on that paper. A paper attributed to Maxwell Taylor, Robert McNamara or Dean Rusk, of the Kennedy era, would not, in almost all instances, have been written by them; but more than likely would have been assembled from information gathered from the Departments of Defense and State and from CIA sources and put into final language by such a man as General Victor H. Krulak, who was among the best of that breed of official writers.

From 1955 through 1963, if some official wanted a briefing on a highly classified subject involving the CIA, I would be one of those called upon to prepare the material and to make the briefing. At the same time, if the CIA wanted support from the Air Force for some covert operation, I was the officer who had been officially designated to provide this special operational support to the CIA.

If I was contacted by the CIA to provide support for an operation which I believed the Secretary of Defense had not been previously informed of, I would see to it that he got the necessary briefing from the CIA or from my office and that any other Chief of Staff who might be involved would get a similar briefing. In this unusual business I found rather frequently that the CIA would be well on its way into some operation that would later require military support before the Secretary and the Chiefs had been informed.

During preparations for one of the most important of these operations, covered in some detail in this book, I recall briefing the chairman of the Joint Chiefs of Staff, General Lyman L. Lemnitzer, on the subject of the largest clandestine special operation that the CIA had ever mounted up to that time: and then hearing him say to the other Chiefs, "I just can't believe it. I never knew that."

Here was the nation's highest ranking military officer, the man who would be held responsible for the operation should it fail or become compromised, and he had not been told enough about it to know just how it was being handled. Such is the nature of the game as played by the "Secret Team."

I have written for several magazines on this subject, among them the *Armed Forces Journal*, *The New Republic*, the *Empire Magazine* of the Denver Sunday *Post*, and *The Washington Monthly*. It was for this latter publication that I wrote "The Secret Team," an article that appeared in the May 1970 issue and that led to the development of this book.

With the publication of the "Pentagon Papers" on June 13, 1971, interest in this subject area was heightened and served to underscore my conviction that the scope of that article must be broadened into a book.

Within days of *The New York Times* publication of those "Pentagon Papers," certain editorial personnel with the BBC-TV program, "Twenty-Four Hours," recalling my "Secret Team" article, invited me to appear on a series on TV with, among others, Daniel Ellsberg. They felt that my experience with the Secret Team would provide material for an excellent companion piece to the newly released "Pentagon Papers," which were to be the primary topic of the discussions. I flew to London and made a number of programs for BBC-TV and Radio. Legal problems and the possible consequences of his departure from the country at that time precluded the simultaneous appearance of Daniel Ellsberg. The programs got wide reception and served to underscore how important the subject of the "Pentagon Papers" is throughout the world.

I have not chosen to reveal and to expose "unreleased" classified documents; but I do believe that those that have been revealed, both in the "Pentagon Papers" and elsewhere, need to be interpreted and fully explained. I am interested in setting forth and explaining what "secrecy" and the "cult of containment" really mean and what they have done to our way of life and to our country. Furthermore, I want to correct any disinformation that may have been given by those who have tried to write on these subjects in other related histories.

I have lived this type of work; I know what happened and how it happened. I have known countless men who participated in one way or another in these unusual events of Twentieth Century history. Many of these men have been and still are members of the Secret Team. It also explains why much of it has been pure propaganda and close to nationwide "brainwashing" of the American public. I intend to interpret and clarify these events by analyzing information already in the public domain. There is plenty.

Few concepts during this half century have been as important, as controversial, as misunderstood, and as misinterpreted as secrecy in Government. No idea during this period has had a greater impact upon Americans and upon the American way of life than that of the containment of Communism. Both are inseparably intertwined and have nurtured each other in a blind Pavlovian way. Understanding their relationship is a matter of fundamental importance.

Much has been written on these subjects and on their vast supporting infrastructure, generally known as the "intelligence community." Some of this historical writing has suffered from a serious lack of inside knowledge and experience. Most of this writing has been done by men who know something about the subject, by men who have researched and learned something about the subject, and in a few cases by men who had some experience with the subject. Rarely is there enough factual experience on the part of the writer. On the other hand, the Government and other special interests have paid writers huge amounts to write about this subject as they want it done, not truthfully. Thus our history is seriously warped and biased by such work.

Many people have been so concerned about what has been happening to our Government that they have dedicated themselves to investigating and exposing its evils. Unfortunately, a number of these writers have been dupes of those cleverer than they or with sinister reasons for concealing knowledge. They have written what they thought was the truth, only to find out (if they ever did find out) that they had been fed a lot of contrived cover stories and just plain hogwash. In this book I have taken extracts from some of this writing and, line by line, have shown how it has been manipulated to give a semblance of truth while at the same time being contrived and false.

Nevertheless, there have been some excellent books in this broad area. But many of these books suffer from various effects of the dread disease of secrecy and from its equally severe corollary illness called "cover" (the CIA's official euphemism for not telling the truth).

The man who has not lived in the secrecy and intelligence environment—really lived in it and fully experienced it—cannot write accurately about it. There is no substitute for the day to day living of a life in which he tells his best friends and acquaintances, his family and his everyday contacts one story while he lives another. The man who must depend upon research and investigation inevitably falls victim to the many pitfalls of the secret world and of the "cover story" world with its lies and counter-lies.

A good example of this is the work of Les Gelb and his Pentagon associates on the official version of the purloined "Pentagon Papers." That very title is the biggest cover story (no pun intended) of them all; so very few of those papers were really of Pentagon origin. The fact that I had many of them in my office of Special Operations in Joint Staff area, and that most of them had been in the files of the office of the Assistant Secretary of Defense for International Security Affairs did not validate the locale of their origin. They were "working copies" and not originals. Notice how few were signed by true military officers.

It is significant to note that the historical record that has been called the "Pentagon Papers" was actually a formal government-funded "study of the history of United States involvement in Vietnam from World War II to the present" i.e. 1945 to 1968. On June 17, 1967 the Secretary of Defense, Robert S. McNamara directed that work. A task force consisting of "six times six professionals" under the direction of Leslie H. Gelb produced "37 studies and 15 collections of documents in 43 volumes" that were presented on January 15, 1969 to the then-Secretary of Defense, Clark M. Clifford by Mr. Gelb with the words from Herman Melville's *Moby Dick*:

"This is a world of chance, free will, and necessity, all interweavingly working together as one: chance by turn rules either and had the last featuring blow at events."

As you may recall, this treasure trove of TOP SECRET papers was delivered to *The New York Times*, and other newspapers in mid-June, 1971, by a then-unknown "Hippie" of that period. His name was Daniel Ellsberg. What few people have learned since that time is the fact that both Daniel Ellsberg, who pirated these highly classified papers, and Leslie Gelb the Director of that Task Force, had worked in that same office of International Security Affairs (ISA).

The "misappropriation" of those documents was not the work of some "true patriots" as Noam Chomsky wrote in 1972. Rather it was an inside job. That ISA office had been the home of many of the "big names" of the Vietnam War period, among them Paul H. Nitze, John T. McNaughton, Paul C. Warnke and William Bundy, among others. The fact that I had many of them in my office, that I had worked with them, and that I had written parts of some of them proves that they were not genuine Pentagon papers, because my work at that time was devoted to support of the CIA. The same is true of General Krulak, William Bundy, and to a degree, Maxwell Taylor among others.

To look at this matter in another way, the man who has lived and experienced this unnatural existence becomes even more a victim of its unreality. He becomes enmeshed beyond all control upon the horns of a cruel dilemma. On the one hand, his whole working life has been dedicated to the cause of secrecy and to its protection by means of cover stories (lies). In this pursuit he has given of himself time after time to pledges, briefings, oaths, and deep personal conviction regarding the significance of that work. Even if he would talk and write, his life has been so interwoven into the fabric of the real and the unreal, the actual and the cover story, that he would be least likely to present the absolutely correct data.

On the other hand, as a professional he would have been subjected to such cellularization and compartmentalization each time he became involved in any real "deep" operation that he would not have known the whole story anyhow. This compartmentalization is very real. I have worked on projects with many CIA men so unaware of the entire operation that they had no realization and awareness of the roles of other CIA men working on the same project.

I would know of this because inevitably somewhere along the line both groups would come to the Department of Defense for hardware support. I actually designed a special office in the

Pentagon with but one door off the corridor. Inside, it had a single room with one secretary. However, off her office there was one more door that led to two more offices with a third doorway leading to yet another office, which was concealed by the door from the secretary's room. I had to do this because at times we had CIA groups with us who were now allowed to meet each other, and who most certainly would not have been there had they known that the others were there. (For the record, the office was 4D1000—it may have been changed by now; but it had remained that way for many years.)

Another group of writers, about the world of secrecy, are the "masters"—men like Allen W. Dulles, Lyman Kirkpatrick, Peer de Silva and Chester Cooper. My own choice of the best of these are Peer de Silva and Lyman Kirkpatrick. These are thoroughly professional intelligence officers who have chosen a career of high-level intelligence operations. Their writing is correct and informative—to a degree beyond that which most readers will be able to translate and comprehend at first reading; yet they are properly circumspect and guarded and very cleverly protective of their profession.

There is another category of writer and self-proclaimed authority on the subjects of secrecy, intelligence, and containment. This man is the suave, professional parasite who gains a reputation as a real reporter by disseminating the scraps and "Golden Apples" thrown to him by the great men who use him. This writer seldom knows and rarely cares that many of the scraps from which he draws his material have been planted, that they are controlled leaks, and that he is being used, and glorified as he is being used, by the inside secret intelligence community.

Allen Dulles had a penchant for cultivating a number of such writers with big names and inviting them to his table for a medieval style luncheon in that great room across the hall from his own offices in the old CIA headquarters on the hill overlooking Foggy Bottom. Here, he would discuss openly and all too freely the same subjects that only hours before had been carefully discussed in the secret inner chambers of the operational side of that quiet Agency. In the hands of Allen Dulles, "secrecy" was simply a chameleon device to be used as he saw fit and to be applied to lesser men according to his schemes. It is quite fantastic to find people like Daniel Ellsberg being charged with leaking official secrets simply because the label on the piece of paper said "TOP SECRET," when the substance of many of the words written on those same papers was patently untrue and no more than a cover story. Except for the fact that they were official "*lies*," these papers had no basis in fact, and therefore no basis to be graded TOP SECRET or any other degree of classification. Allen Dulles would tell similar cover stories to his coterie of writers, and not long thereafter they would appear in print in some of the most prestigious papers and magazines in the country, totally unclassified, and of course, cleverly untrue.

Lastly there is the writer from outside this country who has gained his inside information from sources in another country. These sources are no doubt reliable; they know exactly what has taken place—as in Guatemala during the Bay of Pigs era—and they can speak with some freedom. In other cases, the best of these sources have been from behind the Iron Curtain.

In every case, the chance for complete information is very small, and the hope that in time researchers, students, and historians will be able to ferret out truth from untruth, real from unreal, and story from cover story is at best a very slim one. Certainly, history teaches us that one truth will add to and enhance another; but let us not forget that one lie added to another lie will demolish everything. This is the important point.

Consider the past half century. How many major events—really major events—have there been that simply do not ring true? How many times has the entire world been shaken by alarms of major significance, only to find that the events either did not happen at all, or if they did, that they had happened in a manner quite unlike the original story? The war in Vietnam is undoubtedly the best example of this. Why is it that after more than thirty years of clandestine and overt involvement in Indochina, no one had been able to make a logical case for what we had been doing there and to explain adequately why we had become involved; and what our real and valid objectives in that part of the world were?

The mystery behind all of this lies in the area we know as "Clandestine activity," "intelligence operations," "secrecy," and "cover stories," used on a national and international scale. It is the object of this book to bring reality and understanding into this vast unknown area.

L. FLETCHER PROUTY
Colonel, U.S. Air Force (Ret'd)

PREFACE TO THE SECOND EDITION

Like it or not, we now live in a new age of "One World." This is the age of global companies, of global communications and transport, of global food supply and finance and . . . just around the corner . . . global accommodation of political systems. In this sense, there are no home markets, no isolated markets and no markets outside the global network. It is time to face the fact that true national sovereignty no longer exists. We live in a world of big business, big lawyers, big bankers, even bigger moneymen and big politicians. It is the world of "The Secret Team."

In such a world, the Secret Team is a dominant power. It is neither military nor police. It is covert, and the best (or worst) of both. It gets the job done whether it has political authorization and direction, or not. It is independent. It is lawless.

This book is about the real CIA and its allies around the world. It is based upon personal experience generally derived from work in the Pentagon from 1955 to 1964. At retirement, I was Chief of Special Operations (clandestine activities) with the U.S. Joint Chiefs of Staff. These duties involved the military support of the clandestine activities of the CIA and were performed under the provisions of National Security Council Directive No. 5412/2.

Since this book was first published in 1973, we have witnessed the unauthorized release of the "Pentagon Papers," "Watergate" and the resignation of President Nixon, the run-away activities of the "Vietnam War," the "Arab Oil Embargo" that led to the greatest financial heist in history, and the blatantly unlawful "Iran-Contra" affair. All of these were brought about and master-minded by a renegade "Secret Team" that operated secretly, without Presidential direction; without National Security Council approval—so they say; and, generally, without Congressional knowledge. This trend increases. Its scope expands . . . even today.

I was the first author to point out that the CIA's most important "Cover Story" is that of an "Intelligence" agency. Of course the CIA does make use of "intelligence" and "intelligence gathering," but that is largely a front for its primary interest, "Fun and Games." The CIA is the center of a vast mechanism that specializes in Covert Operations . . . or as Allen Dulles used to call it, "Peacetime Operations." In this sense, the CIA is the willing tool of a higher level Secret Team, or High Cabal, that usually includes representatives of the CIA and other instrumentalities of the government, certain cells of the business and professional world and, almost always, foreign participation. It is this Secret Team, its allies, and its method of operation that are the principal subjects of this book.

It must be made clear that at the heart of Covert Operations is the denial by the "operator," i.e. the U.S. Government, of the existence of national sovereignty. The Covert operator can, and does, make the world his playground . . . including the U.S.A.

Today, early 1990, the most important events of this century are taking place with the ending of the "Cold War" era, and the beginning of the new age of "One World" under the control of businessmen and their lawyers, rather than the threat of military power. This scenario for change has been brought about by a series of Secret Team operations skillfully orchestrated while the contrived hostilities of the Cold War were at their zenith.

Chief among these, yet quite unnoticed, President Nixon and his Secretary of the Treasury, George Schultz, established a Russian/American organization called the "USA-USSR Trade and Economic Council," in 1972. Its objective was to bring about a union of the Fortune 500 Chief Executive Officers of this country, among others, such as the hierarchy of the U.S. Chamber of Commerce, with their counterparts in the Soviet Union. This important relationship, sponsored by David Rockefeller of Chase Manhattan Bank and his associates, continued through the Carter years. The bilateral activity increased significantly during the Reagan/Shultz years of the Eighties despite such "Evil Empire" tantrums as the Korean Airlines Boeing 747 Flight 007 "shootdown" in 1983.

It is this "US-TEC" organization, with its counterpart bilateral agreements among other nations and the USSR, that has brought about the massive Communist world changes.

The Cold War has been the most expensive war in history. R. Buckminster Fuller has written in *Grunch of Giants*:

> We can very properly call World War I the million dollar war and World War II the billion dollar war and World War III (Cold War) the trillion dollar war.

The power structure that kept the Cold War at that level of intensity has been driven by the Secret Team and its multinational covert operations, to wit:

> This is the fundamental game of the Secret Team. They have this power because they control secrecy and secret intelligence and because they have the ability to take advantage of the most modern communications system in the world, of global transportation systems, of quantities of weapons of all kinds, of a world-wide U.S. military supporting base structure. They can use the finest intelligence system in the world, and most importantly, they are able to operate under the canopy of an ever-present "enemy" called "Communism." And then, to top all of this, there is the fact that the CIA has assumed the right to generate and direct secret operations.

—L. Fletcher Prouty
Alexandria, VA, 1990

PREFACE: "THE SECRET TEAM II" 1997

Like it or not, we now live in the age of "One World." This is the age of global companies, of global communications and transport, of global food supply and finance and . . . just around the corner . . . global accommodation of political systems. In this sense, there are no home markets, no isolated markets and no markets outside the global network.

It is time to face the fact that true national sovereignty no longer exists. We live in a world of big business, big lawyers, big bankers, even bigger money-men and big politicians. It is the world of "The Secret Team" and its masters. We are now, despite common mythology to the contrary, the most dependent society that has ever lived, and the future of the viability of that infrastructure of that society is unpredictable. It is crumbling.

As one of the greatest historians of all time, Ibn Khaldun, wrote in his unequaled historical work *The Muqaddimah* of the 14th Century:

> God created and fashioned man in a form that can live and subsist only with the help of food. . . . Through cooperation, the needs of a number of persons, many times greater than their own number, can be satisfied.

As this One World infrastructure emerges it increases the percentage of our total dependence upon remote food production capacity to the mass production capability and transport means of enormous companies operating under the global policy guidance of such organizations as the Chartered Institute of Transport in London, and the international banking community. As individuals, few of us would have any idea where to get a loaf of bread or yard of fabric other than in some supermarket and department store . . . and we are all dependent upon some form of efficient transport, electric power, gasoline at the pump, and boundless manufacturing capacity and versatility. Let that system collapse, at any point, and all of us will be helpless. A cooperating, working system is essential to survival; yet over-all it is a system without leadership and guidance.

At the same time the traditional family farm, and even community farms and industries, have all but vanished from the scene. This has created, at least in what we label, the advanced nations, a dearth of farmers and of people who have that basic experience along with that required in the food and home products industries. Furthermore, as this trend is amplified, the transport of farm produce has become increasingly assigned to the trucking industry, which has its overland limits . . . mostly as applied to the tonnage limits of rural bridges, and the economical availability of petroleum.

As a result, something as simple as a trucking industry strike that keeps trucks out of any city for seventy-two hours or more, will lead to starvation and food riots. None of us know where to get food, if it is not in the nearby supermarket; and if we do have a stored supply of food locked in the cellar, we shall simply be the targets of those who do not. Food is the ultimate driving force. Under such predictable conditions, there will be waves of slaughter and eventually cannibalism. Man must eat, and the only way he can obtain adequate food supplies is through cooperation and the means to transport and distribute food and other basic necessities. This essential role is being diminished beyond the borderline. The lack of food supplies has already resulted in a form of covert genocide in many countries. Other essential shortages unavoidably follow.

As Rudyard Kipling has said: "Transport is Civilization." The opposite is equally true, "Without reliable transport we are reduced to the state of barbarism."

These are fundamental statements of fact. In such a world, the Secret Team is the functional element of the dominant power. It is the point of the spear and is neither military nor police. It is covert: and the best (or worst) of both. It gets the job done whether it has political authorization and direction, or not. In this capacity, it acts independently. It is lawless. It operates everywhere with the best of all supporting facilities from special weaponry and advanced communications, with the assurance that its members will never be prosecuted. It is subservient to the Power Elite and protected by them. The Power Elite or High Cabal need not be Royalty in these days. They are their equals or better.

Note with care, it is labeled a "Team." This is because as with any highly professional team it has its managers, its front office and its owners. These are the "Power Elite" to whom it is beholden. They are always anonymous, and their network is ancient and world-wide. Let us draw an example from recent history.

During the Senate Hearings of 1975 on "Alleged Assassination Ploys Involving Foreign Leaders," Senator Charles C. Mathias' thoughts went back to November 22, 1963 and to the coup d'etat brought about by the surgical precision of the death of President John F. Kennedy, when he said:

> Let me draw an example from history. When Thomas Becket (Saint Thomas Becket, 1118–1170) was proving to be an annoyance, as Castro; the King said "Who will rid me of this man?" He didn't say to somebody, go out and murder him. He said who will rid me of this man, and let it go at that. (As you will recall, Thomas Becket's threat was not against the King, it was against the way the King wanted to run the government.)
>
> With no explicit orders, and with no more authority than that, four of King Henry's knights, found and killed "this man," Saint Thomas Becket inside of his church. That simple statement . . . no more than a wish floating in air . . . proved to be all the orders needed.

Then, with that great historical event in mind, Senator Mathias went on to say:

> . . . that is typical of the kind of thing which might be said, which might be taken by the Director of Central Intelligence or by anybody else, as Presidential authorization to go forward . . . you felt that some spark had been transmitted . . .

To this Senator Jesse Helms added:

> Yes, and if he had disappeared from the scene they would not have been unhappy.

There's the point! Because the structure, a "Power Elite," "High Cabal" or similar ultimate ruling organization, exists and the psychological atmosphere has been prepared, nothing more has to be said than that which ignites that "spark" of an assumed "authorization to go forward." Very often, this is the way in which the Secret Team gets its orders . . . they are no more than "a wish floating in air."

This book is about a major element of this real power structure of the world and of its impact upon the CIA and its allies around the world. It is based upon much personal experience generally derived from my military service from mid-1941 to 1964: U.S. Army Cavalry, U.S. Army Armored Force, U.S. Army Air Corps and Army Air Force, and finally the U. S. Air Force; and more specifically from my special assignments in the Pentagon from 1955 to 1964. At retirement, I was the first Chief of Special Operations with the U.S. Joint Chiefs of Staff. All of these duties, during those Pentagon years, were structured to provide "the military support of the world-wide clandestine activities of the CIA." They were performed in accordance with the provisions of an Eisenhower era, National Security Council Directive No. 5412/2, March 15, 1954.

Since this book was first published in 1973, we have witnessed the unauthorized release of the Defense Department's official " history of United States involvement in Vietnam from World War II to 1969" popularly known as the "Pentagon Papers," "Watergate" and the resignation of President Nixon, the run away activities of the "Vietnam War," the "Arab Oil Embargo" that led to the greatest financial heist in history, the blatantly unlawful "Iran Contra" affair, and the runaway banking scandals of the eighties. Many of these were brought about and master minded by renegade "Secret Team" members who operated, without Presidential direction; without National

Security Council approval so they say; and, generally, without official Congressional knowledge. This trend increases. Its scope expands . . . even today.

I pointed out, years ago in public pronouncements, that the CIA's most important "Cover Story" is that of an "intelligence" agency. Of course the CIA does make use of "intelligence" and its assumed role of "intelligence gathering," but that is largely a front for its primary interest, "Fun and Games" . . . as the "Old Boys" or "Jedburghs" of the WW II period Office of Strategic Services (OSS) called it.

The CIA is the center of a vast, and amorphous mechanism that specializes in Covert Operations . . . or as Allen Dulles always called it, "Peacetime Operations." In this sense, the CIA is the willing tool of a higher level High Cabal, that may include representatives and highly skilled agents of the CIA and other instrumentality's of the government, certain cells of the business and professional world and, almost always, foreign participation. It is this ultimate Secret Team, its allies, and its method of operation that are the principal subject of this book.

It must be made clear that at the heart of Covert Operations is the denial by the "operator," i.e. the U.S. Government, of the existence of national sovereignty. The covert operator can, and does, make the world his playground . . . including the U.S.A.

Today, in the mid-1990's, the most important events of this century are taking place with the ending of the "Cold War" era, and the beginning of the new age of "One World" under the control of businessmen and their lawyers, rather than under the threat of military power and ideological differences. This scenario for change has been brought about by a series of Secret Team operations skillfully orchestrated while the contrived hostilities of the Cold War were at their zenith.

Two important events of that period have been little noted. First, on Feb. 7, 1972, Maurice Stans, Nixon's Secretary of Commerce opened a "White House Conference on the Industrial World Ahead, A Look at Business in 1990." This three-day meeting of more than fifteen hundred of the country's leading businessmen, scholars, and the like were concluded with this memorable summary statement by Roy L. Ash, president of Litton Industries:

> . . . state capitalism may well be a form for world business in the world ahead; that the western countries are trending toward a more unified and controlled economy, having a greater effect on all business; and the communist nations are moving more and more toward a free market system. The question posed during this conference on which a number of divergent opinions arose, was whether 'East and West' would meet some place toward the middle about 1990.

That was an astounding forecast as we consider events of the seventies and eighties and discover that his forecast, if it ever was a forecast and not a pre-planned arrangement, was right on the nose.

This amazing forecast had its antecedent pronouncements, among which was another "One World" speech by this same Roy Ash during the Proceedings of the American Bankers Association National Automation Conference in New York City, May 8, 9, 10, 1967.

> The affairs of the world are becoming inextricably interlinked . . . governments, notably, cannot effectively perform the task of creating and distributing food and other essential products and services . . . economic development is the special capability and function of business and industrial organizations . . . business organizations are the most efficient converters of the original resources of the world into useable goods and services.
>
> The flash of genius, the new ideas, always comes from the marvelous workings of the individual brain, not from the committee sessions. Organizations are to implement ideas, not to have them.

As a Charter Member of the American Bankers Association's Committee on Automation Planning and Technology I was a panelist at that same convention as we worked to convert the 14,000 banks of this country to automation and the ubiquitous Credit Card. All of these subjects were signs of the times leading toward the demise of the Soviet Union in favor of an evolutionary process toward One World.

In addition to the 1972 White House Conference on the Industrial World Ahead a most significant yet quite unnoticed action took place during that same year when President Nixon and his then-Secretary of the Treasury, George Shultz, established a Russian/American organization called the "USA-USSR Trade and Economic Council." Its objective was to bring about a union of the Fortune 500 Chief Executive Officers of this country, among others, such as the hierarchy of the U.S. Chamber of Commerce, with their counterparts in the Soviet Union. This important relationship, sponsored by David Rockefeller of Chase Manhattan Bank and his associates, continues into the "One World" years.

This bilateral activity increased during the Reagan/Shultz years of the Eighties despite such "Evil Empire" staged tantrums as the Korean Airlines Boeing 747 Flight 007 "shootdown" in 1983.

It is this "US-TEC" organization, with its counterpart bilateral agreements among other nations and the USSR, that has brought about the massive changes of the former Communist world. These did not go unnoticed. During a speech delivered in 1991, Giovanni Agnelli, chief executive officer of the Fiat Company and one of the most powerful men in Europe, if not the world, remarked:

> The fall of the Soviet Union is one of the very few instances in history in which a world power has been defeated on the battlefield of ideas.

Now, is this what Nixon, Stans, Shultz, Ash, Rockefeller and others had in mind during those important decades of the sixties, seventies and eighties. For one thing, it may be said quiet accurately, that these momentous events marked the end of the Cold War and have all but shredded the canopy of the nuclear umbrella over mankind.

The Cold War was the most expensive war in history. R. Buckminster Fuller wrote in *Grunch of Giants*:

> We can very properly call World War I the million dollar war and World War II the billion dollar war and World War III (Cold War) the trillion dollar war.

The power structure that kept the Cold War at that level of cost and intensity had been spearheaded by the Secret Team and its multinational covert operations, to wit:

> This is the fundamental game of the Secret Team. They have this power because they control secrecy and secret intelligence and because they have the ability to take advantage of the most modern communications system in the world, of global transportation systems, of quantities of weapons of all kinds, and when needed, the full support of a world-wide U.S. military supporting base structure. They can use the finest intelligence system in the world, and most importantly, they have been able to operate under the canopy of an assumed, ever-present enemy called "Communism." It will be interesting to see what "enemy" develops in the years ahead. It appears that "UFO's and Aliens" are being primed to fulfill that role for the future. To top all of this, there is the fact that the CIA, itself, has assumed the right to generate and direct secret operations.

—L. Fletcher Prouty
Alexandria, VA, 1997

PART I

THE SECRET TEAM

CHAPTER 1

THE "SECRET TEAM"—THE REAL POWER STRUCTURE

The most remarkable development in the management of America's relations with other countries during the quarter-century since the end of World War II has been the assumption of more and more control over military, financial and diplomatic operations at home and abroad by men whose activities are secret, whose budget is secret, whose very identities as often as not are secret—in short, by a Secret Team whose actions only those implicated in them are in a position to monitor and to understand.

For the purposes of this historical study, the choice of the word "Team" is most significant. It is well known that the members of a team, as in baseball or football, are skilled professionals under the direct control of someone higher up. They do not create their own game plan. They work for their coach and their owner. There is always some group that manages them and "calls the plays." Team members are like lawyers and agents, they work for someone. They generally do not plan their work. They do what their client tells them to do. For example: this is true of agents in the Central Intelligence

Agency. It is an "Agency" and not a "Department" and its employees
are highly skilled professionals who perform the functions their craft
demands of them. Thus, the members of the highest level "Secret
Team" work for their masters despite the fact that their own high
office may make it appear to others that they, themselves are not only
the Team but the Power Elite. This recalls a story related by the Rt.
Hon. Lord Denning, Master of the Rolls, of Great Britain, during
WW II.

Winston Churchill had left the Admiralty to become Prime
Minister. Frequently he would come down to the Admiralty basement on his way from #10 Downing Street, to his underground,
bomb-proof bedroom. He made it his practice to visit the Officer
in Charge for up-to-date Intelligence and then stroll into the Duty
Captain's room where there was a small bar from which he sometimes indulged in a night-cap, along with his ever-present cigar.

On this particular night there had been a heavy raid on
Rotterdam. He sat there, meditating, and then, as if to himself, he
said, "Unrestricted submarine warfare, unrestricted air bombing—
this is total war." He continued sitting there, gazing at a large map,
and then said, "Time and the Ocean and some guiding star and
High Cabal have made us what we are."

This was a most memorable scene and a revelation of reality that
is infrequent, at best. If for the great Winston Churchill, there is a
"High Cabal" that has made us what we are, our definition is complete. Who could know better than Churchill himself during the
darkest days of World War II, that there exists, beyond doubt, an
international High Cabal? This was true then. It is true today, especially in these times of the One World Order. This all-powerful group
has remained superior because it had learned the value of anonymity.
For them, the Secret Team and its professionals operate.

We may wish to note that in a book "Gentleman Spy, the Life of
Allen Dulles" the author, Peter Grose cites Allen Dulles response to
an invitation to the luncheon table from Hoover's Secretary of State,
Henry L. Stimson. Allen Dulles assured his partners in the Sullivan &
Cromwell law firm, "Let it be known quietly that I am a lawyer
and not a diplomat." He could not have made a more characteristic

and truthful statement about himself. He always made it clear that he did not "plan" his work, he was always the "lawyer" who carried out the orders of his client whether the President of the United States, or the President of the local bank.

The Secret Team (ST) being described herein consists of security-cleared individuals in and out of government who receive secret intelligence data gathered by the CIA and the National Security Agency (NSA) and who react to those data, when it seems appropriate to them, with paramilitary plans and activities, e.g. training and "advising"—a not exactly impenetrable euphemism for such things as leading into battle and actual combat—Laotian tribal troops, Tibetan rebel horsemen, or Jordanian elite Palace Guards.

Membership on the Team, granted on a "need-to-know" basis, varies with the nature and location of the problems that come to its attention, and its origins derive from that sometimes elite band of men who served with the World War II Office of Strategic Services (OSS) under the father of them all, General "Wild Bill" William J. Donovan, and in the old CIA.

The power of the Team derives from its vast intragovernmental undercover infrastructure and its direct relationship with great private industries, mutual funds and investment houses, universities, and the news media, including foreign and domestic publishing houses. The Secret Team has very close affiliations with elements of power in more than three-score foreign countries and is able when it chooses to topple governments, to create governments, and to influence governments almost anywhere in the world.

Whether or not the Secret Team had anything whatsoever to do with the deaths of Rafael Trujillo, Ngo Dinh Diem, Ngo Dinh Nhu, Dag Hammarskjöld, John F. Kennedy, Robert F. Kennedy, Martin Luther King, and others may never be revealed, but what is known is that the power of the Team is enhanced by the "cult of the gun" and by its sometimes brutal and always arbitrary anti-Communist flag waving, even when real Communism had nothing to do with the matter at hand.

The Secret Team does not like criticism, investigation, or history and is always prone to see the world as divided into but two camps—"Them" and "Us." Sometimes the distinction may be as little as one dot, as in "So. Viets" and "Soviets," the So. Viets being our friends in Indochina, and the Soviets being the enemy of that period. To be a member, you don't question, you don't ask; it's "Get on the Team" or else. One of its most powerful weapons in the most political and powerful capitals of the world is that of exclusion. To be denied the "need to know" status, like being a member of the Team, even though one may have all the necessary clearances, is to be totally blackballed and eliminated from further participation. Politically, if you are cut from the Team and from its insider's knowledge, you are dead. In many ways and by many criteria the Secret Team is the inner sanctum of a new religious order.

At the heart of the Team, of course, are a handful of top executives of the CIA and of the National Security Council (NSC), most notably the chief White House adviser to the President on foreign policy affairs. Around them revolves a sort of inner ring of Presidential officials, civilians, and military men from the Pentagon, and career professionals of the intelligence community. It is often quite difficult to tell exactly who many of these men really are, because some may wear a uniform and the rank of general and really be with the CIA and others may be as inconspicuous as the executive assistant to some Cabinet officer's chief deputy. Out beyond this ring is an extensive and intricate network of government officials with responsibility for, or expertise in, some specific field that touches on national security or foreign affairs: "Think Tank" analysts, businessmen who travel a lot or whose businesses (e.g., import-export or cargo airline operations) are useful, academic experts in this or that technical subject or geographic region, and quite importantly, alumni of the intelligence community—a service from which there are no unconditional resignations. All true members of the Team remain in the power center whether in office with the incumbent administration or out of office with the hard-core set. They simply rotate to and from official jobs and the business world or the pleasant haven of academe.

Thus, the Secret Team is not a clandestine super-planning-board or super-general-staff. But even more damaging to the coherent conduct of foreign and military affairs, it is a bewildering collection of semi-permanent or temporarily assembled action committees and networks that respond pretty much *ad hoc* to specific troubles and to flash-intelligence data inputs from various parts of the world, sometimes in ways that duplicate the activities of regular American missions, sometimes in ways that undermine those activities, and very often in ways that interfere with and muddle them. At no time did the powerful and deft hand of the Secret Team evidence more catalytic influence than in the events of those final ninety days of 1963, which the "Pentagon Papers" were supposed to have exposed.

The New York Times shocked the world on Sunday, June 13, 1971, with the publication of the first elements of the Pentagon Papers.[1] The first document the *Times* selected to print was a trip report on the situation in Saigon, credited to the Secretary of Defense, Robert S. McNamara, and dated December 21, 1963. This was the first such report on the situation in Indochina to be submitted to President Lyndon B. Johnson. It came less than thirty days after the assassination of President John F. Kennedy and less than sixty days after the assassinations of President Ngo Dinh Diem of South Vietnam and his brother and counselor Ngo Dinh Nhu.

Whether from some inner wisdom or real prescience or merely simple random selection, the *Times* chose to publish first from among the three thousand pages of analysis and four thousand pages of official documents that had come into its hands that report which may stand out in history as one of the key documents affecting national policy in the past quarter-century—not so much for what it said as for what it signified. This report is a prime example of how the Secret Team, which has gained so much control over the vital foreign and political activities of this government, functions.

---

1. This is a gross and crafty misnomer [Pentagon Papers], since all too few of those papers actually were *bona fide* military papers. They may have been written under Pentagon headings; they may have been signed by "military" officers or "military department civilians," but for the most part they were not actually military papers. They represent the papers of a small group of civilians, some of whom worked in the Pentagon, and their military [real and cover] counterparts.

Most observers might have expected that the inner group of men who had worked so closely with President Kennedy for three years would have lost heart in those days following his tragic death. On the contrary, they burst forth, as though from strong bonds and fetters and created this entirely new report, thus shaping the future of the Indochina conflict. Their energy and their new sense of direction seemed almost to rise from the flame of Kennedy's tomb in Arlington.

During those hectic months of late summer in 1963 when the Kennedy Administration appeared to be frustrated and disenchanted with the ten-year regime of Ngo Dinh Diem in Saigon, it approved the plans for the military coup d'état that would overthrow President Diem and get rid of his brother Nhu. The Kennedy Administration gave its support to a cabal of Vietnamese generals who were determined to remove the Ngos from power. Having gone so far as to withdraw its support of the Diem government and to all but openly support the coup, the Administration became impatient with delays and uncertainties from the generals in Saigon, and by late September dispatched General Maxwell D. Taylor, then Chairman of Joint Chiefs of Staff (JCS), and Secretary of Defense McNamara to Saigon.

Upon their return, following a brief trip, they submitted a report to President Kennedy, which in proper chronology was the one immediately preceding the remarkable one of December 21, 1963. This earlier report said, among other things, "There is no solid evidence of the possibility of a successful coup, although assassination of Diem and Nhu is always a possibility." The latter part of this sentence contained the substantive information. A coup d'état, or assassination is never certain from the point of view of the planners; but whenever United States support of the government in power is withdrawn and a possible coup d'état or assassination is not adamantly opposed, it will happen. Only three days after this report, on October 5, 1963, the White House cabled Ambassador Lodge in Saigon: "There should be . . . urgent covert effort . . . to identify and build contact with possible alternate leadership." Knowledge of a statement such as this one made by the ostensible defenders and supporters of the

Diem regime was all those coup planners needed to know. In less than one month Diem was dead, along with his brother.[2]

Thus, what was considered to be a first prerequisite for a more favorable climate in Vietnam was fulfilled. With the Ngo family out of the way, President Kennedy felt that he had the option to bring the war to a close on his own terms or to continue pressure with covert activities such as had been under way for many years. Because the real authors were well aware of his desires, there was another most important statement in the McNamara-Taylor report of October 2, 1963: "It should be possible to withdraw the bulk of U.S. personnel by that time [the end of 1965]." This statement came at a key point in time.

Like the others, it was written by Secret Team insiders who knew the President's mind and how far they could go in setting forth ideas which he would accept and yet be acceptable to their own plans. Reports such as the October 2, 1963, document were not written in Saigon and they were not written by the men whose names appeared on them.

This pivotal report was written in Washington by members of the ST. Although it contained a lot of updated material from Saigon (some of which had been transmitted to Saigon verbatim for the express purpose of having to then re-transmitted back to Washington for inclusion in the report—with the all-important Saigon dateline), one may be certain that this report contained a skillful mixture of what the President wanted to hear and what its authors in Washington wanted the President to read. Therefore, when it included the blunt and unequivocal statement that "it should be possible to withdraw the bulk of U.S. personnel by that time," the authors, cover and undercover, were in tune with the times. They knew the President was favorably considering means to extricate the United States from Vietnam.

---

2. The Pentagon Papers' account and the subsequent NBC-TV presentation of the assassination of the Ngo brothers are both excellent representations of what happened during those grim days in Washington and Saigon. The only problem is that neither one is a complete and accurate account of what really took place, especially in Washington.

The ST had had its day with Kennedy on the beaches of the Cuban Bay of Pigs. Kennedy had minutely reviewed that debacle, and from that time on he was ever alert for the slightest sign of any undercover operation that might expand and get so out of hand as to involve this country in any more such disasters. The Team had come a long way since that dismal period in April 1961, and had learned well how to use and thrive with Jack Kennedy, in spite of his caution. One way to do this was to be certain to spell things correctly—meaning hewing close to his line while retaining ST initiative. It is a safe bet to say that this forecast of personnel withdrawal by the end of 1965 was the maneuvering time they wanted and what Kennedy would accept, in their language, so that he too would have time to get re-elected and then carry out his own decisions as he had related them to Senator Mansfield. It appears that Kennedy felt that with the obstacle of the Diem regime out of the way, he would have the opportunity to disengage this nation from the war that he had so far been able to keep from becoming a runaway overt action. Up to the end of 1963, all U.S. Army troops in South Vietnam, with the exception of a small number in the Military Advisory and Assistance Group (MAAG) and a few other such positions, were there under the operational control of the CIA. This was flimsy cover and it was a poor device to maintain that the United States was not overtly involved in military activity in Indochina; but the device did achieve its purpose of keeping the level of the war to a minimum.

Within thirty days of the Taylor-McNamara report, Diem and his brother were dead. The Government of South Vietnam was in the hands of the popular and powerful General Duong Van "Big" Minh. Minh was a strong enough man to have made Vietnamization work. But within another thirty days President Kennedy was dead, and the Government of the United States was in the hands of Lyndon B. Johnson. "Big" Minh may have been the man Kennedy wanted in Saigon, but he did not last long with the new Johnson Administration. Four days after Kennedy's death, on November 26, 1963, President Johnson issued an order reaffirming United States policy in South Vietnam and at the same time referring to the new Government of General Minh as a "provisional government," presaging and assuring the inevitability of another change in the near future. President Johnson's advisers wanted a "benevolent" military regime in Saigon, and they wanted one which would be more suitable than Minh's. Kennedy would have had Minh rally around him a popular and strongly independent Vietnamese administration. After Kennedy's death, U.S. policy called for leadership in Saigon which would accept continuing United States participation in the internal affairs of that Government.

Less than fifteen days after the death of Kennedy, Secretary of Defense McNamara was on his way back to Saigon to assess the situation under General Minh and to report to the new President of the United States. This time, the McNamara report was, to quote *The New York Times*, "Laden with gloom." His assessment laid the groundwork for the long haul and included decisions to step up the covert war against North Vietnam in early 1964 and to increase American aid to South Vietnam. Within ninety days the Government of "Big" Minh was eased out of office and replaced by the more tractable General Nguyen Khanh.

There are those who say that because he had approved certain covert operations in Indochina, President Kennedy was planning to expand the war. It is true that accelerating cover operations is like stoking the fire; but we should weigh Kennedy's actions against the fact that the United States had been actively involved in clandestine operations in Indochina since 1945 as well as in other areas of the world for many years, and that these activities did not signify that the administration concerned had embarked upon a course leading to open warfare.

The paramount condition underlying any approval for clandestine operations is absolute control at the top. The ST will come up with operational schemes all the time and will seek approval for as many as it believes it can get away with. The only way to cope with this is for the President to make it clear that there will be no covert operations without proper approval and that he will always be in a position to cancel or disapprove of any and all operations as he sees fit. Truman and Eisenhower knew this and practiced it. Kennedy learned it at the Bay of Pigs. Eisenhower had terminated major operations in Tibet, Laos, and Indonesia without escalating them into open war. Until his death Kennedy had held the line at the limited level of covert activities in Indochina, and American participation there was restricted to an advisory capacity. (Of course, we all recognize that this advisory role was, in many cases, pure combat.)

Clandestine operations that are small and strictly controlled with a fixed and time-limited objective can be terminated at any time, whether they succeed or fail. However, clandestine operations that become large, that are permitted to continue and to be repeated, that become known or compromised—and yet still continue, as in Laos—are very dangerous and can lead to open hostilities and even war. Thus, when the ST proposed a vastly escalated covert campaign against North Vietnam in December 1963, they were laying positive plans for the major military action that followed in 1965.[3] Within thirty days after Kennedy's death all of this changed drastically. In his report of December 21, 1963, McNamara stated: "Viet Cong progress had been great during the period since the coup. We also need to have major increases in both military and USOM (United States Operations Mission) staffs."

Later, he added, "Our first need would be immediate U-2 mapping of the whole Laos and Cambodian border, and this we are preparing to do on an urgent basis." And then, "One other step we can take is to expand the existing limited but remarkably effective operations on the Laos side, the so-called Operation HARDNOSE. . ... Plans to expand this will be prepared and presented for your approval in about two weeks." And further, "As to the waterways, the military plans presented in Saigon were unsatisfactory, and a special Naval team is being sent a once from Honolulu to determine what more can be done."

---

3. McNamara used to make the distinction that the war against North Vietnam was "sophisticated." Whereas the war in the South was "unsophisticated." The feeling was that there was an element of design and control over the war in the North which was not possible in the South. Walt Rostow had his own term for this. He liked to say that the war in the North was a sort of game of tit-for-tat. His idea was that if they hit us, we'd hit back. This type of game is all the more "sophisticated" when we hit clandestinely; they strike back overtly and then we strike back, claming they hit first!

Then he noted: "Plans for covert action into North Vietnam were prepared as we had requested and were an excellent job. . ... General Krulak of the JCS is chairing a group that will lay out a program in the next ten days for your consideration." All of these statements were evidence of typical, thorough ST groundwork.

McNamara closed out this report—which was so vastly different from the earlier October 2 one that he and Maxwell Taylor had submitted to President Kennedy—by saying: "We should watch the situation very carefully, running scared, and hoping for the best, but preparing for more forceful moves if the situation does not show early signs of improvement."

This was not the report of a group that was planning to wind down the war. It was a report that delineated various avenues of endeavor and that looked well into the future. This was the first such report made to President Johnson, and it was not designed to be reassuring. On the same day that the McNamara report was being handed to President Johnson, a former President was writing a totally different statement for the readership of the general pubic. President Harry S. Truman, observing the turn of events since the death of President Kennedy, and pondering developments since his Administration, wrote for the Washington *Post* a column also datelined December 21, 1963:

> For some time I have been disturbed by the way the CIA has been diverted from its original assignment. It has become an operational and at times a policy-making arm of the government. . ... I never had any thought that when I set up the CIA that it would be injected into peacetime cloak-and-dagger operations. Some of the complications and embarrassment that I think we have experienced are in part attributable to the fact that this quiet intelligence arm of the President has been so removed from its intended role that it is being interpreted as a symbol of sinister and mysterious foreign intrigue and a subject for cold war enemy propaganda.

Truman was disturbed by the events of the past ninety days, those ominous days of October, November, and December 1963. Men all over the world were disturbed by those events. Few men, however could have judged them with more wisdom and experience than Harry S. Truman, for it was he who, in late 1947, had signed unto law the National Security Act. This Act, in addition to establishing the Department of Defense (DOD) with a single Secretary at its head and with three equal and independent services—the Army, Navy, and Air Force—also provided for a National Security Council and the Central Intelligence Agency. And during those historic and sometimes tragic sixteen years since the Act had become law, he had witnessed changes that disturbed him, as he saw that the CIA "had been diverted" from the original assignment that he and the legislators who drafted the Act had so carefully planned. Although even in his time he had seen the beginning of the move of the CIA into covert activities, there can be little doubt that the "diversion" to which he made reference was not one that he would have attributed to himself or to any other President. Rather, the fact that the CIA had gone into clandestine operations and had been "injected into peacetime cloak-and-dagger operations," and "has been so much removed from its intended role" was more properly attributable to the growing and secret pressures of some other power source. As he said, the CIA had become "a symbol of sinister and mysterious foreign intrigue."

There can be no question that the events just prior to this statement heavily influenced his arriving at these disturbing conclusions. It is possible, but quite improbable, that Harry Truman knew about the McNamara report of the same date. But the coincidence between the appearance of Truman's commentary and of McNamara's report is compelling, especially since McNamara's report was the first selected by *The New York Times* for publication in its expose of the Pentagon Papers.

Now that the McNamara report has been published and has emerged from the depths of security, it can be added that this pivotal report was not written by McNamara; it was not even written in Saigon. This report, like the one dated October 2, was actually written by a group of ST and near-ST members and was drafted by them solely to impress upon the new President their idea of the increasing gravity and frightful responsibility of the war in Indochina. It was not for nothing that the *Times* noted that this report was "laden with gloom" and that it offered nowhere any easy or quick panacea for early victory in Indochina. It was not untended to do so. In fact, it did just the opposite. It left no room for any course of action other than eventual escalation of the war. This report and the ones that followed close upon it were carefully and skillfully written to instill into the new President an indelible belief that the war in Vietnam was the greatest issue facing the Free World. They hammered home the fanciful belief that if South Vietnam fell before the onslaught of Communism, the whole world would be engulfed.

As was common with reports such as this one, the first time McNamara saw it was during a few days stopover in Honolulu on his return trip from Saigon. It had been put together from many sources and drafts, primarily from the CIA and other secret-operations related areas, by the office of the Special Assistant for Counterinsurgency and Special Activities (SACSA) in the Joint Staff under the skilled and dedicated direction of Major General Victor H. Krulak. General Krulak was the same man who was designated in the body of the report to chair "a group that will lay out a program of covert action in North Vietnam in the next ten days."

In Pentagonese for highly classified matters, General Krulak's office in the Joint Staff was described as being responsible for serving as the JCS point of contact, in his field of interest, with related activities in the Military Departments, the Office of the Secretary of Defense (OSD), and other agencies of the government. This was the unclassified way of saying that his office was the point of contact within the DOD for the CIA. His contacts in this select circle in the OSD were such men as Major General Edward G. Lansdale, who was McNamara's special assistant for all matters involving the CIA and special operations; William Bundy, who appears throughout the Pentagon Papers as one of the key men of the ST and was at that time a recent alumni of the CIA, with ten years in that Agency behind him; John T. McNaughton, another member of the ST and a McNamara favorite; Joseph Califano, who moved from OSD to the White House; General Richard G. Stilwell of the White House Special Committee (details to follow), and others.

The preparations for and the writing of such influential reports as this one attributed to McNamara was a work of skill, perseverance, and high art. Whenever it was decided that McNamara would go to Saigon, select members of the ST sent special messages to Saigon on the ultra-secure CIA communications network, laying out a full scenario for his trip. The Secretary of Defense and his party would be shown "combat devastated villages" that had paths and ruts that had been caused by the hard work and repeated rehearsals—not battles—that had taken place in them between "natives," "Vietnamese soldiers," and Americans. McNamara would be taken on an itinerary planned in Washington, he would see "close-in combat" designed in Washington, and he would receive field data and statistics prepared for him in Washington. All during his visit he would be in the custody of skilled briefers who knew what he should see, whom he should see, and whom he should not see.

In many cases even the messages relayed from Saigon, ostensibly written by and for McNamara while he was there, had been sent to Saigon from Washington before he had arrived there. When a total communications system such as that available to the ST exists all over the world and is concealed by secrecy, it is not difficult to yield to the urge to "play God" and make everything come out as desired.

While McNamara was on his trip, the Special Assistant for Counterinsurgency and Special Activities and his staff, augmented by CIA and others, were working around the clock on the report. There were times when General Krulak himself stayed at his desk for thirty-six hours or more to keep a full staff going while secretaries and typists were shuttled to and from their homes for rest periods to get the massive report done in time.

While all of the writing was under way, cartographers and artists were working on illustrative material for the final report and for the big briefing charts that became a part of McNamara's personal style. The final report, perhaps two inches thick, was printed and bound in a legal-size, black goatskin cover, with the name of the President engraved in gold on it.

The finished report was rushed by helicopter to Andrews Air Force Base, about twenty miles from the Pentagon, and placed aboard a military jet fighter for a nonstop, midair-refueled flight to Honolulu, where it was handed to Mr. McNamara and his staff. He familiarized himself with the report while his jet flew him to Washington, where he disembarked at Andrews Air Force Base, trotted (with the report tucked under his arm) to the waiting Presidential helicopter and was whisked to the White House lawn to be greeted by the President. As soon as he got into the White House, an aide distributed the closely guarded and controlled copies of the report to those who had the need to know, and discussions began.

This recapitulation is worth setting forth in detail because it underscores not only the resourcefulness of the ST but its ability to perform super-miracles in an age when mere miracles are commonplace. The ST always fights for the minds, the time, and the attention of the top-echelon men. It moves fastest and most adroitly when others are off guard. This report of December 21, 1963, was absolutely crucial to the interests of the ST. Twenty-five years of driving, devoted work by ST members through a whole generation of critical events culminated in the Vietnam war. Never before in all the long history of civilization was a country to devote so much of its resources, its men and their lives, its money, and its very prestige in so strange an event as that which is called "The War In Vietnam." It made the coups d'état in Guatemala and Iran, the rebellion in Indonesia, the escape of the Dalai Lama and the underground war in Tibet, the Bay of Pigs, and the wasting war in Laos all pale before its magnitude.

President Johnson, for all his experience and native ability, had not yet been singed by the fire of experience as had Jack Kennedy in Cuba or Eisenhower by the U-2. Johnson was a natural "wheeler dealer," with courage and a flair for getting things done; but he had not yet learned how to say "No" and make it stick, rather, he had the inclination to defer the issue to a later day. This was the ideal formula for the ST, and they struck while the iron was hot.

There is another important factor to weigh in considering the agility and cunning of the ST. In bureaucratic Washington, few things are worth more than prior information. If a subordinate knows now what his boss is going to know tomorrow, he is in the same position that the gambler would like to be in if he knew which horse was going to win in a future race. The ST has set itself up through the use and control of intelligence data, both real and manufactured, to know now what its bosses are going to know later. This applies most significantly in such events as the McNamara report.

As anyone who has perceived the full significance of the routine described earlier will realize, the ST knows what the report of the Secretary of Defense is going to be even before he does, and therefore, before all the rest of official Washington does. This twenty-four to forty-eight hour lead-time of critical and most influential knowledge is a most valuable commodity. Many staffs who have no real responsibilities in the covert activities of this nation break their backs for a glimpse of what the ST is doing, and for this special privilege they pay one way or another.

At other times the Team will extract from a report such as has been described a few paragraphs that will be skillfully leaked to the press and to selected businessmen. Background briefings are held, most frequently in some quiet conference room in the New State Building or perhaps in the big executive dining room Allen Dulles had in the old "E" Street headquarters of the CIA; and there a sub-staff of the ST will pour over the language of a brief item designed especially for "Periscope" in *Newsweek*, or perhaps for its old favorite, Joe Alsop.

In any event, advance top-level information is a most valuable and saleable commodity. But nowhere is it more valuable than in the White House itself and in the offices of the Secretary of Defense and of the Director of Central Intelligence. McGeorge Bundy, Mike Forrestal, Joe Califano, Maxwell Taylor, and the others always looked good when they could sit down, calm and composed, with the President and with Rusk and McNamara, already knowing what was in the reports these men were pouring over page by page. McNamara would give one of his classic "fully charted" briefings of his trip, utilizing for his purpose the originals of the artwork in his report, and have the President and other Cabinet officers hanging on his every word—words he had been learning and rehearsing while he sped by jet from Honolulu. At the same time, the ST members were secure in their knowledge that they already knew every word that McNamara was going to say and that they had staff studies and Presidential messages already drafted to send to the Ambassador and the commanders in Indochina.

It may seem strange to readers of the Pentagon Papers to note how often a report from the chairman of the JCS to the Secretary of Defense would be followed the next day by one from the Secretary of Defense to the President—and then almost on the same day, by a lengthy message to the ambassador in Saigon. What may seem even more strange is that the reply from the ambassador would follow, with all of its detail, within twenty-four hours. This was not a miracle. This was preplanning by the ST. The whole thing was done at the same time, and even the reply from the ambassador had been anticipated by a closely guarded message via CIA channels to a CIA man on the embassy staff in Saigon, giving him the language to use for the ambassadors reply almost as soon as the President's wire arrived. The ST seldom left anything to chance, and since they had the means of the "Connecticut Yankee in King Arthur's Court," they made it a way of life to use it.

The Pentagon Papers reveal in the total listing of names of the principal writers of those papers a good compilation of key members of the ST at that time. However, it would be very misleading to accept this list as complete and meaningful for anything more than this one area of activity. Furthermore, some of the most influential members of the Team are not even mentioned in those pages. There were and are many men who are not in government who are prime movers of Secret Team activity.

Only one month after McNamara's report, General Maxwell D. Taylor, then Chairman of the JCS, kept the ball rolling with a report to Secretary McNamara, dated January 22, 1964. It is important to keep in mind that Maxwell Taylor was on the same trip to Saigon with McNamara that resulted in the October 2, 1963, report, the one that contained the "home by end of 1965" theme. Now, less than four months later, he was saying: "It would be unrealistic to believe that a complete suppression of the insurgency can take place in one or even two years." And further, "The United States must make plain to the enemy our determination to see the Vietnam campaign through to a favorable conclusion. To do this, we must prepare for whatever level of activity may be required and, being prepared, must then proceed to take actions as necessary to achieve our purposes surely and promptly."

"The JCS believe that our position in Cambodia, our attitude toward Laos, our actions in Thailand and our great effort in South Vietnam do not comprise a compatible and integrated policy for Southeast Asia. U.S. objectives in Southeast Asia cannot be achieved by either economic, political or military measures alone. All three fields must be integrated into a single, broad U.S. program for Southeast Asia."

Later, we shall deal in more detail with this new "military" line, which Taylor was here expounding. But while we are weighing these words, we should note that the U.S. military—more precisely, that part that was closely affiliated with the CIA (and by 1964, General Taylor must be considered to be among them)—was underscoring here in the United States as well as overseas the new political-social-economic role of the Army. This subject is only inferentially introduced in Taylor's report; but as we shall see later, it had become a dominant theme in the peacetime-operations Army procedure of this period.

At the same time it should be noted that Taylor, operating most certainly under the provisions set forth by President Kennedy in his National Security Action Memorandum #55 of June, 1961,[4] is strongly announcing his support of covert actions against North Vietnam. This would have been quite uncharacteristic and unthinkable in the Army before this time. It became Secret-Team-type doctrine, because the Team knew all too well that covert operations of sufficient size and volume could be exploited.

Like the carbon rods in a nuclear reactor, to raise or lower the level of "radioactivity" or to heat up a latent insurgency situation to the level desired, this has been done in Laos for fifteen or more years. The policies that have been used in Indochina create and generate

---

4. See clarification on pages 115 and 401.

more combat than they quench. It has been said that the Vietnamese war is one of "re-counter," the idea being that if you hit someone—even little, starving, terrorized, and homeless natives—long enough, they will eventually fight back with whatever bits of remaining strength they have. Thus, Taylor's following words take on certain special significance:

> It is our [JCS] conviction that if support of the insurgency from outside South Vietnam in terms of operational direction, personnel and material were stopped completely, the character of the war in South Vietnam would be substantially and favorably altered. Because of this conviction, we are wholly in favor of executing the covert actions against North Vietnam which you have recently proposed to the President. [These were the covert actions which the group chaired by General Krulak had developed.] We believe, however, that it would be idle to conclude that these efforts will have a decisive effect on the Communist determination to support the insurgency; and it is our view that we must therefore be prepared fully to undertake a much higher level of activity, not only for its beneficial tactical effect, but to make plain our resolution, both to our friends and to our enemies.

Following this statement, which like others was written by his special staff and by his CIA associates, General Taylor listed ten activities which he said the United States must make ready to conduct in Southeast Asia. One of these was to". . . commit U.S. forces as necessary in support of the combat action within South Vietnam." He added, "The past few months have disclosed that considerably higher levels of effort are demanded of us if U.S. objectives are to be attained."

In the inner chambers of the Government, where secret operations are cloaked in sufficient cover-story language to keep even the experts and top echelon leaders in a state of unreality, nothing ever more closely approached the "emperor's new clothes" syndrome than did the ST's work on Johnson, Rusk, McCone, and McNamara.

Townsend Hoopes, who spent years in the Pentagon in this awesome environment, wrote in the Washington *Post* of August 17, 1971, "The altered alignments in the Communist world were much clearer in 1964 than in 1960, making it, again in theory, easier for Johnson to take a fresh look. But the abrupt and tragic way in which he had come to the White House, the compulsions of the 1964 presidential campaign, and his own lack of a steady compass in foreign affairs (not to mention the powerful and nearly unanimous views of his inherited advisers) effectively ruled out a basic reappraisal of our national interests in Vietnam. Like each predecessor, Johnson decided, as one analyst put it, "that it would be inconvenient for him to lose South Vietnam this year."

There is a fine point to add to Mr. Hoopes' perceptions. Johnson not only did not make "a basic reappraisal of our national interests in Vietnam," but he did not check out the compass to assure himself that the Ship of State was on the same course that it had been sailing before he took the helm of office. He never took the time nor made the effort to check out the ST. He just took it for granted that it was on the same course after Kennedy's death as before. This was his first big oversight.

The point is subtle, and the change was at each turn slight; but the long-range course was being altered dynamically. Each report he received gave the semblance of normalcy, and each report was a reasonable part of the pattern with which he was somewhat familiar. No one would deny that Lyndon Johnson was not an intimate of Jack Kennedy's and that, especially in matters pertaining to Vietnam, he really did not know the Presidents mind. The fact that he had been to Vietnam may actually have been more of a cover story and a handicap for him than a view of reality.

Brainwashing was the business of the ST in South Vietnam. No less than Robert McNamara, Robert Kennedy, Vice-President Johnson, and John McCone were thoroughly indoctrinated on South Vietnam by hardheaded experts who thought nothing of sharpening the scenarios skillfully drawn for consumption by top-level officials. Allen W. Dulles meant it when he called his book *The Craft of Intelligence*. To him and his inner ring of confidants and paramilitary experts, big-time intelligence was craftily managed. As a result, these carefully drawn reports told the President that things were getting much worse in Southeast Asia and that there was a strong possibility of a Communist take-over of all of South Asia if South Vietnam and Laos and then Cambodia succumbed to the insurgency which, the Team said, was running rampant there.

After the reports and briefings of December 1963 and January 1964, it became evident that Johnson was giving way before the pressures of the CIA and the "military" who were working with the Agency.

It is essential that the term "military" be clarified for use throughout this book. Many military men are regularly assigned to the CIA, in their primary roles as intelligence experts, for their own experience and training and to flesh out areas where the Agency can use them. These are legitimate military assignments, and such men are openly identified with the CIA. There is another group of military men who are fully assigned to the Agency, meaning their pay and allowances are reimbursed to the parent service by the CIA, but they appear to be with regular military units or other normal assignments so that their assignment to the CIA will not be revealed to those unwitting of their real task.

These men are on cover assignments. Some of them are completely detached from the service for the period of their assignment although they will get promotions and other benefits similar to those of their contemporaries. Then there are other military personnel working with the CIA who are really Agency employees but who are permitted to wear the uniform and rank or grade of their Reserve or National Guard status. And lastly, there are other CIA personnel who for special reasons are permitted to assume the uniform or at least the identity of one of the military services, with rank as is necessary, even though they have no real service connection.

There are few of these latter individuals; but they do exist. It is also true that for certain practical purposes nearly all CIA personnel carry the identification of the Department of Defense or some other government agency in order that they will have simple cover for such things as credit cards and banking accounts so they will not have to reveal their employment with the CIA. This category is simply a technical expedient and is not intended in the first instance to be used for clandestine purposes.

This strong military bias of the Agency plays a very important part in the operations of the ST and will be discussed more fully in later chapters. It probably played an impressive role in the winning of President Johnson's mind soon after be took office. He no doubt, as did most others, looked to such men as General Maxwell Taylor, General Victor Krulak, General William Rosson, General Edward Lansdale, General William Peers, General Richard C. Stilwell, General William Dupuy, and many, many others as straight-line military officers. Although without question they all were military men, they all also had assignments of various types that made them effective CIA operators. By the very nature of their work, they worked with, for, and in support of the CIA. It was their first allegiance. Those mentioned above form but a brief list of the great number of senior officers in this category.

After these first reports of December 1963 and early 1964, the next round of Secret Team maneuvers was planned as they worked to up-grade the war. It became time for McNamara to bring things up to date with the White House. On March 16, 1964, he made a report to the President, "On Steps to Change the Trend of the War." This report was long and discursive. It even included the line, "Substantial reductions in the numbers of U.S. military training personnel should occur before the end of 1965." Notice how the words were put! This report had the ring of the old "home by the end of 1965" report of October 2, 1963, but with a significant difference. In October, Taylor and McNamara had said to Kennedy that it should be possible to withdraw the bulk of U S. personnel. The key word is "personnel," as opposed to the March 16 "military training personnel."

The Vietnam war has always been a most unusual one from the standpoint of its being a non-typical war. A very large number of U.S. personnel in this war were not military. There were thousands from other government agencies. There were tens of thousands of civilian workers of all kinds. The helicopter maintenance support alone required fantastic numbers of civilian maintenance personnel and contract workers. Kennedy knew this, and when he was told that "U.S. personnel" would be coming home, he knew that meant a comprehensive and meaningful number. However, when McNamara told

Johnson that "substantial reductions in . . . military training personnel" would take place, he was talking about a small slice of the pie.

Even if all of the training personnel came home, there would still be a lot of U.S. manpower there. The distinction was meaningful. It was brainwashing and misleading, and intentionally so. Lines such as this were added simply for flavoring. The ST writers would not expect the President to notice the difference. He would hear the words "reductions" and "personnel" only.

Meanwhile, the ST had a safety valve in their report in the event they had to account for this report at a later date, something they always planned for, but seldom, if ever, had to do. After all of the words, recent history of Indochina involvement, and some philosophizing continued in this lengthy McNamara report, the final paragraph held the meat of the proposition:

> 12. To prepare immediately to be in position on 72 hours notice to initiate the full range of Laotian and Cambodian "Border Control" actions beyond those authorized in Paragraph 11 above and the "Retaliatory Actions" against North Vietnam, and to be in a position on 30 days' notice to initiate the program of "Graduated Overt Military Pressure" against North Vietnam.

This was another big step forward on the way to inevitable escalation. It is one thing for a nation to plan for a clandestine operation with an agent or agents and to arrange for its success, or in the event of failure, to totally deny involvement. All such activities are planned in such a way that the nation taking the action may be able to disclaim plausibly to the entire world that it had anything to do with such an action. But the action above is serious international business, because at the very root of the plan is the intent to violate the sovereignty of another nation. Wars have been started by such events. When a nation feels that it must resort to clandestine activities, it does so with great caution and then only with agents who are specially prepared for such work. In no case, or in the very rarest cases, are members of the diplomatic service and of the uniformed military service ever used for such acts. Honor and honesty in the society of nations demand that the diplomatic corps and the military services be beyond reproach. The paragraph quoted above from McNamara's March 16 report not only proposed more or less routine covert activity against Laos, Cambodia, and North Vietnam, but it added that the United States should plan for "overt military pressure" against North Vietnam, thus carrying through the momentum of action initiated with his December 21, 1963, report. The die was cast. The Gulf of Tonkin incident occurred on August 4, 1964, and from that time on to the President's announcement of the massive build-up of forces, there could be no doubting the course laid out for the United States in Indochina.

This course was set by the winds of change as this Government responded to and reacted to various intelligence-data inputs from as far back as 1945. Vietnam was not so much a goal as it was a refuge and backlash of everything that had gone wrong in a quarter-century of clandestine activities. There can be no questioning the fact that Vietnam inherited some of the Korea leftovers; it inherited the Magsaysay team from the Philippines with its belief in another Robin-Hood-like Magsaysay in the person of Ngo Dinh Diem; it fell heir to the Indonesian shambles; it soaked up men and materials from the Tibetan campaign and from Laos in particular, and it inherited men and material, including a large number of specially modified aircraft, from the Bay of Pigs disaster. In its leadership it inherited men who had been in Greece in the late forties or during the Eisenhower era and who felt that they knew Communist insurgency when they saw it. The nation of South Vietnam had not existed as a nation before 1954, rather it was another country's piece of real estate. South Vietnam has never really been a nation. It has become the quagmire of things gone wrong during the past twenty-five years.

In the August 7, 1971, issue of *The New Republic*, the Asian scholar Eugene G. Windchy says, "What steered the nation into Vietnam was a series of tiny but powerful cabals." What he calls a sense of tiny but powerful conspiracies, this book puts all together as the actions of the Secret Team. That most valuable book by David Wise and Thomas B. Ross calls this power source "The Invisible Government," and in the chapter on the various intelligence organizations in the United States they use the term "Secret Elite."

The CIA did not begin as a Secret Team, as a "series of tiny but powerful cabals," as the "invisible government," or as members of the "secret elite." But before long it became a bit of all of these. President Truman was exactly right when he said that the CIA had been diverted from its original assignment. This diversion and the things that have happened as a result of it will be the subject of the remainder of this book.

CHAPTER 2

THE NATURE OF SECRET TEAM ACTIVITY: A CUBAN CASE STUDY

The call was from Miami and was placed to a covert CIA phone drop in Washington. It came from a Cuban underground contact point on the campus of the University of Miami. The control point there had just received a call from an undetermined location in Mexico. The call had been made by the pilot of a Cuban crew that had been lost and had made a forced landing. The crew was safe and the plane was intact . . . but in Mexico.

An old C-54, a former U.S. Air Force four-engine transport, had taken off the night before from the secret Cuban training base at Retalhuleu in Guatemala. It was flown by a Cuban crew, and their target had been a drop-zone in the Sierra Madre mountains of Cuba. Everything had gone wrong. The dropzone had been cleared and approved by Washington just a few hours before take-off yet, it had been hostile. Either intelligence had been bad or the Cuban ground reception party had been captured. The signals from the ground had been right, luring them in with confidence; but as soon as they began the drop, the whole mountainside had erupted with small arms fire. They had been ambushed, and they had been lucky to get down safely over the waves and back across the Caribbean.

Hours later, somewhere over Central America, in pre-dawn darkness they had circled over a heavy layer of clouds, watching their gas gauges, waiting for the sunrise, and hoping for a break in the clouds so they could let down. Fearful of the mountains and with their radio navigation equipment unreliable, they dared not let down until they had clear contact with the ground. At that point they cared little for all of the precautionary instructions of the Agency mission commander that had been given them during their briefing before they took off all they wanted to do was to find a safe place to land. They knew the plane was stateless; that it was unmarked and had no insignia. It did not even have a legal call sign. In fact, the big transport was very special. Although it looked like any other C-54 or DC-4, a trained observer would have noted those things, and that it had unusual radios, no engine decals, and no manufacturer's labels. It was "clean," a non-attributable air plane. It had been "sanitized" and was the pride of the clandestine operators' art.

It could have been flown anywhere in the world, and if it had been lost on some clandestine mission, the finder—whether he was Cuban, Congolese, or Russian—might have assumed that it had been operated by Americans, but he would not have been able to prove it. In other words, the U.S. Government, if required, could have plausibly disclaimed ownership of the plane and that it had had anything to do with the plane, its crew, and its cargo.

This plane had been on many flights along the Iron Curtain borders, on leaflet drops and on electronic intelligence missions. It had been used for paradrop missions in Greece and in Jordan. It had been to the Congo and had delivered "black" cargoes[1] to the Katangese

---

1. In Special Operations, black flights deliver black cargo into denied or unwitting areas. "Black" in this sense is usually synonymous with clandestine. A black cargo would not go through customs, USA or foreign. A black cargo, might be a defector from the communist world being flown to a safe house in the USA or other host country. If the black flight crossed the ocean, it would be known as a "deep water" flight. Clandestine shipments are made by all modes of transportation, including submarines and PT boats.

even while other U.S. Air Force C-130 aircraft were flying Congolese troops and supplies against the rebels. It had been to Clark Field near Manila, flying Tibetans to and from operational training sites. It had often been to the old World War II B-29 Superfortress bomber bases in Saipan where Southeast Asians were being trained in sabotage tactics and paramilitary civic action programs. But on this flight its crew had been Cuban.

A former Cuban airline pilot was at the controls, and one of his old co-pilots was with him. The Navigator had at one time trained with the Cuban Air Force; and the radioman, also a Cuban, had been trained at a U.S. Air Force school under cover as a member of a "Nicaraguan Training Mission." The crewmen were all natives of Cuba, and all were working with the CIA at that secret base that had been cut out of the open country of western Guatemala.

In keeping with clandestine operational procedures, the crew had been frisked before they got on the plane and had been given "sanitized" uniforms for the trip so that they would have no identification with them in the event they fell into enemy hands—in this case a somewhat meaningless precaution, but routine anyhow.

However, in typical old-school pilot fashion the pilot had written certain radio frequency numbers on his wrist with a ball-point pen, and some of those numbers were a code for the telephone number of the contact office in Miami.

Later that morning, after sunrise, they had flown further to the north seeking a clearing in the clouds through which may could descend. As soon as they found one, they let down into a broad valley and found a small, marked airfield. They landed, and skidded across the field into a nearby farm. The first thing they did was to look for a telephone. While they were placing that call, the airport manager and his apprentice came out to see what had happened. After a few moments of eavesdropping, the manager had all the information he needed. The old Mexican drew a gun and the crew was captured "somewhere" in Mexico. They were not heard from again until after their Cuban friends had attacked the beach at the Bay of Pigs, had been imprisoned by Castro, and ransomed by the United States. It was only after all of these events that the Mexicans released the crew and permitted them to return to Florida. However, their phone call had started some frantic work in Miami and in Washington.

The weather map had shown that the heavy cloud cover over Central America gave way to broken clouds further north in Mexico. The CIA called the Pentagon and asked for assistance, and a call was made to the air attaché in Mexico City. He inquired among his Mexican friends about a transport plane but learned nothing at first. Then, several days later, he heard a rumor that a large transport had made a forced landing at a very small southern airfield. He and a CIA man who worked in Mexico City under the cover of a cargo airline made a quick trip to that field. As they approached they saw the telltale marks of the skidding stop which had been made by the DC-4 in the fresh turf. The plane was gone. When they landed, the airport manager met them. He told them enough to confirm that the plane they were looking for had been there, that the Mexican air force had flown it away, and that this Mexican and his apprentice knew all there was to know about the incident.

Some time later, the attaché was invited to call upon Mexican air force headquarters. He learned that the Mexicans had looked this plane over carefully and did not want to keep it. However, the Mexicans added that they were sure the Americans would be willing to exchange this special plane for another just like it. Not long after that, the old black-flight DC-4 was returned to its operational base at Eglin Air Force Base in Florida. The CIA arranged for the Mexican air force to receive a good-as-new DC-4 from the U.S. Air Force, and far to the south an airport manager, his apprentice, and his son (the husband of the telephone operator who had heard the whole story too) all sported brand-new 1961 Ford Thunderbird automobiles from some unknown donor.

This true story is not really important except that it raises certain questions that will shake most Americans. For example: How does one government agency "buy" a U.S. Air Force transport aircraft, convert it to a civilian aircraft, and then give it as tribute to another country in exchange for one which was lost on a clandestine mission? Or, how does a government agency purchase three new 1961 Ford Thunderbird automobiles and deliver them to a remote site in Mexico and give them to some Mexicans? Who makes such decisions? Why Thunderbirds? Why pay tribute to Mexico for the airplane that quite obviously, once it had been identified, belonged to the United States? (Its very strangeness made it easier to identify if desired and harder to identify if disclaimed.) It would have been stateless only if the United States had disclaimed it. When the United States claimed it, why didn't this Government expect the Mexicans to give it back? Who decides such things? And how is all this done in total secrecy?

Then to the next level of questions. Who in the Government believes that once tribute is paid to another country such as Mexico the problem ends there? Does it not occur to these same officials that Mexicans speak to Guatemalans and to Nicaraguans and even to Vietnamese—and perhaps to Russians and Chinese as well? Who kids whom? Does the gift of a DC-4 close the case and really buy silence, or does it more likely escalate the problem? And then what does all of this behind-the-scenes duplicity do to foreign relations? Doesn't it raise some international eyebrows and make some people wonder who is running the foreign affairs of the United States in the first place? Isn't that exactly what Mr. Khrushchev wanted to know when he challenged Eisenhower either to reveal those who had sent the U-2 over Russia without the President's permission and authorization or to accept the blame himself, signifying that United States foreign policy included the authorization of covert operations?

If the Mexicans received tribute for one such mistake, would it be surprising to learn that the Indonesians had demanded even more tribute for a bigger mistake? Or when government leadership shifts back and forth as has happened several times in Laos, doesn't anyone stop to think about the tales that are told by those on both sides to their new "friends"? What are the Indians telling the Russians about us now in 1972 concerning our actions there in 1962? Or what have the Pakistanis been telling the Chinese concerning their participation in the former U-2 operations or in the Tibetan-support activities that had been launched from Pakistan? Doesn't all of this make it seem rather insincere and even hypocritical for some Americans to charge other Americans with security indiscretions when officials in the Government have been telling thousands of foreign people—officials and peons—that the United States has been playing the clandestine game to the hilt? How can anyone honestly charge Jack Anderson, *The New York Times*, The Washington *Post*, the Boston *Globe*, Daniel Ellsberg, or anyone else with serious violations of security when some of these same sacrosanct individuals who point the finger have themselves approved of such things as the payment of tribute for our clandestine indiscretions and misdeeds all over the world?

All of these questionable operations have begun from such small first steps. In the beginning of the Cuban exercise the CIA had made contact with the Ydigoras family in Guatemala for the use of a large tract of farmland for a training site and an airfield. This site was developed to include a full-sized airport, from which heavy transports, bombers, and training planes operated on a very heavy schedule. Although this site was remote, it was certainly not secret. The extent of the activity that took place there was such that it did not take long before there was no secrecy and no possibility for denial that something very special was taking place. The whole world knew that a major clandestine operation was under way and that the United States and Guatemala, at least, were involved. Who paid Guatemala for all of this? And was it paid to individuals or was it all paid to the Guatemalan Government? These questions give clues to some of the characteristics of the CIA and ST operations.

The ST members have become so powerful and ambitious that sometimes they no longer respect the basic fundamentals of their profession. As far back as 1948 the CIA had been given limited authority by the National Security Council (NSC) to carry out only those clandestine operations that the NSC directed. This authority is contained in a series of documents, the first of which was issued in the summer of 1948 and was called NSC 10/2. When the NSC granted this authority, it did so with the firm stipulation that any such special operation must be truly clandestine, that it must be performed in such a manner that if the exercise failed or was otherwise discovered, the U.S. Government would be able plausibly to disclaim its role in the operation, and further—what would seem most obvious, but was added for emphasis—that it must be truly secret and concealed.

These basic parameters, as established by the NSC, have never been officially retracted, although they have been badly abused by oversight. During the Truman and Eisenhower years "clandestine" meant clandestine, and the ability to disclaim the operation plausibly meant that, too. But as operations became more frequent and increased in size and scope, as they did against Castro in 1960 and 1961, the CIA became forgetful of these strictures upon its methods of operations. From time to time even Presidents have permitted a relaxation of their stringent application. The Pentagon Papers reveal how this doctrine had been disregarded especially with regard to the OPLAN-34, the so-called "covert" raids against Laos, Cambodia, and North Vietnam.

By 1961, the CIA had succeeded in building such a broad base within the bureaucracy of the U.S. Government that any meaningful reference to the CIA must take into consideration the existence of this vast infrastructure and must not be limited to the legal or "Table of Organization" CIA. Most references to the CIA and to the Secret Team's book are to that part of the CIA that is not under the Deputy Director of Intelligence.[2] He is responsible primarily

---

2. *DCI*—Director of Central intelligence; *DDCI* is his Deputy. below these men are three other Deputy Directors:
   DD/I—Deputy Director of Intelligence (responsible for the real and overt intelligence activity of the Agency.)
   DD/P—Deputy Director of Plans (responsible for the clandestine activity of the Agency. By far the largest and most complex portion of the Agency in the Special Operations part of the business.)
   DD/S—Deputy Director of Support (responsible for the logistics support. This is the most effective part of the Agency and makes the others look good.)
   (*DD/A*—Deputy Director of Administration—no longer a part of the Agency.)
   Note: To an Agency man DD/P can be used as an adjective, as in: "I'm going to Europe with some of the DD/S guys on that new DD/P project."
   The same applies with Divisions, Directorates, and Sections. The CIA is very loose about these things. For example: You can say something was done by Special Operations without ever having to say that it was a special operations division (there is no special operations division in the Agency).

for intelligence production and not for covert activity. By 1961, the non-intelligence, the clandestine, and the support sectors of the Agency had become so large and so predominant that they far outnumbered the professional band of intelligence specialists assigned to the DD/I both at home and abroad. By 1961, it had become apparent that the CIA played a split- personality role to suit its own purposes. It would speak of CIA reports which said one thing, when it would be doing exactly the opposite with its undercover, covert sections. This, too, becomes readily apparent to the diligent reader of the Pentagon Papers.

Lest the tremendous significance of such a change taking place within the U.S. Government be insufficiently regarded, consider the words of Arnold Toynbee, the eminent British historian and friend of the United States, as set forth in *The New York Times* of May 7, 1970:

> "To most Europeans, I guess, America now looks like the most dangerous country in the world. Since America is unquestionably the most powerful country, the transformation of America's image within the last thirty years is very frightening for Europeans. It is probably still more frightening for the great majority of the human race who are neither Europeans nor North Americans, but are Latin Americans, Asians and Africans. They, I imagine, feel even more insecure than we feel. They feel that, at any moment, America may intervene in their internal affairs with the same appalling consequences as have followed from American intervention in Southeast Asia."

For the world as a whole, the CIA has now become the bogey that Communism has been for America. Wherever there is trouble, violence, suffering, tragedy, the rest of us are now quick to suspect the CIA had a hand in it. Our phobia about the CIA is, no doubt, as fantastically excessive as America's phobia about world Communism; but in this case, too, there is just enough convincing guidance to make the phobia genuine. In fact, the roles of America and Russia have been reversed in the world's eyes. Today America has become the world's nightmare.

When an uncontrolled and perhaps uncontrollable team can flaunt the historic and traditional codes of civilization by disregarding the honor and sovereignty of other countries large and small, by intervening in the internal affairs of other countries for reasons real and contrived, the rest of the world does fear for its own welfare and for the future of this country. When President Eisenhower accepted the responsibility for the U-2 flights over the Soviet Union, no one would have questioned that he did this for correct and honorable reasons. National Aeronautics and Space Administrator (NASA) Keith Glennan had already made a public statement that the U-2 was operating out of Turkey as a NASA high-altitude, flight-research aircraft and had strayed over Russian territory inadvertently in high winds. Then, Nikita Khrushchev produced the wreckage of the U-2 deep in Russia near Sverdlovsk, it made a mockery of the NASA cover story; and when he produced the pilot alive and well, it demolished the rest of the plausible disclaimer. The CIA was caught without a plausible cover story, and the President had to choose. He could either discredit Allen Dulles and the CIA for operating that clandestine flight and a long series of flights without his knowledge, or he could, as Eisenhower did, stand up and take the blame himself on the basis that he knew of and had ordered the flights and was in complete control of everything done in the foreign arena by this Government. The latter choice would mean that the President of the United States is Commander in Chief during peacetime clandestine operations as he is in time of war. This is a totally new doctrine born of the vicissitudes of the Cold War.

Many have considered this a very noble stand on the part of President Eisenhower, and it was. However, this public admission by the Chief of State that he had directed clandestine operations within another state is exactly the type of thing that reduces the prestige and credibility of United States in the family of nations to the condition described by Arnold Toynbee. Interference in the internal affairs of one nation by another is an unpardonable violation of international law and custom.

The entire Bay of Pigs build-up and operation went much further in flaunting this international code of ethics. At least the U-2 operation on a worldwide scale had been managed in such a manner that the chances for success were great. That the flights were operated in small units with great secrecy and the stipulation that they be strictly clandestine and plausibly disclaimable in the event of failure was not outwardly flaunted until, perhaps, the Gary Powers flight. But the Cuban program was otherwise.

By the time Cuban operations had been expanded to the point that they had become the beginnings of the bay of Pigs operation, activity of all kinds had been discovered and compromised by the press of the world. There were no more secrets. The participation and support of the United States was known to be taking place in Puerto Rico, Panama, Guatemala, and Nicaragua, in addition to some unscheduled action in Mexico. Yet the ST continued to launch an increasing number of special operations without regard for real secrecy.

There was not only a breakdown in the traditional ethics of international relations but there was also a serious degradation of the usual high standard of technical operational methods within the Government. The flights from Guatemala themselves were not tactically sound nor were they politically effective. Most of these flights not only failed miserably to accomplish what the CIA thought they would do, i.e., put in place underground cadres of guerrillas and provide equipment and communications material for other underground groups in Cuba; but as a result of their amateurism and failures, they played into the hands of Castro. They never did become a rallying point for anti-Castroites. On the contrary, they exposed and compromised them and led to many unnecessary firing-squad deaths. The flight paths, by their crossing and recrossing, pinpointed and exposed ground-reception parties, which were mopped up by Castro's troops; in other cases, aircraft were lured over drop-sites that proved to be ambushes. The whole series of operations exposed the weaknesses of CIA's tactical capacity. The CIA cannot properly direct large operations. It has led many small ones successfully; but has failed miserably in a number of large ones.

An important oversight inherent in such activity was mentioned by David Wise and Thomas B. Ross in their book, *The Invisible Government*. They reported The Chiefs (U.S. Joint Chiefs of Staff) were told that the invasion was not a Pentagon operation and that they could give advice only when called upon. Because of the secrecy involved, they were not allowed to take their staffs into their confidence; this of course, cut down on their overall effectiveness.

This was only a part of the story. The Chiefs were told to keep hands off, yet the Agency was operating down through all services to the tactical level, taking supplies, arranging training, utilizing all forms of transportation. However, few if any military personnel even knew enough of what was really going on to give proper advice had they been asked. This is one of the greatest weaknesses of the ST's classified method of operation.

Because the ST acts in response to intelligence-data inputs, it does not operate in compliance with or in support of a plan or policy. It creates an umbrella or catch-all policy such as "anti-Communism," then declares that all of its operations are anti-Communist, and attempts to justify what it does solely on that basis. To clarify by example:

A Cuban reported to another Cuban who was in touch with a CIA contact man in Miami that he had friends back in Cuba who were willing to blow up a major sugar refinery, but they had no munitions or other equipment necessary to do this. The CIA Cuban reported this to his contact. A meeting was arranged right away in a "safe" house—for example, in the Latin American Geological Survey offices somewhere on the campus of the University of Miami. The first Cuban showed on a map where his friends were and explained what they planned to do. The CIA contact man proposed that the first thing to do would be to establish contact with them and then to place a clandestine radio with them. To test the zeal and veracity of the informant, it was suggested that this be done by putting him ashore at night near the target. He agreed, on the assurance that he would be picked up the next night. He was taught how to use the clandestine radio and was provided with a special kit of munitions. He was put over the beach and directed to bring one Cuban out with him for further training. All went well to that point. At no time in this almost automatic-response process did anyone in the CIA ask, "Why are we doing this?" The simple Pavlovian animal-instinct to go ahead and do it because it was an anti-Castro move was all the agents needed at this stage of activity.

But this is where it always starts. Of course, the ST members would have right on their side in their almost religious missionary zeal to do good. The first agent would not only have heard that the Cubans planned to blow up the sugar refinery; but they would have flavored this with ideas of the injustice there and with accounts of the brutality of Castro's police. And they would have pledged that the reason they wanted to kill Castro was that they want to bring democracy to their homeland and to all Cuban people.

The "fun and games" must always be founded upon sanctimonious grounds. At the same time lip service is paid to do-gooder causes, there is scarcely ever any practical consideration of whether or not such an action, or those that will follow whether the initial action succeeds or fails, are really in the best interests of the United States.

The exfiltrated Cuban was given rudimentary demolition training at a remote site in Florida and was taught to use signal lights and panels, as well as the radio. Less than a week later, he was back in Cuba at work with his neighbors in the sugar refinery gang.

Although everything seemed to have gone well, these inexperienced though patriotic Cubans had no understanding of the Castro operated, Communist-perfected block system that was in effect in Cuba and that blanketed the entire island. No one in the CIA had warned them about this, if the thought had ever crossed their minds. As soon as the first Cuban had been exfiltrated, his absence was duly noted by the "system." He had not appeared for work at the refinery, but not a word was said there. A teacher at school was tipped off to make a discreet inquiry of the man's child: "Could your father come to school to see your pretty drawings?" "Well no, teacher, you see my father is not feeling well. He's sick." Then a state medical technician stopped by his home and asked to see the father "because it has been reported he is sick." The mother explained that he was not really sick; it was his uncle in Santiago who was sick, and he had gone to see the uncle. So the net was drawn tighter. Even before he had been returned to Cuba, a Castro agent had been infiltrated into the refinery work crew, and by the time the patriot returned, Castro's men were ready. They waited, alert. They listened to all of the plans. Perhaps they joined in encouraging the plans.

Then, on the night of the raid on the refinery everything went wrong. The whole cabal had been rounded up, and in no more time than it took for the radio operator to flash an emergency signal to Miami, it was all over. The reaction to the first information input by that first CIA agent had doomed those men to death, and their families and friends to lives of misery. Castro's control, rather than being weakened, had been strengthened by the brutal elimination of a few more men of blind courage and the example of that same fate for others who might wish to conspire with the Yankees.

In this example, which is a true case, if the attack had been successful, what good would it have done? Do such random bits of vandalism and sabotage actually further the foreign policy goals of the United States? Is this kind of anti-Castroism really pro-American? The very little harm to Castro and his Government, if any, that might possibly have been done, could not conceivably generate enough benefit to the United States ever to compensate for the loss this country suffers when such activities fail, as they so often do. This brings to mind the prophetic words from the *Rubáiyát* of Omar Khayyam:

> I wonder often what the Vintners buy
> One half so precious as the stuff they sell.

Nevertheless, the ST takes even such a gross failure as a challenge. They interpret it as some sort of Castroite dare, and they leap into action again to gamble with other men's lives. In Miami and in Washington the failure of this first raid was only the beginning. Word was flashed to CIA that a Castro attack had wiped out an anti-Communist underground cell. Instead of leaving the blown operation at that, the CIA readied the next step. No mention was made of how the initial contact was begun nor of the agent-assisted first attempt, which was the provocation to Castro. Instead, it was made to look as though Castro's attack upon the people was entirely unprovoked except by their anti-Communism.

As the next level of reaction, the CIA suggested an attack over the beach against that sugar refinery in reprisal for Castro's so-called "brutal attack upon the anti-Communist Cubans." It would be added as part of the "line" that one of the reasons for this next attack would be to show "the Cuban people that the United States was right behind them." A briefing along these lines was prepared and delivered to the Special Group of the NSC as much for intragovernmental public relations and flag-waving as for the approval the CIA felt it should get for this covert operation which was expected to be closely supported by Americans. In this manner small clandestine operations escalate, even though there may have been no real foreign policy guideline for such courses of action.

The CIA selected a team of Cubans from one of the major training sites in the United States or Central America and trained and equipped them for the major reprisal raid against the Castro provocation against innocent Cubans. The U.S. Navy was requested to provide offshore assistance limited to action in international waters. The Navy would launch and recover a small, fast boat which would make the actual landing. A date during the dark phase of the moon was picked, the weather checked, and the small boat with the special Cuban team aboard was launched. They were crack demolitions experts, familiar with the Navy SEAL team method of high-speed operation. They made a successful landing and approached the refinery. The block system was already alerted and had been waiting. Sentry dogs picked up the men as they moved ashore, and the whole team was wiped out. Their rafts were found hidden on the beach, and when the sentry boat returned for the preplanned recovery, the correct light signals, beaten from the team by Castro's experts, lured the fast boat near the beach into an ambush. In the sky above, Castro's planes, alerted to the position off shore, observed the waiting U.S. Navy vessel and confirmed that this action had official U.S. Government support.

Again, things did not stop there. The challenge was greater.

Americans had been involved closely in that activity. The urge to outwit and to whip Castro was strong. The next round of attacks was to be even greater effort, until the ultimate invasion at the Pay of Pigs. This type of scenario happened many times and in varying target areas and with new characters and new supporting casts. Some of them were successful to the extent that the teams participating accomplished their assigned tasks, or said they did, and returned safely. Others were lost, as this first one was. And in every case it may be certain that success or failure resulted in massive punitive action against the local population. It wasn't long before all Cubans prayed that they would not be the "lucky and fortunate anti-Communists" selected by the benevolent Americans for the next anti-Castro strike.

The CIA's greatest strength derives from its ability to activate various parts of the U.S. Government, usually the Defense Department, with minor inputs designed to create reaction. It finds a minor fact, which it interprets and evaluates to be Communist inspired, or inspired by some other favorite enemy (Trujillo or De Gaulle), then it feeds this item into the White House and to Defense, where a response re-action takes place predictably and automatically. To carry this to the next level, the CIA, by utilizing its clandestine facilities, can stir up the action it wants for further use in turn to stir up a re-action response within the U.S. Government structure. Although such actions and re-actions usually begin on a very small scale, they escalate rapidly as in Indonesia, Tibet and Greece. (They went completely out of control in Southeast Asia.)

It is the type of game played by the clandestine operator. He sets up the scene by declaring in many ways and over a long period of time that Communism is the general enemy and that the enemy is about to strike or has begun a subversive insurgency campaign in a third country. Then the clandestine operator prepares the stage by launching a very minor and very secret, provocative attack of a kind that is bound to bring open reprisal. These secret attacks, which may have been made by third parties or by stateless mercenaries whose materials were supplied secretly by the CIA, will undoubtedly create reaction which in turn is observed in the United States. (This technique was developed to a high art in the Philippines during the early Magsaysay build-up to the point where the Huks were actually some of Magsaysay's own troops disguised and set upon the unwary village in the grand manner of a Cecil B. De Mille production.)

The next step is to declare the enemy's act one of "aggression" or "subversive insurgency," and then the next part of the game is activated by the CIA. This part of the operation will be briefed to the NSC Special Group, and it will include, at some point, Americans in support. So it will go, as high and as mighty as the situation and authorities will allow. It is not a new game. It was practiced, albeit amateurishly and uncertainly, in Greece during the late forties, and it was raised to a high state of art under Walt Rostow and McGeorge Bundy against North Vietnam, to set the pattern for the Gulf of Tonkin attacks. In fact, a number of the leading actors in the cast of key characters in the greatest scenario of them all, "The War in Vietnam," received the earliest training in the Greek campaign of the forties. All of the mystery surrounding those actions was unveiled in the Pentagon Papers with the revelation of such things as the covert OPLAN-34.

Operations arising in this manner and from such sources are, unfortunately, frequently the result of the endeavors of the overambitious, the irresponsible, and the ignorant. They are often enmeshed with and enhanced by the concealed drives of the special interest groups like the Marines who wanted a share of Vietnam in 1964, the general-contractor interests who wanted to dig a big hole in the shore and call it "Cam Ranh Bay," the Special Forces Green Berets who wanted to resurrect the doughboy, and many others who simply wanted to sell billions of dollars worth of armaments. Such operations are carried out by those who either do not care about the results or who do not see far enough ahead to understand the consequences of what they are doing.

This is a delicate subject and needs much understanding. Many innocent and totally loyal men become involved in these activities; but the trouble is that they come upon the scene after the first provocations have been made, and they are generally unaware of them. An allowance must be made for the fact that the provocation can come from either side. Neither side is all right or all wrong. But the fact remains that most of the men who become involved in these activities do so after there has already been some clandestine exchange. They are trying to correct what they believe has been a serious abuse. They do not know where the real action began; to put it simply, they don't know whether they came in on the first or the second retaliation strike. Very few would ever be party to striking first in any event. So the first strike takes place in deep secrecy. No one knows this hidden key fact. This is a fundamental game of the ST.

They have this power because they control secrecy and secret intelligence and because they have the ability to take advantage of the most modern communications system in the world, of global transportation systems, of quantities of weapons of all kinds, of a worldwide U.S. military supporting base structure. They can use the finest intelligence system in the world, and most importantly, they are able to operate under the canopy of an ever-present "enemy" called "Communism." And then, to top all of this, there is the fact that the CIA has assumed the right to generate and direct secret operations.

When we stop and think what the real struggle is and what we have been doing, we are faced with the stark realization that what has been going on is not anti-Communist, nor is it pro-American. It is more truthfully exactly what those wise and wily chess players in the Kremlin have hoped we would do. They have been the beneficiaries of our own defense-oriented, reaction prompted, intelligence-duped Pavlovian self-destruction. How can anyone justify the fact that the United States has lost fifty-five thousand men in Indochina and that the Russians have lost none and then call that anti-Communist—or worse yet, pro-American?

How can anyone note that we have poured more than $200 billion into Indochina since 1945 and that the Kremlin may have put up somewhere between $3 and $5 billion as their ante to keep the game going, and then call that tragic ratio anti-Communist and pro-American? How can anyone believe that after more than twenty-five years of clandestine and overt engagement in Indochina that finds ourselves wasted and demoralized and precariously degraded in the eyes of much of the world, including our friends, we have accomplished anything that is really anti-Communist and pro-American? What do words have to mean and what do events have to prove to wake us all up to the fact that pro-American actions are those that strengthen this country and that anti-Communist actions are those that weaken Communism.

It certainly bothers the Kremlin not at all to see Americans dying in Asia and to see Asians dying at the hands of the Americans.

There are tens of thousands of loyal, dedicated, and experienced men in the DOD, both military and civilian, who have the type of experience it takes to make an operation effective. In matters of tactics and logistics there are few men in the world who know more about the subject than they do. However, the ST operates behind such a shield of secrecy that they keep facts of what they are doing from these experts as well as from the enemy. As a result, all of these people who could help are left out. The very men who by their experience and ability could make these operations succeed, or who would have the good sense to say that they have no hope of success, are ignored and excluded from participation at the very time when they are needed the most. Once these minor actions are set in motion on the basis that they are anti-Communist, whether they succeed or fail they escalate unless specifically halted by top-echelon authority, and then the whole pattern of events is locked in as anti-Communist whether or not this really is so. Furthermore, these very difficult operations are left in the hands of the inexperienced, the irresponsible, and the ignorant.

Whenever an operation grows to the extent that the Bay of Pigs project did, the President and at least the NSC must insist that the finest men in the country be brought in to assist with the planning, the tactical details, and the essential logistics, and that these men should have the right to veto the project if need be, not just to remain silent, as has happened in the case of men as high as the chairman of the Joint Chiefs of Staff. Such silence even in the face of the CIA[3] is inexcusable, even though the men involved in stating their case might be fired, as happened to one of the military chiefs after the Cuban rocket crisis of 1962.

---

3. If a military chief of staff did disagree so deeply with a plan briefed to him by the CIA that he decided to discuss his views with others, it is more than likely the CIA would charge him with a security violation or withdraw his clearance, or both. The Agency would attack him on security grounds, not on substantive grounds or on the merits of the case.

Everyone understands that a certain amount of secrecy, used properly and applied with an eye to the impact which the normal erosion of time plays on events, is essential. However, when secrecy becomes a means of existence itself, when operations take place that never should have been permitted had they been fully revealed, when operations take place that grow out of all proportion to the action originally proposed and briefed to higher authority, and when all of this is veiled in unnecessary secrecy applied within the U.S. Government and against some of the people whose assigned responsibilities would most qualify them to know what was going on, then this type of secrecy is totally wrong and leads to the ghastly and insidious situation that has been quite honestly and accurately described above by Arnold Toynbee. And lest there be those who wish to brush aside Toynbee as an old meddler, let us recall the wise words of Harry S. Truman when he wrote that the, "CIA is being interpreted as a symbol of sinister and mysterious foreign intrigue and a subject for cold war enemy propaganda."

When one of our own Presidents feels that he must warn that the CIA, which he created, has become a tool of enemy propaganda against the United States, it is time to underscore that things are not as they should be.

The very fact that the CIA would not allow the Joint Chiefs of Staff to take their staffs into their confidence regarding the Cuban invasion is one of the deepest problems such an *ad hoc* type of operation creates. This is a two-edged problem, however. No chairman of the JCS, especially not the very experienced and able Lyman L. Lemnitzer, should ever have permitted such a thing to have happened. If what Wise and Ross wrote is true—and we don't question it—and if it was known to the chairman of the JCS that he could not use his experienced staff as they have stated it, then it certainly must have been the duty of that chairman to make this known to the Secretary of Defense Robert S. McNamara, and to President Kennedy. The law gives him that right and it gives him that duty. The chairman is quite properly in the position to take such matters to the President, and he could at any time have done so. Why didn't he?

It would seem to have been an easy solution, but as with other things in this confusing area, it was not that simple. For one thing, there was so much he did not know about the total plan. If he knew the whole operation and then did not speak to the President, that would be one thing: but if he knew only fragments of the plan and if he had been told by his higher authority, namely the Secretary of Defense and the President that an invasion was not contemplated, then it would be an entirely different matter. It should be recalled that early Cuban action began during the Eisenhower Administration and that these early projects did not involve an invasion. In fact, all of the Eisenhower-era schemes were extremely modest when it came to actions against Cuban soil and property.

Furthermore, President Eisenhower, having been sorely hurt by the U-2 affair and all that it did to his plans for a summit conference and a final peace crusade, had positively directed that overflights and clandestine operations be curtailed. He did not want the next administration to inherit anything in that category from his regime.

However, immediately following the election of John F. Kennedy things began to move; stalled activities began to stir. This all took place very secretly and most certainly without instructions or approval from the President and his Secretary of State Christian Herter and Defense Secretary Thomas Gates. It was not unknown to the Secretary of Defense and to his deputy; but the extent of their knowledge may have been unclear, since they had no reason to believe that such things had been rekindled without Presidential direction. (We shall see later the language of the law involved and the distinction between the terms, "by direction" and "with approval.")

As a result of these unusual events it was not until the middle of January 1961 that the chairman of the JCS heard his first reasonably accurate and complete briefing of what the CIA was contemplating on the shores of Cuba. This was a strange time for such a briefing, because in less than a week the Secretary of Defense would have departed and a new one would have taken office, and in that same week the Eisenhower team would have left and John F. Kennedy would have become President. Therefore, even if the chairman had seen fit to carry this information to the Secretary of Defense and to the President, he could scarcely have expected either of them to have been in a position to have done much about it just at that time.

This business of the exploitation of the right moment by the ST is interesting and has been quite apparent in other situations. We have earlier discussed the crucial ninety-day period just before and after the assassination of President Kennedy. This was another such time.

In the Bay of Pigs project the Secretary of Defense or his deputy was briefed almost daily. Furthermore, the same briefing that was given to them would usually be given to the chairman of the JCS or to his executive officer. However, these briefings were piecemeal, arising from events day by day and not from a plan, and they were often colored and fragmented by cover-story inserts. In retrospect, the view of the Bay of Pigs which a man like General Lemnitzer or Robert McNamara[4] had was something like what would happen if someone showed a long movie to them a few frames at a time each day. As a result of this technique, who can blame a busy Secretary of Defense or Chairman if he is not able to piece all of these things together to find the central theme or plot.

This may sound unreal, but in the helter-skelter of activity in official Washington this is exactly what happens, especially with secret operations.

When an operation begins as a minor action, as did the first steps of the Cuban activity, no one knows what may evolve. At that point, with only tenuous bits of information, it seemed ridiculous to take each item to the President, the Secretary of State, and Secretary of Defense for their edification and approval. Yet, because clandestine affairs must be so closely held and because of the limits of the need-to-know restrictions, this is what happened. These busy men received the minor briefings along with the major ones. It became a question of either tell them or tell no one. Thus, as each day's moves

---

4. To add to this confusion, Mr. Thomas Gates was Secretary of Defense and Mr. James Douglas his deputy until January 20, 1961 (Kennedy's inauguration, and then Mr. Robert McNamara and Mr. Roswell Gilpatric followed them. Mr. Douglas told the author on January 19 at 4:30 p.m. that there had been no transition briefing between them.

occurred, the CIA and the Focal Point Offices agreed either to tell no one or to tell only the top men. This decision did nothing to overcome the fact that these top men were getting the story piecemeal.

Later, there were some relatively major steps, such as planned over-the-beach sorties involving the U.S. Navy in offshore support of CIA and Cuban saboteurs. Only then was the Secretary of Defense told that the CIA was going to put some men into Cuba to blow up a refinery the following night. Such briefings were complete with charts, maps, and pictures from U-2s or other such sources. If the Secretary of Defense questioned any part of the plan with respect to approval, the briefer would say, for example, "This is all part of the 'training and arming authority' for Cuban exiles that was approved by the NSC 5412/2 committee on March 17, 1960." The usual reply at that point from the Secretary would be, "O.K., but be sure Lemnitzer and Burke [Admiral Arleigh Burke, former Chief of Naval Operations] know about it." Then the mission would be ordered into action. By this process, such missions were not so much approved as they were not specifically disapproved.

The ST knew that it could use and depend upon Allen Dulles to gain approval for the big steps along the way by having him get an O.K. for an overall amorphous project, such as "training and arming exile Cubans." Then they could take it from there bit by bit. From that time on, everything they did in conjunction with the Cubans was to be attributed to that initial blanket approval. Their control over all events by means of secrecy kept anyone else from knowing the whole plan. Most of the time they did not really have any plan anyhow. Each event was derived from an earlier one or from a new bit of intelligence data input.

The Air Force, for example, protested the utilization of active-duty personnel on a full-scale basis in Guatemala, but did agree to permit aircraft and crews to fly in and out of Guatemala regularly with supplies and to deliver Cubans there. The Air Force was aware of the uncertain condition of the Ydigoras Government then precariously in power and did not want to have its personnel "sheep-dipped" (a cover category which meant that they would be non-attributable to the Air Force and thence technically stateless in Guatemala).

The Air Force held out for official accreditation of its own men to the U.S. Ambassador in Guatemala before it would permit them to remain at the Cuban/Guatemalan base. It received a signed agreement from the Department of State acknowledging the cover status of its men as "civilians" while on duty in Guatemala. (The State Department does not like to do this, because it automatically includes that department in the clandestine game.) These men then lived at the training base at Retalhuleu and trained Cubans to fly the C-46, C-54 (DC-4), and the combat-ready B-26 medium bomber. There were from eight to sixteen World War II B-26s at Retalhuleu. By Latin American standards this was the equivalent of a major air force.

As the Air Force had suspected, there was an attempt to overthrow Ydigoras. At first the coup group appeared to be victorious. Then the CIA and Air Force men realized that if the rebels took over the government, they and everyone else at Retalhuleu would become hostages of the rebel government and might even end up in Cuban prison camps. They were in a desperate position. Their choice was either to fly back to Florida and leave the Cubans, or to fight. The Air Force pilots were all combat veterans of the Korean War. They chose to fight. They got target information from loyal Guatemalans who flew with them to Guatemala City, where they bombed and strafed the rebel headquarters. Caught completely by surprise, and defenseless against this unexpected force, the rebels surrendered. Troops loyal to Ydigoras, and others who swung back to him in the face of this great show of power, cleaned up the remainder of the opposition, and the rebellion collapsed. Ydigoras was back in power, with Yankee help born of desperation. This was the only victory of the invasion task force.

Here again, the CIA had gotten in over its head. If that force of Americans, Filipinos, and Cubans who were at Retalhuleu, along with all of their equipment, had been captured by the rebels, their ransom—like that exacted quietly by the Mexicans of the downed DC-4—would have been stupendous. As it was, the United States had to pay heavily for the invasion's failure in other ways.

At Puerto Cabezas in Nicaragua the CIA had gathered all the clandestine aircraft and considerable quantities of supplies and ammunition to support the invasion. Many of these aircraft were lost to Castro's jets; but vast amounts of equipment and some of the planes remained. With the collapse of the invasion, this material was unused. The U.S. pilots returned to Florida with a few planes. Later, the CIA asked the Army and Air Force mission personnel in Nicaragua to gather up and return all of this equipment. These officers were told by the Nicaraguans very politely and firmly that there was not a thing left at Puerto Cabezas. Since it was all black cargo, it was stateless and it was title-less. The United States never got any of it back. And this was only a fraction of the loss.

All Latin American countries keep a very close eye on the apportionment of U.S. military aircraft, ships, and other material made available to other Latin American states. The formula for the balance of forces is very complex, and this arrangement is a most delicate issue.

Other nations soon observed that Nicaragua had been given a large force-supplement of B-26s and C-46s. The B-26s were specially modified and carried much more firepower per aircraft than those that had been given to other Latin American nations. The other military supplies, guns, rockets, and mountains of ammunition were also noted. The Nicaraguan Government would not reveal how it obtained this unscheduled largesse and the U.S. Government could not. The other governments guessed, and no doubt knew; but they too played the game. They just kept the pressure on.

Needless to say, the U.S. Government had to make similar equipment available to a number of Latin American countries. The cost of all of this, plus the logistics support of this equipment, which goes on year after year, is another of the many high cost-factors that should be added to the total cost of the Bay of Pigs fiasco. Again, because of security—secrecy from Americans, not from the enemy—these facts have remained undeclared, along with so many others over the years.

Early in 1960, President Eisenhower had authorized the secret training and arming of Cuban exiles in the United States. Thousands of able-bodied Cubans had fled their homeland, and many of them were dedicated to fighting their way back in and throwing Castro out.

Eisenhower's approval was very general and nonspecific; it in no way contemplated anything like the invasion. It was understood that any special operation which would involve Cuba, planned at any time, would have to be cleared by the DCI in accordance with existing directives. This meant presenting the operation to Special Group 5412/2.

In what appeared to the DOD as a separate and certainly inconspicuous action, the CIA began to utilize a portion of Ft. Gulick, a de-activated U.S. Army base in Panama. Gradually, a group of Cubans, identified in Panama only as Latin American trainees in a Military Assistance Program (MAP), began to increase in size and activity there. The CIA soon found that this burgeoning camp needed military doctors. In accordance with an agreement between the CIA and the DOD, the Agency asked the Army for three doctors. At that time the Army had a shortage of doctors, so it turned down the request for support from the CIA. Then the Navy was asked; it too turned down the request, on the basis that Navy doctors on an Army post would be conspicuous and would not fit into the cover story. The CIA did not need flight surgeons; so it did not ask the Air Force for doctors.

With these refusals in hand, the CIA made a direct appeal to the office of the Secretary of Defense and won support for its request. This was the very first covert action in the long chain of events that ended in the invasion of the beach at the Bay of Pigs on April 17, 1961. At the time of the request for these doctors, no one anywhere in the Government of the United States ever dreamed that the little mound that was being built would ever become that mountainous disaster which finally resulted. It is characteristic to note that the CIA's request was honored and then directed from the Office of the Secretary of Defense. At that top echelon the Office of Special Operations acted as the liaison between the CIA and the DOD. What most people in Defense were totally unaware of was that in the very office that was supposed to serve the military departments and shield them from promiscuous requests, there were concealed and harbored some of the most effective agents the CIA has ever had. Their approval of CIA requests was assured. The amazing fact was that their cover was so good that they could then turn right around and write orders directing the service concerned to comply with the request.

There may have been some mention of the end-use of these doctors for the Cuban training program. But if there was any mention, it would have meant little or nothing to those who had not been briefed.

The Secretary of Defense and the chairman heard many more such requests during the next twelve months, but the complexities of the veil of secrecy woven by the Secret Team around the project was such that no one ever saw the whole plan. The use of the control device of need-to-know classification made this possible. As this control is generally practiced, the CIA accepts that a group of men have "the clearances" after a very thorough review by its own resources and, as requested, those of the FBI.

Always, in the case of CIA work, this clearance begins at the top secret level. Beyond this, men are cleared for individual areas of information. A man may have a top secret clearance and a "North Side"[5] clearance, meaning that he may be given both classifications of information. However, those in control of North Side may decide arbitrarily that certain men may not have some of the information even though they have the necessary clearance. The control team simply states that those men do not have a need to know, and from that time on, unless they are reinstated, they are excluded from all, or part of the project. There are, of course, some sensible and reasonable reasons for such practices; but that is not what is important here. The fact is that this exclusionary process is used as a tool, arbitrarily.

One way to make sure that there is little opposition to a proposed activity is to exclude possible opponents on the basis of lack of need-to-know. Thus, even though men are in high-ranking, policy-making jobs and have the appropriate top secret and other special clearances, they may be kept in the dark about ST plans, and they will never know it—at least not for a while. Thus Adlai

---

5. A hypothetical name in this instance. Such code names are given in great numbers to all operations and even to various phases or segments of classified operations.

Stevenson, Ambassador to the United Nations at the time of the Bay of Pigs, was not informed about the projected plans until the very last minute, when rumors and news releases appearing in *The New York Times* were being spread everywhere. Even then, Tracy Barnes, the CIA man sent to brief Stevenson, gave a vague and incomplete picture of the operation.

The CIA could, if pressed, prove that the OSD and the JCS had been briefed almost daily from early 1960 until the very day of the invasion. But in spite of this kind of bit-by-bit briefing, it was not until just before John Kennedy's inauguration in late January 1961 that the JCS got any kind of a reasonably thorough briefing. By that time it was much too late. The ST had strong armed the early Eisenhower authorization of the training and arming of Cubans into an invasion of a foreign country, during the "lame duck" period of his administration.

Need-to-know control can also be bent in the other direction in order to secure the support of potential allies and further those allies' careers. Members of the Team who strongly favored the election of John F. Kennedy over Richard Nixon played a very special role in the 1960 election campaign. Nixon presided over the NSC and therefore knew in detail the plans that were intended to have been carried out under the earlier Eisenhower authorization. For one thing, he knew that such authorization did not include anything like the invasion of a foreign country. At the same time it was assumed that Senator Kennedy, as an outsider, did not know those highly classified details. However, he did know. In his book, *Six Crises*, Nixon wrote that Kennedy was told about the invasion by Allen Dulles during the traditional CIA briefing for candidates. But there was more than that to the story, too, it appears.

A former staff member from the OSD recollects that during the summer of 1960 he was sent to the Senate Office Building to pick up and escort to the Pentagon four Cuban exile leaders, among them one of the future commanders of the Bay of Pigs invasion forces, who had been meeting with the then-Senator Kennedy. Those men— Manuel Artime Buesa, Jose Miro Cordona (first Premier of Cuba under Castro), Manuel Antonio de Varona (former Premier of Cuba before the Batista regime) and the fourth man, who may have been

Aureliano Sanchez Arango (former Foreign Minister of Cuba)—were all supposed to be under special security wraps. They certainly were not expected to be exposed to members of Congress, least of all to a Senator who was close to being nominated as the Democratic flagbearer. However, certain CIA officials had introduced them to Kennedy, thus making sure that he knew as much about the plans they were contemplating as did Nixon. In fact, Kennedy may have learned more than Nixon as the result of this personal meeting—an opportunity Nixon did not have—with the Cuban refugee front and with its American secret sponsors.

Throughout this period in 1960, Eisenhower had directed that the Cuban exiles' training and arming be kept at a low level. He felt that he should not bequeath to the incoming administration, whether Republican or Democratic, any such clandestine operations, small as they were under the limited proposal which he had approved. As a result, any plans for expansion of Cuban activities were made to appear by the ST to be the Cubans' alone. The CIA carefully saw to it that the Cubans had the means to travel to and visit such activist headquarters as the American Legion convention and other avowedly anti-Castro strongholds. As the political campaign picked up momentum so did the Cuban exiles' activities, with John Kennedy playing a strong, quiet role on their behalf. His support further endeared him to the CIA, because the anti-Castro project was their biggest special operation at that time since the Tibetan and Laotian projects had began to wane.

When the candidates appeared on television together during the crucial campaign debates, Nixon, abiding by security restrictions which, in his case, he could not disavow even if he had wished to, limited himself in his discussion of the Government's plans for Cuba. This official control did not publicly apply to Kennedy. Since he had been briefed by Allen Dulles, he could have been warned about security violations; but the CIA can be quite liberal with respect to security when it is to that Agency's advantage. As a result, Kennedy could and did openly advocate the overthrow of the Castro Government, and for the strong position he won popular support from a great number of the voters.

Nixon's frustration and anger at Kennedy's calculated tactics were clearly evident on the television screen. As television audiences have learned in the years since those famous debates, when Nixon feels frustration and anger on television he shows it, and when he felt both during the Kennedy debates the audience knew it, and Kennedy made points. Many observers believe that that confrontation over Cuba was one of the peak moments during the debates, when Kennedy scored most heavily—and of course most observers credit Kennedy's performance during the debates with his narrow margin of victory in the election. Few knew that his carefree television position on Cuba was in reality Nixon's official stand in time security-bound NSC record.

That Kennedy's connection with the Cuban refugees before his election was anything but casual or fortuitous was demonstrated nearly two years later. On December 29, 1962, in the Orange Bowl in Miami, before a national television audience, at a welcome-back celebration for the ransomed prisoners of the Cuban Brigade, before a thundering ovation from the jammed stadium, the President spoke informally with the Brigade and with the tens of thousands of Cubans who came to pack the stadium. At one point during the ceremonies, the President walked among the former prisoners, chatted with them, and then threw his arm over the shoulders of one of them. If those watching in the stadium and on TV thought he had chosen the man at random, they were mistaken. The Cuban he embraced was his old friend who had visited him in his Senate offices during the summer of 1960 and also at his West Palm Beach home. This man was Manuel Artime, a leader of the invasion.

One of the most significant aspects of ST work is its control of operational planning by need-to-know secrecy. And as we stated earlier, such control seriously limits the level of competency that can be brought to a major operation such as the Bay of Pigs. The CIA never really knew what to do about Castro and Cuba. During the latter days of 1958, the CIA assembled a staff of Cuban 'experts' under the leadership of its old Western Hemisphere Division hands such as Colonel J. C. King. But the real inside men, those who had responsible roles in these operations and in their so-called planning, are never discovered. The first somewhat obvious reason usually given is that of course those names would not show up because the Agency very wisely kept them concealed under proper security.

This may be part of the answer, but it is more probable that they never would have been linked with the exercise for two other reasons. First, they were truly faceless and practically meaningless participants in the action; they were in their jobs simply to see that things rolled along. Second, because once such an operation has been briefed to the NSC and the lower, middle level of the Agency's operations and support staffs know that the green light is on, they begin to move in all directions, and from that time on there is very little real leadership. Money becomes obtainable, equipment is made available, travel is abundant, the horn of plenty spills over, and all is hidden in secrecy. Partly by plan but mostly by the simple fact that no one at the top restrains the action of these activists at the lower levels. Everything begins to happen everywhere at the same time. There is a special sort of Murphy's Law about clandestine activities once they have received an initial and very general approval: "If anything can happen, it will." The U.S. Government is simply not constituted to become aware of and to control such faceless and random activities as those that take place under the shield of secrecy once the game has been discovered and perfected by the often amorphous ST. Nothing demonstrates this better than the single bitter underlying reason for the failure of the Bay of Pigs operation.

The Bay of Pigs effort failed for the lack of effective leadership, and for no other reason. It could have worked and it could have succeeded. Everything was there that had to be there. The goals were not so grand that they could not have been achieved: "To maintain an invasion force on Cuban territory for at least 72 hours and then to proclaim the free Government of Cuba there on that bit of territory." After that, it would have been up to the Organization of the American States and the United States to support them. But the Bay of Pigs operation did not have leadership when it was most needed. Allen Dulles, the man at the helm, was not even in Washington. Perhaps he thought the invasion could run by itself. For whatever reason he had in mind, Allen Welsh Dulles was not even in the United States at the time of these crucial landings.

As poorly planned as this over-the-beach operation was, it could have been a success within the original parameters of the effort. Jose Miro Cordona had been told that when the invasion forces had been on Cuban soil for seventy-two hours, had raised the Free Cuba flag on Cuban soil, and had proclaimed themselves to be the new government, he would be delivered to the beachhead. Then, when he appealed for assistance from the Organization of American States, the United States would give his "Government of Free Cuba" the assistance it needed

It was expected that once such a government had been established, albeit on the flimsiest grounds, Cubans would flock to its support, and that once U.S. Government assistance was visible and real—such as U.S. warships off the coast, U.S. aircraft flying unopposed all over Cuba, and even U.S. Marines at the beachhead—then the decay of Castro's Cuba would be certain. In essence, this is what the Cubans believed. It may have been what the CIA had in mind as it got caught up in the fervor of the training and arming authorized by President Eisenhower. However, no one could say that Eisenhower, the tough and experienced commanding general of the greatest invasion force of all time, had ever suggested or approved the invasion of Cuba clandestinely with a force of less than two thousand Cuban exiles. Whatever the Cuban project had grown to in the hands of the CIA took place after election day in 1960.

The leadership on the beach was competent enough for the job at hand. The Cubans themselves were good. The tactical leadership back in Nicaragua both for the invasion and for the small air strikes was adequate. The substratum of U.S. military personnel attached to the CIA to bring some order out of the training program was competent, especially the U.S. Marine Corps colonel who worked so hard and effectively to see that the little band of Cubans had some idea of what to do when they hit the beach. The U.S. Air Force officers attached to the CIA who pulled together the small hard-hitting air force of World War II B-26s and C-46s were skilled and combat qualified. But above them leadership was practically nonexistent.

No proper official would have approved of the Bay of Pigs operation unless there was a guarantee that Castro would not have been able to give it any effective air opposition. The few close-in, hard-core officers who knew the real plan would never have given any support to the plan if they did not have assurances that Allen Dulles would be able to guarantee that Castro's few combat-ready aircraft would have been bombed out of existence before the men hit the beach. This was the fundament upon which the operation was established; it was its failure that sealed its doom.

Before the first Cuban exiles' B-26 attacks on Castro's aircraft, U-2 pictures detailed exactly where Fidel's planes were and how many there were. The first wave of B-26s hit those planes and destroyed them, with the exception of the three T-33 jet trainers, two B-26s, and a few old British Sea Furies. In modern air-weapons-system technology the T-33 is a very low-order combat aircraft, and actually it has very little combat capability. However, it is a big jump better than the B-26 bomber in air-to-air combat. Therefore, until these three T-33s had been located and destroyed, there was to be no invasion. The B-26s and the Sea Furies could be handled and ignored. Castro's B-26s were not nearly as effective as the newly modified ones of the Cuban exiles.

It had just happened that the three T-33 jets had been flown to a small airfield outside of the Havana area for the weekend. The chance removal of these planes saved them from the first attack.

The Bay of Pigs instructions called for additional air strikes to get all of Castro's planes if this was not accomplished by the first strikes. This prerequisite was simple and necessary. Damage assessment photos not only showed that the T-33s had escaped, but they showed where they were, lined up on an airfield near Santiago. With this knowledge, a flight of B-26s at Puerto Cabezas in Nicaragua was loaded with bombs and fueled for the long flight to the target. These were excellent B-26s, which had been modified by the CIA to have a cluster of eight 50-caliber machine guns firing from the nose. This gun-pack is most lethal and unsurpassed for the type of operation contemplated. The guns could have made mincemeat of Castro's T-33s on the ground. In the air, the T-33s would have chopped them up. Thus the plan was for these planes to leave Puerto Cabezas at an early hour to assure undetected arrival at the target at sunrise and to permit them to sweep in over the airfield with the sun low and at their backs to give them as much groundfire protection as they could get.

As late as one thirty that morning the CIA agent who was in charge of these planes in Nicaragua had not received the expected message from Washington that would authorize their take-off. Later, acting on his own initiative and to keep the excited and ready-to-go Cubans quiet, he permitted them to start their engines on condition that they wait for his signal for take-off. Meanwhile in Washington, heated arguments had arisen over the air strikes. There was so much opposition to the second strike that those who sought the authority to release these planes were unable to gain approval.

On the one hand, General Cabell, the Deputy Director of Central Intelligence, and Richard Bissell, the Deputy Director of Plans, and the man who was responsible for the entire operation, were second-level officials. They were unable to release the planes on their own authority, and they were opposed by others, some of whom were of Cabinet level. It became a question of who would awaken the President at his Glen Ora retreat in Virginia in an attempt to get his approval. Neither Cabell nor Bissell had the authority to do that, and Allen Dulles was not in Washington. At this crucial time when his agency was faced with its most momentous crisis, a crisis of leadership, Dulles had left Washington to go to Puerto Rico to address the convention of the Young Presidents Organization. He was the man who could have given permission for the planes to go, or who could have gone to the President himself for that authority. On that fateful night the CIA was leaderless. The opposition stood its ground, and the air strike was not ordered to attack the jets at Santiago. This was the key to the failure of the whole operation. Those three jets destroyed no less than ten B-26s, along with some ground equipment, and sank the vital supply ship offshore.

Perhaps if one CIA agent had taken a short bicycle ride, the whole invasion would have been a success. The Cuban pilots in those B-26s on the ground at Puerto Cabezas, with their engines running, were on the point of mutiny. They were going to go without word from Washington, except for one thing. The agent who had the sole authority there to release them had told them that Washington was making a last-minute check of the target photographs and that they had better wait until he got the word. They half believed him. Later, his own faith in the system wavered badly, and he knew that as the moments ticked away the last chance the B-26s would have to get to the target airfield before sunrise would be gone. After that, Castro's jets could be expected to be gone.

Nearby, the agent had a bicycle that he used for his trips back and forth to the operations shack where the circuit to Washington was. During those last few moments he looked at that bicycle, certain that if he just got on it and rode away toward the shack the Cubans would go without waiting for his signal. The temptation was great. He had worked with some of those Cubans for two years; he knew how badly they wanted the operation to succeed. But his own discipline was stronger, and he did not take that ride. Finally, it was too late. The crews shut down the engines and got out of the planes.

Far across the Caribbean the small invasion fleet approached the shore secure in the belief that Castro's planes had been destroyed. They hit the beach shortly after sunrise, and it wasn't long before they came under heavy air attack. They knew then that their time was limited. To add to this tragedy, the same B-26s that were to have wiped out the jets were ordered over the beach to give the invasion troops some firepower against ground opposition. The B-26s were shot down by those jets which only a few hours earlier they could have destroyed. And in sunny Puerto Rico the DCI entered a convention hall to give a speech to a group of young businessmen. This was the kind of elite group he liked. He was at his best among them, and he enlisted their support on behalf of the Agency, which was "saving the world from communism." Many of those same men have since traveled throughout the world on matters concerning business, wearing around their necks the mark of the Agency—the shoulder strap of a new camera. These same men eagerly went from country to country as special agents for the CIA. But when the chips were down and those brave Cubans had been landed on the beach by the

CIA, Allen Dulles was not there. He was perhaps the one man in Washington, had he been there, who could have sent those bombers out that morning for the purpose of destroying Castro's jets.

The Bay of Pigs operation serves as an excellent example of what is good and what is bad about clandestine operations and about the way they are developed, supported, and managed by the ST. From the first assistance to the first small group of Cubans in Miami, from the first light plane touchdown on a remote road in Cuba to exfiltrate one or two men to the huge operation involving thousands of men and tens of millions of dollars worth of equipment, to the tragic failure on the beach and the imprisonment and eventual payment of ransom tribute to Castro, the Bay of Pigs operation was nothing but a somewhat related series of escalating events which, simply stated, just got out of hand after the election of John F. Kennedy.

Some peripheral incidents that have not been apparent are worth a word. After Castro took over Cuba, he nationalized industry and kicked all Americans out of the country. Those companies that had been doing business in Cuba suffered heavy losses. Among the worst of these losses were those felt by the sugar companies. The stock of some of these firms traded at very low rates, if it could be traded at all. With the Cuban support program moving into high gear after the election of Kennedy, a large number of CIA personnel made heavy purchases of these deflated stocks, and word spread to some of their friends that a flyer in sugar stock might be worth the gamble. So orders to buy sugar stock went out all over the country.

The stockbroker community in Washington is most sophisticated. Over the years they see a lot of inside buying for reasons they have no way of knowing. In an attempt to ferret out some of these deals, they have developed their own expertise in divining what is going on. When the sugar purchases were at their peak, some of these brokers called their sources in the Pentagon on the assumption that if something was going to happen in Cuba the military would know about it. Of course, very few military knew about the invasion, and those who did would not have the temerity to let anyone know, most of all a broker. So the brokers were not getting much help in the usual channels. However, one broker who happened to hit on an idea, called a certain mutual fund group where he had reason to believe that there was some more than routine contact with the secret areas in the government. He was able to learn that they had been buying a little sugar stock. He put two and two together and inadvertently started a small buying spree among his and his company's clients.

Needless to say, the sugar balloon burst on those beaches in Cuba; but there have been many other times when the very special inside scoop the ST is able to control has led to some very good investments. More will be said about this as more is learned about the early days of the Indochina affairs during the past ten years. It does not take anyone long to become an avid ST booster once he has sipped the elixir of certain and easy money derived from an inside tip on a sure thing.

PART II

THE CIA: HOW IT RUNS

CHAPTER 3

AN OVERVIEW OF THE CIA

SECTION I: Intelligence versus Secret Operations

What other agency of the U.S. Government has ever had as much blame heaped upon it as the CIA? President Truman wrote that it was being interpreted as a symbol of sinister and mysterious foreign intrigue and a subject for Cold War propaganda. Arnold Toynbee wrote: "For the whole world, the CIA has now become the bogey that Communism has been for America." John F. Kennedy said, "Your successes are unheralded, your failures are trumpeted." Tibetans once supported by the CIA had been left to fend for themselves against the Chinese. Hungarians armed and urged to fight on for their freedom were left to fight by themselves. Cubans stranded on the beaches of the Bay of Pigs were left for Castro's jails. Tens of thousands of people who have contributed to Radio Free Europe and to CARE on the assumption that they were private organizations have learned that the CIA was using them for its own devices. And during the summer of 1971, Congress was faced with a ground swell of indignation over the actions of the CIA in the wake of events in Indochina and as a result of revelations contained in the Pentagon papers. The frequently asked questions are: How responsible is the CIA? How is the CIA permitted to operate independent of national policy and of the general standards of conduct expected of the U.S. Government?

In seeking to solve the dilemma of the CIA, it is important from the beginning to understand the intimate language of the Agency and of the intelligence profession. Intelligence professionals become so accustomed to using and living with cover stories, cover language, and code terms that they use them interchangeably with their normal, or dictionary, usage. Thus the outsider has little opportunity to break through this fabric to get to the real thing.

In the beginning, when Roosevelt assigned Donovan to the task of Coordinator of Information, there was a belief that the United States had within its resources reasonably adequate intelligence organizations in the Army, Navy, and Department of State, but that the gross intelligence product was sadly lacking in coordination. As a result, the President felt that he was not getting the best Intelligence. Thus his insistence that the new chief of intelligence should be a coordinator. This view of the role of the Director of Central Intelligence has persisted through the years, and it is still the primary statement of his mission and responsibility as contained in present law.

The other key word is "information." In 1941, President Roosevelt felt that he required coordinated information, and because of certain unacceptable connotations for the profession of Intelligence, the word "Intelligence" was not used at all. It was not too long before that time (1929) that the then Secretary of State, Henry L. Stimson, had downgraded Intelligence, actually that special part pertaining to cryptoanalysis, with the statement: "Gentlemen don't read other people's mail."

The profession of Intelligence always is beset by one characteristic problem. It is a staff function. It is the kind of effort that can succeed only insofar as it is accepted and used by the leadership. If the commanding general trusts his Intelligence people and makes use of their product, he will generally have good intelligence. If a business leader uses his Intelligence people as a real adjunct to his operations and provides them with the resources they need, he will have good Intelligence. And if the President of the United States uses intelligence as intelligence, and demands a really professional product, he will get the best intelligence in the world. But leadership is often prone to disparage the intelligence product. At one time, in 1939, Winston Churchill said the following about Intelligence: "It seems to me that Ministers run the most tremendous risks if they allow the information collected by the Intelligence Department and sent them, I am sure, in good time, to be shifted and colored and reduced in consequence and importance, and if they ever get themselves into a mood of attaching weight only to those pieces of information which accord with their earnest and honorable desire that the peace of the world should remain unbroken."[1]

The profession of Intelligence before World War II was not well thought of, and it was not very good. There can be no question that the two go hand in hand. Had there been more real demand for good Intelligence, there would have been more funds and personnel provided for its support, and as a consequence, intelligence services would have been better. But history is full of incidents citing very poor intelligence service, under Hitler, Stalin, and the Western powers.

I was at Fort Knox, Kentucky, at the time of the attack on Pearl Harbor. This attack came as such a surprise and with so little preparation or understanding in the United States Army that although that attack occurred more than four thousand miles away, the Commanding General of the Armored Force headquarters at Fort Knox ordered tanks and heavy guns out in a perimeter defense of Fort Knox and of the U.S. gold reserves that were stored there. No one knew what to expect the Japanese to do next after they had hit Pearl Harbor.

A few years later, during World War II, I was the pilot of a large transport plane being sent on an emergency mission deep into the heartland of Russia from Tehran, Iran. Since this was to be one of the first unescorted U.S. flights deep into the Soviet Union, I was called aside by a military intelligence staff officer and told that the

---

1. Sanche de Gramont, *The Secret War*, New York, G. P. Putnam's Sons, p. 29.

maps he had to give me for the flight were of very little value and would I please keep a careful log of everything I saw as I flew some eighteen hundred miles into Russia in order that mapping information and other data might be improved. Then, as I left this briefing, he more or less apologetically wished me well because I had to find my way into Russia without the aid of reliable maps. Before I left Tehran I managed to obtain the maps that had been used by Wendell Willkie's pilot and had been hand annotated. They were the best available at that time.

It was not surprising, then, that President Roosevelt directed that Colonel Donovan be Coordinator of Information (COI). By 1942, Donovan had made some headway, and the war had become better organized. He had built up the reputation of intelligence activities and he had been successful in refining the problem. At the same time, he had learned that the role of coordinator was unworkable, untenable, and undesirable—in other words, hopeless. General MacArthur had preempted the intelligence role in the Far East—that is, those intelligence activities which were not under the control of the Navy—and the FBI had been given the responsibility for intelligence operations in Latin America. As a result, in 1942 the COI became the Office of Strategic Services, (OSS), and the task of that new organization was broadened to include collecting and analyzing information and planning and operating special services. On that day Donovan no doubt put his intelligence hat on the shelf and concentrated on his first love, special services.

In pursuit of the business of definitions in this most elusive of professions, few terms have been so confused and misused as *"special services."* These two words simply mean *clandestine operations.* General Donovan's office was called Strategic Services, and his duties were described as special services. It was all the same clandestine operations. As the intelligence profession has labored through its first quarter-century since World War II, these terms have acquired additional synonyms. Clandestine operations are also known as *covert operations, special operations,* and *peacetime operations* or *peacetime special operations,* and *secret operations.*

There are two other terms that need clarification here in order that they not be confused with the above. *Secret intelligence* is the deep penetration of the enemy by secret agents and other devices. It is more specifically *clandestine intelligence*, as differentiated from the more open and more academic type of intelligence. This leads to *intelligence operations*, which may or may not be clandestine, but are operations carried out to obtain intelligence, and not operations carried out to achieve a certain objective as a result of the gaining of certain intelligence input data. In the former, the operation is carried out to get intelligence, and in the latter the operation is carried out using intelligence input data.

Then there are *secret intelligence* operations, which are deeper and more clandestine operations carried out to get deep-secret intelligence data. It can be said that it is the business of secret intelligence operations to get information required in the making of foreign policy that is unavailable through routine and overt intelligence channels.

The fundamental dichotomy that has always divided Intelligence community and which in the long run has given it its bad reputation is that the Intelligence operator just cannot keep his hands and his heart out of operations. This same affliction leaves its mark on the entire community, not just on individual agents. Established for the legitimate business of intelligence, the Agency has become deeply involved in clandestine operations; yet to maintain its status and reputation in the structure of this open government, it must continually give the appearance of being nothing more than an Intelligence Agency while it keeps itself covertly occupied with special operations on an ever expanding scale.

Nowhere has this attempt to be legitimate been more apparent than in the revelations of the publication of the Pentagon Papers. One of the primary objectives of that inner group (who directed the compilation of that fantastic massive reconstruction of the history of the United States' role in Indochina) was, without doubt, to make certain that the role of the CIA always appeared in a most laudable and commendable manner, to be that of an intelligence organization and no more. Thus the product of the intelligence staff has been extracted from the great mass of records available and portrayed most favorably, while at the same time the role of the CIA, special operations, or clandestine organization as a sinister and secret operational activity has been submerged. In retrospect, the CIA, that part which publishes intelligence reports, always appears to have come up with the correct analysis and evaluation.

On the other hand, this review as it appears in *The New York Times* publication, almost totally conceals or fails to identify the records of the covert activities of the clandestine organizations. When it does present accounts of that action it reveals them under the label of cover organizations either as part of the military establishment or of some other apparatus. Interestingly, the CIA can't help doing both things at the same time, and its leaders are seldom, if ever, concerned with the fact that what they are doing may be at cross purposes. They are duty bound to perform the former and they much prefer to become involved in the latter, secure in the knowledge that their control of security within this country even more than elsewhere is nearly absolute. In fact Allen Dulles and other following DCI's were fully aware of this discrepancy, yet would authorize the publication of intelligence reports saying one thing at the same time they were authorizing clandestine forces to do exactly the opposite.

One aspect of the Pentagon Papers that makes them suspect of not being exactly what they are purported to be, that is, an expose of the role of the Pentagon in the United States' involvement in Vietnam (this is an oversimplified definition of them, but it will serve here) is that they laud the role of the CIA and the overall intelligence community while they disparage the rest of the Government, especially the Pentagon. The following extract is from *The New York Times'* book of the Pentagon Papers, in an introductory and formative early chapter, page 6:

> The Pentagon account discloses that most of these major decisions from 1950 on were made against the advice of the American intelligence community. Intelligence analysts in the CIA warned that the French, Emperor Bao Dai and Premier Diem were weak and unpopular and that the Communists were strong. In early August 1954, for example, just before the NSC decided to commit the U.S. to

propping up Premier Diem, a national intelligence estimate warned: "Although it is possible that the French and Vietnamese even with firm support from the U.S. and other powers, may be able to establish a strong regime in South Vietnam, we believe that the chances for this development are poor and moreover, that the situation is more likely to continue to deteriorate progressively over the next year." The NIE continues. Given the generally bleak appraisals of Diem's prospects, they who made U.S. policy could only have done so while assuming a significant measure of risk."

And *The New York Times* goes on to editorialize: "The Pentagon study does not deal at length with a major question. Why did the policy makers go ahead despite the intelligence estimates prepared by their most senior intelligence officials?"

These brief statements are truly amazing and in some respects may be among the most important lines in the entire *New York Times* presentation of the Pentagon Papers. They show how deeply the clandestine, operating side of the CIA hid behind its first and best cover, that of being an intelligence agency. How can the *Times* miss the point so significantly? Either the *Times* is innocent of the CIA as an intelligence organization versus the CIA as a clandestine organization, a highly antagonistic and competitive relationship, or the *Times* somehow played into the hands of those skillful apologists who would have us all believe that the Vietnam problem was the responsibility of others and not of the CIA operating as a clandestine operation. Let us consider an example:

A few pages after this statement, the *Times* version of the Papers tells us that Edward G. Lansdale went to Saigon with a team in August 1954. This date may be one of the correct dates, but the facts are that plans for Lansdale's move to Saigon from Manila, where he had engineered Magsaysay's rise from soldier to President, were laid long before he actually went there with his team. (The author was a frequent visitor to Manila and Saigon from 1952 through 1954 as the commanding officer of a Military Air Transport Service squadron which provided much of the military airlift between those cities in those days, and on more than one flight carried as special passengers members of the Lansdale team, both U.S. and Filipino personnel, to and from Saigon).

These plans, which were made for the development of a United States presence in Vietnam to replace the French after their defeat at Dien Bien Phu and to create a new leader to replace the French puppet, Bao Dai, had been primarily developed by the operational CIA, almost as a natural follow-on of their production of Magsaysay.

Ngo Dinh Diem was a selection and creation of the CIA, as well as others such as Admiral Arthur Radford and Cardinal Spellman, but the primary role in the early creation of the "father of his country" image for Ngo Dinh Diem was played by the CIA—and Edward G. Lansdale was the man upon whom this responsibility fell. He became such a firm supporter of Diem that when he visited Diem just after Kennedy's election he carried with him a gift "from the U.S. Government," a huge desk set with a brass plate across its base reading, "To Ngo Dinh Diem, The Father of His Country." The presentation of that gift to Diem by Lansdale marked nearly seven years of close personal and official relationship, all under the sponsorship of the CIA.

It was the CIA that created Diem's first elite bodyguard to keep him alive in those early and precarious days. It was the CIA that created the Special Forces of Vietnamese troops, which were under the tight control of Ngo Dinh Nhu, and it was the CIA that created and directed the tens of thousands of paramilitary forces of all kinds in South Vietnam during those difficult years of the Diem regime. Not until the U.S. Marines landed in South Vietnam, in the van of the escalation in 1964, did an element of American troops arrive in Vietnam that were not under the operational control of the CIA.

From 1945 through the crucial years of 1954 and 1955 and on to 1964, almost everything that was done in South Vietnam, including even a strong role in the selection of generals and ambassadors, was the action of the CIA, with the DOD playing a supporting role and the Department of State almost in total eclipse. Thus, when *The New York Times* asks, "Why did the policy makers go ahead despite the intelligence estimates prepared by their most senior intelligence officials?" it has asked an excellent question, because it must include in the "most senior intelligence officials" the Director of Central Intelligence and others of the Agency. This makes one wonder at what point a man like Allen Dulles stops playing the role of intelligence official and sees himself in the mirror as CIA clandestine commander in chief.

These examples have to make certain aspects of the release and publication of the Pentagon Papers deeply suspect, especially since the man who says he released these vast volumes to the newspapers, Daniel Ellsberg, was ideally suited for this role by virtue of his Vietnam experience with the very same Edward G. Lansdale. No matter what one might wish to believe the intentions of Ellsberg were when he did this, it would be most difficult to accept that he of all people did not know all the facts. And if he did know all of the facts I have described, why did he want to make it appear that it was Pentagon policymakers who went ahead "despite the intelligence estimates prepared by their most senior intelligence officials"? Why has so much care been taken to make it appear that these are papers from the Pentagon that he has dumped on the news media's doorstep? Why has no one made the proper distinction that the majority of these documents were not really Pentagon originated at all, but were originated in, among other places, the CIA (Covert side)? Certainly if his facts, as well as those presented by *The New York Times*, are right, the CIA (Covert side) was in a much better position to heed its own CIA (Intelligence side) warnings and advice than any other department or agency in Washington.

The answer to these questions becomes obvious. The CIA uses its intelligence role as a cover mechanism for its operational activities. Furthermore it uses its own secret intelligence as an initiator for its own secret operations. This is what pleased General Donovan when President Roosevelt unleashed him with the OSS and it is what has been the driving force behind the hard core operational agents within the intelligence community since that time.

Allen Dulles himself helps us to define General Donovan's new title in 1942 in his own words: "Special Services was the cover designation for Secret Intelligence and Special Operations of all kinds and character." To the old pro the new designation was an important step forward in the evolution of the intelligence profession in the

United States. One could almost see him hunching up to his desk to write a few more memoranda to the President about the development of the intelligence services. It was no mistake when Dulles entitled his book *The Craft of Intelligence*. He was the crafty professional in a fast-growing profession.

During 1943, General Donovan did his best to extend the OSS into all those parts of the world left to him by the Navy, General MacArthur, and J. Edgar Hoover. At one time in 1943 he got a bit overambitious and went to Moscow. There he met with his counterparts in the intelligence profession and was so won over by their good fellowship that he came back to Washington to propose that there be an exchange program between the Russians and the Americans. Donovan proposed that their hand-picked agents be brought to this country to learn all about Intelligence and special operations with Americans, utilizing new techniques and equipment that we had. To those who recall the same General Donovan on countless platforms ranting about the "communist threat" only a few years later, this proposal of his must seem to have been part of a soft-headed era. In any event, others such as J. Edgar Hoover and Admiral Leahy overruled Donovan's gesture of hospitality to the Russians.

The OSS did set up a Guerrilla and Resistance Branch, which operated from Europe to Burma and was patterned after the highly successful British Special Operations Executive (SOE) model. But General Donovan never got over the blows he suffered from MacArthur and Hoover. His wartime disappointment led him on many occasions to recommend that there be a single top intelligence director who would be placed within the immediate Office of the President and that this director be a civilian who would control all other intelligence services, particularly most of the military. By 1944, his views were so firm that he wrote to President Roosevelt:

"I have given consideration to the organization of our intelligence service for the postwar period.
"Once our enemies are defeated the demand will be equally pressing for information that will aid in solving the problems of peace.

"This requires two things:

1. That Intelligence control be returned to the supervision of the President.
2. The establishment of a central authority reporting directly to you."

On careful scrutiny, this is a most unusual memorandum to be written during time of war to the Commander in Chief of the greatest military force ever assembled. First there is the assumption, and perhaps even an implied criticism, that the control of Intelligence was not under the President, or that the President had lost control of that aspect of the military effort world wide. (Later historians may be able to probe the depths of Donovan's feelings about General MacArthur by delving into the meaning of such papers as that memo.) The other veiled criticism was his proposal that the central authority be made to report directly to the President. By this, Donovan hoped that Roosevelt might establish such a central authority, that would be himself, and that he might thereby gain ascendancy over his arch rivals, J. Edgar Hoover, the Navy, and most of all, General Douglas MacArthur.

The germ of these ideas lived throughout the following quarter-century. Even today, there are those who still propose that the DCI be assigned to the immediate Office of the President. The zeal within the "silent arm of the President," as the intelligence service is fondly called by its own, is so strong that they have created a special meaning for the phrase, "the immediate Office of the President." It might generally be considered that the Cabinet is part of this office, but what the Intelligence buffs mean is that the DCI would be above or, to put it more precisely, equal to and separate from the Cabinet. From General Donovan's day down to the present time, it has been the goal of a good segment of the intelligence community to install their Director next to the President. They always claim that the reason for this is so that the President may always have at his elbow the best and most current intelligence available. This, too, is a master cover story. Just like General Donovan and his clan, what they really want is the place at the elbow of the President, unfettered by the Secretaries of State and Defense, in order to have their way with the function of Special Operations. Of course, what follows from this is what would amount to having the ability to make and to control the foreign policy and military policymaking machinery of this country. We shall have more to say about this. It suffices now to point out where and when the seed was planted.

Shortly after the war had ended, President Truman dissolved the OSS. On September 20, 1945, certain functions of the OSS were transferred to the Departments of State and of War. Although the United States did not delay in disbanding her military might as soon as the war had ended, no group was terminated faster than the OSS. Some of the pressure to dissolve this agency came from the FBI, the Department of State, the Armed Forces, the Bureau of the Budget, and from President Truman's own belief that the "fun and games" was over. He felt that there would be no need for clandestine activities during peacetime, and he meant to devote his time to winning a peace of lasting duration for the generation which had fought its way through the worst depression in history and then through the most terrible war in history.

In this rapid divestiture of its clandestine wartime service, only two sections were saved. The Secret Intelligence Branch and the Analysis Branch were tucked away among the labyrinth of the departments of State and War, where a few dedicated veterans labored quietly through a precarious existence to preserve files and other highly classified materials. Had it not been for the professionalism and zeal of this group of responsible men, these files that had been created during the war would have been lost. Had they been lost or destroyed, or most serious of all, had they been compromised, they might have occasioned the deaths of hundreds of agents who had risked their lives for the United States and who lived in constant fear lest they be exposed in their homelands, which had fallen under Soviet control. Fortunately, these records, along with irreplaceable talent, were saved. Thus ended an era of war-time inspired clandestine activity, the contagion of which was sufficient to infect a new generation of intelligence professionals for the next twenty-five years.

SECTION II: Origins of the Agency and Seeds of Secret Operations

By the end of World War II it was abundantly clear that the U.S. must have a central intelligence authority. The mistakes which were made, more by omission than by commission, by the intelligence community during the war were serious. This country could never again afford the luxury of overlooking the need for reliable intelligence. The witch hsunt that took place right after the war in an attempt to fix the blame for the disaster at Pearl Harbor was indicative of the depth of the problem. After the war, it became clear to many that we had seriously overestimated the strength of the Japanese and that we had as a result seriously overrated the task that confronted the Russians in moving their eastern armies across Manchuria against the Japanese at the end of the war.

In addition to these rather obvious criticisms, there was the fact of the atomic bomb. It had been developed in great secrecy under the Manhattan Project; but once it had been demonstrated at Hiroshima and Nagasaki, it was no longer a secret. Scientists all over the world would be attempting to solve the bomb's problems, knowing now that it was entirely feasible and practical, and their own intelligence and spy networks would be trying to steal the secrets of the bomb from the United States. This put another serious burden upon the intelligence community.

Not long after the cessation of hostilities, the first measures toward the establishment of a central intelligence authority were announced. Less than six months after the end of the war the President set up the Central Intelligence Group. *The New York Times* on January 23, 1946, reported that President Truman established a National Intelligence Authority composed of the Secretaries of State, War, and Navy. It was to be headed by a Director of Central Intelligence. The DCI would have at his disposal the staffs and organizations of all government intelligence units, including those overseas, and would undertake "such services of common concern as the National Intelligence Authority determines can be more efficiently accomplished centrally." This provision would enable the Director to operate his own staff for top secret and high priority missions, while utilizing the production of all other Agency staff operations for general intelligence production.

The plan was devised by the Joint Chiefs of Staff as a modification of one submitted by Major General William J. Donovan at the time of the dissolution of the OSS. It deviated from Donovan's suggestion in several important particulars, however. First, it placed the Central Intelligence Group and its Director under the jurisdiction of the Secretarial triumvirate. In the accepted plan this triumvirate retained authority over the Central Intelligence Group instead of placing the Group directly under the President. Second, it provided that operating funds for the organization would be obtained from the Departments of State, War, and Navy rather than directly from Congress as had been provided for by Donovan's plan. As a consequence, the Group was responsible not to Congress but to the Cabinet members making up the top authority. In his directive, the President ordered that "all Federal and foreign intelligence activities be planned, developed, and coordinated so as to assure the most effective accomplishment of the intelligence mission related to the National Security."

Thus, less than six months after the end of World War II, the battle lines for a major internal war had been drawn.

Most of the problems and the failures of the past twenty-five years can be attributed directly to inadequate and improper decisions made during these struggles within the Government during this immediate postwar period and to the impact they have had upon the welfare of this country since that time.

On one side were the tradition experienced planners who believed in the power of this great nation, all who felt that our future course lay in the increase of our own strength and of the beneficent impact of this strength upon the rest of the world. These men believed in the American way of life and in the ability of our economy to cope with world competition and of American diplomacy to plan our course of action wisely and to carry out effective national policy. They further believed in the capabilities of American military might to back up our diplomats and businessmen. To put it bluntly, these men were not afraid of the Communist bogeyman. They respected Communism for what it was, and they respected the power and strength of the Russian people. At the same time, they were willing and ready to plan for a common world future and an undivided world at peace.

The other side, however, wished to create a sort of Maginot Line of intelligence people around the world, separating the Communist world from the Free World. Then they would peer out at the rest of the world through a veil of secrecy plugged in to data inputs of the intelligence gathering sources wherever they were and supported by a military machine in a defense posture, ready for "reaction" at all times. In essence, this latter point of view of foreign policy operations is passive and reactive, implemented not by plan but only by response to the initiatives of others.

This is well stated by Allen Dulles in his book, *The Craft of Intelligence:* "The military threat in the nuclear missile age is well understood, and we are rightly spending billions to counter it. We must similarly deal with all aspects of the invisible war, Khrushchev's wars of liberation, the subversive threats orchestrated by the Soviet Communist party with all its ramifications and fronts, supported by espionage. The last thing we can afford to do today is to put our Intelligence in chains. Its protective and information role is indispensable in an era of unique and continuing danger." The key word, "counter," appears in the first sentence.

This final and summary paragraph of the old master's book is the best sample of the intelligence team's view of how to live in the modern nuclear age. They would have us establish the most extensive and expensive intelligence network possible and then develop a feedback capability that would automatically counter every threat they saw.

Although Allen Dulles does not say it in his book, his concept of Intelligence is about 10 percent real Intelligence and 90 percent clandestine operations. In other words, he would have us busy all around the world all of the time countering "all aspects of the invisible war." By this he means intervening in the internal affairs of other nations with or without their knowledge and permission. (This leads to a serious danger, which will be treated at some length later.) It is what the United States has been doing in an increasing crescendo of events, beginning with such actions as the involvement in Berlin and Iran in the 1940s and culminating in the terrible disaster of Vietnam that began as a major intelligence operation, went on into the clandestine operations stage, then got out of hand and had to become an overt activity during the Johnson era.

Traditionally, the foreign policy of the nation has been planned, and to the extent possible, has been openly arrived at. On those occasions when diplomacy has failed, the armed might of this country has been exploited overtly to back up foreign policy, or in the last resort to accomplish what diplomacy has been unable to do, by going to war. In the view of foreign policy action and the role of Intelligence as stated by Allen Dulles, however, intelligence would be the device used to set foreign policy actions in motion to "counter . . . all aspects of the invisible war." If this is not clear, he emphasizes, "The military threat in the nuclear missile age is well understood, and we are rightly spending billions to counter it." The idea is that intelligence is the catalytic element that triggers response and that this response will be covert, operational, and military as required.

With the advent of a strong Intelligence community and with the ascendancy of that voice in the higher echelons of the Government, the Government has slowly but positively moved from an active course of following plans and policies to the easier and more expedient course of the counterpuncher. The Government has become increasingly adept at reaction and response. A simple review of what this Government really found itself doing in the Congo or in Laos or Tibet during the sixties would be enough to clarify and support the argument that the Government responded to action inputs and "did something," instead of turning to plans and national objectives, which it did not have. Further support of this thesis that the Government has been weaned away from plans and policy in favor of the easier response mechanism activated by intelligence is apparent in even a cursory look at the degradation of the roles of the once prestigious Departments of State and Defense. Lately, the Army has found new worlds to conquer under the cloak of the Green

Berets who operate with the CIA. Even the Air Force welcomes the utilization of the once proud B-52 strategic bomber in a function that is totally degrading—the blind bombardment of Indochina's forests and wastelands on the assumption that there are worthwhile targets on the Ho Chi Minh trail. The only reason State and Defense can give for what they have permitted themselves to become engaged in is that "the intelligence reports" say the "enemy" is there. No one asks, What is the national objective in Indochina? No one has a national plan for Indochina. We have become counterpunchers without a game plan, and we have become that because we take our cues from raw intelligence data.

In our form of government this is a fairly recent approach. In 1929, when Secretary of State Stimson said, "Gentlemen do not read other people's mail," he was voicing the conditions of another era. We have come a long way since the days of 1929, and nations do read each other's mail because it is easier to do now than it used to be and because the dangers that exist today are much closer to home. We need to know as much as it is possible to learn about Russian capabilities and Russian intent. Total destruction is only about forty-five minutes away.

But there was another reason Stimson made that statement. In an open society we do not develop the same wiles that are necessary in a world in which everyone reads everyone else's mail. Therefore, if you are going to defend yourself by reading the other man's mail, you had better know what he means by what he has written in his letters. He knows you are reading his mail, and he will bluff you right out of the game. And what is more important, we must carry out our own policies in such a way that he cannot keep us from our own goals.

It is this point that looms larger when a government such as ours carries out its foreign and military affairs on a response basis. Such action over a period of time denies us all initiative and leadership and virtually precludes the possibility of bluff or skillful design. One cannot very well bluff or use surprise when he has been set in the pattern of response for twenty-five years. In military terms, the employment of proper tactics and strategy must be tempered by surprise when needed. In the great contest that has been going on between the major powers today, one can see that our course in response to such things as "Communist-inspired subversive insurgency" has cost us hundreds of billions of dollars and tens of thousands of lives; it has cost the same Communists we proclaim we are "countering" almost nothing. The response method of anything is a trap. The most frustrating and debilitating thing about it is that we have no objectives, no goals. We simply have an inertial drift into whatever direction the men in the Kremlin lure us. It is important to realize that if the highest echelons in government become preoccupied and preempted by intelligence inputs, voluminous reports, and other briefings, they do not have the chance to get planning done to weigh alternatives and to see that policies are effective.

General Donovan and Allen Dulles made a career of trying to have the Director of Central Intelligence assigned to the immediate Office of the President for just the reason outlined above. They wanted to be placed in the dominant position in this Government. They knew that with modern techniques, with modern communications and effective controls, all supported by money and equipment wherever needed, Intelligence was capable of running the Government and its foreign affairs. The Kissinger example is a case in point. This was the danger that the legislators saw in Donovan's early proposal. It is why the President, acting on his own authority, placed the Director under the jurisdiction of the three Secretaries.

To emphasize his intent and to make sure that it would work his way, President Truman directed that "operating funds for the organization would be obtained from the Departments of State, War, and Navy instead of directly from Congress." The Donovan plan had proposed the opposite. If the DCI was required to get his money each year through these other departments, he would be subservient to them and he would carry out their wishes.

These were the surface reasons for this decision. The real reason for this relegation of the DCI to a subordinate position was to prevent the Director and his organization from participating in clandestine operations without the express direction and authority of the Secretaries and the White House. As we have noted, President Truman planned for the CIA to be the "quiet intelligence arm of the

President." He and those of his Administration never intended that it become an autonomous operational agency in the clandestine field.

Because of the general secrecy that surrounds such things, this debate did not become public. The establishment of a "National Intelligence Authority" by Truman was considered an interim arrangement. The day after he set up the group, the President announced the appointment of Rear Admiral Sidney Souers as the first Director of Central Intelligence. At the same time, the President established a precedent that has continued to this day, by designating Admiral William D. Leahy to represent him as a member of the National Intelligence Authority. Before his appointment to his new job, Admiral Souers had been the deputy chief of the Office of Naval Intelligence.

It was learned concurrently that President Truman had ordered that "all federal and foreign intelligence activities be planned, developed and coordinated so as to assure the most effective accomplishment of the intelligence mission related to the national security."[2]

The President's directive contained further instructions to the Director of Central Intelligence. They were:

1. Accomplish the correlation and evaluation of intelligence relating to national security and provide for appropriate dissemination within the government of the resulting strategic and national intelligence.
2. Plan for the coordination of such of the activities of the intelligence agencies of all departments as relate to the National Security and recommend to the National Intelligence Authority the establishment of such overall policies and objectives as will assure the most effective accomplishment of the national intelligence mission.

---

2. Note that from the beginning the Agency was considered a coordination center, and that it was not empowered to be a collection agency. The original plan was that the agency simply coordinate all of the intelligence that was readily available from other government departments. As the agency grew during the following twenty-five years, it expanded its role bit by bit from this first limited charter, and it did so by its own zeal and initiative, not by law or direction.

A few weeks later, *The New York Times* published an article by Hanson Baldwin, its Military Affairs columnist, saying: "The establishment of a National intelligence Authority is a very important move. It is more important than the proposed merger of the War and Navy Departments. In all parts of the world today intelligence is most emphatically the first line of defense." This is an interesting use of this term "first line of defense." It appears many times later in the writings and speeches of such men as Allen Dulles and General Donovan. To them, intelligence was not limited to information. It was very much an operational organization and function.

Baldwin went on to say that the new Intelligence Authority under Admiral Souers "will at most just collate and analyze intelligence. Later on it may take over the job of collection of intelligence, and later its agents will supplement the normal intelligence sources of the military services." He added, "The State Department's new Intelligence service under Colonel Alfred McCormick will continue but will probably be somewhat more restricted in scope than it has been." Both of these statements were prophetic and indicate that Baldwin had obtained his information from Donovan-Dulles sources. It was the "party line" that Intelligence would take over the task of collection, whether Congress and the Administration had that function in the law or not.

In the heat of this major behind-the-scenes power play, there was bound to be an explosion. It is quite possible that this development, which occurred during the first week of March 1946, did not carry with it at that time the same significance that it does in retrospect. On the first day of March 1946, General Donovan gave an impassioned and hard-hitting speech before the Overseas Press Club in New York City. He stated that there had been numerous times when faulty and inaccurate intelligence had done great damage to this country's prosecution of the war. But the main burden of his speech concerned the new intelligence Authority. He said that experience had shown that we could obtain tested knowledge only through a coordinated, centralized, civilian directed intelligence service independent of other departments of the Government. Here he was taking a direct slap at General MacArthur and the JCS as well as at the Administration. He agreed that the new Central Intelligence Group established by the President was an advance over anything we had previously had in peacetime, but it lacked civilian control and independence.

Donovan voiced displeasure over any intelligence setup that did not dominate the scene. While Admiral Souers was setting up his new organization, Congress was working on the National Defense Act. The public was interested in and aroused over the provisions of this Act as it pertained to a new Department of Defense. The big word at that time was "unification." Feeling had run strong during World War II that the military services should have been more unified. It was claimed that they would have been more efficient, and there might have been less confusion and waste. At the same time, there were a number of advocates of an independent Air Force. Up to that time, the Air Force had always been a part of the Army. What was called unification at that time seems more like separation today, because the new law, when it was enacted, established a separate Army and Navy and a new Air Force. As we know them today they are still far from unified. In the heat of all this discussion, there was little public airing of the provision for the Central Intelligence Agency.

Those were troubled and confused times. The war was less than one year past, and people who looked back at it forgot all of the worldwide campaigns and remembered only the shock and terror of the atomic explosions at Hiroshima and Nagasaki. With fear of the unknown always more deadly than fear of a conventional shooting war, there was no chance to relax from the tensions of world struggle, safe in the knowledge that another war could not start up at any time, as we had believed after World War I. On the contrary, the threat of atomic warfare, even though it might be sometime in the future, was so terrifying that many felt the potential danger of nuclear weapons in the hands of the Soviet Union represented a graver peril than all the battles of World War II. As a result, with the war only six months behind them, Congress and the Administration turned to the serious problems of defense.

Thus, on the same day that General Donovan had spoken to the Overseas Press Club, Secretary of State James Byrnes also addressed that group. It is most revealing to look back at the major differences between the two speeches. Addressing this group as the official spokesman of the administration, he said that there was one thing that was very important: "The question is what can we do to make certain that there will never be another war?" Then, citing problems of the war, he went on, "Our relief and our gratitude for victory are mixed with uncertainty. Our goal now is permanent peace, and certainly we seek it even more anxiously than we sought victory. The difficulty is that the path to permanent peace is not so easy to see and to follow as was the path to victory." He said that "because we know that no nation can make peace by itself, we have pinned our hopes to the banner of the U.S." Byrnes added, "If we are going to do our part to maintain peace in the world, we must maintain our power to do so. We must make it clear that we will stand united with the other great states in defense of the charter of the UN. If we are to be a great power, we must act as a great power, not only in order to insure our own security but in order to preserve the peace of the world." Continuing, he said, "It is not in accord with our traditions to maintain a large professional standing army, but we must be able and ready to provide an armed contingent that may be required on short notice. We must have a trained citizenry ready to supplement those of the armed contingents." After making these statements, Byrnes added a very interesting comment that has special significance and applicability today. He said, "Our tradition as a peaceloving, law-abiding democratic people should be an assurance that our forces will not be used except as they may be called into action by the Security Council, and cannot be employed in war without the consent of Congress. We need not fear their misuse unless we distrust the representatives of the people."

In view of what has transpired in the Vietnam war, Byrnes' last statement takes on special meaning. As he continued his speech he made another most interesting remark: "So far as the United States is concerned, we will gang up against no state. We will do nothing to break the world into exclusive blocks or spheres of influence in this atomic age. We will not seek to divide a world which is one and indivisible." This "oneworld" view, this idea that no nation should do that which would destroy hopes for world unity and harmony, was the official policy of the Administration at that time. It was the national policy of a people dedicated to the proposition that this country was strong and able enough to stand upon its own feet and make its own way in the world. It was a positive and active policy that would plan for the future; yet only five days later another speech of another kind did more to turn the minds of the world, and especially of the United States, and to blight our future than any other speech in the following quarter-century.

It is startling and most significant to recall that the then leader of the Loyal Opposition in the British House of Commons, Sir Winston Churchill, only five days after Secretary Byrnes' speech made a speech that was just the opposite. He declared: "Beware . . . the time may be short. . . . from Stettin in the Baltic to Trieste in the Adriatic, an Iron Curtain has descended across the continent."

In this famous Iron Curtain speech Churchill, like many others, was driving the tip of the wedge between the great powers of the world, while at almost the same time the Secretary of State had said, "We will do nothing to break the world into exclusive blocks or spheres of influence in the atomic age. We will not seek to divide a world which is one and indivisible." Here again was the classic contest. The active overt planner, Byrnes, versus the passive covert reactivist, Churchill.

These were not simply the comments of one man. They were typical, and they were indicative of the thinking and of the intentions of the official, elected leaders of the United States right after the end of World War II, and of their deep-seated opposition. Great forces were working to divide the world—to set up one half as Communist, and the other half Free World and anti-Communist. There was the inertial drift that was transferring the initiative to the Kremlin.

The source of most of our problems of the past twenty-five years and certainly of the grave problems that beset our country today, lies in this schism between those who believed in the traditional school of national planning and overt diplomacy and those who believed in a passive role of reaction to a general enemy (Communism). This latter school would operate in response to intelligence inputs, without plans and without national objectives, would hide everything it did in secrecy, and would justify its actions in all instances as being anti-Communist. On the other hand, there were those who believed that the United States was the new leader of the world and that its responsibility to its own people and to those of the rest of the world lay in making a better world for all mankind along the lines of the example of the United States' tradition. At its best, this represented the dreams of free men for liberty and individual freedom under law and justice.

The maintenance of such a world and the expansion of such conditions to other parts of the world would require planning and great effort. The original concept of the Marshall Plan was an example of the best that such endeavors can accomplish in the face of Communist threats and opposition. Communism was met head on in Europe right after World War II and was defeated in France and Italy without resort to war and without response mechanisms. Communism was beaten by superior U.S. planning and policy. However, this kind of international effort requires dedicated leadership and great effort. One of the most difficult things for any government to do is develop and carry out long-range plans. That takes a certain inspired vision and rare leadership that is not often available.

On the other hand, it is easier and more typical to react and respond to outside pressures than to act in accordance with approved plans. In a modern government vested with immense capacity and advanced communications, it can be made to look more effective to set up and operate from a feedback system that will respond almost automatically to inputs, most of which are derived from a new style comprehensive intelligence information system fed by bits of data from everything including agents to satellite photography and other sophisticated sensors. The government in this case defines a threat, real or imagined, and responds to each data input from the threat and the danger.

This is what has been developed, and at this stage of the system this has become the normal course. Therefore, since it was all but inevitable that there would be a power struggle of some kind between the two great power centers on earth, even without declared hostility, the intelligence community proponents said that it would be easier to begin our national defense posture by delineating the source of all concern and danger, i.e. world communism, and then to draw lines for a never-ending battle, sometimes called the Cold War. The line so constructed was, in the beginning, the Iron Curtain. Although one might expect that the battles would be waged by our forces on their side of the curtain, and the skirmishes by their forces would be on our side, it has not turned out that way. The battles that have been fought since 1947 for the most part have been fought on our side of the Iron Curtain. It had to happen this way because the intelligence community has gained the initiative, and the response technique will not work on the other side. This was the great contest and although the principals on both sides of the argument, which was of such vital concern to the foreign policy and defense posture of this country, might deny it, this was the basis for the contention that the Central Intelligence Group should be assigned to a position subordinate to the Secretaries of State and Defense and under their direction.

These two pressure groups have vied for power repeatedly since 1946. It is entirely possible that the leak of the "Anderson Papers" in December 1971, and January 1972, was current evidence of an outbreak of this continuing struggle. Henry Kissinger is the titular head of the intelligence community's clandestine operations reaction faction. His appearance as a one-man power center is simply due to the fact that he fronts for the Secret Team and the secret intelligence community. Thus, he vies with the Secretary of State, the Attorney General, and certain others in the "traditionalist" group, who would like to see a return to national planning, strong diplomacy, and moves toward peace through successful conferences between the United States and other countries of the world.

The traditionalists had finally found a long-awaited opportunity to exploit Kissinger's weakened position in the India-Pakistani War, to expose him. Such events will occur repeatedly with the ebb and flow of power between these two positions.

As we continue with the development of the CIA and the ST in the following chapters, we shall see many more examples of the "active" versus "passive" contest.

SECTION III: A Simple Coup d'État to a Global Mechanism

For nothing is hid that shall not be made manifest, nor anything secret that shall not be known and come to light . . . take heed then how you hear . . .

Luke 8:17–18

A MODERN PARABLE . . . The jet airliner had just left the runway with the ex-president of Gandia aboard and was winging its way high over the snowballed Andes. In less than two hours it would land in the capital of Pegoan, where the ex-president had been assured of asylum and safety.

In a remote office in Washington the watch officer awaited the expected word from the agent who had arranged this flight, confirming that the departure had taken place. It was too soon to expect the collateral news that General Alfredo Elciario Illona had secured the reins of the Government of Gandia. This news he would get as soon as a second agent arrived in the capital with the new president. Desk officers had worked all night preparing releases for the news media and sending instructions to its operatives, readying them to support General Elciario's new government.

In distant Gandia all was quiet in spite of the sudden coup d'état. It may have been the quiet before the storm. For the time being all had gone well.

In the cabin of an old converted transport C-47 (DC-3) General Elciario was sleeping off the effects of a heavy drinking bout, on an army style cot that had been fitted into his modest VIP airplane. As soon as the plane had landed on its return from the frontier outpost, the pilot had parked it behind the U.S. Air Force surplus World War II hangar. The General and his closest friends had not even left the plane. Their party had continued on through the night in the plane. The pilot and friend of the General, a U.S. Air Force

Major, had sent the others home while he stayed until the General had slept it off.

As he tidied up the plane he recalled similar days in Greece and Iran, where he had worked as the mission commander on other exercises for "Acme Plumbing."[3] But this was the first time that he himself had been the key agent in the making of a President. It had been hard work, and now all he could do was wait for the brilliant mountain sunrise and word from the embassy that all was well and that the city was under control. In a few hours the General would be awakened and prepared to enter the capital as the new President. Now, as he lay there on that crude cot he did not even know that the coup d'état had already taken place and that it had been completely successful.

The Major had been in Gandia for slightly more than one year. He had come to join the U.S. Air Force mission there after six months of accelerated training at Eglin Air Force Base in Florida. He had flown little since his duty in Korea, but it had come back quickly with the intensive program the CIA had scheduled for him there. At Eglin he had learned new paradrop techniques and had worked closely with the newly formed Special Air Warfare Squadrons. One squadron had been sent to South Vietnam, another had gone to Europe, and the one he was to join had flown to Panama. There he had received further operational training exercises with the U.S. Army Special Forces troops in Colombia, Venezuela, and Ecuador. Other operations had taken him on an earthquake mercy mission to Peru and a medical team paradrop exercise into a mining town in Bolivia. It was while he was in Bolivia that the western hemisphere division (WH) had contacted him through the embassy and told him to report to Gandia.

Not long after he had arrived in Gandia, he met General Elciario. The General had been working with a specially equipped transport plane doing paradrop work over the mountain forests of the eastern

---

3. One of the most frequently used unclassified code names for the CIA; in general conversation by employees and those familiar with their intimate jargon. Note how the White House/Watergate Affair Group called themselves "the Plumbers," showing their CIA lineage.

frontier. The General was from a leading family of Gandia and could trace his ancestry back to the days of Simon Bolivar. Yet he was proud of the fact that he was Gandian and made slight reference to his Castilian ancestry. He loved the squat, barrel-chested mountain people. He was one of them. He was a man of the people, and he was the most famous flyer in the country. He had flown serum to stricken villages during an epidemic, and he had airdropped tons of relief supplies after an earthquake. The people of the villages loved the General, even though he was not a favorite in the capital. As in most Latin American countries, the government was centered in the capital. What took place in the capital was important; what took place in the villages could be ignored. When the General was made the chief of staff of the Gandian Air Force, the old President thought he had made a safe assignment. The General was part of no clique in the city, and he was no threat to anyone.

From the first, the General and the U.S. Major got along fine. The Major preferred the men of the villages to those in the capital, and in no time at all he was popular. Wherever he went the General, too, was popular. In this remote site the Major had become the friend of everyone in the village and in the Gandian Air Force unit. The General had noticed that the units the Major worked with always seemed able to get supplies and favors, which had been hard to get before from military aid channels. The Major must have had some special influence with Washington. On the other hand, whenever the Major distributed these hard to get items, he always credited the General with getting them. This "magic" was simply a part of the long reach of the Secret Team.

The "major" was on a CIA cover assignment, and although everything he did had the appearance of normal U.S. Air Force duty, he was in Gandia to gather intelligence. He was part of a very normal inside operation. He knew who was on General Elciaro's team, and he knew who was not. He knew which elements of the government worked with the Air Force and which were aloof or antagonistic. When his routine reports, which he filed daily through his contact in the embassy and not through Air Force channels, revealed that he was getting quite close to the General, they were passed on by the

Deputy Director of Intelligence to the Deputy Director of Plans, and thence to Western Hemisphere. From that date on, WH monitored all traffic to and from the "major," and from time to time would feed him special instructions and other data. WH wanted to know exactly whom the General trusted and who in the government he worked with on official matters. In Gandia as in many other countries this could mean, "Who does he share his cut of government funds with and who shares theirs with him?"

One day, General Elciario told the major of his growing displeasure with the Government of the old President. This was passed on to WH. Day by day the Major increased the scope and coverage of the civic action training exercises that the U.S. Air Force and the U.S. Army Special Forces troops were interested in and that gave special credit to General Elciario. He was seen everywhere with new projects to build rural schools. He was seen delivering water pipe to a remote village from an Air Force transport. His fighters roared over distant cities and towns, letting the people know that the Air Force was everywhere. General Elciario opened the new U.S. satellite tracking station, and he was at the dedication ceremony of a new U.S. mining company's mountain airfield. And everywhere the General went the Major was somewhere in the background.

The Major found ways to be helpful to the General, and he gave the General an opportunity to widen the gap between himself and his government. Before long, the General was led to believe that the U.S. Government also was displeased with the old President. Although nothing was ever said, General Elciario was quite certain that if he made a move to take over the government, the U.S. Government would not make a move to support the present regime.

Note the formula: There was no commitment of any kind to support a coup d'état. On the contrary, the formula calls only for tacit agreement not to support the incumbent. As a matter of fact, the "major" had been sent to Gandia to look out for subversive insurgency. The possibility of a coup had developed quite spontaneously. And once it became a possibility, it was nurtured. As soon as the General realized this, he began to see himself as the person in power.

The lure was undeniable. He began to create his own team, and he began to count his chances.

It was not long before he came to the Major with the outline of a well planned scheme that purported to see a real and immediate requirement for a big civic action exercise in a remote province. This exercise would require a special consignment of weapons, ammunition, and perhaps silver bullion to buy off some of the dissident tribesmen. General Elciario made a good case for his plan and assured the Major that the natives would be properly stirred up at the right time to make it seem to everyone that this exercise was not only the real thing for training purposes but that a government show of force in that area would help put down rampant "Communist inspired subversion" in the area. The only problem would be the weapons. The General had no way to get that much material without arousing suspicion. The incumbent government kept all munitions under close control in secured magazines. Otherwise, not a word was said about even the remote possibility of a coup d'état. But both men, the U.S. Major and the ambitious General, understood each other.

That night the messages from the embassy to WH were highly classified and loaded with instructions to include the requests for munitions and airlift. WH was quick to respond. The neighboring country, Pegoan, had been scheduled to receive a normal, large shipment of military assistance munitions. The CIA arranged to have these delivered ahead of schedule and to seed the order with extra items for General Elciario. The U.S. Air Force was directed to make available four medium transport aircraft for the Gandian Air Force's "Civic Action" timing exercise. When all was in readiness, two large C-130 heavy four engine transport planes took off from Panama, bound for Pegoan. However, they filed a devious flight plan in order to make some "upper altitude weather tests for NASA." This gave them extra time en route. They landed in Pegoan on schedule; but unknown to that Government they had touched down on a remote mountain airstrip long enough to dump off a number of pallets loaded with munitions for Gandia. The two C-130s were able to get back in the air with only a thirty minute delay and to make their scheduled arrival time at their original destination. No one knew that they had delivered this cache of arms for the rebels in Gandia.

At the barren air strip, there had been only four men, all from the USAF. They had arrived unnoticed and unannounced in one of the U.S. Air Force Special Air Warfare U10 "Helio" light aircraft. This rugged light plane was especially designed to land in short distances on rough terrain. Yet it could carry six men, or four men and a cargo of special equipment. These men had set up panel signals to show the C-130s where to land. Then they had driven a number of heavy crowbars into the ground. To each one they affixed the loop end of a long nylon rope with a hook at the end. As soon as the first C-130 had landed, they directed it to turn around and open its huge rear end cargo doors. The lines were passed in to the crew and attached to pallets on which ammunition was firmly strapped. Then, as the C-130 gunned its engines for takeoff, the ropes pulled each pallet out of the plane and left a string of cargo on one side of the clearing. The process was repeated with the other C-130 on the other side of the clearing. No sooner had the C-130s left than four smaller C-123 medium transports arrived from Gandia, flying low over the mountain ridges to escape detection. The first plane landed short and spun around ready for take-off. It carried a small forklift unit that was used to load all four planes. The whole operation had taken less than an hour, and just before the four men left in their Helio, one of them drove the forklift over the cliff at the edge of the runway. The C-123s hedgehopped to the remote airfield in preparation for the civic action exercise.

Two U.S. Army Special Forces "advisers," working with the tribes in the exercise area, staged a pre-dawn "attack" using "fire fight" packages, along with a team of Gandian Army Special Forces who were told that they were on a training exercise.

The villagers were told this was a hostile attack, and the chieftain dutifully reported subversive insurgency to the district police headquarters in the nearest town. News spread to the capital, and this sector was reported to be in rebellion. General Elciario's field headquarters reported they would put down the trouble and that all would be under control. The increased activity was overlooked in the capital as one of those occasional native outbreaks. Then, under the cover of this "emergency," the incumbent government was served with an ultimatum. A well armed force of paratroopers disembarked at the main airport and began to take over the national radio station and other government centers. Since they were heavily armed, the president assumed that they included men upon whom he had relied and who had keys to the ammunition magazines. He called in his United States CIA friend who "reluctantly" confirmed that this was the case and that safe passage could be arranged for the president and his immediate family in a Fawcett Airlines plane, which "happened" to be at the airport. In a matter of hours, the old president was on his way, and a courier drove onto the Gandian Air Force Base to inform the Major that he could prepare Elciario for his victory march into the capital and to the Presidential Palace.

Elciario served his country for several years, and he may have been replaced in the same manner. Meanwhile the "major" has left for other duties. If the General had had the opportunity to visit the Guatemalan airfield, which was constructed on the ranch at Retalhuleu for the purpose of training Cuban air crews, he would have seen his old friend the "major" busy with those ex-Cuban airline pilots, trying to teach them how to fly the latest and most lethal model of the old B-26. Or he could have seen the "major" a while later at his primary support base in Arizona, where T-28s and other aircraft were being outfitted for Laos. Such men are members of a small and highly competent group of professionals who prepare the way for the operations dreamed up by the ST in any part of the world.

The real day to day operational work of the ST and of its principle action organization, the CIA, is so different from that of any ordinary arm of the Government that it would be worth the time and space here to define it and explain it as it is revealed in the scenes just outlined. The coup d'état described was a composite of real ones although the names of the countries involved and the name of the General are changed. Oddly enough, the General did become president after an all night party, and the "major" did have his hands full trying to get him ready for his victorious entry into town.

The CIA had a full-time man in the embassy who was responsible for what might be called routine intelligence. It was noted that there was increasing opposition to the incumbent President, so an Agency man was introduced into the country as an Army Colonel. He was a Special Forces officer and well known in the U.S. Army as an instructor at Fort Bragg. Actually, he had been at Fort Bragg in the John F. Kennedy Center on a CIA cover assignment. He had been in the Army during World War II and he had a bona fide Reserve commission. Technically, he was recalled to active duty; but he was paid by the CIA, and he was not on the basic Army roles except as a cover assignment.

When this special requirement in Gandia arose, the CIA got him transferred to the Army mission in Gandia by suggesting that the incumbent Army colonel be called back to attend the National War College. This excuse satisfied the Army headquarters in Panama and enabled the "cover" colonel to take over the mission without delay.

No sooner had this Colonel reported for duty than the ambassador began a buildup program for him so that he would have a chance to meet the president frequently and to talk with him sufficiently to win him over to the U.S. Army doctrine on civic action and to convince him that this could be applied to the "rebellious" areas in the border outposts. In this manner he became a confidant of the president and was very useful later during the coup d'état.

At about the same time that the "Army Colonel" arrived in Gandia, an American businessman, who was president of a small independent airline with its main offices in Panama, came into the capital city to open a one-man office to represent his airline. He rented a small space at the airport and hired a clerk and a young mamma who had been working with the well known Latin American airline, Fawcett Airways. Ostensibly to assure the success of his new venture, this man remained in Gandia for several months and visited all major companies in an attempt to sell them special air services which his company, by using small aircraft and one or two old World War II Flying Boat PBYs, could provide for them. He became a regular figure in town and was accepted as a hardworking, friendly businessman who knew Latin America and who could speak fluent

Spanish. Otherwise, he stayed in the background and was rarely seen in the official American community. He seemed to know no one at the embassy, and they were never seen with him. He was gathering intelligence, and he was an old professional. He had a drop for routine messages, which the Agency communications man sent through the special CIA transmitter in the embassy; but even the CIA people in Gandia did not know that he had his own network for highly classified messages out of Pegoan. He would fly there frequently, so that when he had important messages his sudden departure would not be noticed by the Gandians or the Americans.

Meanwhile, the U.S. Air Force "major" had been introduced through Air Force channels. He was technically an "overage" in Gandia and was carried on temporary duty status there for the duration of the civic action exercises, which were scheduled to last throughout the year. He was assigned to the U.S. Air Force Special Air Warfare unit in Panama. He was a longtime CIA employee who had served in many countries and was one of their best career pilots and blackflight specialists.

Although firm intelligence had shown the possibility that the old president was apt to be overthrown because of incipient developments, there were no reliable indications which would identify a possible successor. This left the Agency with the option of waiting to see who might rise to power by his own ability, or of stepping in with an attempt to create a man who could take over when the president's position became dangerously weakened. The former choice was poor because it left the door open for other interests, always considered to be Castroite or Communist, to step in with their own man. Since the Agency believed the fall of the present government to be about as certain as such a thing can be, it was decided to use the "Magsaysay formula" and to create the next president by making him the hero of the people throughout the country as a first step. It would be the job of the major to groom the man they had selected for the role.

The "major" did not know the American businessman who was president of the small airline, and had never come across him during his Agency career. The airline president did not know him either. The Agency planned to keep them working independently so that it could cross-check their reports. The "major" had met the Army

Colonel during airdrop exercises at Fort Bragg, but he thought he was a real Army Special Forces instructor and did not know that he, too, was a CIA career man. The Agency gave him clearance to work with the Colonel very closely and cleared the Colonel similarly. The "major" did not know of the Colonel's role with the old President and the Colonel did not know the "major's" assignment. Each man was to play his role straight.

The ambassador was fully informed of the Agency's plan, since he was the recipient of its secret intelligence reports, and he knew that one of the men in his communications room was an Agency man. He had never made an attempt to determine which man it was because he thought his charge d'affaires knew; also, it would be better for him to keep his fingers out of that kind of thing. He did not know that the "major," the Colonel, and the airline president were CIA men. He did not see their message traffic, although the Agency took pains to make sure that he received "cleaned" copies of their dispatches, which he assumed had been culled from attach reports and other more or less normal sources. The ambassador was not interested in intelligence; he had been in the country only one year, and if he could keep things calm, he hoped to be transferred at the end of the second year. He was a political appointee and not a career man.

The "major" spent a considerable amount of time setting up elaborate civic action exercises in all areas of the country. These were staged like carnivals, and at the climax of every operation, General Elciario would fly in and address the village and local tribesmen. There had been a few native uprisings, and some operations were directed into those areas to impress the villagers with the power of the new air force. The "major" found a few villages that lived in fear of bandit tribes. Here he took a page from the Magsaysay book and rigged some early morning "attacks" by what he called the Red team. These attacks were always repulsed by a Blue team, which just happened to be in the area. In every case, Elciario would show up leading the victorious "anti-guerrillas." The unwitting natives took this as the real thing, and the fame of General Elciario as the greatest guerrilla fighter since Simon Bolivar spread throughout the country.

This kind of script calls for the utilization of equipment "borrowed" from the U.S. Armed Forces, along with personnel to carry out such missions. It also calls for the liberal use of a blank checkbook, which the General is urged to use to win over those who might be useful.

Up to this stage of the action, most of what the CIA has been doing falls in the category of intelligence, with only a preparatory stage of clandestine operations. As its agents report a worsening position for the old President and general disillusionment on the part of key businessmen and other leaders, along with a growing national awareness of General Elciario, WH puts together the outline of a proposed operation to be briefed to the DD/P (clandestine services) and thence to the DCI. Following this briefing, and with the approval of these men, the Agency will brief selected key people in Defense and State to see how they feel about the situation and whether or not they are ready to see a change of government in Gandia.

Throughout this period, the Agency will have been sending special messages to its man in the embassy. He will use these to brief the ambassador, or perhaps to have the Army Colonel brief the ambassador to guide him in this situation. Some of the very messages the Agency will have sent to Gandia will come back over the embassy network as intelligence input, and at the same time will be transmitted by the attaches to the Defense Department. Thus a wave of messages, all corroborating one another, will fill the "In" baskets in State, Defense, and the White House. In his role as intelligence coordinator the DCI will prepare his own analysis of all of this and will prepare to place this business on the agenda of the next NSC Special Group meeting; he will present the current situation *only*, and propose a special operation.

By this time, the Agency and a number of the Secret Team operatives will have just about decided that the only thing to do in Gandia is to go along with General Elciario and permit him to exploit the situation. They will have convinced themselves that if the government is that shaky in the first place, they had better be on the winning side rather than on the "Communists." A special group meeting will be held, and the designated substitute for each NSC member will attend. The consensus of the meeting will be to go ahead with the "major's" program but to hold up until each member has had an opportunity to inform his principal of the action.

The DCI will offer to visit the President and will get his approval; this makes the visit to the Secretary of State and Secretary of Defense purely informational.

This account of developments may seem somewhat unreal. Anyone who has carefully read the Pentagon Papers will recognize most of the above. In fact, most people who have read the Pentagon Papers will see that this is what was done in the case of the Diems in South Vietnam. The significant point is that the CIA may have sent the "major" to Gandia in the first place simply to see how things were going there and perhaps to have him ready for action in a neighboring country if needed. But the "major" is an old firehorse, and when he hears the bell, he cannot help getting into harness. The scenario is somewhat like the movie *Fahrenheit 451*, in which the firemen were the men who started fires rather than the men who put them out.

It is so easy to topple over a government in most small countries simply by finding the key to control. If all arms and equipment are kept under close control, then the armed forces and the police have few useful weapons at any given time. Thus, if the leader of the rebellion all of a sudden shows up with a large and unaccounted for supply of weapons, he may be able to take the government over without a shot, simply by the fact that he has them outgunned before they start. Thus it is not too difficult for a man with boundless resources such as the "major" could command to be able to arrange things almost effortlessly. At that point, all he has to know, and all the man he is supporting has to know, is that the United States will not make a move to support the incumbent. Then, when the tide begins to turn, the incumbent finds himself alone with no one in a position to help him. Like so many things the ST does, this is more a negative coup d'état than a positive action.

It is not to be presumed that a program such as this can be fully implemented in a short time, or that it is set in motion with the objective of causing and supporting a coup d'état. As a matter of fact, the characteristic of the ST that supersedes all others in such a situation as this is that events should take their natural course, with some covert help.

A document that was circulated from the CIA through other government agencies and extra governmental organizations such as the RAND Corporation and the Institute for Defense Analysis shows how this is done. Once a country is included on the "counterinsurgency" list, or any other such category, a move is made to develop a CIA echelon, usually within the structure of whatever U.S. military organization exists there at the time. Then the CIA operation begins Phase I by proposing the introduction of some rather conventional aircraft. No developing country can resist such an offer, and this serves to create a base of operations, usually in a remote and potentially hostile area. While the aircraft program is getting started the Agency will set up a high frequency radio network, using radios positioned in villages throughout the host country. The local inhabitants are told that these radios will provide a warning of guerrilla activity.

Phase II of such a project calls for the introduction of medium transport type aircraft that meet anti-guerrilla warfare support requirements. The crew training program continues, and every effort is made to develop an in-house maintenance capability. As the level of this activity increases, more and more Americans are brought in, ostensibly as instructors and advisers; at this phase many of the Americans are Army Special Forces personnel who begin civic action programs. The country is sold the idea that it is the Army in most developing nations that is the usual stabilizing influence and that it is the Army that can be trusted. This is the American doctrine; promoting the same idea, but in other words, it is a near paraphrase of the words of Chairman Mao.

In the final phase of this effort, light transports and liaison type aircraft are introduced to be used for border surveillance, landing in remote areas, and for resupplying small groups of anti-guerrilla warfare troops who are operating away from fixed bases. These small specialized aircraft are usually augmented by helicopters.

When the plan has developed this far, efforts are made to spread the program throughout the frontier area of the country. Villagers are encouraged to clear off small runways or helicopter landing pads, and more warning network radios are brought into remote areas.

While this work is continuing, the government is told that these activities will develop their own military capability and that there will be a bonus economic benefit from such development, each complementing the other. It also makes the central government able to contact areas in which it may never have been able to operate before, and it will serve as a tripwire warning system for any real guerrilla activities that may arise in the area.

There is no question that this whole political economic social program sounds very nice, and most host governments have taken the bait eagerly. What they do not realize, and in many cases what most of the U.S. Government does not realize, is that this is a CIA program, and it exists to develop intelligence. If it stopped there, it might be acceptable but intelligence serves as its own propellant, and before long the agents working on this type of project see, or perhaps are a factor in creating, internal dissension. Or they may find areas of ancient border contacts, or they may run into some legitimate probing and prodding from a neighboring country, which may or may not have its origins in Moscow, just as our program had its origins in Washington. In any event, the intelligence operator at this point begins to propose operations, and use clandestine operations lead to minor "Vietnams" or other such bleeding ulcer type projects that drain United States resources, wealth, and manpower on behalf of no meaningful national objective.

The CIA maintains hundreds of U.S. military units for its own purposes. Many of these units become involved in this type of operation. After these cover units have been in existence for several years, the military has a hard time keeping track of them. The military system is prone to try to ignore such abnormalities, and the CIA capitalizes on this to bury some units deep in the military wasteland.

The CIA also maintains countless paramilitary and pseudobusiness organizations that weave in and out of legitimacy and do business much as their civilian counterparts would. The small airline alluded to in the Gandia example actually exists and very capably operates in Latin America. It operates as a viable business and competes with other airlines of its type. The only difference is that the officials of the other airlines, who have a hard time meeting the payroll at times, wonder how their competition is able to stay in business year after year with no more volume than they have. At such a point, most of the competition will rationalize that the cover airline must be in some illegitimate business like smuggling and the drug trade, or else that it is connected with the CIA. They could be right on both counts. Most of these cover businesses have to be closed out and reestablished from time to time to support their usefulness. (It may be interesting to note that in September 1963, none other than the Secretary of the Senate, Bobby Baker, got mixed up with one of these cover airlines, Fairways Incorporated, without knowing it, and that the exposure resulting from his accidental charter of this small airline played a part in bringing down his house of cards.

Part of the Gandia coup d'état demonstrates that the ambassador will be briefed on most things that happen in his country, and if he is alert and insistent, he may be on top of most of the things the ST is doing there. In actual practice, however, there may be quite a bit of communications traced that he will know nothing about. The CIA will have its own communications network, and in addition to that, agents who come and go will be sending messages outside of the country that he may never know about. It would be an unusually adept ambassador who would catch all of the by-play in the incoming messages and the outgoing traffic. Most ambassadors would be surprised to learn that some of the staff messages that are proposed to them for authorization to transmit were received from the ST almost verbatim in the form which his "staff" have given him to send back to Washington. This is a useful device for the ST because it gets a message of unquestioned authority from the ambassador into the Department of State and usually into Defense via attach channels.

By this innocent appearing device, the ST is able to create intelligence inputs that are then used for clandestine operations feedback. This becomes a possible ploy, because the Team can separate the people who know about the outgoing messages from those who know about the incoming messages by the "need to know" and "eyes only" restrictive methods. Such methods are not commonly used, but they are used when someone on the ST feels that the desired end will justify this means.

In this example we saw that the Agency had operatives working in Gandia who were unaware of each other's presence. It is entirely possible that the ambassador may not have known either that all of the CIA men working on this project were CIA men. He would have had available to him a list of all Americans in Gandia if he had wanted to research it; but in operational exercises such as this, it is most likely that he would not know all the agents. This is a most touchy area, and there have been times when the CIA's own chief of station, its senior man in the country, was not aware of the fact that other CIA men were working in his country. This can create some very complex problems. In one case of record it resulted in a very serious altercation between two CIA factions, with the result that the chief of station demanded that the other men leave or that he would leave. In that instance, the chief of station left.

Another way the ST gets around the special operative problem is to employ non U.S. citizens to assist in countries where an over-scrupulous ambassador or cautious chief of station have given trouble. A number of such personnel have been used by the CIA in Indochina in a variety of roles, and in some exceptional cases, they have been used on special assignments in Latin America.

The Gandia incident shows another special facility in the hands of the ST. In order to equip General Elciario with an abundance of arms and ammunition, the CIA arranged with the Air Force to airlift these munitions to a remote site. In order to do this the two large C-130 aircraft had to depart from the U.S. Air Force base in Panama with cargo manifests that showed only the actual cargo that was being delivered to the final destination in the capital of Pegoan. This meant that a deal had to be made with customs in order to get out of Panama. The landing in Pegoan had to be clandestine, and the chance of discovery had to be gambled. There have been incidents where such illicit cargo drops were made and then discovered before they could be picked up. In such cases, the cargo had to be abandoned, and the finder was so much the richer;

the U.S. Government could not make a move to identify itself as owner of the property.

The pickup flights also had to be clandestine in that they left Gandia and entered Pegoan without clearance or flight plan, made their landing, pickup, and return with no manifested cargo in Gandia. This part of the operation may not seem important, but should there have been exposure of any of those illicit flights, it could have led to exposure of the entire plot, and a coup d'état by the opposite side may have taken place or the old President may have had sufficient warning to take strong measures to remain in power. Certainly if he did learn of this business, he would no longer be a friend of the United States.

We have mentioned the Magsaysay incident before. The way in which the ST was able to build up Magsaysay from an unknown Army captain to a national hero and eventually to president was so appealing that the technique has been attempted in other countries. One of the gambles with that game is that a situation has to be developed, preferably in some remote area where it can be alleged that there is a pro-Communist activity—in the case in point, Huk (Communist sympathizers) activities. In the beginning there may be an incipient outbreak of banditry caused by crop damage or other hardship. The natives will attack other villages for food and other plunder, usually for the sole purpose of staying alive. As this situation continues and spreads it will come to the attention of the national police or the border patrol. They may not have the means to cope with the uprising and may ask the government to help them. At this point the armed forces may recall their civic action training at Fort Bragg or in Panama and they may ask the U.S. military mission personnel to assist them. No country likes to admit that it has some internal problems, so they quite readily call the banditry "subversive insurgency" and imply that it may be Communist-inspired.

This puts the flame to the wick. Nothing will get a rise out of Special Forces—both Army and Air Force—faster. In short order they will be on the spot to see what can be done, and in every case the CIA will have men seeded in the units. At this point this is still a CIA effort, and it may stay in that category as far as the ST is concerned until the disorders have receded or have flared higher. Usually, the breakpoint occurs when it is discovered that the rioting is being blamed upon the incumbent administration. Then the CIA looks for the possibility of a coup, from there on it is the familiar pattern. Such events—and there have been so many during the past fifteen to twenty years—show how easily intelligence becomes clandestine operations, and how clandestine operations are usually the result of a reaction or a response mechanism and are not a part of any planning or policy.

This is the great danger. The leaders of CIA and important members of the ST have protested countless times that the CIA does not enter into policy making. In this they are correct on most counts. The problem lies in the fact that they are not policy making, and on top of that, the operations they carry out are not in support of policy, either. They simply grow like Topsy, arising out of a feedback from intelligence data inputs; in some cases there is no reason at all for the action. In other words, there may be no national objective other than the loose coverall or blanket observation that the operation is anti-Communist.

Another special area in which the ST excels is that of logistics support of clandestine operations. They always seem to operate out of a boundless horn of plenty. In the Gandia example, the CIA was able to call for and have delivered a large quantity of munitions, and to have it delivered in heavy aircraft, all of which cost someone a lot of money. We shall have a general discussion of logistics support in a later chapter and will not go unto detail here, but it should be noted that it is one thing to be able to move such a cargo in and out of various countries without customs and other controls, and it is another thing to get the cargo in the first place. Most of us have been led to believe that the Armed Forces are required to account for each and every item they have procured with the taxpayer's dollar. Then how does the CIA manage to get so much, so easily? All munitions have to be transferred from control depots to transportation points, and all such transactions are under control and regulation. To get around this, the ST has developed a system of its own storage depots and has them so interlaced with the military system that not even the military can track down some of the transactions.

These transactions are often written off with the comment, "It's all in the government"; but there is one area of imbalance that adds appreciably to the cost of such extracurricular activities. In the foreign aid program, there are very careful balances in aid maintained between different countries, especially neighboring countries or countries in the same sphere of influence. If we give one country a new series of Army tanks, then we must be prepared to give the neighbor the same. This will repeat itself like a row of dominoes, and the next thing we know we have to re-equip a whole series of countries with the newer equipment, because we started with one. This situation is expensive, and it is hard to control. A delivery to Pakistan of equipment not delivered to India will set off a most unpleasant round of talks with India. During India's border problems in 1965, offers were made to deliver a large shipment of arms to India. Although Pakistan was also involved to a lesser degree in the border problem, this was forgotten in the argument over the imbalance which the former delivery would create between India and Pakistan. In the end, Pakistan did increase its contact with China and became less friendly to the United States.

This system is very complicated and few would have the temerity to interfere with it. However, the CIA has from time to time created situations where munitions delivered to one country, ostensibly for a clandestine operation have ended up in the hands of the central government and have created a gross imbalance within the same sphere. An example of this occurred after the Bay of Pigs operation, when Nicaragua took possession of aircraft and other valuable munitions that had been stockpiled at Puerto Cabezas and had not been used. The advanced model of the B-26 bomber being prepared for the use of the Cubans was a much more lethal aircraft than any neighbor of Nicaragua had in its own inventory. This set off a whole round of arguments about increasing the aircraft inventory of the other countries. Though these examples are limited and incomplete, they serve to point out the nature of clandestine operations.

The principle reason why the creation of the CIA within the framework of our free society has caused very serious problems is because the intelligence function, as it has been operating under the DCI and the rest of the community, almost inevitably leads to clandestine operations. The law intended otherwise, but general practice during the past twenty-five years has served to erode the barriers between Intelligence and clandestine operations to the point where today this type of thing, unfortunately, has become rather commonplace. And why has it become so commonplace? The most basic reason is because nations' ills of all kinds are highlighted by instant global communications and then are generally attributed to the Communist bogeyman. This is not to say, of course, that some ills may not be caused by Communist pressures, just as some are caused by American pressures. (In fact, the benefits of being charged with so many actions are so tremendous for the men in the Kremlin that they would be less than skillful if they did not stir up a few obvious cases now and then to keep the pot boiling. When a small contribution to the effort in Indochina on the part of the men in the Kremlin can get fifty-five thousand Americans killed and $200 billion wasted versus no Russians killed and only a few billion dollars invested, the Kremlin cannot be blamed for using this tactic to its advantage.)

In the Philippines, lumbering interests and major sugar interests have forced tens of thousands of simple, backward villagers to leave areas where they have lived for centuries. When these poor people flee to other areas, it should be quite obvious that they in turn then infringe upon the territorial rights of other villagers or landowners. This creates violent rioting or at least sporadic outbreaks of banditry, that last lowly recourse of dying and terrorized people. Then when the distant government learns of the banditry and rioting, it must offer some safe explanation. The last thing that regional government would want to do would be to say that the huge lumbering or paper interests had driven the people out of their ancestral homeland. In the Philippines it is customary for the local regional government to get a 10 percent rake-off on all such enterprise and for national politicians to get another 10 percent. So the safe explanation becomes "Communist-inspired subversive insurgency." The word for this in the Philippines is *Huk*.

In the piece of real estate we now call South Vietnam, the refugee problem that resulted in rioting and incipient banditry was derived from three sources. The huge French rubber plantation holdings and lumbering interests, the mass movement of hundreds of thousands of Vietnamese from north of the 17th parallel, and the complete collapse of the ancient rice economy, which included the destruction of potable water resources during the early years of the Diem regime—all came at about the same time to create a terroristic situation among millions of people in what would otherwise have been their ancestral homeland. Again this was attributed to subversive insurgency inspired by Communism.

This is a familiar formula in Latin America, too, and is found to be at the root of the problem in the emerging nations of Africa. In following chapters we shall see how the new U.S. Army doctrine that has been developed at the White House by a special Presidential committee is designed expressly to meet such situations and to create in those countries a military center of power bracketing all political-economic and social activity.

In the context of "Army" policy this committee's two major contributors and authors were both U.S. military generals who were actually the spokesmen for the CIA. The policy that they developed has become the CIA's most effective tool during the "Counterinsurgency era," which began in about 1960–61.

CHAPTER 4

FROM THE WORD OF THE LAW TO THE INTERPRETATION: PRESIDENT KENNEDY ATTEMPTS TO PUT THE CIA UNDER CONTROL

Beside the towering mountains the field looked more like pastureland than a hidden airfield. As a result, it was not surprising to see mud-covered water buffalo grazing in the shade beneath the wing of the old World War II B-17 Flying Fortress. Low rambling sheds, some of them stables and others supply shelters, were scattered along the perimeter of the field. A full stand of grass and small underbrush had grown up through the mesh of the pierced steel plank that had been laid on the ground to form a parking ramp for a collection of clandestine aircraft.

Coils of barbed wire had been spread everywhere in a cleverly concealed random pattern, with wild flowers growing through it in abundance. Yet for all its appearance of tranquility, this remote airfield was the center of a most active clandestine air activity. The pastoral scene camouflaged the muted industry of teams of Chinese Nationalist specialists who prepared the B-17s for deep flights over the mainland. Agent information told of trouble deep in China that was being exploited by leaflet drops from the old bombers. Skilled crews, who flew low to use the terrain as cover from radar, pinpointed the trouble cities on each flight because they were natives of the area.

Upon return, one crew reported the city ringed with searchlights probing for the planes through the murky sky. The pilot had dropped through the clouds and actually flown the B-17 in a tight circle inside the ring of searchlights, right over the heart of the ancient city, spraying leaflets all the time. As soon as his leaflet cargo had been dropped, he brought the plane down into the dark path of the river and flew at tree-top level back to the sea coast.

One morning, just after the sun had burst above the eastern peaks of Formosa, I saw two of these aircraft drop into the pasture for a safe landing after an all-night mission. As they taxied to a halt on the steel plank the Chinese ground crews swarmed around the planes, thrilled at the return of the crews and the success of the night and eager to hear how everything had gone. Then I noticed a few American technicians systematically removing tape and film canisters and other specialized equipment from in the planes to the laboratory for development and processing. I couldn't help but ponder the significance of these flights upon these two professional groups and the meaning of the word *clandestine*, as well as the nature of the policy that accounted for these flights.

To these Chinese the flights were a return to the homeland. They were probes at the remaining weak spots in the Chinese Communist shield. They were a serious attempt designed to arouse mainland Chinese, to demonstrate that the old regime still cared and that the Western World was still with them.

For the Americans these flights were entirely different. I had traveled to Taiwan with a CIA career man, after having completed eight months of concentrated staff work devising and designing an elaborate logistical system for special operations work all over the world. We had flown to Taiwan to see some of the field operations that were supported by this system. As I watched these two distinct elements work, supporting the same mission, from the same base, I saw at first hand a truth that had not been evident back in the Pentagon. The Chinese were very proud of these flights and of their part in doing something for their own people. To the Americans this was just a job, and it was one in which they could not become identified. If a mission failed, as some did, and the crew and the plane were lost, the Chinese Nationalists would honor their gallant men. If a mission was lost, the Americans would have to ignore it and deny they had played any part in the operation at all. In that sense, warfare is honorable and part of an ancient and respected tradition. On the other hand, clandestine warfare is never honorable and must always be denied. With this in mind, why were Americans themselves involved in these operations and others like them all around the world?

The answer is complex. The more intimate one becomes with this activity, the more one begins to realize that such operations are rarely, if ever, initiated from an intent to become involved in pursuit of some national objective in the first place. It would be hard to find an example of a clandestine operation that had been developed from the beginning solely in support of some significant national objective.

The lure of "fun and games" is addictive, and it is most powerful. There would be no intelligence problem at any level within the community if it were not for the inevitability of the desire to divert intelligence operations into secret operations. There would be little complaint and few problems if the CIA was limited to include secret intelligence and no more. In this day of three-dimensional capability with electronic snoopers and satellites, there is no place to hide anyhow, and concealment and secrecy are time-limited devices at best.

It used to be that if a nation defended its borders and saw to it that no one entered its territory, it could keep secret its actions, its maneuvers, and its intentions. It was the secret development of the simple iron ramrod that gave the armies of Frederick the Great of Prussia such a predominant margin of superiority in battle. Today, such singular and distinct advances might occur, as with the atom bomb. But the secret—if it is a secret at all—cannot be kept. There is no way to hide it and no place to hide. High-flying aircraft and satellite observation platforms provide us with accurate photographic information sufficient to identify and distinguish such an object as a round card table from a square card table. Special sensors give evidence of crop yields, thermal output variations, and many other areas of information. Nuclear weapons plants can be observed on a regular schedule and activity gauged quite accurately by several methods. Various electronic and communications monitors provide much more valuable information that even the satellites cannot get. Sophisticated economic studies provide volumes of essential and very precise information that cannot be hidden except at great cost and inconvenience. The very fact that modern industrial production methods require numbering, marking, and serial coding of products and parts manufactured plays directly into the hands of the vigilant intelligence operator. There can be few real secrets, and even these become fewer as soon as a little time is involved.

A good secret will last only a short time at best. Even the secret of the atom bomb and of its delivery system was more than 50 percent compromised once the bomb had burst over Hiroshima and Nagasaki. As Norbert Wiener had said in his book, *The Human Use of Human Beings:* "When we consider a problem of nature such as that of atomic reactions and atomic explosions, the largest single item of information which we can make public is that they exist. Once a scientist attacks a problem which he knows to have an answer, his entire attitude is changed. He is already some fifty percent of his way toward that answer." And of more particular relevancy to the field of intelligence is another quote from Wiener: "The most important information which we can possess is the knowledge that the message which we are reading is not gibberish." In this context he is talking about the problem of codebreakers; but this is also applicable to many other areas of interest involving data acquired from numberless sources in tremendous quantities. The responsibility lies heavily upon the intelligence system itself to assure that it has been able to separate the wheat from the chaff. Data may not be gibberish as it comes in, but if it is not processed and evaluated properly, it may be useless when it comes out.

It is always of paramount importance to know that the information we have is not planted, false or a product of deception. So even the quest for secret intelligence may not exist as a major requirement to the extent that the CIA purists would like to make it seem. But this is not the real problem. The real problem is with clandestine operations In peacetime that have been mounted in response to intelligence data inputs that might have been deceptive or misinterpreted in the first place

During World War II there were reasons for clandestine operations, and much essential information was obtained by such means. However, as many students and researchers in this area have discovered, the value of such clandestine means was relatively small. As soon as World War II was over, President Truman dissolved the OSS to assure that clandestine operations would cease immediately. Six months later, when he founded the Central intelligence Group, he expressly denied a covert role for that authority and restricted the DCI to a coordinating function. During the debates leading up to the passage of the National Security Act of 1947 (NSA/47), proponents of a clandestine role for the CIA were repeatedly outmaneuvered and outvoted in Congress. In his book *The Secret War*, Sanche de Gramont reports: "The NSA/47 replaced the CIG with the CIA, a far more powerful body. From the hearings on the NSA/47 it is evident that no one knew exactly what the nature of the beast would be." At that time a member of the House, Representative Fred Busby, made the prophetic and quite accurate remark: "I wonder if there is any foundation for the rumors that have come to me to the effect that through this CIA they are contemplating operational activities." That congressman knew what he was talking about, and as we look back upon a quarter-century of the CIA it seems hard to believe that he wasn't sure that was exactly what they were up to in the first place.

When the law was passed, it contained no provision whatsoever either for collection of intelligence or for clandestine activities. However it did contain one clause that left the door ajar for later interpretation and exploitation. The CIA was created by the NSA/47 and placed under the direction of the NSC, a committee. This same act had established the NSC at the same time. Therefore, the CIA's position relative to the NSC was without practice and precedent; but the law was specific in placing the agency under the direction of that committee, and in not placing the Agency in the Office of the President and directly under his control. In conclusion, this act provided that among the duties the CIA would perform, it would:

> ... (5) perform such other functions and duties related to intelligence affecting the National Security as the NSC may from time to time direct.

This was the inevitable loophole, and as time passed and as the CIA and the ST grew in power and know-how they tested this clause in the Act and began to practice their own interpretation of its meaning. They believed that it meant they could practice clandestine operations. Their perseverance paid off. During the summer of 1948 the NSC issued a directive, number 10/2, which authorized special operations, with two stipulations: (a) Such operations must be secret, and (b) such operations must be plausibly deniable. These were important prerequisites.

The CIA really worked at the achievement of this goal toward unlimited and unrestrained covert operations. In its earlier years the directors, Admiral Souers and General W. B. Smith, were preoccupied with the task of getting the Agency organized, with beating down the traditional opposition of the older members of the community, and with performing their primary function, that of coordinating national intelligence. However, with the advent of the Allen Dulles era, ever-increasing pressure was placed on the restraints that bound covert operations. Dulles succeeded in freeing the Agency from these fetters to such an extent that five years after his departing from the Agency the retiring DCI, Admiral Raborn, was so conditioned to the CIA "party line" that he could not quote the law correctly.

In reply to a question put to him by the *U.S. News and World Report* of July 18, 1966, asking what was the specific charter of the CIA, he said," . . . to perform such other services as the NSC may direct . . . That fifth assignment is the Agency's charter for clandestine activities . . . "This is a very small deviation from the exact language of the law, but it is fundamental, and it shows how the Agency and even its DCI in 1966 believed and wanted others to believe that the NSA/47 did in fact give the CIA a clandestine activity charter, whereas it did not. The Act carefully stipulated that the CIA could perform such other activities as the "NSC would from time to time direct." That "time to time" stipulation clearly limits the Agency's "other services" to intermittent matters and does not give the Agency any clear authority to perform clandestine activities. As a matter of fact, many other actions, as we shall see, took place to prevent the Agency from getting any such automatic and routine authority.

Another statement of Admiral Raborn's is equally slanted. In response to a question about clandestine activity, he states that the Agency "must have the prior approval—in detail—of a committee of the NSC" before it can carry out such activity. Again there is but a shading of the language of the law; but again it is most fundamental. The law says that the Agency is under the direction of the NSC. In terms of how the Agency should, in accordance with the law, become involved in clandestine activity, the law follows its "from time to time" stipulation by saying that the Agency will perform such activity "by direction of the NSC." There is a distinct difference between winning approval of something and doing it by direction of the NSC. The distinction is in the area of the origin of the idea. The laws sees the NSC as responsible for the origination of the idea and then for the direction of the Agency. The Agency sees this as being something that it originates, ostensibly through its intelligence sources, and then takes to the NSC for approval. This was not contemplated by the law. Furthermore, the law did not authorize the creation of a "committee of NSC" for such important matters. It was the intent of the Congress that the NSC itself direct such things.

It should be noted also that Admiral Raborn got carried away in this interview with another statement. In response to the question, "Would the U.S. ambassador in the country concerned know about your activities there?" Raborn replied, "CIA's overseas personnel are subordinate to the U.S. ambassadors. We operate with the foreknowledge and approval of the ambassador." The reader may have his choice in concluding that Admiral Raborn either made an untrue statement, or that he did not know how his clandestine services operated. I choose to believe the latter. In either case, there are countless instances in which the ambassador does not know what the CIA is doing. Kenneth Galbraith's *Ambassador's Journal* is all anyone needs to read to see that. Or would someone like to say that Ambassador Keating in India knew what Henry Kissinger and his Agency friends were doing in Pakistan and India during the December, 1971, conflict? Another case would be that of Ambassador Timberlake in the Congo.

It would be unthinkable that the DCI, in this case Admiral Raborn, would intentionally make untrue statements in a national publication such as the *U.S. News and World Report*. The least he could have done would have been to avoid the question entirely. The deeper meaning of this interview is that Admiral Raborn, after more than a year of duty as DCI, simply did not know how his operating agents worked. He thought he had a clear ticket for clandestine operations, and he thought that arrangements were such that ambassadors would know about the actions of the CIA's clandestine operators. This is a clear example of how far the Agency has gone in getting around the law and in creating its own inertial drift, which puts it into things almost by an intelligence-input-induced automation system, without the knowledge of its own leaders and certainly without the knowledge of most higher-level authorities.

In times of peace it would have been unthinkable for one nation to interfere openly in the internal affairs of another without some prior understanding. All such occurrences otherwise are met with disapproval from all over the world. It must be admitted at the present time such fine points are sometimes overlooked for various emergency reasons; but these are the exceptions and not the rule. Even in South Vietnam, where there has never been a really independent government and where the United States, for all its sacrifice and assistance, might be expected quite understandably to have some rights, we find that the ambassador leans over backwards, at least in appearance, not to interfere in the internal affairs of that beleaguered nation. And that is a rather extreme example.

In the world family of nations, sovereignty is one of the key conditions of existence, and sovereignty is inviolate. Even if we talk about some small country such as Monaco or Luxembourg, the code of nations regards their sovereignty to be as precious as that of the United States or the USSR. The day this code breaks down will be the beginning of the end of world order and of a return to the rule of brute force. Liberty begins as the aspiration of the individual, and sovereignty is the measure of the absolute power of a state. As we look around us today, we see an erosion of this fundament of international society. It is for this reason that we must look into this situation and consider how important it is to the world community to uphold principles that we hold to be essential and priceless assets of our civilization.

Since sovereignty is priceless and must be inviolate, it is fundamental that no nation has the right to do that which if every other nation did likewise, would destroy this fragile fabric of civilization. We all agree in 99 percent of the cases that no nation has the right to infringe overtly upon the sovereignty of another. Since there is no higher court or other jurisdictional body empowered as final and absolute arbiter over the nations of the world, judgments in such cases must be left to the honor that exists among nations. When this fails, the only other alternative is for all nations large and small to form power blocks and alliances that in one way or another result in dependence upon brute force and sufficient leverage to demand compliance with the doctrine of sovereignty. Such moves in themselves result in the sacrifice of some measure of sovereignty. The price of alliance is generally some form of agreement and limitation of sovereignty that binds each party to assist the other even to the point of maintaining troops on the other's soil, or some other such measure. But for lack of other means, all nations must in the final issue seek their own security as best they can, and somewhere in this fabric the common good directs that all nations honor and respect certain unassailable rights.

Since no nation would then resort to overt infringement of sovereignty without being ready to face up to a war with that nation—perhaps a war of major proportions involving nations in alliance with that nation—then overt infringement is for all practical purposes out of the question. In all respects overt violation of the sovereignty of one nation by another would be a more difficult decision to make than a covert or clandestine infringement of sovereignty. If one nation believes that it has so much at stake that it must infringe upon the sovereignty of another nation, it will resort to clandestine means as the lesser of two evils.

Choosing a clandestine act leads to a rich dilemma: either the operation will be successful and it will never be discovered, or it will fail and the guilty nation may be found out. And then, realizing that such operations are directed and manned by human beings and that failure is inevitable, the NSC added a second most important stipulation, to the effect that in the case of failure the U.S. Government must be able to disclaim plausibly any part in such an operation. These safeguards take none of the gravity away from the nature of the operation; they simply serve as a precautionary and stringent guidelines to remind the Agency that clandestine operations directed by an agency of the U.S. Government are serious business.

Lest anyone think that the only barriers to the conduct of covert operations are those that reflect upon honor, prestige, and other gentlemanly intangibles, we should not overlook the other side of the coin. The U.S. Government has been blackmailed to the tune of hundreds of millions of dollars in goods, materials, and preferential trade agreements as a result of the failures of clandestine operations in Cuba, Nicaragua, Greece, Indonesia, the Congo, Tibet, Pakistan, Norway, and other nations. This is one of the seldom noted and rarely announced hidden costs of such activities.

At the time the NSC published its guidelines in 1948, they were heeded with great care. One of the most important characteristics of a covert operation, in addition to the fact that it must be secret, is that it be very small. There is no such thing as a successful big clandestine operation. The bigger the operation, the less chance there is that it can be secret. This issue was one of the most serious matters to come out of the personal review of the Bay of Pigs failure that was made by President Kennedy and his brother. Although the law states that the CIA is under the direction of the NSC, there have been times, usually after the failure of a major operation, when the President has had to accept publicly the responsibility for the operation. It is obvious to anyone that the President as the elected leader of this nation is responsible for all activity of the Government. It is even more evident that the President as Commander in Chief of the Armed Forces of this country bears the final and sole responsibility for all military action; but nothing in the traditional military doctrine provides for the role of the Commander in Chief when involved in peacetime covert operations. A nation is not supposed to become involved in covert activity—ever. Therefore its commander in chief is not—ever—supposed to be involved either in the success or the failure of such action. Recent CIA failures such as the U-2, Indonesia, the Bay of Pigs, and more recently, Indochina, have involved the Commander in Chief.

At this point when a covert operation has failed and has become public knowledge, the President is faced with a most unpleasant dilemma. He must accept the responsibility for the operation or he must not. If he does, he admits that this country has been officially and willfully involved in an illegal and traditionally unpardonable activity. If he does not, he admits that there are subordinates within his Government who have taken upon themselves the direction of such operations, to jeopardize the welfare and good name of this country by mounting clandestine operations. Such an admission requires that he dismiss such individuals and banish them from his Administration.

However, by the terms of the definition of clandestine activities, no one should be put in a position of having to admit responsibility for such operations. It is always agreed before the operation is launched that should it fail it will be disowned and denied. If this is not done and if extreme care has not been taken to assure the secrecy, success, and then if necessary, the deniability of each operation, no clandestine operation should ever be launched. If clandestine operations that do not meet these stringent requirements are set in motion they should not be pursued. They are falsely clandestine if they do not meet these requirements and thus enter the realm of open and inexcusable overt operations, disguised as it were as clandestine operations, or finally, in the last analysis, they are the product of shallow hypocrisy and callousness. During the past fifteen years things have gone that far, and there have been so-called clandestine operations that were in reality bold-faced overt activities carried out within another country without its consent. Most such events have resulted in coups d'état, some of which have been successful and some failures; but in all cases the open "clandestine" activity was rationalized on the basis that the old government was undesirable, that it was going to be overthrown and a little intervention was necessary anyhow.

The Bay of Pigs invasion and all of the other operational evens that accompanied that ill-fated exercise were more or less in that category. The whole campaign was much too large to have been clandestine. It had been too long and too open in the preparatory stages, and there had been too many leaks of what was going on. Secrecy was an hypocritical sham. To top this all off, what secrecy there was—what real deep and deceptive secrecy existed—existed within the U.S. Government itself. More effort had been made by the ST to shield, deceive, and confuse people inside the Government than took place on the outside. And since the great thrust of the program came after the Kennedy election in November 1960, the great bulk of the build-up in secrecy and under elaborate cover story scenarios took place right in the White House, the Pentagon, the Department of State, and other agencies that might have been expected to have known what was being planned. The result of all of this was that no one outside of a very few men at the heart of the ST in and out of the CIA had access to all of the facts. I use the words "had access to" intentionally, because even though a small team of men were in a position to know all that was going on by virtue of their being on the "inside" of the ring of need-to-know, they did not know all that was going on because they were not in a position to encompass the entire operation, nor did they comprehend all that they did see. Such an operation, once it begins to grow, takes on a corporate existence of its own, and unless there is unusually competent leadership at the top, the kind of leadership that can tighten things up by saying "No" at the right time and for the right reasons, the whole operation blooms by itself and runs on like wildfire. As we have said earlier, Allen Dulles did not even attempt to apply such leadership, and his chief lieutenants were not in a position to provide it. Thus it was that the Bay of Pigs operation went off pretty much by itself and foundered.

It was only after its failure that Kennedy really began to see the scope and magnitude of the problem. Kennedy was not experience in this type of thing. He had very little useful military experience that would have stood him in good stead here, and he had not been on the inside of a clandestine operation development before. This is a special knowledge that is not learned by equivalent experience in other walks of life, and he had not suspected the problems that he would inherit with this failure. But President Kennedy was also not the type to permit such a thing to hit him twice. He was smart, tough, and politically alert. He saw no other way to quiet the situation after this dismal failure then to accept total responsibility and to try to make the best of a tragic situation. On April 3 he appointed a committee to investigate the entire operation, and on April 4, 1961, the White House issued the following statement:

> "President Kennedy has stated from the beginning that as President he bears sole responsibility for the events of the past few days. He has stated it on all occasions and he restates it now so that it will be understood by all. The President is strongly opposed to anyone within or without the administration attempting to shift the responsibility."

This statement was reminiscent of the blanket statement issued by Eisenhower after the U-2 failure in Russia on May 1, 1960. Once the Government is caught in a "blown" and uncovered clandestine activity that has failed, there can be no other out but to admit that the Government of the United States, for reasons of its own, had planned an intrusion into another government's sovereign territory, and then accept the consequences and see what can be made of a bad situation.

The committee appointed by President Kennedy consisted of Allen Dulles, General Maxwell Taylor, Admiral Arleigh Burke, and the President's brother Robert F. Kennedy. This was a most fortuitous group for many reasons, and it is worth a few lines here to discuss these men and their selection.

Allen Dulles had the special knack of being able to move forward in adversity. He could shed problems and move into the next series of ventures while the Government, the public, and the newspapermen were sifting through the ashes of a past failure. He was confident in this ability because he knew how to make secrecy work for him and how to compartmentalize so that few people, even within his inner circle, really knew which way he was going to move. It would be perfectly correct to point out that this ability to move within a cloak of secrecy comes not so much from some inner wisdom as from the persistent small force, not unlike gravity, that leads the ST from one operation to another for no other reason than that they find a new bit of input data and their built-in feedback system begins to respond like water finding a new course around a temporary obstacle. Thus, Allen Dulles was in an ideal—for him—situation when he was appointed to this committee. Immediately, he began to set the committee up for his net venture, and he maneuvered the hearings to bring about the most gain for the ST and his Agency, even though he no doubt realized that he would not last much longer as the DCI under Kennedy.

It was important to him to see that his chief of clandestine operations, Richard Bissell, was placed properly in another quiet and influential post and that Bissell's successor would be one whom he could rely upon to carry out the goals of the Agency. Bissell was maneuvered into the job of director of the Institute of Defense Analysis (IDA), a high powered think-tank that works directly for the Office of the Secretary of Defense and for the Joint Chiefs of Staff. IDA is also a frequently valuable conduit for CIA proposals that it wants introduced without attribution to the Pentagon, the Department of State, and the White House. In such situations, the CIA will pass a paper to IDA for its processing. IDA will put it on its letterhead, and an IDA team which may include an agent on cover assignment, will take the project to the Pentagon. Then, instead of going into the Pentagon in the usual prescribed manner in which CIA matters are handled, IDA will meet with officials, for example in the prestigious office of the deputy director for Research and Engineering. From there the paper may be staffed throughout the rest of the Office of the Secretary, the JCS, and the Services. This assignment of Dick Bissell to IDA was most helpful to the CIA. And although he was being publicly removed from the Kennedy Administration and banished from the public sector, he was a close as ever to the activity of the Agency in a think-tank totally sponsored by government money. Subsequently, Allen Dulles moved Richard Helms into the position vacated by Bissell.

Dulles' next goal was to rebuild the influence of the CIA in the White House. He accomplished this masterfully by seeing to it that Bobby Kennedy heard all the things he wanted him to hear during these hearings. He won him over without the appearance of catering to him or doting upon him. Therefore, he saw to it that Bobby was left to his own thoughts as each day's witnesses entered the committee rooms in the windowless confines of the inner JCS area of the Pentagon. All he did was to make certain that the train of witnesses was so selected that their testimony would be patterned to present the Agency in its best light and to inconspicuously transfer blame to others, such as the JCS. But most of all he arranged for witnesses who would provide background briefings of the new Agency drift into counterinsurgency. The broad plan for counterinsurgency as a marriage of the CIA and of the U.S. Army had been laid down during the last months of the Eisenhower Administration. It remained for its proponents, mostly men of the ST, to sell it to the Kennedy team.

Throughout this complex process his primary target for conversion to the CIA was General Maxwell Taylor. Here was the right man at the time for Allen Dulles' exploitation and for the use of the ST. Dulles was very good at this kind of thing. He had used General Edward G. Lansdale this way many times, to the considerable personal benefit of Lansdale and for the immeasurable benefit of the CIA. Lansdale had had good fortune in the Philippines in making a president out of the unknown Magsaysay; but it had been Allen Dulles, with skillful assistance from Admiral Radford and Cardinal Spellman, whose bottomless blank-check tactics made the whole thing work. Now Dulles was playing for bigger stakes, and his man was to be General Taylor. Dulles needed a man like Taylor in the White House to rebuild confidence in the Agency after the Bay of Pigs fiasco.

General Taylor's career was interesting. He always seemed to be displeased with the way things were going, and he always seemed to be pushing some "cause" against a real or imagined adversary. Years ago he had followed in the high-speed wake of Admiral Arleigh Burke in attacking the Air Force over the intercontinental bomber B-36 issues and the related strategic concept of massive retaliation. He surrounded himself with a coterie of young hotheads and let them stir up the dust while he pounded the table. In a most characteristic scene, he rose up out of the sound and fury of the post-Suez era in 1956, when Khrushchev had threatened London and Paris with rockets, to sound his trumpet for an intermediate-range ballistic missile. At that time this created quite a stir in Washington and eventually led to the replacement of the Secretary of Defense because of the friction generated by the Army and Air Force protagonists over a missile that nobody needed in the first place. It had just happened that Khrushchev's rockets, to have been effective, would have to have had a range of about fifteen hundred miles. The Taylor and Medaris (Army General Medaris) version of the tactics involved to counter them would then require an American missile with an intermediate range, judged by them to be about fifteen hundred miles. And the Army believed it had just the missile, a rocket called Jupiter. The details of this great debate are not important here; it is simply useful to point out that it is typical of General Taylor to leap into a cause, frequently with a hotheaded team of firebrands, and to joust with the windmill. He got nowhere in the B-36 debates, and he forced an unnecessary showdown over the intermediate range ballistic missile, which went counter to the best interests of the Army.

Later, Taylor had other arguments with the Eisenhower Administration that caused him to resign in a huff in 1959. Immediately, he set out to write a book, *The Uncertain Trumpet*, which purported to show the fallacy of the massive retaliation strategy, but which was more a polemic on the Eisenhower administration's relegation of the Army to a reduced role in national military planning. With this background he was an ideal figure for Allen Dulles to cultivate to act as a front man for the CIA in the White House.

The CIA had learned how to turn the restrictions of the NSC directives around to their advantage with respect to the promotion and approval of clandestine activities. Since the CIA was bound to win the approval of the NSC before it could mount such exercises, the best thing to do was to create a group of participants in the NSC structure itself who would always perform as Allen Dulles wanted them to perform. This left him with a few things to get set up his way.

As we have noted, the law states that the CIA is under the direction of the NSC; and further it states in the escape clause, which is interpreted to suggest that the CIA may get into the clandestine business, that the CIA may perform such other activities as the NSC may from time to time direct. The first thing that the ST did was to wear down the meaning of the word "direct." In the original context it was the intent of the Government that there be no clandestine activity whatsoever except in those rare instances when the NSC might see something so important that it would "direct" an agency, presumably the CIA, to perform the operation. In the strict sense of this interpretation, the only time the CIA could become involved in the preparation of any clandestine activity would be when "directed" by the NSC and not before.

Under the erosion process used by the ST, this idea of "direction" became "approval." Once the CIA had become involved in a series of clandestine operations, it then would make a practice of going back to the NSC, to the Special Group 5412/2 as it was in those days, and ostentatiously brief the next operation as a series. As they hoped, after a while the important and very busy members of the NSC or of the NSC subcommittee would plead other duties and designate someone else to act for them at the meetings. This diluted the control mechanism appreciably. Further, the CIA saw to it that men who would always go along with them were the designated alternates.

This is another part of the special expertise of the ST. The CIA would use secrecy and need-to-know control to arrange with a Cabinet-level officer for the cover assignment of an Agency employee to that organization, for example to the Federal Aviation Administration. The Cabinet officer would agree without too much concern and quietly tip off his manpower officer to arrange a "slot" (personnel space) for someone who would be coming into a certain office. He would simply say that the "slot would be reimbursed," and this would permit the FAA to carry a one-man overage in its manning tables. Soon the man would arrive to work in that position. As far as his associates would know, he would be on some special project, and in a short time he would have worked so well into the staff that they would not know that he was not really one of them. Turnover being what it is in bureaucratic Washington, it would not be too long before everyone around that position would have forgotten that it was still there as a special slot. It would be a normal FAA-assigned job with a CIA man in it.

Then the CIA would work to beef up the power of that position until the man was in a situation that could be used for membership on various committees, boards, and so on. In the case of the FAA, the actual CIA slotted men are in places where they can assist the ST with its many requirements in the field of commercial aviation, both transport and aircraft maintenance and supply companies.

This same procedure works for slots in the Departments of State, Defense, and even in the White House. By patient and determined exploitation and maneuvering of these positions, the Agency is able to get key men into places where they are ready for the time when the ST wishes to pull the strings to have a certain man made the alternate, or to designate someone for a role such as that of the NSC 5412/2 Special Group. This is intricate and long-range work but it pays off, and the ST is adept at the use of these tactics. Of course, there are many variations of the ways in which this can be done.

The main thing is that it is done skillfully and under the heavy veil of secrecy. Many key CIA career men have served in such slots as agents operating within the United States Government. There is no question about the fact that some of these agents have been the most influential and productive agents in the CIA, and there is no doubt that the security measures utilized to cover these agents within our own government have been heavier than those used between the United States and other governments.

Thus the CIA has been able to evolve a change in the meaning of and the use of the control word "direct" and then to get its own people into key positions so that when they do present operations for approval they are often presenting these critical clandestine schemes to their own people. The Pentagon Papers detail much of this, and we shall discuss it later. One reason why Bill Bundy appears so frequently in the Pentagon Papers is because he was a long-time career CIA man, and he was used as a conduit by the CIA to get its schemes for Vietnam to and past such men as McNamara and Rusk.

In this manner Allen Dulles worked to create a role for the army "black sheep," Maxwell Taylor. It was in Dulles' interest to get Taylor into the White House, and it was very much in Taylor's personal interest to get back into a position where he expected to be able to press some of his old ideas, or what was more likely, where he would be useful as the front man for some of his former staffers. Taylor's approach. when confronted with an explanation or a proposal that varied from his own, was usually a brusque, "Get on the team." In other words, if you were not with him, you were against him, and if you were not on the "team" you would be dropped summarily. Many a good Army Officer of that era was brushed aside simply because he tried to point out other views than those held by Taylor.

In Taylor's book, *The Uncertain Trumpet*, he cites his method of operation when he was in opposition to the chairman of the JCS and the other Chiefs: "I arrived carefully prepared with a written rebuttal drawn up with the help of some of my ablest staff officers. I took the offensive at the start of the session, attacking the unsoundness of the proposal from all points of view—military, political, and fiscal." On the face of it there is nothing wrong with such a method, and all of the Chiefs do that, but General Taylor made a career of charging into meetings with the "written rebuttal" of some of his firebrand of officers and of getting knocked flat on his face. This would not be so unimportant an observation if I had not witnessed JCS meetings with and without General Taylor present at the time when he was the chairman himself. And it would not have become so public a bit of information if some of these written works that he cites had not been published in all their unbelievable candor in the Pentagon Papers. Goethe's statement that "There is nothing more frightful than ignorance in action" may be very true, and we have the war in Vietnam to prove it; but that statement can be topped. There is nothing so frightful and so self-righteous as an otherwise intelligent and experienced man who, to serve his own ends, will champion the cause of the ignorant in action.

Allen Dulles was able to get Maxwell Taylor into the White House as personal military adviser to President Kennedy. There was much public discussion about the propriety of placing a general in such a capacity in the White House, ostensibly overseeing and perhaps second-guessing the lawful chairman of the Joint Chiefs of Staff. The CIA had its cake to keep and to eat on this point because not only did it gain Maxwell Taylor as a principal ally at the seat of power, but it finessed a good share of the Bay of Pigs blame upon the JCS without so much as saying so. Most people were willing to read into this key appointment what they thought was the President's own view that there must be something to the allegations that the JCS botched up the Bay of Pigs if Kennedy himself, with all he knew after that investigation, brought General Maxwell Taylor into the White House to keep an eye on the military.

It must have delighted General Taylor to let the rumors and the conjecture fly. He could play it either way. He could second-guess the chairman, General Lyman Lemnitzer—as capable a chairman as there has ever been—or he could settle down to his new role of advancing ST schemes, along with his newly-won friends, the U.S. Army Special Forces, the Green Berets. This sort of Army was much to his liking, and this sort of Army was already up to its neck in operations with the CIA. Maxwell Taylor was not the White House military adviser in the regular sense; he was the CIA's man at the White House, and he was the paramilitary adviser.

Through all of this board of inquiry investigation, Allen Dulles orchestrated the rest of the committee members into his plan. Admiral Arleigh Burke, without question the ablest admiral to serve as Chief of Naval Operations since World War II, had chaired many JCS meetings during the period when the Bay of Pigs operation was being developed, and since much of the planning involved the Navy and the Marines Corps (the top military man on the CIA staff was a most able and experienced Marine colonel) he was the logical member of the JCS to sit on the committee. His position on the committee, however, must have caused him quite a bit of concern, because as he witnessed the unfolding of the operation as Dulles unwound the scheme he must have wondered if what he was hearing in that room could possibly have had anything to do with the operational information that he had heard during briefings.

One of the really secret techniques of the ST is to cellularize and play by ear the development of some scheme. It would be hard to say that they planned it that way, because one of the things that the Team understands and practices the least is planning. But as an operation develops they assign one part of it to one group and another part to another group. At certain levels of the hierarchy these come together. It would be nice if such things were done with PERT chart or Network Charting precision and effectiveness; but they are not. So as an operation develops, it grows haphazardly. When the CIA needs something from the Navy it will have a certain man call upon the Naval Focal Point Office and request the item. Depending upon how easy this detail is put over, the briefer may or may not tell the Navy what he plans to do with it. The Navy may press him and say, in effect, "We cannot send two Navy doctors on temporary duty to Panama for Project XYZ unless you tell us exactly what Project XYZ is and why you need two Navy doctors." The Navy knows that if the doctors were to be used on an Army post this would not look right, even in Panama, and the Navy might be left holding the bag in the event the operation were to be compromised. At this point the CIA man might tell the Navy the real story, or he might tell them a cover story (a lie) and see if he can get away with it. In either case, if the Focal Point officer is doing his job, he will gain sufficient time to call upon the office of the Chief of Naval Operations (CNO) to mention this request to the "cleared" executive officer there. At this point, the executive officer may or may not choose to inform the CNO.

In this rather hit-and-miss manner, the CNO, in this case Admiral Burke, may or may not have ever gotten a thorough briefing on the whole Bay of Pigs operation. Since no one else did, it would be surprising if Admiral Burke did. Furthermore, as he filled in for General Lemnitzer only from time to time, he could not possibly have ever received a full and comprehensive Bay of Pigs briefing in his capacity as a member of the Joint Chiefs of Staff.

This is not to say that the JCS may not have demanded and then have received a formal briefing. The JCS did have a briefing of sorts during January 1961, just before the Kennedy inauguration. It was their one-time introduction to what the CIA was doing. But such briefings are themselves not comprehensive. They suffer first of all from the limitations of the briefing officers, who may not know all that is being done, and who for their own parts, have not been told all that is under way.

Therefore, even though someone as important as a member of the JCS may insist upon a briefing in full, the very fact that he is so important will embolden the ST to endeavor to give as little information as they are pressed to serve up, because they can be sure he has been too busy to become familiar with all prior activity.

As a result, it would be surprising if Admiral Burke could have recognized little more than one-third of what he heard during the committee meetings in those hectic days in the Pentagon of April and May 1961.

Furthermore, Allen Dulles had other trump cards. No one on the committee and few people, if any, anywhere really knew who all the responsible men were at the core of this operation. In his very excellent book, *The Bay of Pigs*, Haynes Johnson tells of his interviews with the Cubans to find out what they were asked at these meetings and what they said at these meetings. But he found no one else with whom he could discuss the operation. He did not know whom to ask, and no one else would know the right ones either. Allen Dulles was not at all interested in bringing to the committee hearings the men responsible for and most familiar with the operation. As a matter of fact, as far as he was concerned, that operation was over, it was a mess, it was not to be resurrected. He arranged these hearings so that Maxwell Taylor and Bobby Kennedy could hear as much as possible about the ways and means of the ST, not in the past, but in the future. As a result, Allen Dulles marched an endless column of men in and out of the committee rooms who had either nothing or very little to do with the real Bay of Pigs operation. The most important thing was that a whole host of men who had a lot to do with the operation were completely ignored. Again using the need-to-know principle, Dulles could do more by excluding knowledgeable men from the meetings than he could by parading platoons of men who knew only one phase or another.

Typical of the style of questioning was that in which General Taylor discussed with certain Cubans the tactics they had used on the beach. This led to a wider discussion of Green Berets and paramilitary-type tactics and of the military role in civic action programs, all of this away from the main subject. Mr. Dulles found in his patient hands some putty in the form of Bobby Kennedy and Maxwell Taylor.

No one should underestimate the role played by Bobby Kennedy. Nothing in his strenuous career had prepared him to become a military strategist or battlefield tactician; but few men in this country were more experienced in the ways of the Government, and few men were tougher than Bobby Kennedy. He may have been won over on the Green Berets' side because at that stage of development their doctrine was uncluttered by later horrible events in Vietnam and because this doctrine was an idealistic mix of Boy Scouts, military government, and Red Cross. But the evidence is that Bobby Kennedy was not misled in his appraisal of the real problems underlying the serious and tragic failure of the Bay of Pigs operation. He came very close to seeing how terribly significant the real meaning of clandestine operations is and how gross an impact the failure of such operations can have upon national prestige and credibility. It is entirely possible that had John Kennedy lived to serve until re-elected, sometime during his Administration the genie of clandestine operations would have been put back into the bottle and the CIA might have been returned to its legally authorized role of an intelligence agency and no more.

The committee hearings ended in May 1961. No report of these hearings has ever been published. It is possible that if it were to be published it would be a most misleading document. It would contain all manner of irrelevant testimony, and it would be devoid of solid inside information. However, somewhere in the inner sanctum of the Kennedy White House there were some very hard-hitting and valuable meetings concerning the future of clandestine operations by the United States Government. These meetings must have been attended only by the Kennedy "family team," not by the President's official staff. Out of these meetings came three most interesting and remarkable documents.

Kennedy did not utilize the structured NSC he inherited from Eisenhower; yet, from time to time he had to issue very important directives that affected the national security. Thus he issued what were called National Security Action Memoranda (NSAM). By June of 1961, some fifty or more such memoranda had been published, and the Department of Defense had established procedures for the processing and implementation of these major directives. Then, shortly after the Bay of Pigs committee had completed its hearings, the White House issued three NSAM of a most unusual and revolutionary nature. They prescribed vastly limiting stipulations upon the conduct of clandestine operations. NSAM #55 was addressed to the chairman of the JCS, and its principle theme was to instruct the chairman that the President of the United States held him responsible for all "military-type" operations in peacetime as he would be responsible for them in time of war. Because of the semantic problems inherent in dealing with this subject, it is not always possible to be as precise in writing about clandestine operations as one might like to be; but there was no misunderstanding the full intent and weight of this document. Peacetime operations, as used in that context, were always clandestine operations. The radical turn of this memorandum came from the fact that the President was charging the chairman with this responsibility. It did not say that the chairman should develop such operations. In fact, accompanying directives clarified that issue to mean that clandestine operations were to cease, or at least to be much restricted. What it did do was to charge the chairman with providing the President with advice and counsel on any such developments. This NSAM therefore put into the chairman's hands the authority to demand full and comprehensive briefings and an inside role during the development of any clandestine operation in which the U.S. Government might become involved.

The usual NSAM was signed by one of the senior members of the White House staff, and this changed from time to time depending upon the subject matter of the directive and the addressee. NSAM #55 was most singular in that it was addressed only to the chairman of the JCS with an information addressee notation for the DCI, the Secretary of State, and the Secretary of Defense; and this order was signed personally by President John F. Kennedy. There was to be no doubt in the minds of any of the inner group of the Kennedy Administration concerning the President's meaning and intentions. The fact that the DCI received his copy as "information" was alone sufficient to heavily underscore the President's message.

Coming as it did on the heels of the committee's intensive though inconclusive and somewhat misleading investigations, this document more than any other emphatically underlined the importance of the role of Bobby Kennedy. He may have been the passive member of the committee as he soaked up the action but if nothing more came out of the hearings than this one directive, his presence on that committee would have been well worthwhile. It had become clear to the Kennedys and to their inner "family" that CIA lack of leadership in the Bay of Pigs had been the cause of its failure. The total lack of on-the-spot tactical leadership was the first element Kennedy attacked once the hearings had concluded. This document more than anything else sealed the fate of Dick Bissell and Allen Dulles. When the chips were down, they had not been there, nor had they made their presence felt.

NSAM #56 was not a significant document and was more intended to fill a small chink in the leaking dam than to reroute the whole stream of events. But what it lacked in thunder was more than made up in NSAM # 57. We have been saying much about clandestine operations and of the very peculiar nature of this type of business. When it has all been reviewed, one of the principal conclusions must be that the United States Government is inherently and operationally incapable of developing and successfully carrying out clandestine operations, primarily because they run at total opposites to our basic way of life. Americanism means an open society, and clandestine operations are the desperate efforts of a closed society.

Fletcher Knebel, in his excellent and very popular book, Vanished, has his principal character, President Roudebush, say after a heated session with his DCI, Arthur Ingram, "We've been over this ground before. He can't see that if we adopt Communist methods in our zeal to contain them, we wind up defeating ourselves, war or no war. What is left of our open society if every man has to fear a secret government agent at his elbow? Who can respect us or believe us?" We have no way of knowing whether or not Knebel had Kennedy in mind as his fictional president; but if he had been a member of the inner Kennedy team at that time he could not have come up with a more topical comment. Kennedy knew that he had been badly burned by the Bay of Pigs incident, and by June 1961 he and Bobby knew that he had been let down by the ST. (I carefully switch to the ST label here, because in all fairness to the CIA, it was more than the CIA that really created the unfortunate operation. For example, the overeager blind participation of certain military elements gave the whole operation a weird and unbalanced character, which doomed it before it got off the ground. Then the lack of leadership, which really is the name of the game in clandestine operations, provided the coup de grâce. It was the whole ST that built a totally unexpected and totally unplanned operation out of the smaller, more nearly clandestine units that might have had some measure of success.) Therefore, Kennedy did feel and did know that such clandestine operations had no place in the U.S. Government. This led him to direct the publication of the most important of these three memoranda, NSAM #57.

NSAM #57 was a long paper as those things go, and we shall make no attempt to recall it in great detail. When "The Pentagon Papers" series was published by *The New York Times*, it was noticeable for its omission. It is this sort of "educated" omission that makes the Pentagon Papers suspect in the eyes of those who have been most intimately connected with that type of work. Any gross batch of documents can be made to mean one thing or quite another, not only by what the news media publishes but by what they delete from publication. NSAM #57 is a controversial document that has not been released to date.

The principle behind NSAM #57 is absolutely fundamental to the whole concept of clandestine operations. It not only restates the idea that clandestine operations should be secret and deniable, but it goes beyond that to state that they should be small. It plays on the meaning of "small," in two areas of interest: First, unless they are very small they should not be assigned to the CIA; and second, if they are not as small as possible they have no chance of remaining secret and therefore have no chance, by definition, of being successful clandestine operations.

This latter issue flies right in the face of the CIA, which had been working for years to define all sorts of operations, large and small, secret or not, as clandestine in order that they would then, by arbitrary definition, be assigned to the CIA. This was an erosion of the principle, but it had been going on for so long and the CIA had used the game so blatantly for so long that it had become almost a matter of course. The CIA managed to declare in 1962 that the training of the border patrol police on the India-China border was a clandestine activity; then, because it was "clandestine," the whole job was assigned to the CIA.

The CIA got itself deeply involved in the Katangese side of the Congo venture, and defined its work as clandestine to keep it under Agency control, whereas everyone in Africa and most of the world knew that the Katangese did not have the clout to operate huge C-97 four-engine Boeing transport aircraft and all the other airlift that became immediately and mysteriously available to Tshombe.

It becomes ridiculous to equate activities in Indochina to any useful definition of clandestine; yet the CIA continued to clamp high-security classification on what it was doing there simply so that the Agency could remain in control of the things it had stirred up. In Vietnam this became so blatant and such big business that the United States Government has always had to retain an operational ambassador there, not because an ambassador could add anything to the situation, and not that the Government wished to depart so far from historical administration in time of war, but because there have always been two equal commanding officers in Vietnam. There has always been the CIA commanding officer and since 1964 there has been an Armed Forces commanding officer. Those generals who served there before 1964 were simply figureheads, although some of them may not have fully realized that themselves, even to the end. The role of the ambassador has been to referee and arbitrate between the Armed Forces and the CIA. For anyone who may find this idea a bit new or rash we would propose that he search for a precedent for the retention of a full and active ambassador in the battle zone in time of full war—and recall, this is by many counts the second most costly war in all of our history.

Thus, by the very size of its activities in so many areas, the CIA had exceeded all reasonable definitions of clandestine. This new Kennedy directive hit right at the most vulnerable point in the ST game at that time. No sooner had this directive been received in the Pentagon than heated arguments sprang up, wherever this order was seen, as to what was "large" and what was "small" in clandestine activities. Oddly enough the rather large and fast-growing contingent of DOD officials and personnel who had found a most promising and interesting niche in the special operations business were the loudest in support of "small" being "large." In other words, they were much in support of more Bay of Pigs operations, and even by June 1961 there had been really significant moves of Bay of Pigs men and equipment from Latin America and the bases in the States to Vietnam. For them, it was onward and upward. What was a small Cuban failure or two? Indochina offered new horizons.

There is no point in pursuing the argument further. It was never really settled, anyhow. Allen Dulles and his quietly skillful team had foreseen this possibility and had laid the groundwork to circumvent it. Opposing Dulles was like fighting your adversary on the brink of a cliff. He was willing to go over as long as he brought his opponents with him. He believed the handwriting on the wall, and he had sounded out the Kennedys. He knew that they had learned a lot from the Bay of Pigs; and he now knew where the Kennedys' Achilles' tendon was, and he had hold of that vital spot.

It would be worth a full chapter or perhaps a full book to be able to recount in detail what really happened to NSAM #55 and NSAM #57. For the purposes of this account we can discount NSAM #56. I was responsible for the action on NSAM #55 and for whatever use it might be put to. Thus its briefing to certain "eyes only" selected senior officers can be accounted for. NSAM #55 was briefed and in detail (it was a very short paper) to the chairman of the JCS. It was "Red Striped," as the JCS terminology goes, meaning that it was read and noted by the Chiefs of Staff.

While General Lemnitzer was the chairman of the Joint Chiefs of Staff and while John F. Kennedy was President, NSAM #55 provided a strong safeguard against such things as the Bay of Pigs. If Lemnitzer was going to be responsible to the President for "operations in peacetime in the same manner as in war time," the best way to fulfill that responsibility in the eyes of General Lemnitzer would be to have no peacetime operations.

Then, President Kennedy made a most significant move, one perhaps that has had more impact upon events during the past ten years than any other that can be attributed to him or to his successors. He decided to transfer General Lemnitzer to Paris to replace General Lauris Norstad as Allied commander of NATO troops. Lemnitzer was eminently qualified for this task, and it was a good assignment. To replace Lemnitzer as chairman of the JCS, Kennedy moved Maxwell Taylor from the White House to the Pentagon. By that time the Kennedys had espoused the new doctrine of counterinsurgency and had become thoroughly wrapped up in the activities of the Special Group Counterinsurgency (Cl) as the new clandestine operations group was called. Although it had not totally replaced the old Special Group (5412) in scope and function as the authorizing body for all clandestine affairs, it had created quite a niche for itself in the new counterinsurgency game. It used to be that anti-Communist activity was carried out against Communist countries, governments, and territory. There had been a gradual drift away from that. The new counterinsurgency philosophy and doctrine meant that anti-Communism would now be waged in non-Communist countries.

Shortly after the Bay of Pigs investigation, Secretary of Defense McNamara, in conjunction with General Earle Wheeler, who at that time was the director of the Joint Staff, agreed to establish in the Joint Staff an office of the Special Assistant for Counterinsurgency and Special Activities. This office, among other things, worked directly with the CIA and the White House. The incumbent, Marine Major General Victor H. Krulak, became the most important and most dominant man on the staff. He carried more weight with Secretary of Defense McNamara than any other general and was always welcomed by the White House, where he frequently and most eloquently preached the new doctrine of counterinsurgency.

This created an ideal platform for General Taylor. He was by that time the chief proponent of counterinsurgency, the Army's Green Berets, and the CIA. In a most fortuitous assignment for the CIA and the ST, he became the chairman of the JCS, and all of the pieces fell into place. With McGeorge Bundy in Taylor's old job in the White House, responsible for all clandestine activity; with Bill Bundy as the principle conduit from the CIA to McNamara (later in State), and with Taylor on top of the military establishment, the ST had emerged from its nadir on the beaches of Cuba and was ready for whatever might develop in Vietnam.

And to further assure this success, Kennedy's own strict directive, NSAM #55, was now in the hands of the very man who would want to use it the most and who would have the most reason to use it, Maxwell Taylor. In the hands of Lemnitzer, NSAM #55 meant no more clandestine operations, or at least no more unless there were most compelling reasons. In the hands of Maxwell Taylor, this meant that he was most willing to take full advantage of the situation and to be the President's key adviser during "peacetime operations as he would be during time of war."

One further factor played into this situation. It is quite apparent that Kennedy did not fully realize the situation he had unintentionally created. To him and to his brother, Maxwell Taylor was the model of the down-to-earth soldier. He looked like Lemnitzer, like Bradley, maybe even like Patton—only better. He was their man. They did not realize that even in his recent book, *The Uncertain Trumpet*, he had turned his back on the conventional military doctrine and had become a leader of the new military force of response, of reaction and of undercover activity—all summed up in the newly coined word "counterinsurgency." Kennedy was not getting an old soldier in the Pentagon. He was getting one of the new breed. Taylor's tenure would mark the end of the day of the old soldier and the beginning of the Special Forces, the peacetime operator, the response-motivated counterinsurgency warrior who has been so abundantly uncovered in the conflict of the past ten years in Vietnam.

This was the climax of a long bit of maneuvering within the Government by the ST and its supporters. To accomplish their ends, they did not have to shoot down the Kennedy directives, NSAM #55 and #57, in flames like the Red Baron; they simply took these memoranda over for their own ends, and ignored them when they were in conflict with whatever it was they wanted. They buried any opposition in security and need-to know and in highly classified "eyes-only" rules. Then, with all the top positions covered, they were in charge, they were ready to move out to wherever secret intelligence input would find a soft or intriguing spot. Historians will be amazed when and if they are ever able to find some of those basic papers. They will discover that the "access lists," meaning the cover-lists of all those who have read the document, and which are so closely guarded, will on some of these most important papers list only a few people, most of whom were no more than the clerks who processed the classified inventories. So very few people have ever seen the real documents, and fewer have acted on them.

More real control can be put on the Government from the inside by not doing and not permitting to be done those things which had

been instructed and directed to be done than by other more conventional means. One of the best examples of this is what happened
to this most important document, NSAM #55. Nowhere else was
Kennedy's strong desire for control more in evidence that in that
paper and the ones that followed it, like NSAM #55. Thus it was
that events marched relentlessly on toward Vietnam. The only ones
who stood in the way were the President and his closest intimates—
and they had been neatly outmaneuvered.

CHAPTER 5

"DEFENSE" AS A NATIONAL MILITARY PHILOSOPHY, THE NATURAL PREY OF THE INTELLIGENCE COMMUNITY

Following the establishment of the National Intelligence Authority, about eighteen months passed in which the DCI was deeply involved in setting up some organizations that could effectively coordinate national intelligence. This was easier said than done. The old scars of the war period had not healed, and nothing Admiral Souers could do would heal them. At the same time, the subordinate organizations were undergoing their own postwar organizational problems. The Department of State had set up an intelligence section under Colonel McCormick, and then, when Congress severely cut his funds in favor of the new Central Intelligence Group, he resigned and left things in bad shape. But some headway was made, and important legislation was pending that if passed would provide for the creation of an agency of some merit.

At this point, the in-fighting got pretty heavy. It would be hard to recreate the hopes and the very real fears of those postwar years. It is one thing to win a major war and to end up victorious as the greatest military power ever created, it is an entirely different thing to realize that this great military force had been suddenly made obsolete by a totally new weapon of major proportions. During the long evolution of warfare, changes in the art of war had come about rather slowly. A thrown rock extended the range of hostility over the bare fist; then the sling gave the rock thrower more range. The sword made the right arm more lethal, and then the spear gave more range to the sword. Changes in weapons and changes in tactics were generally matters of degree. During World War I, the advent of the armored tank vehicle ushered in mechanized warfare, and the utilization of massed rapid-fire weapons made the proximate lines of the hostile perimeter between two powers a veritable and literal no-man's-land. Before the end of World War I, the airplane had extended the range of reconnaissance and air battles, and aerial bombardment gave evidence of the path of the future for aviation and for warfare in three dimensions. During the years between World War I and World War II, the greatest debates on military strategy and tactics were fought over the use of the new air weapon system. It was typical that the land and sea arms wished to cling to tradition and felt it necessary to play down the role of aviation. World War II cleared up these arguments, and by the end of that global encounter the airplane had become, if not the primary weapon of warfare, at least the major weapon of the war arsenal of the nation. Then, just as a quarter-century of sometimes violent argument over the establishment of an independent air force came to an end and the whole world became accustomed to conventional warfare, the atomic bomb threw a new dimension into the picture. No longer could any major warfare be conventional in the sense of that which had taken place during World War II. If all of warfare, if all of the techniques, weapons, and tactics of the ages were to be arranged into one spectrum of forces and then this total force matched against the atomic bomb alone, the bomb would have made all prior weaponry seem like a rock and a club. World War II ended unknowable, and the unthinkable, or so it seemed to many.

In this climate, the postwar years were not relaxing. The aging men who had brought the country through the Great Depression and then who had led it through the greatest of wars were now weary and suddenly old. They had hoped to leave to the world a legacy of peace and prosperity. Many years earlier Wendell Willkie had preached the concept of one world. He, like Charles A. Lindbergh, had traveled the world and had seen that if there was to be lasting peace, men would have to think and practice one world. But that dream faded into the dawn of the war as the world was broken into two armed camps representing the Western world and the Axis powers. And in this case the Western world included the Soviet Union, which the Roosevelt Government had recognized back in 1933, and which it had joined during World War II in the total struggle against Italy, Germany, and Japan.

With the war over and with Harry Truman wearing the mantle of peacemaker, his Secretary of State, James Byrnes, was again preaching one world and was trying to convince the world that the United States would never divide it and the day would never be seen again when mankind would have to resort to war. He was not only echoing the feelings of the prewar dreamers but he was attempting realistically to face the Nuclear Age. Nothing that had occurred before throughout the history of mankind had ever overhung the entire human race as portentously as did the atom bomb. There could be no letdown from the global responsibility, which had become as heavy a burden in peacetime as it bad been during the war.

During 1946, the United States was grimly aware of the fact that it was the sole possessor of the bomb, and that this was to be for only a fleeting time. Scientists knew, even if the statesmen and politicians did not wish to know, that the secret of the bomb had already ended on the day it had been exploded over Hiroshima and that it was inevitable that Russia and other countries would have the bomb within a few years. Therefore, on the one hand there was a great rush to establish and structure the in as man's last best hope for peace. At the same time there was the beginning of a great and growing witch hunt in the United States concerning the protection of the secrets of the atomic bomb. Related to this was a demand for information from all over the world to make it possible for the United States to know the exact status of the development of the bomb by other powers. And related to all of these problems was the growing awareness of the danger that would arise from the growth and spread of Communism. Some of these concerns were real, and many were imagined.

I recall having been in the Soviet Union during World War II. I had entered the country by way of Tehran, Iran, and flown mountains near Baku. Then our course took us further north over Makhachkala and northwesterly along the Manych River to Rostov. Although I had seen many bombed and burned cities during the war—from Italy to Manila and Tokyo—I had never seen anything to compare with the absolute devastation of Rostov. From there we flew toward Kiev to the city of Poltava, where we landed and remained for a few days. Our return was over essentially the same route. Since I had been free to fly a varied course, I flew at about five hundred feet above the ground for the entire trip and wandered off course right and left as random cities and towns came into view.

The major lesson from such a flight was that the war areas of Russia had been terribly destroyed by the German onslaught and by the Russian scorched-earth policy. The other outstanding factor was that over this fifteen-hundred-mile area of the Russian heartland there were absolutely no roads. There were trails and horse or farm-vehicle paths, but no roads of any kind. There were a major railroad and the great Manych Canal. In 1944, one could observe that Russia was going to have to recover from a devastating war and was going to have to make a major effort to develop its backward economic base, which without modern road transportation would certainly be limited in its growth.

It was clear that when the great anti-Communist hue and cry began only two years later, it was founded more on the potential danger of Russia as a developer of an atom bomb capability than it was on Russia's potential threat to the United States. The result of the "Communist threat" emotionalism was to create in the minds of Americans and others in the Western world the image of a Soviet monster, which was only part flesh and mostly fantasy. However, it was just this sort of thing that played into the hands of those alarmists who supported a movement to create a strong central intelligence authority with clandestine operational powers.

There were then several factors that came together in support of the creation of a central intelligence agency. The Administration had seen the woeful deficiencies of uncoordinated intelligence as practiced during World War II. Also, the Administration saw the real importance and necessity for a strong intelligence arm of the President as a result of the new pressures of the Nuclear Age. However, the early Truman Administration was trying to provide leadership for the one world defined by Secretary of State James Byrnes and to keep the world from being torn into armed camps again so shortly after the war. In spite of their efforts, the resounding warning issued by the great wartime orator, Winston Churchill, took its toll, and within one year after he had delivered his "Iron Curtain" speech, lines had been drawn, and the issue became one of Communism versus anti-Communism. The events that turned all of this around during 1946 and 1947 are not the subject of this book; but certainly the British notification to the United States that it was going to withdraw its support of the Greeks and Turks "in their struggle for survival against Communism" did as much as Churchill's speech to raise the banner of the Truman Doctrine and to extend Churchill's wall from the Balkans across the Northern Tier. By 1948 the Truman Administration was no longer advocating what it had preached in early 1946.

All of these pressures—and they were great pressures at that crucial time—played a major part in the decision to create the Central Intelligence Agency and in the behind-the-scenes battles that were incidental to the passage of the law. By the time the lines had hardened, few would deny the necessity for central coordinated intelligence, and nearly everyone was convinced that the quality of national intelligence must be improved. However, as strongly as these measures were supported, the majority also denied the proposals that would have given the Intelligence Authority its own clandestine branch and the means to support such activities. General Donovan, Allen Dulles, and others took to the rostrum and spoke publicly and privately of the need, as they saw it, for an agency with special "operations" powers. To confirm this need and to inflame the public with this issue, the supporters of the clandestine operations proposition became the greatest firebrands of the anti-Communism theme. It was this same group that picked up the banner hurled by Winston Churchill and that saw Communists under every rock. It was during these crucial days that the opposition, no matter who the opposition was, was painted pink or red with the label of Communist. A beginning of this form of public and political blackmail was made during these debates, and it reached its zenith less than a decade later in the infamous days of Senator Joseph McCarthy.

In the quarter-century that has followed this debate, this country and the world have become somewhat accustomed to the polemics of this terrible issue. What began perhaps as an honest effort to alert this country to the fact that the Soviet Government did in fact have the potential to unleash the secrets of the atom and thus to build atomic bombs, gradually became a powerful tool in the hands of the irresponsible and the agitators. All opposition for whatever reason was branded as Communist or pro-Communist. Gradually, this dogma of anti-Communism was extended into the entire world, and by the time of the publication of the Truman Doctrine, the entire world had been divided into Communist and anti-Communist along the lines of the Iron Curtain, the Northern Tier, and the Bamboo Curtain. Once these Lines had been drawn, it remained only for time to run its course and for the Soviet Union to follow natural growth and scientific achievement to obtain not only the atomic bomb, but the hydrogen bomb and then the intercontinental ballistic missile. As many have said, these decisions and pressures, which first appeared during the years immediately following the end of World War II, have contained some of the most serious and grievous mistakes of this quarter-century. Certainly this blind anti-Communism can be listed as one of the most costly, especially when reviewed in terms of the waste and senselessness of the action in Indochina.

The first great fault with the drift of opinion at that time became evident in the very shift of emphasis with regard to the national military establishment. Throughout our history the idea of war had been treated as a positive action. War was that last resort of a nation, after all means of diplomacy had failed, to impress its might and its will upon another. And throughout our proud history we never had faced war as something passive or re-active. But somehow in that postwar era this nation began to think of war as defense and then as defense alone. In other words, in this defense philosophy we were not telling the world that the most powerful nation in the world was showing its magnanimity and restraint; we were saying that we would defend only. And to the rest of the world that meant that we were going to play a passive role in world affairs and that we were passing the active role, and with it the initiative, to others—in this case to the men in the Kremlin. We not only said this as we disestablished our traditional War Department but we have done it throughout the intervening twenty-five years by developing the capability to search out the action of an enemy and then by responding. This defensive posture of our military and foreign policy has been a terrible mistake, and it opened the doors for the newborn intelligence community to move in and take over the control of U.S. foreign and military policy.

Despite the heat and pressure of the intelligence lobby in 1946 and 1947, the National Security Act of 1947 did not contain specific authorization for the new agency to become involved in clandestine operations. In July of 1947 Congress passed the National Security Act, and when President Truman signed it into law, this Act became effective on September 18, 1947. It was the most important piece of legislation to have been passed since World War II. More money has been spent, more lives influenced, and more national prestige and tradition affected by this one law than anything that has been done since that date—and all in the futile and passive name of defense. In this single Act, Congress established the Department of Defense with its single civilian secretary, and it established a new military organization joining the old Army and Navy, with an independent Air Force and a Joint Chiefs of Staff. It also set up the National Security Council, which consisted of the President, the Vice President, the Secretaries of State and of Defense, and the director of the Office of Emergency Planning. It provided for the

Operations Coordinating Board to assure that decisions arrived at within the NSC were carried out as planned and directed. And not to be overlooked, this same act created the Central Intelligence Agency and very specifically placed it, "for the purpose of coordinating the intelligence activities of the several Government departments and agencies in the interest of national security . . . under the direction of the National Security Council. . ."

In a law that already invited the creation of some power center to arise and take over the direction of the military establishment, because that organization was by definition passive, the Congress left the door wide open, by placing the precocious new baby under the direction of a committee. In the context of the period, there could have been no doubt that it was the intention of the Congress and of the Administration that this new central intelligence authority was to perform as its primary function the role of coordinator of information, and no more. Agency protagonists, many of whom have made a career of stretching the language of the law, have always attempted to belittle the significance of the restrictive and delineating language.

Lyman Kirkpatrick, the long-time very able executive director of the CIA, speaks for this very parochial school of thought in his excellent book, *The Real CIA*, as follows: "Many of those who believe that the CIA has too much power, or does things that it should not do, claim that this clause shows the intent of Congress that the CIA should only coordinate the activities of the other agencies and should not be engaged in collection or action itself." This is a shrewd way to put it. He would have his readers believe that only "those who believe that the CIA has too much power . . ." are the ones who read the law properly. The truth of the matter is that anyone who reads the law and who also takes the trouble to research the development of the language of the law will see that Congress meant just what it said, that the CIA was created "for the purpose of coordinating the intelligence activities of the several Government departments and agencies . . ." And no more! When the greatest proponent of a central intelligence authority, General William J. Donovan, prevailed upon President Roosevelt to establish such an organization in 1941, the office that was established with General Donovan as its head was no more than the Office of Coordinator of Information. This office paved the way for the wartime Office of Strategic Services. At the end of the war, President Truman abolished that office and shortly thereafter set up another National Intelligence Authority in January 1946, again for the purpose of coordinating intelligence. It will be noted that the specific duties assigned to the new agency (CIA) specifically itemized most of the standard tasks of Intelligence, with the exception of "collection." It would seem that a Congress that had debated the subject so long and so thoroughly would not have overlooked the function of collection. It is more likely that Congress fully intended what it stated—that the task of the CIA was that of "coordinating" intelligence.

The duties of the CIA were set forth in the law as follows:

1. to advise the National Security Council in matters concerning such intelligence activities of the government departments and agencies as relate to national security;
2. to make recommendations to the NSC for the coordination of such intelligence activities. . . .;
3. to correlate and evaluate intelligence relating to the national security, and provide for the appropriate dissemination of such intelligence within the government . . . provided that the Agency shall have no police, subpoena, law-enforcement powers, or internal security functions. . . .;
4. to perform, for the benefit of the existing intelligence agencies, such additional services of common concern as the NSC determines can be more efficiently accomplished centrally;
5. to perform such other functions and duties related to intelligence affecting the national security as the NSC may from time to time direct.

For those familiar with that language used in legislative writing, it should be very clear that Congress knew exactly what it was doing when it set up a central authority to coordinate intelligence and when it further delineated the responsibilities into those five brief and explicit paragraphs shown above. Yet few such uncomplicated and simple lines defining the law of the land have ever been subject to so much misinterpretation, intentional and accidental, as have these.

Anyone who has read the books of Allen Dulles and of his executive director, Lyman Kirkpatrick, will find that they just cannot bring themselves to quote these simple lines verbatim. They have to paraphrase them and cite them with brief but absolutely essential omissions of key words, or add to them explanations that are certainly not in the language of the law.

Let us look at a few of these important details. The law established the Department of Defense as a full and permanent part of the Government, with a continuing corporate existence and full power and authority to budget for its own funds and to expend them for its own use year after year. The law very specifically placed the CIA under the direction of a committee, the NSC, to serve at its direction. In this sense the NSC was to be the operating body and the CIA was to serve it. This may appear to be a small distinction, but had things worked out this way and had strong and continuing leadership come from the NSC, including the Office of the President, the Agency would not have become what Harry Truman has called, "a symbol of sinister and mysterious foreign intrigue."

The distinction is one of leadership. It may have seemed in 1947 that a committee consisting of the President, Vice President, Secretary of State, and Secretary of Defense would be strong enough to keep the fledgling Agency under control. But no committee is stronger than its weakest, or in this case its busiest, member(s). As planned, the Agency was supposed to become involved in clandestine activity only at the direction of the NSC, if ever. It was not considered that the Agency would get involved in clandestine activity "by approval of" the NSC. However, as the Agency found this weakness and began to probe it, it remained for the members of the NSC to have the strength of their convictions and the courage to say NO. The record shows that this was the case on several occasions in the late forties; but as the Agency grew in size, power, and wiliness it found its way around the committee's horse-collar.

If the Congress had any intention of permitting the CIA to evolve into a major operational agency, it certainly would not have placed it under the direction of a Committee. It is not enough to say that its choice of the NSC was made because this would mean that the CIA would then be safely under the eye of the President. This is what General Donovan wanted; but he and the other strong operational CIA proponents did not want even the NSC (Secretary of State and Secretary of Defense) between the CIA and the President. By assigning the CIA to the NSC, Congress was attempting to make of the NSC itself an operational organization for this limited purpose. It may not have intended this, since we feel strongly that Congress did not visualize any clandestine operations under any setup, but when it gave the NSC the responsibility to direct the CIA it left the NSC with the task of directing the Agency if the time ever arose when clandestine operations were to be mounted. And as history reveals, that time was not far away. The Agency saw to that itself.

Later events underscored the major significance of the NSC responsibility for the CIA. Truman and Eisenhower utilized the NSC as a personal staff. The uses these Presidents made of it were individual and distinct from each other; but they did utilize it along the general conceptual lines inherent in the National Security Act of 1947. Eisenhower used it as a strong military-type staff and then leaned upon the Operations Coordinating Board (OCB) to see that directives were carried out in accordance with his desires. When Kennedy became President he almost totally ignored the NSC and abandoned the OCB. Either he threw aside the NSC because he thought of it as an Eisenhower-era antiquity or he simply may not have completely understood the function of that kind of staff operation.

Whatever his reasons, he certainly left the door wide open for the CIA. With no NSC, there was a major reason why Kennedy never received the kind of staff support he should have had before the Bay of Pigs and why he was unable to get proper control afterwards. It even explains why Kissinger's role has become so dominant in the Nixon Administration after the long years of the unfettered Maxwell Taylor and McGeorge Bundy residency in the White House as key men for the CIA, operating almost without an NSC in control. As time and events have eroded and shaped the application of the interpretations of this law, the Agency has tended to be decreasingly effective in the area of coordinating national intelligence, especially since the emergence of its greatest rival and counterpart, the Defense Intelligence Agency; and it has become increasingly operational as it has succeeded in working itself out from under the strictures of the NSC.

The success or failure of the next four listed duties of the CIA as set forth in the Act are related (often inversely) to the activity of the Agency under whatever type of NSC existed during the administrations of the several Presidents. According to Harry Howe Ransom in his book, *Can American Democracy Survive the Cold War?*, within the Act itself Congress specified that the NSC should "advise the President with respect to the integration of domestic, foreign and military policies" among the various government departments and agencies, including the military; and "to assess and appraise the objectives, commitments and risks of the United States in relation to our actual and potential military power." To show how the NSC was created within the atmosphere of that time, Ransom[1] states, "... the principal role specified for NSC in the statute was not to make final decisions, but to advise the President; to make his national security policy and administrative task more efficient. But whenever the bureaucracy is institutionalized and centralized, there is the risk of minimizing the discretion and flexible maneuverability of the Presidency. And this in turn can adversely affect both the common defense and the fulfillment of the democratic ideal. Many see too much unchecked Presidential power as the main threat to freedom, but this does not appear to be the real danger in modern American government, with the important possible exception of Executive control over the flow of information. It is the President's inability to rise above the decision-making machinery and to exert

---

1. Harry Howe Ransom teaches political science at Vanderbilt University and is one of the Foremost authors on the subject of the Intelligence Community. He has taught at Harvard, Princeton, Vassar, and Michigan State University. He is author of *Central Intelligence and National Security*.

responsible leadership in the national interest—perceived from the highest level—that places the basic democratic idea in doubt."

As Ransom points out, "At the first meeting of the NSC in 1947, President Truman indicated that he regarded it as 'his council,' that is to say, as a purely advisory body. Later President Eisenhower, although inclined to regard it as 'the council,' made clear nonetheless that NSC was absolved of any responsibility per se for national decisions." The NSC advises; the responsibility for decision is the President's, insisted Eisenhower. President Kennedy came to office with an apparent bias against the kind of use Eisenhower made of NSC. Borne into office on a great chorus of rhetoric about the need for purposeful, energetic Presidential leadership, Kennedy "at first made little use of the Council" as a formal advisory body. Following the 1961 Cuban fiasco, however, "the NSC was restored somewhat."

In a very prescient paragraph, Ransom shows how important this grasp for power by an inner secret team was becoming as far back as 1952. Even as the NSC was getting started, a struggle for control of that body was under way; and the control was to be elected by gradually making that advisory committee into an operating power center. Ransom's comment is worth repeating here:

"Early in NSC's life, according to President Truman, 'one or two of its members tried to change it into an operating super-cabinet on the British model.' Truman identifies the members as his first two Secretaries of Defense, James Forrestal and Louis Johnson, who would sometimes, Truman recounts, put pressures on NSC's executive secretary to use NSC authority to see that various governmental agencies were following NSC policy. The executive secretary declined to do this, on the ground that his was an advisory staff rather than an executing 'line' function. Truman fought to keep the subordinate nature of NSC clear to all, emphasizing that Congress had in fact changed the title of NSC 'Director' to 'Executive Secretary.' Forrestal had, Truman notes, advocated using the British cabinet system as a model for the operation of postwar American government. To change to this system, wrote Truman, "we would have to change the Constitution, and I think we have been doing very well under our Constitution."

Nowhere was this behind-the-scenes struggle more significant than it was in the attempt to make of the "quiet intelligence arm of the President" an operational and extremely powerful secret agency. During the Eisenhower years the NSC, which at times was a large and unwieldy body, was reduced for special functions and responsibilities to smaller staffs. For purposes of administering the CIA among others, the NSC Planing Board was established. The men who actually sat as working members of this smaller group were not the Secretaries themselves. These men are heads of vast organizations and have many demands upon their time. This means that even if they could attend most meetings, the essential criteria for leadership and continuity of the decision-making process simply could not be guaranteed. Thus the subcommittee or special group idea was born, and these groups were made up of men especially designated for the task. In the case of the Special Group, called by many codes during the years, such as "Special Group 5412/2," it consists of a designated representative of the President, of the Secretary of State, the Secretary of Defense, and the DCI in person. This dilution of the level of responsibility made it possible for the CIA to assume more and more power as the years went by, as new administrations established their own operating procedures, and as the control intended by the law became changed.

As the years passed, the basic concept of the NSC's role in the direction of the Agency became reversed, or at least greatly diverted. Whereas the law charged the Council with the direction of the CIA and would account for consideration of such things as clandestine operations from "time to time" and then only by Council direction it became the practice of the DCI not only to deliver essential intelligence briefings to the NSC, but to request a limited audience in order that he might inform them of and seek approval for some operation he felt might be derived from his intelligence data.

In the earliest of such instances we may be quite certain that the operations so presented were reasonably modest. The NSC undoubtedly overlooked the variance in procedure and felt that its approval of such minor requests was tantamount to "direction" of the Agency. As time passed and as the DCI exploited his position, it might have seemed to be rather reasonable to suggest the establishment of a small special group to take this "burden" from these senior officials and to provide men who could more readily attend to such matters, minor as they were, in the place of the busy Council principals. Thus the establishment of the first Special Group.

As things progressed, the Special Croup 5412/2 became not just the working group of the NSC but rather a select group that had assumed the responsibility for clandestine activity. Certainly, each designated Special Group member reported back to his principal, but by that time it was not so much for direction as it was for "informational approval"; in the language of bureaucracy this meant, "If he doesn't say a clear NO, it's O.K."

By that time in the course of events, a new process had evolved, and the DCI felt perfectly at liberty to prepare all the clandestine operations his intelligence sources would support and to present them to the Special Group for nothing more than approval. But even this was not enough. The next step was to have Agency-affiliated men in the Special Group itself, or at least to have them working with the Group as special advisers. This is why the President's appointee has always been so important to the DCI. Since the appointment of Maxwell Taylor in that position after the Bay of Pigs, the DCI has had men in that position whom he could count upon as a two-way conduit. When the DCI wanted to get information to the President he would use this man, and when he wanted the President's approval on something, he would use him for that, too. The same has been true with the representatives in State and Defense. During much of the crucial build-up years in Indochina, men such as Bill Bundy and Ed Lansdale have represented State and Defense on this committee. Of course, both of these men were CIA alumni, and as a result the DCI could always count upon them to grease the way for any of his proposals to the NSC.

This has been a significant evolution away from the language and the intent of the law. It has meant that the sole authority established as a final resort to oversee and control the CIA has become no more than a rubber stamp for all clandestine operations. And throughout all of this the ST has been able to carry out its desires under a cloak of secrecy that has kept its moves shielded from the highest officials of this Government. For example, in those crucial early years of Vietnam, did McNamara and Rusk look upon Lansdale and Bill Bundy as Defense and State men under their command and control, or did they recognize them as CIA agents under the direction of the DCI? Or when the Special Assistant for Counterinsurgency and Special Activities from the Joint Staff was called to the White House, did President Kennedy and others look upon this man, General Krulak, as a member of the military establishment because he was wearing a uniform, or did they recognize him as a key spokesman for the interests and activities of the CIA?

This shift of command control over the Agency from under the direction of the NSC was undoubtedly as important a move as has occurred in any part of the Government since the passage of the National Security Act of 1947. It explains why the CIA has operated so free of effective and ironclad control during the past ten to twelve years.

The CIA, even working within the limits of the 1947 Act, has a distinct advantage. It is a true "Dr. Jekyll and Mr. Hyde" agency. The CIA has the responsibility to advise the NSC on matters of intelligence affecting the national security. It therefore is in a position to demand the time and attention of the NSC, including the President, to present its views on every situation facing the nation on a regular and frequent basis. It performs these functions in the name of Intelligence. Thus it is in a position to make the President and his principal advisers virtually its prisoners, in the sense that it has a legal claim to their valuable time. Day by day the CIA tells these men what it wants them to hear, what it thinks they should hear. At the same time, its select audience is in the position of never knowing whether the information it is hearing is no more than Intelligence or whether it may be some special Secret Intelligence primed to prepare the Special Group for another clandestine activity. Certainly, this is a matter of judgment for both factions concerned; but the Agency would be less than human if it did not consider those choice bits of Intelligence, which it thought worthy of clandestine support, to be more important than others. Thus the CIA as an intelligence agency on the one hand, can and does take one position, and as an operational and policy-making organization on the other hand, may benefit from the representations of its other half. Note how this shows up repeatedly in the Pentagon Papers.

Nothing bears this out better than the transition from the Eisenhower Administration to the Kennedy team. Kennedy had his own way of operating within the organizational staff of the Government. He placed friends and long-time associates all over Washington in all sections of the Executive Branch who were unquestionably loyal to him and who worked for him first and for their new organization second. This resulted in a sudden degradation of the value and importance of the NSC, as has been stated in the remarks quoted earlier of Harry Howe Ransom. Since the law requires the NSC to direct the CIA, this meant that the CIA direction was almost nonexistent. It followed then that it was during the Kennedy Administration that the CIA, with the ST opening doors for it everywhere, began its runaway move into special operations with the Bay of Pigs operation and climaxed it with the conflict in Indochina.

This situation might not have been so abrupt and of such magnitude had it not been for the fact that Allen Dulles was one of the few holdovers from the Eisenhower Administration. Had the DCI been a Kennedy appointee, it is possible that he could have provided an element of control over the operational agency. However, Dulles' drive and zeal, given this recognition by Kennedy, accelerated into full speed and power; and unfettered by the NSC, he used it. Great problems arose from this situation, because he used this power without limit both from the point of view of his personal actions, and more importantly, from the fact that the ST was unleashed. Whereas Allen Dulles can be called a responsible official, there were many who were not, as a reading of the Pentagon Papers will demonstrate and confirm.

The best evidence of how unrestrained the ST became lies in the record of the great proliferation of the concept of counterinsurgency (CI). Almost as soon as the Kennedy Administration got under way—certainly as it entered its second year—the CIA, the White House, and certain elements of the DOD added one country after the other to the counterinsurgency list. To the believer in the blind anti-Communist doctrine, it sounded almost preordained that he should search for and then route out all "Communist-inspired subversive insurgency" wherever it was found. In rapid succession, one country after another was added to the long list of counterinsurgency countries, and a new special group was formed, the Special Group CI (Counterinsurgency), which was simply a front within the U.S. Government, to make it possible for the ST to operate in almost any country. The old restraints of a traditional awareness of the meaning of national sovereignty and of the absolute importance of this inviolable principle fell away as if they were of no merit in the zeal of the CI-breed to wipe out so-called Communist-inspired subversive insurgency wherever they thought they saw it.

This flimsy disguise for clandestine operations brought together men who had little experience in the type of operation being developed and even less idea of the political situation in the countries involved. It was a shattering experience to attend some of these meetings and to hear men, some high in the councils of government, not even-able to locate some of these countries and to pronounce their names. The CIA, reveling in this situation, would work up a proposal practically from a mimeographed boiler-plate of other exercises and forward it to some friend, perhaps an Agency man on assignment outside of the Agency, who was working in a think-tank group such as the Institute of Defense Analysis (IDA). The man in the Institute would then make copies of this "operational concept." In normal times this concept would have been highly classified and revealed to a very few cleared officials; but during this Kennedy-inspired CI period it was not necessary to bother with that bit of detail.

To carry on our example, the IDA official would then convene a meeting with representatives of the Office of the Secretary of Defense (OSD), the JCS, State Department, the White House, and even some of the same CIA officials who had initiated the idea and sent it to IDA in the first place. The others would not know that this proposal had begun with the CIA. The main purpose of their meeting would be to discuss this operation, designed to combat the influence of "Communist inspired subversive insurgency" in the country listed. After such a meeting, this *ad hoc* group would propose that either the CIA or OSD work up the operational concept and present it to the NSC Special Group CI for approval. The Special Group CI, noting that this idea had already been well staffed and that it was just about the same thing as others already under way, would rubber stamp its approval and assign the project to the CIA for accomplishment. At this point in the evolution of the ST it would not occur to anyone that such an operation that violated the sovereignty of another country or that was patently a case of "interference in the internal affairs of another nation" should not be carried out without some formal sanction from the host government. The idea of fighting Communism had become so blindly accepted that they began to forget that such activity was properly a "clandestine operation" and should not be performed lightly. The feeling of urgency and of an almost missionary zeal to combat and root out real or imagined subversive insurgency anywhere was such that the great importance of national sovereignty was all but overlooked. "Subversive insurgency" meant third-nation involvement; so the Secret Team just assumed the right to become a party to the action in any country without even asking. What had been covert operations only a few years earlier were then considered perfectly acceptable under the definition of counterinsurgency. This did not mean that they were not concerned with the need for secrecy in the United States to keep the knowledge of what they were doing elsewhere from the public and Congress; it only meant that they worked openly and almost unrestrictedly in the host CI country.

The Army, Navy, and Air Force all had developed many units of Special Forces, Special Air Warfare squadrons and SEAL (Sea, Air, Land) teams, and these were sent into any country that would accept them. These teams were heavily sprinkled with CIA agents, and most of their direction in the field was the operational responsibility of the CIA.

As we develop this further, it will be seen how the CIA was able to work around and out from under the law, which at first saw the Agency as only a coordinating authority and secondly had provided that the NSC would at times have the authority to direct the CIA into other activities in the national interest. The Congress had been so certain that the Agency would not become operational and policy-making that it was content to place it under the control of a committee. Congress knew that the Agency would never be permitted to become involved in clandestine operations and therefore that the NSC would never have to direct it in an operational sense.

Before we leave the subject of the Agency development, we should look at one more aspect of the subject. Much of what the CIA is today, it has become because of Allen Dulles. From the days of World War II, when he was active with the Office of Strategic Service until he left the Agency as it moved to its magnificent new headquarters building in Langley, Virginia, in the fall of 1961, this kindly look-ing gentleman did little else than devote his life to the cause of the Central Intelligence Agency. Whether one met him in the old office building overlooking Foggy Bottom, glasses in his hand, pipe nearby, settled comfortably in his big leather chair with his feet informally shod in old slippers; or at his Georgetown mansion to find him dressed in white tennis shorts and vee-necked sweater, Allen Dulles always had that quiet yet alert look of a man who knew exactly what he was doing. He may not have known at all times what some of the boys in the back room were doing; but don't let anyone ever tell yo u that he did not know precisely what he as doing and what his plans were.

Thus, when Congress enacted the National Security Act of 1947, he accepted it as a major milestone on the road which he knew he would follow. It was not a barrier to him and it was not a handicap. It was simply a place to start. Typical of his method is the way in which he organized his book in 1962. The only intelligence function of general significance not covered in the language of the National Security Act of 1947 was that of collection. Characteristically, the only intelligence function given any chapter heading emphasis— and it is given two chapters—in his book, *The Craft of Intelligence*, is collection. This was so typical of the man. He would have every-one believe that if he repeated something often enough and if he pounded something out often enough, sooner or later everyone else would give up, and he would have what he wanted. His book would convince anyone that the most important Congressional mandate to the CIA was that of collection; yet that function was not named and was specifically omitted in the law. The CIA most certainly did get into the collection business and has augmented the collection capability of the military and of the State Department.

It was this same bulldog ability of Allen Dulles that brought the CIA into the clandestine operations business, and once in, that made it the primary business of the Agency. Here he was, working against all of the constraints that had been set up against him. He simply worked like the Colorado River in the Grand Canyon; he eroded all opposition. We shall find more to say about this in later chapters. The other regular duties of the CIA were spelled out in the law and have generally been clear and noncontroversial, until we get to the provisions of subparagraph 5, which are discussed in detail later.

CHAPTER 6

"IT SHALL BE THE DUTY OF THE AGENCY: TO ADVISE, TO COORDINATE, TO CORRELATE AND EVALUATE AND DISSEMINATE AND TO PERFORM SERVICES OF COMMON CONCERN . . ."[1]

Admiral Luther H. Frost, former Director of Naval Intelligence, paid a very open and informal visit to Indonesia in 1958, at the same time that his boss, Chief of Naval Operations Arleigh A. Burke, found himself in a most ambiguous position. U.S. Navy submarines were operating clandestinely close to the southern coast of Sumatra, the main island of Indonesia, putting over-the-beach parties ashore and providing certain supplies and communications for the CIA-led

---

1. Composite quote from the National Security Act of 1947.

operation against the Government of Prime Minister Sukarno. At the same time, Admiral Burke balanced his unenthusiastic support of the CIA by putting his close confidant and able intelligence chief on an informal and social temporary assignment to Jakarta.

Then to further bracket the situation, Admiral Burke assured for the Navy the chairmanship of a high echelon committee set up by the Secretary of Defense for the purpose of providing support to the CIA during this special operation by placing a three-star admiral on the committee, while the other services were represented by officers several grades junior to him. The Air Force had a retired general working with the CIA as a coordinator of all air action in this operation, and the Army had a number of generals, some on active duty and others either on assignment with the CIA of called up from retirement for similar reasons. But no service so ably circumscribed the moves of the CIA as did the Navy under its most able CNO, Admiral Burke.

Although this was an operational activity carried out in deep secrecy, it may be used as an example of how the intelligence community functions. Over the years it has become customary to speak of the various intelligence organizations within the Government as members of "the community." This word is quite proper, because there is little cohesion and homogeneity within this vast infrastructure which has cost so much and which performs so many varied and separate functions. The members of the community are the CIA, the Army, Navy, and Air Force as separate divisions; the Defense Intelligence Agency; the FBI; the Atomic Energy Commission; the State Department; and the National Security Agency. All are by law brought together by the Director of Central Intelligence, or DCI. His title is not "the Director of the Central Intelligence Agency"—although he does head that Agency for the purpose "of advising the NSC in matters concerning such intelligence activities of the Government departments and agencies as relate to National Security."[2] This is the DCI's first duty as prescribed by law. He is

---

2. The National Security Act of 1947.

to advise the NSC of the activities of the other departments and agencies.

Partisans may take sides as they wish, but it is quite clear that it was the intention of Congress that the role of the CIA was to coordinate all of this intelligence and then to advise the NSC, including the President. There is nothing in this language that would suggest that the Agency sshould become operational or that it should enter the collection business itself. Although the CIA has, during the past quarter-century, usurped powers that are not included in the law, it is this literal interpretation of the law that permits all of these disparate intelligence sections to operate with a high degree of independence. Thus we find strong leaders such as Admiral Burke using his own intelligence arm his own way, while at the same time the Navy was rendering support to the CIA in an operation that was very much on the other side of the coin. It was not in the interest of the Navy to become covertly engaged in Indonesia.

In addition to its independence, the intelligence community does not have its own pecking order. Much has been written about the behind-the-scenes friction and massive power struggle between the CIA and the DIA (Defense Intelligence Agency). The director of the DIA sits on the board with the rest of the community under the chairmanship of the DCI; but this does not in any manner mean that he works for and is subservient to the DCI or to any part of the CIA. The DCI serves at the direction of the NSC and the President, and the director of the DIA is responsible to the Secretary of Defense, who is by law one of the members of the NSC and in that capacity is also one of the DCI's bosses.

As recently as September 1971, during a meeting with a prominent and important member of the House of Representatives, I was asked, "What is the chain of command to the director of the Defense Intelligence Agency?" From this man, who serves as chairman of a key unit of Congress, this was no artless or idle question. And other than citing the obvious, that the director of the DIA serves the Secretary of Defense, there is no other way to answer that question, if anyone would try to find a niche for that director under a hierarchy headed by the DCI, he would be wasting his time. We find then, nearly twenty-five years after the creation of the CIA, that it has remained as the coordinator of information and little more—as long as we are talking about intelligence as an advisory and staff function. When we come into the field of clandestine operations and the inner and more secret pecking order of the ST, we find a totally different situation. This is as Allen Dulles planned it. His biggest cover story of all was the fact that he served as the DCI and that his most able agents were not in the field waging an active campaign against the enemies of the United States but were serving inside the Government of the United States and inside of many greatly influential non-government areas, to create a ST that dominated the entire operational activity of the U.S. Government in peacetime.

The use of the word "peacetime" in this context is fraught with danger and does not mean what might be expected. There are those who say that we have been "at war" since 1945 in a great worldwide cold war struggle against Communism and other enemies of this nation. But that is not the way the term peacetime is used in the ST's clandestine activity dictionary. The rules of war are traditional and are quite clear and uncontroversial. When the nation goes to war legally by Act of Congress and in accordance with these rules, there can be no question about the pecking order and who is in charge of things. The President is the Commander in Chief, and everyone else from the President on down to the private in the uniformed services and the industrial and civilian defense worker has his neat role and position in the chain of command as the emergency law may prescribe. But when this nation is not at war, there are no such rules. Historically, if the nation is not at war, it is enjoying peacetime. Therefore, in time of peace, all foreign planning, foreign policy, and foreign operations are supposed to be the responsibility of the Secretary of State and are managed in accordance with overt political and diplomatic guidelines. To avoid complications on this theme, we shall accept that there are many other departments of the Government that have strong and vital international roles during peacetime, such as the Department of Transportation in the areas of world aviation and commerce, the Department of Labor, the Department of Agriculture, Treasury, and so on. But at the heart of the matter, the Secretary of State is the single Government official primarily responsible for the foreign policy of this nation, and the ambassador who serves under the Secretary of State is the single senior official and head of the country-team in each country throughout the world.

In accordance with custom, International Law, and social tradition, when a country is not at war it is at peace, and the rules of war, which include certain considerations of the necessity for clandestine operations, do not apply. However, in the Cold War era that has persisted since the end of World War II, there is the feeling that we are engaged in a life-and-death struggle with world Communism that verges on real war. At least this is the doctrine of those activists who make a career of promoting anti-Communism. Before World War II there was a wave of anti-Communism, but it was more an expression of choice between the Fascism of Italy, Germany, and Japan or the Communism of Russia. It was fanned to a strong flame during the Spanish Civil War, when the loyalists were for the most part on the side of Communism and the rebels were the supporters of General Franco's version of one-man rule. Since World War II, Communism has become a term that is often applied to almost anything, anyone, and any nation, which in the eyes of the zealous pro-American, is opposed to his views of what is American. Thus "anti-Communism" is an epithet hurled at all kinds of opponents, real and imagined, and at all kinds of targets, from groups of people to individual political foes. Thus, to these activists, we are living in a special state of war.

Inside the ST this kind of thinking has created the phrase, "peacetime operations," which has its own meaning. A peacetime operation is almost always what anyone else would call a "peacetime military operation," or since this is an obvious anachronism, a clandestine operation. By using this special term, the ST keeps the command and direction of such operations from the military, where it would be if it were a real and not a covert operation; and keeps it from the State Department by putting it in the classification of a military activity, even though calling an operation in peacetime a "military operation" does not make sense.

All of this explanation may sound to the uninitiated like a lot of muddy logic or contrived magic. But in spite of the difficulty that exists in trying to explain how the ST rationalizes itself into a position of power, this narrative would be less than honest and less than complete if an effort were not made to delineate the unusual and very contrived paths of reasoning that have been built up through the years.

Perhaps this can best be described by an example. Since the early post-World War I days, the king of Jordan had been served by an elite guard, usually trained by the British. Several years ago, the few remaining British departed and King Hussein found himself in the precarious position of having to trust a close in personal palace guard, not only to protect himself but also to assure compliance with his orders and commands to his military and government officials. In a manner quite normal in many other countries since the end of World War II, King Hussein accepted military aid from the United States, and with it he had in Amman a small number of U.S. military officers whose task was to see that his men were properly trained on the equipment that was given to him. These men worked to raise the standards of competency of his elite troops and recommended that they be given paratroop training so that they could be used anywhere in the country quickly in an emergency. The King was pleased with this proposal, and some U.S. Air Force C-130 transport aircraft were detached from the European Command to support the training program. Selected American Army and Air Force officers arrived to set up the training that would be required. They worked closely with the King, who is a good pilot, and especially with his trusted palace guard.

In Washington, the State Department was informed of this program and approved it as a worthwhile project to increase understanding between the two countries, especially at a time when United States and Arab relations were badly strained. The Department of Defense was pleased to promote this program, because it provided a much-needed contact in the Arab world that might bolster the sagging Middle East defense structure. But neither the State Department nor the Department of Defense, except in very limited offices, knew that among the "military" training personnel were a number of CIA military and paramilitary experts.

As recent history has proven, this high-caliber training for the palace guard has paid off, and undoubtedly was responsible for saving the life of King Hussein, or at least for making it possible for him to remain in the country and in command of his armed forces during the critical refugee uprisings of 1970.

In the case of such operations, the State Department is told that this special training program is part of the Military Aid Program, and unless the ambassador happens to have his suspicions aroused by something unusual, nothing more will be said of it. Most ambassadors never attempt to look into any of these things. They take the view that what they don't know won't hurt them, and even if someone did try to brief the ambassador, he would probably ask not to be told anything covert because that would not be his responsibility; it would be the responsibility of Washington. This usually results in Washington's thinking the ambassador knows what is going on; so it does nothing. And the ambassador thinks the Washington desk knows what the CIA is doing, so he does nothing. The covert activity takes place, then, with no awareness on the part of the Department of State, in spite of what some DCIs have said.

In the Defense Department, the CIA will have asked for support of a training project in Jordan, without much elaboration. Then they will go to the Air Force for planes and to the Army for men and perhaps to both for the equipment they plan to use. In this manner, the CIA gets involved in a peacetime operation that really is not clandestine in the regular sense of the word, because the King will know that this was not part of his regular Military Aid Program, and he will have been contacted by a man who identifies himself as being from the CIA. In most cases, this pleases the King or other principal, because he knows he will be getting something special and usually a lot better and a lot easier than what a comparable Military Aid Program would cost him if it were to be done in the normal manner. So this project is not covert in Jordan. The King will not tell his military leaders what he has agreed to, but that part of the project would not be clandestine anyhow.

This project could be covert to keep it from the Israelis, from other Arabs, or from the Russians. But when considered realistically, this is not so, because aircraft like the C-130 are too big and too peculiar to be seen operating in Jordan for months without giving away the fact that something special was under way. Anyone observing their coming and going would know that the U.S. Air Force was involved in something in Jordan. So the usual classification criteria do not apply. This is where the term "peacetime operation" is most aptly employed. It is simply a device used within the U.S. Government itself to make something appear more highly classified than it really is, in order that it may be directed by the ST and not by State or Defense, where it might normally be assigned.

Of course, to give itself a reason for getting into such activities, the CIA will state that the men it has in Jordan on such an exercise are really there on intelligence business and that their activities as training personnel are simply their cover arrangement. Thus the CIA is always able to provide a story for any exercise it wishes, once it has obtained the charter to collect intelligence and to enter into secret intelligence operations. This example serves to show the unusual nature and usage of the term "peacetime operations." This is no smalltime business, and though this example pertains to the kingdom of Jordan, there have been similar projects in countless other nations.

Any attempt to unravel the chain of command of the Secret Team and more explicitly, of the intelligence community, must take into consideration that it is not what it seems to be and it is not what it was supposed to be. Certain of the most important activities which occur are so concealed within security wraps and so disguised within the intricacies of the special usage of language, such as "peacetime operations," that the uninitiated and inexperienced person has no way to interpret what he finds. Only the dominant elite know what they mean, and what their objectives are when they talk about foreign military training programs, or what they mean by a reconnaissance project or a satellite activity. Beneath all of this, the sinews and nervous system of the whole system run through the entire government almost effortlessly.

So while the intelligence community continues to function as a loosely knit group with each component serving its own master, it does come together at the top and does provide the DCI, and through him the NSC and the President, with advice in matters pertaining to the national security. Under this cover arrangement, the CIA gives lip-service to this mechanism while it goes along a channel it has carved out for itself in the direction of the peacetime operations of the Government. The CIA has an unsurpassed group of dedicated and devoted intelligence experts within its Directorate of Intelligence (DD/I). However, even these men and women feel sometimes that they are not part of the real CIA, so remote is their attachment to the major part of their own organization.

I have spoken to DD/I men many times about certain areas of interest—careful to protect the security boundaries set by their DD/P (Clandestine Operations) brothers—to find that the men in DD/I knew nothing at all about things that were under way in another wing of the building. Nothing has underscored this distinction more than the chance release of the Pentagon Papers.

Coordination of Intelligence, the Major Assigned Role of the CIA

The second major duty of the CIA as prescribed by the law is to make recommendations to the NSC for the coordination of intelligence activities. This has been a continuing concern of the Presidents who have been in office since the passage of this act, including President Truman. And it has been a major concern of most of the other members of the NSC since that time. It has also been the subject of many special committees and other groups assigned to study the intelligence community and to come up with such recommendations themselves. However, even to this day there has been little real coordination of intelligence activities, and it seems that at this late date there is going to be less coordination instead of more. In 1948, President Truman asked Allen Dulles to head up a committee of three to report to the President on the effectiveness of the CIA as organized under the 1947 Act and the relationship of CIA activities to those of other intelligence organs of the Government. The other two members of this committee were William H. Jackson, who had served in wartime military intelligence, and Mathias F. Correa, who had been a special assistant to the Secretary of the Navy, James Forrestal. The Dulles-Jackson-Correa report was dated January 1, 1949, and was submitted to President Truman upon his re-election. No report on the broad subject of intelligence in this country has ever been more important than this one was. The report itself was published and bound in either ten or twelve copies. (Not too many years after its publication, efforts were made to collect the few copies that were not then in the CIA, and they were destroyed.) One copy remained in the Office of the Secretary of Defense for many years; but it was typical of such important and such controlled documents that the access sheet that had been with it since its initial distribution contained only the names of various administrative personnel who had handled it during top secret inventory reviews and of a very few others, none of whom were really in top level decision-making offices. It is interesting to note that William H. Jackson was appointed deputy director of Central Intelligence after his work on this report and that Allen Dulles followed him as deputy DCI in 1950. Mr. Dulles remained with the CIA for the next eleven years. It is much more interesting and pertinent to note that this report, which was originally chartered to study the "effectiveness" of the CIA and the "relationship of CIA activities to those of other" members of the community, really did not waste much time on those mundane subjects. This report laid the groundwork for the entrance of the CIA into the "fun and games" of special operations, peacetime operations, and all the rest. And in leaving this brief discussion of the second duty of the CIA, one may come away with the distinct impression that the CIA has never made a very high score for its recommendations to the NSC for the coordination of intelligence activities.

Correlation, Evaluation and Dissemination of Intelligence: Heart of the Profession

The third duty of the Agency is one that has been done well and which, if it had received the priority that has been given to the "fun and games," would have provided the President at all times with the best intelligence in the world and would have made the CIA of great importance and of real value to the other members of the Security Council. The law charged the CIA with the duty "to correlate and evaluate intelligence relating to the National Security and to provide for the appropriate dissemination of such intelligence within the government . . . provided that the agency shall have no police, subpoena, law enforcement powers or internal security functions."

There is no questioning the fact that this country has the best intelligence capability in the world. It also has the best collection system in the world, and all members of the community span the scope of information-gathering to such an extent that we ought never fear the existence of an intelligence void. Yet there have been gross oversights, and there have been many poor estimates and analyses of situations. With all that the intelligence community has going for it, it is remiss in not applying itself more to intelligence, to coordination, and less to special operations. Here also, the community's preoccupation with senseless security measures has reduced the area of study and review of many subjects to small groups that do not represent the most qualified men available. Furthermore, these small groups are shot through with irresponsible individuals whose primary interests are not related to the production of quality Intelligence. On top of all this, the Intelligence professionals have to cope with monumental masses of raw product, much of which is excellent. As a result, vast quantities of this material are buried in security-locked warehouses and have never been looked at and never will be.

During the past twenty years there have been many times when the Secretary of Defense or other military official has stated that the United States needed to go ahead with the development of a new bomber, a new submarine, or even a new missile system, because Intelligence had acquired information which indicated that the Russians had such a bomber, submarine, or missile and that if we did not get moving to stay ahead or to close the gap, our defenses would be less than the best. Such a comment has recently been made by Secretary of Defense Laird with respect to a new supersonic bomber the Russians have. Since Mr. Laird believes that the Soviets have such a bomber, he believes that Congress should authorize the Department of Defense to go ahead with a new B-1 supersonic bomber for the U.S. Armed Forces. Years ago, some of these estimates were found, upon review, to have been somewhat premature. (Critics have pointed out that the military often gave the appearance of working up some story attributed to intelligence in support of a weapons system they wanted or to support the annual budget, which may have been under consideration at the time of the release of the new information.)

This whole area is one in which billions of dollars are involved, and in the final analysis, our very defense posture is involved. Yet the facts are seldom revealed, even to Congressional committees, and huge expenditures have been made on partial information. In the past this may have been necessary, but at the present time there can be no excuse for the withholding of such vital information. Any objective and practical reflection upon this subject would confirm the conclusion that such secrets either were not really secret in the first place or that they cannot be kept for very long if they had been secret.

Since Gary Powers went down in the Soviet Union in 1960 the whole world knows that we have been operating high altitude photographic aircraft. The follow-on XR-1 has been photographed and shown to the public many times. At various times U-2 photographs that have been shown reveal the capability of the cameras of these planes.

It is no secret that the United States has been launching satellite observatories for many years and that one of the primary purposes of these missiles has been to take real, not television, photographs of the earth's surface. We know that the film capsules are regularly recovered, usually in the Pacific Ocean areas. We also know that the Russians are doing the same thing, although their photography may be limited to television-type transmittal and reception. But in any event, there can be little in such a mechanical process that warrants the withholding of this vital information from Congress and from the public for alleged security reasons. If Mr. Laird says that the Russians have a supersonic bomber and that it has been observed, then he should show actual, incontrovertible pictures and evidence of such a plane. Certainly, a development project that will cost $11 billion is so important that it should be initiated on real and valid facts and not on some estimate alone.

This is one area where the ST has held to itself and its own devices, information that should be made public, when there is no actual need for the control of such information. The problem is even deeper than this. The information that is obtained by the many intelligence organizations of the United States is so voluminous that not even a small portion of it is properly evaluated. It is possible to read-out mountains of information by a computer scanning process, and most of the photographic material that does see the light of day, from that which was originally obtained by aircraft or satellites, has been so processed. But there is so much more that never even gets looked at.

Satellite pictures are very good, and yet they have some very real limitations. For example, the big Chinese nuclear plant up in north central China has huge open drying flats south of the plant. When the plant is in full operation, most of these large areas are wet and in a photograph can be seen darkened by water. When the plant is shut down or operating at a reduced rate, fewer drying areas are wet, and the change can be observed. Thus, a programmed pattern of satellites scheduled to orbit over this nuclear plant at regular intervals can produce accurate information about the operation of the facility. The photographs themselves are much more accurate than this. It is possible to enlarge these pictures in such a way that small areas no bigger than a bridge table can be identified. For a camera operating in an observatory 110 miles over the target area, this is good photography. Since this photography is so good and since it is easily and abundantly available, there can be little excuse for not making it available to Congress and to the public in order that an informed public—and especially an informed Congress—may know better how to deal with the real facts of the modern world. The law does say that the CIA is responsible "for the appropriate dissemination of such intelligence within the government." If more time and much more money and effort were spent in correlating and evaluating this type of information and then in making proper distribution of the product, we would know a lot more about the rest of the world than we do now, and what we know would be based upon solid supportable fact and not someone's estimate. The work of Intelligence professionals, although hindered by the misplaced emphasis on special operations, has accomplished remarkable things. The diversion of operating funds to clandestine activities has been serious but it is almost insignificant when weighed against the losses which have taken place because of overemphasis on security. If the legislators of this country, and if the general public could only know the things which Intelligence has learned, and which could be used to keep the Free World versus Communist World struggle in proper perspective, we could be confident in our achievements, proud of our successes and understanding of international affairs. One of the best examples of how much we have been able to accomplish in this field of Intelligence is the field of aerial reconnaissance.

The Iron Curtain doctrine played right into the hands of the aerial reconnaissance intelligence system. Not long after Churchill had sealed off Europe, the curtain was extended all the way from the Arctic Sea on the one end across Europe, thence across Greece and Turkey over the Northern Tier, including Iran, Pakistan, and India and on to the Pacific Ocean, skirting the Bamboo Curtain south of China. With the Communist world thus neatly hemmed in, the intelligence community was given the task of penetrating this curtain as much and as far as they could. One of the first things done was the establishment of a perimeter flying capability.

At a busy airport just outside of Frankfurt, Germany, and on the nearby Wiesbaden Airport, an assorted fleet of planes was accumulated; these planes had the ability to fly for miles along the border of the Iron Curtain, taking pictures of the denied areas by slant-range or oblique photography. These planes were also equipped with electronic intelligence equipment designed to listen to as many wavebands of information as possible. All of this was taped and read-out when the plane landed. At that time, there was a close relationship between the intelligence units in the field and the Psychological Warfare Offices that were spread through the European Command. The psychological warfare folks wanted to use these same planes to drop leaflets into the denied areas. They would get together with the CIA units and with the meteorological offices along the routes to be flown and study wind currents. When they found a favorable wind they would send out a plane that was going to take pictures and listen for electronic information (ELINT), and then piggy-back their equipment and leaflets aboard. Sometimes they would carry these leaflets for very long distances into the Communist world and at other times the fickle currents would swirl around and drop them in all the wrong places.

In this world of gray secrecy one idea begets another, and soon the Psychological Warfare people were tying leaflets to small balloons and letting them fly deep into the denied areas, wafted by the winds and a small amount of hydrogen in each balloon. The small-balloon-phase did not last long. The weathermen with whom these psychological warriors were working told them about the huge weather balloons they sent up regularly for high altitude weather analysis. This opened new vistas, and the potential of huge balloons carrying thousands of leaflets deep into the heart of Russia captured the imagination of these clandestine operators. Soon the CIA was using more weather balloons than the weather services, and they were launching them with every turn of the winds, hoping to sprinkle all sorts of leaflets behind the Iron Curtain.

Meanwhile, border flying was getting more sophisticated, and some of the most modern planes in the Air Force and the Navy had been converted to do this legal border snooping. These aircraft, modified for long flights and equipped with electronic sensing equipment and other gear, would leave primary bases in Germany or England, fly to forward bases in Norway, Greece, and Turkey for refueling, and then fly border-skirting routes to gather information. Some of the most bizarre headlines of the 1950s were made by the loss of some of these planes, which strayed too close to Soviet territory or became lost in a wind shift that took place in bad weather and then were shot down by Soviet fighters.

Although border flying, if properly carried out, was perfectly legal, attempts were made to keep these flights secret, and all kinds of cover stories were created to attempt to explain the missions of these units. At times, a marginal penetration was flown in an attempt to photograph some target or to get a rise out of some suspected radar that was known to be in the area but had not been pinpointed. Other flights were flown in the Berlin Corridor, utilizing hidden cameras and concealed electronic equipment. But none of these efforts were really big game.

The balloon projects led to a strange development. It was learned that the very high altitude winds over the Soviet Union blew from east to west and that they were reasonably predictable. Very large high altitude sounding-balloons were tested on launches from the Pacific areas and then were relocated over the Atlantic and even over North America after having drifted across Asia.

The next step was to equip these huge balloons with cameras and other sensing devices. This whole project was an extension of the other border sounding projects and seemed to offer potentialities not found before. A large number of these very large balloons were launched, carrying cameras and other devices. Some of them made the trip and were recovered, others fell in the Soviet Union, and others just circled around, coming down almost anywhere. The information gathered by such unpredictable devices was at best of very little use. No one knew ahead of time when to activate the cameras, and even if they could have been activated on some predictable schedule, the weather was a serious factor. But these strange spy balloons did serve a real and most meaningful purpose. They had softened up the authorities to whom the ST would turn to make the next requests by laying a foundation for covert border crossing.

Once border crossing had become accepted, even though it had been accomplished on the wings of the unpredictable winds of the upper altitudes, it was not as difficult to present a program for a better upper altitude information-gathering system. Thus, all that had been done with aircraft, leaflets, psychological warfare, electronic equipment, and cameras came together in the U-2 project. Like so many things that the ST has done, there was not a plan so much as it was that opportunity knocked and the team took it from there.

The Air Force had a very successful early jet fighter called the F-80. As the F-80 got older, other types of planes and newer equipment seriously outdated it. The Lockheed Corporation, manufacturer of the F-80, came up with an F-90—a more advanced version of the tried and true F-80. But as so often happens, the timing was not just right, and the Air Force did not order the F-90. There were several other planes in the air at the time, and the newer Century Series planes were on the way. However, Lockheed had done well with the F-9O and had made a trainer from that plane known as the T-33, which outsold all others of the time. At the same time, Lockheed had been successful in selling an F-94 interceptor to the Air Force for the Air Defense Command. So Lockheed dropped the F-90; but Kelly Johnson, the shrewd vice president of Lockheed, hated to see all that work and development effort go by the wayside. He made one more pitch to the Air Force. He proposed that a highly modified "glider" version of the F-90, with a new high altitude engine, would make a superior high altitude reconnaissance aircraft. He brought his high-powered, very successful briefing team to the Pentagon and gave his pitch to Air Force Operations.

The Air Force was sold on this idea, and its reconnaissance personnel were delighted at the prospect of having a special all-reconnaissance plane developed for once, rather than having to convert other types of planes for that purpose. But as this "hot" briefing worked its way up through channels, it became apparent that the Air Force could not locate the funds to purchase a reconnaissance plane, because the Air Force did not have anything it could do with the plane at that time. It was one thing to take a strategic bomber B-47 from the Strategic Air Command and fly it along a border in the "open skies" for the purpose of getting some electronic information input; but it was an entirely different deal to develop a brand new plane for a mission which at best would be clandestine, except in time of war, and even then would be most hazardous.

However, many of the reconnaissance officers of the Air Force had been working closely with the CIA on these border flights, and they knew men in the CIA who might want to hear about Kelly Johnson's proposed new "glider." A top-level Air Force team gave the CIA a briefing on the plane, and during this briefing it was brought out that this ultra-high-altitude plane had the capability to fly across Russia at an altitude that would most likely be above the ability of the Russians to do anything about, even if they did happen to find out it was there. The rest is history. The Air Force agreed to develop the plane, and the CIA agreed to operate it. As a result, most of the money, the people, and the facilities that went into the project were contributed by the Air Force. The CIA operated the project as a "peacetime operation." This was a classic example of how a project that should have been military, because it was too large to be clandestine, became covert simply as an expedient. The reasoning was that in peacetime it could not be military, because it was clandestine, so it was to be directed by the CIA, the typical Secret Team tautology.

A really magnificent camera capability was developed for this plane, along with an entirely new engine, and before too long the U-2 was operational. The Air Force and the CIA went through all the motions of keeping the whole project a secret; but all over the world, wherever it was seen, this strange plane with the big drooping wing attracted attention. The minute something new in the field of advanced aviation is discovered, all the experts—intelligence, military, and manufacturing—go after it; it would have been most unlikely that anyone who wanted to know about the U-2 did not know all he needed to know by 1955 at the very latest.

Sometimes, little things turn out to have a big and unexpected impact on such a project. It was known that a plane that flew so high would have a most difficult time if the engine should ever flame out, i.e., if the flame, which continually burns the fuel, should be extinguished for any one of several reasons. Since "flame-out" was such a major concern, it was then most important that every effort be made to keep the flame burning. It was discovered that if a small quantity of pure hydrogen was trickled through the engine's burners at all times, this would keep it burning, and the danger of flame-out would be much reduced. This meant, then, that everywhere the U-2 operated, provision would have to be made for the availability of liquid hydrogen. This gas, which is so common in its natural state, is most uncommon when liquid, and to remain liquid, it must be kept in a cryogenic state at some 240° Centigrade below zero. As a result, it is not easy to provide liquid hydrogen wherever in the world one might wish to fly a U-2 or two.

The Air Force had the job of provisioning the U-2, and it went to elaborate measures to assure the availability of liquid hydrogen. Although the movement of these planes and of their crews and other special paraphernalia was most highly classified, no one had thought to classify the movement of these special quantities of liquid hydrogen. Not too many people were actively involved in the movement of this most volatile material, but it did require the special efforts of a good number, and they soon realized that every time they were asked to deliver some liquid hydrogen to a certain remote area, the U-2s would be operating there. To a lesser degree, the same was true of the crews. They were a special breed of Air Force personnel who had agreed to be sheep-dipped and then had taken "civilian" jobs in the program. This altered status—from military pilot to civilian pilot—made them stand out everywhere they went, because nowhere is there a more closely knit clan than that of the fighter pilot. Once others saw them in Germany or in Japan, the fact that they must be flying something special could scarcely be hidden. Their old buddies knew they were not about to be flying some charter airline's slow transport. Thus it was that even the pilot situation made concealment of this project very difficult.

At this point, the U-2 project, under the very capable Richard Bissell, became a very large, very active, and really global program. However, it was still maintained as a small clandestine operation, because if it were not a controlled clandestine operation it would have had to have been a military program, and everyone knew that the military could not operate such a military program in peacetime. By this time, the ST was getting powerful enough to control major projects, even though there was no chance of calling them truly clandestine and "plausibly deniable," as the old directives had said.

In spite of all this, the U-2s did gather some of the best information ever acquired on a gross basis. The photography obtained by the U-2 camera system is in many ways still unmatched. When some really good pictures are needed anywhere in the world even today, it is probable that the U-2 will be given the mission.

I had attended a meeting in the old headquarters of the CIA one day shortly after I had returned from a special Rand Corporation presentation on missiles. Not long after the "missile-gap period," the Rand Corporation had been asked to put on a full missile orientation course for top echelon officials of the Government. There was so much about this new age of missiles that was not known. With all the emphasis the Government brought to bear in that field, it was realized that not too many top military officers and other high officials knew much about these new weapons and the new technology involved in their manufacture and operation. When Rand had this course ready to go, that excellent organization decided to give it a dry run for the benefit of the instructors and administrative staff who would support it. A list of officers was made for the purpose of attending this dry run, and I happened to be one of those selected. The course was excellent, and later was given to a great number of people; then the whole curriculum, properly censored, was entered into the Congressional Record. Many unusual things happened during those missile-gap days.

Having just returned from this course and having attended a meeting with the Deputy Director of Central Intelligence, who at that time was General Cabell, I got into a discussion with him about the advisability of having certain high level CIA officials take that course. In the discussion, and more or less to make my point, I suggested that the CIA ought to move their cameras from the cockpit of the U-2 into the nose cone of a missile in order to place them in a surveillance orbit. I doubt that I could claim to have originated the idea, but only a few days later he called me and asked that I see about getting some spaces in the course for officials from the CIA. Not too many years later, the satellite observatories were a fact.

Because of the height at which they orbit the earth, their pictures require very special treatment, but they do have the advantage of taking pictures through very clear space until they reach the heavier layers of the atmosphere and weather below. However, on that score they have no more trouble than high altitude aircraft, because most of the obstructions are no higher than sixty thousand feet. The principal problem with the use of satellites is that they enter a fixed orbit as soon as they are launched, and they transit certain predetermined sites on a rather random schedule. Nothing can be done to change this orbit and the schedule they fly once they are put in orbit. (There could be some limited repositioning by using additional burst of rocket power to accelerate or decelerate the satellite.) As a result, satellite observation from any given platform will not suffice to take a picture of any target at any time. The pictures must be taken at a time determined by the prearranged orbit and the time of day or night, and with some consideration of the weather. But these problems are being overcome, and it may be possible to get some information from almost any part of the earth at any time, day or night, weather or no weather, as the canopy of observation platforms increases in size, scope, numbers, and versatility.

Missile technology places a great responsibility upon the Agency to collate all information from so many sources and capabilities. The read-out problem is massive, and once these data are put in some readable form they must be indexed and made accessible through some form of retrieval system. As we pass from an era of agent activity into the newer era of machine technology, there should be little information we need that is not available to us at all times. With this as a firm prospect, the responsibility falls upon the system to prepare the data properly and to disseminate it as broadly as possible. There is a tendency within the intelligence community to over classify and to hold information from all but a few readers. As a result, much that would be useful to many is never known in time or at all. This tendency must be corrected and put to work for the country as a whole. A free society cannot remain free if information is locked from it by its own government.

Services of Common Concern: An Attempt at Efficiency

The fourth duty of the Agency is "to perform for the benefit of the existing intelligence agencies, such additional services of common concern as the NSC determines can be more efficiently accomplished centrally." These are the functions that serve all the components of the intelligence community and can best be undertaken centrally. To more or less sum this up, the principal responsibility of the Agency is to gather information that relates directly to national security.

The distinction is made between information and intelligence: "Intelligence" refers to information that has been carefully evaluated for accuracy and significance. The difference between information and intelligence is the important process of evaluating the accuracy and assessing the significance of such information in terms of national security. In this context, when a raw report has been checked for accuracy, and analyzed and integrated with all other available information of the same subject by competent experts in that particular field, it is "finished intelligence." When, in addition, it represents the conclusions of the entire intelligence community, then it is "national intelligence."[3]

---

3. Extracted from a typical USNWR question and answer review, July 18, 1966, Adm. Raborn, interviewee.

CHAPTER 7

FROM THE PINES OF MAINE TO THE BIRCHES OF RUSSIA: THE NATURE OF CLANDESTINE OPERATIONS

A light plane skimmed the tree-tops of the dense hardwood forest of northern Maine. It dipped from view, and was gone. To anyone who might have been watching, the lake where the plane landed was too small for any pontoon equipped plane. However, the landing was safe, and the plane taxied toward two men sitting in a small inflated boat. One of them had been winding the hand crank of a small generator. The other was tuning a transceiver. As the plane approached, the pilot cut the throttle, and the men paddled to the nearest float and climbed aboard.

The pilot reported that he had picked up the homing beacon several times at distances of from thirty to sixty miles. He could have gotten more range, but the flight plan called for a low altitude flight, so he had to do the best he could from tree-top height. The beacon,

newly modified to give a stronger signal, satisfied them. Further testing would take place at Norfolk. The men stowed the gear aboard
the plane and deflated the raft. The co-pilot, who spoke no English,
helped them up. The pilot restarted the engine and gunned the
throttle to take them to the far side of the pond.

With everything ready for take-off and the plane heavy with four
men aboard, the pilot waited for a slight breeze, which would put
ripples on the water and help them get off more quickly. A technician would have noted that large leading-edge slats on this plane
were extended before take-off and that the large trailing flaps were
also down for maximum lift. With the breeze, some steady ripples,
and a full throttle, the pilot let the plane accelerate for about twelve
seconds and then lifted it clear. Once off the water, he began an easy
spiral climb to get up and out of the tree-lined valley.

A month of special training had paid off. The new Helio "Courier"
had proven itself to be the best and most rugged short-field plane
available. The floats were not too heavy, and the plane handled well
on the water. Most important, the new co-pilot had transitioned
quickly and had handled the plane like an old pro. He needed
more instrument work for weather flying, and he needed some
navigational experience. He would get that training at Norfolk.
He had liked flying in Maine, and he reported that "it looked like
my homeland." After a short hop, the plane landed on Moosehead
Lake, and everyone went back to Greenville to prepare to close the
camp.

In Germany, hundreds of thousands of displaced persons and
repatriated refugees had been interrogated and debriefed as they
came through the military processing centers. A small fraction of
this horde of people, fleeing the Communists and the reprisals of
their own countrymen, possessed information that was useful intelligence. This select group was turned over to professional interroga-
tors who worked for military intelligence and the CIA. Only the very
best were reserved for CIA questioning; and these were screened
carefully to assure accuracy and integrity and to spot the inevitable
planted agent. Among this group, the Agency had found several
who had given evidence of a military buildup by the early 1950s,

of a very special nature far north of Moscow. This intelligence had been screened, evaluated, and analyzed to see what it meant. About the best that the refugees and defectors could provide was that new interceptor fighter bases were being built farther north than ever seen before and a vast array of radars, indicating the development of a sophisticated air defense network, was being installed.

One day, a young Polish defector, who claimed to have been a pilot, turned himself in, and after careful screening and background checking, he was brought to the "safe house" not far from the I. G. Farben building in Frankfurt for further interrogation. In the course of this work, he said he had made several trips as a co-pilot delivering cargo to the new construction sites at these fighter bases in the Soviet northwest. As if to prove his point, he said he could find his way back there anytime.

Clandestine operations take form through such small and unexpected leads. The agent who had been working with this pilot was not on the Directorate of Intelligence side. He was a member of the Central European staff of DD/P, the special operations staff of the Agency. Up to the time of that last statement he had been interested only in a secret intelligence project designed to obtain all the information it could get on Soviet air defenses. That evening when he stopped at the officers club in Frankfurt, he met a few other agents who were visiting from Washington. He mentioned the chance remark of the Polish pilot.

A few months earlier, there had been a meeting in the Pentagon in the Air Force Plans offices, where the vast Air Resupply and Communications program was managed. These special Air Force units, called ARC Wings, were stationed in strategic locations all over the world. Included among their special classified missions was the task of providing wartime support of the CIA. Several CIA men attended the meeting in the Pentagon, and when it broke up, one of them stayed behind to ask the Air Force pilots what they thought was the best light plane for rugged, special-operations-type business. One of the officers reported that a small company, consisting for the most part of ex-Massachusetts Institute of Technology aeronautical engineering men, was building and flying a plane called the Helio

Courier. If it was really as good as it was reported to be, it might be the plane the CIA wanted.

About one week later, a man reported to the Helio Aircraft Corporation in Norwood, Massachusetts, to learn more about this plane. He gave his true name, showed the identification of a U.S. Air Force civilian employee, and said he worked in Air Force headquarters. He spent several days with the Helio company and returned with an enthusiastic report. He actually worked for the Air Division of the DD/P in the CIA, and his boss at that time was an Air Force colonel on duty with the CIA.

After proper testing and evaluation, the CIA decided to purchase several of these aircraft. However, the Air Force had none of these planes, and the plane could not be purchased by the Air Force for the CIA because it could not be "covered" unless there were others like it in the Air Force. The CIA decided to buy these planes anyway and set up a civilian cover unit for them putting them under commercial cover. At the same time the agent in Frankfurt was talking with the Polish pilot, these same aircraft had just been delivered to the CIA and were being shaken down for special operations work.

Thus it happened quite by chance that this agent told his friends in Germany that the CIA had just the plane that could make the flight, if they could get the Polish pilot sufficiently trained for it and if they could get the operation approved "through the Old Man." They knew "Air Division" would back them. It wanted more action than border flying and training exercises. They counted on the approval of Richard Helms and Frank Wisner (both men at that time were in DD/P; Wisner was the chief) and felt sure General Cabell would go along with the idea, since the Air Force could use any information it could get about the Russian air defenses, to support the growing B-52 strategic bomber flight budget. They knew the ultimate decision would be up to Allen Dulles.

During the next weeks the agent in Frankfurt worked very hard with the young Pole to see just how much he knew, whether he really knew the Soviet Union, and whether he really could fly an airplane. Everything seemed to work out, the information the Pole gave him checked out with everything the Frankfurt station could get.

With this under way, the Frankfurt station agent kept a friend in Washington informed of all developments. Between them, they kept feeding "business" messages, designed to heat up the subject of "new Soviet air defenses," into intelligence channels. Everything possible was done to increase intelligence communications traffic on this subject. The Air Force intelligence office at U.S. Air Forces, Europe headquarters (USAFE), in Wiesbaden was put on the task. It quite willingly picked up the ball because that headquarters had a very active border flying activity, and this would give them something to do besides dropping leaflets and furnishing tens of thousands of weather balloons. USAFE increased its traffic on this subject to the U.S. Air Defense Command in Colorado Springs and to the Strategic Air Command headquarters in Omaha.

At the same time, the Frankfurt station agent arranged to have the Air Force group at the Wiesbaden air base set up a light-plane flight reorientation course for the Polish pilot. An Air Force light plane was made available and to the relief of everyone, the Pole proved to be a good pilot. It was easier get him through the refresher course than it had been to get the plane for him.

If this mission were to operate into the Soviet Union, the pilot must never know who was supporting him. Therefore, he was told that a German air operator had a Polish pilot and a plane and that they would give him some refresher flying so that he could seek employment. He was never told that he was being prepared to fly to the Soviet Union. The Air Force plane was put into the hangar and stripped of all USAF identity. Then German instrument decals were put in the cockpit and a Polish pilot, one whom the Agency had ready at a special billet in Greece, was transferred to the Frankfurt station.

Every day, the Polish defector would be driven to the airfield for his lesson. The older, CIA "stateless" pilot, not only gave him transition flying but tried in every way to test the newer man and to break his story. But the facts held up, and the young pilot proved to be sincere and reliable.

With this success, the idea of the project had begun to take shape. Air Division plotted several flight plans from a secret location in

Norway into the Soviet Union. Because the Courier performed so well on water, and a water landing at an "unknown" destination seemed to offer the most chance for success, it had been decided to operate from a water departure point to a water destination. Also, each flight plan called for a low "under radar canopy" tree-top level pattern.

Long-range, low-level navigation is difficult because visibility pilotage purposes is reduced to a narrow track. This was doubly true for this flight, because any radio aid that might exist was limited and hostile. Border electronic information flights had pinpointed some radio fixes that could be used; but even at best these were quite unreliable. A Loran navigation fix would be ideal; but none was in operation that far north. This was overcome by having the U.S. Navy agree to put a Loran-carrying ship in the far north as part of a "NATO exercise." This would give a good, reliable, and secret navigational and code signal system for most of the flight. The mission plane would not be required to make any transmissions in order to use Loran for navigational purposes. It would simply receive the signals it needed.

Meanwhile, Air Division did not wish to pin all of its hopes on the young Pole. He would fly the plane, but an agent would be trained to help him navigate and to serve as a helper for the two-man team that would be infiltrated into Russia. A series of long-range navigation missions was set up and all systems thoroughly tested.

By this time DD/P had accepted the proposal and had become its sponsor. The U.S. Air Force and Navy had been fully sounded out, and they went along with the idea. At that point, a meeting was set up in the OSO/OSD[1] office to soften up any possible opposition and to prepare for the crucial vote of the Secretary of Defense in the NSC Special Group meeting. Since the operation would have a vital military intelligence tie-in, the OSD vote was just about assured. This was the period of the Allen W. Dulles-John Foster Dulles partnership; so no meeting was scheduled at the Department of State. "The Old Man will handle that" was sufficient to assure that vote at

---

1. Office of Special Operations, Office of the Secretary of Defense.

the NSC. With all of this preparation, it was no problem for DD/P Wisner to sell the idea to General Cabell. The way was cleared for the meeting with Allen Dulles.

The agent from the Frankfurt station flew into Washington on a "deep water" flight—a clandestine flight with a cover flight plan and no customs intervention—on a CIA-owned U.S. Air Force C-118 transport, with the Polish pilot as a passenger. The Pole was kept at a "safe house" near Andrews Air Force Base, just a few miles from Washington. The Frankfurt station agent attended the meeting with Dulles, as did General Cabell, Wisner, and a few others. The idea was accepted by Mr. Dulles, and he asked his executive to put it on the agenda for the next Special Group meeting. That evening, before his usual tennis game on his backyard court, Allen Dulles dropped by his brothers secluded house just off Massachusetts Avenue and discussed the operation with him. Foster agreed that Eisenhower would go along with it. He walked over to the wall lined with book shelves and picked up the special white telephone that connected directly with the White House operator. All he said was, "Is the man busy?"

Foster Dulles opened with, "Boss, how did you do at Burning Tree today? . . . well, six holes is better than nothing . . . Yes, I've been talking here with Allen. He has a proposal he wants to clear with you. He feels it is very important, and it will lift the morale of Franks [Wisner] boys. You know, since Korea and Guatemala you haven't had them doing much. Will you see him tomorrow morning? Fine. How's Mamie? O.K. boss, I'll speak to Allen . . . 9:30 . . . Thank you; good night." There was not much left to do. The flight would be scheduled.

First, the Polish pilot was given a briefing on his cover story. He was "being employed by a foreign company to do some bush-flying, and he would get some training with one of their men in the United States." The "company" man was the CIA agent from Air Division; he would be the mission commander. Shortly after their first meeting they were flown to Maine, where they met the pilot—also an Agency employee—of the Courier. The plane had a cover company name on it and a special FAA registry number, which would never show on official FAA records if it were to be challenged. The flight indoctrination concentrated on float techniques, short-field landing and take-off, and low-level, long-range navigation. The Agency mission commander had been trained to take the Loran fixes for navigation.

When the pilot had passed all of his flying tests, he was introduced to the two-man "stay-behind" team. These men would be infiltrated on one flight and then recovered on another. These "passengers" went about their business by themselves and were always, except on the flights, accompanied by a case officer. It seemed that they did not speak English, and they made no attempt to speak to the Polish pilot. If this mission failed and any of them were interrogated, they would know nothing about one another.

At Norfolk, the final phase of training took place. A secluded cove near the mouth of the York River on Chesapeake Bay had a very small section roped off to simulate the tiny landing area they expected to find in Russia as target of this infiltration mission. Day after day, the pilot practiced from that tree-bordered cove so that he would be instinctively used to flying that way. Short take-off and landing (STOL) flying is a real high order skill, and he needed all the training he could get. The next thing he needed was long-range navigation experience—much of it over water and out of sight of land. Flight plans, as much as possible like the one he would fly from Norway into Russia, were set up. He flew these at extended range day after day until he could hit his target accurately. The Agency man helped him with Loran navigation and taught him how to fly in such a manner that he would conserve his fuel. On the real flight he would have to get in and out of Russia without refueling, and he would have very little reserve. The next step was to ask the Frankfurt station liaison officer, who had contact with the British intelligence service, to set up a meeting somewhere in England for the Polish pilot and a very reliable, high-level Russian defector who was being debriefed secretly at that time. The British agreed to the meeting and suggested it be held at the CIA sub-base near the U.S. Air Force base of the Air Resupply and Communications Wing stationed in

England. Thus the meeting would be very secret and could be covered adequately by the Royal Air Force and the U.S. Air Force.

Finally, everything was ready. The Courier was left at Norfolk because another new plane had been built for this flight, one with absolutely no identification markings of any kind—no paint, no decals, no serial numbers. Even the tires, battery, radio parts, etc., were either stripped clean or had been purchased from various foreign sources. If this plane were lost in Russia, no matter what the Russians might try to charge, this Government would say nothing at all, and if pressed, would deny everything. The plane had been totally sanitized from the start.

The new plane had its wings removed and was placed aboard a U.S. Air Force transport plane. All of the mission personnel were placed aboard the same plane and flown from Andrews Field on a black flight to England. There, at the same base where the pilot had first met the Soviet defector, a final briefing was held. At this time the pilot was told what he was really going to do. He agreed to go ahead and was briefed by the Russian, along with Agency personnel. Later, the same Russian briefed the two passengers separately. They knew what to do.

A few days later, the whole team was flown to an airfield in northern Norway. The Oslo CIA station chief had cleared the operation with the contact man in the Norwegian Government. He was told about the flight and given only a cover story about the real reason for it. Foster Dulles had told the American ambassador as little as possible; he had simply been "informed." If by some chance any of the stateless personnel were compromised by a take-off crash or other incident, the ambassador would be prepared to act. Otherwise, he had no role to play.

The mission commander led the whole team through the entire exercise on several dry runs until they all knew their roles perfectly. The U.S. Navy, British Navy, and a Norwegian ship or two were participating in a NATO northern exercise. Fleets of transport aircraft flew from various northern bases back and forth over the Arctic, making obvious use of the Loran network. All was in readiness. Border reconnaissance flights were intensified out of Athens and Wiesbaden. RB-47 high altitude flights were stepped up off

Murmansk. Then, with a report of good weather and clear skies, the Courier left Norway with its four occupants and secret equipment.

For hours the plane skimmed the waves, staying below radar surveillance. U.S. ELINT monitors listened for increased "alert level" activities. All were silent. Suddenly in the Loran carrier wave, a final "all clear" signal was given. It was a simple code flashed in microseconds and unintelligible to all but the most sophisticated equipment. Then the Courier turned to the southeast and toward landfall. The barren coastline rose quickly. A heavy, dark forest grew right to the sea. The horizon was low and rolling as the plane sped on its way. Although the plane lands at a very slow speed, it cruises at a relatively high speed, even with floats. Just as dawn broke gray and heavy, they neared the destination. The only identifiable landmark they had passed was a single-track railroad cutting a long straight furrow through the forest. After the railroad there was a stream that led to the pond where they would land. The pilot made only the slightest half-turn pattern, cut the power, dropped full flaps, and slipped over some pine trees and landed with an easy splash. They were down. The Maine short-landing techniques had paid off.

With the engine off they paddled the plane to the shore, where they hastily concealed it with netting and evergreen branches. The stay-behind team unloaded all of its gear and moved well into the woods. The pilot and the mission commander slept. Later in the twilight of the brief northern day, the crew waved to the men on shore, and the Courier flashed across the pond, up over the trees, and away into the darkness. An hour after crossing the coastline, the M/C flashed a simple signal on the carrier wave. Right away, a "welcome" flash came back on Loran and an "all clear" radio signal, which meant destination weather was all right. A few hours later, the plane landed in Norway.

The training had paid off. Ten days later, the stay-behind team was recovered. This time they had helped the pilot by using the hand-cranked generator to put out a signal to guide him to the pond. All four men returned to the base in Norway. The M/C was debriefed in England, with certain British agents present. Then he flew back to Washington. The two infiltrated team men were not seen again by anyone of the early group, and the young Pole was transferred to his new civilian job in Athens.

The instrument team made their secret intelligence report to the appropriate staff sections of DD/I in the old CIA buildings near the reflecting pool beside the Mall in Washington. Their report was properly evaluated, analyzed, and disseminated to the military. They had heard, aurally and electronically, much fighter aircraft traffic and had picked up radar signals, which they had recorded. This team and the M/C received—silently—the highest award the CIA can give. In their profession the fact of the award was known; but elsewhere, even the award itself was a classified subject.

Meanwhile, certain very closed and select meetings were being held in the Agency's inner sanctum in a nondescript office building in the "H" Street NW area of downtown Washington. Designated need-to-know staff members from the CIA, the White House, Defense, State, the NSA, and the AEC (Atomic Energy Commission) had a number of sessions with the men who had been in the USSR. Their report was of great value. This whole fighter-base-radar-defense operation was real. But it was itself all part of another layer of cover story. These two men of the stay-behind team had recorded a Soviet nuclear explosion. They had, by unexpectedly lucky timing, actually witnessed the faraway glow of that tremendous explosion, and they had left in Russia very sensitive earth-sounding sensors, which would give limited but valuable signals whenever they were activated by further Soviet nuclear tests.

As in the case of other CIA undercover missions, most of what was known, even by those who knew that a plane had been flown into and back from Russia, was a cover story. State and Defense had benefited from the Air Defense intelligence. The real story, all of the facts, were reserved for the inner team of the CIA and for their co-workers secreted throughout the Government. This flight into Russia was for them simply a step on the road to Indonesia, to Cuba, to Tibet, and ultimately to Vietnam.

This had been a well-rehearsed and well-developed small operation, in the style and manner of true covert intelligence work. When the leaders of the U.S. Government use such operations for positive purposes, they may be expected to do some good. When they are repeated too frequently, when they grow too large, and when they are poorly developed and directed, they are harmful and they destroy any good that might ever come from them.

The operation described was real; but it was not a single operation and it did not happen exactly as described. Even though it took place many years ago and the significance of that project has been lost in time, some of the people involved are still in the business and some of the places used may still be used from time to time. It serves to demonstrate how a really professional special operation can be done, as contrasted with some of the haphazard and careless missions that are often carried out by some of the irresponsible non-professionals who so easily slip under the cloak of secrecy.

For example, we have said that the country involved was Norway. This was selected because the U-2 did not use Norway on certain flights over the Soviet Union. In most cases, the host country is told the truth, or at least all the truth that is known at the time of the first briefing. In a case such as this one, the station chief in Norway would tell his counterpart that we were preparing an operation in which a plane would be sent into Russia with a team and then would return there ten days later to pick them up.

Since the Norwegians share NATO secrets, it is possible they would be promised some of the data acquired. In this case, where the flight had more than ordinary significance, the Norwegians might only be told about the Air Defense mission and not about the nuclear weapons test. The host country might wish to have a representative at the scene before departure to satisfy itself that should the plane crash in Russia and be found there, nothing on it should give evidence that it had taken off from Norway.

The Norwegian Government would be asked to participate in the NATO exercise that was laid on to provide cover for the use of LORAN navigation equipment and generally to soften up the Soviet attention to activity in the area. For this the Norwegians would be permitted to bill the United States for all out-of-pocket costs incident to such activity. In other words, the United States would pay for any part of the exercise that the Norwegians could not have paid for had they not participated in it. This can run into an appreciable amount of money and equipment.

Norway might ask for and could expect to be granted assurances that in the event the exercise was uncovered for any reason, the United States would positively ignore and if necessary deny any participation in it and would guarantee that no mention be made of Norway in any event. (This did not happen in the case of the Powers U-2 flight, and Norway and Pakistan were forced to make their own embarrassing public statements.) It might also require that, in the event the plane was detected and had to flee the area, it would fly away from Norway to an alternate landing near a U.S. ship or submarine. In other words, Norway or any other host country would have a lot to say about their own involvement.

This, of course, varies a lot with the country and the situation. If by some chance we were helping one country against a traditional enemy and our special operation was inadvertently discovered, the country being helped would be glad to have its enemy know that the United States was helping it. As a matter of fact, such a situation usually leads to a so-called "inadvertent" disclosure, so anxious is the first country to let the second country know that the United States is on its side. But this would not have been the case in our example.

There would also be some arrangements that involved the minor participation of the West German Government and the British. Each of these countries would be handled separately, if possible, to keep the primary mission from being exposed. This is not possible sometimes, and the responsible agent may have to brief his counterpart in West Germany and in England.

None of these matters alone seems too important. The ST usually briefs the higher staffs of the Government piecemeal, and so they rarely get to see the whole picture as it accumulates. The opposite is true overseas. In this rather modest exercise, three foreign countries plus the Soviet Union were involved—and we perhaps should add a fourth, because certain crewmen had been kept in security isolation in Greece. In many ways knowledge by other countries is as important a consideration as any other. From that date on which they become involved on, each of those countries will know that the

United States is actively involved in clandestine operations and that it is willing to involve other countries with it in these endeavors. From that day on, it will be impossible to convince any one of those countries again that the United States does not become engaged regularly in such actions.

As time went on, and other countries were involved in other minor events, such as the use of a seemingly clean national commercial airline to do some camera spying or other clandestine project, the list grew, until by 1971 there were very few countries anywhere in the world that had not at one time or other been somehow engaged in clandestine operations with this Government. The significant thing here is that though all these other countries know this, and the Soviet Union and its community of nations know it too, the shield of secrecy spun by the ST here in the United States keeps much of this information from our own eyes, ears, and minds. Then, when we hear other nations speaking quite openly of the things this Government does that are not exactly aboveboard, there are those who would say, "Those foreigners are always saying untrue and malicious things about us." In reality, they are doing nothing more than referring to things that each of them knows we have done, because each of them has at one time or other been involved with us.

This brings up another facet of this kind of operation. In many of these countries, governments are overthrown in fast succession and quite unpredictably. What happens to the members of the inner circle of a government that was once in power and shared secrets with us, now that it has been overthrown, and these same men are in exile or at least powerless in their own country? Do they just forget all these past events? They not only remember those events, but they capitalize on their knowledge in many ways. Some are quite sophisticated, and they bide their time until they have a chance to contact the man who used to contact them when they were in power. Now they whisper that the new "in" government is "Communist-oriented" and that with a little help they can get back in power.

Others are less sophisticated and more direct. They make deals where they can to uncover other actions and networks in what they think is a loyal effort to help their old cause against the current government, not caring about the exposure of the United States, whether that matters to them at all or not. And there are others who use their information for open blackmail. Some collect, and some disappear.

The same is true of those who are voted out of office. They have known the inner workings of government. When someone tries to say that things were not quite as they were, many of these men, hoping to make a political comeback, are forced to reveal things that they have known.

There have been a number of cases where this information about third government participation with the United States in special operations has led to subtle, legal blackmail. Each government gets foreign military aid according to a carefully worked out schedule. A number of governments have used the CIA relationships they have established to plead for and to gain by heavy-handed methods hundreds of millions of dollars worth of equipment that they could not have gotten otherwise.

In summary, there are few if any men in government, from the NSC on down through the executive branch, or in the Congress, who have had the opportunity to put enough of these events together to see how heavy and oppressive twenty or more years of accumulated clandestine operations can be. When a new Assistant Secretary of Defense or Assistant Secretary of State can say in public something like, "The United States has no combat troops in Laos, and it has not had any there, and it will not have any there," at least fifteen or twenty other nations can listen and *recall* that they have at one time or other directly participated in actions that involved American combat troops in Laos; or, since this is intended as an example only, in some other country. In many such cases the person who makes such a statement is known either to be uninformed or lying.

There is a good story about American Army troops in Laos. About fifteen years ago an agreement had been reached whereby the U.S. Government would take over certain training functions and the French would leave. Some French were to remain as advisers in government and as a training cadre with the armed forces of Laos. By a local agreement worked out with the Government of Laos and with the senior French officials there, a Military Aid Program was established, calling for the delivery of large quantities of U.S.-manufactured military weapons. However, the use of many of these weapons was dependent upon a degree of training and sophistication beyond the ability of the Laotian army. The American ambassador volunteered that he could arrange for American civilian training personnel to come to Laos for the sole purpose of training the armed forces of that country on American equipment. This offer was accepted, and it was broadened to include military matters, which at that time were included in the general concept of civic action. This gave these U.S. training personnel broader responsibilities, to include such things as irrigation, village hygiene and sanitation, rudimentary school-building construction, and related tasks, all in addition to the regular weapons orientation. It also included basic electronics work and communications indoctrination of a low order of skill. By the time this whole program had been packaged, the requirement for instructors had grown to several hundred. Although this entire endeavor had the appearance of being entirely overt and coming under the responsibility of the ambassador, it was his invisible staff of CIA men who had worked up the idea to counteract French influence, which was admittedly at a low ebb following the defeat at Dien Bien Phu. In those days there was as much animosity between the CIA and the French as between the CIA and the Pathet Lao. The CIA team got the military assistance program approved and the equipment destined for Laos. The next thing was to get the civilian instructors. To accomplish this task, they beefed up their own staff with a number of new men and then turned to the Army for volunteers, who would be sheep-dipped and sent to Laos as "civilians."

(The term "sheep-dipped" appears in *The New York Times* version of the Pentagon Papers without clarification. It is an intricate Army-devised process by which a man who is in the service as a full career soldier or officer agrees to go through all the legal and official motions of resigning from the service. Then, rather than actually being released, his records are pulled from the Army personnel files and transferred to a special Army intelligence file. Substitute but nonetheless real-appearing records are then processed, and the man "leaves" the service. He is encouraged to write to friends and give a cover reason why he got out. He goes to his bank and charge card services and changes his status to civilian, and does the hundreds of other official and personal things that any man would do if he really had gotten out of the service. Meanwhile, his real Army records are kept in secrecy, but not forgotten. If his contemporaries get promoted, he gets promoted. All of the things that can be done for his hidden records to keep him even with his peers are done. Some very real problems arise in the event he gets killed or captured as a prisoner. There are problems with insurance and with benefits his wife would receive had he remained in the service. At this point, sheep-dipping gets really complicated, and each case is handled quite separately.)

In this instance the Army readied several hundred sheep-dipped officers and enlisted men for duty in Laos. They were hired by a private company created by the CIA, and they were called "White Star" teams. The total number of men involved was kept a secret from all parties, and the teams were infiltrated and entered the country at the airport in Vientiane. Others came in overland by other points of entry. Some came in on clandestine cargo flights. Finally, the last group made a ceremonial entrance into Laos by commercial air, most likely on the prime ministers own airline, Air Laos. They were met at the airport by an official party from the American embassy and were accompanied by Laotian and French officials. This small overt party contained all of the higher ranking White Star party. In customary order of precedence—reverse order of rank—everyone had disembarked from the plane except the senior official who, of course, was known simply as a civilian. Then he appeared at the door of the plane and looked out over the scene and at the welcoming party at the foot of the stairs. His eyes rested on American officials he had known before, during the long days of his special training and indoctrination, upon Laotians he had heard of by name but whom he was to meet for the first time, and upon French officials whom he had not expected to see at the plane. He expected that the White Star teams under his leadership would replace the French in the favor of the host Laotians in a short time. And then he saw the figure of a ranking French officer. Their eyes met for the first time in more than a decade. Of all the men, this sheep-dipped Army colonel, John A. Heintges, could have met at the steps of a plane in Vientiane, Laos, the one whom he saw was the same French officer with whom he had spent years in a German prisoner-of-war camp. Months of preparatory cover work went up in smoke. French intelligence there were able to match the cover story "official record" of this "civilian" with his known true role with the U.S. Army Special Forces once they discovered his identity. The White Star team bubble burst even before it got started.

Here again is an example that adds up, along with so many others, to prove that what may be called clandestine and what may be treated with deep secrecy in the never-never land of "Secret Team Washington" is really not so secret and so undercover out in the cold factual world. There have been so many generals and admirals from the U.S. Army, Navy, and Air Force who have either been serving on assignment with the CIA, or who were really CIA career men serving on a cover military assignment, or mixes of both, and who have worked in Southeast Asia during the past twenty years, all as a primary duty with the CIA, that it would be no wonder at all that the officials of governments from Korea to Pakistan could certainly be excused for not knowing whom or what they were dealing with every time they came upon a senior-grade military man.

This is no place to name their names, but even a quick scan of the Pentagon Papers will fill a whole page with these names. For example, Air Marshall Ky of Vietnam may not know to this day that some of his closest early friends in the U.S. Air Force were not really with the USAF; and Colonel Thieu, now President Thieu, could be excused if he never really knew whether most of the generals who were closest to him were really Agency men or U.S. military men on Agency assignments. The record is now so public about Ngo Dinh Diem's tutelage at the hands of Magsaysay's creator Edward G. Lansdale that it certainly may be redundant to point out that Lansdale was serving the CIA in the Philippines and in South Vietnam. His case was quite special even in that role, because he served a special inner sanctum of the Agency and not the regular Agent section. Some of his greatest problems in Southeast Asia were the result of mix-ups, not with Communists or with the French, whom he detested and who had similar feelings for him, but with other members of the Agency's clandestine staff, who either did not know who he was at first, or if they did know, would not accept him. The little "White-Star" team episode was very modest with respect to its attempt at the big game of clandestine operations.

Two former Commanders in Chief, Pacific Armed Forces (CINCPAC), have served with or are now serving as directors of Air America. This huge overt/covert airline is properly listed in Dun and Bradstreet and in many public telephone books; so it is not unusual to find high-ranking admirals serving on its board of directors. However, when some of these directors call on old friends in the DOD at times when Air America is bidding on a U.S. Air Force aircraft maintenance contract or on a Navy air transport contract carrier contract in the Pacific, they attend the meeting as Admiral this or Admiral that, but when the chips are down someone adeptly slips the word that the "CIA is asking no favors, remember, but all it does ask is a fair competitive position." These admirals do their job for the CIA like any other agent. By the same token, when ranking officers travel throughout the Pacific on what appears to everyone, and of course especially to officials of the host countries, to be U.S. defense establishment business, no one should be surprised if, in later years, these same host countries begin to wise up and think that almost everyone they meet must be CIA.

This is not a sometime thing; it involves a large number of senior officers up to and including those wearing four stars. It certainly prime exponent stretches credulity not to expect that in this whole string of Asian nations, not one of which can ever be faulted on the grounds of being both clever and wily, someone would take advantage of the CIA-versus-the-overt-military-establishment-routine for his own ends. Chiang Kai-Shek has been the prime exponent and recipient of the many advantages of this game. Marshall Sarit of Thailand was not far behind, and Ngo Dinh Diem knew how to play both sides against each other for his own ends, until finally even his own creators let go of the string, and he fell.

The example of the small flight operation into Russia shows something else that enters into peacetime special operations as carried out by the ST. The law and the NSC directives that followed did not authorize the CIA to build up forces sufficient to carry out such operations. However, when the NSC did direct an operation, there were no such limitations on that senior authority concerning money, manpower, and materials. The NSC could stipulate that the Agency perform such tasks with civilian resources. It could further stipulate that the CIA perform the operation with civilian mercenary non-U.S. personnel. Or it could permit the Agency to utilize the obvious resources of the U.S. military establishment up to the point of the actual flight. This became a customary procedure, at least in the days up to about 1955 or 1956.

During these fledgling days, the precocious Agency made good use of the military. As in this flight, it gave them all kinds of tasks as enumerated. Not only would the CIA enlist direct assistance with the words that "NSC 5412/2 has directed this exercise and its support by the military"; but it would convene meetings in the Pentagon, in the Paris headquarters of U.S. Forces in Europe, in Army headquarters at Heidelberg, Air Force headquarters in Wiesbaden, and Navy headquarters in London, all to churn up the idea and let these headquarters vie with each other in seeing how far they could go out of their way to "support" this exercise, which they knew only as a code name or at best as a plausible cover story. In response to the magic of the CIA relationship, the services would come up with all kinds of support, often beyond the dreams and expectations of the Agency. This had a double-barreled effect. It made a given clandestine operation much larger in its overt supporting areas than originally visualized. It led also within all of the services to a growing capability, often overlapping, which had the effect of creating a very large submerged infrastructure, ready, willing, and eager to become involved again and again with the glamorous CIA. We shall go into this in more detail later.

There are things in every really clandestine exercise that must be done in an expert manner. In the example, we saw that the Agency used non-U.S. nationals for certain hard-core assignments. One man, the pilot, was in a sense fortunate. The CIA happened to find him among thousands of displaced persons. However, one of the pilots who trained him was a real stateless or "multi-national" person. Also, the two infiltrated instrumentation experts were non-nationals. This type of person places a real burden on the Agency, and special attention is given to them and to their welfare and maintenance. It is one thing to use a young Polish pilot for one air mission; but what does the Agency do with such a man year in and year out? Such people do exist, and such people do some important and very specialized work. It may not be "James Bond" all the time; but it has its moments. In between these moments, there are many problems to be solved—among them such things as a place to live, marriage, family, schools, vacations. Saying that they exist is sufficient for the purposes of this book. What is done with them both during operations and during the dull intervals in between would take another book.

Another area of activity that lies underneath much of the commonplace activity of the Agency has to do with the interminable processing, evaluating, analyzing, and utilization of intelligence of all kinds. It is important to query hundreds of thousands of displaced persons and to get warehouses full of information, only if that information can be used. There are times when the Agency is nonplused by its own cleverness and resources.

There are countless other facets of clandestine operations. It is ridiculous for the Agency and for the rest of the Government to deny them, and it is equally erroneous for those who know nothing about them to speculate about their real character and meaning.

It may appear to be an oversimplification to say it; but an Agency career develops a thick skin, which is occupational, and this thick skin includes an extra set of eyelids which pop over the eyeball of the mind when the man discovers himself in a situation where he finds he should not be.

It is said that the tens of thousands of Japanese who live on one block in a city such as Tokyo develop the ability to live in close proximity, separated one house from the other, usually by no more than a few scant inches and by rice-paper walls and windows. Without question, families in a given area hear each other and all the usual household noises; yet they all maintain that they hear nothing of what goes on in the neighbors' house. The idea is that they are supposed to hear nothing; so they hear nothing. This same mental process that permits the disciplined brain to separate out sounds one from another is not unusual in many other cases. It applies in a sense to people who spend their lives in highly classified work. They actually learn to shut out and to avoid seeking out what the other person is doing. As a result, many of the real agent careerists and the staff personnel who support them really do not know what other offices are doing, and they don't care to know.

This blocking-out process may not apply in a majority of cases, but it is true in many. In other cases, there are men who have spent their lives in the Agency who have never really had any direct contact with actual missions because of the nature of their work and because those who were involved in operations kept such information from them. Therefore, some of these old-timers really do not know what is going on. They may think that they do because they have always been aware of activity of one kind or other, and they have heard the usual rumors of what has been taking place. This is often more of a handicap than a help, because if the man has not actually gotten out on the operation he may have heard a very well laid out cover story and thought it was real. He would have no way to know otherwise. Examples of this in other walks of life are not hard to find. When Ford changes its model lines and is introducing some really new design or engineering feature that it wants to keep secret, it will put several teams at work designing the next model car. At certain check points of development, these teams are told, "Fine, now go ahead with what you are doing, to the next stage." Thus, unknown to each other and to the fairly large staffs who support them, more than one team believes its new model is the one that the company has selected. Only at the last moment, when it is too late for them to continue the bluff and too late for a competitor to gain from discovery of the new design or feature, is the unneeded team told that their model has not been selected and that their work was necessary cover to conceal the real design. It is better to have some teams actually living and believing the cover story than to have some just play-acting the cover story. This leaves the final operational go-ahead options open until the very last moment and assures that if there are leaks, the other side will have the problem of finding out whether the operation they have discovered is real or planned deception.

This situation was practiced quite widely during the Bay of Pigs operation. Some units thought they were going to be involved in the exercise, but they never were. This had one odd result right in the office of the Joint Chiefs of Staff. A team of ranking officers thought that they were working on part of the Cuban operation. They were very active and thought that the things they were doing were really happening and that their work was being used by the CIA. It turned out that all the things they did were dummy activities and that the Agency never even intended to use them. It was a sort of Agency cover and deception operation against a part of our own forces. The military were never told that what they had been working on was not used, and later during the review of the Bay of Pigs operation, the senior officers of that task actually appeared before the Presidents Review Board and testified concerning what they had done. Their testimony was so realistic that it was taken as the real thing, and no one ever spoke up to clarify the matter. Apparently, it was in the best interest of the ST to let it go as it did; it only served further to implicate the military in the Bay of Pigs, when in reality they had very little to do with any part of it. This was a very strange turn of events, and exposes another aspect of the strange ways of clandestine operations. When this country permits itself to enter the dream world of covert operations, it creates a national Frankenstein of such proportions that major factions within the Government do not know how something happened, who authorized it, and why it was done. The system begins to run itself from the moment of data input. From the agents first bit of information to the emergence of a clandestine operation, everything is constructed entirely out of response-mechanisms to the ever-claimed threat of Communism. Therefore, the system must do something anti-Communist. Nowhere was there anything built in to say "Stop."

Lyman Kirkpatrick[2] writing so intelligently and from an inside position of real administrative experience said that "President Kennedy paid for the abandoning of the NSC at the Bay of Pigs. He had allowed himself and his principal advisors to be made the captives of the proponents of the plan. . . . If the President had insisted that the deliberations on the operation be conducted within the framework of an NSC system, with appropriate staff work and review, there would have been a much greater chance that he would have received a more realistic appraisal of its chances for success [or failure]."

This could not have been set in words with more truth and impact. Again we see the bugaboo of CIA secrecy—it precludes the employment of normal and experienced supporting staff action. In the area of covert operations it is especially important to have someone of high authority in the position to say "No" when "No" is called for. President Kennedy did not convene the Security Council, which might have helped him, and President Johnsons greatest failing was that even though he may have from time to time convened the Council, it was by that time made up of few responsible men and several irresponsible people who more than frequently tended to go along with the ST on everything and left the final decision up to the President who could not and did not say "No."

The discussion in this chapter is intended to serve as an introduction to the world of clandestine operations. We have discussed at some length the first four duties of the CIA as spelled out in the language of the National Security Act of 1947. It remains to look at the fifth duty, the one that the Agency and the ST use to establish that it was the intention of the Congress and of the President to permit the Agency to become involved in the area of clandestine operations as a regular function.

---

2. *The Real CIA*, New York: The Macmillan Co., 1968.

CHAPTER 8

CIA: The "Cover Story" Intelligence Agency and the Real-Life Clandestine Operator

The CIA likes to publicize itself as it wishes to be seen; it tries consistently to maintain its cover story. These facts would not be publicly admitted by the agency; but they are facts. It is only fitting to note that when Allen Dulles died, he was writing a book about "Communism and Subversion." This was his first love, as it was J. Edgar Hoover's. This was his occupation. Intelligence was his avocation. When he was writing about Communism and subversion, he was writing, of course, about the real work of the CIA. He liked to write about the CIA and he liked to see that others wrote about the CIA.

After his retirement from the Agency in the fall of 1961, he wrote a very interesting book entitled *The Craft of Intelligence*. This book is good reading. It contains a lot of folklore about the peripheral world of intelligence; but it says almost nothing useful about the CIA. In fact, as he intended it, it tells a great many things about the CIA that were designed to create the picture of a noble CIA, one that really does not exist. This was typical of Allen Dulles.

Other CIA men have written about the CIA. The most able Lyman B. Kirkpatrick, Jr., long-time career Intelligence stalwart and Executive Director of the CIA, wrote a book, too, which he called *The Real CIA*. This is unquestionably the best book written by a CIA man about the CIA. It is as forthright and as honest a book as any career man has written or may ever write. Later authors will have missed the great pressures and inner violence of the early struggles, from the days of the OSS and its internecine battles with the Navy and with MacArthur, through the days of the post-World War II hiatus, and then to the struggles from 1947 to the Korean War. This was the truly formative period, and this was the time which spawned the giants.

Lyman Kirkpatrick has written an elegant book; but it leaves much to be said. This is not to suggest that considerations of security have intervened, it is rather to suggest that those career professionals who have devoted their lives to this cause and who have totally lived the party line just cannot bring themselves to see some things as they appear to others, and then admit it even if they should. There is much about a life in the Agency that is like a religious order or a secret fraternity.

After these men, numberless others have written about the CIA. A great percentage of this latter group has written about the CIA at the bidding and urging of the Agency. An organization such as the CIA, which exists in a true never-never land, needs to have someone write about it so that there will always be a plethora of material available and so that this vast stew-pot of material will be what the Agency wants the world to believe about it. The Agency does not answer writers, whether they attack it or not. But it works doggedly and brilliantly at times to bury anything not the party line that is written about it. Thus the Agency has a whole stable of writers, its favorite magazines and newspapers, its publishing houses, and its "backgrounders" ready to go at all times.

Allen Dulles had twelve or thirteen regular members of the news media who would be invited to join him frequently for lunch in the beautiful old dining room he maintained in East Building across from his office. Many an agent or military officer who had been invited to his offices to meet with him or with his deputy, General Cabell, to discuss matters of utmost secrecy, would be astounded at lunch with them to find the room filled with these well known writers and commentators. And then, as lunch proceeded, the same subjects that on the other side of the hall had been so carefully shrouded in secrecy would become table gossip with these men of the press. Dulles believed that if he kept these men well informed, they would then be able to draw that fine line between the CIA party line and its security limits.

Even as Dulles regularly placed himself at the mercy of the lions, he played a bigger game. If he gave them a bit of insight into the workings of the Agency, he also gave them a heavy mixture of that special brew, which he was so good at concocting. He fed them the CIA point of view all the time, just as he fed so many others, from Presidents on down, and as he has fed the readers of his book.

His greatest bit of writing in this special field is regrettably hidden away under heavy security wraps, although by now there cannot be a thing in it that would warrant classification. The report written by Allen Dulles, Mathias Correa, and William Jackson in the latter part of 1948 was a small masterpiece. It clearly and precisely outlined what Allen Dulles was going to do; and to his credit, he did just that and more. During that busy summer of election year, 1948, Allen Dulles was officially the speech-writer for the Republican candidate, Governor Thomas E. Dewey of New York. All through the campaign it had been generally accepted that Dewey would defeat President Truman. Allen Dulles, his brother, John Foster Dulles, and the others of that Dewey team fully expected to move into Washington on the crest of a wave with the inauguration of their candidate.

In this context then, the Dulles-Correa-Jackson report takes on a special meaning. Although this select committee had been established by President Truman, they had timed their work for delivery to the President during his—they expected—"Lame Duck" period. Then they planned to use it as their own plan of action in the new Dewey administration. In one of the greatest political upsets of all time, Truman beat Dewey, and the Republicans were forced to wait another four years. Thus it happened that this crucial report on the national intelligence community was reluctantly delivered into Truman's more than hostile hands on January 1, 1949. Due to other circumstances, Allen Dulles did spend eleven years in the service of the CIA, and at least ten years prior to that in endeavors directly related to intelligence. It was not until he left government service in late 1961 that he began his book, published in 1963, *The Craft of Intelligence.* This book, which he was to leave to the world as his public definition of the agency, says very little that is real about the Agency and very little that is real about intelligence. It contains all manner of contrived concepts designed over the years to make people believe that the CIA was what he was saying it was and that all of the authority he said it had did exist. Any reader who thought the CIA was anything like the description contained in the book will be excused for his thoughts, because if ever a subject was painted in camouflage and in words of guile, this was it. This really is not a light matter. Not only did Allen Dulles portray the CIA in public as something that it most certainly was not; but he had done so for many years within the U.S. Government. Let us see how Allen Dulles presents the subject of secret intelligence and clandestine operations.

He opens the book with a "Personal Note." He wants to take the uninitiated reader into his confidence at once. (Those who have seen him operating with such public figures as Joseph Alsop have seen the same approach. The fatherly figure couldn't possibly be weaving a web of connivance around the unsuspecting fly, whether he be a well-known writer or an unknown reader.) By the time he gets to page 6 he says, "CIA is not an underground operation. All one needs to do is to read the law—the National Security Act of 1947—to get a general idea of what it is set up to do. It has, of course, a secret side and the law permits the NSC, which in effect means the President, to assign to the CIA certain duties and functions in the intelligence field in addition to those specifically enumerated in the law. These functions are not disclosed."

Without delay, Mr. Dulles begins to soften up the innocent reader. First the blunt statement, which means nothing: "The CIA is not an underground operation." The trick here is that he is saying bluntly what is fact. It is not an operation. But he intends to lard the book with as much justification as he can muster to support the contention that the CIA is entitled to operate underground.

Then he neatly says that in reading the law a person will get a "general idea" of what the Agency is supposed to do. Right away he has the reader thinking that if the law only sets forth the "general idea" of what the Agency "is set up to do," then there must be some other "law" that gives it other powers. Of course, there is no such other law.

Next he says, "It [CIA] has, of course, a secret side . . ." True again, like the opening statement; but that is not because of the law, although he hopes the reader thinks that the law provides for the "secret side." Then, as if to lift the edge of the curtain to let the uninitiated see a bit of the promised land, he adds, ". . . the law permits the NSC . . . to assign [note the use of the word 'assign' rather than the word which is in the law, 'direct'] to the CIA certain duties and functions in the intelligence field in addition to those specifically enumerated in the law." Here, he has set up the idea, "secret side," in the mind of the reader and then proceeded to weakly paraphrase subparagraph 5 of the list of duties, quoted above. Notice also that he says, ". . . the NSC, which in effect means the President . . ." This is a subtle and most meaningful suggestion when one recalls that this book was written in the Kennedy era, from 1961 to 1963. It is true that President Kennedy did all but abandon the NSC, and that in doing so, the NSC became only the President, nearly in fact. This reveals much more than it says when one recalls that the young President had selected only two of the Eisenhower appointees to remain in his Administration. One of them was Allen Dulles. Thus we see that if Allen Dulles had personally briefed the new President on the way the CIA worked, he might very well have done it just as he is doing in his book. He is the one who most probably put the cap on the views of the new man that really the NSC was simply an Eisenhower idiosyncrasy, carried over from the Truman years, and that he might as well abandon it. As Dulles' own Executive Director, Lyman Kirkpatrick, has ably pointed out, this "abandonment of the NSC" by Kennedy led directly to the Bay of Pigs and its great failure, and most likely, to other things that followed, including the Vietnam initiatives.

It is not hollow word play to read into the Dulles book these deeper, almost sinister, meanings. Anyone who has had the privilege of having read both publications, the 1948 report and this book, will be able to confirm the subtle and premeditated structuring of Dulles's powerful course of action. Dulles was an able disciple of the Goebbels school of propaganda. Mr. Dulles's enlightening paraphrase of the fifth duty from the National Security Act is as close as he gets to that bit of the law through the whole course of the book, until six pages from the end. Then he cleverly runs the fourth duty and the fifth duty together in such a way that the reader will most likely not even recognize them for what they are, and Allen Dulles will have purged his conscience by being able to say that he covered all of the law "verbatim." That he did; but it was a masterful job of obfuscation and of mind-bending. If ever the technique of brainwashing has been put to good use, it has been done by Allen Dulles and others of his ilk.

Having used this much mind-bending at the start of his book, he then follows with forty pages of interesting anecdotes and history, after which he comes right back to the same brainwashing, saying, "A Republican Congress agreed [with General Donovan—which in fact it did not] and, with complete bipartisan approval, the CIA was established in the National Security Act of 1947. It was an openly acknowledged arm of the executive branch of the government, although, of course, it had many duties of a secret nature."

Here again, he used the techniques of the ST by associating the public language of the law, quite incorrectly, with the idea that "it had many duties of a secret nature." As we know from our review of the law, above, it did not have duties of a "secret nature." At least it did not have them in the law. He went on to say: "President Truman saw to it that the new agency was equipped to support our government's effort to meet Communist tactics . . ." This is at variance with Truman's own words about this quiet intelligence arm of the President. What Truman himself said was, "I never had any thought when I set up the CIA that it would be injected into peacetime cloak and dagger operations." Truman, the man who signed the bill into law, says that it was never his intention that the CIA would have such duties. Again Allen Dulles brushes such things aside to make a case for the Agency he did so much to change from the "quiet intelligence arm" into the most powerful peacetime operational force ever created.

Dulles continued with his ritualistic chant by adding, "Its [CIA] broad scheme was in a sense unique in that it combined under one leadership the overt task of intelligence analysis and coordination with the work of secret intelligence operations of the various types I shall describe." He employs the technique of beginning with a thought that is correct—intelligence analysis and coordination—and then, when the reader is trapped, he continues into an area he wants the reader to think is equally correct—the work of secret intelligence operations. Characteristically, he has not bothered to define "secret intelligence operations." Even inside the Government, where such terms are used with some frequency, there is much controversy about the real meaning of that phrase, "secret intelligence operations." As a further clue to where Mr. Dulles is planning to take the reader, notice his use of the word "operations," and then recall his blunt, though meaningless early statement, "the CIA is not an underground operation." He is already back at that theme and beginning to work it around so that the reader will believe that the CIA and operations are wedded.

Only a few times farther on, he says; "CIA was given the mandate to develop its own secret collection arm, which was to be quite distinct from that part of the organization that had been set up to assemble and evaluate intelligence from other parts of the government." He continues his clever intertwining of fact with fact to create a pattern that, when woven further with his own contrived designs, is totally at variance with the original. The only mandate he had mentioned to this point in the book was the law of 1947. The "mandate" to which he is making reference in this context, however, was contained in a National Security Council Intelligence Directive (NSCID) 10/2 of August 1948. This directive did authorize the CIA to develop a secret division to perform certain secret activities; but it was a far cry from what Allen Dulles is describing.

The law did not authorize secret or clandestine activities. However, Agency protagonists continued to put pressure on the Executive Branch to permit the CIA to collect "secret intelligence." The argument most frequently given was that since the United States had always been lily white in the area of foreign policy, there was no organization that could "fight the Communists in their own dirty way." It was proposed that since the CIA, which had re-assembled some of the former OSS operators, possessed the demonstrated know-how to carry out secret intelligence operations, it should be permitted to form a unit for that purpose. In the beginning, this idea was avowedly limited to secret intelligence. The CIA disclaimed any intention of using secret intelligence as a bridge to secret operations.

Finally, the NSC consented and published its directive 10/2. However, anyone who had had the opportunity to have read the directive would have been amazed to find what lengths the NSC went to in order to restrain the CIA from going too far in this direction. Absolutely contrary to Mr. Dulles' contention that the CIA was given many duties of a secret nature and then equipped to perform these duties, the NSC directive did authorize the CIA to set up an Office of Policy Coordination (OPC), which would be prepared to engage in secret intelligence activities. However, the director of that office had to be selected by the Secretary of State and approved by the Secretary of Defense. The personnel of that office was to be CIA employees, but their boss was hired and fired by the Secretaries of State and Defense. This was done to keep the DCI from having control over him and thus over the clandestine activity of that office.

This was a partial victory for the clandestine operations activists, but it was an unhappy solution. At that time, the Secretary of Defense was Louis Johnson. He had embarked upon a rigid budget-cutting program by direction of President Truman. Another part of this NSC directive prohibited the CIA from having the funds to carry out clandestine activities. It stated that if and when the NSC directed such action, it would, as a function of its directive, state how the activity would be manned, equipped, and paid for. In the beginning, Congress had not found it necessary to put any special restraints upon the CIA for budgeted and approved funds. Since Congress intended that the CIA would be an overt coordinator of intelligence, it made no plans to hide CIA money in various secret accounts. However, the NSC provided that the CIA was not to use intelligence funds for clandestine activities, but was to be allocated funds from other sources whenever such operations were directed. In this manner, the custom of having CIA funds buried and hidden in the allocations to other departments and agencies began. The intent at first was for this to be a control device over the Agency's activities and not a full flood tide of money pouring without check or constraint into a horn of plenty to support CIA clandestine operations.

Again, there are few who had the opportunity to see these working papers; but in 1949 a most excellent bit of staff work produced a long letter to the DCI over the signature of Secretary of Defense Louis Johnson. It contained a full outline of how such funding would operate, how it could be moved unseen from one department and agency to another in accordance with the provisions of a little noticed law, the National Economy Act of 1932, as amended in the Legislative Branch Appropriation Act 1933, of June 30, 1932. It also stipulated how the gaining agency would be required to reimburse the losing agency for all expenses and especially for those that were clearly out-of-pocket. This control was much more effective in those days because the CIA had very little money it could put into costly clandestine operations. As a result, the CIA was very restricted in what it could do as long as the Secretary of Defense required that the DOD be reimbursed. In later years, this stipulation was reversed, and there occasionally were hints from the CIA that it would seek compensation from the DOD for the intelligence it provided.

Another factor of importance was that at that time there were a number of qualified, competent, and top-echelon men who were familiar with the provisions of the National Security Act of 1947 with the NSCIDs, and with the implementing directives derived from all of them. They knew very well that all of this was being done to keep the CIA under control and to prohibit it from going ahead with any clandestine operation or secret intelligence without clear and specific authority. But no one would ever know this from reading Allen Dulles' book. (In a later chapter more will be said about the financial arrangements to include the Central Intelligence Agency Act of 1949.)

Just a few lines after his statement about the CIA's "mandate," Mr. Dulles makes another point designed to have the reader believe that clandestine operations were a very matter of fact thing: "One of the unique features of CIA was that its evaluation and coordinating side was to treat the intelligence produced by its clandestine arm in the same fashion that information from other government agencies was treated." That sentence really does not mean a thing pertinent to what he had been saying in his book, with the one big exception. He is including the clandestine arm idea again with an otherwise true and correct statement—its evaluating and coordinating side—to make the reader believe that because one statement has the ring of truth, the other must be true also. Then he continues with one of his boldest and most brazen statements. There would be no reason to call it "bold and brazen" except for the fact that he is making all of these remarks in the part of the book he calls the "Evolution of American Intelligence." The use of the word "evolution" connotes a theme of chronological development by sequence. He has been manipulating the chronology to make what he is saying appear to be a part of the law or of other true directives, when in fact they did not develop in quite that order. Thus the next statement is most significant: "Another feature of CIA's structure, which did not come about all at once but was the result of gradual mergers which experience showed to be practical and efficient, was the incorporation of all clandestine activities under one roof and one management." The statement is not untrue as it stands; but it is true not because of the law, or of directives which created the CIA as it is today. The final roll-over of the evolutionary process was a runaway situation created more by the ST itself, in which even the Agency was one of the tools in the greater action, than it was by law and design of the normal channels of the Government.

This whole issue has been made needlessly complex by those who have been unwilling to submit to and comply with the law and to NSC directives as they have been written. We have said earlier that one of the most important facts of the law is that the CIA was created "under the direction of the NSC." We see again that the fifth duty says that the CIA will "perform such other functions and duties . . . as the NSC may from time to time direct." There is a world of difference in saying that the CIA will do what the NSC directs from saying that the CIA may do what the NSC authorizes. It is one thing to take a proposal to a committee and win their approval and thereby to gain the authority to perform the requested activity. It is an entirely different thing to be called to a meeting of so eminent a body as the NSC and to be "directed" to perform an activity.

On this simple and clear point the CIA protagonists have rebelled and argued and connived for almost twenty-five years. Through a succession of skillful internecine maneuvers the CIA, working within the ST and shielded by secrecy and the systems and pressures that heavy secrecy make it possible to utilize, has been able to either plant people in the NSC who are really CIA agents or men who will work at their bidding, or to so brief and brainwash the NSC representative or his designated alternate so that he will believe the CIA explanation of what the law and the directives mean.

This is why it has been important to read the Dulles book line by line. This book is no more nor less than a final compilation of all of the soothing syrup and old wives' tales Allen Dulles concocted and poured over the fevered brows of men in high office and high public and private position for twenty-five years. The book shows how the CIA has been "sold" to the inner staff of the Government and to others, such as writers and commentators, businessmen and educators, both in this country and all over the world.

One would like to speak as kindly as possible and to say that these misinterpretations that cropped up in this book were no more than mistakes and that they can be attributed in part perhaps to ignorance of all the facts; but this could not possibly apply here. This cover story and fairy tale about the "evolution of American intelligence" had been fabricated by highly intelligent men and has been honed to a fine edge through years of skillful manipulation and practice. It is not the result of ignorance or lack of comprehension. This cover story is the planned scheme of a team of men who wish to present the CIA as a benign and well-controlled organization operating under law and directive, and doing nothing except intelligence, when for the most part and in actual practice it is not.

The Agency is very much aware, too, that it cannot look back, because fate is creeping up on it. The tremendous pressures in this country that have built up during the long tragic years of the conflict in Indochina are driving researchers, politicians, and other concerned Americans to search for the origins and sources of responsibility for that disaster. This is bringing them closer and closer each day to the curtain of secrecy that has effectively veiled these areas from sight for more than a decade. This pressure is now forcing Agency and ST supporters to begin a serious program of rewriting history, in a massive effort to protect and shield the Agency while shifting the search into other avenues. We have already said that the work of Daniel Ellsberg and the number of people who helped him may have been the first major step in this effort. The released Pentagon Papers do much to portray the CIA as it is supposed to be, while doing all it can to shift any censure of the CIA as an organization primarily concerned with clandestine operations, to the military, the National Security Council, and the White House.

Now a second salvo has been favored in an attempt to go further along this same road for the purpose of whitewashing the Agency. As the sometimes prestigious *Foreign Affairs*, the quarterly review of the Council on Foreign Relations, enters its fiftieth year, it has published an article entitled "The CIA and Decision-Making," by Chester L. Cooper. The author is listed as the "Director of the International and Social Studies Division, Institute of Defense Analysis; Special Assistant to Averill Harriman in planning the U.S. negotiating position on Vietnam, 1966–1967; Senior Staff Member, National Security Council, 1964–1966; author of *The Last Crusade: America in Vietnam*." The review does not add that he was and may still be a member of the CIA. This contribution to current history is a most astounding bit of writing and reweaving of events. It appears to be Phase II, or at least a part of Phase II, of the whitewashing of the CIA in Indochina. This article is a most expert and ideal example of what is meant by saying that the CIA likes to see itself in front, as long as it can control the pen.

It begins most suitably by pointing out that Allen Dulles selected the motto, which is chiseled into the marble at the entrance to the new CIA building in Langley, Virginia, from the words of St. John: "The truth shall make you free." And with this fresh in mind, the article goes on to say, ". . . one of his [Allen Dulles's] greatest contributions in nurturing the frail arrangements he helped to create [was] to provide intelligence support to Washington's top-level foreign-policy-makers." Then it gets down to the serious business of trying to show how ardently the CIA (Intelligence) has worked during the Indochina conflict, wholly ignoring the other, and major side of the house, CIA (Clandestine Operations) and CIA (senior member of the Secret Team).

To set the stage, it dwells upon the responsibility of the CIA to turn out the National Intelligence Estimates. "When PRAVDA has been scanned, the road-watchers' reports from Laos checked, the economic research completed, Pham van Dong's recent speeches dissected, radar signals examined, satellite observations analyzed and embassy cables read, the estimators set about their task . . . it is likely to be the best-informed and most objective view the decision-makers can get. . . . [they] brood about the world's problems and project their views about how these problems are likely to affect America's national security interests." All of this is to laud the intelligence side of the house, and this praise is most deserved. However, the intelligence staff has had its problems, and in mentioning some, this article attempts to use them as a means of shifting some blame to other parties, as in the following: ". . . the Office of National Estimates had a thin audience during the Johnson Administration." In other words, if the Johnson Administration did not take advantage of this excellent intelligence, then certainly the CIA can't be blamed for what befell that Administration; or at least this is what this author would like his readers to believe.

Then to enlarge the scope of his case he adds, "Nixon's Administration . . . relegated the National Intelligence Estimates to but a tiny fraction of the studies, analyses, position papers, contingency plans, research reports and memoranda generated by the large new NSC staff..." Again he implies that if the Nixon Administration failed to heed the National Estimates, it was its own fault and not that of the CIA.

Having set the stage and prepared his case, he goes directly to the heart of the matter: "Most Americans concerned about foreign affairs have long had to accept on blind faith that our government takes pains to provide its highest officials with the best possible intelligence guidance—and then to squirm under our private suspicions that this advice is, all too often, regarded with indifference. Thanks to Daniel Ellsberg, those of us who have not seen a National Intelligence Estimate for many years, or who have never seen one, can address the matter with somewhat more confidence than we could have a few months ago. Although it probably did not cross Ellsberg's mind when he released the Pentagon Papers to *The New York Times*, he succeeded in doing what the Agency, on its own, has rarely been able to do for more than twenty years: he made the CIA 'look good' through what inhabitants of the Pickle Factory themselves would call a 'highly credible source.'"

To those well steeped in the ways of the real CIA, and unfortunately there are too few who are, the above statement fits the pattern. Here is an Agency partisan praising Daniel Ellsberg. This does much to support our earlier contention that one of the real reasons these papers were delivered to the public was really on behalf of the CIA and the ST and not the other way around. Then the article goes on to say ". . . the Pentagon Papers tell us little about what actually happened in the White House Cabinet room, they do reveal much about the intelligence guidance made available to the policy-makers." He is still working on the major premise in an attempt to show that everything the CIA did was right, by showing from the included extracts how excellent its intelligence product was during those trying years. Let's look further into this propaganda, as an example is selected from among the many available.

"By mid-summer, the issue of American support for Diem's fledgling and untried government was high on the NSC's agenda. The CIA was requested to prepare an Estimate on the viability of a Western-supported, anti-Communist government in Vietnam. According to the Pentagon Papers, the National Intelligence Estimate of August 3 (1954) warned that 'even with American support it was unlikely that the French or Vietnamese would be able to establish a strong government and that the situation would probably continue to deteriorate!' The NSC, nevertheless, recommended American aid for the frail and untried Vietnamese government, a recommendation that was soon followed by President Eisenhower's fateful letter to Diem offering American support.

"This estimate had long since been validated and it seems clear that the United States would now be better off if President Eisenhower had paid more heed to that warning and less to the strong pressures that were being exerted by his Secretary of State and hard line members of Congress."

This voice of the CIA is saying that the CIA National Intelligence Estimate "has long since been validated" and "the United States would now be better off" if the President had listened to it and not to John Foster Dulles and "hard-line members of Congress." Remember, as we review the record further, that this NIE, as reported by *Foreign Affairs*, was dated August 3, 1954.

During this very same period when such NIE were establishing a cover story for the clandestine side of the CIA, the record shows that the Director of Intelligence, Allen Dulles, was working through his clandestine channels to keep knowledge of his activities from other officials of the Government and at the same time to establish a vast clandestine operational presence in Indochina. To compound this deception, the *Foreign Affairs* article of January 1972 presents a bold attempt to further conceal the duplicity of the CIA by hiding these facts and at the same time blaming members of Congress, John Foster Dulles, and President Eisenhower for things that were being done, not by them at all, but by Allen Dulles and his clandestine staff. There can be no other way to interpret this action to cover up the role of the Agency during the early and formative years of the Indochina conflict than to expose it as a premeditated effort to rewrite and restructure history by hiding the operational role of the CIA under its Intelligence cover.

This is one of the most compelling reasons why "secret intelligence" and "secret operations" should not be placed under the authority of one agency.

In spite of what the Office of National Estimates was saying during 1954, on January 30, 1954, during a meeting of the President's Special Committee on Indochina, Allen W. Dulles inquired if an unconventional warfare officer, specifically Colonel Lansdale, could not be added to the group of five liaison officers to which General Navarre had agreed. In other words, as early as January 1954, Allen Dulles was moving into the action in Indochina with his crack team of agents, among them Ed Lansdale.

Then, by April 5, 1954, the conclusions of the report of this same Presidential Committee included the following: "The United States should, in all prudence, take the following courses of action . . . to give vitality in Southeast Asia to the concept that Communist imperialism is a transcending threat to each of the Southeastern Asian States. These efforts should be so undertaken as to appear through local initiative rather than as a result of U.S. or U.K. or French instigation." This action was assigned to USIA, (United States Information Agency), the State Department, and the CIA.

It was to be the job of the CIA, among others, to see that the "concept" of the "threat to each of the Southeast Asian States" was to be made to appear to be "Communist imperialism." This was the direct charge of a committee on which Allen Dulles served and is a blunt definition of how anti-Communism is hoisted to the top of the mast whenever it is needed as a rallying symbol. As the theme of the "transcending threat" in Indochina, it was in the direct line to the later Communist-supported-war-of-national-liberation theme and then to the Communist-inspired-subversive-insurgency theme of the Kennedy era. There can be little wonder why, in the minds of most Americans, South Vietnam is so intricately tied to the idea of Communist subversion. Words such as the above show clearly the role of the initiative taken by the CIA in Indochina as far back as 1954, even while the Office of National Estimates was saying otherwise.

And while all this was going on, Admiral Arthur W. Radford, the chairman of the JCS, gave a memorandum to the Secretary of Defense which included the following extract: "The JCS desire to point out their belief that, from the point of view of the USA, with reference to the Far East as a whole, Indochina is devoid of decisive military objectives, and the allocation of more than token U.S. armed forces in Indochina would be a serious diversion of limited U.S. capabilities." This was the view of the top military man as presented at the same time Dulles was sending his teams into action there, under the cover of military men.

While this was happening, the Geneva Conference was under way. Although the *Foreign Affairs* article chooses to heap blame on John Foster Dulles, we should recall that Dulles had not attended that conference since its organizational meetings. In his place he had sent his Under Secretary, Walter Bedell Smith, who had been the DCI before he went to the Department of State. Certainly John Foster Dulles, whose brother was the DCI and whose principal assistant was a former DCI, was well aware of the views of the Office of National Estimates on the one hand, and of the actions of the clandestine side of the house on the other.

Then the Saigon Military Mission (SMM) ("military" only in the sense that it was a cover arrangement) entered Vietnam on June 1, 1954. This mission "was to enter into Vietnam quietly and assist the Vietnamese, rather than the French, in unconventional warfare. The French were to be kept as friendly allies in the process, as far as possible. The broad mission for the team was to undertake paramilitary operations against the enemy and to wage political-psychological warfare. Later, after Geneva, the mission was modified to prepare means for undertaking paramilitary operations in Communist areas rather than to wage unconventional warfare . . ."[1] By its own statement of mission this team was not to aid the French and was to wage a paramilitary campaign against the "enemy." This left it with only

---

1. *The Pentagon Papers* (*New York Times* ed.) 1971.

one real mission, "to assist the new government of Ngo Dinh Diem." And Allen Dulles sent this clandestine team into South Vietnam in August of 1954, exactly the same month of the NIE, which the *Foreign Affairs* article says the CIA published as guidance for this country. Dulles' covert actions and his overt NIE were in direct conflict. He was saying one thing and doing another.

There is only one conclusion that can be drawn from such writing, and it is derived from one of two alternatives: Either the author did not know about the existence of and the mission of the Dulles directed Lansdale SMM team; or if he did, he was attempting to cover up the CIA role in such activity, which had more to do with the course of events in Indochina since that time than anything else done by any of the other participants.

Here again we see the ST at work. It is most interested in covering up its role in Indochina during the past twenty years, and in so doing it is skillfully working to shift the blame wherever it can. It is trying to charge that if the military, the diplomats, President Eisenhower, President Johnson, and President Nixon all had heeded its advice as contained in the National Estimates, they would not have gotten this country into such trouble. Their efforts even go so far as to attempt to hide behind their intelligence position by using the "transparent" Pentagon Papers. The *Foreign Affairs* article would have its readers believe that the NIE is the only real CIA and that such things as the Saigon Military Mission, because it was called a "military" mission, will be discovered not to be the CIA at all.

We have been saying that the release of the Pentagon Papers by the former CIA agent and long-time associate of Edward G. Lansdale, Daniel Ellsberg, may have been the opening attack by the CIA to cover its disengagement not only from the physical conflict in Indochina, but also from the historical record of that disastrous event. In this effort, the CIA appears to be trying to hide behind its own best cover story, that it is only an intelligence agency and that its fine intelligence work during the past twenty years on the subject of Southeast Asia is all that we should remember.

Now we find in Cooper another CIA apologist using the *Foreign Affairs* review to follow up and to praise Ellsberg. In fact, Cooper's exhilaration in his task gets the better of him when he says, "Thanks to Daniel Ellsberg . . ." He means it! This near-endorsement of Ellsberg by a CIA writer in the publication of the Council on Foreign Relations is all the more significant when one learns that this Council is supported by foundations which are in turn directed by men from the Bechtel Corporation, Chese Manhattan Bank, Cummins Engine, Corning Glass, Kimberly-Clark, Monsanto Chemical, and dozens of others. Not long ago, the political scientist Lester Milbraith noted that "the Council on Foreign Relations, while not financed by government, works so closely with it that it is difficult to distinguish Council actions stimulated by government from autonomous actions." And while we appreciate that *Foreign Affairs* states clearly that "It does not accept responsibility for the views expressed in any articles, signed or unsigned, which appear on [its] pages," its record and especially its list of authors over the years, from John Foster Dulles in its first issue, speaks for itself.

This whole plot thickens to the point of near-hypocrisy when Cooper cites the August 3, 1954, National Intelligence Estimate. The same Pentagon Paper from which he quotes also contains a report on the year-long activity of the Saigon Military Mission. This report, written by Edward G. Lansdale of the CIA, began in that same month of August 1954. While the NIE was speaking disparagingly of Ngo Dunh Diem, the SMM was supporting the Diem regime during the days after the French defeat at Dien Bien Phu. This team and all of its efforts were CIA originated, CIA supported, CIA manned, and CIA directed. From 1954 through 1963, all American activity in Vietnam was dominated by the CIA. Although Lansdale and his key men, such as Charles Bohanon, Lucien Conein (the U.S. go between at the time of the Diem coup d'état, Bill Rosson, Arthur Arundel, Rufus Phillips, and others were listed in the Pentagon Papers with military rank, they were all in the employ of the CIA and were operating as CIA agents.

This is what the Pentagon Papers reveal as happening in 1954 and 1955. Now the CIA would have us believe that it was an objective and blameless intelligence agency all through those horrible years of the Vietnam build-up. However, it was the CIA that hid behind its own cover and that of State and Defense to fan the flames of a smoldering conflict. To add insult to injury, the CIA would have us believe that Eisenhower's Secretary of State, John Foster Dulles, the DOD, Lyndon B. Johnson, and Richard M. Nixon were all to blame because they would not read and heed their NIE. Where were the CIA officials of the clandestine sector when their own men were writing these National Intelligence Estimates?

The big question is, if the National Estimates produced by the intelligence side of the CIA were so good, then why didn't the men in the clandestine operations office read and follow the advice of their own estimates? Yes, the CIA likes to write about itself, and the CIA likes to have others write about it, as long as what they write is laudatory and skillful propaganda.

How can the CIA rationalize the fact that at the very same time it was sending its most powerful and experienced team of agents into action in Indochina, after its successes with Magsaysay in the Philippines, it was writing NIE for the President saying exactly the opposite? It is alarming enough today to put the Ellsberg releases and the Cooper tales together, but what did the CIA have in mind in 1954 when it was doing such disparate things? What did the CIA expect President Eisenhower and John Foster Dulles to believe: The NIE that said we couldn't win with the "frail Diem regime," or the SMM clandestine operation that was designed to support the same Diem regime? Or could it have been that they either did not know about the secret operation or were improperly briefed? This is the very heart of the matter. This is what this book is all about.

To put this in another context, when Eisenhower was planning for the ultimate summit meeting in May 1960, did the NIE say that all was going well and nothing should be done to upset the chances of success of that most important mission; and did the DD/P come in with his briefing for the U-2 flight at the same time? Or perhaps was there an NIE and no briefing about the U-2? How did the ST handle that one?

Or to carry this same theme over to early 1961, did the NIE correctly foretell that the Cubans would not rise up and support an invasion of so few troops without United States troops and air cover; and how did the DD/P brief the secret operation to President Kennedy to perform an invasion operation that was patently diametrically opposed to the NIE?

To drive home the point of this duality farther, Cooper states: "In November 1961, shortly after General Taylor[2] and Walt Rostow returned from their trip to Vietnam recommending, inter alia, that the U.S. 'offer to introduce into South Vietnam a military task force,' an NIE warned that any escalation of American military activity in Vietnam would be matched by similar escalation by Hanoi. . . . the North Vietnamese would respond to an increased U.S. commitment with an offsetting increase in infiltrated support for the Viet Cong."

Again the Intelligence Directorate of the CIA plays the lily white role. At about the same time, July 1961, the Pentagon Papers show that a report, again by Edward C. Lansdale, at that time a brigadier general assigned to McNamara's staff and still, as ever, a strong supporter of the CIA, lists the very considerable amount of unconventional warfare resources in Southeast Asia, which were supported by and operating under the CIA. These military and paramilitary forces added into the tens of thousands of armed men and were liberally supported by American men, American money, and American equipment, all put in place under the direction of the CIA. The Deputy Director of Central Intelligence, General Cabell, had just ordered the CIA-operated United States Marine Corps[3] helicopter squadron from Laos, where things had turned from bad to worse, into South Vietnam, where things were going to turn from bad to worse. They were flown into the Camau Peninsula by Americans,

---

2. At that time, General Taylor was Special Military Advisor to President Kennedy—that was the overt title. He was the CIA clandestine operations man closer to Allen Dulles than to anyone in the Pentagon. He was in the office later held by McGeorge Bundy and currently by Henry Kissinger, who by the way has long been a key spokesman for the Council of Foreign Relations.

3. The helicopters had been obtained from the USMC but there were no Marines in the organization flying them, or on the ground. *The New York Times* report of The Pentagon Papers, Nov. 8, 1961, p. 148.

and they were supported by Americans for the purpose of airlifting the Special Forces Elite troops of Ngo Dinh Nhu for action against the citizens of that terrorized area. This was another example of what was going on in the covert field at the same time that Intelligence was putting out an Estimate to the contrary. We have Cooper to thank for the "nice" story and Ellsberg to thank for the "not-so-nice" story. Who was President Kennedy to believe—the man who came in with the NIE, or the man who came in to brief him about the tremendous clandestine and paramilitary operations? Or did they tell the President about both?

Today, the CIA would like us to believe that it had challenged the validity of the hallowed Domino Theory by advising Lyndon B. Johnson that, with the possible exception of Cambodia, it is likely that no nation in the area would quickly succumb to Communism as a result of the fall of Laos and South Vietnam. Furthermore, a continuation of the spread of Communism in the area would not be irreparable.

In 1961, the same time as this quote, Maxwell Taylor, the White House spokesman of the clandestine side of the CIA, informed President Kennedy that "the fall of South Vietnam to Communism would lead to the fairly rapid extension of Communist control, or complete accommodation to Communism, in the rest of the mainland of South East Asia and in Indonesia. The strategic implications worldwide, particularly in the Orient, would be extremely serious."[4] In those days, Maxwell Taylor expressed more properly the views of the CIA (DD/P) than those of the DOD where he was held in awe and suspicion after his return from retirement to become a member of the Kennedy "inside" staff.

General Taylor continued to espouse this view even after he moved to the Pentagon as chairman of the Joint Chiefs of Staff. On January 22, 1964, in a memo to Secretary of Defense Robert S. McNamara, he said, "A loss of South Vietnam to the Communists will presage an early erosion of the remainder of our position in that subcontinent." Even though he had moved to the Pentagon, Taylor's memoranda on South Vietnam were written by the Special

---

4. *The New York Times* report of The Pentagon Papers, Nov. 8, 1961, p. 148.

Assistant for Counterinsurgency and Special Activity, an office within the confines of the Pentagon, but an office that had been created to work with the CIA, and which by that date had become a regular conduit for CIA thought and action.

Then, McNamara picked up this same "party line" in his memo to President Johnson (at that time his memoranda on this subject were written either by Lansdale or Bill Bundy, both CIA men) of March 16, 1967. "... Southeast Asia will probably fall under Communist dominance, all of Vietnam, Laos and Cambodia ... Burma ... Indonesia ... Malaysia ... Thailand ... Philippines ... India ... Australia ... New Zealand ... Taiwan ... Korea and Japan." By now, everyone was putting all pressure possible on Johnson, and as noted, they used all of the dominoes. Yet the CIA today would have us believe they were only the voice of the DD/I and not the DD/P speaking, through SACSA, to Maxwell Taylor, thence to McNamara, with input from Bundy and Lansdale, and on to Rusk and Johnson. No wonder the CIA wants men like Cooper and Ellsberg writing for them.

The final irony is discovered when the Cooper story begins to pit the National Estimates against other Ellsberg data in 1964–1965. He states that the NIE of late 1964 claimed that, "... we do not believe that such actions [against the North] would have crucial effect in the daily lives of the overwhelming majority of the North Vietnamese population. We do not believe that attacks on industrial targets would so exacerbate current economic difficulties as to create unmanageable control problems [for the Hanoi regime] ... would probably be willing to suffer some damage to the country in the course of a test of wills with the U.S. over the course of events in South Vietnam."[5] Then, as if to place the blame on the military, he adds, "As the Pentagon historians note, this view had little influence on the contingency papers which emerged."

The most remarkable thing about this paragraph from *Foreign Affairs* is that it is directly the opposite of the views presented in the Pentagon Papers as the "William Bundy memo" on "Actions Available to the United States after Tonkin," which is dated August 11, 1964.

---

5. *Ibid*. p. 148.

Bill Bundy was at that time no longer sitting in the Pentagon; he was working for the ST as Assistant Secretary of State for Far Eastern Affairs. However, overriding that position, Bill Bundy was always the ready spokesman and puppet, in both the Kennedy and Johnson Administrations, for the CIA. He had been with the CIA for ten years, was the son-in-law of Dean Acheson, and has been reported, as of this writing, to be in line for the position of editor of *Foreign Affairs.*

In this utterly fantastic memo, CIA spokesman Bill Bundy listed pages of "dirty tricks" and increasing pressures that were to be brought to bear against Hanoi, including the Rostow favorite, "tit for tat" actions. By late 1964, military escalation had begun, and the role of the CIA did not diminish—it was just overshadowed by the greater military magnitude. The flames that the CIA and the greater ST had ignited were faced by the military. However, even this huge force was never able to snuff them out; it just had to stand there and let them burn themselves out.

Then the Cooper account presents Dr. Sherman Kent, the long-time chief of the Board of National Estimates saying: "The nature of our calling requires that we pretend as hard as we are able that the wish is indeed the fact and that the policy-maker will invariably defer to our findings . . ." He feels that his associates' concern about their influence is misplaced: ". . . no matter what we tell the policymaker, and no matter how right we are and how convincing, he will upon occasion disregard the thrust of our findings for reasons beyond our ken. If influence cannot be our goal, what should it be? . . . It should be to be relevant within the area of your competence, and above all it should be to be credible."

Sherman Kent is an old pro. He knows his business and is one of the very best in his field; but how strange the context of this *Foreign Affairs* essay must seem to him. While he did prepare these NIE, his own associates in clandestine operations and his own boss, the DCI, were fanning out all over Southeast Asia under the cover of his professional expertise, not only oblivious and unheeding of his work, but making mockery of it. Such are the ways of the ST.

When a National Estimate is presented by the same house that presents the collateral and usually opposite view of Special Operations, the Agency pulls the rug from under the feet of its own best achievements and the men responsible for them. Allen Dulles was wrong when he wrote in 1948, along with Jackson and Correa, that the two broad functions of Intelligence and Special Operations should be under the same man and in the same agency. There is nothing wrong with the NIE system and with men like Sherman Kent, Ray Cline, and Bob Amory. The evil is on the other side; and in spite of the vigorous efforts of Agency zealots, who have attempted to rewrite the history of the past quarter-century, we cannot but take some faith in those words of Saint John that Allen Dulles chose for the entrance way of the new CIA building: "The truth shall make you free." This attempt to warp the truth will not.

It might also have been well if the Agency and its disciples had reconsidered their own "more appropriate choice" for a motto: "Look before you leap." The American public and the world for which Arnold Toynbee speaks, prefer Truth.

CHAPTER 9

THE COINCIDENCE OF CRISES

The National Security Act of 1947 was brewed in a cauldron under great heat and pressure, with the flavoring of spices from many sources. The year 1947 was one of great pressures that simmered and smoldered below the surface of national events. 1946, so close to the end of the great war, had begun as the year of "one world," with faith in the charter of the United Nations. On the first day of March 1946, barely six months after the end of World War II, Truman's Secretary of State, James Byrnes, had said, "So far as the United States is concerned we will gang up against no state. We will do nothing to break the world into exclusive blocks or spheres of influence in this atomic age. We will not seek to divide a world which is one."

Then, only four days later, the great hero of Britain's war days and the leader of the Loyal Opposition in the British House of Commons, Sir Winston Churchill, speaking in Fulton, Missouri, with President Truman at his side, said: "Beware . . . the time may be short. . . . From Stettin in the Baltic to Trieste in the Adriatic an Iron Curtain has descended across the continent." At about the same time, George F. Kennan, one of the Russian authorities of the U.S.

Department of State said, "If Europe was to be divided, the blame should be placed on the Russians and not ourselves."

Under the pressures brewing at that time, it took only a short time to depart from the dream of one world at peace and to plant the seeds of rupture and divisiveness. The one world had in a brief span become bipolar, with the atom bomb hanging as the sword over the heads of mankind, and Communism as the dread enemy of the Western world.

Following quickly upon the dismemberment of the victorious military might of the U.S. and upon the dissolution of the OSS came the transfer in January 1947 of the great nuclear weapon technology to the new Atomic Energy Commission. This momentous project had no sooner been set up than a great tumult arose in Congress about the loyalty of two of the leaders of this program, David E. Lilienthal and J. Robert Oppenheimer. Already, Communism, or more properly, a new banner and call-to-arms, "anti-Communism," had raised its head. This issue played an important part in the philosophy behind the development of the CIA.

The United States had a nuclear monopoly in 1947. At least, it was the only country in the world with weapons on hand, with the means of delivering them, and with the production know-how and capacity to increase the nuclear stockpile. Therefore, it became a matter of great national interest first of all to protect those weapons, the delivery system, and the production techniques from other nations, from their spies, and from those who might aid those nations by giving away our secret. And secondly, it became most important that we have the intelligence capability to learn, without delay, the status of the state-of-the-art in any other nation that might be attempting to build nuclear weapons. Our scientists and other practical men knew that once we had exploded a bomb over the sands of New Mexico and over Japan, other scientists would be well on their way toward duplicating this feat, since they now knew that such a thing was possible. Thus, development of the atomic bomb by another nation would be no more than a matter of time and intention; it would not be helped too much by either the activity of spies or interested parties from within our own country.

The interplay of these most important factors created great pressures for the realization of a central intelligence capability of much greater capacity and effectiveness than anything that had existed before World War II.

To add more fuel to this raging conflagration, the British announced on February 21, 1947, that they could no longer provide financial support to the weak governments of Greece and Turkey to enable them to continue their battles against Communist aggression and subversion in the form of strong rebel activity. The sudden departure of the British from this crucial portion of Eastern Europe left a serious vacuum that had to be filled by someone else without delay. Only three weeks after the unexpected British announcement, on March 12, 1947, President Truman proclaimed the Truman Doctrine, which in effect established a stout barrier between the world of Communism and the Western world along the northern borders of Greece and Turkey.

Churchill had specifically drawn the line from "Stettin in the Baltic to Trieste in the Adriatic." Now Harry Truman had extended that line from the Adriatic to the borders of Iran. It had not taken long to totally reverse course from Secretary of State Byrnes's, "We will not seek to divide the world which is one" to the lasting division which continues even today, after twenty-five Cold War years. To strengthen this position and to drive home the full intentions of the United States, the new Secretary of State, George C. Marshall, announced in July of 1947, the plan for all of Europe, designed to help those countries that had been ravaged by war and were "threatened by the onslaught of Communism" to recover sufficiently to stand upon their own feet.

In this test of history, while charges of "Communism" were being hurled back and forth among adversaries who in the great majority of cases had nothing whatsoever to do with real Communism, Congress was debating and writing the National Security Act, which on the surface was primarily concerned with the military establishment, but was beneath the surface, where the real pressures were most at work, fundamentally concerned with the creation of a central intelligence agency. It was in this highly charged atmosphere that the philosophy of the military posture of "defense" emerged. Throughout the history of this country, there had been a great respect for and tradition of the honorable resort to arms in time of war. As a result, this country had a long and proud heritage, which supported the existence of a Department of War and a Department of the Navy with its proud Marine Corps. All men knew that the United States would resort to war only when diplomacy and all other efforts had failed. Yet no one misunderstood the full meaning of such a tradition. The heart of war and its only sure way to victory lies in the concept of the "offense," carried out in pursuit of clear national military objectives, under superior leadership both in uniform on the field of battle and in mufti in the White House. Somehow, under the pressures of the great debates during 1947, this tradition and heritage broke down, and in the face of the responsibilities incumbent upon this country in the Nuclear Age and in the face of a growing "Communist menace," the American military posture became one of defense.

This was a significant mutation in the dominant cell structure of the life blood and soul of this nation. The very word "offense" connotes action and the existence of a plan of such action. A country that is in command of all of its facilities and has the vigor to shape its own destiny does so in accordance with a plan, a great national plan, and with the sense of action that is the very essence of life and liberty. Liberty itself is a difficult word to encompass within a single definition. But certainly there can be no liberty if there is no action, because one is not free to act if frozen in the posture of defense, waiting to counteract the free action of his adversaries, real and imagined. For the greatest nation in the world suddenly to assume the role of a defensive power is a certain signal of some major change in national character. One would hope to discover that this was to be interpreted as a symbol of magnanimity and understanding while the nation was in sole and undisputed possession of the atomic bomb; but events of the past twenty-five years make it difficult to accept that position.

This national defense posture places even greater emphasis upon the role of intelligence. If any nation goes on the defensive, then by its very nature it must be—it is forced to be—totally dependent upon intelligence. If a man is adequately armed, and he is hiding behind a wall reasonably secure from his adversary, the one thing he needs most is information to tell him where his adversary is, what he is doing, whether he is armed, and even what his intentions are. In that unusual year, 1947, the great pressures upon Congress and the Administration somehow impressed upon the Government of this country the beginnings of a belief in reliance upon a major intelligence structure to be backed up by a powerful Department of Defense.

It takes a long time, as Darwin made very clear, for an evolutionary process to make itself known. For many years, this nation of veterans, and mothers and fathers of veterans, along with the sisters and brothers of veterans, has looked upon the post-1947 Army, Navy, and Air Force, not as they were becoming, but as they had known them at first hand at Normandy and Iwo Jima, at the Battle of Midway and the undersea services, in the Eighth Air Force over Fortress Germany, and with the B-29s of the Twentieth Air Force flying back from a fire-ravaged Tokyo.

Thus it was that while the country was caught up in the great debate about "unification," about the new role of nuclear weapons and about anti-Communism, it failed to note that our military establishment was being diverted from an active role as an essential element of national planning to a response position of re-action to the inputs of intelligence. This was not evident during the remaining years of the forties. Its first indication became apparent at the time of the Korean War, and what was not prominently apparent in the more open and overt military establishment certainly was scarcely noticed in the early days of the CIA.

In support of this low-key first blush of a defense posture, the CIA was placed under the direction of an admiral who had as his deputy a general. Both of them supported the idea that for the new CIA, intelligence was to be business as usual. As had been expected, and in strict compliance with the language of the law, the CIA was developed along military lines. In fact, little thought was given to organizing it any other way by those who were given the responsibility of getting things started. As Lyman Kirkpatrick wrote, "most of the senior positions in the Agency at that time were held by military personnel who had been detailed for a tour of duty. Some of these were well qualified, but many were not. In any event they were in key positions."

These were the type of men who believed that intelligence was a supporting staff function only and that the object of an intelligence organization, whether it was in the field with a fighting outfit or at the seat of government serving as the "quiet intelligence arm of the President," was simply to coordinate, evaluate, and analyze information and to provide it to the President and his Cabinet members for their own use as they saw fit. They did not view their job as secret operations, to be set in motion by the intelligence agency itself. Not only was this the outlook of men in the key positions of the Agency; but this was also the way the President saw it. President Truman looked upon this new agency as his staff section for information, and no more; and there were many others in Washington who wanted it that way too.

Although a central intelligence agency had been created, under law, and had been accepted within the already existent community as essential for the purpose of coordinating national intelligence, there were many who wished to keep its role to a minimum. None of the traditional intelligence organizations wanted to give up anything to the CIA. They agreed to share with it the role of formulating "national intelligence," but that was it, as far as they were concerned. As a result, they all participated, more or less evenly, in manning the fledgling agency and in seeing that it got under way in a manner sufficient to accomplish its primary assigned task, and no more. Within this group there was little desire to make the CIA into the agency it is today, nor was there any desire to see the Agency enter into clandestine activity of any kind. They believed that if such a task was required by higher authority and in support of a national plan of supreme importance, then the new NSC would, with approval of the President, direct that it be performed by any of several possible organizations, one of which might be the CIA. This was a more or less routine assumption, and it was about as far as any of those officials at that time wanted to go.

It should also be noted that among the early military assignees to the Agency there were those who had personal ambition and plans to work up in this new organization, bypassing the conventions of their old units to achieve some personal goal, which in some cases included the desire for a "fun and games" career. As the years passed, many of these men were able to do just that, and they formed a nucleus within the Agency, which for a variety of reasons, strove to exploit the covert side of the house.

It was from among this group that the first activists emerged to begin the covert process of using the Agency to utilize and later to dominate the military. We shall see beginnings of this in this chapter; it will be more fully developed later. These agents employed covert methods not always to conceal their actions from the "enemy," but more often to keep the inroads they were making in the actual exploitation and use of our own military from being discovered. One of the better examples of such activity has been the "mutual" development of a method of operations between the CIA and the U.S. Army Special Forces.

There were other men in Washington at that time who opposed the way military men in key positions were developing the Agency. They were actively and vociferously opposed to the Agency development as it was being performed by the military men in the key positions. Chief among these critics and self-interested agitators was the former head of the OSS, General "Wild Bill" Donovan. He went up and down the country, preaching the doctrine of active anti-Communism and demanding that the CIA be made the first line of defense of the country in the Cold War. General Donovan was always clamoring for "civilian control" of the intelligence establishment—an unusual stipulation, considering his long military background; but more importantly, he spoke of the CIA role as an active and operational role. He was less interested in intelligence than he was in clandestine operations. This, even though he did not link up the two conditions at any one time, he would, if he had had his way, have used the CIA to develop and direct operations that would have been fleshed out by the military establishment.

At the same time, Allen Dulles and John Foster Dulles were actively engaged in international affairs of a somewhat chameleon-like nature, with religious groups, international societies, the Council of Foreign Relations, and others. After one special Council meeting in early 1947, the Under Secretary of State, Robert Lovett, said that he had been convinced that ". . . it would be our principal task at State to awaken the nation to the dangers of Communist aggression." Of course, there are various ways in which a statement such as this may be interpreted. There can be the straightforward approach, which takes such action as a result of bona fide Communism aggression and to awaken the country to such a danger; or there may be the interpretation, more properly borne out by the events of the past twenty-five years, that "the task . . . to awaken the nation" would be one akin to the operation of a propaganda machine. When we recall some of the comments made in earlier chapters about stirring up such visions in Indochina and omens like that, the real intentions of such words bear close scrutiny. In any event, the men of whom mention has been made above, were among the most ardent advocates of a stronger CIA, one to be developed as a bulwark against Communism and to be prepared for operational tasks of secret intelligence collection and clandestine operational activities.

The pressures in public and upon the Administration were so great that even before the CIA had been in existence for one year, the President was persuaded to appoint a select committee to "report on the effectiveness of the CIA as organized under the 1947 Act and the relationship of CIA activities to those other intelligence organs of the government."[1] It was quite unusual to have so new an organization so suddenly on the carpet. But 1948 was an election year, and the Governor of New York, Thomas E. Dewey, had been selected by the Republicans to carry their standard against the old and war-weary Roosevelt team, which had the doughty Harry Truman at its helm. While Truman declared he would "Give 'em Hell," Dewey calmly and with great assurance and confidence told the country that it was time for a "new rudder on the Ship of State" and for "a new man at the helm." The country believed that Dewey would be elected easily. He had been a renowned crime-fighter, and his campaign was

---

1. Allen Dulles, *The Craft of Intelligence*, New York: Harper & Row, 1963.

built on the idea that he would be a superior Communist-fighter. Meanwhile, the issue of Communists in government plagued the Democratic party incumbents as a result of campaign tactics attributable to Allen Dulles and his clan.

It was, then, most surprising to learn that the men whom Harry Truman chose to put on the Intelligence Review Committee were none other than Dewey's chief speech-writer during the campaign, Allen W. Dulles, along with William H. Jackson and Mathias Correa. There is no doubt that these men were qualified and competent, but they could hardly have been accused of being objective. Certainly, the President must have known that Dulles was strongly committed to the Dewey campaign, which was in action at the same time that he was to be working with Jackson and Correa. And he also knew that Dulles had been opposed to the provisions of the National Security Act of 1947 since the beginning.

William H. Jackson's career in Military Intelligence dated back into the early days of World War II, and he was known to favor the "military" side of the issues that confronted the committee; but he had been very active in the "new intelligence" picture, in spite of this parochial background. The other member of the committee, Mathias Correa, was also experienced in intelligence and had worked closely with the former Secretary of the Navy and first Secretary of Defense, James Forrestal. However, there can be no question about the fact that this committee was dominated by Allen Dulles.

Another factor that did much to shape the course of these events was the fact that by the summer of 1948 the NSC itself had published certain directives that delineated the functions of the Agency. One of these, published in August 1948, was NSC Intelligence Directive 10/2 (NSCID, commonly known as "Non-skids"). This regulation authorized the CIA to create a small section that would have the ability to carry out secret intelligence operations, and that at some point might contemplate the pursuit of secret operations.

The issuance of this directive did not mean that the NSC was encouraging the CIA to enter into the world of secret operations. In fact, the real language of the NSCID was so restrictive that had it been faithfully followed there would have been few such operations under any conditions. The Council took this first step with extreme caution. The new section, which was to be called the Office of Policy Coordination (OPC) was to be a part of the Agency. However, its director was not to be under the control of the DCI. The NSC directed that he would be selected by the Secretary of State and seconded by the Secretary of Defense. The first man appointed to be director of the OPC was Frank Wisner, a former OSS agent and at that time an official of the State Department. Although Wisner had been with State, his assignment there was a matter of convenience for him, as it was for several other old OSS hands while they awaited the creation of the CIA. While they were with State, these men took care of certain records and other valuable assets of the OSS, which had been handed down from World War II.

As a result of this NSC action, by the end of 1948 the DCI did have a secret operations potential, but it was so rigged that he did not have full control of that office, and he could not take things into his own hands if he wanted to. He had to await directions from the NSC. This was unwieldy; but it was the only way the Council would agree to the establishment of such a function. It was a small first step which led to others. It was another part of the pressures building up under the surface while the Agency was busying itself with organizational matters and the task of coordinating national intelligence.

This was the background that led up to the time of the Dulles-Jackson-Correa report. No single report on the subject of intelligence, and perhaps even on any subject, has had a greater impact upon the past twenty years in this country than that work of Allen Dulles. Throughout the closing months of the 1948 election campaign, John Foster Dulles was acting as personal liaison representative between Thomas E. Dewey and the State Department. Not a word appeared in the press about the Dulles-Jackson-Correa report, although the principals were busy reviewing drafts and working on the broad subject before them. One can imagine with some interest the position Allen Dulles found himself in, writing for Dewey as he campaigned all over the country and then busily engaging himself in his real labor of love—the intelligence report. Undoubtedly he saw this report, which he expected to complete just after the election, as the stepping stone to reaching the office of the DCI. It is inconceivable to imagine that he worked so hard on a report that would be submitted to Harry Truman as President for a new term. He fully expected to hand it in to a lame duck president. As it happened, Truman surprised the entire country by being re-elected.

The Dulles clan had to wait another four years before they rode into power with General Eisenhower. But this very delay may have made things much easier for Allen Dulles when he did become the DCI. Dulles wanted to expand the Agency and so stated in his report; yet the years following the 1948 election were years of government austerity. He could not have done it then. Dulles was not a strong administrator, and he would have had real problems getting all of his plans into operation. But he was an expert at getting things done by a special kind of secrecy-shrouded wheeling and dealing. This would not have worked during Truman's administration, with Louis Johnson as the Secretary of Defense.

There was in the official files of that time a long and very detailed letter to the DCI signed by Secretary of Defense Louis Johnson, which stated that the Agency should not become involved in any operational activities that involved any part of the DOD unless the Agency was fully prepared to be able to disclaim the role of the military and unless the Agency was prepared to reimburse the Defense Department for all actual and out-of-pocket expenses it might incur. Asking the CIA to be prepared to disclaim the role of someone else who gets caught in a CIA operation is one thing; but asking the Agency to pay for what it uses and expends is entirely different. The Agency gives lip-service to the former and cringes at the latter. The latter is the only effective control there is over the Agency, and this is something the Congress should do more thinking about today.

In 1949 and 1950 this letter from the Secretary of Defense to the DCI was the normal way of handling such matters. Staff officers in the late sixties and early seventies would be shocked at such language from the Office of the Secretary of Defense in an official letter to the DCI. Allen Dulles could not have attained his goals under that type of "cooperation" from his biggest benefactor. The time was just not ripe. Thus it may have been another one of those favoring coincidences, which have always seemed to crop up at the right time for the CIA to pave the way for later developments.

With the surprise election of Truman, there was nothing to do but to turn in the report to those in charge of the Agency. It is inexcusable that security impediments can bury such letters and reports as we have mentioned, for so many years. The Dulles-Jackson-Correa report was the CIA *Mein Kampf*. In this study, Dulles described exactly how he would lead the Agency from a low-key intelligence coordination center to a major power center in the U.S. Government, and in the process, how he would become the closest adviser to the President. He foretold the existence of a vast secret intelligence organization, a top echelon clandestine operations facility at White House level, a hidden infrastructure throughout other departments and agencies of the Government, and the greatest clandestine operational capability the world had ever known primarily based upon the exploitation of military manpower, money, and facilities all over the world.

For all the dynamite contained within its pages, the report was practically ignored when it was given to President Truman early in January 1949. (It was dated January 1, 1949.) The major elements of the report were so arranged within its chapters that the military men who were at that time in command of the Agency would not notice them for what they were. What caught their eyes were the page after page of charges against their stewardship of the Agency. There were few things being done in the Agency that this three-man committee had approved. Therefore, all the men in the Agency glanced at when they received the report was that portion that concerned them directly. As Lyman Kirkpatrick has said in his book, ". . . most of the senior positions in the Agency at that time were held by military personnel who had been detailed for a tour of duty. . . . they wrote the reply to the report, which, needless to say, was not very responsive." And no one should know that better than Kirkpatrick.[2]

For about a year this report remained in the files, and nothing was done about it. As a piece of information and as a working document,

---

2. *The Real CIA*, New York: The Macmillan Co., 1968.

the report never was the center of action. It was so cloaked in security that few people have ever seen it, and fewer have read and studied it; but because Allen Dulles spent eleven years with the CIA, nine of them as its director, the report is most important as evidence of his thought and techniques and because it so comprehensively records his thoughts from the 1947–48 period. It is an essential document of government lore and subsurface action for the years from 1951 to 1961.

Dulles was not a planner. He was not the type of man who would be a great chess player, seeing his objective clearly, planning his own tactics, and weighing all of that against his opponent's options. He was a counterpuncher and a missionary. He was a meddler. He thought that he had the right and the duty to bring his pet schemes into the minds and homes of others, whether they were wanted or not.

His system was like a maze full of mousetraps all set to snap and placed side by side carefully over every inch of his domain. When he heard a trap snap, and then another, he would quickly sense that something was happening and would know where the activity was. Because his sounding devices were mousetraps, he would have already prepared his defenses for mice and would throw his anti-mice operations into action immediately. He would not maintain a force of mice-fighting equipment himself but he would get his organization to throw all of its force into the fray in response to his mousetrap information. His trap sensors were the catalytic activators of the greater resources of his entire organization . . . his country.

Dulles was the personification of the intelligence operator, as contrasted with the intelligence staff officer. He created systems that would respond to inputs from intelligence sources. He did not work with others to establish objectives; he did not make plans to achieve those objectives and then to drive toward the achievement of those goals without permitting himself to be diverted by other irrelevant influences. Rather, he would create a vast mechanism that would sound out bits of data which could then be used to activate response operations, all in the name of the common enemy, Communism. He was proud, and he was proud for his agency. He did not like being the low man on the totem pole, as he was when he first became DCI. As a matter of fact, Lyman Kirkpatrick reports, "The *U.S. News and World Report* of October 18, 1957, ranked Allen Dulles thirty-fourth on the Protocol List." He goes on to report that after John McCone had been made DCI, his position was raised to the level just under the Cabinet officers. Allen Dulles had always thought that he should work directly for the President and that the Agency should be responsible only to the President. He did not enjoy the position assigned to him by law under the "direction of the NSC," which meant that he was well below a committee of Cabinet officers and a relative thirty-fourth in rank. Such things were very important to him not just as a personal matter but because of the ranking it gave to the Agency.

We shall see the impact of this report further as we continue with this account. Another event of these times was having a great impact upon the Agency and would be fundamental to its role in Indochina many years later. In Greece, a civil war was under way, and it was evident that the Communist neighbors of Greece—Yugoslavia, Bulgaria, and Romania—were providing safe haven for the Greek rebels and, on their own part, were assisting the rebels with supplies and arms. At the end of World War II, the United States had a strong force in Greece, which had been there since the Germans had been driven out in 1944. The Americans, mostly Army but with a number of CIA personnel, played an active role in assisting the Greek Government against these rebels. A good number of the CIA men, and U.S. military men who worked with the CIA or on assignment to the CIA, became a closely knit cadre of Communist rebel fighters. They learned their trade on the proving ground of Greece and later went on to play the same role in other countries such as Iran, Guatemala, Thailand, and especially Vietnam. If one were able to discover the real names of the CIA personnel, including the U.S. military personnel on assignment to the CIA who served first in Greece and then years later in Southeast Asia, he would find some very striking and significant parallels. This Greek experience was very influential on the fledgling agency. Men like John Richardson, who was the station chief in Saigon during some very crucial times, was also station chief in Athens. Ambassador Puerifoy played an important role in Greece and then went on to Thailand, where he died in an automobile accident. General Marshall Carter, at the time aide to Secretary of State George Marshall, served briefly but importantly in Greece and later was the DDCI. Henry Cabot Lodge, while Ambassador to the UN, became much involved in the Greek rebellion and of course played a most important role in Vietnam, where he was Ambassador on two different occasions. The list is long and most significant. The Agency obtained some of its first field experience, much on the wartime OSS pattern, in Greece and then applied the same formula to many other countries, using the same paramilitary-trained men.

By 1950, the DOD had reached its lowest ebb since World War II, and it looked as though the Agency would do likewise. Then two most important things happened. Again the coincidence that saved the Agency when all looked like a lost cause came to the rescue. First of all, the Korean War snapped the military out of its lethargy and provided the impetus for a major build up and rebuilding of forces. This gave the CIA a chance to play an active role, along with the military, as sort of a wartime "Fourth Force" during the Korean War. The other event that had a great impact upon the Agency was the assignment of General Walter Beedle Smith as DCI following Admiral Hillenkoetter. This dramatic change took place in October 1950, four months after the start of the Korean War.

The "Fourth Force" concept was influential in the expansion of the CIA in a way that was never intended and which has been quite unnoticed, even to this day. As we have mentioned, one of the dominant forces behind the requirement for a national intelligence authority was the existence of the atom bomb and all that it meant. It goes without saying that the atomic weapons system totally obsoleted most of the concepts of World War II. There may never have been a time in all of the evolution of warfare when the introduction of one weapon had so suddenly and so totally overwhelmed all other weapons and all other tactics and strategy. World War II was the major war of all time, and the weapons systems and the tactics and strategy employed by the U.S. military forces during this war were the supreme high water mark of battle effectiveness. Whether we credit the massive system of over-the-beach invasions, or strategic bombardment or carrier task forces, or armored blitz warfare, or others for the supremacy of U.S. forces is not the point. The remarkable thing is that even before that great war ended, a new weapon that completely changed the whole concept of warfare with one great big bang came into being.

This change was so dynamic that even though the United States and its allies were victors by virtue of the unconditional surrender of the vanquished, and thus were total masters of the field, they could not rest upon their laurels once another country had unlocked the secret of nuclear weapons systems. The great fact in this realization was that there could be no peacetime relaxation and no resting upon the fruits of victory, secure in the knowledge that we were masters of the world.

As a result, in the dim halls of the Pentagon and in the many major and overseas commands of the U.S. and allied military forces, the war planners worked long hours to rewrite basic war plans. This is well worth a story by itself. No two groups agreed exactly on what warfare in the future would be, and no two groups were willing to admit that their services were not made obsolete by the nuclear weapons system. As a matter of fact, as late as 1955, the new Joint Staff school, the Armed Forces Staff College, was just beginning to include a nuclear weapons system annex in its classical War Plan. Even up to 1955, they had not agreed sufficiently upon nuclear weapons and how to use them to permit the inclusion of such weapons in war games and school exercises.

In spite of all this, it was generally accepted that World War III would be a nuclear war, that it would be a brief war during the nuclear exchange period, and that it would be followed by a long, protracted, and very complex post-strike campaign in which the least devastated nation would try to mount forces sufficient to occupy the territory of most of the damaged nation and to bring about some order in what would most certainly be a totally devastated area. Such plans visualized that there might very well be strong cells of more or less conventional forces and other cells of varying degrees of local political power that would have to be taken over and organized in the enemy's homeland.

During World War II, the military had developed a most useful Civil Affairs and Military Government Command (CAMG). It had done an exemplary job in moving in behind the advancing army and getting the civilian population back on its feet, as well as in assisting local political leaders to begin the process of setting up some form of basic government. The new war plans began to expand this role and to see a major task for the CAMG forces. As a result, the CAMG school at Fort Gordon, Georgia, was kept in operation, even though many others had been closed, and a number of CAMG reserve units were kept active throughout the country to retain the experience that had been so laboriously created during World War II. A major issue facing President Truman during the 1948 campaign year was the attack upon the lack of preparedness of the Armed Forces, particularly the reserve forces, which had been allowed to reach a low ebb. In spite of this, the CAMG program had been kept very much alive.

What had kept it alive was the increasing responsibility of its role in war plans. At the same time, a number of the military men who were serving with the CIA also recognized that if CAMG work was to succeed and if it was to have any chance to even begin to operate, something must be done during peacetime to prepare for this exigency during wartime. This brought about some serious studies of what could be done in eastern Europe and even in the Soviet Union to establish contacts, agents, and stay-behind networks, which would help to form the essential cadres for the CAMG troops who would be parachuted into certain selected areas immediately following a nuclear exchange. Such plans required that certain areas of any potentially hostile country must be left untouched by atomic warfare in order that radioactivity from direct hits and from the much more unpredictable fallout patterns would not become a retarding factor. Various studies were made of meteorological patterns and other known physical factors in order that war plans could be drawn that would leave certain selected uncontaminated pockets in the target countries.

With this basic work under way, the next thing to do was to see what might be done about building up the number of agents and cadre personnel in those areas. For one thing, the vast refugee and displaced personnel programs, which resulted in a flood of millions of persons from the eastern European countries into western Europe, provided a great opportunity to ferret out certain people who knew about these areas and perhaps knew individuals who were still there and might be contacted and trained to be cadre personnel, on the promise that in the event of such an all out nuclear war they would be saved. This was a most appealing prospect to certain selected individuals who had loved ones remaining in some of these pocket zones. (In this connection it is interesting to note that in the intelligence business people leaving one area to take up residence in another are called *defectors*, *displaced persons*, *refugees* and the like. In other times and other places, these people have simply been called *emigrants*.)

The military and the CIA were working together on the refugee and displaced person program. The military then asked the CIA to participate in top-level war planning. This was a foot in the door for the CIA, and it was a most logical move on the part of the military. After all, the military and the OSS had worked together, although precariously, during World War II. During the late forties and early fifties many of the key personnel of the CIA were active military personnel or veterans of World War II who had converted to civilian status and had become career employees of the new agency. They were well qualified for service with the military in these top-level war planning assignments. To do this, the CIA went through paperwork cover assignments with the military department to have these men called back on active duty in their reserve grades and then assigned to the headquarters concerned.

Few of the officers of the commands involved knew that these men were CIA agents, and most thought that they were routine military assignees. Care was taken to see that the personnel manning tables of these headquarters were increased by the two or three spaces necessary to cover these men. As a result of this precautionary step, personnel administrators and others such as the finance department personnel had no way of knowing that the men in these positions were not real military personnel. In time, these jobs bred their own supporting requirements, to the extent that civilian secretaries and other staff were added by the same or similar means. Only in some Focal Point offices would the true identity of these personnel be known, and then more for the purpose of protecting their identity and assisting them than for any military considerations of the role they were playing.

These war-planning military and pseudo-military agents worked on the post-strike part of the war plan, and more specifically, on that part which pertained to the development of safe areas, agents and agent lines, and other CAMC-type matters. At that phase in the development of the war-planning philosophy and strategy, this was a new role for the military and one they quite willingly turned over to these hard-working men who seemed so dedicated to the task. Their offices were usually identified by such titles as Subsidiary Plans, Special Plans, or even the more normal Psychological Warfare and Unconventional Warfare designations.

Once these annexes of the war plans had been accepted by the remainder of the staff and approved by the commanding general, they became officially part of the war-planning structure of that command and then of its day-to-day mission for operational and supporting logistics functions. If the command was expected to provide forces for the immediate post-strike task, it would have such forces earmarked and trained for that job. They not only had to be ready but they had to have equipment, vehicles, communications, printing presses, aircraft, and all the rest of the tools of their very special trade.

Here again, the CIA men became prime movers. They drew upon the World War II experience of men in their Washington staff and worked out elaborate tables of equipment and tables of organization, in the best World War II fashion, and presented these to the local command for their guidance. Since most of the real military staff officers had done little work in this special area, and most of them had more than enough work to do in their own fields of specialization, they were delighted to have these helpful members of the staff come to them with such finely drawn staff work. Without too much red tape and delay their figures and tactical proposals were accepted as part of the requirement of that command and were inserted into the new budget planning. This is a slow process covering years of prodigious effort, but once this level of accomplishment has been achieved, the rest is practically automatic, and the opportunity to increase such figures from year to year is almost equally automatic.

The timing for this sort of skillful surgery was just right, and the CIA made the most of it. The military, too, was getting swept up in this kind of thinking. It matched with some of the Cold War ideas, generally new to war planning, that derived from new thinking about the role of nuclear weapons and from the urgent pressures of the new anti-Communism. In the eloquent words of Adlai Stevenson, this was the time of ". . . a coincidence of crises . . . that brought together the flames of war, the atom's unlocking, and the emergence of aggressive Communism." It was the time of a world torn by the predominance of military thought, not only by professional military men but by scientists, professors, and other amateurs and by the high emphasis placed on secrecy. In this turmoil the issue of secrecy was ultimately related to the issue of military control. This was the external mix of issues into which the CIA and later the ST maneuvered, under the cloak of secrecy, to enhance and greatly enlarge its control over elements of the military establishment—elements that with the growth of the ideas summed up best by the word "counterinsurgency," became dominant over the rest of the establishment. Who in the years from 1949 to 1955 would ever have visualized the use of the hydrogen bomb-carrying strategic bombers and the Navy's nuclear carriers in a war in which the principal adversary was the little, terrorized brown man in the forests of his wasted homeland. Yet this type of war was all but preordained as the CIA gained increasing control over the military during the fifties and early sixties through the tactics described above. A whole generation of military men trained, hardened, and honed by World War II experience believed in the principles of Clausewitz and others who stated that when diplomacy failed, it was time to go to war; but on the other hand, while diplomacy was being tested and while diplomacy was the name of the game, the military should do no more than plan and train for the possibility of war. The most warlike action that the military would be prepared to take during peacetime would be a show of force or an emergency relief action in some ravaged country.

This was the convention; this is what was overthrown by the new coincidence of crises. Throughout the late forties a new wave of ideas began to spread, and some of these involved military plans and military utilization in peacetime. The idea of the Cold War was making peacetime seem more like a kind of warfare than previous conventional military planning had ever envisaged. For example, at Mitchel Field on Long Island, New York, in 1949, a new commanding general, directly returned from the postwar staff of General MacArthur in the Far East, General Ennis C. Whitehead, called together the staff of his new command, the Continental Air Command, and in a brief but hard-hitting speech told them that they might have thought that the world was at peace; but they were wrong. Every day, he said, the Russians were sending bombers into the skies of the Arctic, and every day they were coming closer and closer to North America in waves that, if not a direct threat, were at least a symbol of the threat that was always present. And day by day, American interceptor fighter pilots were being sent aloft to investigate these targets that appeared on radar. Some day, he said, and not too far in the future, one of those young lieutenants is going to have to make a major decision. He is going to have to decide on his own, up there in his lonely cockpit, whether the bomber he has in his gun sights has made a hostile act or an act of hostile intent, or whether he is only carrying out an acceptable training mission. Should the lieutenant decide that the Russian is hostile, he will be under standing orders to shoot, and he will knock down a Soviet bomber over North America. At that time World War III will not have begun; it will simply have reached its climax. In the words of General Whitehead, one of the outstanding air combat leaders of World War II, World War III was already under way, and none of those officers assembled to hear him should ever forget that.

For those officers trained in the history of war and experienced in the fires of World War II, this was strong talk. Only a few months later about half of those men present that day transferred with General Whitehead from Mitchel Field to Colorado Springs to set up the new Air Defense Command. In so doing every one of them knew that he was a member of an elite military unit that was already committed to victory in World War III. They knew that they were at war every day; all they were waiting for was the day when the Strategic Air Command (SAC) would be given the same orders which they already had received and would join the war actively against the Soviet Union.

Of course, there was a tremendous difference between the missions of the two commands. The battlefield of the Air Defense Command was limited to the skies over North America. The battlefield of the SAC was in foreign skies, but this type of thinking was changing ideas about the conventional role of the military in the Nuclear Age. And into this evolutionary period came the CIA and those of the military who specialized in what came to be called the "unconventional war" or the war against Communist-inspired subversive insurgency.

High over Italy in a plushed-up old World War II B-17 Flying Fortress, the man who was the Chief of Staff of the U.S. Air Force, the same man who had been Director of Central Intelligence just prior to the appointment of Admiral Hillenkoetter in May 1947, General Hoyt S. Vandenberg, wrote to his second in command a most significant letter. It has been preserved in Air Force files; it is quite distinctive because it is on plain white paper and in the handwriting of General Vandenberg.

Vandenberg, recalling his Intelligence experience, and thinking about the new area of unconventional warfare and of the heated-up Cold War, wrote to General Thomas D. White that the Air Force should have a full-sized Psychological Warfare Air Command to be the equal of the Air Defense Command, the Tactical Air Command, and the Strategic Air Command. He proposed that the problems of the Cold War were such that they should not be left to the normal forces, but should be dealt with by experts and by highly skilled men who would be in a position to apply and to utilize military strength and influence during the Cold War. He had particularly in mind psychological activities, but he also took into consideration the role of reconnaissance and other technological developments that are commonplace today. In other words, General Vandenberg was proposing that the military should get into the business which the CIA was working its way into and is in today to a considerable degree—in fact to a degree that even General Vandenberg would have been appalled to witness now.

The Air Force was not the only service thinking along these lines at that time. At Fort Gordon, Georgia, the Army was still very active with its Civil Affairs and Military Government school. Later, we shall look into some of the language of their doctrine and training manuals to see how influential this material became later in the hands of the ST. Not only at Fort Gordon but at Fort Bragg the Army was nursing along the tiny detachment of Special Forces, which had all but gone out of existence. However, by late 1949 and into the 1950s these small first stirrings became major forces.

Thus, these three things played into the hands of the CIA as it began to move into areas which it knew best and in which it could make moves unseen and unobserved by others in the Government. The CIA was moving like spilled water. It was not exactly sure of its course and direction but it was following the line of least resistance, aided by its own law of gravity, which in this case was its banner-waving allegiance to the cause of anti-Communism of any kind.

By the late forties the Air Force had established by General Psychological Warfare Air Command visualized by General Vandenberg, but other units known as Air Re-Supply and Communications Wings (ARC Wings). These were very large organizations. They consisted of a variety of aircraft, all the way from small specialized light planes to the super-bombers of World War II—the B-29, or the later version, the B-50. These mixed units had everything from flying capability on a global scale to printing presses and leaflet dispersal units. Once they had been created and shaken down during training exercises, they were deployed all over the world at such places as Clark Field near Manila, at Okinawa, Great Britain, and Libya. Elements of these units became heavily involved in the Korean War,

and specialized sections worked with the CIA all over Europe, the
Middle East, and parts of Asia.

In accordance with war-planning practice, these Wings had a
wartime mission that was highly classified and infrequently discussed, save by those few who knew what it was. Because of the
high classification of the mission of these units, something had to
be said for their existence and why they seemed to be so busy when
they had nothing "officially" to do. As a result, they became actively
involved in a whole array of peacetime missions. They engaged in
frequent military maneuvers and training exercises, and if there was
an earthquake somewhere and a backward nation found itself with
a major tragedy on its hands, a detachment from the Wing would
show up and begin the process of bringing in as much aid and assistance as could be arranged. Such activities became the cover for the
Wing and more or less explained its existence for those who did not
know and did not need to know about the war plan requirement.

The same was true of the Army Special Forces components. Their
wartime mission was highly classified, yet they were a large organization, and they had to have some cover reason to exist that would
more closely tie them in with the rest of the parts and they took part
in other exercises with NATO forces, from Norway south to Greece,
Turkey, Iran, and Pakistan. They added experienced manpower to
disaster relief and to other underdeveloped "nation building" work.

All of these things resulted in a large, active, and consuming military organization. These big units all had to be funded, manned, and
maintained by the military. In the days of real austerity this created
many problems, but because these units existed under heavy cover
and secrecy, no one in the apparent parent services knew how to get
to them to cut them back. Thus, they were sustained. Behind the
scenes the CIA smoothed out many of these problems, and this vast
organization grew. The Korean War saved the day for all of these
activities, and for several years in the early fifties there was money,
manpower, and plenty to go around for all such units.

It was in this manner, through the innocent-appearing device
of working with the military war planning staffs, that the Agency
acquired a vast quantity of equipment, men, and base facilities all

over the world, even to the extent of major aircraft and other heavy equipment. Though the NSC directives stated that the CIA could not create an organization to accomplish clandestine activities, and even though the President had said that the CIA must come to the Council for any such equipment, the CIA managed to create a huge capability that cost them nothing and that was ready to do its bidding at the drop of a hat.

Many have wondered how a small agency, such as the CIA was in the late forties, could have grown so fast and have had so much physical influence and impact upon foreign and military policies. It was this great military war plan-earmarked organization in all of the services which was used by the CIA quite innocently and which gave it its great unsuspected strength. As a matter of fact, the servicemen who became involved in this pseudo-military work enjoyed their special freedoms and the inevitable "fun and games." Even if they did not participate in them, they at least worked close to and in the aura of the big game. There were many like General Vandenberg, the former DCI, who thought that the peacetime military forces should become much more proficient in this type of operation. And once they got into these organizations, they actively and eagerly supported their CIA counterparts. Many of these men accepted duty assignments with the CIA. These units all over the world became the havens for a large number of CIA cover assignment men. These CIA people served as military personnel easily in the pseudo-military units.

This, too, was a significant departure from the original plans. It was early agreed that military intelligence experts would serve freely and voluntarily with the CIA, and from the beginning a great number of jobs, including many top-level key jobs, were assigned to active duty military personnel, and as we have shown, CIA men served in the military by agreement in the war planning spaces. But it had never been visualized that hundreds of military men would serve with the CIA in its clandestine sections in order to work in support of such units as the Army Special Forces and the Air Force ARC Wings. Nor was it ever envisioned that hundreds of CIA men would cross over into the military to serve with the line military units, such as these were supposed to be.

Thus it was that while the fledgling agency was getting itself organized, and while it was beginning to be able to perform some of its assigned functions, it was also laying the ground-work, skillfully and in a major effort, for the future when it would use thousands of men in huge clandestine operations such as the Bay of Pigs, the Indonesian support project, and eventually, the prelude to South Vietnam.

What had begun as a simple central intelligence organization charged with the responsibility of coordinating all elements of the national intelligence community had become the center of a power system.

This system, through secret and covert channels within the Federal Government's structure—and beyond that into industry and the academic world, and the world of the media and publishing houses—had developed a tremendous unseen infrastructure consisting primarily of the vast resources of the national military establishment all over the world. The central intelligence idea that had been born in the realization of the failures of World War II and in the postwar "one world" era became the precocious fledgling of the "Communist threat" protagonists. Then the Central Intelligence Agency, which was more or less the caboose of the National Security Act of 1947, began gradually to work itself around to becoming the hand at the throttle on the greatest peacetime military power ever maintained by any great nation . . . a military force that had been emasculated and reduced to one of response, ever on the defensive, and therefore ready for manipulation and control by an action group such as the ST.

CHAPTER 10

THE DULLES-JACKSON-CORREA
REPORT IN ACTION

The great significance of the thought and content of the National Security Act of 1947 can only be understood after a careful review of the emerging events of that period. We have already mentioned many of those great and growing pressures. One that was fundamental to that time was the idea of "cybernetics," as propounded by the great Massachusetts Institute of Technology mathematician, Norbert Wiener, in his book of that name, published in 1948. Wiener, along with many others, had worked during World War II to develop radar, projectiles, and methods of solving problems of fire control, principally in the employment of massed anti-aircraft weapons.

Another segment of the scientific community was involved in the development of nuclear weapons and related activity. These two pioneering groups became greatly involved in the developing age of the computer. It is quite possible that the move from development of the atomic bomb to the creation of the thermonuclear (hydrogen) bomb would not have been achieved without the assistance of the advanced MANIAC computer and others that were being assembled.

As a result of the strategic role played by so many brilliant, though perhaps overly specialized men, there was a great overlap in the field of strategic planning, involving the conventional military professionals, political leaders, and these advanced scientists. The military men of that time believed that they held the key to the control or neutralization of the world because they had just completed the destruction of the forces of Japan and Germany in the greatest of all wars and because they had sole possession of the atomic bomb and of its means of delivery over great distances, as had been demonstrated at Hiroshima and Nagasaki.

On the other hand, the politicians, recognizing the unmatched power of this country, looked ahead with a certain magnanimity upon the long-sought era of world peace, which seemed to be within reach if they could but continue the One World postwar climate of exhausted euphoria which any great victory brings.

Meanwhile, the scientists, who were much closer to a true realization of the facts of the situation, saw that this was no time to relax. They knew, if others were unwilling to admit it to themselves, that nuclear supremacy was not permanent and that there was no way to make it so unless the United States was willing to dedicate itself to the difficult, costly, and massive task of moving ahead.

One group of scientists felt very strongly that the atomic bomb was a sufficient "ultimate" weapon and that this country should dedicate itself to the manufacture of more and better atomic weapons until a stockpile of incontestable superiority had been obtained. This goal, positively and technically attainable, meant that this country would have to continue its nuclear production at a wartime pace or face the chance that Russia or some other country might surpass it within the next critical decade. Although the goal of these scientists was the lesser of the two general proposals, it was not an easy one, and supremacy was not assured without great effort.

Other scientists insisted that the only way in which this country could maintain its leadership in the great nuclear race was to drive directly at the mysteries of the thermonuclear weapon. These scientists, who could not guarantee ultimate success in a venture so difficult, maintained that even the shreds of hope which their experience held out to them were so important that if some other country solved the secrets of the fusion explosion before we did, it would from that time on wrest world power leadership from us.

The thought of doing both simultaneously was almost beyond comprehension, and a great struggle raged within all three worlds—political, scientific, and military. Needless to say, with such grave matters under consideration the traditionally normal concepts of diplomacy and military policy had been outmoded almost overnight. Diplomats long accustomed to the fine points of balance of power and to the value of alliances were faced with the fact that there was no such thing as a balance of power, even if all of the rest of the world's nations were to be balanced against the nuclear superpower. In the years 1946 and 1947 the world-power pecking order began with the United States; number two on the list was almost immaterial.

The same situation of shattered tradition faced the military. Army generals who had just driven their forces over the remnants of the once great German army refused even to think of how they would deploy forces against an enemy equipped with nuclear weapons. It was years before the senior war colleges would even permit a nuclear annex to be included in their master war plans.

Somewhere in the flux of all of these ideas and great conflicts there began to grow a fear, a real national dread, of the potential of that "enemy" who would gain the atomic bomb first. In those early days it was not even necessary to put a name on the country that might loom up over the horizon armed with the bomb. That was the "enemy" and that nation would be the ultimate enemy of all enemies of all time. And along with this idea came the play on the threat. Those who believed that our only road to salvation lay in greater stockpiling of atomic bombs, those who argued that it must be the hydrogen bomb, and those few who said it must be both, all perhaps without common intent, began to create the idea of the "enemy threat." It was coming. It was inevitable. The things that have been done since that period in the name of "anti-enemy" would make a list that in dollars alone would have paid for all of the costs of civilization up to that time, with money to spare.

Such an enemy is not unknown. Man has feared this type of enemy before. It is a human, and more than that, it is a social trait, to dread the unknown enemy. This enemy is defined in one context as the Manichaean Devil. Norbert Wiener says, "The Manichaean devil is an opponent, like any other opponent, who is determined on victory and will use any trick of craftiness or dissimulation to obtain this victory. In particular, he will keep his policy of confusion secret, and if we show any signs of beginning to discover his policy, he will change it in order to keep us in the "dark." The great truth about this type of enemy is that he is stronger when he is imagined and feared than when he is real. One of man's greatest sources of fear is lack of information. To live effectively one must have adequate information.

It was in this great conflict that the National Security Act of 1947 was brewed. And man's demand for information pervaded and surmounted almost every other move he made. Thus a great machine was created. All of the resources of this country were poured unto a single Department of Defense—defense against the great Manichaean Devil which was looming up over the steppes of Russia with the formula of the atomic bomb in one hand and the policy of World Communism in the other. Our statesmen foresaw the Russian detonation of the atomic bomb in 1949 and the concurrent acceleration toward the hydrogen bomb as soon thereafter as possible; so they created the Atomic Energy Commission in January 1947 and then the Defense Department in September 1947, and gave them both the eyes and ears of the CIA to provide the essential information that at that time was really the paramount and highest priority. The CIA was ordered to achieve both goals—the second-to-none atomic bomb stockpile and the hydrogen bomb, and the DOD was ordered to create the global force that would defend this country against the giant of the Soviet Union and all other nuclear powers.

This then created its own great machinery. To fight this great, and mostly unknown devil, it was necessary to create a truly defense establishment, which would have the ability to spring up against attack of any kind, of any nature, and from any place. It was to be truly a massive machine. "Defense" was no social or polite term to be held up like a banner in order that the rest of the world might believe that the United States was forever denouncing the use of force and was therefore forever denouncing that paramount doctrine of military strategy, the power of the offensive. This was the real thing. Defense was to be defense; and the national defense establishment was to be the greatest force we could create and maintain for just that purpose.

This meant that the military policy of the United States was to become more like the concept of the chess player than that of the brilliant tactician. Everything was done to guard against making a mistake that would give the alert adversary that advantage that would enable him to defeat the defender. Thus the chess player is governed more by his worst moments than by his best moments. The worst calamities of defense policy since 1947 have been those resulting from being caught off guard, such as the Korean War and the Sputnik period, when the entire nation felt endangered by the stark realization that the Soviet Union had launched an orbiting body before we had.

This realization resulted in the creation of a defense establishment machine much like that proposed by Dr. W. Ross Ashby and recounted by Wiener. It was a great, "unpurposeful random mechanism which seeks for its own purpose through a process of learning . . ." Such a machine is designed "to avoid certain pitfalls of breakdown [and will] look for purposes which it can fulfill." These brief quotes taken from men who were writing and lecturing during this period are now most prophetic. Not only was this monstrous machine created for the defense of the United States; but it was so established that it was looking for purposes it could fulfill.

In other words, this great defense establishment was ready to go, looking for opportunity, and all it needed was to have someone throw the switch and give it a little direction.

Evidence of this exists in the beginnings made by the Agency with the participation it volunteered in the war-planning functions of the major overseas military commands, especially in Europe. This war-planning work led to the stockpiling of considerable amounts of war-making materiel earmarked for the CIA and stored in military warehouses, both real and cover units, all over the world. These supplies could be called out then whenever the CIA had any requirement, even at a time when the NSC thought that it had the CIA well under control because they had prohibited it from having men, equipment, and facilities for operational purposes. This was the start. The Agency worked itself into key positions within the defense establishment, and then orchestrating its data inputs to create highly classified requirements, it began to develop great power within the U.S. government and around the world.

The year 1950 was an important one for the CIA. Again all of the pieces began to fall into all of the right slots. First of all, the war in Korea began on June 25, 1950, and although the intelligence community—CIA and all—was caught unprepared for the attack just as it had been years before at Pearl Harbor, the failure of national intelligence to assist with such a major prediction spotlighted what must be done if the United States were ever to have a worthwhile intelligence capability. While the war was getting under way and the U.S. armed forces were picking themselves up off the mat, almost as they had had to do after the attacks on Pearl Harbor, Truman looked around for a stronger man to pull the Agency together and to give it a sense of mission. Meanwhile, strong-agency proponents argued that the fault had not been the CIA's. On the contrary they attempted to show, if the President had been briefed properly, on a daily basis by the CIA as the Dulles-Jackson-Correa report had recommended, he would have known that an attack was imminent.

This was an important recommendation of the Dulles-Jackson-Correa report, and these activists took this opportunity to promote the issue at the cost of the incumbent DCI and his military-dominated staff.

It should be recalled that it was Truman's refusal to deal directly with the intelligence arm but to have them instead brief the NSC, and then to make his Cabinet members responsible for keeping him informed, that stirred up this issue in the first place.

This was continuing evidence of the old fight between those who saw Intelligence as the primary force in the Government, responsible only to the President, and those who believed the function of

Intelligence was to keep the President and his Cabinet informed in the true staff sense. Both of these views were made more at odds with each other by the pressures generated by the Manichaean Devil syndrome.

The U.S. Ambassador to Moscow for several years preceding the Korean War had been General Eisenhower's old Chief of Staff, the brilliant and tough Walter Beedle Smith. He was very well qualified, by his World War II experience with Eisenhower, for a major assignment; and in a special sense he was well qualified to become the new DCI by virtue of the fact that he had been in Moscow for so long. So many of the intelligence clan had been exploiting the cause of anti-Communism for so long that it seemed that bringing in the one man who really ought to know at first hand what Communism was all about would be the best move to counteract those who were saying that the Administration was soft on Communism. As we look back at this appointment, we may have forgotten the great crisis which had been stirred up by Senator Joe McCarthy over the issue of Communists being everywhere. This was no small issue, and the appointment of a man as highly regarded as General Smith was an ideal choice.

In spite of this, the McCarthy movement swept him up in its fervor. Soon after his appointment he was called to appear before McCarthy's committee, and in response to a question as to whether he thought there were Communists in government, specifically in the CIA, he replied to the effect that he thought it was quite possible that there were Communists in the CIA. This statement was a real shocker, and it made instant headlines. At that time and in the special context of those days this was a most amazing statement whether it was factual or not. The general had been the DCI for only a brief time and he was more or less excused for the statement on the grounds that he had not had time to really know the Agency. For any other man but General Smith, in that position and at that time, to have given a similar reply would have resulted in having him ridden out of town by the rabid McCarthyists.

Smith replaced Admiral Hillenkoetter who had been DCI since the days of the central intelligence group, before the Agency had been created. The failure of the CIA to give proper warning of the probable or at least highly possible North Korean attacks, and its failure to evaluate the nature and strength of that attack may well have been contributing factors in hurrying President Truman's decision to replace Hillenkoetter. He had done his duty and played his role as the script was written. He had been charged with running a military-type CIA, and he did just that. The brief encounters the Agency had in such places as Greece, Iran, and along the perimeter of the Iron Curtain were simply postwar OSS-type games, and they never amounted to very much.

However, there was one major characteristic of CIA operational efforts during Hillenkoetter's time that began to change with the Smith era. During its first years, when the CIA did something anti-Communist it was something done against the real Communists. For example, the fighting in Greece also involved Bulgarians, Yugoslavians, and Romanians. All of the work the CIA did along the Iron Curtain and in Greece and Iran was directly concerned with close and tangible Russian influence. In those days the CIA did not go to the Congo or to the Philippines to seek out the subversive influences they then called Communist. The CIA worked nose-to-nose against the Russians wherever they found them in reality. This point cannot be underscored too heavily. Most of the CIA clandestine effort since 1955 had been against supposed Communists or subversive Communism or some such third country target. In other words, the "Communism" the CIA finds and goes after in its operational efforts during more recent years has been that which it finds on the soil of non-Communist countries. In the beginning the skirmishes of the Cold War were fought on or near real Communist territory. Since that time Communism had been fought on the soil of our own circle of friends, in such countries as Vietnam, Laos, India, the Congo, and the Dominican Republic, to name a few. This change in the focus and direction of the pursuit of Communism is important.

At the time General Smith became the Director of Central Intelligence in October 1950, events in Korea looked very bad. The greatest military power in the world only five years earlier was being pushed into the sea near the southern tip of the Korean peninsula, and the CIA shared a certain amount of the blame with the military establishment. Smith moved suddenly to put an end to the bad image of the Agency.

One of the first things he found in his files was the Dulles-Jackson-Correa report of January 1, 1949. It had been gathering dust and had resulted in very little effective change. This had not been because of the language of the report. It was tremendous. It attacked what it thought was wrong without hesitation; it made firm recommendations for the changes it sponsored. However, because the men it had attacked so vehemently had been in a position to bottle it up, nothing it recommended had been accomplished. General Smith took the report out, and when he had read it, he got on the phone and called William H. Jackson. He asked him to leave his business and come to Washington at once. Jackson, who had already devoted much of his life to intelligence service, came immediately and was appointed the Deputy Director of Central Intelligence. Smith dialed the phone again and called the prestigious law firm of Sullivan and Cromwell in New York City and asked for Allen Dulles. In short order he had Dulles in the fold as chief of foreign operations. There is no official explanation of what the duties of the foreign operations section were, but it would take little imagination to figure them out. Then he called another old friend, Murray McConnell, and asked him to come to Washington to be his Deputy Director for Administration.

In a busy six months the CIA had become reasonably well-organized and sported four strong deputies: Deputy Director intelligence, Deputy Director Administration, Deputy Director Support (Logistics—in the broadest sense), and Deputy Director Plans (Clandestine Operations—the "fun and games" side of the house.)

Meanwhile, Smith began to put into effect the functional proposals of the Dulles' *Mein Kampf*." He was amazed to learn that the director of OPC (Office of Policy Coordination) was not "his" man but was tied up in that bureaucratic red-tape device prescribed by NSCID 10/2 and intended by the council to keep him from running free into the arena of clandestine operations. When General Smith learned that this important deputy was appointed by the Secretary of State and seconded by the Secretary of Defense, he went right to the root of the problem. He called the Secretary of State and then the Secretary of Defense and informed them that from that date on the director of OPC was to be under his own control and that if they had any objections they were welcome to talk with him about them. If either one had objections in the heat of a messy war in Korea, he kept them to himself.

From that date on the CIA had its own clandestine operations division, although it was still required by law to remain out of that business until directed by the NSC to develop an operation.

The CIA had made various minor incursions into the special operations field during the late forties, but all of them were carefully phrased and gingerly submitted to the NSC for approval in strict compliance with the law and with the provisions of NSCID 10/2. Now that the DCI was in control of the special operations section, he felt that it was his to use as he saw fit.

This move was very timely. It would have done little good for him to have gained the clandestine staff if he had possessed no resources in the form of the military men, equipment, and facilities that had gradually been laid at his disposal as a result of the tedious years of war planning. However, just as he took over the OPC (Office of Policy Coordination) he found that the CIA had access to a vast military organization in the Army and Air Force and that he would have very little trouble using the exigencies of the war in Korea as an excuse to put into motion certain large and important special operations in that country. These operations were directed at Taiwan, Okinawa, and the Philippines, in addition to Japan and Korea, and led to the development of Agency interests in all of Southeast Asia.[1]

There were other similar moves made during this period as the emerging ST began to make itself felt in Asia as it had been in

---

1. It should be recalled that General Donovan of OSS fame had been the Ambassador to Thailand and that he was followed by the former Ambassador to Greece, John Peurifoy. Both men were, of course, CIA-type operators, and it was their expertise that accounts for so much of the relationship that has existed in Thailand during the past twenty years.

Europe. All of this was done initially under the cover of the Korean War, and significantly, most of these events took place after the removal of General Douglas MacArthur, who among others had always been a foe of Donovan and the hard-core Intelligence clan.

As the Korean War drew to a close, the French were heavily engaged in a losing battle in Indochina. The CIA was operating there in both the north and south of Vietnam during that time. When the Government of the United States finally permitted large twin-engine transport aircraft to operate in Indochina and to fly to the besieged battlefield of Dien Bien Phu, a hearty band of civilian pilots who worked for the CAT Airline (precursor of Air America, Incorporated) did the flying—not military pilots. They had been hastily trained by the Air Force to fly the C-119 aircraft. The actual flights into Indochina, culminating in heavy air-drops at Dien Bien Phu, were made by these civilian CIA contract pilots. Even at this early date the CIA was well inside the door of Indochina.

Back in Washington the election campaign of 1952 had been heated with the unpopular war as a major issue. General Eisenhower had agreed to run on the Republican ticket against Adlai Stevenson, who had picked up the mantle of the Democratic party from the gallant old warrior, Harry Truman.

After Eisenhower won the election, he kept his promise to visit Korea and to bring the war to an end. He also found himself heir to many of the old stalwarts of the Thomas E. Dewey team from the campaign of 1948. He appointed John Foster Dulles to be his Secretary of State, and because Allen Dulles wanted the job of DCI. Ike prevailed upon his old crony and longtime Army companion, Walter Beedle Smith, to accept the post of Under Secretary of State and to give up his Intelligence chair to Allen. William Jackson had stayed in the Agency as Smith's deputy for less than a year, and in August of 1951, General Smith had appointed Allen Dulles to be his deputy director in Bill Jackson's place. The trip to Washington, which Allen Dulles had made back in October 1950, and which was supposed to have lasted for no more than a week or two, now was on its way to becoming an unbroken eleven-year stint for the Agency to which he had already given so much of himself.

Dulles found many of the things that he had hoped to get done well under way. General Smith had taken another hurdle for him after he had gotten the director of the OPC into the fold. As we have said many times, President Truman had a firm policy concerning what the intelligence staff meant to him. He looked upon the Agency as his "quiet intelligence arm" and no more. Having this interpretation, he felt that the Agency should evaluate and analyze information and disseminate it to the staff, primarily to his Cabinet, and that they should all use it in the formulation of national plans and policy. This meant that unless he called for some specific matter, he did not expect intelligence to be brought to him daily, weekly, or at any fixed time. He was content to know that it was there, that it was available equally to his Cabinet and to him when needed.

This did not satisfy Allen Dulles, and he had so stated in his report. He felt that it was the responsibility of the DCI to brief the President daily, if not oftener when the subject warranted a special or an emergency meeting. General Smith agreed with this approach. General Smith was accustomed to the military staff procedure whereby a smoothly oiled staff meets daily and briefly with the commanding general and keeps him informed. This is a good system during a war because the General has nothing else to do but to get on with the war, and he needs the current inputs from all of his staff. But for a President with countless other demands upon his time, any fixed schedule such as that visualized by the Dulles report would result in a gross imposition upon his time and with the burden of certain responsibilities and decisions that he might best attend to after his Cabinet and other special staff members had had the chance to come up with their own decisions.

However, Smith moved in with the Dulles proposal and got it accepted. It always seems to work out that when the Agency has fallen down on one job it gains strength from the resultant adversity and pops up somewhere else stronger than before. The Agency had failed to give a proper warning and evaluation of the Korean attack. They now turned this failure into a maneuver to get their foot into the office of the President on a regular and daily basis. Linked with the acquisition of (1) special operations, old OPC and new DD/P, and (2) the massive special military strength in the Special Army and Air Force forces, this third step was most significant, and should be discussed in some detail.

This third major development was the establishment of an office and a system designed especially to handle current intelligence. General Smith felt that his most important job was to keep the President fully and promptly informed of everything going on in the world that affected United States interests. He made arrangements with the President for such briefings, and he wanted the best support possible for this task. As much as anything else done during these formative years of the CIA, this was a most important step that has been best described by Lyman Kirkpatrick, who took part in all phases of this change. In his book, *The Real CIA*, he says:

"This [establishment of the Current Intelligence Office] requires explanation. Not even all of the policy-makers of the government understand the current intelligence process and consequently fail to use its product as it should be used. I know that the American people, who should appreciate what they have in Washington—and want to know about it—have no realization of this aspect of intelligence work. . . .

"General Smith . . . wanted a daily intelligence report that he could hand to the President which would succinctly summarize in a very few pages the important developments in the world that affected U.S. interests . . . this report to be all-source . . . press reports and radio broadcasts to the most secret information from the most sensitive sources available to the government . . . the report to be carefully analyzed and evaluated by the most competent experts on the subject or area . . . to be done immediately upon receipt of the information, right around the clock, twenty-four hours a day, and seven days a week. If the information was urgent it should go forward to the policy level immediately upon evaluation. If it was important, but not critical, it could go into a regular daily report . . . so well written and attractively presented that the recipients would be sure to read it.

"The office . . . would have as many experts as could be recruited or trained and persuaded to make a career in current intelligence. And it would have all of the production facilities necessary for a publication designed for the President of the United States . . .

"The production facilities and the people required to man them constitute an important aspect of the success of any such office. Working under intense pressure that at times makes the wire desk of a major newspaper during a national catastrophe calm by comparison, the experts need top-flight help at every level. If the girl who types the final copy doesn't know Danang from Nhatrang or Ouagadougou from Bamako, and doesn't care, errors can creep in that could help destroy the credibility of the entire item or even of the publication. Maps, charts, and other graphics have to be produced quickly and accurately, and the document must be printed and delivered at dawn. Of course everybody touching it has to have the highest security clearance, and every sheet of paper must be accounted for. Everybody in the office from the typist to the top supervisor realizes full well that hundreds of large-eyed officials at the top of the government will catch the slightest mistake. . . . An intelligence report has nothing to sell it but consistent credibility. Anything that tends to lessen this credibility means that the report will not receive the attention it should . . .

"Unfortunately, intelligence is a very uncertain profession. It is never possible to have all of the information on any subject that one would like to have before telling the President of the United States about it. On some occasions one could assume that 90 percent of all the facts would be on hand, and the balance would be obvious. On other occasions the percentage would be much smaller, diminishing at times to only a hint or a clue. On both of these occasions it is the expert analyst who makes the difference and insures that the information presented is the best available.

"There are two ingredients that go into this expert analysis. The first is the quality of the analyst, and the second is the availability of the necessary information. The first is attainable. The second may not always be possible.

"Some have likened the current intelligence process to the production of a daily newspaper, but the analogy is inaccurate. With all due respect to our excellent press, it is not composed of specialists who are experts on the areas on which they report, with of course some well known exceptions. The current intelligence analyst is a man or woman who starts with a good academic background, including advanced degrees on the area of responsibility, spends years studying every scrap of information received in Washington on that country, and becomes increasingly expert with the passage of time. What is not generally understood even inside the government is that when an intelligence report is received and before it is passed on to the policy level it is analyzed and evaluated against every bit of information available on the same subject that has ever been received by the U.S. Government.

"This process is one of the best safety valves against the government's acting on inadequate information or a false report that perhaps had been deliberately planted as a deception measure. One of the truly great dangers in passing intelligence to the policy level is that somebody will start pressing buttons based on partial information, and in my opinion the passage of unevaluated reports to the top of government is always unwise. When it happens, an inevitable flap occurs and a lot of government time and money is wasted."

This statement is an accurate reflection of exactly what was taking place and was written by a man, who but for physical impairment brought about by infantile paralysis, which struck him at the peak of his career, might well have been appointed DCI. Among the inner group of top Agency careerists, he was a moderate and a most dedicated man. As a result, his statement takes on a very special meaning. It is an example of the blind statement of faith found in a religious order. The great error and the great damage, however, from this kind of thinking arises in the fact that it is predicated upon the belief that the leaders of the Agency can do no wrong.

When the same organization is given the authority to develop and control all foreign Secret Intelligence and to take its findings, based upon the inputs of this secret intelligence, directly to the last authority, the President—not only to take it to him regularly but to preempt his time, attention, and energies, almost to the point of making him their captive—and then also is given the authority and the vast means to carry out peacetime clandestine operations, that agency has been given the power to control the foreign operations of the Government on a continuing day to day basis.

Note carefully in this calm and apparently objective account by Lyman Kirkpatrick the germ of ridicule and distrust of the press. It is said explicitly nowhere in the statement, yet it conveys the thought when it says, "There are two ingredients that go into this expert analysis. The first is the quality of the analyst, and the second is the availability of the necessary information. The first is attainable. The second may not always be possible.

"Some have likened the current intelligence process to the production of a daily newspaper, but the analogy is inaccurate. With all due respect to our excellent press, it is not composed of specialists who are experts on the areas on which they report, with of course some well known exceptions. The current intelligence analyst is a man or woman who starts with a good academic background, including advanced degrees on the area of responsibility, spends years studying every scrap of information received in Washington on that country, and becomes increasingly expert with the passage of time."

Note that the reference to the press is sandwiched between two strong paragraphs that laud the intelligence analyst, and then by loaded inference downgrade the press.

It is not the statement by Kirkpatrick which is so much in contention as it is that the ST has used this kind of damning with faint praise to downgrade any outsider, whether he be press or, at times, Cabinet member. When such downgrading is done behind the cloak of secrecy, the person and persons so attacked are silently slandered and surely destroyed. They have no way of finding out that they have been the object of such attacks, because they have been quietly left out from a circle where exclusion means extinction.

This has been no idle example. *The New York Times* had a most able and knowledgeable young correspondent, David Halberstam, in South Vietnam during the earlier days of the fighting there. He had devoted himself to the problems of Indochina and knew the area, the people, the history, and almost everything else about Indochina as well as or better than nearly anyone else, including what we might call the "intelligence analysts." At that time his crisp reporting frequently came up with items that went at cross purposes with most of the men who are mentioned so frequently in the Pentagon Papers. At first his reports were given the usual treatment. They were said to be inaccurate and slanted. Then they were ignored. But as they became more and more popular among those readers who found in them the stark ring of truth, an element of the ST caused a small office to be set up in a remote corner of the Pentagon where "information" could be fed to a staff who had nothing else to do but crucify this writer every day for the "eyes only" of the President of the United States.

It was the function of this small staff to clip that author's column from the paper each day it appeared and to paste it on one side of an open scrapbook-type of album. Then they would create a carefully worded rebuttal column of their own, which would be pasted on the other side of the open album. The rebuttal data arrived from many sources and usually was the subject of urgent telegrams from Washington to Saigon and back, in order to find every possible way of attacking the works of that author. Not too many weeks passed before the President was reported to have called the publisher of *The New York Times* and made a suggestion to the effect that it might be better for that newspaper to change its correspondents in Indochina. In due time that young and skilled reporter, easily superior in terms of knowledge of his subject to most intelligence analysts, many of whom had not ever been to Indochina, was transferred to Poland so that he might no longer offer competition with the production of the analysts.

This is an example of the real significance of the Kirkpatrick statement—not so much his statement, which is honest and realistic, but what his statement means in practice. When the powers within the ST believe that the President is better informed, every single day and without the cushioning intervention of other able staff members, such as his Cabinet officers and their top-level staff personnel, by the product of their own parochial analysts, they fall

victim to two unpardonable sins. First and most obvious, these
analysts may not be actually as experienced as they are perhaps
educated. Their research may turn up the material all right; but they
have not experienced it. Oftentimes they are not in a position to
interpret it adequately, and their research falls short. One of their
greatest and most obvious weaknesses is that their motivation is
derived from random input. Their input is more or less a mechanical process whereby the intelligence data is acquired randomly and
in many cases unexpectedly, and it is not the result of a plan or of
a planned objective. They are simply responding to something that
came into their hands from any of numberless sources. The force
that drives them is not their own.

Even with the most able and experienced analyst it would always
be best to put him into the heart of the staff, as an intelligence expert
should be, and then to permit the rest of the staff to work with him
so that his analysis might benefit from their varied and considerable
experience in all other staff areas.

The second and most portentous danger that lies within the
system outlined by Kirkpatrick is that such a procedure is susceptible
to influences and even malevolent abuses. Again, if one believes that
the Agency leaders can do no wrong, one grants to these leaders an
element of infallibility and rests his whole system on faith in their
honor and total integrity. One may not question honor and honesty
in any public official but one may properly show considerable interest in shades of influence. If the President of the Unites States is to
open his eyes each day upon a world painted by an artist who is a
realist, he may get a fair picture of the affairs of the world as seen by
that artist sometime during the deep hours of the preceding night.
However, if he is to open his eyes upon the work of other artists who
during the same long night have created a scene that in their eyes
was honest and true but still may have been very much influenced by
the sources of the intelligence data, then who is to tell the President
that what he has viewed is not really the shape of the world that
morning? Once access has been gained through the portals of the
office of the President, there is no other authority to visit. However,
if the final authority remains one echelon aloof from the day-to-day

processes, he then has the option to work his way through a selection of views in his lonely search for truth.

We opened this accounting of the ways of the ST with a look at the first report The New York Times selected to publish in its presentation of the Pentagon Papers. Let us emphasize once more that even though 99.9 percent of the people who have read that newspaper account or subsequent book of the same name have been led to believe that the report cited was really a McNamara trip report, the facts are otherwise. The report was actually another ST—directed staff production created right in Washington, D.C. Isn't this just what we are talking about? This report created by trained analysts was given to President Johnson. Is there any record that anyone at all had an opportunity to explain to and clarify for President Johnson that he was really being briefed on a homespun staff report, and not a trip report made on the spot in Vietnam?

Even as we point out the way this report was written, we are very much aware of the fact that it would be entirely possible for trained and experienced men in Washington to turn out a report as good as one that McNamara and his party could have done from Saigon. And it is also recognized that with the excellence of communications as it is in this day, such a report can be written in Washington as easily and as adequately, from a substantive point of view, as it could be in Saigon or on the official airplane on the way back. The content of the report and the intent of the authors in writing it as they did is significant in this place and in the context of the subject of this chapter. There is great power in the hands of those who can develop and utilize secret foreign intelligence, interpret it daily, and present it by standard procedure directly to the President each day, and who at the same time possess the authority to carry out secret clandestine operations either in pursuit of more intelligence or in response to the data inputs of that intelligence.

As Kirkpatrick reports, a huge current intelligence organization was established by General Smith, and it was manned and supported without regard to budget. It soon became a major interest of the Agency. Whereas the General began with the idea of publishing daily current intelligence in a publication, the process has since become even more direct and refined. The daily intelligence has become a daily briefing that is second to none in perfection. The same care and perfection planned for the publication go into this truly superior presentation. It may very well be that new Cabinet members and the President and Vice President themselves are awed at this most elaborate presentation; and that they begin to find it easy to downgrade the Huntleys, Brinkleys, and Cronkites if for no other reason than their familiarity with the sheer excellence and the superior content and quality of the daily intelligence briefing.

We have seen otherwise sophisticated men attend these briefings regularly, and for the first few times come away with a look of awe and wonder. It is very heady stuff to look at the world from a satellite or U-2, or to see the whole world laid out before you in the unscrambled maze of global electronics deciphering.[2]

When a reporter can casually step to the podium and say that the Russians said this or that to one another down the missile range, or that traffic analysis from China shows such and such, all this is most eye-opening. At this point, even the top-echelon men in Government, who after all find this as new during their first days and weeks in office as would anyone else, are so awestruck by this fabulous display that few question it at all. These first impressions set the tone for the months and years that follow. There can be no question that Robert McNamara's first daily briefings during those December and January days before Kennedy's inauguration did a lot to shape his thinking on Indochina, thinking that he could never break away from it. Similarly, skilled experts planned the brisk briefings and the concomitant global traveling to which John McCone was immediately subjected upon his taking over as DCI. He too got a lasting and most powerful impression of Indochina, which stayed with him throughout his tenure. These are the things the ST is good at. And much of this process began with the Dulles-Jackson-Correa report and with the fortuitous

---

2. Deciphering performed by computers from material picked up by global listening posts.

implementation of its key features by the skilled administrative expeditor, General Walter Beedle Smith.

Allen Dulles inherited the fruits of his own cultivation, harvested for him by a most able man who at the time he was performing these tasks was doing them honestly and objectively simply because he unquestioningly thought that it was for the good of the cause.

When elder statesman Harry S. Truman looked back upon those years and said that the CIA had been "diverted," if he had been in a position to have seen what really happened as a result of the Dulles-Jackson-Correa report he had commissioned, he might have felt some inner surprise at the realization that it was his own pen that gave authority to a good bit of that diversion. Then when President Eisenhower came upon the scene, he had no reason whatsoever to question the work of his own closest military assistant or to question the position of two brothers who had for the most part played no active role in the Truman Administration. As a result, when Allen Dulles became the DCI he had everything going for him, and he just turned to the next pages of his report to maintain the momentum.

PART III

THE CIA: HOW IT IS ORGANIZED

CHAPTER 11

THE DULLES ERA BEGINS

The old, pastel yellow brick east building on a hill overlooking Foggy Bottom, on what is now the site of the Kennedy Center for the Performing Arts and the Watergate Buildings, was just the place for the scent of pipe tobacco and the quiet shuffle of worn leather slippers. The high-backed chair and elongated office were also right for its new tenant. Allen Dulles moved into a place that already seemed to bear his trademarks and characteristics. Unpretentious as the East Building was, it seemed right for a daily stream of jet-black, chauffeur-driven limousines to pull up the hill, over the winding narrow driveway, and then down into the garden circle where no more than three or four cars could stop at any one time. Typically, the VIP cars pulled over onto the grass to permit the little old bottle-green buses to shuttle from one hidden CIA building to another. All these buses seemed at some part of their wanderings to find their way past the home of Mr. Dulles, as though anyone who worked for him should be kept aware of the fact that he was sequestered somewhere up there on the dim second floor overlooking the Potomac.

The Agency had a good chance of being secret without making much effort. Either by design or by a hand-me-down procedure, the CIA inherited the most motley group of buildings imaginable. Someone in the General Services Administration with a real sense of humor must have made out the CIA allocation in the Greater Washington area. At the north end of the Fourteenth Street (Rochambeau) Bridge and to the north of the Bureau of Engraving and Printing, where not less than 70–80 percent of all tourists who scramble through Washington each year find their way, there is a red brick building that looks like part of a converted stable. The Agency was in there. Further north on Sixteenth Street, across from the Statler-Hilton Hotel and next door to Washington's own Gaslight Club, is another nondescript building, not too far from the Soviet Embassy. CIA was there. On Connecticut Avenue, in what is now the heart of the business district, there used to be a building that had floors that sagged so much that tenants shuddered each time a big truck went by down below. CIA was in there. CIA was crammed into every one of the fairly well kept, but seriously over-crowded World War II Tempo Buildings along the south side of the Reflecting Pool east of the Lincoln Memorial Across the parkway, near the cherry tree Tidal Basin, in buildings named "Alcott" and "Barton" for their World War II Army WAAC tenants, the CIA was tucked in too. In fact, the CIA was so scattered that there was scarcely a part of Washington that did not have CIA offices hidden away. And of course, it was very simple for anyone who wished to find out where the Agency was to follow the little green buses, which trundled all day long in never-ending circles, some clockwise and some counter-clockwise, from building to building.

Things like this did not bother Allen Dulles. It is entirely possible that he never found out where all of his agency was anyhow. Such details were not for him. As a matter of fact, one of the first things he did when he became the Director was to abolish the office of the Deputy Director of Administration. In a city renowned for its bureaucratic administration and its penchant chant for proving how right C. Northcote Parkinson was, Mr. Dulles' first act was more heretical to most Washingtonians than one of Walter Beedle Smith's first actions—the one in which he told the McCarthy hearings that he thought there might well be Communists in the

Agency Washington—was not as upset about the Communists as it was to learn that a major agency of the Government had abolished Administration. Mr. Dulles took the view of the intelligence professional that it was much more dangerous and therefore undesirable to have all kinds of administrators acquiring more information than they should have, than it was to find some way to get along without the administrators.

While the public was mulling over that tidbit from the CIA, the real moves were being made inside the organization, where no one could see what was going on. The Deputy Director of Intelligence, strengthened by the addition of the current Intelligence organization and other such tasks, was to be responsible for everything to do with intelligence, and more importantly, was to be encumbered by nothing that had to do with logistics and administration. This was the theory. In practice, the DD/I has a lot of administrative and support matters to contend with as does any other large office. However, as much of the routine and continuing load as could be was set upon the Deputy Director of Support.

At the same time, the new and growing DD/P (the special operations shop) was similarly stripped of all encumbrances and freed to do the operational work that Dulles saw developing as his task. This left the DD/S (Support) with a major task. He was responsible for the entire support of the Agency, support of all kinds, at all times, and in all places. At the head of this directorate for many, many years has been the most unsung hero of the Agency and perhaps its ablest deputy, L. K. White. He is better known as "Red" White, a former Army colonel and a most able manager and administrator. He has made things work.[1]

---

1. The Agency makes a specialty of covering its people with code names as they travel around the world. Thus the message traffic will he gibberish to most people when a list of names of the Agency's key men appear. Many years ago, "Red" White and another executive from Mr. Dulles' office made an extended trip through the Pacific. They were given code names just before they left. Some genius in the cover department gave "Red" White the code name "Ballew." As he traveled from station to station it was "Red, White, and Ballew," like the flag.

The CIA as an intelligence agency offers no unusual elements on most counts. It is pretty much what it seems to be. Special operations has been exposed one way or another so many times that there is not too much guesswork about its role. But researchers have been unable to work their way into what it really is that makes the Agency what it is today. This distinctive characteristic is its superior logistics support. If an agent working in Greece needs some Soviet-built rifles of a certain vintage to equip some agents for a border or cross-border assignment, all he has to do is get his request to the station chief. He will in turn put it on the Agency line direct to Washington, where DD/S will process it. Within hours, one of their men, posing as an Air Force man in "X" country, will leave his office and drive out with an Air Force pickup truck to a small building on the far side of the base. There he will unlock a wire-anchor fence, then step unto a "go-down" storage tunnel until he comes to a row of heavy boxes. There he will look for a special mark that describes the guns he wants.

He will drive, with the nondescript box, across the field to another building, where a normal-looking Air Force supply office is located. In what looks like the usual supply room and storage area, he will find a shop filled with special tools and machinery. In short order, he will have the guns unpacked, removed from the heavy coatings of cosmolene and lead foil, and in an hour or so these guns will have been repackaged and labeled "P-84 Wing Tank" or some such cover name. Then an Air Force transport plane on its way to Naples and Athens will take this boxed "Wing Tank" to the Air Force Military Assistance Advisory Group section at the military airfield outside of Athens. There an Air Force MAAG man will take the box and see that it gets to its destination. That same day a small single engine plane will fly low over a remote, mountainous site and gently airdrop that box onto a set of camouflaged panels that mark the site for the trained pilot.

Nothing is difficult for the DD/S. The above order and action are examples of the routine. What was not routine was the establishment and maintenance of the system that made that possible. Someone had to get those special guns into the hands of the CIA in the first place. Then an elaborate global network of supply and support bases had to be established, not only as functional bases, but also with the double role of looking like one kind of facility and doing the important task of another.

A closed World War II airfield in England, once the home of an American fighter wing, was found to be an ideal site for DD/S operations. The Navy is "Prime" (the U.S. military department assigned the task of working with the British on all matters pertaining to the support and housing of Americans on the British Isles) in England. The Agency asked the Navy to establish some reason for asking the British to permit the limited reopening of this base. The CIA and the Navy agreed on their cover story and then met with the British, who of course were told the real reason for the request, but also were expected to maintain the cover story.

With some small show of normalcy, the British reopened the base. The most obvious evidence that the base had been reopened in that country neighborhood was the appearance of British uniformed guards at the gates on a twenty-four-hour basis. The Navy set up a "supply facility." It had a real U.S. Navy base designation. The base commander arrived in uniform, and his staff and enlisted men followed soon after. The base hired local British people, some as secretaries and others to run the kitchen and other facilities. In actual practice, the base had not a single real Navy man. All of those at the base were CIA men carefully accredited to the Navy and sent overseas as naval personnel.

The base gradually was loaded with "Navy" equipment, and at the proper time it was announced that the Navy was going to maintain some highly classified gear at the base in addition to the regular items and that certain buildings would be off-limits to all unauthorized personnel, British and American. By that time DD/S had a major storage and maintenance site in a most convenient and secure location.

If anyone knew that this site had been created for more than met the eye, he might note that it was not far from the huge operating base of the U.S. Air Force Air Resupply and Communications Wing that was assigned to England. The Agency site would actually be a satellite base to the huge Air Force operation with which it was linked. It is this formula that has made it possible for the CIA, with the appearance of only a little in the way of support and logistics on its own, actually to command boundless equipment, manpower, and facilities, including aircraft from the ever ready and always eager Air Force sister unit. The law and the directives and the other limits that have been put upon the Agency in an attempt to keep it out of major operations seemed to most observers—and in this business there were few witting observers—to be working well; but for the knowledgeable, the Agency was fast becoming, by the mid-fifties, a major peacetime power.

It was in 1955 that the then new Senator Mansfield, among others, attempted to get a law through the Congress that would establish a strong watchdog committee to oversee the CIA. One of the principal reasons this law did not pass was that such CIA stalwarts as Senator Russell and Senator Saltonstall affirmed that there was no need for such committees. The Congress, in their words, needed no more committees than it had at that time. They went on to say that they were always informed about everything the Agency was doing and that they could see no reason why the whole Congress should be brought in on such things when there was no need whatsoever for such action.

I have worked closely with Senator Saltonstall, and many others who were on those committees, and except in rare instances, they never knew that the CIA was so huge. They knew how big the CIA was within the bounds of the "real" or intelligence organization; but none of them knew about its tremendous global base capability, and what is much more important, none of them knew the intricacies of the Agency's supporting system that existed in the name of the Army Special Forces and the Air Force Air Supply and Communications Wings. Again there will be some who say, "Oh yes, Senator John Doe visited that base, and he saw this, and he was told that the whole business was highly classified. He said he knew what it was." Such things usually can be said, and such things may have happened; but no one man or no one group of knowledgeable men had ever had the opportunity to see the whole picture. As I have heard Senator

Saltonstall say, "Now don't tell me about that classified material. What I don't know about it won't hurt me." That has been a general attitude on Capitol Hill. In discussions I have had with responsible committeemen on the Hill, I have found this to exist as recently as September 1971. This situation has not changed much. There are no Congressmen and no Senators who really know about the Agency and about what the Agency is doing.

As a result of the war planning role of the CIA, it was easy for the CIA planners to enter in the plans of all armed forces, requirements for wartime equipment, vehicles, aircraft, and facilities that had to be earmarked and stockpiled for use by the Agency in the event of war. Once such requirements were listed in the war plans they could be requisitioned along with all the other war-plan material. This meant that the cost of this equipment would be worked into the military budget, and then in due time each item would be purchased and delivered to the advance base site where war plan material was stockpiled. Warehouse after warehouse of "military equipment" is stored in the Far East, in Europe, and throughout the United States for the eventual use of the CIA. The cost of this material and of its storage, care, and conditioning is inestimable.

To handle all of this material the Agency has large bases in Europe, Africa, Southeast Asia, Okinawa, Japan, Panama, and the United States. These supplies are kept in good shape, and reconditioned and rotated in stock with those that are used. Thus, whenever a requirement arises, the Agency has what it needs or can get what it needs from other sources.

Some of the war-plan equipment has a brief shelf-life, which requires that it be exchanged, used, or at least rotated with items in service. The Agency does not have sufficient demand for some of these things to permit it to keep up with such practices, so it has worked out rotation schedules with the services to let them have what it has in storage and then to get new replacement equipment when it is available. Also, the Agency has become a stopgap source of supply when something is needed as for a military assistance project or some other such emergency. As the years passed and as the Agency's "military" role became more a matter of custom and generally accepted, Agency military cover units became so deeply covered that their neighboring military units did not know, or forgot, that the unit near them was not a regular military unit. By that time, requisitions from these CIA units were as readily acceptable as any others and the units became easily self-supporting without any Agency funding input.

There are so many CIA cover units in the military that no accounting system can keep up with all of them. The military System also permits easy requisitioning between the services. As a result, an Army unit may requisition from a nearby Navy or Air Force unit and vice versa. A Navy CIA cover unit, for example, will requisition from an army or Air Force unit that will never question the right of that unit to draw the supplies it wants, but will simply make out cross-servicing accounting tickets and file them. The service that gave up the material will gather the supply tickets at its supply centers and then, depending upon how sophisticated its accounting system is and upon the instructions it may have received from its CIA Focal Point Office, it will either turn them in for reimbursement or pay them itself and forget about it. At all staff meetings on the subject, the CIA will protest that it pays all bills that are presented for reimbursement by the DOD and other agencies of the Government. This may be true, but the important thing is that few of the other government offices ever sort out all of these cats and dogs to the point where they are able to tally them up and render meaningful statements. As a result, the CIA gets millions of dollars of equipment each year without any attempt to collect on the part of the losing organization.

After World War II and, more importantly, after the Korean War, the military services had counted millions of dollars worth of surplus equipment in storage. One of the biggest tasks of the military logistics branches was to find some legal way to get rid of this surplus, most of which was new and unused. The laws that governed the disposal of such material required that it be made available first to the other services. Materials not wanted by the other services would then be offered on the basis of a priority list to other government agencies and departments, to state and local governments, colleges and universities, and so on, until any remaining surplus would be put up for public sale or auction.

The CIA found that it could beat this system easily by setting up certain cover units that appeared to be military units. These cover units would requisition copies of the surplus lists, would go over them carefully, and then would claim the items in the quantities desired and take delivery of them at some service base, where they would be prepared for transshipment to a military facility under CIA control. In this manner, or through variations of this method, the CIA was able to stockpile mountains of equipment.

Some of the variations on this system were rather subtle. For example: If a country that had certain elements who were working with a U.S. military unit that was really a CIA organization wanted certain items of military equipment not authorized by the mutual aid program or other such assistance plans, it might in the normal course of business ask the men in the unit what they could do to help. The unit would pass this word on to the CIA station chief, who would contact the DD/S staff to see if the equipment desired could be obtained, perhaps through surplus.

The DD/S would alert one of its cover units, and they would screen the surplus lists to find the items. In most cases, they would find them or they would find that the Army could be persuaded to list the needed number of those items as surplus, as long as they knew that they were going to be cross-requisitioned by the "Air Force," and as long as they had thus been assured that the items would not slip past the surplus lists and reach public sale. Thus the CIA would get what it wanted, free and in the quantity it wanted. They would be delivered to the CIA's own military cover supply depot and from there they would be processed to the overseas unit. All packaging, crating, and shipping would be kept within military channels and would be paid for in most instances by the military, since it would not know that the two units, the gaming one and the shipping one, were both cover units. In due time, the equipment the foreign government wanted would arrive at the "military" unit there, and that government would either have the use of the equipment or would be given the equipment as soon as transfer arrangements could be made.

It takes a lot of study of these processes and a lot of familiarity with the system to clarify how it works and how these things can happen without an exchange of funds. However, it would be incorrect and unwise to attribute to the CIA the idea that the Agency improperly uses the cover system to acquire valuable equipment without properly paying for it. It would be equally incorrect and unwise to create the idea that the military services do not account properly for the equipment they have on their inventory rosters. In normal cases, the military is quite precise about transfer of property, and there is seldom more than an occasional malfunction in the supply system. Also, the CIA has been scrupulous when it has been possible for it to pay for, by reimbursement, any equipment that the military services have furnished and for which it has been billed. The breakdown comes in the application of secrecy. Few supply people in the huge defense supply organizations know that the CIA has military units, and most of them, if they thought that the CIA was involved with some shipment, would never say a word to anyone about it. Then when the statement drawn upon a cover unit that was unfunded was not paid properly by the transfer of funded sums, the supply agency would simply pay it off from some available account rather than break security. They may be wrong to do this; but they choose this rather than taking a chance on exposing a CIA activity that might be important.

On the other hand, the CIA will state at the time they requisition items of equipment that they will pay all bills rendered. In some cases, they have put money in what amounts to an escrow account so that the DOD may draw against it. However, again the existence of such funds is usually cloaked in security, and it is seldom that the account is drawn upon. I knew of millions of dollars in such accounts that were never used, and they were lost to both organizations as they returned unclaimed to the general treasury. There is a feeling that "it is all for the Uncle anyhow," so why account for such transactions.

This may be all very well and may be a suitable reply; but when one reflects that the President and the Congress had taken great precautions to preclude the growth of an operational agency and to do this by prohibiting the Agency from building up just such supplies of equipment, this whole process becomes more important on that score than it does from the point of view of the money involved. The CIA was not supposed to have money, men, materials, or global facilities. The ease with which the Agency got around these restraints was remarkable, and it explains why so few knew at the time it was being done. One of the only tried and tested methods by which any government can control its subordinate organizations is through the purse-strings. When an organization finds ways to get around the restraints of money control and grows from within in a parasitic manner, it becomes very difficult for the usual controls to operate. Add to this the thick screen of security that has kept most of the other normal review authorities from seeing what the Agency was doing, and it is not too surprising to find that neither Congress, the President, nor the American people had realized that by 1955 the CIA had become, right before their eyes, the largest and most active peacetime operational force in the country.

Some of these actions worked in strange ways. And some of these actions were subject to the same irregularities that plagued the rest of the operations that were kept from the eyes of the public and from the controls normal to an open government. The irresponsible step in from time to time and get away with things that would be discovered in normal activities.

At one overseas base heavily involved in air activities in support of the Agency and of the foreign nationals the Agency was assisting, there were a number of aircraft of doubtful ownership commingled with other aircraft that were on "loan" from the Air Force. These aircraft were flown and maintained for the most part by a civilian facility that had the appearance of being a civilian contract carrier; but there were also a number of Air Force and Navy personnel with the unit in various capacities. The primary base unit was under Navy cover and had been for years, as a result of an earlier mission. With such a mix of personnel and equipment it was all but impossible, and certainly impractical, to attempt rigid controls in the manner customary on a real military base.

One of the planes assigned to this unit was a small transport aircraft common to all three services and built by the Beech Aircraft Corporation. This plane was flown by the officers of the staff and was used for shorter administrative flights. One of the pilots who flew it regularly came in to land in a bad crosswind one day and momentarily lost control of the plane after it had touched the ground during landing, in what is called a "ground loop." He recovered in time to keep from doing very much damage and no one was hurt. The plane needed minor repairs to be as good as new. However, this pilot, who also had maintenance authority at this conglomerate base, ordered that the plane be hauled out behind the main hangar and covered with a large protective tarpaulin. It was left there for months, and unknown to others on the base, a report was filed to Washington that it would cost more to fix the plane than it was worth; so the plane was scheduled for what the military calls "salvage." This means it is put up for sale to the highest bidder for scrap, or whatever.

No one on this base, which was primarily managed by the CIA, gave this a thought, and after a while the plane was not even missed. During this time the pilot, a major who was actually a career CIA employee serving in his Air Force reserve grade, was transferred back to an assignment in Washington at CIA headquarters. He had not been there long when he located the paperwork on that plane and made a bid in his own name and that of a friend to purchase the plane for scrap prices. Since no one else even knew where the plane was (and even if they had they would not have wanted to go to that remote place to get it) and of course, since any other bidder would have believed that the plane was a total loss, there were no other bidders. The major bought the plane in a perfectly legal maneuver.

He then applied for a brief vacation. Dashing back to the overseas station, where he was well known, he arranged with the local maintenance crews to have the plane fixed at very little expense to himself, and in no time he and his friend shipped it back to the United States. Their profit on the deal was many times more than the actual money they had invested, and no one ever knew about it because all of the records had been kept in highly classified channels.

Secrecy can be used for many purposes, and this was just one of the uses to which it can be put by those of the team who know how to get away with it.

Emboldened by this success, the same man arranged a few years later to be the project officer on a rather large air operation in Antarctica. He and his companions worked up a team that was going to accomplish some very special work on that remote continent. They had two Air Force twin-engined transport aircraft heavily modified and modernized, and then got together millions of dollars' worth of special electronic and photographic equipment. They filled the planes with equipment and still had so much left over that they had to have the Air Force fly it to Panama, where it caught up with the Navy's regular shipments on the way to McMurdo Sound. They had this priority-classed equipment put aboard, even at the cost of off-loading some of the Navy's own equipment.

Everything was brought to Antarctica, where these men established their own base satellited upon the Navy from McMurdo Sound. Whereas most of the Navy's supplies for Antarctica are either ship-borne via the Panama Canal or airborne from Christchurch, New Zealand, this group flew down the coast of South America to Argentina, and then took off from there, with elaborate assistance from the Argentine navy.

After their project had been completed for the year, they reported that one of the planes could not operate because of some sort of engine trouble, and that since the dangerous trip back with only one plane would be too hazardous, they planned to leave both aircraft and all of their equipment cached in the Antarctic. All personnel were flown out by the Navy and returned to the United States. It just happened by coincidence nearly one year later that a U.S. military officer stationed in Argentina reported the arrival of a civilian who was working with contacts in the Argentine navy to see if arrangements could be made, privately, to bring those planes out of Antarctica. This chance tip was followed up, and it was learned that the same man had decided that if he could get away with one plane, he might as well try to get away with two much larger aircraft and with the millions of dollars' worth of equipment, which was, in his mind, fair salvage somewhere on the ice cap of Antarctica. With the excellent cooperation of the Antarctic project officers on the White House staff and with the support of the Navy, all of this equipment and the planes were recovered and returned to service.

These are special cases and do not reflect upon the system so much as they do upon the actions of a few individuals. The problem is that the U.S. Government is not properly constituted to deal with such actions when they are cloaked in heavy security wraps, and the incidence of such happenings is far greater than it need be, since in most cases there should not have been any security over any of the projects. The cost of allowing the ST to operate in secrecy is high.

There are a number of aircraft that have been completely scrubbed of all usual identification, and they are operated by the services for the CIA. For those unfamiliar with the complexities involved in maintaining aircraft, it will be worth a partial explanation to show what problems arise. The huge radial engines on these large transports are all carefully marked with serial numbers, decals, and other special identifications, which are so coded and catalogued that the men who do the heavy maintenance on them in the major depots of the services can work from drawings and instructions that are in turn coded to match the engine series involved. When engines are made non-attributable, for CIA use, all of these markings are removed or changed. This means then that only certain crews can work on these engines, and they have to be cleared to know that the aircraft are special.

Sometimes, something will happen to an engine when the plane is far from its regular base. In such instances, a message is sent to the nearest Air Force base commander, and he is told to fly a maintenance crew there to get the engine and to "melt," or destroy it. Instead of working on the engine and revealing that the plane and its intended mission were classified, a costly engine is destroyed. Then that engine must be replaced by another identical non-attributable engine before the plane can continue its flight.

Sometimes things will happen to the plane itself. The Air Force had a number of special aircraft in Europe that had been converted to use for certain classified projects, although from outward appearances they were perfectly normal four-engine transports. One time, one of these aircraft had a simple nose-wheel problem. It should have been an easy thing to have it worked on at the base and returned to fight operations. However, some of the simpler maintenance work had been turned over to native teams. One such activity was the repair of nose wheels. To keep this problem from the natives, a CIA crew chief took a torch and cut several of the main electric cables in the plane, then grounded it for serious maintenance problems. He thought that this would get him the authority to hire an American contract crew that could work on the nose wheel as well as on the cables.

Since the inspection report showed very severe damage to the plane, the reviewing authority in the United States would not authorize a team to fix the plane, and instead ordered it to be salvaged. In the salvaging process, the alert CIA had one of its civilian units bid for the plane, and in a short time it was back in the air, in good shape, as the property of a civilian airline, which put it to work in its own interest and incidentally for the CIA whenever requested. This could be called an inadvertent windfall. But in any event, it was very costly and had it not been for the security measures that made the whole thing unwieldy, the damage could have been repaired easily and the Air Force would still be flying that plane.

By the late nineteen-fifties, the CIA logistics system had all it could handle all over the world. It could deliver such unit shipments as forty thousand arms by airdrop in the period of a few days or it could send aircraft and helicopters into Laos and move tens of thousands of Meo tribesmen from one part of the country to another with ease. By that time, the CIA had no less than eight hundred to one thousand units, all cover units within the DOD. This was a huge and intricate system.

The Agency did not man all of the units. Many of them were no more than a telephone number with someone to answer the phone and give information or receive calls. If, for example, a group of military personnel from a foreign country were passing through Washington on their way home after a school on a Military Aid

Program quota, and they had been told to get in touch with a certain contact, they could call a number in Washington and their contact would answer the phone and tell them where to meet him, where they were to stay, and so on. If a defector had been flown to the States, was living in some safe house, and was not permitted to leave unless he was escorted for his own safety, he could call a certain number in Washington and ask for a certain military officer, who would give him instructions of one kind or other.

Some of these "phone-drop" organizations were used for nothing more than to requisition supplies from another service. The supplying service would never know that the requisitioning outfit did not really exist. Of course, the Agency would go through the details of making certain that the units it was using were listed in the supply catalogues, in the regular military postal catalogues, and in other normal references.

Other units were manned with many people and served as active training units, storage sites, or operational facilities of one kind or another. In such cases, the manning would be either all Agency in the cover of military, or Agency and military blended together, or it might be all military supporting the Agency. In the latter case, the unit might be an Air Force Squadron that had aircraft and other equipment maintained in readiness complete with well-trained crews ready to fly out for the Agency on any of a great number of special missions. Everything possible would be done to make it appear to be a real Air Force unit.

Few people, even among those who are supposed to know all about the Agency's relationship with the DOD, have ever known exactly how many such units exist, and what is more important, what these units really do.

One day back in 1960 or 1961, it was necessary for me to brief the chairman of the JCS on a matter that had come up involving the CIA and the military. Such briefings, when they have been put on the regular agenda of the day, take place in a sort of reverse pecking order. Each item that comes before the Chiefs is briefed by its staff-supporting office from the least sensitive to the most highly classified. On this day there were a number of briefings on all sorts of subjects. The room where the Chiefs met was full and the anterooms were packed with briefing teams. One by one the teams were called in to give their briefings. As they finished, they would be dismissed, and if the Chief of any given service had any of his top-level staff there with him, he might dismiss that officer along with the briefers. (Sometimes, when one service is briefing, a Chief of another service will want to have one or more of his senior assistants there to hear the briefing with him.) As a result, as the briefings progress from least classified to most highly classified, the whole group begins to thin out. This is done with a very precise control, verging on the ritualistic.

Finally, the briefings on atomic energy matters, missiles and space, and other highly classified matters took place. Then the Chiefs began to hear some of the more closely held intelligence matters. The last item was the one that pertained to the CIA operational information. As I was ushered into the room I noted that everyone was leaving except the chairman and the commandant of the Marine Corps. The chairman was General Lyman L. Lemnitzer, and the commandant was General David M. Shoup. They were close friends and had known each other for years.

When the primary subject of the briefing had ended, General Lemnitzer asked me about the Army cover unit that was involved in the operation. I explained what its role was and more or less added that this was a rather routine matter. Then he said, "Prouty, if this is routine, yet General Shoup and I have never heard of it before, can you tell me in round numbers how many Army units there are that exist as 'cover' for the CIA?" I replied that to my knowledge at that time there were about 605 such units, some real, some mixed, and some that were simply telephone drops. When he heard that he turned to General Shoup and said, "You know, I realized that we provided cover for the Agency from time to time; but I never knew that we had anywhere near so many permanent cover units and that they existed all over the world."

I then asked General Lemnitzer if I might ask him a question. He said I could. "General," I said, "during all of my military career I have done one thing or another at the direction of a senior officer.

In all of those years and in all of those circumstances I have always believed that someone, either at the level of the officer who told me to do what I was doing or further up the chain of command, knew why I was doing what I had been directed to do and that he knew what the reason for doing it was. Now I am speaking to the senior military officer in the armed forces and I have just found out that some things I have been doing for years in support of the CIA have not been known and that they have been done, most likely, in response to other authority. Is this correct?"

This started a friendly, informal, and most enlightening conversation, more or less to the effect that where the CIA was concerned there were a lot of things no one seemed to know. It ended with those two generals asking me about matters that they had unwittingly participated in during earlier years that they had never been told about.

It was amazing, very basic, and very true that a great number of operations, some of them quite important in terms of foreign policy, and usually involving one or more foreign nations, had taken place in the guise of military activities when in reality they were not. Since the military had been used for support purposes, first in the context of war planning and later for more open and more active roles, as the CIA and the ST became more powerful and bold, the military had continued to believe that whatever it had been asked to do must have been sanctioned from above by someone.

This brings us back to the Dulles-Jackson-Correa report. One of the major undertakings of that report was to place the CIA quietly within the structure of the entire U.S. Government, ostensibly to obtain more complete secrecy when necessary. For example: It was necessary for the CIA to arrange for aircraft to enter the country quite frequently without the usual customs check that all military aircraft must undergo. In the earlier years the CIA would arrange directly or through State or Defense to have customs waive inspection of a plane with classified cargo or carrying a defector or on some other highly classified mission. Then, when such things had become more or less commonplace, the CIA would politely offer to provide a few men to work with the regular customs personnel to take the burden for such activity from them. This was the way it was put in the first place, and the customs office would gratefully accept the assistance. The CIA would go through all the necessary steps to get authorization for increasing the manpower allocations in the customs service by the number of men it planned to put there and then to make arrangements to reimburse the customs office for the payroll and other costs of the office.

This latter step would always be taken, because it would be best for the customs office to go through all of the normal motions of paying these men, including promoting them and paying for their travel or other usual expenses, so that their assignment would appear to be completely normal to all others in the office. Then, by special accounting procedures that would take place in the main office, the CIA would reimburse the Treasury Department for the money involved.

In the beginning this would all be done with elaborate open-handedness, even to the point where the new agency men would receive training and other prerequisites of the job. However, as the years passed, most of this procedure would be forgotten, and few would recall that those special assignments had even originated with the Agency. Accountants who had known how to transfer the funds would have been transferred themselves, and the Treasury Department might no longer bill for the costs involved. But the Agency men would stay on, their replacements would be carefully fitted into the manning tables, and few would even notice that they were there.

This has happened quite extensively in a great many places all throughout the Government. There are CIA men in the Federal Aviation Administration, in State, all over the DOD, and in most other offices where the CIA has wanted to place them. Few top officials, if any, would ever deny the Agency such a service; and as the appointive official departed, and his staffs came and went, the whole device would be lost with only the CIA remembering that they were still there.

Many of these people have reached positions of great responsibility. I believe that the most powerful and certainly the most useful agent the CIA has ever had operates in just such a capacity within another branch of the Government, and he has been there for so long that few have any idea that he is a long-term career agent of the CIA. Through his most excellent and skillful services, more CIA operations have been enabled to take place than can be laid at the feet of any other, more "legitimate," agent.

This was the plan and the wisdom of the Dulles idea from the beginning. On the basis of security he would place people in all areas of the Government, and then he would move them up and deeper into their cover jobs, until they began to take a very active part in the role of their own cover organizations. This is how the ST was born. Today, the role of the CIA is performed by an *ad hoc* organization that is much greater in size, strength, and resources than the CIA has ever been visualized to be.

There is another facet to this type of organization that has had a major impact upon the role of secret operations in this Government. With the spread of the influence of the CIA into so many other branches of the Federal Government, the agents found it very easy to make friends and win willing disciples in their new surroundings. There is a glamour and allure to the "fun and games" of Agency work that appeals to many people, and they go out of their way to provide support above and beyond what the CIA has ever asked for—or thought to ask for.

As a case in point, consider the U-2 project. The Lockheed Company came up with the plane, but the Air Force knew it could not use it in peacetime and thought that it might be able to get it into use by offering it to the CIA. The CIA picked up the idea and operated the whole project, provided—and this was a major "provided"—the Air Force paid for it and actively supported it with men, material, and facilities. A proposal that began as a plan to get a new aircraft on the production line for Air Force reconnaissance purposes thus became a project to get the plane flying for CIA photographic intelligence purposes. As the photographs began to come in, the input data from them began to dictate new operations that arose not from some foreign policy or national planning staff, but from intelligence sources. Intelligence input began a cycle that supported intelligence itself. A new machine, which required more and more support of its own actions, was born within the Government.

By the time of the Bay of Pigs operations, the CIA was part of a greater team, which used the Agency and other parts of the Government to carry out almost any secret operation it wanted. By that time this organization had the equipment, the facilities, the men, and the funds to carry out clandestine operations that were so vast that even on the basis of simple definition they were no longer truly secret, nor could anyone hope that they might be.

The availability of supplies and facilities made it possible for all of this to come about. The growth of the CIA and of the greater ST has resulted more from the huge success of the DD/S side of the Agency than from either the DD/P or the DD/I. When Allen Dulles had abolished the DD/A (Administration) he had put nearly everything that was not intelligence and that was not secret operations into the DD/S division. The DD/S became responsible for the function of budget and comptrollership; for personnel and for the special personnel function that is most important in the Agency, personnel cover; for communications; for research and development including that very special Agency shop that is responsible for the development of all of the very special gadgets and other devices so important to the trade of intelligence; for transportation; for facilities—a special resource so vast that few people even know 50 percent of what exists; for supply, and for maintenance.

Many of these functions, which are normal to any major enterprise, take on special meaning in the CIA. In fact every one of these general headings has buried somewhere deep in its staff special arrangements that make the Agency what it is.

Research and development is a most interesting enterprise as carried on by the CIA. For example, let us say that the CIA has a modified aircraft that it flies along the border of the Iron Curtain, or for that matter anywhere it wants to listen to electronic traffic. This monitoring airborne system is as sophisticated as the military can make it, and in many instances the CIA has been able to have even the newest military system modified to give it some special characteristics of particular use to the Agency.

In the normal pursuit of its mission, the plane cruises at altitude on a prearranged course and listens to every thing that it hears on all wavebands. After the flight, the plane lands at its Air Force home base, and the tapes it made during flight are immediately taken from the racks on the plane, sealed in shipping containers, and put on the first jet to Washington. Within twenty-four hours these tapes are processed in a special readout laboratory that might involve computerized read-out as well as human listening. As a result of this process, there might be found a certain signal that appeared as perhaps no more than a bit of static on some normal-appearing carrier wave. More detailed study of this signal reveals that it is unlike the usual static and that there is a chance that this split-second blip is something special; but there is no known system for interpreting such a signal.

A review of other tapes made in the same area might reveal that similar blips have been occurring on some of them. The CIA takes this up with the Air Force experts who designed the system and through them learns that the equipment was designed by a certain team working for a well-known manufacturer of electronic equipment. The Air Force, of course, has a contract with this manufacturer. The CIA goes to the manufacturer under the guise of the Air Force and asks what might be done to identify and if possible to read out the blips.

The manufacturer agrees to take on the problem as an overrun to the original development contract with the Air Force. The Agency people, known to the manufacturer only as Air Force people, agree. In due course, the manufacturer finds a scientist at Stanford who has experimented with a remarkable tube that seemed to promise some solutions to the problems involved. A subcontract is let, and further work is done on the tube. Finally, the manufacturer is able to demonstrate a receiver that is able to find these blips, which are actually hidden at all wave channels, and to get them recorded on tape. They are now able to get this new equipment to stretch these blips to the right length in terms of sound waves, and before long these blips are shown to contain decipherable data.

Now the development contract is terminated, and the receivers are put into production, also on the Air Force contract. As things turned out, the Air Force is able to use some of these fabulous sets itself, and it increases the production order. By this time, a small development project to which the CIA had agreed to contribute about sixty thousand dollars had grown into a total development project of more than one million dollars, with a long manufacturing and procurement contract on top of that.

The important thing in situations like this is that through this method, even when it was used honestly and properly, the services can pay out millions for the Agency without realizing it. Most of the Air Force intelligence and electronics technicians involved in this case—which though hypothetical, has its basis in fact—were not also procurement experts and had no experience in the intricacies of such financial matters. As a result, they went along thinking someone else was taking care of the money. The Agency went along, protesting that if someone sent them the bill, they would pay it. The bills were rarely if ever sent.

Such actions soon became known, and others who want work done for other reasons find the way to use this same technique. To cite a case: An Army project officer who had trouble getting his service to approve a new gun that he had been shown by a manufacturer found that a fellow officer, on a classified project, was interested in it. They demonstrated the new gun to a group, much as if it were a real Army demonstration. The manufacturer, willing to do anything to sell his new weapon, participated fully in these demonstrations and tests. He may have thought it odd that the tests had been scheduled at the Army Chemical Warfare station at Fort Detrick instead of at the Aberdeen Proving Ground where most tests are usually held; but he was selling, not asking questions, so he eagerly went along. After the tests at Detrick, there were meetings in a special section of the office of the Secretary of Defense, located near the office of the Deputy Director for Research and Engineering (DDR&E). The DDR&E representative was a prominent career civilian who had recently been made head of that office after a long tour of duty in the Office of Special Operations, where CIA matters were usually processed. In other words, this man was less an engineer than a special operations man; and he was less an Army or military counterpart than he was an Agency collaborator.

At this meeting, there were many Army officers, and there were Air Force officers. There may have been Marine and Navy officers, and there were many civilians. The manufacturer's representatives could not be faulted if they believed that they were selling their new weapon to a most highly qualified group. In fact, the main sponsor of the weapon, an Army Lieutenant Colonel in uniform, gave all appearances of being the Army representative, which he was not. The meeting ended with a consensus that the gun should be purchased in trial numbers by the Air Force for security reasons "for use by the Air Force Air Police units." Later, the Air Force did purchase tens of thousands of the new weapons, and they disappeared into the security-covered inventory of the CIA. This is a part of the story of the M-16 rifle of questionable repute in the Vietnam operations.

With the passage of time, the Agency has become more adept at getting any supplies and support it needs and in getting them supported, stored, and transported. (The story of the Agency transportation capability will be told later.) All military equipment is controlled by an elaborate supply system, and the funds that are required to develop, procure, and maintain this vast store of equipment all over the world are detailed in the budget. Anyone can easily make a case for occasional errors in such a vast system. There have been those who, along about budget time every year, show how the Air Force has purchased $.15 nuts and bolts for $28 each, how the Navy has procured 5,400,000 shrimp forks, and how the Army has been paying three times as much as the Navy for a common hospital blanket. In spite of all of this, the logistics services of the military establishment do an amazing job, and no military services in the world have ever had the support that they have provided. It is within this fabulous system that the CIA logistics experts, most of whom are retired military personnel themselves, have learned to create miracles.

There is on the books of Congress and in the Law of this country an old bit of legislation called the Economy Act of 1932. It remains in force, as amended. In theory, it is simple and important. During the early years of the depression it was found that a considerable amount of money could be saved if the Congress would permit the various departments and agencies of the Government to trade among themselves when one had a surplus that the other wanted. It used to be that each department had to keep rigid accounting of what it had and that it could not transfer what it had to another department. This Economy Act, among other things permits one department, say Agriculture, to let the Army, for example, buy desks that it may have in excess for a price to be agreed upon by both departments. This law has worked well, and it has permitted savings among all parts of the Government.

Early in its history, the CIA looked at this law and found that it could be used for some interesting purposes. The CIA might like to purchase some equipment that it could not afford or more likely, that it did not want anyone in the Government to know it had acquired. It would have one of its people, most likely "covered" in some other department, meet with the owning department and sound it out about the purchase, "in accordance with the provisions of the Economy Act of 1932, as amended." Usually, the Agency would know beforehand that the equipment was available and that the selling department would practically give it away. The Agency would then conclude the action and buy this material with funds of the department under whose cover it had entered into the agreement.

In certain cases, the buying department would require the Agency to reimburse it for the cost of the transaction; but increasingly this became a doubtful process. At other times, the CIA would approach another department, through a cover cut-out, to an office where it also had another cover arrangement.[2] These offices, bickering with each other as separate departments, would arrive at an agreement that they would actually staff through other sections to make it appear to be scrupulously legal and authentic, and then the CIA would end up with what it wanted without the expenditure of any funds.

Even the retelling of some of these arrangements sounds ridiculous, and the reader may be excused for wanting to believe that this could not have happened. Not only have things like this happened;

---

2. A cover cutout is some device or process that has been set up to circumvent or otherwise bypass normal procedure so that the connection with the CIA cannot be discovered in the normal course of business.

but some that are even more portentous. The Agency will go to any ends when it has convinced itself that it is doing so on the grounds of security. The Agency, at the constant reminder and conditioning of Allen Dulles, always believed that anything it did was all right as long as it was carrying out the will of Congress to protect its secret sources and methods.

After decades of logistical endeavors of all kinds and of all types, the Agency has acquired more than enough in hardware, in facilities, in transport and warehousing to perform all the peacetime operations it could ever dream of. And if it should come up with a specially large project, it would easily supply itself from within the hoards of other departments and agencies. To the Agency, cost is no barrier. When things can be delivered by air, they are delivered by air, regardless of cost differential. When equipment can be obtained new, it is purchased new rather than surplus, when new is available. It is not so much that the Agency was always that way; but it became spoiled, because since Louis Johnson's time, just before the Korean War, there has not been a Secretary of Defense who really concerned himself with the cost of supporting the CIA. There has not been a Secretary who knew enough about what the CIA was really doing to believe that the volume of material warranted concern over the cost. So the Agency found its pipe attached to the boundless sea, and it learned to make the most of just letting it flow in.

The same can be said of the Congress. There are no members of the House or the Senate who have ever contemplated in anywhere near exact amounts the great volume of men, money, and materials the Agency has been able to acquire and to expend without observation by those normally charged with that responsibility. The Agency excuses its own actions on the basis that it employs these methods secretly for the good of the country; thus, it does not have to expose its sources and methods as it requests men, money, and supplies in the usual manner. Once the Agency has become accustomed to this form of rationalization, there are no limits to what it and its peripheral operators will be perfectly willing to do "for the good of the country" and for the cause, always unquestioned, of anti-Communism.

CHAPTER 12

PERSONNEL: THE CHAMELEON GAME

An Australian scientist waiting at the counter of the Military Air Transport Service passenger service desk at 3:00 am felt ill at ease in these unfamiliar surroundings. He had been assured that his travel through to Washington had been arranged and that he would be met when his plane arrived from Manila at Travis Air Force Base in California. All he had in the way of instructions was a small note that said, "Major Adams will meet you upon arrival at Travis. If he should not be there, call him by base telephone, number 12–1234." The WAF on the other side of the counter could find no Major Adams listed anywhere in the Travis telephone book; but she volunteered to ring that number anyhow. A sleepy voice answered, "Special Support Squadron, Airman Jones speaking." The contact was made. "Airman Jones" appeared shortly at the passenger service desk in civilian attire and announced himself as Major Adams. The Australian had met his contact and would soon be on his way to South San Francisco airport for his commercial flight connection to Washington.

In Washington he was met again by another contact and spent two or three days at a hotel where from time to time he met various scientists and their companions. They discussed with him the meetings he would attend in Rotterdam, then later in Moscow, to join with the world's top radio astronomers in observing the latest massive antennas that were being used in Europe and in the Soviet Union. Nothing in the United States approached the sophistication of the Soviet equipment, and the Australians were far ahead with their own work. After a few days with his new friends in the scientific world, with whom he met on the basis that they were from the National Science Foundation, the Australian flew to Europe and thence to Moscow. In Europe he had more meetings with American scientists, and after the Moscow meetings he willingly discussed the advanced equipment and techniques he had seen and worked with there. He even talked about a totally new antenna concept of his own for which he hoped to get funds in Australia and which had been enthusiastically accepted by the scientists in Europe and Russia as a great advance over present fixed-parabola technology.

In return for free air travel and other amenities, this Australian had been willing to spend time with American scientists whom he knew or knew of and with certain of their friends and fellow workers. He was unaware of the fact that among those "fellow workers" were CIA personnel eager to learn all they could about the technology of the Russians. Advanced radio antenna work used in astronomical observations could, with minor changes, also be used in radar antennas for an advanced air defense system.

The recruitment of personnel for such special and fleeting requirements is one of the many skills of the Personnel Division of the CIA under the leadership of the DDIS. It is another of the logistics functions of that Directorate that performs major miracles for the CIA and even for the ST.

In the beginning, when a new organization is formed in the Government, such as HEW (Health, Education and Welfare), HUD (Housing and Urban Development), and others, it is customary to flesh out the unit with staff and resources from other organizations assembled for that purpose. Since the CIA was a totally new organization, this normal process could not be relied upon to build a professional staff in the period of time required for the Agency to become effective. Former OSS alumni from World War II were pulled in from wherever they were at the time and they were augmented as rapidly as possible by personnel from other units within the Government who had the special training for intelligence type of work. This meant that the FBI was "raided" to the point that its director called upon the DCI to ask that such raids be halted. Many other early personnel came from World War II military resources of all kinds. The straight-line intelligence personnel went into DD/I and a large number of logistics specialists went directly into the DD/S.

It was startling to see them take on new life as they began to realize that they no longer worked under the routine red tape and restraints of the military service in which they had been trained. Men who had fought to keep supply levels up to authorized quotas now found that they could exceed quotas with abandon. Men who had watched budget figures year after year to build little caches to take care of essential needs found that they could draw upon funds that never seemed to run out. The same was true for personnel needs, for transportation, and for communications. It was not long before the Agency was quite adequately manned, and wherever there were shortages, it was able quite easily to find military personnel who would voluntarily accept an assignment. As a result, thousands of military men served with the Agency from its inception.

This turned out to be fortunate. No long range organization can prosper with most of its employees in the same general age bracket. The Agency, having been born in the immediate postwar era, inherited people who were generally in the same age group. The men at the top and the men in lesser jobs all were about the same age. This meant that as the years rolled on, the openings at the top would be few and the log jam of those in lower grades would be terrific, stifling career development. The overhead of "disposable" military personnel helped clear up this problem. Therefore as all personnel, military and civilian, rose to higher positions, there became fewer of these higher positions. The military could be returned to their services and the overhead easily weeded out, leaving room for the more senior careerists. This helped, but it was not a total solution.

The Agency put into operation a Junior Officer Training program (JOT) something like an ROTC program. In fact, JOT drew many of its men from the college ROTC resources. As these men filtered into regular jobs they replaced military men who went back to their parent services. Meanwhile, the Agency pushed an "early-out" retirement program and other projects to clear up the age-bound overhead.

This had an interesting and perhaps unintentional bonus effect. A large number of men who had served with the Agency as volunteers had rotated back to their own military services, and in some cases, back to other government departments to pursue other tasks. However, the lure of "fun and games" is great, and most of these men still retained much of the old desire to play the intelligence game. The Agency found itself with willing alumni in all parts of the Government, and they made use of these men in every way possible.

This can be illustrated in the Pentagon Papers since that is an available source of names and other statistics. A quick survey of the Pentagon Papers as published by *The New York Times* reveals a random listing of military officers of general and admiral rank, all of whom in one way or other took part in the early activities in Vietnam. Some of them served with the Agency for a number of years and went back and forth from Agency assignments to military assignments. And in most cases the military assignment was simply an Agency cover assignment under which they served at the direction of CIA superiors. It is a most important fact that most of the political and military leaders of Asian countries from Korea to Pakistan could easily be sympathized with for not being able to discover whether the "military" officers with whom they were dealing were military or were CIA. Most of the generals mentioned in the Pentagon Papers were involved in CIA activities while they were in Southeast Asia and were not under the operational control and direction of the DOD.

When Marshall Sarit of Thailand met with an American Army general to discuss the buildup of the Thailand border patrols on the

Laos border, he may have believed that he was talking with a U.S. Military officer and that the results of their talks were going to be achieved with the direct assistance of the U.S. military. He had no way of knowing that the results of his talks were going to be carried out by "U.S. military" under cover who were working under the direction and operational control of the CIA. The same can be said for such talks with Somanna Phouma and Phoumi Nosavan in Laos and for Generals Thieu and Ky in Vietnam. The Diem regime, far back in those early and formative days of the Vietnam operations, never did know who they were talking with, and Ngo Dinh Diem had to rely upon the few real American friends he had, such as Ed Lansdale, a bona fide U.S. Air Force general, but also a man who worked solely for the CIA for more than a decade. Diem could unravel some of the deals he became involved in by calling his friend Lansdale in Washington; but he could not get similar help from the contacts he had in Saigon. The string of generals who appeared in Saigon from 1954 through 1964—who were really not generals— would have been enough to confuse anyone. In fact, real generals stayed away from Saigon for fear of being labeled "CIA" by their contemporaries back in Honolulu or Washington.

The other side of the coin was equally significant. Military men found the CIA an easy means to promotion. As a result, they longed to get more of that valuable duty. Men who would have retired as majors, lieutenant colonels, and colonels found that the CIA was the easy road to generals' stars. There are a great number of generals, even up to the full four-star rank, who would never have made that grade, and who never would have made general at any level had it not been for their CIA assignments and the role they played in the development of the Vietnam operations. There were a great many of these men; this force alone has had a considerable impact upon the nature of Vietnamese events and upon the escalation of activities in Vietnam back in the days when small but catalytic events propelled the early actions into a massive campaign.

The same thing was happening in Washington. As men who served under Allen Dulles went out into other parts of the Government— into the Institute for Defense Analysis, the Rand corporation, certain

key university jobs, into select businesses and major foundations—
Dulles found that he had a massive instrument upon which he
could orchestrate events as he wished. It was not his technique to
lay deep plans and to use all of these resources in pursuit of these
plans. Rather, it was his game to continually call upon the vast and
continuing resource of secret intelligence to supply him with input
data, with the raw events that he could then toss upon the keyboard
to sound their own chords across the field of foreign relations.

This may sound a bit weird at first telling; but how else can anyone
explain the random series of events that has happened in the names
of foreign affairs and anti-Communism since 1955? All personnel
who had trained with the Agency had learned enough about its
ways, its freedoms, and its ability to circumvent normal bureaucratic
red tape, and were somewhat spoiled. Later, when they had gone out
into other departments and agencies of the federal government, they
would find themselves, at times, frustrated in their everyday activities. They tended to return to their Agency affiliations and found
that they could still get things done through Agency channels. They
also served as Agency conduits for things which the Agency wanted
done where they now worked. This developed a loose but effective
network, with tentacles that reached out in all directions.

There was a group that was utilized as airline operators. They went
into various countries such as Ethiopia, Iran, Jordan, Laos, Vietnam,
and many others and worked to establish airlines, many of which
ostensibly were national air carriers. These airlines were put together
by common interests, part civilian business and part clandestine
operations. In such cases secrecy was not really very deep; but it was
used to shield the identity of the interests concerned from other
parties in the U.S. The host government certainly knew who was
behind the airlines, and they knew that there was more money being
spent than was coming in through commercial revenues.

These airlines and their supporting bases, which in many countries
were relatively costly enterprises, became increasingly modern. They
began with what were called World War II surplus aircraft, such as
the old C-46 and the C-54. Then they began to get hand-me-down
Constellations and DC-6 and DC-7 aircraft, which had been the

backbone of the U.S. airline fleet before the advent of jet transports. Most of these countries did not have the pilots and other personnel essential to the operation of modern aircraft, so the Agency cover units filled these spaces. Soon, national pride dictated that these airlines have the finest modern equipment in order that their neighbors would not outshine them. It was not long before a number of these small and impecunious airlines began to flaunt their new jets before the public, from Manila to Tehran.

These operations all began as modest havens for personnel who had been affiliated with the Agency or who were still with the Agency but gave the appearance of having left. By 1960 the CIA had grown very large in comparison with the figures that had been projected and with the figures that various controlling authorities thought the Agency had. By the time of the Congo problems and the uncertainties of other emerging African nations, the CIA had not less than forty stations scattered all through that continent, all of them very active and all of them manned with everything from U.S. military to non-attributable civilians of all kinds. The agency that Harry Truman thought would be his quiet intelligence arm had become a vast organization, which no one could control for the simple reason that the Agency was no longer the finite organization that had been created by law and then built with properly appropriated funds. It was now a tremendous force, using its own funds as an ante to open the big game, and then playing the big game with money belonging to most of the rest of the Government.

In the Government, people (or as the bureaucratic euphemism goes, "bodies") are controlled by the appropriation and then authorization of funds. Thus, any Government organization is permitted to have precisely so many people; and to exactly control that number of people, the Congress appropriates only enough money to pay that number and no more. This is usually an effective method of control, provided measures to evade them are not cloaked in security. When the Air Force had the problem of manning the vast space center at Cape Canaveral, it found that it did not have sufficient people for the task but that it could get funds for the maintenance of that huge and fast-growing complex. So the Air Force obtained enough funds to contract the operation and maintenance of that base. Thus several companies bid for the job of operating the big space center, and Pan American Airlines was awarded the contract. By this device the Air Force could man a huge complex, with money and not with people. There are many obvious advantages of this method of performing a housekeeping task.

The Agency witnessed the simplicity and effectiveness of this action and began to use it for its own ends. It would transfer funds to another department of the Government, and in return it would get people. Thus the Army, for example, could truthfully say that it had perhaps forty-two people in the Military Advisory and Assistance Group (MAAG) in Athens, and yet any visitor to the MAAG offices in Athens could easily see that there were more than one hundred people working throughout that big building. As a matter of fact, some visiting Senators noticed this and commented on it. They were told, with a straight face by the local MAAG officials, that the Army did have only forty-two people there and that they would be glad to have the Department of the Army in Washington furnish the Senators with an exact accounting of those people. This satisfied the visitors, and upon their return to Washington they were given audited figures from the U.S. Army, certifying to the fact that the Army had spent no more than "X" dollars on personnel in Athens and therefore could not have had more than forty-two people there.

This is an old story. There are military bases that have been closed by the services. The records, based upon money audits, show that the bases are in fact closed, yet the base had been reopened by the service concerned with CIA funds and for CIA support purposes. There is a small but uniquely self-contained Army base near Washington that was closed in such a manner years ago. It is still open, and it is so active that it has a very lively housekeeping function, including a PX and commissary that services not only the special CIA elements on the base but a select group of senior retired military and naval personnel who live in baronial luxury in the adjacent horse country.

There is also a massive Army post that has been closed many times. No news is ever published to show that it has been opened;

but there is always a fanfare when it is closed. This huge, forested reservation is one of the best hunting preserves in the Washington vicinity, and it is frequented by noble parties of ranking military and other high government officials who travel to their shooting sites on an old Army railroad in quaint old cars—in real luxury attained by few people short of Hugh Hefner and the Onassis set.

There was a time when the late Senator Harry Byrd, father of the present Senator, used to have to intervene on behalf of a few of his select clientele, because he kept receiving letters and telephone calls about bombs and other explosives bursting at a "closed" U.S. Navy station. The Senator had these messages sent to the Honorable Secretary of the Navy, who in turn would pass them to the Chief of Naval Operations and thence on to the proper authorities in the Norfolk area. Time after time the Navy would reply to the good Senator that there were no explosives being detonated in the area and that the base in question was closed and secured by a proper guard force.

This exchange of correspondence went on for about three unpleasant cycles, until the Senator felt that he should bring it to the attention of the Secretary of Defense. Thus started an investigation that finally brought a harried naval officer to the Office of Special Operations at the Secretary of Defense level to ask if by some chance there might be some highly classified activity going on at that "closed" Navy base that the Navy did not know about. It was found that the Agency was in fact doing some demolitions and explosives training with a special group of foreign agents whom they did not want to expose at the Special Forces training site at Fort Bragg, North Carolina. The Agency was taking these men, from time to time, from Fort Bragg to this abandoned Navy base where it had set up some special training for them. Then the Office of Special Operations asked the Agency to move its training to another site, the Navy was given a polite but obtuse answer, from this the Navy wrote apologies to the Senator, and eventually things were settled graciously with the Senator's constituents.

These things, of course, are not earthshaking and are not too different from similar uncoordinated activities that can happen in any large operation. But the Agency had acquired the power to carry out such activities in spite of restrictions and in spite of other plans and policy. It was not just the one MAAG in Athens in which Agency people were hidden, but it was almost every MAAC all over the world. In fact, wherever the military might have some small out-of-the-way outpost in a foreign country where the Agency might wish to install one of its people, it would not take long before the position would be assigned to the Agency so that it could have its own man there. In many countries, the vast Military Air Transport Service network (now military Airlift Command, or MAC) would have only two or three men to handle landing and take-off requirements for a few planes a week. Such small pockets of men in remote places and with little apparent activity became havens for CIA personnel. And when activity grew in such locations, as it inevitably did, the Agency would make funds available to the parent service for more bodies, and the manning would be increased to provide for an invisible military expansion. Later auditing of the strength of the service involved would never show the increase. The Agency would never have to show the increase either, because all it had done was expend dollars and this would not be questioned.

One of the things Allen Dulles achieved shortly after the submission of this report to President Truman was the approval of an amendment of the National Security Act of 1947. The amendment was passed in 1949. Among other things, it gave the CIA much more latitude in the expenditure of and accounting for its authorized funds. As a result, all the DCI had to do was to personally certify that the money had been spent properly, and there would be no further review. It was not thought at the time that money such as this would be used to make major changes in the personnel strengths of supporting Government departments. This device was used, however, and it permitted vast expansion of CIA manning-strength in the guise of other Government department jobs. All of this went without review and audit.

By the time the Agency was ready to participate in an operation as large as the Indonesian campaign of 1958, it had the resources to open foreign bases, to create an entire supporting Tactical and

Transport Air Force, and to demand the services of naval supporting forces. A former World War II air base on a remote Pacific island was reopened and put into commission, and a whole fleet of aircraft was put into major overhaul bases in the States to create an attack force of substantial capability. A rather considerable Air Transport force was able to deliver deep into Indonesia tens of thousands of weapons and the ammunition and other equipment necessary to support such a force, all by airdrop. The CIA had become a major power by 1958 and was ready to enter the world arena as the core of the greatest peacetime operational force ever assembled.

By this time the Agency was not working alone. It was getting the willing and most active support of other elements of the Department of Defense and from the White House and parts of the Government. It was becoming a broad-gauge ST. The CIA was being diverted from its original role by the actions of men who took their motivation from the substance of secret intelligence inputs and turned them into response activities as large as many overt military campaigns. Yet, for all of this, they covered their work in deep security, which of course was a false security, and veiled their true intentions and actions from the rest of the Government, and especially from those whose normal task and responsibility it would have been to carry out such actions had they been so directed by proper policy and authority.

In 1949 the Congress enacted what is called The Central Intelligence Agency Act of 1949, which restated the powers and duties of the CIA as they had been in the National Security Act of 1947, and added some interesting paragraphs concerned primarily with money and personnel. By 1949 it had become apparent that a great number of the personnel assigned to the CIA would be military personnel and that this situation would continue. Thus the new Act spelled out the terms and conditions of such assignments and did this in a manner that would not appear to expose or compromise the system; yet the whole procedure appears in clear text within the law. The clear text is written as though it were a description of the duties of the DCI or of the DDCI only;

however, it is actually applicable to all military personnel on duty with the Agency:

(2) ... the appointment to the office of Director, or Deputy Director, of a commissioned officer of the armed services, and his acceptance of and service in such office, shall in no way affect any status, office, rank, or grade he may occupy or hold in the armed services, or any emolument, perquisite, right, privilege, or benefit incident to or arising out of any such status, office, rank, or grade. Any such commissioned officer shall, while serving in the office of DCI, or DDCI, continue to hold rank and grade not lower than that in which serving at the time of his appointment and to receive the military pay and allowances (active or retired) as the case may be, including personal money allowance payable to a commissioned officer of his grade and length of service for which the appropriate department shall be reimbursed from any funds available to defray the expenses of the CIA. He also shall be paid by the CIA from such funds an annual compensation at the rate equal to the amount by which the compensation established for such position exceeds the amount of his annual military pay and allowances.

(3) The rank and grade of any such commissioned officer shall, during the period in which such commissioned officer occupies the office of DCI or DDCI, be in addition to the numbers and percentages otherwise authorized and appropriated for the armed services of which he is a member.

This is a most important feature of CIA personnel policy. Note that the law states that "the appropriate department shall be reimbursed from any funds available to defray the expenses of the CIA." The CIA is authorized to use money to buy people, and as long as they have the money, they can add people. This is one reason why few people really know how many personnel the Agency has; and why even these few may not know exactly, because so many of the cover people have been lost within the labyrinth of the total Government.

Another key phrase is that in Paragraph 3, wherein it states, "The rank or grade of any such of commissioned officer shall . . . be in addition to the numbers and percentages otherwise authorized . . .

for the armed service . . ."The military services, as other departments and agencies of the Government, are bound precisely to certain total personnel strengths and to the percentage of rank and grade throughout those totals. This is an exact amount, and one that must be maintained and accounted for at all times. However, the CIA is not so bound. Thus the services are permitted to provide as many personnel as the CIA requests and can pay for, to the extent that the services simply deduct those totals by rank and grade from their own strict manpower ceilings. As a result, the services encourage certain personnel to join the CIA, and certainly do not discourage them from leaving the roles of the services for that purpose. In a sense, the more the better. Some five thousand or ten thousand military personnel in the CIA are just that many less for the military budget to account for and just that much more strength for the CIA, which it accounts for by "reimbursement."The Central Intelligence Agency Act of 1949 further underscores this bookkeeping device in favor of the CIA in the following manner:

Par 403j. CIA: appropriations; expenditures.

(a) Notwithstanding any other provisions of law, sums made available to the Agency by appropriation or otherwise may be expended for purposes necessary to carry out its functions, including (1) personal services, including personal services without regard to limitations on types of persons to be employed . . . (2) supplies, equipment, and personnel and contractual services otherwise authorized by law and regulations, when approved by the Director.
(b) The sums made available to the Agency may be expended without regard to the provisions of law and regulations relating to the expenditure of Government funds; and for objects of a confidential, extraordinary, or emergency nature, such expenditures to be accounted for solely on the certificate of the Director.

Not only, then, is the CIA not required to account for the number and grade of all of its people by virtue of the fact that it is authorized to use money to buy people, without regard to other law; but as we see in these latter phrases, the CIA is not required to account for the money it spends either. In 1949 this was a reasonable piece of legislation. The reader may judge for himself whether this same reasonableness applies today and tomorrow.

There is another portion of this Act that touches upon another special facet of the personnel policies of the CIA. It states that "Whenever the Director, the Attorney General and the commissioner of Immigration shall determine that the entry of a particular alien into the United States for permanent residence is in the interest of the national intelligence mission, such alien and his immediate family shall be given entry into the United States for permanent residence without regard to their inadmissibility under the immigration or any other laws and regulations or to the failure to comply with such laws and regulations pertaining to admissibility: provided, that the number of aliens and members of their immediate families entering the United States under authority of this section shall in no case exceed one hundred persons in any one fiscal year." The common basis of understanding of the provisions of this paragraph is usually given as an allowance made for a valuable defector or official who might not otherwise be able to come into the country for such illegal reasons as that he was patently a Communist or at least a native and citizen of a Communist country. Certainly, in arranging for such defections the DCI and his agents must be able to guarantee to the defector that he and his family will be accepted permanently into the United States.

This is the surface reason for this portion of the law. However, we discuss it here in this chapter on personnel because there are many more "illegal" aliens brought into the country who have been recruited as agents than there are defectors. In one sense of the words, "illegal alien" and "defector" may be about the same thing. However, there cannot be much confusing the roles of defector and agent. Most defectors would not submit to becoming active agents and to going back into the world of clandestine intrigue. However, many men serve the United States who are, in a sense, totally citizens of the world. These men are technically United States citizens by virtue of the application of the above cited law, but they also have been given "citizenship" in other countries as cover. These are extremely intricate ploys that require considerable time, money, and effort to maintain, as well as the dedicated daring of the men so occupied. Some of these men are pilots, navigators, and members of other highly specialized professions, and the least of them would titillate a true-life James Bond on most scores.

They are, of course, but a nucleus of a greater segment of the Agency. There are a great number of non-U.S. citizens who work for the Agency in many capacities. Filipinos, for example, appear in the wake of so many CIA operations, including the Bay of Pigs and many Indochina projects, because there are a large number of skilled Philippines citizens in the regular or contract employ of the Agency.

With such a variegated personnel congregation, the CIA has been given very special authority with respect to retirement. This, too, is spelled out in plain language in the CIA Act of 1949, some of which has the same double meaning as the bits which we have dissected above. Retirement is a special thing for the "deep" Agency employee. If by circumstance any such employee must retire for reasons of health or other infirmity, the Agency is burdened to assure that whatever attention and treatment he may get will at no time result in disclosures that might occur during anesthesia, treatment by drugs, or during other periods when the principal might not be in full control of his mental processes. Furthermore, the CIA must remain concerned about the locale in which such people choose to retire, to assure that they are not unduly exposed to dangerous influences. The not-too-infrequent problems with alcohol and even hard drugs place a special burden upon the Agency. All of these men have been involved in many highly classified matters. All of them have at one time or another been "on the black box" (polygraph), and all of them have been debriefed; but these are no more than the routine precautions that a large government agency can take. Much more remains that must be done. A thorough debriefing may underscore the zones of deep security; but it cannot erase memories, the activity of the brain, and the area of human weaknesses. As more and more men reach retirement age, these problems are increasing. One solution for a great percentage of this problem lies in the area of rapid, effective, and continuing declassification of those numberless episodes that certainly have no reason to be classified. As with so many other things, unnecessary security measures crop up as an artificial generator of problems, whereas many of the problems would go away if unnecessary classification could be ended.

The remaining special characteristic of CIA personnel activity is that which is known in the trade as "cover." Except for the true and overt intelligence employee and other strictly administrative and service types, all Agency employees live under some form of cover. The great majority live out their days with the Agency as Department of Defense employees. Many others have other common cover, that cover which is essential for no more than their credit cards, driver's licenses, and other public documents, just so they will not have to say that they are employed by the CIA.

From this base, the vast intricacies of cover become manifold as the nature of the individual's work increases in areas of high specialization and security. Sometimes, cover is changed, and the man must go through a transition period and develop a whole new character, as when he may have served as a Navy man at one station and then must become an Army man at another. Such situations are rare, because of the ease with which such cover is blown with the passage of time.

Some of the deepest and most total cover exists right inside the U.S. Government itself. Some of the most buried of CIA men have been employed by other departments and agencies for years, and only a few know any longer that they are really CIA. This is a special use of cover, but the CIA gets more per capita benefit from these men than from any others of the profession.

There are other deep cover personnel all over the world; but their existence and occupation is not the subject of this book. That they are there is enough. Some of them exist to assure that others in precarious positions can exist, and the rupture of the thin thread that supports them all is fraught with personal danger to them and their networks. These men are a part of the trade, and all countries know about the profession.

Many people have tried to estimate the total personnel strength of the CIA. This is categorically a useless objective pursued by amateurs. First, there are the open, professional intelligence people. Next there is the vast army of support personnel, many of whom are buried as deeply as the "fun and games" types; upon them depends the success of the clandestine side of the house absolutely. This is a very large group, and it is certainly not all within the structure of the Agency. Then there is the DD/P (the Directorate of Plans) and all that it encompasses. In most respects, this operation is the largest by far, and in certain aspects the border between where DD/P begins and DD/S ends is seldom clear.

Add to all of this the great supporting structure behind both DD/P and DD/S, such as that which exists in Air America and other corporate subsidiaries of the worldwide Agency, and this will include tens of thousands of non-U.S. personnel. For example, Air America alone has no less than four thousand employees in Thailand and not less than four thousand more in Taiwan as of 1972.

Beyond these fringes, there are additional thousands of CIA camp followers. There are members of the business world who enroll themselves or who have become enrolled for various reasons in the lure of "fun and games"; there are people from the academic world, the publications field, and so on. And since the limits of the CIA personnel rosters are really only the limits of how much money that Agency can put its hands on, even the groupings herein set forth simply serve to give evidence of what surrounds us. Would anyone wish to conjecture whether the CIA has been on the moon?

CHAPTER 13

COMMUNICATIONS: THE WEB OF THE WORLD

Perhaps the greatest achievement of modern times is the communications revolution. Time and distance are all but obliterated by the speed and totality of worldwide communications networks—even outer space networks. We have witnessed a man stepping onto the moon in the full view of live and instant television. We have listened to the President as he placed a call to the men on the moon and talked with them, just as you and I would talk to other men. As this is being written, a satellite laboratory is speeding through uncharted space on its way to the planet Jupiter and beyond. All of these wonders of physical science and of man's ingenuity are in the hands of the ST. The intelligence community has absolutely unlimited communications power, and there is literally no place to hide from it.

The Russians may wish to test fly a new bomber. To do this, they must arrange an intricate communications system between the crew, the instruments in the plane, monitoring airborne aircraft and other stations. The CIA and its sister agency, the NSA, will hear the communications support of the flight and will interpret all of the coded information almost as easily as the Russians themselves who are monitoring it. The Russians will orbit a satellite with intricate and complicated telemetering equipment aboard, designed only for their own ears. The long antenna of the CIA/NSA, among others— United States and foreign—will monitor this satellite and read it out with ease directly proportional to the skill, technology, and energy they have invested in such things.

A small group of men will meet secretly in a room to discuss the overthrow of a government or to make plans to meet the agent of a foreign power. They will have with them an expert, trained in the high skill of electronic debugging. He will have checked their room and tested the telephone; yet every word they say will be recorded by a gang-monitor at a central switch belonging to the telephone company where all conversations, on any line, being made by anyone with any telephone in that huge network can be monitored with ease.

Soviet messages transmitted by a special device that varies its transmission frequency often and unexpectedly and that has the ability to send a long message in the briefest "squirt" of time will be monitored and recorded accurately. Massive all-wave and all-frequency band receivers with high-speed scanning capability have the means to capture the "squirt messages" and then to draw them out until they are intelligible enough to be turned over to the computers for decoding.

Even infrared signals, sound signals, and earth vibrations, such as are caused by railroad trains and mining operations, are recorded and translated into intelligence. The hum of high energy transmission lines carrying various loads gives indications of peak periods of line usage. There are no secrets.

As Norbert Wiener said years ago, ". . . society can only be understood through a study of the messages and the communication facilities which belong to it"; and ". . . development of these messages and communication facilities, messages between man and machines, between machines and man, and between machine and machine, are destined to play an ever-increasing part." And he adds, ". . . the theory of control in engineering, whether human or animal or mechanical, is a chapter in the theory of messages."[1]

In these modern times it may be added that the theory of control of governments is also another chapter in the theory of messages. That organization that controls the communication system will have in its power the ability to control the government. One of the greatest attributes of the communications system is its use in the development of feedback, the ability to generate future action—usually response—by the sensing of inputs from past performance. The total communications system makes it possible for the intelligence organization to collect and then to grade a great volume of information and to cull from this, those bits that will be made into the daily briefing and the essence of the current intelligence portfolio.

More than anything else, it is this tremendous communications system that makes the Agency operational system what it is. From all over the world, messages of all kinds pour in from agents buried in all sorts of places and making all sorts of contacts. From all over the world, small bits of information gleaned from all kinds of instrumental communications equipment and advanced sensors feed information back into the centers of collection. Behind all of this, there are action officers who evaluate and process the bits that are culled and selected from the gross input from all sources.

Whenever one of these action officers discovers something special, he will do his best to see that it is brought to the attention of his superiors. The system is so constructed that such data moves rapidly from the lower, gaining echelon, to the middle management areas where it is again weighed and evaluated. If the information survives this first sorting process, the action officer will be directed to go back to his source, whether it is mechanical or human, to seek further information to enhance the first bits. The occupational characteristic in this whole operation is that the action begins with the receipt of information. What happens afterwards is generally re-action. The message input becomes a control mechanism itself. The area of interest may build rapidly and require response in hours, or it may cover

---

1. *The Human Use of Human Beings*, New York: Doubleday & Co., 1954.

a period of months or even years. With each round of traffic the overall pattern begins to shape itself, and gradually the little projects become big ones. Then more and more people are put on the job, and responsibility for project development is moved higher and higher up the chain of command, until finally it will be considered for some sort of major action directly under the control of the DD/P and his senior staff.

The fact that information is sought and pursued effectively must not be overlooked or ruled out. When certain events take place, experience teaches that others may follow, and the intelligence machinery will be set in motion to look for such things. This is particularly true in long-range projects. In modern manufacturing, it is impossible to assemble things like television sets or motorcycles without a system of marking and coding the parts so that they may be assembled properly in any plant having that know-how; and so that spare parts may be ordered that will fit the original set properly. Modern manufacturing requires that parts and major assemblies be marked for cost control and inventory purposes. In many instances the marking and coding systems used are very sophisticated. Thus, if a Japanese solid-state transistor radio is put together using "Ten Nines" germanium (the element of germanium pure to .9 to the tenth power), the tiny transistors will be marked with a code that proves they are the genuine product and that they are of that quality.

This not only signifies that the transistors are a quality item; but it also indicates that the Japanese manufacturer has reached that level in the state-of-the-art that permits him to make and use such superior materials and techniques. The same is true for alloys, tolerances, and other things that are essential to quality work. Thus, if an agent buys several television sets in a foreign country and takes them apart to study them, he will find all of the subassemblies, down to tiny bits, coded and marked. If in the process he should find some novel, rare, or extremely precise technique, he will look further into the production methods of that factory and of that country to see what this means.

In a country like the Soviet Union with a highly developed nuclear program and a superior missile and space manufacturing capability, it is to be expected that every so often new telltale discoveries will be made by finding some little item in an exported product that signifies a technological achievement, and perhaps even a new breakthrough. It is almost impossible for any sophisticated manufacturing system to conceal such developments once they have gone into mass production. Furthermore, serial numbers that usually accompany the marking program will show development serially, and one item acquired in an Asian country may carry one series of numbers that link with others found in a Latin American country. Reconstruction of the series which the codes, markings, and numbers reveal will give a quite accurate indication of rate of production, among other things.

From such leads, the system then puts its agents to finding out whether these new metals, techniques, or ideas have developed from the space program, from weapons systems work, or what. The communications system feeds all of this back, and agents all over the world are coordinated in their development of this information speedily and accurately, as if they were assembling some massive jigsaw puzzle.

So all communications bits are not just happenstance; but the distinction usually lies in the difference between intelligence collection and special operations. Since it is our objective to look more closely into the operational efforts of the ST, it is then more in character to see the communications network as a great machine that continually feeds bits of action information into a system that is prepared to respond whenever the "communist-inspired subversive insurgency" button is pushed.

The ambassador to any foreign country is by Presidential appointment the senior official and representative of the Government of the United States. In peacetime, before World War II, his role was relatively uncomplicated, and most of the work done by the ambassador and his staff had to do with the processing of visas and taking care of traveling dignitaries and businessmen. Since World War II, the role of the ambassador has become much more complex. He is still the senior representative of his country, but now he may have with him in the country of his appointment a senior military officer and perhaps even a UN command with U.S. military components. He will have a senior CIA station chief, and he will have many other government officials, such as those from the Departments of Labor, Commerce, Agriculture, and other agencies.

In spite of all of this, the Ambassador is still supposed to be the head of the country team, and all other Americans are supposed to be under his control. Special arrangements have been made where military units have active roles within that country as a part of larger organizations such as NATO. Troops move in and out of the country, and he is informed about such things but he rarely enters into any official contact with them. With the CIA, things are different, although they protest in public that they are always subservient to the ambassador. One of the areas this is most noticeable in is communications. The ambassador has communications channels directly from his post to the State Department. The ambassador has the authority to contact the Secretary of State directly, and some ambassadors, like Galbraith in India, find reason even to contact the President directly. These are exceptions and certainly not the rules of the game.

When an ambassador communicates with State, his messages are received by the geographical-area desk responsible for his country. From there they are processed to the Secretary, Under Secretaries, and wherever else they need to go. Much of this routine is a protocol, which has developed over the years, and much of it is dictated by true security precautions, which demand that diplomatic matters be handled with secrecy and discretion.

In accordance with these practices, the other members of the embassy, such as the labor attach and the agricultural experts, all utilize the embassy communications channels and then rely upon the Department of State to make distribution for them in Washington to their own departments. The same is true of military attach traffic. And in many cases embassy channels may carry certain CIA traffic. But this is not the limit of the CIA capability. In every country the Agency station chief has access in one way or other to direct communications contact with the CIA in Washington and when necessary he has direct contact to the DCI.

The global U.S. military system is without question the most massive, the most powerful, and the most capable communications system in existence. However, the best and most efficacious system in the world belongs to the CIA. In making this statement, allowance should be made for the capability of the National Security Agency, but that is more or less a part of the military system and need not be explored here. The CIA is able to cover the entire world, not like a blanket, but like a rapier. There is no place it cannot reach out to get to an agent or to a busy station chief on its own secure facilities. In doing this, the Agency makes use of all kinds of communications; some are considered rather old and crude but effective, and others are highly sophisticated.

Early in its buildup the CIA obtained the services of one of the military's top communications giants, General Harold McClelland. General McClelland began with a typical military base system and then let brains and technology run their course. He died in 1966 and left behind a superior system and the men to operate it.

When a U-2 is thousands of miles away and all by itself over hostile lands, it is tracked silently by sensitive devices that provide assurance that it is still in operation and on course to a hidden destination. When an agent has made a contact in Istanbul or Koforidua he is able, if he so arranges, to be continually in contact with a back-up agent, either to record his conversation or to provide directions and advice for other activities that may arise. Agents may have effective radios built inconspicuously into a suit coat, antenna and all, and they have motoring pickups (bugs) of fantastic capability and design. But above all this, the most important communications are provided all the time between the station chief—the man who is the prime mover in any given area and his boss in Washington.

One of the most radical things about the CIA network is that it does not have to go through any intermediate echelons. In State, the ambassador goes through the desk man, and woe befall the ambassador who tries to avoid that simple and red-tape structure. In the military the commanders overseas must go through their in-between military joint command chiefs in addition to the various levels of their own service echelons. Not so with the CIA station chief. When he wants to contact the DCI or the DD/P, he gets on the transmitter and he gets his man. Communications travel with the speed of light;

yet many of the finest systems in existence are slowed down by the necessity of going through channels and then of decoding, review action, and encoding for retransmittal. The Agency avoids most of this on its essential traffic. The Agency may have a man who works day and night in a full-time military assignment in India; but when that man has something to send to the CIA, he gets it out through his station chief right to Washington, and none of the military channels will ever see it. The same applies to the ambassador.

There are protests from time to time, and the Agency, for its own bureaucratic well-being, will retransmit a "clear" message by way of State channels or military channels to make it appear that a given wire of the same date and time group was transmitted properly. But when the chips are down, the "hot" message, the one that really got the action done, would have been transmitted by Agency circuits first.

Of course, the reason given for all of this is to provide security over its sources and methods. The same old chestnut appears every time and is swallowed by most of official Washington year after year. There are cases when security for just that reason is essential, but for every one of those occasions that are true and fully justifiable, there are perhaps ten thousand or a hundred thousand times when such security has not been the case, and the CIA separate and direct channel has been used for Agency reasons alone.

For example: There have been times when the Agency wanted to get something done in a certain country but the staff in Washington felt that is should be done on the basis of some agent input of one kind or other and its relationship to other information they had or wanted to use. However, the man in the field, not realizing that Washington wanted it done in a certain manner, did not come up with the exact language the Agency needed to present the idea to the Special Group for action. The Agency would find itself in a position not unlike a player in the parlor game of charades. It was making all the suggestive moves, but the unwitting partner was not getting the idea. On such an occasion the CIA is not averse to getting on its own secret system and canning a message to its contact in the distant country and saying explicitly, "Send us this message with information copies to the Secretary of Defense, the Secretary of State, the White House," and to anywhere else where they wish to make an impression. Then when they call the meeting, which they planned to do all along, they can say, for instance, "Gentlemen, we have a message which we understand you all have too, that leads us to believe there is grave trouble on the borders of India." All the other Government conferees especially gathered on the basis of top secret clearances and the need to know would agree that the situation looked grim. Perhaps the Army representative would say, "Yes, we have that message and we have several more from our attaché, who says that trouble has been brewing for some time and that the Indian army may need help on the border." The White House might concur by pulling out its sheaf of copies of the attaché traffic which also supported the idea that the Indian army was in trouble on the border.

At such time the Agency would ask everyone to look at his copy of message Number 123 from New Delhi Embassy on such a date. That message would say that the trouble on the border was severe; however the group having the problem was the border police and not the army. Since border police assistance would fall under the jurisdiction of the Agency and not the U.S. Army, the Agency would propose that the assistance given to the Indians should be clandestine police support, under the cover of a Military Aid Program project accelerated because of the border problems. Everyone else would have his portfolio of messages and would be convinced that the CIA's view of the situation was correct. The Group would agree that the MAP project should be set up and that the aid delivered should be turned over to the CIA representatives and that the training program should be under CIA operation and direction.

Superior and independent communications makes all the difference in the world at times like these. There are other times when an operator on a special project has the means to communicate with his headquarters in Washington independently of other channels. In such cases, this operator will at times bypass not only the ambassador and military hierarchy, but he may even bypass his own station chief. All of this is excused on the grounds of security and expediency. In some cases the station chief has become incensed over such actions; but, as in the case of the baseball player arguing with the umpire, his anger seldom got him very far. One of the most famous of these differences occurred in the Philippines when Ed Lansdale was operating with Magsaysay, and the station chief, who was on excellent terms with Magsaysay himself, was not aware of some of the operations that Lansdale and his Filipino cohorts had set in motion.

Other instances have arisen where the ambassador and his CIA counterpart have come to grief over message traffic that the ambassador learned of somehow and then demanded from State and CIA in Washington an explanation of what was going on in his country. Such things were more important in the earlier days. As the CIA and the ST have become stronger there are not so many surface problems. Most ambassadors and most military commanders do as the Congress has been doing; they bury their heads in the sand and hope that the peacetime operation will go away so that they will not have to know a thing about it.

When the question "what to do with Trujillo in the Dominican Republic" arose, a great proportion of military and of diplomats in the Department of State defended him. They maintained that Trujillo may not have been the ideal ruler of his country and that his strong one-man government was oppressive and diabolical; but at the same time, he was anti-Communist in the extreme when anti-Communism was supposed to be the epitome of good sense and good character regardless of all else. Why should anyone want to dispose of such a staunch anti-Communist? But several factions converged in the Trujillo case. It became known to those who would overthrow him that if they took action against this island strongman, the United States would not lift a finger.

During this period, there were reports coming from military channels, from diplomatic channels, and from CIA channels. All of these reports came together in Washington in meetings of the highest order, and the fate of the Trujillo regime hung in the balance. It became evident that the United States would not do anything and that the policy would be that if such an overthrow took place, the United States would not support anyone and would not back anyone. However, it also became evident that the United States would not support Trujillo, nor would it warn him or move to protect him. It is this factor that makes a coup d'état possible. It is not so much positive action; it is the understanding that there will be no support of that regime in power by the United States once the uprising begins.

Although the Pentagon Papers do not provide all of the insight, it becomes clear that the Diem regime was toppled not so much by anything the United States did as by the fact that we did nothing. It is this exposure to his enemies that seals the fate of a government leader, as certainly as if the trigger were pulled from the embassy.

One of the key elements in all of these situations is the ability of the Agency to have its own message traffic quickly and deftly in hand while the other major communicators are going through their channels.

In the broad sense, communications involves much more than the means of transmitting messages. In this broad sense the ST has even greater weapons to employ. Even the fastest message system and the most direct routing and processing will not assure supremacy unless the men at both ends of the system are experts and unless they are able to act with the information they have. Here is where the ST excels and where it shows its superiority. An agent in a foreign country can send a message by a select channel with security coding that keeps the information from everyone who does not have the proper clearance and the need to know. This assures that very few people will get that message in the first stage of handling. The basic message will go to a control office in the CIA, and an information copy may go to cleared parties in the White House, State, and Defense. The men who receive these messages in those other departments may very well be CIA personnel who are in cover assignments. This means then that the State, White House, and Defense copies are still in the hands of Agency personnel, even though the record will show that they have been properly transmitted to the other addressees. Thus the control has not been lost, and delivery of these messages will be in strict compliance with and in timing with what the ST wants.

This is why so many messages that have been made public in the Pentagon Papers appear to be part of Pentagon, or more specifically,

JCS activity, when in reality this traffic was between Saigon and the Agency, with the information copy being delivered to the Special Assistant for Counterinsurgency and Special Activities (SACSA). This section in the office of the Joint Chiefs of Staff was manned, for the most part, by military personnel. They did have some normal military functions but most of their work was involved with the support of the CIA. In this capacity they would control communications coming to the Joint Staff and in turn coordinate them with counterpart CIA-support offices in the office of the Secretary of Defense, or to a Focal Point office in each of the military services. During the period described, the OSD offices were those of Bill Bundy, General Lansdale, and others, in such places as the Directorate of Research and Engineering.

To anyone not knowing the process, it would then appear that the Saigon message in question would have been properly staffed to the OSD, JCS, and all services, when in reality it had simply been to all of the CIA control points in those offices. The real military would not have seen it. In cases where action was to follow, it would be up to those persons who received such messages to call them to the attention of the Secretaries and Chiefs of Staff involved. This would be done with care, and yet these senior men seldom had all of the facts and all of the background to be able to see what really was under way since they would be seeing these messages piece by piece and rarely as a whole. Emboldened by knowledge of the fact that they had properly touched base with all parties and offices concerned, the ST would then go ahead with the project, on the assumption that no one had said not to go ahead with it after having been advised.

This was one of the major steps forward taken by Allen Dulles as a result of his report. It looked like a small thing, and it was applied bit by bit; but once the NSC found itself in the position of doing no more than "authorizing" activities of the CIA rather than "directing" them, the roles began to turn 180 degrees, and the ST became the active party. When the NSC was established, it was realized that if such an eminent body of men made decisions and then directed that they be carried out, they would not necessarily be in a position to see that someone actually did carry them out. Therefore, provision was made for an Operations Coordinating Board, (OCB), which would see that the decisions of the President and his Council were carried out. This was effective only as long as the NSC was directing activity. The OCB would require that the NSC staff keep a record of decisions in duplicate, and the Board would ride herd on these decisions and see that they were done. It had trouble doing this when CIA was just getting its proposals "authorized."

When the NSC was divided into a small and elite Special Group for the purpose of working with the CIA on matters that were from time to time clandestine, the task of the OCB became more difficult because of the cloak of security. Still, the OCB tried to keep up with such decisions, if by no other means than to require "blind" progress reports. But when the NSC, through the Special Group, simply sat and listened to outside proposals and then permitted or authorized actions that were highly classified and highly limited by need to know, the role of the OCB became impossible to perform. This was exactly what Allen Dulles wanted. His report had stated that he should be able to initiate operations and to take his proposals directly to the President, and that the President or an authorized representative would then approve what the DCI brought to him. He had not been given that authority by the law, and he could not have done it under Truman because Truman used the NSC and OCB differently from what Dulles visualized. But year by year during the Eisenhower Administration he worked to erode the NSC-OCB pattern until he was able to work through the Special Group 5412/2 almost without interference. Part of his success was due to his effective control of communications, which made it appear all the time that projects had been thoroughly staffed in all parts of the Government concerned and that the approval of the NSC (Special Group) was merely a formality.

By the time Kennedy became President, he was led to believe that the NSC was unimportant, one of those Eisenhower idiosyncrasies, and that he could do without it. If he could do without the NSC, he certainly could do without the OCB. (Since it could be shown that the OCB was not able to perform its job properly because it was unable to find out what the Special Group had approved, there was no reason for OCB either.) Without either of these bodies in session, the DCI was able to move in as he desired, with very little effective control from any Council member. This was a major change brought about by a kind of evolution and erosion. It was certainly a downgrading process; but the trouble was that all too few people had any realization of what had taken place, and those who had were either with the CIA or the ST, and they were not about to tell anyone.

In concluding our review of this function of the CIA communications system, it would be a mistake to overlook what is perhaps the heaviest source of volume. The CIA monitors electronic signals all over the world, and it gathers so much of this that it is practically swamped with taped information. However, it does a most excellent job in keeping its ear to the traffic of the world. There can be little question that an enlightened system of listening can pick up about all of the information any country would ever need, to keep itself well informed of what any other country is doing. In this day and age, almost all major parts of the Government and of industry must utilize and depend upon electronically transmitted messages and data transfer. All of this can be monitored, and even if it is in code it can be read sooner or later. This is one task of the Agency, and it is a major part of its role and responsibility to coordinate all national intelligence.

Perhaps no other function of the Agency so clearly demonstrates the dual nature of the CIA more than does communications. In the intelligence business, communications is absolutely essential to make bits of information available to the collection center. However, by its very nature, the more capacity the communications system has and the more information bits it handles the more it tends to degrade the value of the information. The Agency receives so much information every day that the great proportion of it is never seen, never processed, and never analyzed . . . and most likely should not be.

On the other hand, in this flood of information there is always the good chance that much is intentional deception and gibberish. Just having the information does not insure that it is worth anything. In this country in particular, information on almost anything is becoming something that has a price and can be bought and sold; yet even this does not ensure that it has value.

From the other point of view, a high-caliber communications system makes it possible for the center to go out to all of its outposts and agents with instructions seeking certain information of value. This is certain to produce the best input, since the return product will be what is sought and not some random article. One of the greatest needs of an intelligence system is to know what it is looking for, along with all of the technical know-how in the organization. "Know what" is so much more valuable than know-how.

But, as we said above, communications brings out the duality of the agency. While agents all over the world are seeking information, the operator is always looking for that choice morsel of data that can be used for another operation. In all of the material flashed over the communications network, there are those special bits and pieces— border trouble between two countries, a political slaying, an uprising in a remote village, a student riot on an urban campus—that provide fuel for clandestine operations. Such things provide the "fun and games" people with the fuel for their fires.

When the Agency wishes to pursue one of these leads, it flashes the word back to get more information. It may activate a dormant agent network to see what further information can be acquired. If the situation warrants, agents may be flown in quickly to where the action is. A planeload of guns may be moved to a border area for early airdrop if called for; and so it goes. To the clandestine operators, communications is the lifeblood of the whole business.

One thing is common to both sides. They always wish to keep their information secret. As we have seen, there are many reasons for secrecy, and many of them have little to do with real secrecy—which would keep the information, or the fact that we have it, from the enemy. But both parties should keep in mind that information is a continuing process. The dissemination of all information, all secrets, is only a matter of time. There is no "first line of defense" for the brain. Any idea conceived by one brain and known to a few more is bound to be general information in a short time. The purpose of secrecy is self-defeating. It is much more important for us to have adequate knowledge than it is for us to try to keep some other country from that knowledge. More harm is done every day by keeping essential information from those who should have it than ever is done by those whom we say we are trying to keep from getting it. If more experienced military men had known about the Bay of Pigs operation, it either would not have happened, or if it did, it would have had a better chance of success. On the other hand, the very people whom the cloak of secrecy was supposed to keep from knowing about the operation, ostensibly the Cubans and the Russians, knew all they needed to know about it.

The best communications system in the world is certainly a tremendous asset for any intelligence organization; but in the hands of those who wish to use its information for the creation and promotion of clandestine operations it is another one of those facilities that lead to the type of problems described by President Truman and Arnold Toynbee.

CHAPTER 14

TRANSPORTATION: ANYWHERE IN THE WORLD—NOW

In moonlight so clear that the high Himalayas could be seen one hundred miles away, an Air Force C-130 transport few over the multinational border region of Laos, Burma, and China. In the cargo compartment a small, highly skilled team of Tibetan Khamba tribesmen huddled quietly beside the heavy airdrop pallets that lined the center compartment. Under a dim light in the forward part of the huge cargo area, four Agency men played nickel-and-dime poker while they sipped hot coffee from the plane's airborne kitchen hotplate. The crew peered into the darkness at brilliant stars guiding them on into the vast remoteness of Western China. From time to time the navigator was busy taking star shots to verify the electronic navigation signals he was getting, but which were growing dimmer and less reliable as each hour passed.

The Operations officials of the Agency had directed that the crew fly as low and as close to the horizon as they could with safety, so that that their radar profile would be obscured by ground clutter.

This same low pattern played havoc with long-range navigational signals from remote sites. But this gave the experienced crew little concern. The C-130 was in fine shape, the four turboprop engines purred in their sleek nacelles, and fuel flow was well within the flight-plan parameters. Precise navigation at this point was essential only to verify wind conditions and to warn if major shifts in strength and direction might have an impact upon total effective range. They knew that this mission was going to demand all the range the C-130 had, and a little more. The target for the airdrop of the Khambas and the black cargo was in the vicinity of Koko Nor, deep in the outback of unknown China.

A trainload of olive-drab GI six-by-six U.S. Army trucks had been delivered to a siding in North Carolina. A crew of men had worked for days unloading the trucks and towing them to a small remote dockside facility for loading onto an old, World War II front-loading landing craft. Another old, but newly shipshape, vessel lay at anchor, ready to shove off for the south as soon as the last shipment of trucks had been hoisted aboard. Both ships, with skeleton crews, slipped out of the port quietly and ran southward to Puerto Rico, where they would await orders to join the small armada bound for an unknown beach in the Bay of Pigs region of western Cuba.

The temperature sometimes reached 125 degrees, perhaps even 135 degrees, in the scorching sunlight of northern Libya. The jet fighters lining the runways shimmered in the ever-present mirage that hung over the concrete runways. Men fueling these planes wore heavy gloves, in spite of the intense heat, to protect themselves from burns. Far across this huge base in the remote area reserved for rockets and other armament, a few low outbuildings were the only evidence of a below-ground ammunition and arms cache of a most unusual nature. A steady stream of trucks had been weaving back and forth all day from the huge C-124 transport planes to this dump area to unload heavy cases of guns. These were not the usual World War II leftovers. These were British Enfields, French guns, and most important, they were a good mix of guns from Iron Curtain countries, picked up from many sources, including war-captured booty from the Israeli campaign in the Sinai Desert.

The common thread through all of these anecdotes is the fact that in every case the Agency was operating in its own interest with transportation provided by the military forces. The aircraft belonged to the U.S. Air Force. The trucks and the special flatbed rail carriers were provided by the U.S. Army. And the ships that made the run to Cuba had been U.S. Navy equipment, refitted for use in that operation. The Agency has ready access to all kinds of transportation all over the world in the global transportation system of the Department of Defense. This great network gives the Agency the opportunity to carry out its work behind the screen of regular military movements. This saves the CIA the problem of covering the bulk of its movements, and it saves a tremendous amount of money. Again, this is money that the Agency usually protests it will gladly reimburse to the prime agent of the DOD, provided it is billed for it. Most shipments made by the CIA through the military networks are made to and from Agency cover units using military designations. The cost therefore is not identifiable unless a knowledgeable person intercepts the shipment. This is not likely, because the Agency will protest and the top echelons of the service will support it that the high classification of the shipment precludes such identification. Thus the bulk airlift of tons of guns, which would mean nothing to military shipping clerks, travels without charge under the guise of secrecy.

Much military shipment is made by contract airlift. During the peak Vietnam operation years, the total of military-purchased contract-airlift averaged three quarters of a billion dollars per year. With the CIA responsible for a $1 billion a year "pacification" program in Vietnam, it can be seen that the Agency's share of that airlift could have been appreciable; yet the chances are very good that no one ever knew just which shipments were Agency shipments and what to charge for them or how to collect reimbursement for them. When one reflects upon the early days of the CIA and upon the serious precautions taken to assure that the CIA would not grow beyond the size of a small, truly special operations capability, it is most significant to remember how all of this was done and how it has become such a normal and accepted practice today that at times even the U.S. Army has moved into certain operations under the cover of the CIA.

When the CIA leaves the realm of the DOD and must strike out for itself into non-military areas and into areas where military relationships must be abandoned, it is able to use its own funds to provide its own first-class transportation to meet the situation. Most Agency personnel going overseas do so under one form of military cover or other, and as a result they travel on military aircraft or military contract shipping. This includes their household goods and other equipment as well. But there are times when CIA personnel cannot travel as military personnel, and then they travel as ordinary civilians and utilize all other means available.

In foreign countries, the CIA procures fleets of indigenous vehicles to be able to pass more easily among the population among whom they will be working. It would be unwise for some man, attempting to be inconspicuous in Istanbul, to be seen driving around that crowded city in a new Buick or Chrysler. More than likely, the Agency will see that he has a Volkswagen or Renault, and perhaps one that is a few years old. In like manner, the Agency purchases civilian aircraft and boats of various types and sizes, to meet other special requirements. I have known of CIA personnel traveling in dog-sled parties and in sleek civilian business jets.

The Agency does not want for transportation anytime, anywhere, and of any type, and they get so much of it free or for so little relative cost that what they need over and above the bulk military support, their own funds are more than adequate to provide. The Agency has a very large and special fleet of its own equipment, most of which is covered as commercial equipment. At the time of the Bay of Pigs invasion, the CIA used landing ships of World War II origin, which it had purchased from surplus sources and then refitted for the occasion. In other water moves, the CIA has used special Norwegian-built high speed boats, and it has used small, light canoes. In such instances, the Agency mans these vessels with its own personnel, and augments the agent cadre with experienced men when necessary. Where the Agency excels in this business is with its many clandestine airlines, which are scattered throughout the United States and around the world. The most famous of these is Air America.

Air America, the airline of the flying mercenaries, conjures up stories true and imagined, real and unreal, of the Dragon Lady and Terry and the Pirates and of deep, secret missions into rebel-held territory in countries from faraway Asia to Latin America. Air America, Incorporated, is a worldwide operation, chartered in Delaware and listed solidly in Dun and Bradstreet. Its main offices are within a few hundred yards of the White House, on Washington's posh Connecticut Avenue, and it numbers among its directors many famous names, including several former Navy admirals who have at one time or other been Commanders in Chief, Pacific (CINCPAC). Air America is a most important adjunct of the CIA.

When the travel to Mecca is heaviest with the devout Moslems involved in the hadj, a nondescript old transport aircraft will shuttle pilgrims across the Arabian desert. When summer travel peaks in Europe and thousands of students hire charter planes to take them to an international peace festival in Munich, among these available planes will be aircraft belonging to Air America and flying under one of its countless cover, subordinate companies. If the Agency wishes to make a clandestine cargo drop in some out-of-the-way place like Burma, Pakistan, or Indonesia, a perfectly normal appearing commercial transport aircraft will find itself on business through and around that area for a while, until any suspicion that might be aroused has died down; then on one special flight it will open its rear cargo door and paradrop the supplies, equipment, and perhaps agents over the selected target zone.

The men of Air America are legendary, from the incomparable "Earthquake" McCoon, who lost his life over Dien Bien Phu in an unarmed C-119, to nameless and faceless Chinese and Anzacs, who have flown for Air America on flights that would make fiction accounts tame by comparison.

In the middle nineteen fifties, it became necessary to resupply Agency outposts deep in Laos. The usual DC-3 or C-46 from World War II surplus stockpiles required too much runway for some of these rugged areas. Helicopters lacked the range and load-carrying ability required. The CIA turned to light planes and worked with the native tribesmen to clear landing strips deep in the forested valleys of

Laos. For a short time these strips were useful, until their adversaries found them and showered them with gunfire from the surrounding mountainsides.

Air America came in and selected landing sites in the most precarious positions. It had become expert in the use of a small, special plane used by the Air Force Special Air Warfare squadrons and by the Army Special Forces troops. This plane was called the L-28, or commercially, the Helio Courier. It was as rugged as a Jeep and could land and take off in remarkably short distances. This ability to land and take off in short distances is not by itself sufficient to commend an aircraft to this special use. Almost any light plane can, with a big engine, take off or land from short distances. However, once that same plane is in the air, if it does not have superior control surfaces and other slow flying characteristics designed for really slow-speed control in the air, it will be lethal in regular service. The Agency learned this the hard way when it and the United States Information Agency (USIA) missions attempted to use other aircraft that seemed able to do the job and were a little cheaper. More than 50 percent of those planes crashed in the first year of use. Meanwhile, the Air America planes and experienced crews actually operated from fantastically short and crude airstrips, which had been cleared by the natives on top of the ridge lines of the high, forested mountains of Laos. Even today, the flight handbook for pilots in Southeast Asia speaks of two categories of landing grounds in Laos—regular and Helio. Air America and the rugged Helio have made an unheralded and unequaled record all over Laos.

Air America is not a small unseen company. At two bases alone, one in Thailand and one in Taiwan, it has more than four thousand employees at each. To live its cover as a commercial airline, it flies regular routes and is a major contract carrier airline competing with other airlines of the world for flying business and for aircraft maintenance work.

Years ago, when pilots and ground-crew men of the old Chennault Flying Tiger groups decided to stay in China and to form an airline there, CAT Airlines, the forerunner of Air America and others of that time, operated all over the mainland. They bought a fleet of World

War II surplus C-46 cargo aircraft and set up a big maintenance facility at a Chinese mainland airport. As the fortunes of war drove them from one base to another, someone decided to put the maintenance facility on board a big war surplus ship. Finally, with the defeat of the forces under Chiang Kai-shek, this shop with its facilities and stockpile of equipment sailed to Taiwan and anchored beside a dock in Tainan. There this most unusual aircraft maintenance facility performed maintenance for a fast-growing and very busy fleet of planes for many years.

One could walk through that ship absolutely amazed at the beehive-like activity on board. Hundreds, perhaps thousands, of Chinese worked in that ship on stages, rather than floors or decks, joined by narrow catwalks. Many of those workers worked in small basket-like spaces, barely large enough for a small Chinese. Parts and materials were brought to them and poured into each work space as through a funnel. The worker would finish his special task and then drop the part through a short chute, where it would end up for the next worker to do his part. The whole operation worked on a sort of force-of-gravity basis, with the finished item falling out at the bottom, ready for an alert runner to carry it to the packaging room. Whole sets of aircraft engine spark plugs would be specially treated and then placed into a big slab of plank, drilled out specially to accommodate just enough plugs for a certain type of engine, e.g., twenty-eight plugs for a 14-cylinder engine. This was done so mechanics would not have to check plugs; they simply removed all of them and put in a whole set of new plugs, while the old ones would be returned complete to the shop.

Even instruments were rebuilt, and as they were, the faces and decals were changed to have Chinese or English markings, as required. There were propeller shops and wheel shops. Planes could be completely rebuilt from this one facility. As a matter of fact, the CIA had obtained master transparent film slide sets of the aircraft manufacturers parts and supplies kits, and for such planes as the DC-6, Air America could make every part just about as well as Douglas Aircraft. The CIA justified this irregular and perhaps illegal operation on the basis that it was working with sanitized engines and aircraft and that it could not put such items back in the supply line of the services. As a result, instead of buying from Douglas, through the services, it simply made the parts in its Tainan facility. It is entirely possible that complete small aircraft were made in this manner and that Air America or its subsidiaries ended up with more aircraft in operation than it had had in the first place.

This technique is "justified" by the nature of air registry, which precludes the availability and even the existence of "extra" aircraft. Every aircraft built and flown must be registered. Once it has been registered, that serial number stays with it for the rest of its existence. Therefore, if the Agency wishes to remove all traces of identity and ownership from an airplane in order to make it plausibly deniable, it must also arrange to cover that plane in the registry. This is done in many ways, one of which is to assemble an extra plane from the parts available. To begin with, the CIA may be able to salvage a destroyed aircraft and have it declared discarded. Then from the frame or some other essential part it will rebuild the plane from parts not having any serial numbers at all. This method must be used with larger aircraft; but the Tainan facility had the capability to build smaller aircraft from scratch, just by assembling spare parts, many of which it would have made itself right at the plant.

With this splendid maintenance organization, the Agency faces the necessity to assure it sufficient business to be able to live its cover as a commercial establishment. At this date and time it is doubtful that the cover of Air America is of any real value. Certainly, anyone who needs to know by now knows all about Air America; but in any event, such a plant and all that equipment cannot be permitted to stand idle. As a result, Air America and its subsidiary maintenance components bid actively for commercial airline contracts and especially for U.S. military contracts. It is this military business that actually supports Air America. This is true also in the airline passenger and cargo business.

Air America has a fine record, and on the basis of experience and service it is at least the equal of other contract carrier airlines that bid for U.S. military airlift. However, since the Agency has a proprietary interest in Air America, the CIA feels that the services should give the airline every opportunity to bid, and everything else being equal, the opportunity to be selected for contracts up to the minimum income level the Agency holds is essential to keep the airline in business and give it the added capacity to support ST activities when called upon.

There was a time when contract carrier bidding was very competitive because the Pacific airlift had been cut back and there was very little to go around. After a few cycles of bidding, other airlines noted that Air America was getting business steadily, even if not in large volume. One new and most enterprising contract airline president flew into Washington and presented his views to the proper authorities in the Office of the Secretary of Defense and in the Air Force. At every turn he was assured that the bidding had been perfectly legal and correct, and that Air America was getting no more than its share and that Air America had made valid low bids. This man had heard some stories about Air America's pedigree, stories that were very easy to come by in any bar in Hong Kong where Air America pilots were very popular; so he went into town and hired a lawyer. As his good fortune and, no doubt, his good sense would have it, the lawyer he retained was a knowledgeable individual who among other things had served as Secretary of the Air Force.

Accompanied by this gentleman, the airline president returned to the Pentagon and held a brief meeting with certain aware officials there. By the time they left the Pentagon, this airline had the promise of a contract in the Pacific. The contract saved that airline from lean years, and it would be nice to be able to leave the story there with a happy ending.

Actually, once that airline president had learned the trick, it was only inevitable that he would resort to that game again and again. Middle-level executives and appointive officers in the Pentagon rotate and move on after brief terms. With each generation of new faces someone sooner or later would be confronted by the same "pirate" airline president with the same story. Each time, the heavy cloak of security had kept the new man from knowing the antecedents of the case; so he would have to seek help and advice from the staff. Inevitably he would be told, "Do anything you can to placate the man. That subject is highly classified, and we can't let legal action compromise the real facts in the case." As a result, the president would get his contract again and again. Because he knew that, he had all the high cards in the deck. Today that contract carrier advertises as one of the largest and most successful in the business, and its very successful leader has done very well with his secret formula.

What was involved here was not such a lot of money; but it is indicative of a great weakness in this sort of a system. What works in one case works in countless others. It is a sort of blackmail predicated on not breaking security, and no real consideration is given to whether the security is worth the price or not. This same type of "security blackmail" exists in many forms. If a government does not get the Military Aid Program material it thinks it should get, it will put pressure on the CIA liaison people, telling them it will have to stop supporting a reconnaissance unit or some radar installations, or some similar threat. Then CIA puts pressure on the MAP staff and gets the additional material for them, or may even get it out of its own resources of stockpiled military material. Or, as in the case of the Bay of Pigs operation, the governments that assisted Guatemala and Nicaragua either kept what they "found on base" or bargained for more. This upset other assistance plans because other countries claimed the right to more equipment based upon a balanced formula, security or not.

We see other applications of such blackmail, as in the case of the ransom paid to Castro for the Cuban invaders. This figure in money and heavy equipment as well as in medicine has been quoted as being $53 million or more. It seems pertinent to note that so much money and equipment was paid willingly for captured Cubans and as far as we know, not one cent has been offered, except by certain private citizens, for the release of our own prisoners of war in Indochina.

After the adventure in Indonesia, considerable amounts of equipment and preferential purchasing rights were paid to the Government of Indonesia as a sort of compensation for that misadventure.

In the case of the airline president above, he has made a success of this technique, which has been exceeded only by the success of Air America itself. This is now a very large and honorable company directed and managed by some very able men. It is the excellence and superiority of the men on the logistics side of CIA who have made the Agency look good year after year in spite of some of the problems created by the more adventuresome operators. As Air America has become quite overt, respectable, and above-board, it in turn has had to be the cover unit for much really deep operational work. It has the capacity and the know-how, and it certainly has the people, to perform aircraft support for almost any operation that can be conceived.

In fact, it is organizations such as Air America that show how the Agency could have done things from the beginning, if it had not turned so quickly to the soft touch in the Department of Defense. If the early opportunists had been content to perform truly clandestine missions of a size and expectation that would have had the chance to remain clandestine, then the CIA might have managed to live within its charter and to have limited its operational efforts to those actually in support of intelligence, instead of becoming a vast international operational force. It was the broad-gauge goals set by the Dulles-Jackson-Correa report and the exploitation of the war-planning largesse of the military that launched the Agency upon a runaway operational activity, which resulted finally in the Indochina venture.

CHAPTER 15

LOGISTICS BY MIRACLE

Historians attribute to Napoleon the statement that armies move on their stomachs. In actual practice, it may have worked the other way around. The army's stomach may have been what made the General move. When the great Genghis Khan captured and pillaged a city, his army ate well for a while. However, when the food began to run low Genghis Khan was already looking for the next city to capture. Historians may attribute his conquests to a vast imperial effort; but objective analysis may reveal his sweeping across the cold and hostile land-mass of Asia was due more to the need to feed the growing horde of men behind him than to any other one incontestable factor.

It is logistics that permits armies to move. When the British Army sat at El Alamein holding the Rommel advance at bay, their failure to attack was more a function of logistics than it was of tactics. Montgomery and his great assistant, Alexander, knew all too well that once the army moved, it would be absolutely dependent upon a flow of supplies that must remain unbroken all the way to Tunis. They were not about to give the order to move until that flow of supplies was assured.

When Patton broke out across the fields of France in his dash for the Rhine and the destruction of the German armies, his fate lay in the hands of General J. C. H. Lee, Eisenhower's logistics chief, more than it did in his tactical wizardry.

And so it has been with the CIA. The important thing about the logistics system of the Agency is not that it has so much and that it can do almost anything it wants with its horn of plenty; but that it has achieved this position without specific authorization and quite generally without the knowledge and approval of the rest of the Government, especially Congress. The ultimate control over any agency of the Government lies in the purse-strings that are held by Congress. Yet the Agency grows and grows, and Congress seems to have little to do with it and to know little of what it has created. Of course, everyone knows that the CIA has a fleet of aircraft, tens of thousands of people, ships and trucks, overseas facilities, weapons of all types in vast quantities, and almost limitless funds. Almost anyone, especially any member of Congress can say, "I certainly am aware of the fact that the CIA has secret overseas facilities." And another can say, "I know that the CIA is mixed up with Air America, the contract carrier airline, in some manner or other." Another might add, "I have visited overseas capitals and I have found that the CIA had a number of people there under cover assignments." And some other Congressman might even say that he has heard that the Agency gets plenty of money through various secret channels from other Government sources.

The Agency likes to conceal the fact that it has so much under heavy security wraps. Whether these facts are concealed for real security reasons, or whether they are concealed simply to keep them from the eyes and ears of Congress and of the American public is the big question. Actually, the CIA prefers to keep its wealth under security so that all Americans, including the members of Congress, do not know how much it has and how it got it. There is a very good chance that the other nations of this world have a much better idea of what the CIA has in their countries than we do in this country. They make it their business to know, and we do not. We have just let it happen before our eyes without ever making a real investigation of the facts. If everyone else in the world knows, why shouldn't we? If Greece is the locale of one stockpile and they know what is in it; and if Turkey, Iran, and Jordan all have stockpiles in their countries and know what they contain and where they are, what makes someone here think that they do not talk to each other and compare notes? As a matter of fact, they not only compare notes, they use each other's knowledge to improve their own game. The only ones who don't know what the CIA has in Greece, Turkey, Iran, and Jordan are the American people and their representatives in Congress.

And for all those Congressmen who know about the Agency, there are none who can say that they know all of the things the Agency has of all kinds. Each Congressman may have a smattering of knowledge of some of the things that the Agency has. But the CIA has achieved this vast wealth in manpower, money, and materials, as well as facilities all over the world, without the knowledge of the rest of the Government. This means that the rest of the Government does not know about it in total—all in one place, as in Congress.

Undoubtedly, someone from the CIA and perhaps from the executive branch of the Government may say, "That is not exactly right. We are fully aware of the total inventory of the Agency. We are aware of its manpower resources and of its goods all over the world, and we have an inventory of its facilities and installations, including those in foreign countries." Certainly, there is no need to doubt or to question such a blanket statement of faith. Somewhere there must be a fairly accurate total of what the CIA is supposed to have; but at that point one will be confronted with the tautology, "This inventory of the Agency lists everything the Agency has; therefore, everything that the Agency has is listed in this inventory."

For the CIA, the idea of property takes on a new meaning. Any other agency of the Government that wanted to use one hundred trucks would have to buy one hundred trucks or make some arrangement with another agency of the Government, or with a private organization, to acquire the trucks. And that agency would have to show in its budget the expenditure of a certain amount of its funds for the purchase or lease of the hundred trucks. In other words, its utilization or ownership of property could be verified and accounted for by reviewing or auditing its appropriated funds. The CIA can use and the CIA can acquire and "own" one hundred trucks without any budgeted fund transaction at all.

The CIA has the authority, or at least it is given the authority by other Government agencies, to create cover organization within other parts of the Government. This is one of the key tasks that the old Dulles-Jackson-Correa report set out for the Agency. Having once created such units, the CIA is then able to use those units as though they were real elements of the covering organization and to do with them pretty much what it pleases. So if the CIA wants to use one hundred Army trucks, it may have one of its Air Force cover units (it could use an Army unit; but it is easier to use cross-service channels to conceal such a transaction) duly and properly requisition the trucks. In response to this order, the Army will furnish, and write off, the trucks to the Air Force. However, the Air Force won't really know that one of its units, a cover unit, has acquired these trucks; so the Air Force will not pick them up on its inventory. The trucks are then in a sort of never-never land. They are "owned" by an Air Force cover unit that the CIA has the authority to direct, and those trucks will be used as the CIA wishes and for as long as the CIA wishes. There have been cases where the CIA turned around and transferred such property to another country in a sort of a CIA-MAP project all of its own.

In this manner, only one of numerous variations, the Agency has acquired countless mountains of material, which it stockpiles, uses, loses, gives away, and just plain warehouses all over the world. Even the Agency doesn't know what it all is and where it all is. No one in the Government really knows how much the Agency has. A corollary of this statement is that the Agency has been able to stockpile money in a somewhat similar manner, because if it had money to buy trucks and then was never billed for them, it still has those funds to spend elsewhere.

With these funds that the CIA has stockpiled for its own use, it develops areas beyond those in the realm of the military and other regular branches of the Government. The Agency has a wonderful little shop called "TSS." Few know what TSS really means; but it probably means something like "Top Secret Stuff." This shop makes all kinds of James Bond trinkets. It is the place where they design briefcases that will not burn, that will blow up if someone attempts to open them the wrong way, and that will put out long spidery legs if they are released by the agent who is carrying them. And it is the shop that puts a full-blown tape recorder into a Zippo lighter case or a lady's lip-rouge container.

The TSS shop works on all kinds of unusual and very special weapons, and it works with chemicals that can perform all manner of special tasks. It has the finest bugging devices available and the very best debugging facilities. TSS goes out into industry and has things made without telling the people who have made them what their uses will be. At one time for photographic purposes the Agency wanted to develop a brilliant floodlight that could be carried on the wing-tip of an airplane in a pod. This light required so much energy to operate it that the normal electrical supply of the aircraft could not ignite it properly. The Agency then developed, with the help of a private corporation, a generator driven by a propeller attached to the pod. This small propeller was so efficient that it could drive a generator for the floodlight to illuminate an entire area below the plane.

Although this was a splendid development, it was found that in a tactical situation the worst thing you could do was to send a plane into a hostile situation lit up like the sun. This would be an easy target for ground gunners. The next step was to synchronize the light and the camera shutter to the point that the flash would be so brilliant and so brief that an unwitting ground party would not realize it had blinked.

This created new problems; a whole new automated photographic and lighting system had to be developed. This was done, and Agency aircraft can now approach targets in the dark, even at times in an engine-out or engine-idling glide for silence, and take high-speed pictures without anyone on the ground knowing that they have been photographed. TSS was also able to make another advance in aerial photography. The U-2 had proved that it could fly across denied or unwitting territory without notice or without danger from attack because of its speed, altitude, and range. It was also a relatively small radar target. However, at the flight altitude at which the U-2 operated, any normal aerial camera was being pushed to its limits. The camera lens had to focus on the target area and put what it saw on film as precisely as possible. At some point the lens became better than the film paper. This meant that the image that the lens put on the paper was finer than the grade and grain of the paper. Therefore the process of enlarging such pictures and then enlarging them again and again became limited, not because the lens could not accurately transmit the image but because the paper itself had a grain structure that began to break down the detail after a certain amount of enlargement. By working on this problem, TSS and its corporate research associates were able to create a means by which enlargement could be carried so far, for example, that it could distinguish between an oval table or a roundtable of about four feet in diameter from the operational altitude of the U-2, or even higher.

This became a most useful facility in the days of the U-2; but it had not reached the zenith of its utility until the Agency went into space. Now the Spy-in-the-Sky orbital laboratories park out in space at about 110 miles mean altitude and take very valuable pictures of the earth's surface on predetermined schedules or on signals. For example, such pictures of the Chinese atomic energy facilities clearly delineate between dry drying flats and moist drying flats. The continuing variations give a fairly accurate estimate of the rate of activity at the facility.

These developments have led to policy problems that this country has not faced up to primarily because so few people really know about them. They are hardly secret from our enemies, and for that matter they are not secrets from our friends. They are the kind of secrets we keep from ourselves in order that secret operations may be continued in the hands of the ST. For example, Secretary of Defense Laird has made a strong case before the Congress on behalf of the development of the B-1 supersonic bomber, which the U.S. Air Force states it will need for the defense of the country in the decade of the eighties. As a function of his presentation to Congress, Mr. Laird gave information about a Soviet supersonic bomber, which he said had already been built and flown. As a result of the impact of this information, he drew the conclusion that the United States must get on with a project to build a bomber that would be equal to or even better than the Soviet bomber. In support of what he had been saying about the Soviet bomber he gave sufficient details of that new plane to artists to permit them to arrive at a suitable pictorial representation of it. A copy of this artists' conception of the Soviet bomber appeared in an issue of Time magazine and was used in that periodical as the basis for a strong article in support of a crash program to build an American supersonic bomber without delay. This whole process, which most Americans will recognize as a familiar pattern used for submarines, super-carriers, and for missiles, is intended to make everyone believe that we are behind the Russians and that we must catch up; we must close the bomber gap.

To the tune of an opening request for $11 billion, Congress is supposed to vote for production of this bomber based on the information given in limited fashion and upon a poor picture of an alleged flying aircraft. When the stakes are so high and so costly, it is time that the intelligence community and the DOD give up this facade of secrecy. Everyone knows that the intelligence community uses cameras of great ability and that they use orbiting laboratories from which photographic canisters are dropped for recovery and development. And everyone knows that these orbiting laboratories take pictures of Soviet territory and of any other territory desired. None of these things would be done if the pictures were not excellent and if they were not getting an excellent product. Therefore, if the intelligence community has hard information about a bomber, which includes photographs of that bomber, why should it not show the actual pictures of that bomber to Mr. Laird, to the President, to the Congress, and most of all to the American public and to the whole world? What possible case can be made for keeping such things secret, especially when they are asking for $11 billion? Is the reason they do not show these pictures to Congress the fact that they do not have these pictures? And if they do not have the pictures, why not? Is it because they have been unable to find the bomber and to get a picture of it outside its hangar? Or perhaps their conjecture about the bomber is a bit premature, and the bomber is perhaps only on the Soviet drawing-boards, like too many American bombers?

Of course, there are technical problems. An orbiting photographic laboratory can only take a useful picture of such a bomber at certain optimum times in its orbiting periodic cycles. And an orbiting lab can be tracked by the Soviets, and they can hide the bomber whenever they know a satellite, suspected of being a photographic type, is due to fly by. But, by the same token, there are tactical things the intelligence community can and should be doing to get such pictures anyhow. They are not established to get second-best pictures or none at all. If the long ears of electronic intelligence and of other sensors tell us that the Russians are flying a new supersonic bomber, then there are other ways of getting its picture and of getting so much concrete information about it that we do not have to depend upon incomplete data. This is what an intelligence agency should be for, instead of a lot of other things that it would rather be for.

Such frankness openly discussed and openly aired would give up nothing to our enemies and would in the long run improve the total program. It would be most helpful and it would save billions of dollars. However, so many of these things that the wonders of U.S. industrial capability have developed for the CIA and for its TSS, have been kept under wraps—not so much because some form of security has been established that makes this reasonable and correct, but because the security shield leaves room for maneuvering when the ST needs to create a story that intelligence, for the time being perhaps, cannot actually support. Furthermore, if the huge spy satellite program were to be brought out in the open as a routine technical achievement, which it is, it might better be operated by NASA or one of the services than by an element of the intelligence community.

Much could be said for the merits of the TSS side of the Agency. The ability of the intelligence community to develop truly remarkable equipment and to extend the reach of surveillance and knowledge has been really magnificent. However, just as one would like to commend the community for having done something well, one realizes that the human factor has crept back in and beclouded the issue again by throwing up artificial barriers about these developments and by keeping them under wraps so that the controlling members of the "big game" may be able at one time or another to spring facts as surprises and at other times to spring surprises with or without the facts; and no one anywhere will be in a position to know otherwise, including, as President Truman has said, the very President and Commander in Chief.

What is so miraculous about the Agency's logistics system is that it has grown to such tremendous proportions in spite of the fact that the NSC directives specifically stated that the CIA should not have the men, money, or materials to pursue operations unless and until the CIA had been directed to carry them out by the NSC in the first place. During the early nineteen fifties, the Council was in the process of issuing a directive revision and an updating of the old NSCID 10/2—which would authorize the CIA to carry out special operations when directed by the NSC. A copy of the original draft of this directive used to be in the files of the Office of the Secretary of Defense, and the paragraph that pertained to what might be called the "logistics plan" of this directive had been carefully and elaborately annotated in plain handwriting. The handwriting was that of the President, Dwight D. Eisenhower. He wanted to make it so certain that the Agency could not acquire the logistics base for regular operations that he wrote into this directive his own stipulations.

When the final draft was published, these stringent stipulations were still there, and they required that whenever the Agency was directed to carry out a special operation, it would be instructed as a function of the same decision of the NSC, to request assistance from one Government agency or another, and that this assistance would be granted from "time to time" and would not be kept by the Agency for use from one operation to another. In other words, Eisenhower prohibited the CIA from stockpiling material for clandestine operations.

This philosophy ran at cross-purposes to the course laid down for himself and for his agency by Allen Dulles. Even though his brother was Secretary of State and his friend Ike was in the White House, he found ways to erode and to get around these stipulations. His report had said that a central intelligence agency should have the power to combine the secret intelligence function and the secret operation function under one official—the DCI. He was getting closer and closer to having the authority to carry out special operations; but to go all the way he must have the logistics. This is why the early war planning role of the Agency had been so important and then later why the Army Special Forces and Air Force Air Resupply and Communications Wing concepts had proved so opportune. With ready resources such as these all over the world, Dulles never lacked for equipment, facilities, and personnel. On top of this, he was greatly aided toward his goal by the zeal and initiative of the services themselves. They practically fought with each other to see who could provide the Agency with the most at the lowest cost, or for nothing at all.

It was this latter phase of developments that moved the CIA into a position of sufficiency. By the time of the mid-fifties, so many military men had been rotated through the Agency and had been retained as ardent disciples of Allen Dulles that the military services were shot through with men who were even more zealous for the CIA than some of its own people were able to be. When the Agency had not figured out some way to get something it wanted, or when in its own straight-laced manner—and there were some straight-laced people in the Agency—it could not bring itself to suggest that one of the services should do this or that, it frequently happened that a general or other ranking individual, still carried away by the "fun and games" fervor of his Agency tour, would set up procedures whereby the agency would get exactly what it wanted. In a sense, the whole U-2 program was an outgrowth of such zeal.

Gradually and with security-concealed movement, the Agency advanced toward its goals, and the glacier-like progress was reinforced by the assurance that in its relationship with the DOD the CIA would never lack for logistics support. During the later part of the fifties, the Agency began to set up storage facilities of its own in many foreign countries. Most this equipment was labeled for war-plan-directed utilization and was otherwise concealed as 'military' property. By 1955 the Agency was ready to try for the big game, and by 1955 knew that it had the equipment to move out. Although the directives had not been changed in that respect, no one noticed the movement of the glacier as it slid along toward Dulles-inspired goals. And by 1955 the Agency was more than the CIA—by that year the quiet intelligence arm of the President had been diverted into a vast operational organization and its direction had passed from the limited control by the DCI to the ST.

PART IV

THE CIA: SOME EXAMPLES THROUGHOUT THE WORLD

CHAPTER 16

COLD WAR: THE PYRRHIC GAMBIT

BY THE SUMMER OF 1955 THE CIA had grown to the point where it was ready to flex its wings in areas in which it had never before been able to operate and in ways that would test its intragovernmental potential. The first wave of Army Special Forces support of CIA war-planning initiatives and of U.S. Air Force Air Resupply and Communications activity had waned following the Korean War; yet the major overseas base structure that the CIA had been able to establish under the cover of those units remained. Border flights, leaflet drops, and other Iron Curtain sensing operations were under way both in Europe and Asia; but the CIA had no major projects that it could call its own.

The Agency believed that it had the means and the requirement for advanced operations, which it would support on its own initiatives. One of the first of these would be a worldwide airborne capability for electronic intelligence, radio transmission surveillance, photographic and radar intelligence, and other related activity. TSS had developed many things that could be put to work, and the overseas base structure that the DD/S had created under the "war planning" cover was more than adequate to support operations.

A small team of Air Force officers, some real Air Force officers who were on Agency assignment, and other CIA career personnel who operated under Air Force cover, met with U.S. Navy personnel to make arrangements for the purchase of seven new navy aircraft, known as the P2V-7. The P2V was not a new plane. It had been developed shortly after World War II, and the original model at one time held the world record for straight-line unrefueled long-distance flight. The "Dash Seven" model had, in addition to its two large reciprocating engines, two small T-34 Westinghouse jet engines. These small jet engines gave the plane a powerful jet-assisted take-off capability and a burst-of-speed capability, if such should be needed in any hostile situation. The airframe was rugged and proven, and Navy support facilities were available all over the world. Also, adequate cover for this plane was possible because it was slated to be given to many foreign countries as part of the Military Assistance Program. This meant that if one should happen to be lost on a clandestine mission, the United States could disclaim any connection with the flight on the hopeful assumption that whatever country found the wreckage in its backyard would be unable categorically to say whether it came from the United States or from one of several other countries.

The gross weakness of this type of cover is readily apparent. Any target country, such as China, eastern European satellites, or the Soviet Union, would scarcely even consider that these specially equipped aircraft had been launched on such a mission by Greece, Taiwan, or Japan, even if they did have some P2V-7s as part of their MAP. Furthermore, the appearance of any aircraft of this type in the inventory of any country would be made the subject of an attach report, and any worthwhile military intelligence system would have reported within days the existence of the exact number of such aircraft. Therefore, if one did show up as wreckage in a denied area, all that country would have to do to verify any cover story release would be to check its records against what it knew to be there and determine if a plane had in fact been lost. The loss would be readily apparent.

Such rather simple abuses of cover would usually lead one to conclude that the exploitation of cover was no more sincere than most other security devices, and that it had been designed just to play the secrecy game in this country, whether it had any merit vis-à-vis the world of Communism or not. But in any case, this is the way it all was done.

This latter point, about cover itself, was always made a subject of prime importance by the Agency. Wherever the planes would be operated, they would have to have insignia and special serial numbers; nothing stands out more than an unmarked plane. And they would have to operate as part of some parent, or cover, organization. To be effective cover, these numbers and insignia could not be picked out of thin air. The CIA cannot operate aircraft of its own with a CIA insignia on them. This was one of the prime considerations during the first meetings with the Navy.

Discussions went well up to the point of getting the Navy to agree to provide the worldwide support and cover this operation would require. The Navy could see that if anything ever went wrong with the program, if any one of these planes ever crashed or was shot down over denied territory, it would be the Navy that would have to bear the brunt of the exposure. The Army and Air Force already had a history of going along with the CIA; but the Navy, a service that has created a much stronger sense of tradition, was willing to help; however, it was never willing to "become involved." For a while this impasse brought the P2V-7 negotiations to a standstill.

Finally, the "Air Force" people in the CIA decided that they could find no other suitable aircraft and that they would have to find some other way to get this project going, utilizing their original choice, the P2V-7. They asked for a meeting with the Air Force. It took place sometime in August or September of 1955. It was finally agreed that the CIA would make arrangements with the Navy for the production and purchase of the planes and that they would be delivered to the U.S. Air Force. The Air Force had agreed, at the insistence of the CIA, to try to establish an adequate support program for these Navy aircraft.

Such a support project is not easy. The Air Force had aircraft with similar engines; but everything else about them was different. The Navy maintenance and supply manuals were completely different, and the Air Force might just as well have been supporting a completely new type of aircraft. Parts procurement, which would have to be done with Lockheed, the manufacturer, would require that either the Air Force requisition all parts from the Navy and then have the Navy go to Lockheed, or the Air Force would have to set up a separate supply channel itself to Lockheed. In either case it would be complicated. It is as difficult to support seven aircraft of a new and distinct type as it is to establish procedures to support seven hundred. It would have been easier for the Air Force to have set up a line for seven hundred.

All of these things were worked out, and the CIA "Air Force" officers became the project officers at the Lockheed plant. The seven planes were given production numbers along with the regular Navy production orders, and the project was well under way. Air Force pilots were selected for training in these planes, and Air Force maintenance and supporting men were sent to Navy schools to learn how to maintain these planes. All of these men were eventually informed of the special nature of the project and that the CIA was involved. This meant that all of these men had to be assigned to the CIA and that they were all volunteers for the project.

It was necessary to designate one Air Force base as the prime station for these new planes, for their maintenance and for the basic supply stockpile. At the same time the CIA Air Operations staff and the DDS Air Support staff had come to the conclusion that CIA air activity had reached the point where it should be consolidated on one major base rather than spread out all over the world as it had been. Also, the operational missions of the Agency had reached a level that required worldwide capability instead of local European or Asian capability. The Air Force and the CIA agreed to bring all of this together at Eglin Air Force Base in Florida. In terms of real estate, this was the largest base in the Air Force, and all kinds of special operations could be set up at Eglin without becoming apparent to others.

Also this was the Air Force proving ground, and it was customary to find there aircraft of all types from all services, undergoing operational training exercises. That base was an ideal location for such an organization as the CIA would have once it had been assembled. Agreement upon the CIA base at Eglin facilitated the support of the P2V-7s. They would go to Eglin also. However, there were differences, and there were problems.

One of the things the project officer on a regular Air Force procurement program is responsible for is to see that new aircraft stays within the limits of design specifications and that it does not "grow" in the process. If the design weight was to be eighty thousand pounds, then the project officer must see that it does not begin to exceed that weight as it is developed. This problem of growth usually arises as the result of the addition to the airframe of other components that are to be part of the plane's armament and electronic (avionics) packages. This was not quite the problem with the CIA plane because it would not have armament; but because this project had been shrouded in security classification, the usual specialists who would have been monitoring the work on these planes were not permitted to work on the P2V-7s, and the Agency had its own men on the job. Later in the development of the CIA version of the P2V-7, it was found that the plane had taken on a lot of weight and that if all of the extra gadgets and other components that TSS and other "users" had been adding to the plane were to be put on board, these planes would never be able to get off the ground.

As a result, many of these parts had to be redesigned, and all sorts of compromises and Rube Goldberg schemes were devised to package these additional items. For example, one group of the Air Operations shop wanted the plane to have a very modern leaflet drop capability. A huge device, which took up all of the space in the bomb-bay compartment, was designed. It looked something like an oversized honeycomb. Tens of thousands of leaflets could be stacked in small compartments, and then when the bomb-bay doors were opened and special motors activated, leaflets would be peeled off each honeycomb section and distributed like a computer-programmed snow storm. This was an excellent idea, and the leaflet spreader worked like magic; but it could not possibly be permanently attached to the plane. It was too heavy and it was too cumbersome. It would have meant that many of the other gadgets that were being planned would have to be left off.

This started some internal hostilities in the Agency. To pay for this P2V-7 project, the CIA Air Operations staff had put together the requirements of several offices of the Agency and had pooled their funds. This was all right for the purchase of the plane; but it was not a reasonable solution for a working arrangement. Every shop that had contributed to the purchase of the P2V-7 felt that it had a proportionate right to put equipment aboard the plane. However, all equipment requirements do not divide themselves into equal packages by weight, and some of these minor "piggyback" accessories began to overload the plane. There was no one in a clear position of authority and know-how sufficient to overrule each claimant. As a result, a number of non-operational concessions were made, and each P2V-7 grew like Topsy.

This is not an uncommon problem, and as we shall see later, this overgrowth of technology and the lack of restraint placed upon highly classified projects—because the normal "restrainers," the men whom on normal projects would have known how to deal with such problems, were precluded by security measures from knowing what was going on—caused many projects to go wrong and many others to grow and expand far beyond the original idea.

To accommodate this problem with the P2V-7, the manufacturer and the augmenting-equipment manufacturers reached the conclusion that most of the extra equipment would have to be modularized and made detachable. In this way, the plane could be configured for one set of targets on one flight and for another set the next time. Even with this compromise, certain elements of every system had to be permanently installed, and by the time the planes became operational, they were always overweight.

(At this very same time the CIA bad won approval for the U-2 project, and the Agency was hard at work with its Air Force supporting elements, getting that major program under way. This meant another large Lockheed project on top of the P2V-7 package.

The CIA and the Lockheed Aircraft Corporation have always been especially close. At one time, the CIA was working closely with one group of Navy specialists and with two groups of Air Force personnel, all of them aided by highly skilled technical representatives from the Lockheed Corporation. As Allen Dulles had planned, the CIA would be able to grow operationally by spreading itself into other parts of the Government and into industry and by making itself the catalyst for each project, which to the uninitiated would seem to be a project of the host service and not of the CIA.)

Meanwhile, special crews were being trained at Navy bases from Whidby Island in Washington to Jacksonville, Florida, and support personnel were being made familiar with Navy supply catalogues and procedures. Finally the day came when these special planes could be flown to Europe. Some operated out of Wiesbaden, Germany, for several years, and others went to Taiwan. Eglin Air Force Base became the logistics support base for their worldwide operational mission.

These unusual aircraft served many purposes and many masters. They possessed an advanced low-level photographic capability. They were an operational test bed for highly specialized electronic intelligence border surveillance work. They were perhaps the first operationally successful carriers of the new side-looking radar system, and they had that novel and most effective leaflet scattering system. On top of all that, someone had insisted that they have the capability to drop supplies or personnel, so a hatch had been cut in the underside of the plane, which could be opened in flight for that specialized purpose.

It was not so much the success or failure of the P2V-7 project that is important. The real issue is that after 1955 the CIA had reached the point in its development at which it was prepared to take on major global operational missions on its own using—not just requesting support of—the vast resources of the DOD for its own ends. This was a major turning point in the process that had begun with the passage of the National Security Act of 1947 and that had been moved forward by such other events as the Dulles Report of 1949. By 1955 the CIA had progressed from its assigned role as the "quiet intelligence arm of the President" to become the major operational center of power within the military and foreign policy infrastructure of the Government of the United States. The P2V-7 project was another step on the way and was positive evidence of that stage of development.

The important thing was not the size of the project itself or of the CIA operation relative to the gross size of the DOD. Rather, it was the fact that the CIA project was an active operation. It was in a sense a major part of the battle of the Cold War.

Thus the fact that only seven P2V-7s or a few squadrons of U-2s were involved was not the real measure of the impact of the ST. It was the fact that the ST was operational anywhere in the world, fully supported by any element or elements of the DOD and its supporting industrial complex that the CIA needed for its "fun and games." Thus the Western World versus the Communist World Cold War was made increasingly more real because the ST was actively, though clandestinely, engaged.

There was a French colonel in the nineteenth century named DuPicq who wrote that battles—the great early battles of history— were not quite the massive, total confrontations that historians have portrayed them to be. On the contrary, they were the close-up hand-to-hand clashes of the few men who were on the contiguous perimeter of opposing forces. Although sixty thousand men may have been arrayed on one side confronted by eighty thousand of the advancing enemy, the only men actually engaged at any one time were those in the front line, and then only those that formed part of the front line who actually came into physical contact with their counterparts and adversaries. Thus it was the task of the general, the man on the white horse, to see that more of his men were in position to engage—face to face, hand to hand—the enemy that were on the other side. Yet, the shoulder-to-shoulder mass combat of that time meant only so many men could effectively be crammed into a given area at the same time, and this would roughly be equal for both sides. It was at this juncture that tactics and training began to decide the course of the battle. As men in the front fell others directly behind them had to move into the fray. As the course of battle ebbed and flowed the well-trained, disciplined army would seize the initiative at every turn, not so much demonstrating superior power as superior training, equipment, and morale. Thus the fates of nations and empires rested not so much on huge armies as upon the shoulders of a few men engaged on the perimeter of the battle zone.

In that type of combat, before weapons with longer range—spears, bow and arrows, and then guns—the battle was won on the perimeter by small circles of men face to face, locked in deadly combat, with no choice but to go forward or die, until each adversary fell before the physical onslaught. This was essentially a battle of total attrition, with the victory going always to that force that outlasted the foe. Victory was total. It was won by annihilating the vanquished.

In a certain sense this is how the Cold War is being fought. It is all too inevitable that the two greatest powers on earth should oppose each other. General Motors has its Ford; Macy's has Gimbel's, and in nature, positive has negative. Major forces always oppose each other. This is normal. Even without the incessant reminder of real or imagined, actual or potential Cold War, a massive contest would inevitably exist between the United States and the USSR in all areas of contact. We should not lose all sense of proportion as a result of this realization, any more than they should. This confrontation is a fact of life. Thus the battles, large and small, of the "war" are the local face-to-face skirmishes between small, often unnoticed, elements on both sides. These battles may be social, economic, athletic, political, religious, and military. And no matter how large or small, how deadly or insignificant, there is only one way to tally up the score in the won-and-lost column. It is the same way one scores in chess. The game is won by not losing. As in chess, luck plays no part; the loser loses his own game. The winner is simply the man who is there at the end.

Thus the Cold War is a massive, totally grim game of attrition. The loser will be the one who has dissipated all of his resources; the winner will be the one who remains with his force relatively intact. The great and terrible truth is that in this type of warfare the loser may be the victim of deadly attrition brought about as a result of his own futile actions, as much as or even more than by actions of an enemy. Consider the battles of the Cold War all waged against the enemy, Communism. In the Berlin airlift, for example, there may have been a sort of local victory; but in the true measure of victory in the war between the great powers it was the United States that paid very heavily and the USSR that made little more than verbal onslaughts. On the scale of relative total attrition the United States went down and the USSR went up. In this type of scoring, the "up" is relative.

Or look at the score of the massive special operation into the rebellion in Indonesia. Again the battle was waged against Communism. The cost to the United States was very great, much greater than most people realize because so much of what actually took place was concealed quite effectively from the American people, although it was not unknown to the Indonesians, the Chinese, and the Russians, and for that matter, to any other country that chose to know. As a result of that costly Cold War battle, again the attrition of the United States was considerable and that of the USSR was negligible.

The Bay of Pigs was another such major battle. We made a great investment in resources and in our world prestige. Russia's contribution was again little more than words, and they were more the words of Castro than of the men in the Kremlin. Even after the gross failure of this battle, the United States lost further in the tribute it paid in the sum of more than $53 million for the release of the Cuban patriots who had been captured by Castro. It might be pointed out here that it is not so much monetary and other costs of such a secret operation that are important as it is the fact that like the battles of old, it is the ratio—in the Cuban operation, $53 million to zero—which is so deadly.

This has been the scoring for the Cold War almost all the way along. When Khrushchev no more than threatened western Europe with medium-range rockets after the outbreak of the Suez attack in 1956, he set off a flurry in this country to create a weapon that up to that time had never been considered essential. This led to the hasty and fruitless development of the Intermediate Range Ballistic Missile. Hundreds of millions of dollars were spent on those rockets, and except for their bonus payoff as power systems for certain space projects, the Jupiter, Thor, and Polaris (original model) programs were all hasty tributes to the Cold War threat. Again United States attrition was in the billions of dollars and the USSR loss was little more than the bluster of an angry Khrushchev.

The Cold War has been fought along the perimeter of the zones of Communism and of the Free World, along what is called the Iron Curtain, the Northern Tier, and the Bamboo Curtain. In a very special sense, it has been fought, like ancient wars, by those few who actually brush against the hot spots. If anything was ever a better example of the futility of this type of conflict than the operation in Indochina, which has taken place during the past two decades, it would be hard to find. Here again the contribution of the United States, the terrible attrition of our national wealth, prestige, manpower, and money has been stupendous. It is really unparalleled in the history of warfare. One nation has lost so much and its stated adversary has lost and contributed so little. The United States has lost more than fifty-five thousand men and the USSR has lost none. The United States has lost more than $200 billion and perhaps much more if the gross cost is included in this total, and the Soviet Union has lost a few billions at the most—only enough to assure that we would not lose heart and leave. Unless there is an early realization of these significant facts and with it a major change in the course of events in this country, this massive conflict may well be the last one of this stage of civilization. By all indications now, it is moving on relentlessly to a conclusion of doom for the United States. As in a terrible human chess game, the loser is giving up all of his men as a result of his own errors, and the winner is doing little more than waiting out the game and keeping up the relentless pressures.

This is why it is so important to see how the early small-scale contests between the operational forces under the direction of the ST began to stir the sleeping giant of the Defense Department into an ever-ascending crescendo of Cold War activity. With such minor events as the worldwide program of the P2V-7 and all that it involved, with the much more significant U-2 program escalating from its first tenuous border excursions to that final flight by Gary Powers in

May of 1960, the ST was preparing itself for other operations, each one larger and grander than the one that came before. And each time, as the ST prepared a new operation, it was the catalytic force that spurred the passive, counter-punching military establishment further into the quagmire of massive attrition.

By 1958 things had gone so far along these lines that the CIA was able to get itself involved in its most ambitious foreign operation. Contact had been made with an attach from Indonesia in Washington. This is not an unusual thing, and the CIA, the Department of State, and the Defense Department are frequently in contact with foreign individuals and groups who believe, selfishly in most instances, that with the help of the United States they can take over their own Communist oriented government. In the case of the Indonesian attach, the CIA was willing and ready to sound him out further, because it believed the removal of Sukarno from power in Indonesia would return that major Asian nation to the non-Communist family of nations. The "anti-Communist" war cry looked especially good there.

Rebel leaders from one end of the Indonesian island chain to the other were encouraged to organize and to plan a major rebellion against Sukarno.

Meanwhile, the CIA prepared for its most ambitious peacetime operation. A headquarters was established in Singapore, and training bases were set up in the Philippines. An old World War II airfield on a deserted island in the southwest Pacific was reactivated, and other airstrips on remote Philippine territory were prepared for bomber and transport operations. Vast stores of arms and equipment were assembled in Okinawa and in the Philippines.

Indonesians, Filipinos, Chinese, Americans, and other soldiers of fortune were assembled in Okinawa and in the Philippines also, to support the cause. The U.S. Army took part in training the rebels, and the Navy furnished over-the-beach submarine back-up support. The Air Force provided transport aircraft and prepared the fleet of modified B-26 bombers. The B-26 is a light bomber in modern terms, but it had been fitted with a nose assembly for eight 50-caliber machine guns. This is a power-packed punch for this type of warfare. A small fleet of Korean War B-26s was prepared, and a number of covert crews were assembled to fly them.

In the beginning, rebellion broke out in various parts of the island chain, and loyalist forces were forced to deal with them one at a time. While the Indonesian army, under the command of General Nasution, began an attack upon the rebels on the main island of Sumatra it seemed that the rebel cause would be victorious on the other islands.

However, the inability of the rebels to win decisive victories and to enlist the aid of neutrals or of the regular forces of the Government turned the war back gradually in favor of the loyalist army. The struggle was protracted, and the CIA threw everything it had into the attack. Tens of thousands of rebels were armed and equipped from the air and over the beach, but at no time were the rebels ever able to take the offensive.

Meanwhile, the U.S. ambassador in Jakarta had the difficult task of maintaining the semblance that the rebels were acting on their own, and that the United States was not involved. As if to strengthen his hand, the Chief of Naval Operations, then Admiral Arleigh Burke, sent his chief of intelligence to Jakarta right at that time, as much as if to say that certainly there was no U.S. military involvement in these attacks. It was an unusual rebellion, with the CIA doing all it could to help the rebels and with the overt U.S. Government officials doing all they could to maintain normal relations. Then, during an air attack on an Indonesian supply vessel, one of the B-26 bombers was shot down. The pilot and crew were rescued. The pilot turned out to be an American, and his crew was mixed from other nations. This American, Allen Pope, had in his possession all kinds of routine identification documents, including a set of U.S. Air Force orders that proved beyond any doubt that he was an active U.S. Air Force pilot. The only choice left for the Indonesians was to assume that he was either a U.S. Air Force pilot flying for the USAF, or that he was a U.S. Air Force pilot flying in support of the rebels clandestinely at the direction of the CIA.

Things had not been going well, and other CIA assistance had been compromised. It was not long before rebel activity was limited to remote areas where government control had never been strong in the first place. General Nasution continued a mop-up campaign, and the rebellion came to an end.

There were many who asked, when Allen Pope came up for trial in Jakarta, how it happened that a man who was flying clandestine missions could have been carrying so much and such complete identification with him. Why had he not been subjected to a search and other controls that would have assured that he would have been stateless and plausibly deniable if captured? These same questions were asked after Gary Powers had been captured in the Soviet Union after his U-2 had landed there in 1960.

The usual procedure requires that the aircraft, and all records that might ordinarily have been aboard the plane, and all other airborne materials be sanitized before the plane is used on any clandestine mission. A considerable amount of money had been spent by the Air Force to assure that these B-26 aircraft had been sanitized and that all airborne equipment was deniable.

At the forward base where Allen Pope and the other pilots were operating, the CIA was supposed to assure that all crew members were sanitized. This required that they enter a crew room, strip naked, and then be examined by proper authority. From that room they would enter another bare room, where nothing but the flight clothes they would wear would be available. All personal effects and other identification would be removed and left in the first room. From this second room the crew would be driven directly to their aircraft.

However, all crew members, as all other members of the human race, have a strong sense of survival, and they know very well that if they are captured and declared to be stateless, they will then have no legal means to appeal to the United States or to any other nation and they will be shot as spies in accordance with custom. On the other hand, if they are captured and can prove beyond doubt that they are American, then they become valuable pawns in the hands of their captors. The nation that has captured them can deal privately with the U.S. Government in a form of top-level international blackmail. The lives of the men involved becomes of minor importance by that time to both countries compared to the advantages that the capturing country can wring out of the loser with the threat of exposure of the facts of the case. This is the key factor in the present prisoner-of-war problem with Hanoi. Those prisoners, many of whom were captured under unusual circumstances in accordance with the compacts signed in Geneva, have become a much more valuable asset to the Government of Hanoi than what might be called the usual prisoner of war, as in World War II.

With this in mind, it can be said that every agent takes precautionary measures on his own to see that he has some identifying material with him if he can possibly get away with it. It is entirely possible that the crew of the captured B-26 had their identification hidden in the plane and that they retrieved it once they were in the air. This must have been the case because the official reports from the base where they had departed on that mission stated that they had gone through the inspection process outlined above. In spite of all this, the Indonesian Government was able to produce at Allen Pope's trial copies of his recently-dated Air Force orders, which had transferred him to the Philippines. They had his Air Force identification card and a current post exchange card for Clark Air Force Base Manila, and such other documents. There could be no doubt in their minds that Allen Pope was a current Air Force pilot and that he was flying in support of the rebels and for the CIA. Such evidence is all that is needed to expose the hand of the United States and to lay this Government open to pressures.

Students and researchers of subsequent action in Indonesia may have noted that the Pope case and all that it exposed has cost this Government heavily in the years that followed. Although Pope had been captured in 1958, it remained for Bobby Kennedy, during the Administration of President John F Kennedy, to complete some of the remaining "payoff."

The Indonesian campaign was no small matter. It marked the entry of the CIA into the big time. Its failure also marked the beginning of a most unusual career for the CIA. It seemed that the more the CIA failed, the more it grew and prospered. As a direct and immediate result of this failure, the Eisenhower Administration made a searching review of what had happened. Unlike the Bay of Pigs investigation three years later, this review was not made in public and it was not as gentle on the main participants. The leader of all CIA activity in Southeast Asia at the time of the Indonesian action was Frank Wisner. He was then the Deputy Director of Plans for the CIA. He had gone to Singapore himself to head the operation rather than delegate this important task to someone else. Wisner was relieved of duty with the Agency, along with several other top officials, and the whole team that had worked on that program was broken up and scattered to the four winds of Agency assignments.

This brusque action by Eisenhower, although properly justified, led to certain events that have left their record upon history. The activist in the Eisenhower Administration who had gone along with Allen Dulles and Frank Wisner on this campaign was the Vice President, Richard M. Nixon. Also the man who wielded the cudgel when it came time to clean house was the same Richard Nixon. In the government civil service 'safe haven,' it is one thing to censure and to wring hands; but it is an entirely different matter actually to fire someone and release him from the protective cocoon of government service. Since the Indonesian campaign was, technically anyway, highly classified, most other government workers did not know why all of these 'nice people' had been fired, and since they were cool to Nixon anyhow, they arose in unison to damn him when he ran for President in 1960.

This in turn led to other events of some magnitude. When Eisenhower directed Allen Dulles to brief Kennedy and Nixon equally during the campaign, Dulles had briefed each of them according to his idea of what each needed to know. He knew that Nixon was up to date on such things as the anti-Castro campaign, so he did not have to go into detail on that with him. And when he briefed Kennedy, he gave the same briefing, being strictly fair and equal. This meant that Kennedy had not been briefed as fully on the anti-Castro plans as Eisenhower might have thought desirable. Allen Dulles was able to report, when challenged, that he had briefed them both equally and that he had not gone into the detail of the covert Cuban campaign (later Bay of Pigs—this will be discussed in detail later). However, other CIA officials at a level well below Allen Dulles did see to it that Kennedy knew all there was to know about the anti-Castro campaign and everything else that might help him in his bitter and strenuous campaign against Nixon.

Thus Nixon, who carefully observed the limits of security, was at a considerable disadvantage, and Kennedy, who could take the stance that he was not "officially" aware of classified things of that nature, could use anything he chose against Nixon. The assistance that he got across the board from the multi-million-civil-servant reservoir of good will easily proved sufficient to tip the scales of that very close election in favor of John F. Kennedy. It is interesting to see how proper action at the time of the Indonesian debacle backlashed against the man who carried it out as a member of the NSC.

With one Deputy Director of Plans gone and with the Agency scrambling to find something to do after it had withdrawn from the area in Indonesia, Allen Dulles turned his attention to the U-2, which had become operational on a grand scale. He made the director of the U-2 program the new Deputy Director of Plans for the Agency, thus promoting Richard Bissell to the highest clandestine operations spot in the U.S. Government.

Meanwhile, the P2V-7 project continued to grow and to operate on a worldwide scale, as did the U-2 project. The Agency also got itself involved in lesser activities all over the world. It was active in Iran and in Ethiopia. It stepped up its work in Laos and Thailand, and it was actively supporting the Chinese Nationalists in their penetration operations into the mainland. Then, in May of 1959, the Agency found itself again involved in one of those totally unexpected catastrophes that seem to occur when least expected and least desired.

Chapter 17

Mission Astray, Soviet Gamesmanship

High over eastern Turkey, the big plane tossed fitfully in the turbulent air. Scattered snow-white cloud formations billowed above to thirty-five and forty thousand feet. In the brilliant sunlight and clear air between the clouds the crew could see the distant shores of Lake Van. At Lake Van they would turn to the southeast to cross near Lake Urmia and then on to Tehran. All was going well, and they expected to be in Tehran on schedule or perhaps a little early. The navigator was new in this remote area of the world, but he had noted that the winds were picking up, and he had alerted the pilot to watch for the turn at Lake Van: "You know, if you miss it we'll be in Russia."

Five men were up front in the pilot's compartment, and the others were in the empty cabin, relaxing. One young crew member, enjoying his first visit to the Near East, was taking pictures out of the right side of the plane. He noted one particularly high peak rising all by itself from the knot of mountains around it. The plane was cruising at about nineteen thousand feet, yet this lone majestic peak seemed almost to reach that altitude. Then it was lost from sight because of a cloud and he waited for his next chance to take another picture.

In front of them the pilot saw that they were getting quite close to the big lake, and he was preparing to turn as soon as he reached its near corner. On this highly classified mission, none of them wanted to take any chances of being too close to the Soviet Union. If what was in the heavy briefcases in a tail compartment of the plane ever fell into the hands of the Soviets, the work of many years with the U-2 in the Near East would be exposed, and the participation of those friendly Northern Tier countries would be compromised.

As Lake Van dipped under the nose of the big transport the pilot took the plane off of autopilot, gently banked it to the right, and set a course along the international airway for Tehran, which should have brought him just to the east of Lake Urmia. As he was busy realigning the autopilot he noticed far ahead, under the base of the cumulus clouds, what looked to be the shore of Lake Urmia just about where it should be, slightly to his left. Still thinking of the Soviet Union, he gave the knobs that controlled the autopilot an extra twist to bring the big bird that much more onto the safe side.

The young airman in the rear of the plane was able to get another good view of the big mountain now, off to the right rear, and was preparing to shoot another picture when he saw the first MIG coming up fast on their wing tip. When he saw another MIG and that undeniable Red Star on the big, high slab tail which is the distinguishing feature of the MIG, he dashed up to the cockpit and called to the pilot. At about that time they all could hear the "thutt-thutt-thutt" rapid fire of the MIG's cannon. With MIGs riding just off the right wing tip, the pilot had no choice but to detach the autopilot and veer slightly to the left. Then his co-pilot noticed the Russian pilot motioning them downward. He told the pilot, who cut the power a little and continued to bank left. In this maneuver they began to come full circle, and just as they thought they might be able to slip into a nearby cloud the whole plane shuddered and the men in the cabin saw the left inboard engine burst into flames. Another MIG flying just under their belly had given them a convincing burst of fire in the left engine nacelle.

Without waiting, five of the nine men on board donned parachutes, jettisoned the big main door as soon as the pilot decompressed the cabin air pressure, and bailed out. All of these men landed safely but were burned by flying droplets of molten metal coming from the burning engine. The other four men had no choice but to stay with the plane. With the MIGs flying only a few feet off their wing tips, they gently let the burning plane settle toward the fields below. It was then that the pilot noted a small unfinished airstrip in the farm land. He leveled off and eased the plane toward the only safe haven he could see. As he approached this small landing strip, he noticed that the grass was leaning toward his line of flight and that wind in the few small trees indicated that he would be landing downwind. This meant a fast landing on a small strip; but he did not dare to pull the plane up and try again. He could see the flames in the white-hot inboard engine, and he knew that the wing would fold up and drop off in a few more minutes. He cut his power, dropped the gear, and dropped full flaps, all as fast as he could, and drove the big plane into the ground, planning to bring it to a halt with brakes and luck.

The plane stopped skidding, far out into the field, beyond the end of the unfinished runway. It had been a rough landing, but they were on the ground. Now they had to get out of the plane right away. Because of the tail wind, the fire around the engine was blowing forward and had begun to engulf the entire wing and cockpit area in billowing smoke. The fuel tanks in the outer wing would be the next to go—and that would be some explosion. The four men on the plane didn't wait to put the ladder down from the cabin doorway which was about nine feet in the air. They swung from the emergency rope and slid to the ground, then ran away from the plane as fast as they could. As they ran they saw smoke billowing above the plane. The MIGs swirled above them as much as to say, "Stand where you are. We're watching." Just as they stopped running they saw where the five parachutes had settled to the earth a few miles away. All nine men had landed. All nine wondered where they were.

In Washington I had just been home for about an hour and had started a charcoal fire in the backyard. The steaks were ready, and my wife and I were finishing a drink on the patio when the telephone rang. My young daughter answered the phone and then called to me, "Mr. White wants to speak to you, Daddy." I picked up the phone, and Mr. White turned out to be General Thomas D. White, then the Chief of Staff of the U.S. Air Force. He did not want to discuss the subject on the telephone, but suggested that I go directly to Allen Dulles house and do whatever I could to help him with a grave problem that had arisen.

In a few minutes I was on the way to Mr. Dulles' home. I pulled into his driveway just before dark, and as I walked through the house to his study I noted four men finishing a tennis match on the court in the rear of the house. Allen Dulles had on a vee-necked tennis sweater with white tennis shorts and peaked hat. He quickly introduced me to Dick Bissell and some of the others who were there and then began to tell me about their problem.

American newsmen in Moscow had been saying that a USAF aircraft was down somewhere in the Soviet Union. This report had been coming in from Moscow for more than eighteen hours. No one had been able to confirm or deny it. The President wanted an answer one way or the other without fail. A check of all Air Force aircraft showed that none were missing and that none were known to be anywhere near the Soviet Union. The other services and all other operators of large transport aircraft that might have been in that area were checked. No aircraft were missing. Quiet requests had been made to the CIA station chiefs in other countries to see if there might have been a foreign plane of a U.S. made type that could have gone down in the Soviet Union. For eighteen hours all of these checks had proved to be fruitless; yet the story from Moscow persisted. It was apparent that the Russians knew more than they had released, and that they were letting someone stew over the problem. A picture of a four-engined aircraft was given to the press and had been radio-photographed to the States. It showed a large plane burning in the last stages of destruction. About all that was left was the towering tail section. (Since the wind had blown from the rear, the fire had burned the front and the wings where the fuel cells were located and had left no more than the high tail section.) This gave little to work on; yet it was quite obviously the tail of a DC-6 or military C-118.

After I talked with them for a while and listened to all of the news they had, I excused myself and went to the Pentagon. In my office there was a top secret safe with a special card file on a great number of the seven-thousand-odd men who worked with me all over the world in special activities that were generally related to the support of the CIA. It consisted of a code of names, numbers, and other information that was indispensable. I took this box of cards and went down into the basement of the Pentagon, to the Air Force Command Post. This is one of the finest communications centers in the world. The duty officer authorized me to enter and to take over one of the telephone positions there on a matter of urgency.

In a few minutes I had reached the home, in Germany, of an Air Force officer who might be able to tell me about a C-118 aircraft that was not in the Air Force inventory and which might be the one that was missing. The plane I was looking for was one that belonged to the CIA itself and one of two considered to be Mr. Dulles' personal planes. I had called this officers' home in Germany by private commercial lines to bypass the military center in Frankfurt. There would be time for them later.

It was about four in the morning then in Wiesbaden when the phone was answered by the housekeeper. The officer was not home. I asked where he was and learned simply that he had gone on a flight. This was part of the answer I needed. I called another Air Force officer, one who was a cover type. He told me that the plane was away on a trip. I stopped him there and asked him to go immediately to headquarters and to call me from there on the secure scrambler telephone.

About twenty minutes later the security phone rang, and he told me that General Cabell, the Deputy Director of Central Intelligence, had arrived in Germany a few days earlier in the special C-118. He had authorized a CIA/Air Force crew to take the plane on a very highly classified and important flight to Tehran and Pakistan. Cabell had gone on to England in a smaller plane, and the nine Agency men had taken the big plane to Cyprus, then to Adana, Turkey and thence to Tehran. He was advised to get the names of the nine men involved while I called Adana.

The next call was to the duty officer at Adana. He was asked to check the records there for the C-118. After a few moments he said that no C-118 had come through Adana on the day in question. He was asked to check again and to query the operations office people even if he had to wake them up one at a time. The plane must have gone through there. Fortunately, he started his search by talking with the weatherman on duty. He had been on duty when the C-118 had left Adana. The meteorologist remembered the crew and the plane. Still they could find no record of the flight. Finally, the duty officer checked the on-duty operations officer to see if perhaps he had held out the clearance papers for that flight. This did the trick. A few minutes after I had gotten the complete crew list from my contact in Germany, a call from Adana came in, stating that the pilot of the C-118 had told the operations officer not to file the clearance he had made but to hold it. This was done frequently on such black flights, and it accounted for why no one had missed the plane. Ordinarily, any overdue Air Force aircraft would be the subject of an alarm and search within one hour after its last report of position. The people at Adana did not know where the plane was going and the people at Tehran did not know that it was expected; so once the plane—this plane of all planes—had taken off, no one had monitored the flight at all. Its singular disappearance had gone completely unnoticed, even to the extent that it was not included on the Air Force master inventory or on the DOD master list of all military aircraft.

Having pieced this much together, I called Allen Dulles on the direct line to his home and told him that the plane we were looking for was General Cabell's plane, but that Cabell was not aboard. Within minutes, even at that hour, he was on the phone to his brother, who in turn passed the word on to the White House.

After a few hours rest, I drove back into town and stopped at Allen Dulles' house, picked him up and went to Foster Dulles' house, where we met the Secretary of Defense, at that time Neil McElroy, and the Chief of Staff of the Air Force, General Thomas D. White.

The CIA had confirmed that nine men were on the plane, that it had left Adana for Tehran, and that the men had with them aboard the plane some most highly classified material in heavy briefcases. There was nothing to do but announce that a military transport aircraft on a routine trip had been blown off course on its way from Adana, Turkey, en route to Tehran and that it had landed in the Soviet Union south of Baku. At that time we knew no more than that, and we did not know that the plane had been shot down. The Secretary of State picked up the direct telephone to the White House and spoke with the President. The 'official' version of the story was released with the hope that there would be no necessity to elaborate further. However, this would depend upon the identification carried by the crew members and on whether or not the classified materials and other items that might have identified the CIA would be uncovered.

It was not long before the Russians released the story that the big plane had violated its airspace and that MIG fighters had forced it down as it attempted an escape maneuver, by firing a warning burst into the left wing. What we did not know at the time was that the pilot and other crew members had mistaken Lake Sevan for Lake Van. This meant that a greater than expected tail wind had blown them off course to the left and at the same time had put them ahead of schedule. Because of the clouds they missed Lake Van, and with Lake Sevan in sight they felt no concern. They were sure they were on the right course. The CIA had utilized a crew for this flight who did not know the area well, and confusion is not uncommon for a new crew in a strange place. Then, with Lake Sevan as their mistaken turning point they did see water ahead, which looked like Lake Urmia. Not being familiar with Lake Urmia, a larger lake, they mistook the distant shoreline of the Caspian Sea for Lake Urmia and thought all was well. Actually, on this windblown course, they were well inside the Soviet border, somewhat south of Baku.

The key to their mistake was discovered later, when all of the crewmen were questioned and the young airman in the cabin who had been taking pictures told us about the huge mountain off to their right. That was Mount Ararat, over sixteen thousand feet in altitude and the highest peak in the area. Mount Ararat should have been far on their left, and they should have turned to the southeast before they ever got near Ararat. When the airman revealed that he had photographed Mount Ararat through the right window—looking to the south—before the turn, and then had seen it again through the same right window after the turn—thus to the east—it became indisputably clear that the plane had passed north and then well to the east of Mount Ararat. This was far off course and over Soviet territory.

Another thing we did not know was that as the men in their parachutes were descending they all realized that they were carrying considerable identification, including reference to their USAF "cover" unit that might have compromised them; so they began to clean out their pockets and tear up all they could while going down. Later, they learned that Russian farmers noticed this hail of bits and pieces and that the local police had rounded up scores of people, located most of this evidence, and reassembled it during their captivity in Baku.

Another thing that became evident from the selected pictures the Russians chose to release was the fact that the C-118 did not burn completely; the part that remained after the tail-wind landing was the entire rear of the plane—where the classified briefcases were. Tests on such briefcases had shown that they could sustain considerable heat and some flame without appreciably damaging the documents inside. The chances were very good that the entire classified cargo had been recovered intact.

This may have saved the men from lengthy captivity. Knowing that they were doing nothing more than transporting briefcases, and that most likely they were little more than a crew and not true agents, the Soviets may have reasoned that it was better to release the men early. That would imply they really believed the men were simply transport crewmen, and it would lead us to attempt to find out how much the Russians might have gained through the unscheduled gratuity of the briefcases. The men were held for nine days, and during this time they were questioned continually. The Russians learned all they needed to know and then let the crew go without too much delay.

One episode stands out clearly and supports the idea that they knew quite well exactly what they had captured. Aboard was an Air Force colonel and the senior officer of the USAF cover unit in Wiesbaden, Germany. He was a real Air Force officer and his cover assignment was deep; but not so deep that he would have had great value to the Russians. However, they did not wish to miss any chances. After a few days in Baku the Russians approached the colonel and told him that since he was the senior officer and since it had become obvious to them that he was simply the commander of a transport unit—his cover story—they saw no need to have him attend the strenuous interrogations in which the other men were involved. In fact, they suggested that he might enjoy a few days fishing on the Caspian. They also told him that they had located a teacher who happened to be there on his vacation and that this teacher could speak English.

The colonel accepted this offer, and for several days he joined this male teacher on hiking and fishing trips. During this time they talked a lot about the United States. It seemed that the teacher had been in Washington during World War II and that he had been a member of the Russian Lend Lease staff. The teacher was able to lead the conversation into many fields, and the colonel thought it best to speak unrestrainedly in order to establish a comfortable relationship that might help all of them to gain their release. However, upon retrospection the colonel did realize that the teacher seemed to have a most excellent insight into current American policies and practices; but in his zeal to win his cooperation the colonel tried to answer what seemed to be simple questions, even when they led at times into some areas that put a little pressure on secrecy.

When the men were released nine days after they had been shot down, a special team had been sent to the Iranian-Soviet border to provide transportation to get them back to Germany without delay. In Germany the men went through lengthy interrogations designed to be somewhat superficial so that they might let their guard down. Then when they were flown to the United States they were put through a program of intense and highly professional interrogation by teams of well-trained FBI, CIA, and military men. It was the Washington debriefing that uncovered the Mount Ararat fix, the location of the briefcases, and the fact that they most probably were not destroyed; this debriefing also developed the "school teacher" angle further. By about the fifth day of debriefing, the combined FBI and CIA team[1] was able to lay a set of pictures on the table before the colonel and with apparent ease show him several very good pictures of the "school teacher." This "vacationing school teacher" was none other than one of the top intelligence men of the Soviet Union. He had been with the Russian staff in Washington during the Lend Lease period in World War II. The very fact that this man himself participated in this mild interrogation on the shores of the Caspian made it quite clear that the Russians had found out that they had made a big catch in the capture of this one plane.

This whole incident in some ways presaged the U-2 affair and in some ways offered clues to other events that followed. The CIA was getting to the point where it took operational matters into its own hands. There was no reason whatsoever why the highly specialized and sanitized C-118 should have been used on a mission close to the Soviet border. Any Air Force aircraft could have been used. Certainly the Russians combed the remains of the plane and found a number of odd features, among them totally unsanitized and "unmarked"[2] component parts.

There was no reason whatsoever to utilize an inexperienced CIA crew on this flight, when the Air Force had a number of crews that were very familiar with the Gordian Knot area of remote Turkey. Actually, there is an effective radio beacon homer at the southern tip of Lake Van, and an experienced crew would have used it properly. For example, the navigator on this CIA crew had not been in this area before and another navigator who was with him had not been there for a very long time.

---

1. Headed by the same James McCord later to gain notoriety in the 1972 "Watergate" affair.

2. Industrial components are marked with special numbers, codes and other identifying inscriptions. A thorough intelligence system classifies these things and can gain considerable information from such data. (More later.)

Perhaps the most damaging oversight, which must have confirmed for the Russians that they had caught a pretty special breed of fish, was that the CIA used unnecessary secrecy with respect to fight clearances of the plane. There was no good reason why the plane, which looked just like a regular Air Force plane, should not have used the customary landing and take-off clearances that all Air Force aircraft use the world over. This would have assured that the flight would have been monitored. Under such regulations the Air Force would have noted the silence of that plane within thirty minutes, and in any case within one hour after its last contact with a ground station. This is standard procedure. Had this been done, a search would have been started right away. Then the Secretary of State and the President would not have had to deny that a plane was missing for a full eighteen hours, while the Russians knew all that time exactly what had taken place. They had the men, the plane and the briefcases. It might be added that a normal part of an Air Force clearance requires confirmation that the crew is competent and has been over the route recently.

Failure of the entire U.S. Government to respond to the reported loss of this aircraft certainly signaled to the Russians that this plane must have been on a special mission, if nothing else did. One year later this same thing happened when the U-2 was lost. At first the United States did not know just where the U-2 had been lost. Then, when it was realized that it was down in Russia, it was assumed that the pilot was dead; so a cover story was used, only to have Khrushchev blow it up when he surfaced a live pilot and a nearly whole aircraft, both in Soviet hands.

It goes without saying that the CIA compounded the problems of this incident by permitting a most highly secret cargo to be entrusted to this plane and crew, when it could have set up a more secure and less casual means of transportation even if it had used a normal commercial air carrier. Such disregard for real professionalism, in favor of a growing dependence upon its new-found strength, independence, and size, became more marked as the years passed.

CHAPTER 18

DEFENSE, CONTAINMENT, AND ANTI-COMMUNISM

A decade had passed since Jackson, Dulles, and Correa had submitted their report to President Truman. Allen Dulles, a lawyer trained in the ways and traditions of the law, may well have been familiar with the famous concept of Dicey on "Law and Opinion." "The opinion," according to Dicey, "which changes the law is in one sense the opinion of the time when the law is actually altered; in another sense it has often been in England the opinion prevalent some twenty or thirty years before that time; it has been as often as not in reality the opinion not of today but of yesterday."

With a simple twist that quotation can be made to apply to the eventual outcome of the Dulles report. What he wanted and what he planned to do as a result of his work and his study in 1948—fully expecting that Thomas E. Dewey would be elected President and that he would then become the DCI—had all come about anyhow by 1959. The opinion and hopes of yesterday had all but become the law of the day. If this was not entirely true as early as 1959, it was under way in the glacier-like movement of covert events, as we shall see in the next chapter, and by the winter of 1961 the new Kennedy Administration thought that the methods being used and exploited by Allen Dulles and the ST were, in fact and in practice, the law.

Dulles was the DCI, and his agency had grown to great strength and great power and influence in the Government. As a result of the intelligence oversight at the start of the Korean War, we have seen how his immediate predecessor had been able to turn that gross mistake into an advantage and to establish the concept of the Current Intelligence Estimate, and following that success, to develop the practice of the daily report to the President. Exploited as it was during the following seven years, this device became a most effective tool in the hands of Allen Dulles. By playing on what he called "security," he had been able to limit the National Security Council's working control of the CIA to a small, friendly, and hand-picked Special Group, which instead of "directing" the CIA from "time to time," had easily fallen into the practice of convening its meetings simply to put the stamp of approval on proposals made by the CIA for almost any Secret Intelligence-generated Peace-time Clandestine Operation. By 1959 there were almost no restraints. This permitted the CIA to avoid entirely the scrutiny of the OCB and to work outside the continuing monitorship of that board. In effect, by 1959 the Agency was able to run operations itself as it saw fit.

During this same decade Allen Dulles had been able to accomplish his goal to join within one organization the two power-packed elements of Secret Intelligence and Secret Operations. Dulles knew that when he could combine Secret Intelligence and Secret Operations, he could bring them together under conditions of his own choosing to create a force of unequaled power. By the time he had created an agency, which by bypassing all of the barriers of the law and of the NSC, and with the men, the money, and materials sufficient to carry out any operation anywhere in the world, he knew that he had succeeded in turning the tables completely. He was, for all intents and purposes, in control of the foreign policy and clandestine military operational power of the United States for combat in the Cold War. In this sense the vast military establishment, including much of its industrial supporting complex, had become his orchestra. By 1960, after Eisenhower had seen his hopes and dreams of peace crushed by the untimely disaster of the U-2 flight, he warned of this power and of its abuse.

During this formative decade Dulles had positioned CIA personnel and Agency-oriented disciples inconspicuously through out the Government and in many instances had positioned the CIA throughout the business world and the academic community as well. It will be recalled that many of the new Kennedy team came from some of these founts of power, such as The Center for International Studies at the Massachusetts Institute of Technology. In fact, there were few places where the CIA had not taken advantage of covert positions, at home and abroad, for the ostensible purpose of gathering intelligence, and for the undercover purpose of making it possible for the CIA to mount any operation it chose to direct.

As in the case of the wayward C-118, the support of the rebellion in Indonesia, the paramilitary activities in Laos, and other such activities in Tibet, by the time the Agency had reached this position of power it had become somewhat insensitive to the usual and ordinary restraints that normally apply to covert operations. The Agency lost a plane, compromised a crew and the U-2 operations, and exposed its hand in Indonesia. But instead of halting such risky and fruitless operations, it ordered more planes and looked for more "subversive insurgents to counter." It was this attitude and this type of activity that led to many controversial events that have plagued this Government during the second decade of the CIA.

To understand why the CIA has become so controversial, one must understand its motivations and one must understand what happens when things are done clandestinely—and by this we mean clandestinely within the Government of the United States. Recall that we pointed out how World War II ended with Truman's abolishing the OSS and demobilizing the military as fast as possible. Recall what is more important, that the great war against Hitler, Mussolini, and Tojo had been won with the help of the Russians. No matter how anyone may feel about the ideological distinction between the Soviet Government and the United States, the incontrovertible fact is that the Russian people fought the might of Germany on their doorstep, and those people, with our material help as a factor, utterly destroyed the great German war machine. Those of us who have seen the destruction and havoc caused in Russia by that war can vouch for the fact that no conflict in history has ever been so massive and so total.

Then, with victory it was only realistic to have some feeling still for the people of Russia who had given so much to the common cause during that war. And from this feeling there arose in our Government the official view, stated on many occasions by the Secretary of State, among others, that we must establish peace in this world with the Russians and with all people, and that we must not do anything that would divide the world into armed camps and divisive forces. While the official spokesmen of this Government were pledging their faith in the United Nations and in the "one world" of 1946, only one short week passed until the aging Lion of Britain stood up on that platform in Missouri with President Truman beside him and uttered the great cry of the weak, "Beware!" Here in the greatest country on earth, with the greatest victory ever achieved in a major war, with armed forces equipped with the most advanced technology and production know-how, and with all of this increased by an unbelievable order of magnitude because of the possession of the atomic bomb and the proven means to deliver and detonate it, we were being told to beware of that other ally whose ideology we did not like, but certainly whose strength and even whose intentions could scarcely have been dangerous in that era.

But with that cry others were given heart. General Donovan, the Dulles brothers, and many others, including Clark Clifford, preached the doctrine of containment. Even in those days they saw the Soviet danger as a military threat against the United States. How could they support that openly? Even George F. Kennan, then in Moscow, warned of the Soviet danger; but the great distinction was that he saw Russia as a political threat; and the threat that he saw was, more correctly, that the Marxists expected that the United States would crumble in spite of itself. Their threat was not so much what Communism would do to us as what they expected we would do to ourselves. In other words, the Marxists felt that all they had to do was maintain the political pressure, and we would crumble under the weight of our own weaknesses.

Then, behind the curtain of secrecy, the Donovan, Dulles, and Clifford element began to win the day. No longer did the President stand behind his Secretary of State on that declaration that "we shall do nothing to divide the world into blocs." But now he listened to the counsels of the frightened and the weak as they rigged first the Iron Curtain, then the Truman Doctrine, with its shield over NATO, Greece and Turkey, on to the Northern Tier, and then to the Bamboo Curtain. By the end of 1947 the entire military establishment of this great country was technically, semantically, and philosophically reduced to an uncertain and cowering defensive posture. From this position it became dependent upon the eyes and ears and mentality of the intelligence community to tell it what was going on in the rest of the world and where the next threat was coming from. From that day to this, this country has been engaged in the most massive war of attrition ever fought.

By now, the terrifying truth of the matter is that in this last great total war we have been wiped out in every battle. There is no sense in trying to rate the intangibles such as, "We have made friends in Greece" or "We did pretty well in the Congo." The facts are that even though we say that we are engaged in a war with Communism, which at some point inevitably must mean Russia, we have paid all the losses in tens of thousands of men, hundreds of billions of dollars, and prestige beyond measure. On the other side, the Russians have done exactly what Kennan said they would do—preside over our own demise and demoralization. In a war of attrition, the winner is he who holds his own position while his adversary wastes away. Whether the loser wastes away as a result of strategic moves on the part of the winner, or as a result of his own miscues is of no concern to the historian. All the historian will note is that like the dinosaur, the loser will become extinct in spite of the fact that he seems at the time to rule the world.

The shocking fact is the growth of the power of secret and clandestine actions. The legislators and the Administration that passed into law the National Security Act of 1947, and with it created the

CIA, were the same men who most staunchly protested against and denied to the Agency the right to become involved in clandestine operations. Yet it was patently inevitable that the creation of such an agency would lead to its exploitation for just such purposes.

As the National Security Act visualized, the NSC might "from time to time direct" the Agency to carry out a clandestine operation and no more. Congress expected that there would be clandestine operations; but they saw them only as those operations which the highest echelon of the Government would plan and direct. On the other hand, as General Donovan and Allen Dulles had proposed, the very success of Secret Intelligence would from time to time create its own requirements for subsequent clandestine operations for no more reason than that the intelligence input had detected something somewhere. The legislators knew that clandestine operations would grow out of the findings of Secret Intelligence whether or not there was any national plan or policy to carry out in the first place. This is why the Donovan-Dulles-Clifford school of thought requires the existence, real or imagined, of a constant enemy—Communism. With the constant enemy, every bit of Secret Intelligence that reveals the existence of Communism is its own reason for the development of an operation. Then the counterpunch becomes the action of a machine, not of minds.

Recall the area covered with sprung and set mousetraps we have mentioned before. The traps are there, covering every inch of the floor and every avenue of entree. All the master of the house has to do is wait until a trap has snapped. Then when one trap snaps it most likely activates others, which in turn activate others until all the traps go off. While all of this is going on, the master of the house comes to one preordained conclusion—there are mice in the house and at least one of those mice has just entered his domain. His "machine" is ready to do the rest.

Throughout this period these were two opposing views. The 1st saw requirements for clandestine operations arising only after and as a result of planning and policy—in other words, from a position of confidence and strength; the second saw such requirements as an inevitable result of and response to the product of Secret

Intelligence—or from a position of weakness uncertainty, and re-action. In either case, the resort to the use of clandestine operations would be an extremely serious business.

By 1959 there had taken place a rather sinister refocusing of such operations themselves. As we have said earlier, the impetus behind the creation of the CIA came from concern over the gross failures of intelligence during World War II and worry over the possibility that the Soviet Union might acquire the atomic bomb. When the CIA first started, it concentrated its limited efforts in those primary areas of interest in the heartland and contiguous periphery of the Soviet Union. The CIA in those days worked right along with the military as the military establishment developed its "new generation" war plans. As a result, all early targeting of the CIA was directed upon the Soviet Union as a military adversary and on the Iron Curtain countries as part of the primary target area. In other words, the CIA and the military were deeply committed to the "containment" philosophy and dedicated to the encirclement of the Soviet Union and the Communist world.

This action on a continuing basis taxes the counterpuncher severely. He must be always on the alert, always geared for maximum action, and unhesitatingly diligent lest the enemy make a move. The war of attrition was already beginning to take its toll, even in those early years. It would be impossible to maintain a posture of massive retaliation day after day, forever, and then to maintain an alert air defense force, as well as a total intelligence effort supporting both. The whole "defensive-posture system" needed to find some way to maintain its apparent vigilance, but in such a manner that would permit it to relax now and then.

By the end of the decade of the fifties the CIA had found a way to do this and at the same time to make it appear that it was as much in the center of the fray as ever. It began to find Communism in other areas. Rather than devoting all of its time and energies to the Soviet Union and its neighbors, the CIA began to see "problems" in the territories of our friends. By that time the CIA had spread itself all over Africa, Europe (that part that is in the Free World sector), Latin America, and Asia (again the part that is Free World). The CIA spent less and less time concentrating on Russia and its zone of influence and more and more time looking for the influence of Russia and the influence of Communism in our own back yard. As the host nations, among them most of our friends, became increasingly aware of this intrusion, often an unwitting one, they became more and more concerned over the foreign policy and activity of the United States because it was clothed almost everywhere in the black cloak of espionage and clandestine operations. This had become a serious problem. In time this intrusion looked as ominous and sinister as the possibility of Communist intrusion itself.

The change in the very character and traditional nature of this country bothered our friends. Historically, the United States has always professed to be an open society. This government is of the people, and since the power was in the hands of the people, there has always been a majority who believe there is no need for limiting that power. Even as Franklin D. Roosevelt had assumed more and more power, first to fight a terrible depression and then to fight the greatest war in history, few people believed that this usurpation of power by the President was anything more than evidence of the fact that this power was after all being used for the good of the public. Certainly, the American Dream in the minds of most foreigners, at least until 1960, seemed to mean that we lived in an open society and that the power in the hands of the Government was limited to that which could best be used for the good of all citizens.

But with the advent of the Truman Doctrine we heard the new voice of those who had taken the defensive. "The language of military power is the only language," it said in part, and "the main deterrent to Soviet attack on the United States, or to attack on areas of the world . . . vital to our security, will be the military power of this country." This was something Americans had always believed, whether they had in mind Russians, the Red Coats of the British, or the Blitzkrieg forces of Hitler. But then this traditional policy changed: "In addition to maintaining our own strength the United States should support and assist all democratic countries which are in any way menaced or endangered by the USSR." And then, "as long as the Soviet Government adheres to its present policy the

United States should maintain military forces powerful enough to restrain the Soviet Union and to confine Soviet influence to its present area."

In 1947, as a part of the Truman Doctrine, this was the way the idea of containment was planted as a seed in the minds of the American people. This was followed by such things as the Marshall Plan and then the worldwide Military Assistance Programs of various kinds. What had begun as a plan to contain Russia and Communism with strong military force became not a barrier against Russia itself, but a creeping encroachment upon the sovereignty and territory of our own friends. Whether they wanted them or not, we have kept military forces on the soil of our friends for more than thirty years, and there is no end in sight. But even more important, we have developed in more than forty countries strong clandestine and paramilitary forces far more dangerous to the internal welfare of those countries than encroachment of Communism, which is supposed to be the reason for the existence of such action. And these covert forces exist. The "Communism" they are there to guard against is for the most part no more than an interpretation of intent.

Whether one believes in the inviolability of national sovereignty as the supreme power among nations—unlimited, inalienable, indivisible, absolute, and the very essence of a state—or whether one believes that sovereignty is an antiquated idea, its great importance in the community of nations cannot be disregarded. If the whole concept of sovereignty were to be abandoned, we would of necessity have to fill the void. We would then face the fact that we are dealing with raw power, and what is important in the nature of power is the end it seeks to serve and the way it serves that end. Whether we accept the concept of absolute sovereignty or whether we see a complex world riddled throughout with power centers and other binding, uncontrollable forms of human relationships, we must realize that these rights, in no matter what form, imply certain duties, such as the duty of non-intervention in the affairs of other nations and the duty to respect the rules and customs of international law. Forcible intervention, which was in less civilized times rather common in the relations of states, is now no longer either condoned or justified and is almost always met with violent condemnation, except where crimes have been committed or where international interests of great importance are endangered.

As this nation turned to a broad though quiet and generally covert campaign of worldwide anti-Communism, it pressed its military forces, economic forces, and its intelligence arm upon this group of more than forty countries. At the same time, it turned from the real Communist states such as Poland, Hungary, and others on the periphery, not to mention the heartlands of Russia and China. Thus the struggle took place in remote areas of the rim-land along the traces of the Iron Curtain. The struggle was hidden from the view of most Americans and from those countries where there was no activity at that time; but not from the countries that were active, such as the Philippines, Thailand, Pakistan, or Iran—and certainly these actions were not hidden from the awareness of the Soviet Union. Although we may have cloaked an activity on the border of India in deepest secrecy, who in India and who in Russia would believe that such activity was being supported and directed by anyone else than the covert peacetime operational forces of the United States?

If the Dalai Lama is spirited out of Tibet in the face of an overwhelming Chinese army of conquerors, are the Chinese going to think he found his support in heaven? If the disorganized rebels on the scattered islands of vast Indonesia are suddenly armed with great quantities of modern and effective weapons, including transport aircraft to airdrop such weapons and the bombers to support their attacks, are the Indonesians and the Soviets going to be fooled for even one day by "secrecy" that is supposed to keep them from knowing where this all came from?

The entire position and policy of the United States Government turned to the defensive. It abandoned its position of real leadership in favor of creating a vast intelligence organization and the mightiest peacetime armed force of all time to react to and respond to the activity, real and imagined, of the men in the Kremlin. And we became totally dependent upon the inputs of intelligence from any and all sources, generally quite random, to activate this great force in what, by the time the Kennedy Administration came upon the scene, had come to be called "counterinsurgency."

By this time the entire might of the U.S. military had become a reservoir and magazine operating in support of the operational machinations of the ST and its paramount force, the CIA. Even though at first impact this may appear to be a totally unrealistic picture in terms of the disproportionate ratio of strength of the two organizations, it comes into focus when we consider the analysis by Colonel DuPicq. That is, the only forces that are in combat are those actually on the perimeter—even on the three-dimensional perimeter as was Gary Powers in his U-2 and these forces not only bear the brunt of the action, but they make the victory or the defeat.

Now a small CIA operation in Laos, for example, involving only a few hundred CIA personnel, real and contract, and a few hundred more or a few thousand U.S. military in support, may seem too small an effort to support the statement that the entire might of the U.S. military existed in support of the ST. But if the ST activity becomes a runaway action, such as it did in Indochina, it is inevitable that the few hundred, and then a few thousand, all too easily became five hundred thousand.

Thus, in those crucial ten years, the clandestine activities of the CIA were redirected from those originally aimed at the Soviet Union and its neighboring states to the many nations of our friends, in which we saw the "rampant," dangerous forces of "subversive insurgency." And today they have been even further directed, along with other powerful arms of secret power, to seek the sources of subversive insurgency within this country itself. All during this refocusing of direction, the ST has increased its utilization of secrecy in order to keep the host nation from knowing what was gong on. Throughout this complex series of operations the Agency went out of its way to keep this information from the Congress and from the people of the United States. There is no doubt that the people of Taiwan, of the Philippines, of France, and of many other countries know more about what the CIA has been doing during the past twenty years than we do here in the United States.

Even as Congress debates whether or not it should be given more intelligence information by the CIA it can be seen that those august men are again being misled by the turn of events. Should Congress rule that the CIA must brief it on current intelligence matters, it will find itself more and more enslaved by the system, just as the President has been by the current intelligence briefings which are his frequent diet. Not only will the CIA then take over the daily indoctrination of key members of Congress, but it will also place them under the "magic" of its security wraps. Every day it briefs the Congress, in whole or in part, it will warn that what they are hearing is Super Red-Hot, Top Secret and that now that they have heard it, they must not mention it to anyone. Then, to provide them with a reasonable alibi, since most of those men have an occupational proclivity for free and easy speech, the CIA will provide them with suitable cover stories. Day after day they will hear about happenings around the world, as the ST wants them to hear about them, and day after day they will have less and less time to hear about real world events from any other source. Thus their own ideas and knowledge of the outside world will decrease from day to day. Then to finish what this process does not accomplish, consider what the day-by-day pabulum of cover story after cover story can do to otherwise intelligent and wholly rational men.

The record is full of the names of men appointed to high office who have come under the influence of the daily dosage of current intelligence. Look what it has done to them. At whose doorstep did men like Robert McNamara, John McCone, Earle Wheeler, Maxwell Taylor, and countless others learn about Vietnam. Their briefings came directly, or at the most once removed, from CIA sources, whether they were "in house" CIA men like Tracy Barnes and Desmond Fitzgerald, or "across the river" CIA men like Bill Bundy, Ed Lansdale, and Bill Rosson.

The course of these events did not just happen as a random or natural development. It was guided, sometimes quite deliberately, by the early work of Clark Clifford, or later by such relatively chance events as those that took place during the latter part of the fifties. It may be worthwhile to trace a course of events that played quite a role in this period just before the election of John F. Kennedy to the office of President.

In 1956, just before the Arab-Israeli War, the British, with Selwyn Lloyd in the Foreign Office, and the French, with Guy Mollet, had made covert plans to help the Israelis against Nasser for their own interests. Naturally, General Dayan wanted to defeat and roll back the Egyptians, and the British and French were more than willing to help re-establish some form of control over the Suez and to relieve Arab pressures on Algeria. These three interested partners planned in secret to strike at Egypt, defeat the Egyptian army, and depose Nasser. A French undercover unit of navy commandos disguised as Arabs was in Cairo for the express purpose of killing Nasser. All of this hinged upon careful timing and secrecy. Neither Britain nor France informed John Foster Dulles, the American Secretary of State, of their plans. As events progressed, Dulles played on this lack of formal coordination heavily, assuming the role of an unwitting and appalled outsider. However, Allen Dulles was providing Foster with all the information he needed in the form of regular and most revealing high-altitude U-2 pictures and other ferret-type intelligence. These revealed the arrival and off-loading of the French and British shipping in Haifa and the subsequent removal of these ships to pick up allied forces in Cyprus for the next phase of the operation.

As is frequently the case in such pressure situations, the partners got concerned about one another's sincerity and reliability, and they all knew that the CIA has long eyes and ears. Or perhaps Dayan had been tipped off that Dulles knew what was going on. For whatever reasons, Dayan jumped off against the Egyptians with crushing air attacks about forty-eight hours ahead of the joint plans. This locked the British and French into the action and called their hands. Dayan swept across the desert. Since the Egyptian air force had been utterly destroyed on the ground, he received little opposition from the unprotected Egyptian ground forces. The French navy commando elements operating under the skillful direction of the youngest admiral in France, Admiral Ponchardier, moved in swiftly to do away with Nasser. French and British forces steamed across the Mediterranean at top speed to join the action. It was certain that Nasser would be knocked out in a short time.

At this point several strange things happened. John Foster Dulles, seeing all this before him and knowing, despite his technical protestations, exactly what was taking place, demanded that the British and French stop where they were and ordered Dayan to a halt. Over the other horizon, Khrushchev thundered that if the attack did not stop he would hurl missiles at all hostile targets in Europe. With pressure from Dulles, from Khrushchev, and with the vociferous opposition of the Labor Party in England to contend with also, Selwyn Lloyd and Guy Mollet submitted. They called their troops to a halt. The magnificent plan, which might have done much to change the course of history during the past fifteen years, was shattered. This Suez affair has perhaps been one of the most unfortunate episodes of the past twenty-five years. It prevented the British from re-establishing an enlightened control over the Canal, and it created a situation that made further French action in North Africa untenable. And it has led to fifteen years of unrest on the Arab-Israeli border, not to mention what the weight of its failure had upon events in the Far East. One other thing that came out of this odd situation had a tremendous impact upon the United States.

The United States Army at that time had been going downhill since its glorious days in World War II and its slight though unsatisfactory resurgence in Korea. Then, in the pre-Sputnik era the Army had assembled a team around Werner von Braun in an attempt to regain some of its lost glory in space. Just at this time, Maxwell Taylor, the Army Chief of Staff, heard Khrushchev's threat to hurl rockets across Europe, loud and clear. He and his staff sat down without delay and computed that this meant that the Russians must have in operational weapons delivery system that could deliver a warhead effectively about 1,750 miles. This was derived from the computation of the average distance from Russian launching sites to all European capitals. Using this as their battle cry, they set up a great clamor for an Intermediate-Range Ballistic Missile with about 1,800 miles range. The IRBM battle was under way to win supremacy for the Army over the Air Force and the Navy in the new missile and space era.

In the clamor of this battle the Suez crisis was nearly forgotten while the U.S. Army and the Air Force fought it out in the halls of Congress and before the eyes of the unwary public. The Army came up suddenly with an IRBM called the Jupiter and the Air Force with its own Thor. Actually there was very little difference between the two. In fact, they both utilized the same rocket motor and many other common components. However, the battle was on not only for the Jupiter or the Thor; but to determine which service would have the primary responsibility for IRBM warfare. Behind the scenes those who were in the know were aware that the Army and the Air Force were puppets for much more serious contenders.

All of the services were joined in a struggle that really involved the most powerful segments of the vast military-industrial combine. The war was not so much about which service would be supreme in the missile business; but it was about whether the great American automobile industry would get the majority of missile contracts or whether the powerful aviation industry would get these contracts. The Navy joined in the fray later and quietly, on the coattails of the steel industry and the conventional munitions makers, with its Polaris system. (The prime contract was through Lockheed for the missile structure; but the whole system was dependent upon submarines and submarine base support and with a solid propellant system that would utilize vast quantities of explosives, which would mean huge contracts for the munitions industries.) Forces were joined, and Maxwell Taylor was at the forefront, leading his Army contenders and fronting for the automobile industry. At that time the Secretary of Defense was the former president of General Motors, Charles Wilson. The ensuing decision from which there could be no escape was not for him to avoid or to make. How could a pre-eminent auto maker rule against his industry? On the other hand, how could he rule against aviation and its powerful industry? With every practice missile shot, the tensions mounted, and Maxwell Taylor was demanding a decision. He saw this as essential to the automobile industry, which had always been the friend of the Army; but he saw it more as a chance to spur his old commanding general, now his Commander in Chief, into making a decision in favor of the Army. This was something Eisenhower had not done for a long time.

Finally Eisenhower finessed the decision by accepting the resignation of Secretary of Defense Wilson and appointing a man from the soap industry, Neil McElroy of Proctor and Gamble, to make this decision. After more study and after working out a more or less acceptable compromise on the business front, McElroy ruled against Maxwell Taylor and his Jupiter crowd. This, along with other decisions that had made the Army the least of the three armed forces, weighed heavily on General Taylor. By 1959 he announced that he would resign from the Army before the expected termination of his assignment as Chief of Staff. On the first of July, 1959, General Lyman L. Lemnitzer succeeded Maxwell Taylor as Chief of Staff of the U.S. Army.

This was a most important time. We have discussed how the Agency had grown in size and in capacity so that it had become involved in a really major campaign in Indonesia and in the U-2 global operation. While the CIA grew the Army declined in strength as John Foster Dulles and Eisenhower shaped the world for a grand move toward lasting peace based upon the recognition of the power of nuclear weapons and upon the realization that because they were so powerful no reasonable nation would employ them. Even this was not enough. President Eisenhower was embarked upon a crusade for peace. He had mobilized his Administration with but one objective: to leave as a lasting monument enduring peace. However, there were many small clouds on the horizon.

Castro had come to power in Cuba, and he posed a threat to Latin America. Eisenhower went to Acapulco to meet with the President of Mexico and to win assurance that Mexico understood the Castro menace. De Gaulle had become President of France and had embarked upon a new era, with the Fifth Republic. De Gaulle was occupied with Algeria, which was then a losing cause as a result of the failure to defeat Nasser, and he had little time to work on matters other than French problems. There was continuing trouble in Laos; and each time it flared up the country would authorize more CIA activity and little else.

Early in 1959 the Dalai Lama had been forced to leave Tibet as the Chinese Communists swept across that barren country. This fantastic escape and its major significance have been buried in the lore of the CIA as one of those successes that are not talked about. The Dalai Lama would never have been saved without the CIA.

In the spring of 1959, John Foster Dulles resigned, and shortly thereafter he died of cancer. His successor was Christian Herter, who became Eisenhower's greatest ally in the quest for a permanent peace. At the same time, the Chinese Nationalists and the Chinese Communists worked each other over with aircraft and artillery in a contest for the offshore islands of Matsu and Quemoy. But even this sporadic hostility forecast no real problems for the peace offensive.

President Eisenhower sent his Vice President, Richard Nixon, to Russia to meet with Khrushchev and to make arrangements for the impending summit meeting. It was at this time that Nixon and Khrushchev engaged in the now famous "Kitchen Debate." Then Eisenhower himself went to London and Paris, and by late September he and Khrushchev reported that they had "reached an understanding designed to relieve world tensions." Not long after that Eisenhower further reduced the role of the Army by ordering the transfer of all remaining Army ballistic missile programs to NASA. During November, the United States and the USSR announced "a joint nuclear research program," and a few days later, another joint announcement, this time by the United States, United Kingdom, and the USSR confirmed an agreement "on details of a control organization to be set up, with the signing of the nuclear test-ban treaty."

Then, in December President Eisenhower left on an eleven nation, three-week trip to Europe, Asia, and Africa. For a man of his age, who had suffered through a series of near-fatal heart attacks, this was a major undertaking designed to carry him further toward the pinnacle of his lifelong goal of lasting peace. Everywhere he went he was widely acclaimed. He drew the biggest crowd ever assembled in New Delhi, India. Looking back at such events in the light of present times and conditions makes one realize how far the situation has deteriorated since that time. In those halcyon days, whenever the

President of the United States visited a foreign capital tremendous crowds of friendly people gathered to do him honor. Now, fourteen years later, this is not the case. The Vietnam war has done much to destroy the American Dream.

When Eisenhower returned, the Government announced in a most unusual and significant move a planned series of summit talks to be convened in Paris in late April and early May of 1960. Summit talks have seldom if ever been announced so far in advance, at least not in public and with so much prospect for real success. On Christmas Day of 1959, Khrushchev accepted the invitation, and on New Year's Eve the date for the greatest summit meeting of all was set for May 16, 1960.

Since the collapse of the Indonesian campaign and the serious compromise brought about by the loss of the CIA C-118 aircraft, Allen Dulles had kept the Agency at a low profile. He had lost one of his closest lieutenants with the departure of Frank Wisner in the aftermath of the Indonesian effort. Although neither the Indonesian incident nor the C-118 loss had broken through security bounds enough to expose the CIA, as the Bay of Pigs episode was to do a few years later, he knew and President Eisenhower knew that the Agency had survived two close calls by the slimmest of margins. However, 1959 and 1960 were not quiet years. The CIA and Allen Dulles had a way of surmounting disaster and coming up ahead.

As 1960 began, two great pressure groups collided. President Eisenhower was steering his Administration to the climax of its final term in office. Everything done during the early months of 1960 was dedicated to the task of establishing a foundation for an era of peace and prosperity. The ultimate summit meeting was to be the prelude to his tour, his visit to Moscow and to other capitals of the world on his crusade for peace.

Although all mankind hoped for peace and few would oppose the noble objectives of the aging President, there were still those of the 'fear Communism' school who believed that the Kremlin could never be trusted, in spite of its public willingness to join with President Eisenhower and other leaders. Elements of this underground faction not only raised the banner of anti-Communism, but lived by it and traded upon its power. They played upon the baser motivation of fear that is in all elements of human society. For them it is easier to move men by that method than to attempt it by more noble means. This under ground faction gained strength from three major areas. The Maxwell Taylor school of Army dissidents, along with their powerful industry collaborators, openly opposed the Eisenhower doctrine of military and foreign policy supported by "massive retaliation," and they distrusted the peace offensive.

Another group—ostensibly Army, Air Force, high-level Office of the Secretary of Defense and Executive Office Building (White House) personnel—was working quietly on a vast education and reorientation program of civic action, nation-building, and such other ideas, which were in reality a cover for the extension of covert activities of the ST into the countries served by the Mutual Security Program and such other assistance projects. The regular military assistance program countries were the primary targets. The military cover personnel and their civilian disciples worked on this project with the zeal and energy of dedicated missionaries in support of a new and vital religion. (This is the subject of the following chapter.)

The third group was made up of the hard-core CIA and ST elite activists who were increasingly prepared and able to wage clandestine counterinsurgency anywhere in the world with forces of any size, at any time, and in response to intelligence inputs of all kinds and characteristics. For example, the inputs did not have to be anti-Communist when it did not suit the team. They could see danger to this country in almost any situation. The sudden dislike of the Latin dictator Trujillo certainly had nothing to do with anti-Communism, but he went the way of all "enemies" on charges of a special nature, just as Ngo Dinh Diem did in 1963.

Over the years this group had begun by defining the Soviet Union and World Communism as the enemy. Then it had pressed the idea of global containment of the world of Communism. Having built the wall from Norway on the North Sea to Turkey on the Black Sea, and from Iran on the northeast slopes of the Gordian Knot to India and Pakistan on the high Himalayas, and then on along the tenuous northern borders of Burma, Laos, and the 17th parallel in Vietnam, it began the cultivation and indoctrination of the idea that the real danger lay in the spread of Communism into the peripheral countries by means of subversive insurgency and support of wars of national liberation. To complete this fear-of-Communism syndrome, this movement contained a strong element that saw Communism and Communist subversion seeping into and permeating almost every area of the United States.

One of the greatest non-elective, non-ruling power forces of all time is this anti-Communist fanatic group, which rips through to the very heart and soul of the nation, playing upon fear and ignorance for its own selfish and in many cases ignorant, fear crazed interests. More harm has been done from 1947 through 1972 to the United States and the world by this rabid and ruthless element than the Kremlin could have hoped to have accomplished itself by any other means short of nuclear war.

This combination of power elites did win its tremendous underground struggle against the peacemakers led by President Eisenhower when the U-2 reconnaissance spy-plane flown by Francis Gary Powers crash-landed in the heart of the Soviet Union only two weeks before the Paris summit conference. Powers' flight was a most unusual event. It was not part of the regularly scheduled series of routine U-2 operations. It was launched and directed by a small cell of inner elite for reasons which may never be possible for anyone to determine. If by any chance the thought had ever occurred to the four men who launched it that the failure of this relatively unimportant flight would completely wreck and vitiate all of the hopes and plans of the Eisenhower Crusade for Peace, they could not have chosen a more effective method or time to have done it. The very fact that what was done could have been done so easily according to a sinister plan, not an accident or Soviet act, serves only to fuel the thought that it might have been done on purpose. Such a simple thing as failure to supply the plane with sufficient hydrogen for the flight could have resulted, just as it did, in the certain flame-out of the engine and the subsequent failure of the mission—or success of the mission, depending upon the secret intent of those who dispatched it.

This trend of thought is intriguing, because scarcely had the U-2 crashed into the daisy fields of central Russia than all three power groups mentioned above leaped into the void created by the demise of the Eisenhower initiative, to power a ground-swell upon which the Nixon campaign foundered and the Kennedy team rode to victory. The interesting part of all of this, even the ominous part, was that the ground-swell had started even before the collapse of the peace crusade and the summit conference. It would lead an observer, at least one who was very close to the inside activity, almost to believe that there is a great force somewhere that does not want to see a peace crusade succeed; or, to put it in active terms, that wants to promote professional anti-Communism and all that the term has come to mean during the past inglorious decade in Vietnam.

CHAPTER 19

THE NEW DOCTRINE: SPECIAL FORCES AND THE PENETRATION OF THE MUTUAL SECURITY PROGRAM

The military assistance program had been modestly launched as aid to Greece and Turkey in 1947. It was expanded to include military aid to NATO, Iran, Korea, and the Philippines in 1949. Since 1951 it has been absorbed into the annual Mutual Security Act, which is an omnibus legislative enactment covering military aid, developmental aid, technical assistance, and a contingency fund. Over the years, military assistance has been provided to more than forty countries, and in most, if not all of these arrangements, the CIA has been a key factor.

According to the U.S. Army, it is a basic tenet of American foreign policy that Soviet piecemeal aggression must be stopped wherever it occurs so that the balance of power will not shift to the Communists. The most obvious means of carrying out this policy is providing military assistance to our allies so that they will be able to defend themselves. It is further postulated that a recipient's capacity to contribute significantly to resisting active aggression is maximized by building up adequate standing forces and arsenals, and secondly, that the recipient's capacity to maintain internal order and to control subversion is emphasized.

The Army states that there are various goals for the Military Aid Program, depending upon the country and the general region in which it exists. "Aid to Asia is intended to help Asiatic recipients resist internal subversion and perhaps to a more limited extent to resist open aggression." As an internal matter, the Army looks at Military Aid as a program that "straddles the areas of responsibility of the Department of State and of the DOD. . . . The development of the MAP involves many agencies."

The program in each country was developed and is controlled by a Military Assistance Advisory Group (MAAG). The CIA places both military and civilian personnel within these MAAG offices. In some places the number of Agency personnel exceeds the number of military personnel who were assigned. Of course, if the Agency or the DOD were queried about this by a member of Congress or other Government official, they would deny the existence of these people and justify their denial on the basis that the agents in the MAAG had been "declared to be military" by some paperwork cover, usually kept in a highly classified file back in Washington, in the Agency and the service concerned. Thus they could say, "Yes, everyone in that MAAG is a member of the military establishment." But the truth requires them to add, "and some of them are really CIA employees who are military simply as a function of a cover arrangement." However, they never add that, and no one ever asks them in those specific words.

The important thing about the Military Assistance Program is that it brought with it some new definitions of the role and responsibility of the armed forces of the nation. In the first instance, these definitions seemed quite correct and served to make the Military Assistance Program more meaningful to Americans. However, as the years passed and the MAP work became routine, and as these earlier doctrines became part of the "military language" for both countries involved—the United States and the host country—they began to produce subtle changes in the role of the U.S. military. This led to a very sophisticated form of direct intervention in the internal affairs of the forty host countries, and in some cases, it resulted directly in the separation of that nation's armed forces from its political control through practices that will be explained. In this sense the elaborate statements of mission of the mutual security programs are a refined cover story. The military assistance program becomes the means by which the ST may, whenever it finds or suspects "communist-inspired subversive insurgency," increase its role in the armed forces and political organizations of the host country until the trouble becomes an outbreak of open hostility. Thus the "fireman" becomes the man who sets fires rather than the one who puts them out.

One source of this doctrine was the Civil Affairs School at Fort Gordon, Georgia. This Army school dates back to World War II, when it was the training ground for the Civil Affairs and Military Government (CAMG) program. It was the function of those specially trained men to go into countries like Italy and France, which had been under German military domination for several years, and to assist with the rebuilding of the local government in the war-torn areas. As a result, these men had been trained in political functions more than in the military tactical profession. Their record in World War II was outstanding, and after the war the school, although cut back as was most of the military, continued, prospered, and found a new life in working up a curriculum based upon the post-strike phase of a nuclear war. It was in this phase of work that the CAMG school and its doctrine played so prominently into the hands of the CIA by underscoring the potential of the Agency during peacetime for establishing contact in denied areas and for setting up clandestine contacts with the agent, underground networks that would be established. This led the CIA into the war planning function of all major military headquarters, and from its success with this, into its logistics buildup.

It was not unusual, then, to find the CIA returning to the Civil Affairs School during another trying period in an effort to breathe new life into Agency operations, which had been seriously curtailed after the Indonesia fiasco of 1958. MAP was an ideal place for the Agency to operate. As we have said, the CIA had by 1959 become well entrenched in all parts of the U.S. Government. Through MAP, the Agency now was able to establish itself quietly in up to forty foreign countries in ways that its usual civilian and diplomatic cover would not permit. All assistance programs needed recruiting and the CIA volunteered to take over the task of helping the services with recruiting in the host country. If some Iranians were to be selected to attend an electronics course in the United States for six months, someone had to select the men who would go. MMG military personnel who had been selected for their assignments, usually on the basis of their tactical and professional background, were not generally well informed about the people with whom they would be working. The Agency supplied men who spoke the languages of and wherever possible were experts on the host country and who already may have had underground contacts there. They were ideal, then, to take over the responsibility and the chore of selecting the men from the host country who would go to schools in the United States.

This gave the Agency a valuable tool for exploitation. Whereas the MAAG may have looked upon this selection in purely professional terms, the CIA looked upon it in political and rather pragmatic terms. The Agency knew well that any Iranian selected to go to the United States for six months, with extra pay and other allowances such as the ability to purchase a new U.S. automobile at low "diplomatic" prices, was going to leap at the chance to go. Thus if the selection were made wisely the Agency could make some valuable contacts and friends in that country. Needless to say, many of the men who reported to the electronics school didn't know the first thing about electronics and didn't care.

The CIA parleyed these contacts into close friendships in these countries and became in many instances very close to the chosen recipients of "military aid." The next thing was to cultivate the soil in order that both the military and the Agency would benefit from these windfall relationships. This was done by carefully relating the Military Assistance Program to the old slogan, anti-Communism.

The Civil Affairs School curriculum, which was to provide background information on the Military Assistance Program, began with an elaborate summary of a course called "Communist Techniques of Aggression." It laid the groundwork for reflexive anti-Communism by telling all students that "local Communists gradually took over [these countries] under the threat of the military domination of the Red Army at their border," and went on to tell them "how important a tool military power is for shaping men's minds in conditions of conflict short of open warfare." It further characterized the kind of Communism they were talking about by saying, "Diplomacy is the classic means of carrying out relations between nations, and hence is not a typical Communist technique. . . . the Russian embassy in a foreign country is always used as the center of espionage activity in that country." Then, as the text became more specific in terms of areas of the world where the United States might have an interest, it took into consideration the problem in Vietnam before Dien Bien Phu: "The French did not dare to form an armed force of members of the indigenous population for fear that it would defect to the Communists." This made good instruction as far as the Army was concerned in those formative days. It sugar-coated the cover story. But as we know, the French did try to Vietnamize their war just as we have been trying to Vietnamize ours.

After many more pages of "analyzing" Communism and Communist techniques, the Army lesson goes on to say that in taking over governments, the Communists seek to control "the key positions . . . the Ministry of Defense, which controls the Army, and the Ministry of Interior, which controls the Police. "It adds that the Russians carry on espionage with a worldwide organization: "The information they seek is not only military intelligence but also reports on political and social matters which will guide the Kremlin in its worldwide planning. . . ."

In doing this, the lesson insists that the espionage network operates completely separate from other foreign channels of the Soviet high command, and that "the ambassador, who is the nominal head of the legation, may not even be permitted to set foot in parts of his own embassy."

This legitimate curriculum on the subject of Communism and its ways has been, over the years, lifted almost in its entirety and neatly inserted into other curricula that were used to train United States and foreign nationals how they should operate in a peacetime operation situation; in other words, "Do as they do." When men have been taught that this is the way the enemy does it and the only way we can defeat the enemy at his own games is by copying and emulating him, then it becomes easy to insert into the normal training programs bits and pieces of this doctrine. After years of hearing this material used at first for clandestine orientation and later for less than clandestine operations, these ideas begin to seem right in our own service.

One area with which American servicemen had been totally unfamiliar was what is called the paramilitary organization. A course in such organization has become very formative in the indoctrination of a new generation of military and their civilian counterparts, along with the tens of thousands of foreign military and civilians trained in MAP projects. The following is an official U.S. Army definition of paramilitary forces as extracted from a standard lesson guide.

"We Americans are not very well acquainted with this type of organization because we have not experienced it in our own country. It resembles nothing so much as a private army. The members accept at least some measure of discipline, and have military organization, and may carry light weapons. In Germany in the 1920s and early '30s the parties of the right and the Communists had such organizations with membership in the hundreds of thousands. It is readily apparent what a force this can be in the political life of a country, particularly if the paramilitary forces are armed, when the supremacy of the Army itself may be threatened."

In the beginning these lessons were used to train forces to go out and work with the native forces of other countries, and in many of these other countries the U.S. Army role was submerged and covered in the CIA mechanism. The CIA, rather than train the legitimate army of a host country, would train the paramilitary force to create a structure within the country that could balance the army or even overthrow it.

In many cases the CIA would work with the national police rather than with the paramilitary forces. The results were the same. The thinking as stated by the U.S. Army in this doctrine was that with U.S. guidance and help, the politico-military actions of the [host] armed forces can be decisive in building strong, free nations, with governments responsive to, and representative of, the people." This was the doctrine, but it would be most difficult to find a single case of the armed forces of any such nation being truly representative of, and responsive to, the people. In most cases the situation has been exactly the opposite.

Even as far back as the mid-fifties the U.S. Army doctrine, had a strong overtone of CIA assistance and was preaching "pacification." Pacification, as it is carried on in South Vietnam, can be shown to date back to the Fort Gordon course, where it was taught that "the operational doctrine for the take-over of zones evacuated by the [rebels] was known as Pacification." The doctrine adds, "The two largest pacification campaigns [in Indochina] were undertaken in the early months of 1955, in Camau in the far south and in Quang Ngai-Binh Dinh provinces of the central coast region. . . . As a result of good planning, training, and operations by the military, effective government and security were quickly established in the pacifica-tion areas, much of the war torn economy was rehabilitated, and the Communist organizations left behind were revealed by the popula-tion, along with a great many hidden caches of arms and equip-ment." This was the U.S. Army lesson guide of 1959–1960 about minor operations in 1955, which by now has been proved to have been so terribly wrong.

Remember, this was the doctrine the school was teaching key people who eventually became the MAAG officials in forty foreign countries. This was also the basic doctrine used to rejuvenate the long dormant U.S. Army Special Forces program. As it continued, it wandered far from its original theme of Communist cold war techniques to talk more about American activity and specifically the type of activity that was most unconventional for the American

Army, the use of civilians, foreign nationals, and foreign military in U.S.-sponsored, third-country projects that were essentially clandestine, as extracted from U.S. Army lesson guides.

"During the pacification campaigns, the Vietnamese army learned to work closely with two notable civilian organizations, which are worth mentioning here as an indication of teamwork employed to bring stability to a free nation. The organizations were 'Operation Brotherhood,' involving the International Jaycees, and the Vietnamese Government's 'Civic Action' teams. These two organizations of volunteers brought high morals and ideal, unselfish spirit to the campaigns . . . 'Operation Brotherhood' was originally staffed by Filipino volunteers."

Looking at this with the hindsight of ten to fifteen years of bitter experience in Vietnam, one wonders at the real meaning and intent of such subject matter. As the lesson continues it states that the same Filipinos' Operation Brotherhood was operating in Laos, then it discusses similar projects in Burma. Before leaving the subject of pacification, this Army lesson guide quotes a French officer in Algiers: "The pacification authority cannot be the old one, for the mayors and civilian councilors and some French Moslems, preoccupied with their own interests, are regarded with suspicion by the vast majority of Moslems." The conclusion was that the army must throw out the old regime, the old ways, the old customs, and come up with new villages, new pioneer spirit. "The army turned itself into a social revolutionary forces in the same way that the Chinese Red Army had done during the struggle with Chiang Kai-shek. Every army command started a far-reaching scheme for full civilian employment." In other words, the local army was the new order, and the U.S. Army was being indoctrinated and trained by CIA instructors to do the same thing.

This was heady doctrine for an Army that had just seen its Chief of Staff retire in disgust after what he had termed unfair treatment for the U.S. Army by the JCS, the Secretary of Defense, and the Commander in Chief himself. Finally, the lesson guide with this potent doctrine got to the real subject it had in mind when it started talking about Communist techniques. It ended with a long treatise on the Military Assistance Program. It set forth as an objective of this program, "First, a recipient's [of U.S. military aid] capacity to contribute significantly to resisting active aggression is maximized by building up adequate standing forces and arsenals. [And in this context this doctrine meant paramilitary and police forces as much as it meant military forces.] Second, the recipient's capacity to maintain internal order and to control subversion is emphasized.... Aid to Asia is intended to help Asiatic recipients resist internal subversion and, perhaps to a more limited extent, to resist open aggression."

Before this indoctrination concluded, it made the key point that MAP "straddles the areas of responsibility of the Department of State and of the DOD.... The development of the MAP involves many agencies."

This very long (twenty-nine pages) typewritten, single spaced, doctrinal lesson guide was the work of key men dedicated to the reconstruction of the U.S. Army along lines being visualized by General Maxwell Taylor in his book, *The Uncertain Trumpet*. While he was writing about his problems with the Eisenhower Administration regarding the army and the other services, and while he was outlining his thoughts in terms of what he called "A New National Military Program of Flexible Response," a team of strong-willed and opportunistic men was plowing up new ground for the U.S. Army. This was to nurture the seeds planted by the Army and the CIA along with powerful assistance from the other services and such other places as the Executive Office Building at the White House and from the Department of State.

This Civil Affairs curriculum was taken from Fort Gordon without the knowledge of the intervening next higher command at the Continental Army Command headquarters at Fort Monroe, Virginia, and was brought into the Pentagon where a select team of CIA-experienced officers and civilians worked it over into the new curriculum for the U.S. Army Special Forces school at Fort Bragg, North Carolina.

At the same time, action directly related to the above-mentioned projects was taking place at the highest levels of government. A special Presidential committee had been formed early in 1959 to study

"Training Under the Mutual Security Program" and to "provide instruction [to recipient countries] in concepts or doctrine governing the employment of the military instrument, in peace and in war." The Presidential committee's report went on to note that "the committee's principle concern—and consequently the subject of this paper—is that training objectives have been so severely circumscribed, so inadequately related to the full sweep of our own national interests and of the recipient countries as well." Early on, the committee reported, "The International Cooperation Administration has yet to recognize the potential of the MAP training base for the furtherance of technical assistance objectives." In other words, this committee was laying it right on the line that the Government should be stepping into the Mutual Security program with "military" training, including the development of paramilitary capability in the recipient nations. The only way this could be carried out would be to mount clandestine operations in every country where this was to apply. By this period the CIA knew that it was ready, equipped, and in a position to do this in any "counterinsurgency-list" country, as it had been digging its way firmly into the MAP since the earliest days of the Greek and Turkish aid programs.

The Agency did not take any chances with this vital, to the CIA interests, report. Like the report from Fort Gordon that was being worked on by a team of CIA-experienced officers and civilians, the authors of this report of the President's committee were also CIA-experienced, but not known to be by those with whom they were working. They were under cover within the White House itself! Both primary authors of this report, although recognized throughout this period only as an Army general and an Air Force general, had served for many years with the CIA and then for many more years in service assignments directly supporting the CIA. After they wrote these formative and most influential documents, both of these generals saw considerable service in Southeast Asia, all in conjunction with the CIA. By 1959 and 1960 the CIA was so well entrenched in the Government—and for that matter in the governments of the some forty recipient nations—that it could pull the strings even as far up as in Presidential committees. Once a report as important as this one had appeared, with the imprimatur of the Executive Office Building, the rest of the road was clear sailing. Even Presidents themselves would not question its validity. Actually, its authors were frequently called to the White House as Presidential advisers on such matters.

Early in this detailed thirty-three page report the committee made a key point. It stated that the new training programs would "reflect substantial increases over previous years." The latter included a first entry into the undergraduate study field. Meanwhile, the geographic emphasis of the International Educational Exchange Service shifted away from Europe to the underdeveloped countries. Note that the ST was turning from the direct confrontation of the Communist bloc to the softer underbelly of the underdeveloped world for its action. The Agency and the military had established their positions in and around the recipient countries, and now they were going to exploit those positions at will.

One begins to find the term "subversive" sprinkled throughout these and other related reports. Many have thought that the "subversive insurgency" doctrine was an outgrowth of the Kennedy era. It came to the surface during Kennedy's Administration; but Kennedy and his young, inexperienced staff inherited the whole idea of subversive insurgency and the role of counterinsurgency from this inside dissident group that had begun to surface toward the end of Eisenhower's term, after the U-2 affair and the destruction of the summit conferences. It should be pointed out that this was not a doctrine endorsed by Eisenhower, although the Deputy Secretary of Defense at the time did find himself in the position of unwittingly putting his blessing on some of the activities crucial to the beginning of this new movement.

A broad hint at the new rationale came near the heart of the report itself:

"It is not enough, however, to restrict leadership inputs to United States norms. Except in specifically defined circumstances, our Armed Forces have no operative responsibilities within national frontiers; conforming generally to the precepts of Western democracies, they are not an integral part of the mechanism for maintenance of law and order. The prevailing concept is expeditionary—an instrument of latent power, unentangled domestically, ready for projection abroad should the exigency arise. Not so for the great bulk of the forces of the new nations. Their role has additional dimensions and their missions are actual as opposed to contingent. They are a key element in the maintenance of internal security and are largely determinant of whether stability or instability characterizes the routine of government. The Officer Corps is perforce deeply involved in domestic affairs. Those who lead, or are destined to lead, must acquire qualifications and attributes beyond the criteria which identify the successful commander in combat. "

More important, tens of thousands of Americans served in the MAP programs, which openly taught and practiced this doctrine. To them, this was the only military they knew, and this was the teaching they received. This was American doctrine, not Communist. Recall that more than three million Americans have been rotated through Indochina during the operations there since 1954 most of these men know only the Army of this doctrine. The impact of this dogma and doctrine, and of these changes in traditional military philosophy, has been tremendous. It is beyond estimate and comprehension at this time. It certainly relates to a considerable degree to the problems that exist in the generation of returned veterans that had not existed before, especially with so many Special Forces Green Beret veterans in our municipal and state police forces.

We said earlier that this doctrine proposed that the CIA assisted in the selection of trainees from the recipient countries. This same proposal was framed in the President's Committee report, and it was cloaked in the following language so that the uninitiated would not be aware of it: "MAP can assist in the identification of officers who should be trained for key responsibilities in the civil sector." Since the CIA was well placed in the MAP, it frequently became the function of the Agency to select these officers "for duty in the civil sector." This was usually unknown to the officers so selected, at first. However, on occasion the Agency did share some of its plans with some of the recruits. In this manner men like Nguyen Cao Ky of

South Vietnam and many others who have become quite prominent around the world, got their first real training and made firm friends with American acquaintances. For example, Ky became a fast friend of an Air Force officer who years later "happened" to be in Vietnam when the government was overthrown. He was in a senior position, able to suggest to Ky that he should step forward and assume control. Many of these contacts were of long duration, and the ST saw to it that they remained so. General Loan, the infamous police chief of Saigon, had been so selected for a course at M.I.T.

Of course, things did not always work out smoothly. One afternoon at about 4:00 pm in Vientiane, Laos, the "U.S. Army" contact man with Kong Le[1] left him with a promise to meet later at the officers club. Within two hours Kong Le was leading a Pathet Lao column against the government. Of course, his troops were called "Pathet Lao" because they were the opposition. There was little evidence that Kong Le ever embraced Communism, even the brand of Communism attributed to the Pathet Lao. It was not too long after that when news reports had Kong Le back at the head of "Neutralist" forces marching against the Pathet Lao into the Plaines de Jarres. Kong Le, like so many others, had received U.S. training and CIA indoctrination.

Another part of the President's committee report continued, "The stakes for which we contend justify attention to every possibility to improve the competence and influence the orientation of the officer corps of these nations. The attach personnel should be so instructed; and the special efforts involved [this means the Agency efforts] in securing Presidential determinations [this is a cautious reference to the NSC approval required for training in the U.S. or third countries accepted]." There could be little question that the intent of this project was to direct the efforts of the Agency and the entire ST effort toward the orientation of friendly countries to bring about political, social, and economic ends.

---

1. Captain Kong Le of the Royal Laotian army had been given special training by the U.S. Army, which included familiarization with CIA supporting activities. Later he broke away from his U.S. friends and led a revolt against the government.

Even in the beginning it was contemplated that this program would be massive. Before the document had been put into final form and readied for approval, it said: "A price tag attaches to any such concept—one must think in terms of several hundred million dollars over the next few years." Remember, this was more than a decade ago, and several hundred million dollars was a lot of money. It was spent, and much more with it; and yet this was always a quiet project and generally unmentioned in routine budget activity e.g., as a good case in point, the Fiscal Year 1972 budget for the Pacification Program in Vietnam, a program directed by a senior CIA official, amounted to $1 billion.

As this massive report continued it veered away from nonmilitary training and got down to the real purpose of its existence. In a section headed "New Roles for the Military," it said:

> "In the past year, a number of informed and thoughtful observers have pointed out that the MAP supported military establishments throughout the less developed areas have a political and socio-economic potential which if properly exploited, may far outweigh their contribution to the deterrence of direct military aggression. . . . armies are often the only cohesive and reliable non-Communist instrument available to the fledgling nations.

> "It is not enough to charge armed forces with responsibility for the military aspects of deterrence; they represent too great an investment in manpower and money to be restricted to such a limited mission. The real measure of their worthiness is found in the effectiveness of their contribution to the furtherance of national objectives, short of conflict. And the opportunities therefore are greatest in the less developed societies where the military occupy a pivotal position between government and populace. As one writer has phrased it . . . properly employed, the army can become an internal motor for economic growth and social-political transformation."

At this time almost everywhere in the Government the word was going around that the only real stabilizing, honest, and useful force in these underdeveloped nations was the army. It could be trusted, it was disciplined, and it would keep and hold the country safely within the Western world. These were nice words, and there might have been an army or part of an army like that somewhere; but few armies anywhere, especially in the underdeveloped countries, were much more than brutal and corrupt forces. In fact, many armies are simply poorly trained groups of desperate men, beggars and bandits who have no other recourse than to submit to military service for a little food for themselves and their families. In most countries the army is the most corrupt sector of the government, and as one group governs another plots its downfall only so they can share the loot for a while.

The type of army this study describes is more like the armies pictured in Communist manuals. The Russian army and the Peoples Army of China are depicted in just the terms that are used in the paper of this Presidential committee. It is a glorious and appealing and totally unreal concept. Anyone can look around the world at countries under the control of their armies, and he will find brutalized nations under generally corrupt and backward leadership.

The report continued to try to win enthusiastic support for this new role for the foreign policy of the United States. In describing the role of the local army, it said: "The maintenance of internal security constitutes a major responsibility of these armed forces, whether assigned directly or not." In other words, if this role were not given to the army, it was suggested that the army would take it over. This is in conflict with the fact that most of the nations under consideration have nationwide national police forces whose traditional role is the maintenance of internal security.

Naturally, this philosophy led to many outbreaks in these recipient countries. The MAP-trained army began to take over the internal security role and got into trouble with the national police and with those national leaders responsible for the national police. This situation brought about friction, which frequently broke out as civil war, and of course there was nothing to do but to declare that the national police were the forces of subversive insurgency; thus the head of Communism was reared. Once these labels had been affixed, the United States would join the army's side with the banner of anti-Communism flying.

The writers of this document saw this in the offing, since they noted, "There must be comprehension of the complex nature of the subversive forces at play and of the variegated methods of Communist attack." It is almost as though the training of firemen should dwell more on the setting of fires rather than on extinguishing them.

The report goes on to say:

> "Here is the ultimate test of the armed forces. Their role, in the countries under discussion, is unique. They are at once the guardians of the government and the guarantors that the government keeps faith with the aspirations of the nation. It is in their power to insure that the conduct of government is responsive to the people and that the people are responsive to the obligations of citizenship. In the discharge of these responsibilities, they must be prepared to assume the reins of government themselves. In either capacity—pillar or ruling faction—the officer corps, at least, must possess knowledge and aptitudes far beyond the military sphere."

These are interesting words and interesting ideas. Burma has been ruled for years by a general. Is all well in Burma? Trujillo was in a sense the personification of this model. Who would like to have lived under the rule of Rafael Trujillo? What of the oppression in Greece at the present time under the leadership of some of the very men who received the same training exemplified in this Presidential report? Is Greece a better place to live in today because its officer corps had been trained by the MAAG in "knowledge and aptitudes beyond the military sphere"?

The report of the President's committee was unclassified. The ST frequently does this when they wish to utilize a paper freely with foreign nationals and with others who may not at the time possess Government clearances. It further underscores the fact that the ST makes use of administrative security simply as a device to meet its own ends. In this case, it was easier and much simpler to control this paper by a hand-to-hand technique than to control it by the usual classification. This was also done with the paper quoted nearer the beginning of this chapter, the "Lesson Guide," U.S. Army.

These papers, too, were circulated among those who would be properly impressed by their high-level imprimatur. At the same time, when General Taylor was working on *The Uncertain Trumpet* and coming up with his new National Military Program of Flexible Response, and the Agency was quietly working to rekindle the U.S. Army Special Forces program along the lines of the Civic Action curriculum, the ST was gradually getting more and more involved in subversive identification projects throughout the soft spots of the Free World.

All of this was going on while President Eisenhower was doing everything he and his Administration could to prepare for the fulmination of his two terms of office with the crusade for peace which would begin with the summit conference in Paris in May 1960. Early in January 1960, Khrushchev pledged not to renew nuclear testing unless the United States did. At about the same time, the United States, England, and Russia resumed discussions at Geneva to find ways to limit or stop nuclear weapons testing. Russia announced that it was demobilizing 1,200,000 men from its armed forces. By the end of the month Eisenhower made a statement, which has taken on special meaning in later years, "there will be no reprisals against Cuba or intervention in its internal affairs." This was the President's official position, and it was the position he emphasized within the government where certain anti-Castro actions were being planned. It was not President Eisenhower who laid the plans for what later was to be known as the Bay of Pigs invasion.

During February the President made another statement in which there were some of the seeds of the later Vietnam problem: "The United States would consider it intervention in the internal affairs of the Americas if any power denied freedom of choice to any republic in the Western Hemisphere." Note that it has been this "denial of the freedom of choice" slogan that has become a battle cry in South Vietnam as one of our reasons for being there.

As the time for the summit conference approached, Eisenhower spread more oil on the waters. Secretary of State Herter pledged that the United States would not resume altitude flights in the Berlin Corridor. The Russians and East Germans had objected violently to certain high-altitude flights previously. At about the same time Eisenhower, as if to underscore his position as a lame duck, announced his endorsement of Richard M. Nixon as the Republican candidate for President. Eisenhower made this early announcement for many reasons, none of which, perhaps, was more important to him personally than to assure the world that he was attending the summit conference as a totally nonpartisan President interested solely in the welfare of the whole world.

Then a last minute round of visits, reminiscent of the bowing and scraping in a classic minuet before the main dancing begins, took place. Khrushchev went to Paris to visit De Gaulle. Macmillan came to Camp David to visit Eisenhower. De Gaulle came to Washington for a last visit before the summit. De Gaulle went back to Europe and visited with Macmillan. Seldom have the chiefs of state made so many planned visits and so many formal announcements prior to a major event as took place during the month before the scheduled meeting. Then, as if to allay any other fears, Under Secretary Dillon announced, "Summit agreements will not abandon Berlin."

Everything was in readiness. It was hard to discover anyone in government not vitally concerned with preparations for this most magnificent meeting, and the hand of the President was evident in all arrangements. This was to be the crowning achievement of a long life devoted to outstanding public service. Seven years of work dedicated to this goal drew to a close as an eventful April ended.

On the first of May the Russians gathered in Red Square, as they have since the revolution, for their annual show of military might. Khrushchev was on the majestic podium, along with all of the Soviet hierarchy. However, the man who was supposed to be at his right, Marshal Rodion Y. Malinovsky, was late.

The great festival had begun. All of Russia cheered its leaders, and all of Russia wished them well, for peace at last seemed to be in the Spring air. Then Marshall Malinovsky arrived at the side of Khrushchev, and there was a hasty discussion. Without any delay, the Marshall delivered an impassioned speech on the theme of vigilance. He knew, and at that time Khrushchev knew, that the spy-plane

U-2, with Francis Gary Powers at the controls, had crash-landed in Russia at Sverdlovsk.

Seldom if ever in the history of man had an event of such importance occurred more dramatically. In the following two weeks the course of world history was drastically altered as the hopes and plans of a crusty, earthy son of mother Russia and of a courageous, gallant, and dedicated son of the Great Plains of America were shattered.

CHAPTER 20

KHRUSHCHEV'S CHALLENGE: THE U-2 DILEMMA

As the glow of sunrise illumined the snowcapped peaks of the Western Himalayas, the pilot moved the throttle lever to full power and the heavily laden plane began a lazy roll down the long runway at Peshawar. The engine whined, the rate of acceleration was slow, and with each unevenness of the runway the long downward sloping wings dropped up and down, unable to come to life at that slow speed. And then, with more speed, the wings began to fly. They rose and steadied, the flopping and oscillation dampened out, and they strained to lift the heavy plane into the air. Just before the runway ran out, one last light bump, gentle as the tiptoe leap of a ballet dancer, lifted the plane into the air, and it was instantly transformed into a thing of beauty—a graceful long winged jet.

As speed built up and wheels were retracted the plane sped through the pre dawn haze. The pilot eased the flaps up into the wings and began to climb toward the mountains. High above and to the left was the historic Khyber Pass. On course, there was a pink tinged twenty-five thousand foot peak, and further to the right was Godwin-Austen, over twenty-eight thousand feet, wearing its perennial white plume. The jet was so heavy that the pilot swung it into a lazy turn inside the valley to spiral up and out, gaining altitude as he went, until he was above that famous path of the conquerors through the Khyber and nearly level with the twenty-five thousand foot mountain top. Kabul, the capital of Afghanistan, lay below; to the right, Tadzhik, the first major city inside the Soviet Union, lay ahead with Tashkent beyond. Border crossing was made at Kirovabad in a climb to sixty thousand feet. The sky was clear and dark blue—the sky that only the small band of jet pilots know the world around. At this altitude the weather, whatever weather there was, was a remote thing, noticed only as patches of white cloud below, obscuring the ground. At cruising altitude the cockpit air system had cleared out all moisture, and the canopy was clear and brittle. Visibility was almost limitless. The pilot was a lone soul above the world, above all normal environment, under a simple, burning sun, and tuned to the even silence of the engine and the slow, mushy responsiveness of the controls in the near vacuum of the atmosphere at that height.

In the still early morning at Peshawar, the operational team had just finished flashing their message to Washington: "Puppy 68" was off and on his way to Norway via Sverdlovsk. The watch officer in the special U-2 control office in downtown Washington got that word shortly after 8:30 pm on the evening of April 30. Dick Bissell, the Agency man in charge of the U-2 project, was notified immediately. Then, in short succession four other men were called. One by one they heard the same information, "Puppy 68 is away." President Eisenhower was at his favorite retreat, Camp David, with Prime Minister Macmillan of Great Britain, putting the finishing touches on plans for the summit conference. De Gaulle had just left Washington, and Macmillan and De Gaulle were scheduled to meet again in Paris on May 5. All was well with the world. The aging men who had led the world through World War II and then through the bitterness of the Cold War were preparing to culminate their long efforts in a great summit conference and then, one by one, lay down Khrushchev's Challenge: the mantle of government to a new generation who would reap the benefits of peace—hopefully true and lasting peace.

The fate of the world hung in the balance somewhere between these earnest plans for peace and the miles remaining ahead of that U-2 as it neared Sverdlovsk. This was not the normal U-2 flight. Much was made of the fact that the pilot had with him a vial (needle) of poison; so that rather than expose his native land to charges of willful violation of the air space and sovereignty of the Soviet Union, he could silence himself in death. The code of the spy. Yet little was made of the antithetical fact that the pilot also had a parachute which would save his life. Much was made of the fact, afterwards, that this was a "civilian" aircraft and that it was flown by a "civilian" pilot. Yet this pilot had been permitted to carry with him on this flight his military identification card, complete with name and picture, along with a pocketful of other identifying cards, all of which easily placed him at military installations, in military instrument flight schools, and on military facilities just days before the flight. He was hardly a deniable spy.

Much was made later of the fact that Air Force Captain Powers had resigned from the Air Force and that he was a civilian employee of the Lockheed Aircraft Corporation. He was technically a civilian: But his records were still held by the Air Force, and had he chosen, he could have returned to the Air Force without loss of pay, seniority, and promotion status.

Furthermore, the number of identification items that he had with him made it clear that he was less a true civilian and more a civilian cover spy pilot. He was in the same mold as Allen Pope in 1958, who was captured by the Indonesians, and of the Air Force crew that was shot down in Armenia also in 1958. By that time the Russians had plenty of evidence to know that "civilian" pilots belonged to the CIA by way of the U.S. Air Force.

This course of events had more impact upon the United States than upon the Soviet Union. The U.S. Government made much of the fact that the U-2 was an "unarmed civilian aircraft" and that it was flown by a civilian. However, in his book, *The Craft of Intelligence*, Allen Dulles makes much of the fact that operation of such sophisticated aircraft could scarcely have been kept a secret. It wasn't! As he wrote, "Sooner or later, certainly this would have leaked out." Since this was so certain, then why did the U.S. Government have to give out untrue cover stories? And why did they have to permit Powers to carry so much identification when it would have been better to limit the leak as much as possible? Even if he had died, they would have had all the information they needed. How did it happen that they broke with policy procedures for that special flight by letting him take off loaded with incriminating evidence that proved he was a U.S. spy pilot? Who was it who wanted this special U-2 flight on May 1, 1960, two weeks before the summit conference, to fail and then to become so glaring an admission of guilt when it did fail that it would inevitably doom the summit conference along with it? The incidence of these things, too many things, give weight to the thought that this flight was intended to be something rather special.

Nothing was said that all clandestine operations personnel, and especially the select coterie of U-2 pilots, were required to submit to a complete inspection before takeoff, which included the removal of all clothes and other personal effects and the issue of sanitized, non-identifiable clothing and equipment sufficient only for the flight. Neither pilot nor plane were sanitized on this flight as was required on other flights.

But these are only details that came up after the flight. The special question about this flight and this plane and this pilot was, "Who sent him out in the first place? What was this flight supposed to gain that could have been worth one particle of what it lost?" The Secretary of State, in attempting to justify the flight and as the official spokesman for his Government, said, "Conditions at a latter season would have prevented obtaining very important information. There is never a good time for a failure of an intelligence mission. We believe it unwise to lower our vigilance because of these political negotiations." Then the following three reasons for operating this flight were given:

1. Clear skies had been forecast, which meant clear pictures.
2. May 1 for the Russians is something like the Fourth of July for Americans. It is a national holiday that honors the solidarity of the

working class. In Moscow it is the occasion for a display of armed might in a mammoth parade that winds past the Kremlin where high Soviet officials, including Khrushchev, watch the troops and material go by from a reviewing stand. It was felt in Washington that the Soviet vigilance might have relaxed on May 1 because of the holiday, that perhaps radar and antiaircraft crews would be celebrating to the detriment of their defenses.

3. The CIA had intelligence that a new Soviet rocket twice as large as anything produced by the USA would be on its launching pad for a May Day test. The launching pad, it was known, was at a new missile base near Sverdlovsk industrial complex and noted that the launch points were domed rather than following the herringbone pattern of the older Russian ground-to-air missile sites.

For some reason almost everything about this flight was different, and for some reason it had to go at precisely the time when it would cause the most alarm if it failed. A careful rereading of the objectives of this flight fails to confirm them to be of sufficient significance to override the natural precautions that should have been taken, especially since every top official in the Government knew how important the summit conference was to the President. And only high level officials—or knowledgeable ST members—could have launched that flight. All of the regular launch authorities certainly knew that they were under strictest orders to do nothing that would jeopardize the success of the conferences.

Flights such as this one from Pakistan, Turkey, and Norway were tracked by U.S. radars and other sensitive tracking equipment. The plane did not have to maintain total silence. After all, anything the long range radars from peripheral areas could track from hundreds of miles away the Russians air defense system could track from twelve (the flight altitude) to a few hundred miles. The Soviets would know the plane was there; as we learned later, they knew of almost every flight during the previous four years. They had tracked and forced down countless U.S. aircraft in preceding years. It has been known for decades that Soviet radar is as good as or better than ours. They tracked the U-2 planes, but could not reach them at their extreme altitude. So the U-2 could communicate, not in the usual manner, but with flash, or "squirt," coded transmissions at predetermined times. In spite of the rather strange way in which the news of the loss was announced, there is no reason why we should believe that some authorities in this country did not know that it had occurred, and perhaps they knew exactly why it went down. Yet they ordered the administrator of NASA to give out an unreasonable cover story, which even said the plane had come from Turkey.

When the plane went down, its signals faded and it was lost from tracking radar. The engine had stopped, and Powers was gliding the plane down from its extreme altitude, which was so high that the air's oxygen content was insufficient to support combustion. The normal combustion of the jet engine at that altitude had to be assisted by the infusion of a trace of raw hydrogen from a small liquid hydrogen cryogenic storage bottle. If by some chance the engine either coughed itself out, or if something happened to this slight hydrogen supply and the engine flamed out, it could not be restarted at that altitude. The pilot would have had no recourse other than to let down and see if he could restart the engine at some lower altitude. The evidence that the engine would not restart even at thirty thousand feet indicates that the trouble was most likely hydrogen deficiency and not a normal fuel flameout. Had it been a simple flameout and had there been plenty of hydrogen, the engine should have restarted, as others had in similar circumstances.

When the plane did not restart, Powers was forced to let it continue to spiral toward the earth, and then at a safer altitude either bail out (a high altitude bailout is dangerous and violent) or continue on down to the ground. Actually, some of the early pictures of the U-2 showed an aircraft that was relatively undamaged, when one considers that the Russian story was that it was hit by a rocket in the air and then crashed into the ground. We may never really know whether Powers parachuted because he was hit by Russian rockets or gunfire or whether he parachuted simply to leave a plane that was doomed to crash anyhow. The elaborate pictures of the plane, which the Soviets released at the trial, show neither bullet damage nor rocket fragment damage, although at that point neither would be important; the plane was going to come down. If it had not been on the way down, neither rockets nor bullets would have been able to bring it down in those days.

Those who had been watching the progress of the flight from Washington control soon learned that the U-2 had dropped from surveillance, and they may have received coded information that gave them solid clues as to why the plane did come down. After all, space technology had reached the point by that time that ground tracking stations could tell every minute change and environmental perturbation on a remote nose cone. There was no reason why anyone should expect that the U-2 tracking system was not at least as good as that. Nose cones transit the Soviet Union all the time and are monitored all of that time. The U-2 was most likely monitored in the same manner. Therefore, it was not long before the alerted officials in Washington knew that Gary Powers was down somewhere in Russia.

In spite of this firm knowledge they instructed the CIA to say nothing. By this time the President had returned to his Gettysburg farm, and Secretary of State Herter was in Turkey, continuing his rounds of talks prior to the summit conference. As far as Eisenhower and Herter were concerned, all was well, and the conference was a short two weeks away.

In the belief and the hope that the crash had been unobserved and undiscovered by the Russians, Allen Dulles suggested that the administrator of the National Aeronautics and Space Administration, T. Keith Glennan, release a preprepared cover story. Glennan reported that a high altitude weather research aircraft on a flight from Adana, Turkey, was missing and that "it might have accidentally violated Soviet air space." At that time he added that these aircraft were special U-2 high altitude planes and that they were essential to the space program. It was believed that this frankness would take some of the heat off the flight, especially if the Russians should ever find the wreckage and report it.

This was the initiative Khrushchev had been waiting for. On the fifth of May, five long days after the plane had landed, he reported that an American plane had been shot down over Russian territory. He gave no more detail than that, although he did harangue about American war-mongers, and those Americans who remembered, recalled that the Russians had shot down that innocent U.S. Air Force transport aircraft in June 1958. It began to look as though the barbaric Russians were being trigger-happy again and that they had shot down another innocent weather plane.

Those who knew the real fate of the U-2 remained silent, and those who did not went through the paces like automatons. The official spokesman of the State Department, Lincoln White, came out immediately after Khrushchev's remarks and repeated Glennan's story, and again claimed innocent action on the part of the "disabled" pilot. On the same date, the U.S. Ambassador in Moscow reported that he had picked up some cocktail party gossip in Moscow that implied that the American pilot had been captured and that he was in good health. The 1958 incident was being repeated almost to the line, and hopes began to rise that this "mistake" would be no worse than the last one.

Then, on May 7 Khrushchev moved in for the kill: "Comrades, I must let you in on a secret. . . . When I made my report I deliberately refrained from mentioning that the pilot was alive and safe and that we had the remnants of the plane. We did this deliberately, because had we given out the whole story, the Americans would have thought up another version." He then went on to give the whole story in detail. However, he stopped short of accusing Eisenhower of knowing that the flight had been ordered over the Soviet Union. It is entirely possible, in fact it is most probably the whole truth, that Eisenhower did not know that the U-2 had been dispatched on that fateful flight. Khrushchev offered him an out when he said, "I am prepared to grant that the President had no knowledge of a plane being dispatched to the Soviet Union and failing to return; but that should alert us still more."

The Russian Premier was ready to say, "We are so close to the summit and to peace. I am ready to accept that this was a cruel and terrible provocation made by others without the knowledge of the American President." Let the President stand up and say that he had no knowledge of this flight, and then back up his statement by firing Allen Dulles, Dick Bissell, and those other four men who had pressed so hard for this flight. This was the challenge and that was the price. There was still a chance that Ike could have his long dreamed of summit conference; but now he would have to pay the price. Thus Eisenhower was put to the biggest test of his entire career. Could he clean house? Could he rid the country of those who, as Harry Truman said, "had diverted the CIA to become the center of foreign intrigue," or would he have to bend to their might and their cunning and see his dreams shattered in a cold and cruel awakening? Many years later it was President Richard M. Nixon who said, "When you inherit a nightmare . . ."—and that was as far as he went with his thought. President Kennedy after the Bay of Pigs had the same nightmare. President Eisenhower had come within two weeks of achieving not only the goal of an aging President who had given his entire adult life to his country; but of realizing the hope of the entire country for a lasting and hopeful peace.

No one will ever know just why he turned down Khrushchev's gambit. No one will ever know why he decided to back the ST at a time when it had permitted his plans to be shattered. Did he simply believe that his course was the only honest way out and that someone in his Administration had made an innocent mistake; or did he succumb to a greater pressure?

It was not only the U-2 that had trapped him. The ST had armed and equipped a major force of tens of thousands of Tibetans high beyond the Himalayas; it had thousands of Cubans under arms and in training all over the North American continent, from the Canal Zone to many sites in the United States it was deeply entwined in the politics and economy and rebellions of Africa; and already the United States, which had seldom seen armies in its own streets, was becoming accustomed to the roar of heavy trucks and the march of feet in embattled inner cities. Did Eisenhower really have a choice? Could he just fire Allen Dulles and a few of his top lieutenants and clean house that simply? He knew that he could not. Those other men who had seen to it that all the little things fell into place and that the U-2 had gone aloft on that precise day were men of the ST, and wiping out Dulles and his staff would not touch them.

Furthermore, it was one thing to have the power to see that the U-2 was not stopped from going on a rather routine flight; but it was an entirely different matter to be able to assure that it would come down in the very center and heart of the Soviet Union.

The men responsible for this flight were highly competent and they knew, for instance, that if the all important hydrogen bottle was only partly filled they could count upon the plane's coming down as certainly as if they had only partly filled its tanks with fuel. But fueling was a routine chore done by men who always know the plane must be full; and a pilot knows that he must check the tanks and the caps. Also, on the U-2 you can just about tell how full it is by seeing how much the heavily loaded wings droop when the plane is on the ground. Hydrogen starvation was much more subtle..

As Ike pondered his dilemma it no doubt flashed through his mind how all of these pieces began to fit together. He had heard a little about the training of Cuban exiles. He had heard something of the Tibetan flights and of the training of Tibetans in the United States for deep paradrop missions into far northwest China. He knew of the troubles in Africa, and he knew how inner city problems were welling up in the United States. But he had put all this aside as small matters in comparison to the importance of his great crusade for peace. It is quite evident that these thoughts preyed upon his mind. On May 9 he authorized Secretary Herter to say, "In accordance with the National Security Act of 1947 the President has put into effect since the beginning of his Administration directives to gather by every possible means information required to protect the United States and the Free World against surprise attack and to enable them to make effective preparations for their defense. Under these directives, programs have been developed and put into operation which have included extensive aerial surveillance by unarmed civilian aircraft, normally of a peripheral character, but occasionally by penetration."

To underscore what the Secretary had said and to confirm what had been on his mind, the President himself said: "As the Secretary of State pointed out in his recent statement, ever since the beginning of my Administration I have issued directives to gather, in every feasible way, the information required to protect the United States and the Free World against surprise attack and to enable them to make effective preparations for defense." He was putting together in his own mind all of the bits and pieces of the big puzzle. He had been trapped by his own ST, and all of the things they had been doing now made a pattern.

The United States and the world were not going to have peace; they were going to enter a generation or perhaps even more of numbing cold war in which the inputs of random secret intelligence would provide evidence of subversion throughout all the countries of the free world and the United States would react by attacking subversive insurgency wherever it was discovered.

Now Eisenhower could see what his old comrade in arms, Maxwell Taylor, had meant by his new "National Military Plan of Flexible Response." There is much more meaning in those words than anyone would suspect at first reading. It would have been enough for Maxwell Taylor to suggest a new national military plan; but this was not the idea. He meant that from now on the country would be mobilized in an increasing frenzy to the tune of another trumpet, which called for a military plan of flexible response to Secret Intelligence alarms and cries of subversive (Communist) insurgency.

All of these things took on a new meaning and a totally new warning. The President may have realized that he was not really in charge of events, and he could not honestly say that he didn't know what was going on; yet he had never seen the picture in its totality before. There was no other way out. President Eisenhower did the only thing he could. He announced to the world that he had known about the flight and that it had been his sole responsibility as Commander in Chief of the United States.

With that, Khrushchev had no choice but to face the same facts, his way. How could he hope to reach a peaceful settlement and meaningful agreements with a President who was admitting to the world that at the very time he had been speaking peace he had been plotting overflights and the invasion of the territorial integrity of not only the Soviet Union, but of China and Tibet and Cuba. Khrushchev had no alternative either. All hope for a successful summit conference had gone. The leaders of the world attended the conference individually but all was lost. With this great disaster the fifteen year search for a peaceful settlement in a world menaced by the atomic bomb came to an end. Vietnam lay ahead.

Chapter 21

Time of Covert Action: U-2 to the Kennedy Inaugural

There was no need for post-mortems The great crusade was dead. There would be no thaw in the Cold War. Pressures that had lain dormant while the world waited and prayed for the success of the summit conference broke out more violently than before: in Japan where Jim Haggerty, the President's press secretary and advance man for his trip, was mobbed outside the Tokyo International Airport; in the Congo where Dag Hammarskjöld was to die violently; in Cuba, and especially in U.S.-USSR relationships. The ST moved fast and quietly. Its operators in many of the MAP countries and in other peripheral areas stepped up their activities. Trouble spots, such as countries suffering from crop failures, border disputes, and terrorization by bandits were given particular attention. What had been a lull before the summit now became a ground swell before the storm.

Eisenhower put out an immediate order that there would be no more overflights anywhere at anytime. This brought to an end, for the time being, the U-2 program, the Cuban exile overflight para-drop program, the vast Tibetan project that was entirely dependent upon long-range transport infiltration, and others of lesser merit. But it did not bring about an end to clandestine activity. It simply drove it deeper under cover right here in the United States. By that time so much was going on all over the world that curtailing overflights had only a small impact upon the rest. The ST muffled its more elaborate operations and began to put all its eggs into one basket—the move to counterinsurgency operations in the counterinsurgency-list countries.

More than fourteen thousand Tibetans and remote area tribesmen, nearly all of the active population of Tibet above the high Himalayas, had been armed, equipped, and fed by the Agency. This flow of equipment and activity stopped abruptly with Eisenhower's order. These valiant men were left to their own devices in their hostile homeland. They have, no doubt, been rounded up and many of them slaughtered. All of the equipment destined for them was held at CIA supply points in Okinawa, Taiwan, Thailand, and Laos. The Indonesian campaign, which had ended the year before, had resulted in a windfall of leftover military supplies and aircraft, which were sent to Taiwan, Thailand, the Philippines, Laos, and Okinawa. The Cuban program became less visible and more political. It continued to gather together in strategic locations massive stockpiles of aircraft, armament, and shipping. All of this was being held in readiness in storage in Florida, Guatemala, Panama, and Puerto Rico. As a result, the Eisenhower order, if anything, served to strengthen the operational side of the Agency and place it in a position of being able to move fast with ready equipment and personnel as soon as the Administration changed. That was only six months away; so the ST prepared.

All of this preparation and readiness served to underscore how farsighted and how determined the Agency had been in planning within its own sanctum for its role as leader of the Cold War response mechanism. Whereas its Intelligence chieftains received public accolades for work well done, and its Special Operations (DD/P) agents and operators worked as quietly as they could behind the scenes, none of them were more successful than those of Logistics (DD/S), with emphasis on the men in the comptrollership and budget offices. Somewhere in the early days one of these men, or perhaps one of their friends in the legal division, where Larry Houston has held sway for so many years, observed the special applicability of an old law from the depression days—the National Economy Act of 1932.

For the CIA it has been the big end of the horn of plenty. In layman's language this act states that if one department or agency of the U.S. Government has something which it would like to get rid of, and another agency of the government would like to buy it, then the two agencies are authorized to get together and agree on a buying and selling price to their mutual satisfaction. The sale would be consummated under the terms of the National Economy Act of 1932. The uses to which this expedient can be put to use are infinite and what the agency can do with a few dollars and a few good cover units would in most cases be unbelievable to the uninitiated.

The National Security Act of 1947 was quite strict with reference to money for the Agency, and in many ways the Congress had shown that it did not want the Agency to get much money and that it believed that one sure way it could keep the CIA out of the covert activities business would be to control and restrict its funds. However, by 1949 Congress relented, and although it did not give the Agency a great deal more money, it had let the barriers down. Ever since that law was promulgated, the CIA has had no trouble at all getting adequate funds. But more important than the dollars the Agency gets is what it can do with those dollars to make them cover all sorts of research, development, procurement, real estate ventures, stockpiles, and anything else money will buy, including tens of thousands of people who do not show on any official rosters.

For example: The CIA Act of 1949 says the CIA may "transfer to and receive from other government agencies such sums as may be approved by the Office of Management and Budget, for the performance of any functions or activities authorized . . . and any other government agency is authorized to transfer or receive from the agency such sums without regard to any provisions of law limiting or prohibiting transfers between appropriations. Sums transferred to the agency in accordance with this paragraph may be expended for the purposes and under the authority ... of this title without regard to limitations of appropriations from which transferred."

Such procedures give the CIA an open hand to move funds in and out of other accounts freely. Of course, the language of this law mentions "activities authorized" and such other normal controlling terms. However, under high classification few people know that this is going on, and few want to become involved even if they find out. Also, the Agency works long and hard to get its own people, or entirely sympathetic people, into the key jobs where such things as this take place, and they see that the controls of the law do not bind at any point.

Years ago, in the headquarters of the Air Force there used to be a fine old gentleman in the budget office who had been there ever since the cement in the Pentagon was wet. He knew as much about the intricacies of the Federal budget as any man in Washington. He had previously worked with Jesse Jones in the Reconstruction Finance Corporation during the old days of the Roosevelt Administration. Somehow he had been assigned the job of handling all of the CIA money that flowed through the Air Force, and he did this with more zeal and élan than any of the actual Agency men "across the river."[1] He had in his area of operation a younger and most capable assistant who learned the trade from him. As the years passed, this second man was promoted into the highest budget assignment in the Pentagon, where he served under Robert McNamara, who knew all of the intricacies of the CIA money management, and who saw to it that things always went smoothly. In the case of both of these exemplary public servants, they did their work efficiently and smoothly, and one of their greatest common achievements was that they never let any of these unusual money matters create friction, irregularities, or publicity. Whenever things got to the point just before the boil, they knew how to raise the flag of "security," and the subject would be dropped quietly. This process is one of the key elements in the success of the CIA in matters pertaining to money.

---

1. When the CIA was housed in World War II temporary buildings in the Foggy Bottom and Reflecting Pool part of Washington, the Pentagon was "across the river" from the CIA. Thus, it had a special meaning to both organizations.

It is possible to read the unclassified Public Law on National Security closely, and by careful interpretation, one can see a lot more there than one might see the first time through. By 1959-60 the Agency was able to count on a great deal of money and upon even more tangible things that its money could buy at considerable savings. There were no barriers then to becoming involved in much greater action, and the stage was set for the political moves that would make it possible.

While elements of the ST were keeping Cuban plans alive, other elements were working on the political resurgence of the U.S. Army. Maxwell Taylor had published his book, *The Uncertain Trumpet*, and announced his new National Military Plan of Flexible Response. The plan itself did not so much advocate a new military system as it opposed the system that existed. He made light of the "massive retaliation" doctrine of John Foster Dulles, which was the mainstay of the Eisenhower defense posture. Taylor proposed that the United States be ready to respond anywhere in the world with whatever it would take to defeat the "Communist-inspired subversive insurgency," which he felt lay all around us. His plan was a totally passive and defensive stand, based upon one word, one idea and one strategy—response. It was the embodiment of the idea of "containment" one stage removed from the proposals of Clark Clifford.

With the Taylor proposal as a rallying call, the ST began to rekindle and rebuild the Army Special Forces along new lines. The Special Forces were being turned away from war planning activity and MAP support to an active role against subversive insurgency in the countries of the Free World. This was called "flexible response," but at least in the initial stages, it was direct clandestine intervention by U.S. Armed Forces in other countries.

The Agency and certain other of its close friends obtained the Civil Affairs school curriculum from Fort Gordon, and working with that as a foundation, rewrote it into the new U.S. Army Special Forces doctrine and course outline. These words, which sounded reasonable for the training and indoctrination of selected foreign troops, took on an entirely new meaning and significance when they were taught as part of the doctrine of the U.S. Army. This political-social-economic role for the Army was a far departure from the historic indoctrination of the military forces of a free nation.

Work on this activity took place in the last half of 1960 and was ready for initial action before Kennedy was inaugurated. The timing was important, and it was very cleverly arranged. Ordinarily, any major policy change and curriculum change in the Special Forces school at Fort Bragg would have been processed through the Continental Army Command at Fort Monroe, Virginia—the next higher headquarters. However, this new curriculum was not shown to the Continental Army Command. It was brought to the attention of certain selected CIA-oriented officers of the Army headquarters in the Pentagon so that they might obtain a certain de facto blessing from the civilian top echelons of the Army on the premise that it had been duly and properly "staffed." Then this curriculum was taken directly to Fort Bragg and placed in the hands of selected instructors, some of whom were Agency personnel on cover assignments. They worked rapidly to get an instructor-group trained and ready for the first classes, to be given during December and January of 1960–61. Then, in a very opportune move, the CIA and its friends in the office of the Secretary of Defense set up a visit for the Secretary of Defense to this school. The ostensible purpose of this visit was to enlist his support for the Special Forces who, it was said, needed a morale boost after years of neglect. (Actually, this was made to appear to be the Secretary's formal dedication and approval of this new curriculum and the resurgence of the Green Berets.)

The Secretary of Defense was unable to make this trip, but in his place he designated his most experienced and able deputy, James Douglas. He flew to Fort Bragg to see the rejuvenated Special Forces and the school where Green Beret volunteers and foreign students from all over the world were attending classes featuring the new curriculum.

Mr. Douglas found the Green Berets on the firing range with special light weapons. He saw them practicing with one of the most famous and most lethal weapons, the long bow. Special Forces troopers excelled with the ancient weapon. Others were in outdoor classrooms, learning how to use mines and other explosives for sabotage and demolitions work. Still others were listening to foreign instructors, learning a selected vocabulary of foreign words in the languages of Laos, the Congo, or in Spanish. Then he went into formal classrooms where the U.S. military instructors were lecturing to large classes of U.S. students, into other classes where the students were all foreign, and into still others where foreign and American students attended classes together. This was a stirring sight to the Secretary. He had no way of knowing that as he went from front door to front door a number of students were being hastily shuttled out the back door from classroom to classroom to fill every class he witnessed. The whole scene was polished and fleshed out to a high degree of reality and perfection.

Everywhere in the Special Forces sector of Fort Bragg there was new life and new spirit. The camp was alive and most impressive and convincing. He could not have known that some of those instructors had never seen their notes and lesson guides before that day, and he could not have known that many of the foreign students had been rounded up for that visit, were not enrolled in the school, and had not the slightest idea of what was taking place. He had no way of knowing that the curriculum and the whole show that he had witnessed were part of a major plan to help create the future forces needed by the ST and by the new "flexible response" doctrine of the U.S. Army. What he was doing was participating in the "Selling of the Pentagon"—1960 style. He was seeing the resurgence of the Special Forces, a resurgence that would involve the active employment of U.S. military personnel in clandestine activities throughout the world. In other words, the Army would be operating under the direction of the CIA in overseas areas such as Laos and Vietnam, Thailand and Latin America. The course of events had, since 1947, run full circle. Whereas it had been visualized and contemplated that the CIA might be used as a sort of fourth force in the event of active employment of U.S. forces under the direction of the military commander, now it was the military establishment that was furnishing forces to the CIA to serve under the operational control and direction of the CIA in the covert activities of the Cold War.

When he returned to Washington, Mr. Douglas approved what he had seen and authorized a modest expansion of the Army Special Forces. At a time when the Army had reached its lowest man power levels in two decades, this was a significant event. The Green Berets were looking for new fields to conquer. Their victory over the bureaucracy was celebrated throughout the Army, and there was a special quiet elation among the ST. They were on their way. From the date of the U-2 disaster, the ST had become the dominant force within the Government of the United States, in terms of foreign policy and military affairs short of all-out nuclear war. (That proviso is added only because it has not yet been tried, not so much because it is beyond possibility.)

Men from the Special Forces were sent to Panama and Guatemala to train Cubans for the ST. Others went to Eglin Air Force Base in Florida to work with the Air Force Special Air Warfare units in their supporting mission on behalf of the Cuban program. The Air Force, not to be outdone by the Army, had leaped into the special warfare business with special aircraft and with the Air Commandos. Although they saw conflict on several fronts in the offing, at that time they were all working on the Cuban program. During the political campaign, President Eisenhower had directed that the Cuban operations should come to a halt. He wanted nothing under way during the remaining portion of his Administration to be left for the incoming Administration to perform. The over-the-beach projects were halted, and the somewhat regular overflight paradrop projects were stopped. The Cubans did not accept this quietly, and to keep them occupied, their training program was maintained at a good pace.

Other Special Forces troops were sent into Laos as advisers to work with the Meo tribesmen and with other groups who were fighting with the national forces against the Pathet Lao. For some time the skirmishes in Laos far outweighed anything going on in Vietnam or Thailand in size and scope. United States support was shifted from one strongman to another faster than the army could keep up with it. On many occasions British, Canadian, Philippine, and other than French foreign nationals were brought in to work with this undercover army. The CIA had all sorts of units working there. Air units were mercenaries, "covered" U.S. Air Force, Chinese Nationalists, and Thailand air force personnel. This was the place where the CIA first employed helicopter forces of considerable size. The years in Laos were formative years for the CIA and all of the forces that later became engaged with it in Southeast Asia.

Once the military forces began to get a regular taste of this sort of action, certain elements of the military, such as the Special Forces, went to great lengths to excel their mentors, the CIA, in the pursuit of secret operations. This operational activity gave birth to staff cells back in higher headquarters, such as at CINCPAC in Hawaii and in the service headquarters in the Pentagon. In the beginning this was relatively informal; but as time and experience were gained they became hard-core operational centers, such as the famous SACSA of Kennedy-era fame.

These forces saw action all over the world. No matter where the action arose, the same group of men and the same equipment and tactics went into action. The Air Force was given the assignment of flying into the Congo in support of the Kasavubu government. Meanwhile, the ST had put together an air armada of heavy transport aircraft, along with other mercenary units, to aid the Katanga cause on the other side. In Latin America the Special Forces—both Army and Air Force—were working closely with many countries and were teaching them to act positively and swiftly against rebel elements in remote areas. None of these early experiences were too noteworthy, but they were evidence of things to come.

In previous years, everything the CIA had done had been carefully cloaked in secrecy to avoid detection. Also, the operations of the Agency had been kept small in order that they would be easier to keep secret. However, since the U-2 program the ST had become less and less concerned with security in overseas areas, as long as they could maintain a measure of security within our own government. Secrecy was maintained very closely here, and very few people in government knew what the Team was doing; but overseas the very existence of powerful operations, even though they were generally clandestine, gave evidence of the strong and stealthy hand of the

CIA. This was particularly true of the impending Cuban program. The activity in Panama, in Nicaragua, and Guatemala, and the heightened activity in and around Miami and New Orleans could not be kept secret. Anyone who cared to know, knew that something was under way.

In October 1960, just before the election, Castro charged the United States with aerial aggression. It was true that despite the stand-down directed by Eisenhower, a special interpretation was given for overflights manned by Cuban exiles and to flights from non-U.S. bases. Therefore it was considered by the ST not to be a violation of the President's orders to perform such operational flights from Guatemala to Cuba with paradrops of supplies and ammunition for "supposed" reception parties in Cuba. Few of these flights ever accomplished anything of real value. However, they did much to keep the morale of the volatile Cuban community in the United States from collapsing. Then, on October 30, less than one week before the election, Castro warned his people and the world that the United States was planning and preparing an invasion of Cuba. There can be no question of the fact that Kennedy's stand on the Cuban issues in the campaign and especially on the television debates played heavily in his appeal to many voters, who felt that the country should take a direct course of action against Castro. Therefore, Castro's announcement did little to hurt Kennedy and may have just about finished Nixon's chances of salvaging any votes from the anti-Castro sentiment that ran high in the voting public. John F. Kennedy had foreclosed that issue.

The votes were no sooner counted than the ST began a major buildup of the Cuban program. What had always been known as an airdrop and over-the-beach program now began to be called an invasion. Where hundreds of Cubans had been in training, suddenly the numbers leaped to the thousands, and the camps were filled with Cubans who had volunteered at the recruiting stations in Miami, in New Orleans, and other points.

The heavy logistics elements began to converge on shipping points in North Carolina and Florida, and airlift material was sent down to Guatemala and Nicaragua. The invasion operators in the

Agency saw no restraints with the new Kennedy team coming in that January. Eisenhower made no more moves to limit their action, and they felt that they had Kennedy's tacit approval, or would have as soon as he got a full briefing. All they needed to know was that he would not stop them. Allen Dulles fully briefed the President-elect late in November, and at about that time, Kennedy announced that he would retain Allen Dulles and J. Edgar Hoover as his DCI and FBI director. In moves that may have had some significance later, Edward G. Lansdale left Washington for a long time and was known to be in Saigon with President Diem. Walt Rostow and Jerry Weisner went to Moscow for lengthy visits, before coming back to take up senior positions in the Kennedy Administration. Then, shortly after Robert McNamara was announced as the new Secretary Of Defense-designate, he took up offices in the Pentagon and assembled a small staff who began immediately to accustom themselves to their environment. Most of them had seldom if ever been in the Pentagon before.

While this transition was under way, the ST was moving rapidly with its new concepts and policies. The school at Fort Bragg was being rapidly expanded, and at the many MAAC headquarters all over the world the planned training program for civic action began to be implemented. New troubles broke out in Laos, and things began to look very grave there. There had been a brief attempt to overthrow Ngo Dinh Diem in Saigon. Cuba asked the UN to investigate imminent military aggression against itself by the United States. After a brief recount of votes in Hawaii the official tabulation of votes in the Presidential race was announced as 34,221,531 for Kennedy and 34,108,474 for Richard Nixon. It was the closest election in history. The ST may not have elected Kennedy, but they had defeated Nixon. This had been their objective ever since 1958.

Even before the inauguration Washington, official and non-official, began to realize that the most important turnover of Presidential power since the arrival of Franklin D. Roosevelt was under way. The Kennedy team had been together for more than two years. They had worked, fought, plotted, and hoped for the election of their man. In the heat of that long battle they had learned not only to dislike the Eisenhower Administration and all that it stood for, they had learned to hate it. In most instances, as they approached Washington and assembled in their new offices they were not so sure what they planned to do. But they were very sure of one thing if it had been done by the Eisenhower Administration, it was going to be changed.

As the Kennedy Administration settled into their official chairs, some of them were selected to hear about the Cuban invasion plans, and some were not. The first big move was ready to come on stage. The ST was ready to show the Kennedy Administration how things would be done from that time on for the future.

CHAPTER 22

CAMELOT: FROM THE BAY OF PIGS TO DALLAS, TEXAS

During the afternoon, snow began to fall. It had that windblown, leaden look of a major storm. Those who could, slipped out of their offices early to beat the traffic. Few cities in the world suffer more in snowstorms than Washington. The view from the big windows in the office of the Secretary of Defense, out over the Tidal Basin and the Potomac, was wintry and beautiful. A heavy curtain was falling on the end of an era. Men who had been in Washington since the days of Franklin D. Roosevelt were planning to leave, or at least to retire from the daily commitment to government.

In 1960 Washington had become a rather shabby city. The massive government buildings stood stark and cold. The many parks and monuments had been neglected by the aged tenants, who had grown too accustomed to their appearance. No one noticed any longer how drab the whole city had become. They never remembered it any other way. It was evident everywhere that this was the end of an era. An era of depression and recovery; of major war, victory and hopeful peace; of the atom bomb and of worldwide, instant communications. An era of great depths and an era that had the promise of great heights. But all of its leaders were now old and spiritless. Their great moment, those years of preparation for the ultimate summit conference and for the crusade for peace, had come to a shattering end. Now, in the shambles of that dream, that weary generation was turning over the mantle of government, the greatest government the world has ever known, to a young man who was barely a youngster when they had first come to Washington. And as many of the old stalwarts gathered in the office of the Secretary of Defense to say their farewells to him and to the world of great power they knew so well, they looked for the last time out over the Potomac into the sweeping and deepening snow as the night, and history, closed over them.

As if to presage the change that was taking place beneath the surface of the glittering events, the streets of Washington had been plowed, shoveled, and swept clear of all snow for the inaugural parade, not by the municipal equipment other cities would have used, but by the U.S. Army and its heavy equipment. The Kennedy Administration owed its very inaugural festivities to the might of the U.S. Army, to its stealthy appearance by night into the streets of the city—a United States city. And this was part of the new era, too. Subtle changes, which had been under way, began to burst forth into the open with the inauguration.

From the first, changes were visible. The Kennedy team had been together through a tough and long battle. Their operational procedures were honed and ready. There was a Kennedy way and there was the other way. They changed Washington a lot with the Kennedy way. Eisenhower had been precise in his administrative practices. He had made great use of the National Security Council and of the implementing support of the Operations Coordinating Board. His decisions were the product of open and free discussion in the NSC chambers; and then having been made, those decisions were followed up by the OCB to assure their proper accomplishment within the Government. But Kennedy saw no real need for the NSC method. In the beginning he did not recognize and understand its usefulness and significance. When he wanted something done, he called upon one of his close friends, even upon one of his relatives, and after a brief discussion, they would go out and do what he had directed. This system can work in an operation such as the campaign had been, where the campaign team is the whole organization. However, in any organization as large and as immobile as the ponderous U.S. Government, this system is quite ineffective and leaves much undone and uncontrolled. It tends to leave tens of thousands of lesser bureaucrats on their own and to their own devices. It encourages the stagnation of the bureaucrat, and the catastrophe of the irresponsible in action.

Almost immediately following the inauguration, the ST saw that the door was wide open. With practically no NSC meetings, and therefore no Council to effectively control the CIA, there was no application of those crucial parts of the National Security Act of 1947 that require the NSC to direct the Agency. Without such direction and control, the CIA was practically free to act on its own.

Few men in the new Government had any idea of what was being put into shape for the Cuban invasion. Those who did knew only bits and pieces of the whole plan. These men were not accustomed to the double-talk and undercover language and actions of the Agency. They heard briefings, but they did not know what they really meant. On the other hand, a large number of the new Kennedy team were old CIA hands. They did know exactly what was going on, and they used their special knowledge and experience to further isolate those who did not.

There is a peculiar and dangerous characteristic that derives from the continuing application of secrecy. In an open government such as this country has been accustomed to having, it is only natural to believe that if a man is a fire-fighter, then his job has to do with putting out fires; and if he is a soldier, then his job is being prepared for war. In a simpler sense, Government workers are trained to expect that if the men in the next office are working on the Military Aid Program for Pakistan, then those men are doing that work. Customarily, if they meet those occupants of that next-door office in the snack bar or at the dining hall, they might be expected to ask them how things are going in "Pakistan."

Now if the men who are supposed to be working on the Pakistan aid program are not working on that program at all, but are actually working on a special support program for the border police of India, and the Pakistan aid program is simply a cover story, then whatever they tell their office neighbors is part of their cover story too. In other words, it is false—more plainly, a lie. However, they justify that lie as being permissible, in fact necessary, because they have been told that the "border police project" is highly classified and that they cannot tell anyone about it. So if you are on a classified project, it is all right, in fact it is essential, for you to lie. So you lie, the other man lies, everyone lies. But it is all supposed to be for the good of the cause.

Over a period of time this can develop many strange situations too involved to mention here; but one or two examples may be useful. In the Pentagon there are many offices established to do one thing. They really do not do that thing at all, but something entirely different. As a result, there are hundreds and even thousands of men who either cannot say what they are doing; or if they are forced to say something, they must lie. The polite thing is to say that they are "following their cover story."

This can lead to further complications. Even within the cover Story scheme there will be factions. Some men may be working on a certain project with a cover story, and others may be working on exactly the same project under another cover story; and neither group will know about the other. Later, when the Secretary or some other high official wants to be briefed, he may meet with one group and not the other—simply because the first group did not know of the other's existence. And he will not hear the whole story; he will hear only the first group's version of the activity. So it is not that the new Kennedy team was not properly briefed about anti-Castro activities as it was a matter of the inability of any one briefing officer to give all the facts at one time. There may have been no way to have rounded up all the facts and present them; so much of what was going on was decentralized. In spite of this, each briefing officer may have thought that he knew all the facts and that he was telling the whole truth, as happened when Tracy Barnes was sent to give Adlai Stevenson his briefing at the United Nations.

Other complications crept in. Under the cover of the Bay of Pigs operation, much bigger moves were being made. All over the world the MAP training program was picking up volume and momentum. Thousands of foreigners from all forty countries converged upon the United States for training and indoctrination. The new curriculum was either the one at Fort Bragg or like it. The Army interest in political-social-economic programs, under the general concept of "nation building," was gaining momentum. For every class of foreigners who were trained and indoctrinated with these ideas, there were American instructors and American soldiers who were being brainwashed by the very fact that they were being trained to teach this new doctrine. These instructors did not know otherwise. To them this new nonmilitary political, social, and economic theme was the true doctrine of the U.S. Army. A whole generation of the American Army has grown up with this and now believes, to one degree or another, that the natural role of an army lies in this political field. Also they believe that an army mixes some medical and educational ingredients into this nation building. They believe the army is the chosen instrument in nation building, whether the subject be political—social, economic or military. In many cases, due to the great emphasis the CIA placed on training the police forces of certain foreign countries, a large number of American servicemen who were used for such training became active in what was really police work and not the scope of regular military work.

It was the CIA, with help from a few other agencies, that put together the Inter-American Police Academy during the early Kennedy years, which played such an important part in emphasizing national police power in the nations of Latin America. The CIA brought in police instructors from all over the United States and from the military for this school. The success of this school, operating covertly from an Army base in the Canal of Panama, led to other schools in the United States that have carried on this type of work for police forces in this country. Part of the impetus behind the great buildup in the strength of police force all over the country dates back to this CIA police academy work and to the other schools it spawned. This police work not only involved training but it integrated new weapons, new procedures, and new techniques into American police work, some of which has been good and much of which has been quite ominous.

Anyone who doubts that this nation building and police activity has not become real and very effective right here in the United States need only visit the area around Fort Bragg to find one of these early paramilitary CIA-oriented specialists, General Tolson, sending his American soldiers out into the countryside with nation-building programs for the citizens of the United States. If such tactics continue, it is possible that an enlargement of such a program could lead to a pacification program of areas of the United States, such as the CIA and the U.S. Army have carried out in Indochina.

At the same time this training program was under way, larger and larger civic action teams and other benevolently named organizations spread throughout the world. MAAG units were no longer small logistics and training organizations. They had grown to large size and were frequently and almost augmented by large units on temporary duty in the host country. This Army accounting device of "temporary duty" is always interesting because of the way the Army uses it. The Army may tell an unwitting Congressman or reporter that there are 50 men in the MAAG of a given country, although there may be many more men there. The Army will justify this lie about the total number by claiming that the extra men, sometimes many more than the regular staff, are there on temporary duty. And of course there may even be 100 or 150 more men there, but since they are on the CIA cover payroll, the Army won't report them either even though they are there on Army cover. In that case there will be another justifiable lie to protect the existence of the CIA.

All of this is a game. The secrecy can't mean a thing to the host country, they know exactly how many men are there and it makes no difference to them whether they are Army, Army temporary duty, or Army cover. By the same token, the Soviet embassy, and all other embassies, will know exactly how many Army men are there. And to them, the fine distinction makes no difference. The only people these devices fool are American. American reporters, American Congressmen, American government specialists, and of course the

American public. There was almost no way in which anyone in the United States Government could unravel the whole clandestine business. But at least a beginning was made as a result of a most unexpected series of events and as a result of some very shrewd and clever work by Bobby Kennedy and his closest associates.

What had grown quietly, secretly, and almost totally unobserved within the infrastructure of the U.S. Government was by 1961 so large that it was time to bring it to life and give it some reason for existence. While Jack Kennedy and Bobby Kennedy were seriously pondering what had gone wrong with the Bay of Pigs operation, this new doctrine and new organization was emerging. It remained necessary, then, for the Kennedys to find the master key to all of this activity. It took the Bay of Pigs Board of Inquiry to perform this feat. The day-by-day litany of the Board was designed to indoctrinate Bobby Kennedy and to win him over to this new doctrine of counterinsurgency, flexible response, civic action, nation building, and the rest—and through him, to win over the President. While the Board was meeting day after day in the back room in the Pentagon, something more important than the fate of the Bay of Pigs was being discussed and elaborated upon. As witness after witness filed through the Board's chambers Bobby Kennedy sat there saying absolutely nothing, just soaking up the hearings and searching for cracks in the story. At the same time, Allen Dulles and Maxwell Taylor paraded a hand-picked group of disciples into the room for interviews and questioning. These men were selected to preach the doctrine of the new covert intervention. Their interviews were designed to train, indoctrinate, and to use an overworked term, even to brainwash Bobby Kennedy. What he heard each day was the Maxwell Taylor new-military-plan-for-flexible-response theme, blended with the White House Committee report material, and topped off by Allen Dulles's own theme of secret operations. This was a most heady mixture, and it was effective. Some of the men who were called to talk about the tactics of the Bay of Pigs had not been connected with it at all, but were Special Forces men from the Army Staff or directly from Fort Bragg. Bobby Kennedy emerged from the incessant catechism of the "truths" ready to soak up the doctrine of counterinsurgency. This was to be the new watchword. The Kennedy Administration became hooked on counterinsurgency, and the indoctrination occurred to a good measure right there in the Board of Inquiry process.

Thus the inner Kennedy clan came out of the Bay of Pigs disaster with two strong convictions. Closely held and deeply felt was the conviction that the CIA had somehow done them in and that they had better be extremely wary of anything it did in the future. This was a very deep feeling and only seldom revealed in any official actions. In fact, Jack Kennedy developed a cover story of his own by giving the appearance as much as possible in public that he could go along with the CIA, when private actions and discussions tended to support otherwise.

The second conviction was that the world was being divided sharply into two strong camps in the battle between the "world of choice" and the "world of coercion." It was President Kennedy who said to Chairman Khrushchev, "The great revolution in the history of man, past, present, and future, is the revolution of those determined to be free." The Dulles contribution to this philosophy was the reiteration of the Khrushchev challenge to support all wars of national liberation; and the Maxwell Taylor contribution was the simple reflex of the counterpuncher, the plan of flexible response. Defined in terms of the infantryman, this meant counterinsurgency.

One of the better definitions of counterinsurgency as practiced in the Kennedy era was that written by a general who worked for the Secretary of Defense:" . . . the technique of using, in appropriate combination, all elements of National Power in support of a friendly government which is in danger of being overthrown by an active Communist campaign designed to organize, mobilize and direct discontented elements of the local population against the government." Although counterinsurgency has been generally regarded as a military activity, careful analysis will reveal that it is really more a civilian-controlled action in the paramilitary area of operation. This is a most important consideration as we observe the country moving from the "Roosevelt-Eisenhower" era into the "Kennedy-Johnson" era, which includes the Vietnam episode. Note also how the definition of counterinsurgency, above, written by an Army General closely allied with the CIA and with the authors of the President's Committee report, almost precisely paraphrases sections of that report. In other words, the actions of this Government, which were called counterinsurgency, were not very different from the actions that were attributed to the Communists and called subversive insurgency. As a matter of fact, they seemed to be identical.

This may seem to be a fine point, but it is the key to much that has happened since then and particularly in Vietnam. Note that the same material written by the spokesman for the Office of the Secretary of Defense continues as follows: "A successful counterinsurgency strategy requires, therefore, the integration of all U.S. Government activities in the country concerned, under the central leadership of the Ambassador or [if the local situation had deteriorated to the point where U.S. Armed Forces are actively involved] the military area commander. In the final analysis, the defeat of a Communist-led insurgency hinges largely on the effectiveness of the Country Team. This depends in great measure upon the willing cooperation of the government departments and agencies in Washington."

When one realizes that this was written by a man who was for years the executive assistant to the Deputy Secretary of Defense and in his own right an acknowledged leader in the new Army doctrine, he begins to see that this is another part of the pattern that was changing this country's entire traditional idea of military action. We have a new doctrine at the Special Forces school, we have worldwide MAP training in the political-social-economic spheres, we have the new creed dramatically spelled out by the President's Committee report and then, to tie this all together, we have the definition of counterinsurgency. We find the official version of counterinsurgency is not to be confused with the more or less public idea of counterinsurgency, which assumes that it is a form of anti-guerrilla fighting against Communist-inspired rebels. The official doctrine of counterinsurgency states clearly that it is carried out "under the central leadership of the ambassador." This means that counterinsurgency is intended to be civilian directed, even though it appears to be a military program, and that the senior man is to be the ambassador. He is placed in charge, not actually to be the country-team commander in chief, but to make it possible for him to delegate his authority to the CIA station chief rather than to some senior military officer.

This has shaped the total efforts of the United States in Vietnam for the past decade and more. All of U.S. history prior to the past decade, more or less followed the general principles of warfare which state that in time of peace the Army trains for war, and during this time the affairs of the nations are carried out by diplomats. When diplomacy fails, then the military men take over and accomplish by military means what the politicians had been unable to accomplish. It has always been clear that when war was the only remaining means of accomplishing national objectives, the ambassador and his staff would leave the scene and the generals would take over. Now here was the highest echelon of military power in the United States stating publicly the new doctrine of the Kennedy era to the effect that counterinsurgency (a form of war) would be "under the central leadership of the ambassador."

Why would a ranking U.S. Army general on a special assignment to the White House define the new training program for mutual security, and another ranking U.S. Army general on assignment to the Office of the Secretary of Defense define the new method of warfare designed to counter the Communist support of "wars of national liberation," and both in terms of civilian direction of the military operations of U.S. forces? To anyone trained in the profession of arms, this is heretical. The answer is simple, although it has lain buried under the long years of the horrible disaster in Vietnam. Both of these men were closely affiliated with and had served with the CIA, and both were the type of men who make up the ST. Even though they wear the uniform of the U.S. Army, their primary allegiance has been with the STICIA new method of operations in peacetime. They saw that the time had come for the ST to make its big move and for it to sweep out beyond the DOD and the CIA to form a massive paramilitary international power under para-civilian leadership and a monstrous cloak of security. Their words were so simple and so Boy-Scout sounding; yet they have changed the entire world during the past decade.

They went on to say, "The United States therefore has made the decision to enter the lists early, to throw its national power into the counterinsurgency campaign on the side of our allies, the local authorities. The problem of counterinsurgency now is receiving the personal attention of the President and his senior advisors. A major effort is being made throughout the government, and particularly within the DOD to develop sound doctrine for the conduct of this unorthodox form of warfare. The JCS, for example, have recently established within the Joint Staff a special staff section dealing exclusively with the problem of counterinsurgency.... counterinsurgency is not susceptible to a purely military solution ... it requires the closest possible coordination of political, economic, psychological, and military actions." By the end of 1962 this nation had gone so far down the line following the Agency, the new Special Forces doctrine, the MAP, and the new U.S. philosophy as outlined in the President's Committee report, that it was saying openly it was well on its way to carrying out as top national policy a major clandestine operation so big in fact that the entire government would be involved. Obviously, it could not be really clandestine in the sense that it would be kept secret from our enemies; on the contrary, it was a new kind of "clandestine," so it would be kept secret from all Americans.

When such men stated that the war would be waged under civilian leadership, and then named the ambassador as the commanding and senior officer, they simply were carrying out their usual cover-story double-talk. Any such counterinsurgency would be initiated and directed by the CIA. Of course the generals involved would be real generals; but they would be working inside of and for the CIA—or in some cases not exactly inside of the CIA, but certainly under its direction. Has it ever been properly explained why this country has retained an ambassador in Saigon since the first one was selected by the CIA to go to that new piece of real estate, a new nation called South Vietnam, back in 1954? Why should the longest war in which this country has ever been involved, and the second costliest and second most destructive, have been waged through all these futile years under the direction of an ambassador? Is it because of the above doctrine? Is it because we entered this conflict to support what were, at first, minor CIA operations? Then when these actions grew and grew, there never was a time when the "war" transitioned from the clandestine operators to the military operators. During all of these years the ambassador has remained as a sort of minor commander in chief, one step down from the Commander-in-chief role of the President. And this has been done so that he could serve as a referee between the CIA and the military, the end result being that neither one of them has been really in complete control since 1964, when the first Marines arrived in Vietnam. Before that, the CIA was in control of operations, while the military played a logistics role and perfunctorily acted the part of a military organization.

At that time, 1963–1964, the ambassador could have been withdrawn in favor of the military commander as the escalation went into effect. Then the CIA chief should have been relegated to the Fourth Force role he should have in a wartime situation. As late as the end of 1963, every U.S. Army combat soldier in Vietnam (excepting a few assigned to such offices as the legitimate MAAG section—as differentiated from the oversized cover MAAG section) was under the operational control and direction of the CIA. It was only after the beginning of real escalation that the Army soldiers under Army generals began to take over certain roles and missions and areas in Vietnam. They never did take over full responsibility for what was called a "war." One reason for this was that there never was a real honest to God military objective of this war. There never has been in Vietnam that objective, which when achieved by military force, would have spelled victory. There never has been that battle which, if won, would assure victory. Of course, the counterinsurgency supporters have said, "That's the nature of this type of warfare. You can't beat insurgents that way." That is nonsense. When a nation is ready to demand from its people fifty-five thousand lives and more than $200 billion of its wealth as a contribution to some foreign action, it should at least have an objective that can be achieved in a tangible manner so that one can tell when it has been reached or when such attainment is beyond reach. What has happened in Vietnam is that the CIA got in over its head, and the Army was sent in to attempt to bring some order out of the chaos that existed there after the assassination of President Diem. Only then, when the Marines and the Army arrived, were troops serving under the actual command and direction of their generals.

One of the real reasons the Army got in there in the first place was because when the Marines came in they refused to take the field under the CIA. By that time, General Krulak, formerly the Special Assistant for Counterinsurgency and Special Activities on the Joint Staff, and then commanding general of Fleet Marine Forces, Pacific, knew too much about the CIA and its activities to permit his Marines to hit the beaches of Indochina under any command other than Marine and the U.S. Military Command, Vietnam.

Kennedy undoubtedly saw the beginnings of this serious problem after the Bay of Pigs investigation. At that time he wrote two very powerful National Security Action Memoranda, NSAM 55 and NSAM 57. Both were issued from the White House in June 1961. NSAM 55 was a brief memorandum of greatest significance, which was addressed directly to the Chairman of the JCS and was signed personally by the President. In essence it said that Jack Kennedy would hold the chairman (Lemnitzer) responsible for all action of a military nature during peacetime in the same manner as he would hold him responsible for such action in time of war. In other words, the President was saying that he wanted any and all peacetime operations (military type-clandestine, covert, paramilitary, etc.) to be under the control, or at least under the close scrutiny, of the chairman of the Joint Chiefs. One way to interpret this in light of the then current events would be, "No more Bay of Pigs." This was a powerful memorandum, which set forth Kennedy's views without equivocation. It was in fact more positive as an action against the non-addressees than it was for the addressee, the JCS.

General Lemnitzer, a fine soldier of the old and traditional school and one of the best administrators to serve after World War II, did not take advantage of this memo. He knew exactly what it meant, and he did not intend to abuse it. The best way he knew to have no more Bay of Pigs disasters was to have no more Bay of Pigs. He noted the memo, had the Joint Chiefs of Staff "Red Stripe" (formally approve it), then filed it for future use, if needed. As far as that old soldier was concerned, that memo meant there would be no more clandestine military operations in peacetime and that such things as Indonesia, Laos, Tibet, and the Bay of Pigs were a thing of the past.

I was the officer responsible for briefing this paper to General Lemnitzer and to the other Chiefs of Staff, and that NSAM rested in my files. There need be no misunderstanding about what the memo meant, what the President meant, what Lemnitzer understood and did, and what the other Chiefs of Staff understood.

This was an unusual memorandum because Kennedy sent it directly to the chairman and sent information copies only to McNamara, Rusk, and Allen Dulles. It should also be noted that Robert McNamara, Dean Rusk, and Allen Dulles knew that NSAM well and understood its full meaning and intent; and they knew exactly what President Kennedy meant by it. In other words, President Kennedy by the explicit publication of this brief memo was letting the entire top echelon superstructure above the ST, wherever it existed, know that from that time on there were to be no more such ill-conceived, inadequately planned, and inherently dangerous clandestine operations. If this directive had been followed explicitly and if Kennedy had lived to assure that it was followed as he intended it to be, there is a very good chance that United States involvement in Indochina would never have been escalated beyond the military-adviser level. He had learned his grim lesson at the Bay of Pigs, and as his directive made clear, he was not going to become involved in that type of operation again. If evidence of this is needed, consider how he handled the missile crisis in Cuba a year later. Once he had been convinced of the gravity of the situation, he directed the mobilization of sufficient troops overtly, and challenged the Cubans and the Soviets to comply with his demands. He respected the proper employment of military power and had seen how undercover military power fails.

The second memorandum, NSAM 57, though issued at the same time, was signed, as most NSAMs were, by a member of the NSC staff for the President. Coming as it did paired with NSAM 55 there could have been no misunderstanding that it carried the same thrust as NSAM 55, and that it fully expressed the views of President Kennedy. This memorandum was much longer, and it gave much more detail.[1]

Following the policy of the National Security Act of 1947 and of such other directives as NSCID 10/2 and later NSCID 5412/2, it recognized that there might be requirements for clandestine activity from time to time. Then it went further than those earlier directives and became much more explicit. It said that any small and truly covert type of operation "may be assigned" to the CIA and that any which were larger would be the subject of special study and planning and then "may be assigned" to the military, that part of the military which would be sufficient only to carry out that one operation on a one time basis. It directed that large covert operations would not be assigned to the CIA.

This attempt at clarification provided the opportunity for the CIA and its fellow travelers with a chance to blow up the balloon. They counterattacked with a long and drawn out argument about what was a "small" operation and what was a "large" one. They then proceeded to argue about what happens if the Agency goes into some country with a small operation, and then it expands. At what point will the CIA operation be transitioned from the CIA control to the military solely on the basis of size, since it might be assumed that it might or might not have remained covert. The CIA argued that if it remained covert, regardless of size, no such transition of direction could take place. The whole point of the CIA argument was to

---

1. It may be worthwhile to note that both memoranda were very well written, exceeding by far the usual bureaucratic language of such papers in style and clarity. The writer—Sorenson?—was certainly more than one of the run-of-the-mill memo writers. Since the Pentagon Papers seem not to have contained these memoranda, it may be some time before we can learn who wrote these excellent and extremely significant papers for the President.

invalidate the President's controlling mechanism, which depended upon a scale of size.

This started some very long and heated arguments, and as often happens, since the real career military such as Lemnitzer had very little interest in this subject anyhow, the well drilled opposition made quite a bit of headway. After all the dust had settled, it began to appear that except for NSAM 55 which Lemnitzer had let remain in the file (his being of the it-can't-happen-here school), Kennedy's directive had been turned into an encouragement to the CIA to go out and start small fires and count on the military to bail them out. This may seem an odd conclusion—almost funny—but it is exactly how we got into Vietnam in spite of the directives from the White House. The ST is perfectly capable of turning a No into a Yes by its gift of irrepressible argument.

I have quoted the ranking U.S. Army officer who worked in the office of the Secretary of Defense, with reference to his definition of the term "counterinsurgency." Now I shall add a few lines written almost exactly one year after the NSAM 57 arguments about how big and when to transition to the military, and which take on a special meaning in this relationship. In this one critical year here is exactly how the fight came out: "A successful counterinsurgency strategy requires, therefore, the integration of all U.S. Government activities in the country concerned, under the central leadership of the ambassador . . . or, if the local situation had deteriorated to the point where the U.S. armed forces are actively involved, the military area commander." In this special sense, read "deteriorated" to mean "expanded beyond the ability or desire of the CIA to continue to be involved." This is exactly what was happening in Laos at about this same time. The CIA had become overextended, and things were going very badly. The CIA wrote a letter to the Secretary of Defense, asking relief or suggesting the abandonment of the Meo tribesmen whom they had been supporting.

Recall how the trouble in Vietnam started. The CIA had been involved in a great number of brush fire operations there for a number of years in one way or another since the OSS days of 1945. These raged out of control, becoming a general conflagration by the end of 1963. At that time there were more than sixteen thousand American military personnel there, more or less in the ostensible role of advisory personnel; but all of these were under the actual direction of the country team, which meant that they were under the operational direction of the CIA. (Some parties may wish to deny this in an attempt to maintain the fiction of those earlier days; but the early general officers who were serving in Vietnam at that time were either serving with the CIA under the cloak of CIA or were closely affiliated with the CIA, such as the Special Forces. One more bit of operational evidence is offered by the combat intelligence available in those days. There was none of the real military kind. What was there was a form of CIA village network intelligence, which on most counts was dependent upon the native population. Even as late as the attacks on the villages in the My Lai complex, it was the Agency intelligence functionary who told the military to attack.)

On the "when to transition" concept it will be noted that even ten years later and after the escalation of military manpower had reached the staggering figure of 550,000 men—to say nothing of gross amounts of civilian manpower—the central leadership was never transitioned to the military as President Kennedy's NSAM 57 had ordered. If anyone ever wanted an example of how far the ST can turn things around, this is one of the best. In June 1961 the President stated one thing categorically; by 1962 the Army's spokesman (actually in Army uniform; but a CIA/ST spokesman) had totally turned this around in his counterinsurgency doctrine and definition. Then, after President Kennedy died, the ST retained control of most of the Vietnam war from its earliest birth pangs to the peak of escalation. Even to this day the combat phase of the Vietnamese war, which is called "pacification" and which in fiscal year 1972 cost more than $1 billion, is totally under the direction and control of the CIA.

The key to all of this, the matter that made it so easy for the ST to wrest control of this major peacetime "covert" operation, even from the hands of the President and Commander in Chief, lay in the words of the Army general quoted above: "The JCS have recently established within the Joint Staff a special staff section dealing exclusively with the problem of counterinsurgency." This was a carefully designed move, and it emerged from a formative series of events. Almost from the time of the creation of the CIA, the Secretary of Defense had maintained on his immediate staff an Assistant to the Secretary for Special Operations. Among other things, this man was charged with the responsibility for liaison with the CIA, NSA, Department of State, and the White House. His area of interest was almost totally within the field of clandestine operations, although he was interested in routine intelligence matters and other related functions. For the five or six years prior to the Kennedy inauguration, this office was filled by an extremely able and wise figure, a retired four-star Marine general, Graves B. Erskine. He had served in that capacity longer than any man had ever served in the office of the Secretary of Defense at such a level of responsibility. His tenure had covered service under Charles Wilson, Neil McElroy, Thomas Gates, and for a brief period, Robert McNamara. As he was utilized by the secretaries prior to McNamara, he kept a close eye on all CIA operational activity that involved the military in any way, and whenever in his judgment things were going too far he would inform the Secretary, and in most instances the CIA would be asked to drop its request for military support, which generally was tantamount to halting the project. Erskine's role was one of considerable quiet power; yet he used it sparingly. Then shortly after U.S. Air Force Colonel Edward G. Lansdale came back from Saigon, where he had been working for the CIA ever since the establishment of the Diem regime and immediately before that had been in Manila during the selection and establishment of the Magsaysay regime, he was assigned to General Erskine's office at the specific request of Allen Dulles. Along with a number of other CIA agent cover "plants" in the Office of the Secretary of Defense, Lansdale provided a strong counterfoil to his boss, General Erskine, within the military departments, where he was known, except to a few, only as an Air Force officer on the Secretary of Defense staff. (By 1961 the CIA, partly as a function of the vast U-2 project, was widely and deeply entrenched in the DOD.)

When McNamara became Secretary, he was advised that he really would not need an Assistant for Special Operations. He abolished that office. Then many of the old office staff were dispersed, especially in one sudden move the day after the failure of the Bay of Pigs operation. Those who were left moved to a new location in a new office, which was then headed by General (recently promoted) Lansdale. During this period, I had been assigned to the Erskine staff and was performing a rather special function, which I had been doing for about five years before in the Pentagon, but in a different staff location. Shortly after the new Lansdale office had been established I was asked by General Earle Wheeler, then the director of the Joint State, if that function would not be better applied if it were moved from OSD to the Joint Staff, so that it might he applied uniformly for all the services and for the many major military commands overseas. He discussed this further with McNamara. In a most unusual administrative maneuver, required because of the stringent limitations of the size of the Joint Staff, my office was transferred from OSD to the Joint Staff, along with the necessary manpower spaces and authorization to staff the office with representatives of all services and administrative support. This small staff was joined later by another highly classified group, which performed a somewhat related function. Then, as a progression of this first move, the Joint Staff created an office called the Special Assistant for Counterinsurgency and Special Activities (SACSA). This new office was much larger than the original office that had moved down from OSD, and it brought with it a large staff of CIA oriented personnel from all services. It had several temporary special assistants, among them General Hemtges and General Craig, before it acquired its greatest and most dynamic driving force, U.S. Marine General Victor H. Krulak.

The important thing to understand is that the much-heralded office of SACSA had very few military responsibilities. It was almost entirely CIA oriented. Most of its dealings with the services were in areas in which the CIA was most active. For example, the great proportion of its dealing with the Army was strictly limited to Special Forces activity. With the Air Force it was for the most part limited to Special Air Warfare activity, and with the Navy it was active in the Sea, Air, Land (SEAL) teams. There were other duties of course; but most of them gave the office something it could say it was doing while it performed its primary task of supporting the CIA, the ST, and of breathing life unto the massive Frankenstein called counterinsurgency.

SACSA played another very important role in the highest level policy discussions of this country. It has been said that Kennedy wanted to get out of Vietnam in 1963 but deferred it "until after his re-election," as he told Senator Mike Mansfield, because such a move would stir up a "McCarthy (Joe) wave of sentiment" and would lose him the support of the JCS.

The JCS Kennedy knew best was the voice of SACSA. The one officer he saw from the Joint Staff more than any other during those crucial days was General Krulak. (See how often Krulak's name appears in the Pentagon Papers, and then see if the name of General Dean ever appears. Technically, General Dean should have been the action man—he was the operations director of the Joint Staff—but General Dean was not the CIA/ST man.) This was because Allen Dulles and Maxwell Taylor (at that time the military advisor to the President) opened the door for Krulak, since Krulak's job was to "support the CIA." General Krulak's closest advisors were such men as Bill Bundy, a long-time career CIA man on McNamara's staff at that time; General Lansdale, and other key CIA agents and high officials, whose names will be omitted because some of them are still active. (Some of these highly placed officials were so deeply covered that it is possible that no one in OSD, including Krulak, knew that years ago they had been planted by the CIA. Thus, when he worked frequently with a man in the Department of Research and Engineering, from whom he had been told he could get some assistance, it is quite possible he never knew the man he saw was from Dulles's office.)

Later, when Maxwell Taylor had become the chairman of the JCS, the only JCS John Kennedy knew was even more CIA biased, since Maxwell Taylor himself was by that time more oriented toward the ST than the military, and Krulak was closer than ever to the President.

Thus it was not the real military that Kennedy would have offended if he had withdrawn from Vietnam in 1963. It was the chameleon STICIA military who made him think they would have objected, and who made him think that they represented the military. In this special sense the creation of SACSA and the appointment of Maxwell Taylor as Chairman of the JCS were most influential events. It is no wonder ST writers have made so much of the great importance to them and to the CIA, of SACSA. A careful reader of the Pentagon Papers will see how well documented all of this is, especially if he observes how many "JCS" papers were actually not bona fide JCS papers but were in reality SACSA/STICIA papers, attributed only to the JCS.

As important to the ST as SACSA was, of equal importance was the return to the government and especially to the Pentagon of Maxwell Taylor. After the Bay of Pigs, it was inevitable that Allen Dulles would leave the CIA. His chief lieutenant, Dick Bissell of U-2 fame and of Laos and Bay of Pigs infamy, left the Agency to become the head of the Institute of Defense Analysis, an organization with many interesting functions—among them acting as a conduit for CIA activities. Dulles again showed that uncanny ability of his and of the Agency's to rise above each fiasco on to new heights. During the Bay of Pigs inquiry he ingratiated Maxwell Taylor to the Kennedys so firmly that Jack Kennedy assigned General Taylor to the position of Military Adviser to the President. This was a good cover assignment for General Taylor. For those who thought he might be interfering with the duties and prerogatives of the chairman of the JCS, this assignment caused a few raised eyebrows. Dulles and Maxwell Taylor were content to let those rumors and fantasies spread because they did much to help transfer some of the blame for the Bay of Pigs from the CIA to the military. However, everyone else in the need-to-know clan knew that Maxwell Taylor was in the White House to be the President's liaison man with the CIA. The President may not have known how closely Maxwell Taylor's aspirations and those of Allen Dulles matched each other. During the last days of the Dulles era, Maxwell Taylor served as the Focal Point man between Dulles and his Agency and the White House.

This was a perfect role of Maxwell Taylor. He had quit the Army in a dispute with the Eisenhower Administration and now he was in an ideal position to encourage with all support and haste the urgent development of the new flexible response army, attuned to the trumpet of Taylor's own choosing—counterinsurgency. All the pieces were coming together, and during this formative period a new special group was formed. This was the Special Group (of the NSC), Counterinsurgency, better known as the Special Group CI, or CI. This group presided over the CIA, State and Defense Departments, and others, who hastily put together a host of counterinsurgency nations. It was a watch list, which varied from time to time as intelligence inputs rose and fell with the tides of international events. The Special Group CI list usually ran to about sixteen or seventeen countries, in the order of how deep they were along the path to insurgency and decay. It is worth noting that although the automatic target of CI was Communism, not a single "Communist" country, including Cuba, was on the list. It was characteristic of the new ST focus that the United States was to intervene in the affairs of its friends and not in the affairs of Russia's friends or of China's friends.

This game as it was then played in Washington was a most serious business. As countries were added to the list their military aid programs were hastily escalated, and literally hundreds and sometimes thousands of American military personnel of all types descended upon them. Sometimes they arrived in uniform and sometimes in civilian disguise. They went to work immediately in support of the new political-social-economic doctrine, and before long new schools were being built—by the army; new hospitals were being built—by the army; new farming techniques were under way—by the army; irrigation and water purification projects were under way,—again by the army. Underlying all of the paramilitary and sometimes real military work was the CIA, working with the host government to weed out, to identify, and to categorize all of the subversive insurgents. In countries where the word Communism had never been applied to bandits, beggars, and rebels before, all of a sudden all opposition was given the name "Communist." All the problems were attributed to Communists, and the counterinsurgency action was under way.

These rather amateurish activities were met with all kinds of receptions in the various host countries. Some were cool to this love-your-army doctrine. Some were stunned. It was pretty bitter medicine for many countries, where hatred and fear of the army had been traditional, to find the Americans coming in with a program designed to make the army into local heroes according to the Magsaysay formula of a Robin Hood game. But what were they—the Colombians, Congolese, Laotians, Jordanians—able to say in the face of American "goodwill" and concern? It did a lot of good for the "do-gooders" of counterinsurgency action in the U.S. Government, and if nothing else it served to quickly coalesce the ST. The next move, as SACSA and the Agency consolidated their power and influence in the White House and in the DOD, was to propose the "logical" move of General Taylor to the Pentagon to become chairman of the JCS. As soon as this was accomplished, the Army actively threw itself into the Special Forces mold and set out to win back its position of number one on the defense team.

Thus, all of these pressures and behind-the-scenes efforts piled up before Vietnam, and came to a head in Vietnam. As we have said before, the logistics equipment in huge amounts from Indonesia, Tibet, Laos, the Bay of Pigs, and many other operations all began to accumulate in Vietnam along with the ST personnel, who saw an opportunity to accomplish, almost with abandon, all of the things that they had failed to do or had been unable to do before.

While this was going on quietly and quite subtly before his eyes, President Kennedy did a lot of talking with many old hands about "what has gone wrong with the Bay of Pigs" and "what is the meaning of Vietnam." As has been ably reported by many good writers, President Kennedy was forming his own opinion of what was going on, and the evidence is that he was quite close to the facts and to a real evaluation of what was happening. One of Kennedy's closest friends, Kenny O'Donnell, reports that General MacArthur had "stunned" the President in 1961, after the Bay of Pigs, with his warnings about the folly of trying to match Asian manpower and about the absurdity of the domino theory "in a nuclear age." O'Donnell further reports, "The General implored the President to avoid a U.S. military buildup in Vietnam, or any other part of the Asian mainland. . . ." And Mary McGrory, a reporter, has said, in words more truthful and important than she knew, "President Kennedy, who at the time was caught up in the counterinsurgency mania which had swept the New Frontier, was subsequently startled by the passionate objections of Mansfield. But he told Mansfield privately, after a White House leadership meeting, that he agreed with him "on a need for a complete withdrawal from Vietnam, but I can't do it until 1965 after I get re-elected."

Kennedy had the misfortune, which he was overcoming rapidly, of being young and inexperienced in the inner ways of government, such as those employed by the ST. He could not have realized that Maxwell Taylor, for example, by the time he had returned to the Pentagon as chairman of the JCS, was actually more of a Judas goat, as far as the military was concerned, than the leader of the herd, as he had been when he left three years before. Few great armies have been so vastly demoralized and stricken by an integral campaign as has the U.S. Army since those dark days of 1964 and 1965, when Maxwell Taylor and his ST counterparts led them into Vietnam under the banner of counterinsurgency.

Vietnam is not a simple thing. There were many new forces at play there. It had always galled the Navy and the intelligence community the way General MacArthur had dominated the Pacific during World War II and then later in Korea; and in so doing, he had gained the complete upper hand over all of his adversaries in the U.S. military, especially over "Wild Bill" Donovan of the old OSS. They were violently jealous of him. Admiral Radford, who had been Commander in Chief, Pacific Forces, objected strenuously to any decision that would make Southeast Asia an Army theater of action as MacArthur had made the Korean action an Army show. Radford supported the CIA and Lansdale when they moved into Saigon from Manila. For other reasons the Navy and the CIA had the full support of Cardinal Spellman, since he strongly urged the installation of a Catholic in the President's office in Saigon, and Ngo Dinh Diem and his family were pillars of the Catholic Church in Indochina.

Businesses that had been all but knocked out of the defense contract arena by the end of the Eisenhower regime—some by the sudden and abrupt swing to ballistic missiles and space during the late fifties—saw new light at the end of the tunnel in the resurgence of the foot-soldier army and the ground warfare this new dogma presaged. They could expect to go back to making World War II type munitions again and dumping them on the shores of Asia. Perhaps the strongest support for the Vietnamese war has always come from the national defense industries, which benefited tremendously by this windfall. The helicopter industry, which was on the ropes in 1958–59, became a major supplier of war material for Vietnam. At the beginning of the war in Vietnam the Air Force had very few aircraft that could carry a respectable tonnage of bombs—not because the planes could not carry the load, but because they had all been designed to carry nuclear weapons. As the war became a bombing war—what McNamara called the "sophisticated war" of the North—all of these huge bombers had to be refitted to carry bombs, and the huge munitions industry put back to work manufacturing bombs. There were many periods in the early days of the bombing when the Air Force actually ran out of bombs while the industry was getting out its old tooling and delivering World War II weapons again.

This war halfway around the world was a major bonanza for the transportation industry and especially for the air transportation groups. During peak years, the DOD was spending three quarters of a billion dollars on charter airlift for Vietnam alone.

In the services, military personnel who saw forced retirement facing them during the sixties were looking at the inevitable retirement as majors, lieutenant colonels, and colonels, until a whole new vista opened with the new plan and its return to a ground war of massive troop strength. Men who had lingered in the grade of lieutenant colonel got their colonel's eagles and some of them leap-frogged by way of the Green Berets and CIA recommendation to become brigadier general, major general, and even lieutenant general. There were so many diverse interests, which all came together in the springtide of Vietnam and grew and grew from under a cloak of classification and secrecy. It would be interesting to discover how men like Lansdale, Peers, Dupuy, Stilwell, Tolson, Rosson, and so many others had served with the CIA and also made rapid promotions to the grade of brigadier general and higher as a result of the CIA, Special Forces, and Vietnam. The list is long, and mostly comprised of the men who are listed in the Pentagon Papers, including of course a great number of civilians in the same category.

Few people realized how some of these operations got started, and how important some of these seemingly small things were in the escalation of Vietnam. The Agency brought a squadron of helicopters down from Laos, and immediately these complicated machines needed a great number of skilled men to support them; then these vast agglomerations of men and machines created their own requirements for additional men to protect them and to feed, house, and support them. The first helicopters came in under the wraps of secrecy. No one seemed to know how they got there; but once they were there the great logistics tail that was essential to keep them operating had to be built in the open, without classification. It could not have been kept secret, even if anyone had tried.

On top of this, since the ST was running the beginnings of the war from Washington, they felt that every gimmick they could dream up was worth a try. Even before the escalation, this plan to build up the action in Vietnam was foreshadowed and preordained by official military-type ST doctrine, which stated: "These natural advantages [of the guerrilla] can be largely neutralized by the imaginative employment of modern technological advances which military research and development have been perfecting since the last war . . . night vision devices, lightweight body armor, portable radar for infantry use, invisible phosphorescent dyes, defoliants to deprive the guerrillas of their jungle cover, fast lightweight, silent, shallow-draft boats for river patrol, and tiny reliable short-range radios. . . Practical uses for all these new developments can best be found by establishing combat development and test centers in the country where the counterinsurgency campaign is being waged."

Such centers were set up later in Vietnam and proved to be the modern counterpart of the horn of plenty and the runaway Connecticut Yankee in King Arthur's Court. The center in Saigon was given the highest priority to send daily messages to the Pentagon, and from there every single request, large and small, important or unimportant, was given a high priority to be carried out, all on the assumption that each and every request of the CDTC (Combat Development Test Center) would help win the war of counterinsurgency. The floodgates were open for the zealots, the irresponsible, and the special interests. Such things make small wars grow fast.

The CIA was the first in Vietnam with helicopters. It introduced the M-16 rifle there, and it brought into Indochina the B-26 bombers left over from Cuba and Indonesia and the T-28 trainer aircraft modified as a ground-attack plane. It had the first L-28 utility aircraft, and it brought in the old C-46, C-47 and C-54 aircraft of World War II vintage. It introduced many new ships, such as the Coast Guard patrol ships and the Norwegian-built PT boats. It used the U-2 and had the use of the product of the RF-105 reconnaissance planes. Many of the battlefield tactics used later by the army were first used in the field by the CIA.

By the middle of 1963 it had become evident that either the President was going to have to step in and put a halt to the spread of this counterinsurgency conflagration or it would consume the country. Everywhere the young Kennedy team turned, they came up against CIA and ST specialists. With the sage and powerful General Erskine gone from the staff of the Secretary of Defense, his replacement in this type of activity was either Bill Bundy, a long-time CIA man; Ed Lansdale, a long-time CIA man also, or others too numerous to mention and so well concealed (such as those who really sent the U-2 out on that fateful May 1 mission) that the unaware McNamara had no defense against their continuing pressures. Even in the office that he thought would give him some buffer between the Agency and the military—that special office in the Joint Staff—SACSA, McNamara was getting almost 100 percent CIA action, and when Maxwell Taylor became Chairman even his efforts were expended more in support of the ST, as he saw it, than in regular line military.

This was most discernible to those of us who had been in the Joint Staff for some time. In the days of other chairmen, such as Twining and Lemnitzer, JCS meetings used to be wide-open, entirely professional, and generally constructive. This is not to say there were not some strong differences and stronger language when such men as Arleigh Burke the Chief of Naval Operations, or Curt Lemay, the Air Force chief, did not see eye to eye. In any case, they were marked by discussion. They were not dominated and controlled by the chairman. Then, when Maxwell Taylor became chairman, the meetings were somber and apt to be a one-man-show. Little was ever said by any of the Chiefs pro and con when he was in attendance; but let Taylor be away and the meeting then be chaired by another man, the meetings would be open again.

These top military men who had known Taylor for years, had seen him leave the Army in a huff and had watched him return to the White House, where he cast his lot with the CIA and the ST. They knew that even though he was among them officially as the chairman, he was no longer one of them. He was leading the Army and certain elements of the Navy and Air Force away from their traditional roles and into an opportunistic and uncertain future with the CIA and the ST—into the orgy of Vietnam.

We have seen earlier that President Kennedy's directive NSAM 57, which laid out the ground rules for covert operations and broke them down on the basis that very small was for CIA and the larger ones must be reviewed and probably assigned to the military, had been so turned around that it had become, in practice, almost meaningless on the intangible issue of when to transition from the CIA to the military. To demonstrate how totally this directive has been circumvented, we should note that there has never been a transition in Saigon, even when the force strength stood at 550,000 men. How large does a peacetime operation have to get before the CIA is told to give up its more than intelligence and more than clandestine operations role? How long before the ambassador is withdrawn? before it is placed in the hands of the professional military commanders?

We have not seen what had happened to NSAM 55, the memo Kennedy had sent directly to General Lemnitzer. The General filed that memo and used its silent power to assure that the military would not become involved in covert operations. When Maxwell Taylor became the chairman, he inherited this power. As a prime mover of the inner and security-cloaked ST, he now had the scepter of greater power in his hands. Whereas the President had called upon the chairman of the JCS to advise him in peacetime as he would in wartime, now he had appointed an adviser who was with the other side. The CIA knew that Taylor would not advise against them any more than Lansdale and Bundy would, up in McNamara's office.

Therefore, with the move of Maxwell Taylor to the chairmanship of the JCS, the ST had checkmated President Kennedy on both NSAM 55 and NSAM 57. As the country moved into the crucial summer of 1963 the President admitted to his closest confidants that he could not move against the right-wingers and the ST. As he told Senator Mansfield, "I can't do it until 1965, after I'm re-elected." And as he told Kenny O'Donnell, "In 1965, I'll be damned everywhere as a Communist appeaser. But I don't care. If I tried to pull out completely now, we would have another Joe McCarthy Red scare on our hands." Then in a broadcast on Sept. 2, 1963, President Kennedy gave a hint of his plans for disengagement when he said, speaking of the Vietnamese, "In the final analysis it is their war. They have to win or lose it." Then, as Mary McGrory says, "But Kennedy, like the two presidents who have followed him, was a captive of the Saigon Government." It is typical of reporters and other researchers to give such limited conclusions, because even as close as they are to the Government they are unable to get behind the screen of secrecy and see how the ST really works. Not only was Kennedy captive of the Saigon Government but he and the Saigon Government were captives of the ST.

As we look back to the beginning of this narrative and to those remarkable papers called, quite incorrectly, the Pentagon Papers we recall that early in October 1963, only one month after the above cited broadcast, McNamara and Maxwell Taylor reported to the President that it looked to them, after their visit to Saigon, as though things could be put under control and that we would be able to withdraw all personnel by the end of 1965. Now we can see why they chose that date. This was the date the President had used in his own discussions with his closest advisers. They all knew that he planned to announce a pullout once he had been re-elected. Less than one month after that report, the men who had been running South Vietnam since they had been placed in power there by the American CIA, along with Ngo Dinh Diem and his brother Nhu, were dead, and the government had been turned over to one of the friendly generals who more properly fit the pattern for counterinsurgency and the new plan. If South Vietnam was to be redeemed it would best be saved by a junta of benevolent army generals—or so the new military doctrine went.

Less than one month after that date, President Kennedy himself had been shot dead in Dallas. And what is even more portentous, it was less than one month after that tragic date that the same two travelers, McNamara and Taylor, returned again from Saigon and reported to a new President that conditions were bad in South Vietnam and we would have to make a major effort, including American combat troops and a vast "sophisticated" clandestine program, against the North Vietnamese.

The ST struck quickly. While the echo of those shots in Dallas were still ringing, the ST moved to take over the whole direction of the war and to dominate the activity of the United States of America.

In the face of these shocking and terrifying events, who could have expected a man who had been in the range of gunfire that ended the life of his predecessor, to make any moves in those critical days that would indicate he was not going to go along with the pressures which had surfaced so violently in Dallas? He knew exactly what had happened there in Dallas. He did not need to wait for the findings of the Warren Commission. He already knew that the death of Lee Harvey Oswald would never bring any relief to him or to his successors.

CHAPTER 23

FIVE PRESIDENTS: "NIGHTMARES WE INHERITED"

Five Presidents have been responsible for and have had to learn to live with the CIA. A parade of Secretaries of State have seen their power and influence dwindle and be eclipsed almost to extinction by the CIA. Even the Secretary of Defense, who in 1947 was charged with the responsibility for direction of the unified military force of this country, has witnessed the diversion of those forces from their traditional peace time role and their subjugation to the requirements of the special operations activities of the CIA. The conflict in South Vietnam stands as a costly and frightening example of how United States military force can be drawn into an operation in pursuit of the unconventional paramilitary activities of the CIA, and of intangible objectives not in keeping with those of the once proud and historic traditions of military power. The Secretary of Defense retains control over nuclear weapons and their means of delivery. In the context of this book that part of Defense has not become involved in action in support of the ST—yet.

There have been times when Presidents rode high with the CIA, as with the spectacular escape of the Dalai Lama from beleaguered

Tibet, and the encouraging developments in Jordan and other moves to protect and safeguard the oil resources of the Middle East. There have been times of grave embarrassment, as the untimely loss of the spy plane U-2 deep in the heartland of Russia.

John Kennedy rode into office on the shoulders of strong CIA support, re-appointed Allen Dulles and J. Edgar Hoover, and then crashed against the beaches of Cuba with the leaderless Bay of Pigs operational disaster. This episode, coming as it did at the very threshold of his term, awakened him abruptly to the stark realities, gross ineptitude, and sudden dangers of secret operations; and it caused him to study with great care what had gone wrong and where the inherent dangers lay. Supreme Court Justice William 0. Douglas recalling a discussion he and Kennedy had about the Bay of Pigs said, "This episode seared him. He had experienced the extreme power that these groups had, these various insidious influences of the CIA and the Pentagon on civilian policy, and I think it raised in his own mind the specter: Can Jack Kennedy, President of the United States, ever be strong enough to really rule these two powerful agencies? I think it had a profound effect . . . it shook him up!"

The eminent, experienced, and wise Supreme Court Justice states the problem precisely when he says, "Can . . . the President of the United States ever be strong enough to really rule these two powerful agencies?" Can any President learn about, comprehend, and then believe what he has learned about this whole covert and complex subject? Can any President see in this vast mechanism, in which there is so much that is untrue and hidden, the heart and core of the real problem? Will any President be prepared to confront this staggering realization when and if he does uncover it? Is this perhaps the great discovery which President Kennedy made, or was about to make? It is not just the CIA and the DOD that are involved. It is also the FBI, the AEC, the DIA, elements of State and of the Executive Office Building, NSA and the hidden pulse of secret power coursing through almost every area of the body politic. It extends beyond into governmental business, the academic world, and certain very influential sectors of the press, radio, TV, papers, magazines, and the publishing business. Before any President can rule this covert automatic control system, he must find out it is there—he must be aware of the fact it exists—and he must devise some means to discover its concealed activity.

President Kennedy made a valiant attempt to effect control over this system with his directives, NSAM 55 and 57, as a start. If he had more actively utilized the NSC system, and if he had structured a really strong and effective Operations Coordinating Board or its equivalent, he might have had a chance to grasp control of some segments of this intragovernmental cybernetic machine. As it was, he lacked the administrative experience of Eisenhower, and he did not fully appreciate the power and significance of the NSC/OCB system of effective control. But, as a result of the Bay of Pigs, the inquiry, and the realization by 1963 of how, despite his great efforts, he was still unable to wrest control from and to rule the ST machine, he was beginning to develop an NSC/OCB technique of his own, which by 1965 might have accomplished this task had he lived to perfect it.

Kennedy's battle was not all with the ST. He was going through the same pressures with other groups—not the least of which was his quixotic contest within the immensely powerful and ruthless professional education establishment and the equally powerful parochial Catholic school hierarchy. For those who have been unable to accept the one-man theory of the Warren Commission report of the Kennedy assassination, there is in evidence more than enough pressure from any one of several of these groups, or their more radical subgroups, to support the germ of the idea that a sinister conspiracy may have arisen from these pressures. For these groups realized that Kennedy was gaining real knowledge, experience, and political power and that he had to be removed from office before winning the inevitable mandate from the U.S. public, which was certain to be his in 1964.

If ever one event had greater influence upon the course of recent history than those shots ringing over Dealey Plaza in Dallas on November 22, 1963, it would be hard to discover what it might be. The man who was to become President in 1969 had been in Dallas only two days before that. Richard Nixon felt the tensions of Dallas in the air in November 1963. He was pierced by the great shock of that staggering event. As the Bay of Pigs had seared John F. Kennedy, the tensions of Dallas seared Nixon. The man who would immediately succeed President Kennedy as President was in a car behind the President. He did not have to read the Warren Commission report, which Allen Dulles and others helped write, to understand the voice of the oracle.

Harry Truman had observed what happened in Dallas from a position once removed. He pondered the significance of that hour, and one month later he wrote:

> "For some time I have been disturbed by the way the CIA has been diverted from its original assignment. It has become an operational and at times a policy-making army of the government. . . . I never had any thought that when I set up the CIA that it would be injected into peacetime cloak and dagger operations. Some of the complications and embarrassment that I think we have experienced are in part attributable to the fact that this quiet intelligence arm of the President has been so much removed from its intended role that it is being interpreted as a symbol of sinister and mysterious foreign intrigue and a subject for cold war enemy propaganda."

Who knows the thoughts that passed through his mind during those thirty days from November 22 to December 22 in 1963, thoughts that led him to write those powerful and intense words? What "disturbed" him? Who had "diverted" the Agency? How was it "injected into peacetime cloak and dagger operations"? Who did it? And how was the CIA "much removed from its intended role, having become a symbol of sinister and mysterious intrigue"?

Two wise men, much experienced in the terrible pressures of government, Harry S. Truman and William O. Douglas, came up with similar conclusions, one after Kennedy's searing lesson at the Bay of Pigs and the other after his tragic death in Dallas. Both of them saw sinister intrigue and the extreme power of these two groups, the CIA and the Pentagon. Both saw the various insidious influences of the CIA and the Pentagon, and both wondered as Douglas asked, "Can any President ever be strong enough really to rule?"

A third wise, experienced, and tough man raised his hand in Dallas and accepted the awesome responsibilities of the office of President of the United States. While his ears still rang from the sound of those shots, while the murdered President's young wife stood beside him in blood-soaked clothes, while one of his old friends and political cronies lay seriously wounded in the hospital, and while the body of his young predecessor was lifted gently aboard the Presidential aircraft, what thoughts coursed through his mind? Were they by chance similar to those thoughts of Harry Truman and of William Douglas? We may never know.

Then in the following months, when he was engulfed in the affairs of office, it became quite clear that he had come to some hard, earnest, and inevitable decisions: Hold on, keep the temper of the nation below the boiling point, dedicate all action to the restoration of normalcy, and hope for time and divine assistance and guidance to pull through.

Lest anyone wish to raise the suggestion that Lyndon B. Johnson should have made hard, bold, and decisive moves during those fragile and explosive days, let him recall the frightful days in 1968 after the life of Martin Luther King had been snuffed out by another assassin's bullet. The country was very close to real trouble. Law and order was destroyed, and things were out of control in many major cities. The racial riots inspired by the loss of Martin Luther King were one thing. Any violent recrimination over the sudden death of John F. Kennedy could well have been monstrous. The pressures, the deep tragedy, and the popular unrest were all there. Even though the Warren Report itself really satisfies few serious scholars and investigators, it did serve to get this country through a trying time.

Yet not all the answers are to be found this way. Johnson rode on the popular tide that was running first with Kennedy and then later with him. But all the time, those same great pressures were there. The ST machine, always at its most active and insidious best in adversity, surged forward in the post Kennedy void. The record shows that Lyndon Johnson almost never said "No." The only mechanism in existence designed to control the CIA and other members of the ST consisted of the provisions of the National Security Act of 1947, along with other such legislation and directives. It was designed to curtail, to deny, to stop the CIA's inevitable appetite for self-generated activity. There was no curtailment, no denial, and no strong hand to halt its mad rush into Vietnam. Plans that had been directed toward getting out and home by 1965 were suddenly discarded and never mentioned again. Johnson rode the ship throughout the storm, and the team he inherited steered the course based upon data inputs arising from subversive insurgency inspired sources. The wild force of the cult of the gun, resurrected Manifest Destiny, rampant anti-Communism—ran away with events in Southeast Asia. Even the popular narrative history of the slaughter and extermination of the American Indians and the ruthless *Westward Ho* as related by Dee Brown in *Bury My Heart at Wounded Knee*, is tame and more believable compared to the waste and devastation brought about by the forces of savagery unleashed upon the helpless people of Indochina.

By the time President Johnson had to make his decision, he already knew too much. Now he saw what Truman saw, what Justice Douglas saw, what Arnold Toynbee saw, and what so many others could see. He had no place to go. His withdrawal in 1968 came as a surprise; but if the LBJ of old had been able to gird himself for battle again, as once he had characteristically been able to do, the next four years would have witnessed the battle of the century, and would have been a bigger surprise than his sudden announcement not to run again. He gave evidence of this in the remaining months of his tenure when, for the first time, he reined in the wild horses and began to put some control on the runaway Indochina conflagration.

Thus the fifth President who has had to live with the CIA and these other forces came upon the scene. There could not have been a man more suited by experience, determination, and background to take over this job. Richard Nixon had lived intimately with the growing power and the growing momentum of the ST during the Eisenhower years. His experience was unmatched. It may have been a handicap. His learning, his training, his beliefs were all tempered by those more established years. His miscalculations at the time of the television debates with John Kennedy serve to underscore that he was not prepared, not aware of the really sinister nature and character of this special adversary, the ST.

He had actively lived through the Eisenhower peace offensive era. He had gone to Russia to meet Khrushchev. He had been as shocked and as damaged by the U-2 disaster as Eisenhower, but for different reasons. He had lost his "sure-thing" election to succeed Eisenhower when the shambles of his own crusade-for-peace inheritance turned out to be more a liability than an asset. Furthermore, he had lost some intangible strength when elements of the ST learned that they could hurt him personally as well as at the polls during his campaign against Kennedy.

Above all of these things, however, was his own wealth of experience and his political know-how. Moreover, he was determined to end the war and to give the nation the "lift of a driving dream." Thus, as two years of the Nixon leadership passed, the nation began to evidence real surprise to see that things were not changing as he had promised. The biggest problem was the war. Nixon's strongest promises had been about the war. All other issues paled before that; yet he not only seemed to be no more effective in the face of the war than Johnson had been; he also seemed to espouse the war. The Kennedy-Johnson war had become the Nixon war. What was astounding was that rather than deny this, he actually appeared to accept the mantle. What had happened? As Truman might have said, "How has he been diverted from his original and self-proclaimed assignment . . . What forces a President to change like that?"

Have we now witnessed the real significance of the Truman words, of the Douglas words, or the Toynbee words? Is the President, any President, really capable of ruling these forces of insidious influence? Does he rule and command, or is there another power? Can the ST be harnessed? We have one indelible example after the other which seems to say "No." Before his election, Nixon pledged he would end the war. Early in 1971, assessing the outstanding events of his first two years in office, he declared as follows: "We are on the way out [of the war] and we are on the way out in a way that will bring a just peace, the kind of a peace that will discourage that kind of aggression in the future, and that will build, I hope, the foundation for a generation of peace. That is our major achievement in, I think, the foreign policy field."

In the middle of 1972 the war was raging at renewed intensity, equal to any other time despite the token withdrawal of American troops. What has happened to the "driving dream" and the January 1971 proud "achievement"?

On January 4, 1971, Richard Nixon sat in the library of the White House with four reporters: John Chancellor of NBC, Eric Sevareid of CBS, Nancy Dickerson of PBS, and Howard K. Smith of ABC. It was Howard K. Smith who in a later interview best said what was on the minds of these reporters even at this interview: "Mr. President, 1 understand that this has been the winter of your discontent." That was the tone of this earlier meeting as they came to discuss his first two years in office. The 1970 midterm elections had not quite been a defeat for his party; but they were no great mandate either. After a rather lengthy and cheerless interview and toward the end of the questions, Nancy Dickerson addressed the President: "Speaking of your campaigns, you made the kickoff address in New Hampshire in 196.8 . . . You made a speech how the next President had to give this country the lift of a driving dream. . . . Well, as yet, many people have failed to perceive the lift of a driving dream. I wondered if you could articulate that dream for us briefly and tell us how you plan to specifically get it across to the people in the next two years."

The President is always a most polished television personality, and he is characteristically quick, precise, and alert with his answers. But now, toward the end of a trying session and with the weight of the full meaning of that query heavy on his mind, he did a rather uncharacteristic thing. He hesitated, and he looked almost blankly around the room at the four people there with him, and away from the uncompromising eye of the camera. Then he lowered his head and slowly said: "Miss Dickerson, before we can really get a lift of a driving dream, we have to get rid of some of the nightmares we inherited. One of these nightmares is a war without end. We are ending that war. . . . But it takes some time to get rid of the nightmares. You can't be having a driving dream when you are in the midst of a nightmare."

Five Presidents have been responsible for and have learned to live with the CIA. Five Presidents at one time or another, under varying conditions and events, have all suffered from this relationship. It can be said that Richard Nixon has come as close as any of them to putting into words the soul-rending, brutal reality of the impact of the power and of the burden that this covert force places upon the mantle of government, when he said, "You can't have a driving dream when you are in the midst of a nightmare." Like a terrible, haunting, terrorizing nightmare, the sinister machine pervades every aspect of the government today—and affects all of us, our way of life, and the welfare of the entire world.

We have described the ST. We have talked about who it is, what it does, how it operates. But it would be impossible to uncover everything about it and to attribute to it all that it really is. Likewise, it would be wrong to grant to this cybernetic, automatic-control machine more wisdom, more power, more sense than it really possesses. The worst possible mistake would be to overestimate it. It is not just one finite team of individuals. It is a matrix that changes with the gestation of each new operation. It is a sinister device of opportunity and contrivance. What does exist is the mechanism. What exists is the automatic system, much like a nervous system or an electrical system. More properly, what exists is like a giant electronic data processing machine, on the model of Ross Ashby's idea, which has its own power to grow, to reproduce, and to become more insidiously effective and efficient as it operates.

It is a great intragovernmental infrastructure that is fed by inputs from all sources. It can be driven by the faceless, lobbying pressure of a helicopter manufacturer, or of a giant Cam Ranh Bay general contractor. It can be accelerated by the many small pushes of hundreds of thousands of career military personnel—uniformed and civilian—who see higher rank and higher retirement pay as a goal worth seeking. It can be suddenly activated by almost any "counterinsurgency" area or similar "hot button" initiator.

This great machine has been constructed by such able men as "Wild Bill" Donovan, Clark Clifford, Walter Beedle Smith, Allen Dulles, Maxwell Taylor, McGeorge Bundy, and many others, who have guided and molded it into the runaway giant that it is today. It is big business, big government, big money, big pressure, and headless—all operating in self-centered, utterly self-serving security and secrecy. As C. P. Snow has said, "The euphoria of secrecy goes to the head." And as Allen Dulles has said, perhaps in a slightly different context, this is really the craft of intelligence.

For all its fabrication and apparent unreality, especially in this open society, the ST machine does have a central soul or brain . . . or perhaps . . . holy spirit. It is the evidence of a form of new religion. It has its secrets. It has its divine and unquestioned rights and obligations. It has self-righteous power over life and death. It does not believe in anything. It does not value anything. It is utterly ruthless. Its greatest motivating force and drive is entirely undefined, because it moves by pressure. It reacts. It is therefore blind, meaningless, senseless. It will do anything in the name of anti-Communism. Yet in its greatest anti-Communist war it sees no inconsistency in the killing of one of its most anti-Communist creations—Ngo Dinh Diem. In its zeal to rid the Caribbean of Communism, it leaps at the chance to rid the Dominican Republic of Latin America's strongest non-Communist, Rafael Trujillo. Any person or groups that know how to get to this infrastructure, who have the clearances, who have the need-to-know, can make an input into this ST, and as long as the desired action is anti-Communist, the system will operate.

As Kennedy saw, as Johnson may have seen, as Nixon's "nightmare" may suggest, there is but one way to control this massive ST structure. It must be uncovered. It must be made known. It must be exposed to the light. And then it must be told No. To be effective, this means that Congress must cut its money off, not only at the central source, but at all the hidden nerve centers.

Before it is too late, we Americans must realize that this great cancer exists. We must expose it for pro-American reasons; not as a work of anti-Communism. We have been subjected to so many anti-American and pro-Communist notions all in the name of anti-Communism, that words and facts almost elude us. We must look at all actions—political, social, governmental, and international—in terms of their being pro-American. There is such a world of difference between a truly pro-American positive action, and an anti-Communist passive, or reactive, operation.

It is not pro-American to pay barbaric tribute before the shrine of anti-Communism in Southeast Asia by sacrificing fifty-five thousand young men there. Neither is it pro-American to pay tribute in the amount of hundreds of billions of dollars before false altars of savagery there. There may be some argument, some slight argument, about such central effort being anti-Communist. We have been so brainwashed about the meaning of anti-Communism for twenty-five years that we may have forgotten what it really means. To be anti-Communist should mean that an action does have some effect upon real Communists and Communism; certainly the loss of not one Russian in an anti-Communist war can hardly be hurting the Russians one bit. But regardless of this semantic issue, the fact is that what had been going on in Indochina is not pro-American, and that is what matters the most.

Thus this ST must be exposed, bared, and silenced. Then a new and better way of life must be created. We must end the philosophy of Defense. The alternative is not simply Offense, either. The real alternative is the requirement for a sensible strategic concept to meet American needs, not to counter imagined and suspected Communist threats. We must end the policy of "Re-action" in favor of planned action and positive diplomacy. We must end the exploitation of secret intelligence by clandestine operations.

The first twenty-five years of the CIA have given solid evidence of how important the ideas of those legislators in 1947 were. The CIA should be, must be, the "quiet intelligence arm of the President." Not his nightmare. The CIA should be limited to the function of intelligence—and not a bit more.

APPENDIX I

The following job description, taken from the *U.S. Government Organization Manual, 1959–1960*, page 143, is a typical government definition of the term "special operations." It also defines the work I was in from 1955 through 1963, whether it was with the Headquarters, U.S. Air Force, the Office of the Joint Chiefs of Staff, or the Office of the Secretary of Defense.

Assistant to the Secretary of Defense (Special Operations)

"Assistant to the Secretary of Defense (Special Operations) is the principal staff assistant to the Secretary of Defense in the functional fields of intelligence, counterintelligence (except as otherwise specifically assigned), communications security, Central Intelligence Agency relationship and special operations, and psychological warfare operations. He performs functions in his assigned fields of responsibility such as: (1) recommending policies and guidance governing Department of Defense planning and program development; (2) reviewing plans and programs of the military departments for carrying out approved policies and evaluating the administration and management of approved plans and programs as a basis on which to recommend to the Secretary of Defense necessary actions to provide for more effective, efficient, and economical administration and operations and the elimination of duplication; (3) reviewing the development and execution of plans and programs of the National Security Agency and related activities of the department of Defense; and (4) developing Department of Defense positions and providing for Department of Defense support in connection with special operations activities of the United States Government. In the performance of his functions, he coordinates actions, as appropriate, with the military departments and other Department of Defense agencies having collateral or related functions and maintains liaison with the Department of State, the Director of Central Intelligence and the Central Intelligence Agency, the United States Information Agency, and other United States and foreign government organizations on matters in his assigned fields of responsibility. In the course of exercising full staff functions, he is authorized to issue instructions appropriate to carrying out policies approved by the Secretary of Defense for his assigned fields of responsibility. He also exercises the authority vested in the Secretary of Defense relating to the direction and control of the National Security Agency and related activities of the Department of Defense. The Assistant to the Secretary of Defense (Special Operations) is appointed by the Secretary of Defense."

APPENDIX II

U.S. *Title 50—War and National Defense, Chapter 15—National Security* contains, in one place, a collation of most of the law as it pertains to the Central Intelligence Agency. Most people who write about the CIA and who talk about the CIA—indeed, many who have served with the CIA—have never read this law. It is most significant that the legislation that pertains to war and national defense is the same legislation that includes all reference to the CIA. It is almost as if the bomb contained its own live fuse or the gun came with the trigger cocked for action. As we have seen, during the past twenty-five years the CIA has become the active agent that ignites the military establishment whenever that great mass becomes supercritical.

Fundamental to the whole concept and character of the CIA is the statement of the five powers and duties, which appears in Section 403 (d). This is a precise, clear, and unequivocal delineation of what Congress and the President wanted the Central Intelligence Agency to be. The language of the law has never been substantively altered; yet in practice the CIA and its Secret Team mentors have changed it beyond recognition. (This appendix includes all important material relevant to the CIA from the National Security Act.)

§ 401. Congressional declaration of purpose

In enacting this legislation, it is the intent of Congress to provide a comprehensive program for the future security of the United States; to provide for the establishment of integrated policies and procedures for the departments, agencies, and functions of the Government relating to the national security; to provide a Department of Defense, including the three military Departments of the Army, the Navy (including naval aviation and the United

States Marine Corps), and the Air Force under the direction, authority, and control of the Secretary of Defense; to provide that each military department shall be separately organized under its own Secretary and shall function under the direction, authority, and control of the Secretary of Defense; to provide for their unified direction under civilian control of the Secretary of Defense, but not to merge these departments or services; to provide for the establishment of unified or specified combatant commands, and a clear and direct line of command to such commands; to eliminate unnecessary duplication in the Department of Defense, and particularly in the field of research and engineering by vesting its overall direction and control in the Secretary of Defense; to provide more effective, efficient, and economical administration in the Department of Defense; to provide for the unified strategic direction of the combatant forces, for their operation under unified command, and for their integration into an efficient team of land, naval, and air forces but not to establish a single Chief of Staff over the armed forces nor an overall armed forces general staff. (July 6, 1947, ch. 343, § 2, 61 Stat. 496; Aug. 10, 1949, ch. 412, § 2, 63 Stat. 579; Aug. 6, 1958, Pub. L. 85–599, § 2, 72 Stat. 514)

§ 402. National Security Council

(a) Establishment, presiding officer; functions, composition

There is established a council to be known as the National Security Council (hereinafter in this section referred to as the "Council").

The President of the United States shall preside over meetings of the Council: *Provided,* That in his absence he may designate a member of the Council to preside in his place.

The function of the Council shall be to advise the President with respect to the integration of domestic, foreign, and military policies relating to the national security so as to enable the military services and the other departments and agencies of the Government to cooperate more effectively in matters involving the national security.

The Council shall be composed of—

(1) the President;
(2) the Vice President;
(3) the Secretary of State;
(4) the Secretary of Defense;
(5) the Director for Mutual Security;
(6) The Chairman of the National Security Resources Board; and
(7) the Secretaries and Under Secretaries of other executive departments and of the military departments, the Chairman of the Munitions Board, and the Chairman of the Research and Development Board, when appointed by the President by and with the advice and consent of the Senate, to serve at his pleasure.

(b) Additional functions

In addition to performing such other functions as the President may direct, for the purpose of more effectively coordinating the policies and functions of the departments and agencies of the Government relating to the national security, it shall, subject to the direction of the President, be the duty of the Council—

(1) to assess and appraise the objectives, commitments, and risks of the United States in relation to our actual and potential military power, in the interest of national security, for the purpose of making recommendations to the President in connection therewith; and

(2) to consider policies on matters of common interest to the departments and agencies of the Government concerned with the national security, and to make recommendations to the President in connection therewith.

(c) Executive secretary; appointment and compensation; staff employees

The Council shall have a staff to be headed by a civilian executive secretary who shall be appointed by the President. The executive secretary, subject to the direction of the Council, is authorized, subject to the civil-service laws and chapter 51 and subchapter III of chapter 53 of title %, to appoint and fix the compensation of such personnel as may be necessary to perform such duties as may be prescribed by the Council in connection with the performance of its functions.

(d) Recommendations and reports

The Council shall, from time to time, make such recommendations, and such other reports to the President as it deems appropriate or as the President may require. (July 6, 1947, ch. 343, title I, § 101, 61 Stat. 497; Aug. 10, 1949, ch. 412, § 3, 63 Stat. 579; Oct. 28, 1949, ch. 782, title XI, § 1106 (a), 63 Stat. 972; Oct. 10, 1951, ch. 479, title V, § 501 (e) (1), 65 Stat. 378.)

1949—Subsec. (a) Act Aug. 10, 1949, added the Vice President to the Council, removed the Secretaries of the military departments, to authorize the President to add, with the consent of the Senate, Secretaries and Under Secretaries of other executive departments, to authorize the President to add, with the consent of the Senate, Secretaries and Under Secretaries of other executive departments and of the military department, and the Chairmen of the Munitions Board and the Research and Development Board.

The National Security Council, together with its functions, records, property, personnel, and unexpended balances of appropriations, allocations, and other funds (available or to be made available) were transferred to the Executive Office of the President by 1949 Reorg. Plan No. 4, eff. Aug. 19, 1949, 14 F.R. 5227, 63 Stat. 1067, set out in the Appendix to Title 5, Government Organization and Employees.

§ 403. Central Intelligence Agency

(a) Establishment; Director and Deputy Director; appointment

There is established under the National Security Council a Central Intelligence Agency with a Director of Central Intelligence who shall be the head thereof, and with a Deputy Director of Central Intelligence who shall act for, and exercise the powers of, the Director during his absence or disability. The Director and the Deputy Director shall be appointed by the President, by and with the advice and consent of the Senate, from among the commissioned officers of the armed services, whether in an active or retired status, or from among individuals in civilian life: *Provided, however,* That at no time shall the two positions of the Director and Deputy Director be occupied simultaneously by commissioned officers of the armed services, whether in active or retired status.

(b) Commissioned officer as Director or Deputy Director; powers and limitations, effect on commissioned status

(1) If a commissioned officer of the armed services is appointed as Director, or Deputy Director, then—

    (A) in the performance of his duties as Director, or Deputy Director, he shall be subject to no supervision, control, restriction, or prohibition (military or otherwise) other than would be operative with respect to him if he were a civilian in no way connected with the Department of the Army, the Department of the Navy, the Department of the Air Force, or the armed services or any component thereof; and

    (B) he shall not possess or exercise any supervision, control, powers, or functions (other than such as he possesses, or is authorized or directed to exercise, as Director, or Deputy Director) with respect to the armed services or any component thereof, the Department of the Army, the Department of the Navy, or the Department of the Air Force, or any branch, bureau, unit, or division thereof, or with respect to any of the personnel (military or civilian) of any of the foregoing.

(2) Except as provided in paragraph (1) of this subsection, the appointment to the office of Director, or Deputy Director, of a commissioned officer of the armed services, and his acceptance of and service in such office, shall in no way affect any

status, office, rank, or grade he may occupy or hold in the armed services, or any emolument, perquisite, right, privilege, or benefit incident to or arising out of any such status, office, rank, or grade. Any such commissioned officer shall, while serving in the office of Director, or Deputy Director, continue to hold rank and grade not lower than that in which serving at the time of his appointment and to receive the military pay and allowances (active or retired, as the case may be, including personal money allowance) payable to a commissioned officer of his grade and length of service for which the appropriate department shall be reimbursed from any funds available to defray the expenses of the Central Intelligence Agency. He also shall be paid by the Central Intelligence Agency from such funds an annual compensation at a rate equal to the amount by which the compensation established for such position exceeds the amount of his annual military pay and allowances.

(3) The rank or grade of any such commissioned officer shall, during the period in which such commissioned officer occupies the office of Director of Central Intelligence, or Deputy Director of Central Intelligence, be in addition to the numbers and percentages otherwise authorized and appropriated for the armed service of which he is a member.

(c) Termination of employment of officers and employees; effect on right of subsequent employment

Notwithstanding the provisions of section 652 of Title 5, or the provisions of any other law, the Director of Central Intelligence may, in his discretion, terminate the employment of any officer or employee of the Agency whenever he shall deem such termination necessary or advisable in the interests of the United States, but such termination shall not affect the right of such officer or employee to seek or accept employment in any other department or agency of the Government if declared eligible for such employment by the United States Civil Service Commission.

(d) Powers and duties

For the purpose of coordinating the intelligence activities of the several Government departments and agencies in the interest of national security, it shall be the duty of the Agency, under the direction of the National Security Council—

(1) to advise the National Security Council in matters concerning such intelligence activities of the Government departments and agencies as relate to national security;

(2) to make recommendations to the National Security Council for the coordination of such intelligence activities of the departments and agencies of the Government as relate to the national security;

(3) to correlate and evaluate intelligence relating to the national security, and provide for the appropriate dissemination of such intelligence within the Government using where appropriate existing agencies and facilities: *Provided,* That the Agency shall have no police, subpoena, law-enforcement powers, or internal-security functions: *Provided further,* That the departments and other agencies of the Government shall continue to collect, evaluate, correlate, and disseminate departmental intelligence: *And provided further,* That the Director of Central Intelligence shall be responsible for protecting intelligence sources and methods from unauthorized disclosure;

(4) to perform, for the benefit of the existing intelligence agencies, such additional services of common concern as the National Security Council determines can be more efficiently accomplished centrally;

(5) to perform such other functions and duties related to intelligence affecting the national security as the National Security Council may from time to time direct.

(e) Inspection of intelligence of other departments

To the extent recommended by the National Security Council and approved by the President, such intelligence of the departments and agencies of the Government, except as hereinafter provided, relating to the national security shall be open to the inspection of the Director of Central Intelligence, and such intelligence as relates to the national security and is possessed by such departments and other agencies of the Government, except as hereinafter provided, shall be made available to the Director of Central Intelligence for correlation, evaluation, and dissemination: *Provided, however,* That upon the written request of the Director of Central Intelligence, the Director of the Federal Bureau of Investigation shall make available to the Director of Central Intelligence such information for correlation, evaluation, and dissemination as may be essential to the national security.

(f) Termination of National Intelligence Authority; transfer of personnel, property, records, and unexpended funds

Effective when the Director first appointed under subsection (a) of this section has taken office—

(1) the National Intelligence Authority (11 Fed. Reg. 1337, 1339, February 5, 1946) shall cease to exist; and

(2) the personnel, property, and records of the Central Intelligence Group are transferred to the Central Intelligence Agency, and such Group shall cease to exist. Any unexpended balances of appropriations, allocations, or other funds available or authorized to be made available for such Group shall be available and shall be authorized to be made available in like manner for expenditure by the Agency.

(July 26, 1947, ch. 343, title I, § 102, 61 Stat. 498; Apr. 4, 1953, ch. 16, 67 Stat. 20.)

EX. ORD. NO. 11460. PRESIDENTS FOREIGN INTELLIGENCE ADVISORY BOARD

Ex. Ord. No. 11460, Mar. 20, 1969, 34 F.R. 5535, provided:

By virtue of the authority vested in me as President of the United States, it is ordered as follows:

SECTION 1. There is hereby established the Presidents Foreign Intelligence Advisory Board, hereinafter referred to as "the Board." The Board shall:

(1) advise the President concerning the objectives, conduct, management and coordination of the various activities making up the overall national intelligence effort;

(2) conduct a continuing review and assessment of foreign intelligence and related activities in which the Central Intelligence Agency and other Government departments and agencies are engaged;

(3) receive, consider and take appropriate action with respect to matters identified to the Board, by the Central Intelligence Agency and other Government departments and agencies of the intelligence community, in which the support of the Board will further the effectiveness of the national intelligence effort; and

(4) report to the President concerning the Boards findings and appraisals, and make appropriate recommendations for actions to achieve increased effectiveness of the Governments foreign intelligence effort in meeting national intelligence needs.

SEC. 2. In order to facilitate performance of the Boards functions, the Director of Central Intelligence and the heads of all other departments and agencies shall make available to the Board all information with respect to foreign intelligence and related matters which the Board may require for the purpose of carrying out its responsibilities to the President in accordance with the terms of this Order. Such information made available to the Board shall be given all necessary security protection in accordance with the terms and provisions of applicable laws and regulations.

SEC. 3. Members of the Board shall be appointed by the President from among persons outside the Government, qualified on the basis of knowledge and experience in matters relating to the national defense and security, or possessing other knowledge and abilities which may be expected to contribute to the effective performance of the Boards duties. The members of the Board shall receive such compensation and allowances, consonant with law, as may be prescribed hereafter.

SEC. 4. The Board shall have a staff headed by an Executive Secretary, who shall be appointed by the President and shall receive such compensation and allowances, consonant with law, as may be prescribed by the Board. The Executive Secretary shall be authorized, subject to the approval of the Board and consonant with law, to appoint and fix the compensation of such personnel as may be necessary for performance of the Boards duties.

SEC. 5. Compensation and allowances of the Board, the Executive Secretary, and members of the staff, together with other expenses arising in connection with the work of the Board, shall be paid from the appropriation appearing under the heading "Special Projects" in the Executive Office Appropriation Act, 1969, Public Law 90–350, 82 Stat. 195, and, to the extent permitted by law, from any corresponding appropriation which may be made for subsequent years. Such payments shall be made without regard to the provisions of section 3681 of the Revised Statues and section 9 of the Act of March 4, 1909, 35 Stat. 1027 (31 U.S.C. 672 and 673)

SEC. 6. Executive Order No. 10938 of May 4, 1961, is hereby revoked.

Richard Nixon.

SHORT TITLE

Act June 20, 1949, § 10, formerly § 12, 63 Stat. 212, renumbered July 7, 1958, Pub. L. 85–507, § 21(b) (2), 72 Stat. 337, provided that Act June 20, 1949, which is classified to sections 403a–403j of this title, should be popularly known as the "Central Intelligence Agency Act of 1949."

§ 403c. Same; procurement authority

(a) In the performance of its functions the Central Intelligence Agency is authorized to exercise the authorities contained in sections 151 (c) (1)–(6), (10), (1), (15), (17), 155 and 159 of Title 41.

(b) In the exercise of the authorities granted in subsection (a) of this section, the term "Agency head" shall mean the Director, the Deputy Director, or the Executive of the Agency.

(c) The determinations and decisions provided in subsection (a) of this section to be made by the Agency head may be made with respect to individual purchases and contracts or with respect to classes of purchases or contracts, and shall be final. Except as provided in subsection (d) of this section, the Agency head is authorized to delegate his powers provided in this section, including the making of such determinations and decisions, in his discretion and subject to his direction to any other officer or officers or officials of the Agency.

(d) The power of the Agency head to make the determinations or decisions specified in sections 151 (c) (1), (15), and 154 (a) of Title 41 shall not be delegable. Each determination or decision required by sections 151 (c) (12), (15), 153, or 154 (a) of Title 41, shall be based upon written findings made by the official making such determinations, which findings shall be final and shall be available within the Agency for a period of at least six years following the date of the determination. (June 20, 1949, ch. 227, § 3, 63 Stat. 208.)

§ 403f. Same; general authorities of Agency

In the performance of its functions, the Central Intelligence Agency is authorized to—

(a) Transfer to and receive from other Government agencies such sums as may be approved by the Office of Management and Budget, for the performance of any of the functions or activities authorized under sections 403 and 405 of this title, and any other Government agency is authorized to transfer to or receive from the Agency such sums without regard to any provisions of law limiting or prohibiting transfers between appropriations. Sums transferred to the Agency in accordance with this paragraph may be expended for the purposes and under the authority of sections 403a to 403c, 403e to 403h, and 403j of this title without regard to limitations of appropriations from which transferred;

(b) Exchange funds without regard to section 543 of Title 31;

(c) Reimburse other Government agencies for services of personnel assigned to the Agency, and such other Government agencies are authorized, without regard to provisions of law to the contrary, so to assign or detail any officer or employee for duty with the Agency;

(d) Authorize couriers and guards designated by the Director to carry firearms when engaged in transportation of confidential documents and materials affecting the national defense and security;

(e) Make alterations, improvements, and repairs on premises rented by the Agency, and pay rent therefor without regard to limitations on expenditures contained in the Act of June 30, 1932, as amended: *Provided*, That in each case the Director shall certify that exception from such limitations is necessary to the successful performance of the Agencys functions or to the security of its activities. (June 20, 1949, ch. 227, § 5, formerly § 6, 63 Stat. 211; June 26, 1951, ch. 151, 65 Stat. 89; renumbered July 7, 1958, Pub. L 85–507, § 21(b) (2), 72 Stat. 337, and amended Aug. 19, 1964, Pub. L. 88–448, title IV, § 402(a) (28), 78 Stat. 494; 1970 Reorg. Plan No. 2, eff. July 1, 1970, 35 F.R. 7959, 84 Stat.—.)

REFERENCES IN TEXT

The act of June 30, 1932, as amended, referred to in subsec. (c), is the Legislative Branch Appropriation Act, 1933, act June 30, 1932, ch. 314, 47 Stat. 393, and is classified to section 303b of Title 40, Public Buildings, Property, and Works.

CODIFICATION

Section was not enacted as a part of the National Security Act of 1947 which comprises this chapter.

§ 403g. Same; protection of nature of Agency's functions

In the interests of the security of the foreign intelligence activities of the United States and in order further to implement the proviso of section 403 (d) (3) of this title that the Director of Central Intelligence shall be responsible for protecting intelligence sources and methods from unauthorized disclosure, the Agency shall be exempted from the provisions of section 654 of Title 5, and the provisions of any other law which require the publication or disclosure of the organization, functions, names, official titles, salaries, or numbers of personnel employed by the Agency: *Provided*, That in furtherance of this section, the Director of the Office of Management and Budget shall make no reports to the Congress in connection with the Agency under section 947(b) of Title 5. (June 20, 1949, ch. 227, § 6, formerly § 7, 63 Stat. 211, renumbered July 7, 1958, Pub. L. 85–507, § 21 (b) (2), 72 Stat. 337; 1970 Reorg. Plan No. 2, eff. July 1, 1970, 35 F.R. 7959, 84 Stat.—.)

§ 403h. Same; admission of essential aliens; limitation on number

Whenever the Director, the Attorney General, and the Commissioner of Immigration shall determine that the entry of a particular alien into the United States for permanent residence is in the interest of national security or essential to the furtherance of the national intelligence mission, such alien and his immediate family shall be given entry into the United States for permanent residence without regard to their inadmissibility under the immigration or any other laws and regulations, or to the failure to comply with such laws and regulations pertaining to admissibility: *Provided*, That the number of aliens and members of their immediate families entering the United States under the authority of this section shall in no case exceed one hundred persons in any one fiscal year. (June 20, 1949, ch. 227, § 7, formerly § 8, 63 Stat. 212, renumbered July 7, 1958, Pub. L. 85–507, § 21 (b) (2), 72 Stat. 337.)

CODIFICATION

Section was not enacted as a part of the National Security Act of 1947 which comprises this chapter.

§ 403j. Central Intelligence Agency: appropriations; expenditures

(a) Notwithstanding any other provisions of law, sums made available to the Agency by appropriation or otherwise may be expended for purposes necessary to carry out its functions, including—

   (1) personal services, including personal services without regard to limitations on types of persons to be employed, and rent at the seat of government and elsewhere; health-service program as authorized by section 150 of Title 5; rental of news-reporting services; purchase or rental and operation of photographic, reproduction, cryptographic, duplication and printing machines, equipment and devices, and radio-receiving and radio-sending equipment; purchase, maintenance, operation, repair, and hire of passenger motor vehicles, and aircraft, and vessels of all kinds; subject to policies established by the Director, transportation of officers and employees of the Agency in Government-owned automotive equipment between their domiciles and places of employment, where such personnel are engaged in work which makes such transportation necessary, and transportation in such equipment, to and from school of children of Agency personnel who have quarters for themselves and their families at isolated stations outside the continental United States where adequate public or private transportation is not available; printing and binding; purchase, maintenance, and cleaning of firearms, including purchase, storage, and maintenance of ammunition; subject to policies established by the Director, expenses of travel in connection

with, and expenses incident to attendance at meetings of professional, technical, scientific, and other similar organizations when such attendance would be a benefit in the conduct of the work of the Agency; association and library dues; payment of premiums or costs of surety bonds for officers or employees without regard to the provisions of section 14 of Title 6; payment of claims pursuant to Title 8; acquisition of necessary land and the clearing of such land; construction of buildings and facilities without regard to sections 59 and 67 of Title 40; repair, rental, operation, and maintenance of buildings, utilities, facilities, and appurtenances; and

(2) supplies, equipment, and personnel and contractual services otherwise authorized by law and regulations, when approved by the Director.

(b) The sums made available to the Agency may be expended without regard to the provisions of law and regulations relating to the expenditure of Government funds; and for objects of a confidential, extraordinary, or emergency nature, such expenditures to be accounted for solely on the certificate of the Director and every such certificate shall be deemed a sufficient voucher for the amount therein certified. (June 20, 1949, ch. 227, § 8, formerly § 10, 63 Stat. 212, renumbered July 7, 1958, Pub. L. 85–507, § 21 (b) (2), 72 Stat. 337.)

REFERENCES IN TEXT

Sections 259 and 267 of Title 40, referred to in text, was repealed by Pub. L. 86–249, § 17 (12), Sept. 9, 1959, 73 Stat. 485. See chapter 12 of Title 40, Public Buildings, Property and Works.

CODIFICATION

Section was not enacted as a part of the National Security Act of 1947 which comprises this chapter.

§ 405 Advisory Committees; appointment; compensation of part-time personnel; applicability of other laws

(a) The Director of the Office of Emergency Preparedness, the Director of Central Intelligence, and the National Security Council, acting through its Executive Secretary, are authorized to appoint such advisory committees and to employ, consistent with other provisions of this Act, such part-time advisory personnel as they may deem necessary in carrying out their respective functions and the functions of agencies under their control. Persons holding other offices or positions under the United States for which they receive compensation, while serving as members of such committees, shall receive no additional compensation for such service. Other members of such committees and other part-time advisory personnel so employed may serve without compensation or may receive compensation at a rate not to exceed $50 for each day of service, as determined by the appointing authority.

(b) Service of an individual as a member of any such advisory committee, or in any other part-time capacity for a department or agency hereunder, shall not be considered as service bringing such individual within the provisions of sections 281, 283, or 284 of Title 18, unless the act of such individual, which by such section is made unlawful when performed by an individual referred to in such section, is with respect to any particular matter which directly involves a department or agency which such person is advising or in which such department or agency is directly interested. (July 26, 1947, ch. 343, title III, § 303, 61 Stat. 507; Aug. 10, 1949, ch. 41, § 10(c), 63 Stat. 585; Sept. 3, 1954, ch. 1263, § 8, 68 Stat. 1228.)

§ 407. Study or plan of surrender; use of appropriations

No part of the funds appropriated in any act shall be used to pay (1) any person, firm, or corporation, or any combinations of persons, firms, or corporations, to conduct a study or to plan when and how or in what circumstances the Government of the United States should surrender this country and its people to any foreign power, (2) the salary or compensation of any employee or official of the Government of the united States who proposes or contracts or who has entered into contracts for the making of studies or plans for the surrender by the government of the United States of this country and its people to any foreign power in any event or under any circumstances. (Pub. L. 85–766, ch. XVI, § 1602, Aug. 27, 1958, 72 Stat. 884.)

CODIFICATION

Section was not enacted as part of the National Security Act of 1947, which comprises this chapter.

§ 409. Definitions of military departments

(a) The term "Department of the Army" as used in this Act shall be construed to mean the Department of the Army at the seat of the government and all field headquarters, forces, reserve components, installations, activities, and functions under the control or supervision of the Department of the Army.

(b) The term "Department of the Navy" as used in this Act shall be construed to mean the Department of the Navy at the seat of the government; the headquarters, United States Marine Corps; the entire operating forces of the united States Navy, including naval aviation, and of the United States Marine Corps, including the reserve components of such forces; all field activities, headquarters, forces, bases, installations, activities, and functions under the control or supervision of the Department of the Navy; and the United States Coast Guard when operating as a part of the Navy pursuant to law.

(c) The term "Department of the Air Force" as used in this Act shall be construed to mean the Department of the Air Force at the seat of the government and all field headquarters, forces, reserve components, installations, activities, and functions under the control or supervision of the Department of the Air Force. (July 26, 1947, ch. 343, title II, §§ 205(c), 206(a), 207(c), 61 Stat. 501, 502.)

APPENDIX III

T he document that follows is one of the most influential documents of the past quarter-century. It was written and compiled from the work of many nameless and faceless authors within the government and from other sources close to these men in the academic world and the world of business. It was drafted by an Army General, Richard G. Stilwell, while he was serving as a member of a special Presidential committee. It includes much material written by Air Force General Edward G. Lansdale, among others. Its origins come from the depths of a special source reaching far back into the history of the man. Its twentieth-century manifestation occurs in the Russian Revolution of 1917 and in other revolutions since that time. These paramilitary ideas and methods know no ideology and no creed or code. They are the craft of those who would seek power and of those who would fight wars by technical means, and who would utilize the military organization of the state to gain that power by influencing the minds of the "elite," by engaging in social, political, economic, and almost incidentally, military activity.

As we have said this course of action begins with a high-sounding resolve to improve the lot of the poor "under-developed" nations, using the vehicle of the Military Assistance Program to take over the army of that country. This then is repeated in other countries, as we have seen, becoming evident in recent times in such countries as Greece and Brazil, among others.

If this were all that it meant we might be able to treat it lightly as another evidence of the inherent activity of the "do-gooder" instinct of Western man. However, it is only reasonable to see, in this action, the ominous fact that it is the American soldier who is the teacher of this doctrine; and it is the same American soldier who becomes his own student. Since this action was begun in 1959 tens of thousands—yes, hundreds of thousands—of American military men, a whole new generation, have grown up believing that this is not only the right thing for "those foreigners" but for Americans as well.

The following document begins mildly and almost reasonably. It gets to the heart of the matter smoothly and without alarm. However, as it builds and creates its own crescendo it begins to veer from its scholarly and well-tempered tone and approaches the type of delivery made famous by such men as Hitler, Mussolini, and Joseph Stalin. When highest officials of this Government assert that the majority of the nations of the uncommitted "Third World" would be better off under the control of their military elite, an elite to be selected by Americans, it is time for other Americans to read, to listen to, and to sound the warning on the possibility that this same American elite may not become persuaded of its own role in this country.

Note that this paper was drafted in May 1959. It was drafted during the Eisenhower Administration, and it was a forerunner of such catchwords, generally associated with Presidents Kennedy and Johnson, as *counterinsurgency, pacification, special forces, subversive insurgency,* and the like. These terms had all been introduced before Kennedy's tenure and were simply awaiting their day in the world of the Secret Team.

In keeping with Secret Team practice, this so-called draft was unclassified so that it could be processed through all sections of the elite without control of transmittal or copies.

May 15, 1959
Training Under the Mutual Security Program
(with emphasis on development of leaders)

Contents

    I. Introduction
   II. Present Pattern
  III. New Horizons
  IV. Leadership Programs
         Non-Military Sector
         Military Sector

V.   Development of Indigenous Educational Systems
VI. New Roles for the Military
VII. Development of Values
     U.S. Training Environment
     Role of the Advisor
VIII. Requirements and Recommendations

I—Introduction

The Committee has thus far placed primary stress on defining the quantitative threshold and material guidelines of a continuing mutual security effort. Yet the Committee is mindful—and indeed so stated in transmitting its Interim Report—that an adequate United States contribution to the security and growth of our Free World associates, and particularly the less developed countries, involves much more than the provision of military hardware and economic capital, vital though these ingredients be. The indispensable complement, and a clear third dimension of United States programs, is the development of requisite institutional frameworks, managerial organizations and individual talents to effectively use the physical resource inputs. The Committee has had reports, from all quarters, that the severe shortage of trained executives, administrators, and other categories of decision makers is a major impediment to balanced economic growth in the less developed areas. It is conscious that arms alone do not an army make; that leadership, collective motivation, and identification with the aspirations of countrymen are equal determinants of a military establishment adequate to its tasks and compatible with its environment. It is impressed with the magnitude of the tasks which face the fledgling nations in the quest for symbols to replace those no longer valid; in the adaptation of cultural heritage to new settings; in the development of political, social and ideological foundations; and in meeting today's manpower deficiencies while laying the educational base for the future.

One is impelled to speak out on this subject because the record demonstrates that, far from receiving major attention, human resources development has been relegated to secondary importance.

II—The Present Pattern

Admittedly, there are impressive statistics as to the numbers of foreign personnel who have received training, under auspices of the Mutual Security Program, in the United States, in their own countries, or in third areas. But the concept and the approach have been largely mechanistic. While there has been a measurable shift in the past year, the bulk of ICA training programs are still "project-oriented": designed to meet the specific administrative, technical, and professional skill requirements generated by the concurrent ICA developmental activities. Likewise, the thrust of the massive training programs of the U.S. military departments has been determined by the materiel aspects of the MAP: production of specialists, technicians and junior tacticians to handle the equipment and systems furnished.

Certainly, these instructional efforts have been essential. Certainly also, such programs must continue, and probably at an expanded rate.

In the military area, new technical training dimensions are explicit in the second round of arms aid involving provision of advanced weapons systems for the NATO nations and an accelerated rate of modernization elsewhere. They are also explicit in the commendable new emphasis on improvement of indigenous logistic apparata and operating techniques. The Committee is confident that the minor obstacles to expansion will be surmounted and that the Defense agencies will press on to develop and implement programs of requisite scope in these categories.

In the civil sector, one need only contemplate the staggering estimates of skill deficiencies throughout Afro-Asia to appreciate the magnitude of the gap. Unlike the military, the ICA's ability to meet any measurable portion of this widening gap, at the technical level, is limited by the general inflexibility of its operational base—built of direct hire personnel and a system of contract which demand detailed governmental administration, planning and supervision. There is a need to change the nature of the base, to bring the tremendous strength and unparalleled competence of our non-governmental institutions to bear on this training problem and, concomitantly, to shift the government role to the more suitable tasks of broad planning, support, and arrangements vis-à-vis the foreign authorities concerned. The modalities of this shift have been explored in other committee papers.

The Committee's principal concern—and consequently the subject of this paper—is that training objectives have been so severely circumscribed, so inadequately related to the full sweep of our own national interest and of the recipient countries as well.

The Shortfalls

Review of what is being done, and projected, in the training, educational and related fields by the combined efforts of the Department of Defense, the International Cooperation Administration and the International Educational Exchange Service reveals many shortfalls. The following are representative:

(1) the scale of orientation visits and hand tailored courses for key government or opinion leaders has been much below feasible norms; as indeed has exploitation thereof by the agencies concerned.

(2) all too few foreign military officers, of middle and upper rank, have been provided instruction in concepts or doctrine governing the employment of the military instrument, in peace and in war. Equally conspicuous is the absence of training in management above the unit level.

(3) procedures for the identification and grooming of future leaders are lacking.

(4) analyses of the trained manpower implications of country economic development goals are incomplete; comprehensive plans for meeting deficiencies are non-existent; and U.S. actions to stimulate either are half-hearted.

(5) higher educational opportunities available through the aggregate of ICA, IES and other non-military programs are below minimum thresholds, lack depth and present serious imbalances and gaps. The fields of under-graduate study is largely uncovered; trainees from the public services and the private

profession sector are few; and the potential of ICA university contracts inadequately utilized.

(6) the substantial technical level and short term programs now in progress have not been paralleled by comparable efforts to accelerate the growth of basic educational systems within cooperating countries.

(7) effective coordination among the different programs has been wanting; and has resulted in loss of mutual support opportunities. ICA has yet to recognize the potential of the MAP training base for the furtherance of technical assistance objectives.

And of overriding moment has been the near universal failure to understand and accept concomitant responsibility for the political and psychological orientation and motivation of the trainee, the participant, the counterpart. There has been no guidance or concerted approach in the sensitive but vital area of inculcating, or testing for, compatible precepts of public morality, social responsibility and personal ethics. Notwithstanding the intensity of the struggle for the allegiance of the "middle billion," influence on the thought, habit and attitudes of these peoples, and on the institutions that bind them together, has been left to chance.

Confronted with these broad deficiencies, the Committee can only conclude that the Executive Branch has grasped neither the measure of the challenge nor the inestimable potential inherent in the human side of development.

In rendering what is tantamount to an indictment, two tempering considerations have been recognized. The first is a series of factors, cumulative in effect, which serve to place finite limits on the pace and scope of the corrective actions implied by the foregoing compendium of criticisms. The second involves several initiatives, independently pursued unfortunately, with the aim of improving the direction, the depth and the substantive payoff of activities in the human resources field. Neither was sufficiently weighted to invalidate the basic conclusion. Both, however, have had an impact on the proposals to be presented subsequently. They therefore merit treatment in general outline.

The Limitations

The formidable obstacles to rapid expansion and improvement of these activities include such diverse factors as political sensibilities and attitudes, legal restrictions, availability and qualification of trainees and trainers, capacity of facilities, and financing problems. Moreover, they are so intermeshed that all must be attacked concurrently. Among the more significant:

(1) National educational systems and manpower problems involve such politically sensitive considerations that U.S. initiative and aid are not automatically accepted by local governments; nor does full cooperation necessarily follow acceptance. And in the first instance, the less developed nations simply do not have either statistics or plans and are therefore faced with major, time-consuming efforts to produce both.

(2) Under the provisions of Section 451c of the Mutual Security Act, a special Presidential determination is required before military training can be extended to any country with whom a bi-lateral agreement has not been negotiated.

(3) Important strictures surround the present selection base for overseas training for high-level personnel. One is the requirement for a working knowledge of English or third country language, coupled with the limited availability of such instruction. Another is divergence in criteria applied by the cooperating country and by the U.S. agencies in determining candidate qualifications. Still another is reluctance to release individuals for extended instruction abroad, given the competing demands for their services locally.

(4) Appropriately qualified U.S. personnel for staffing overseas educational, advisory or training projects are in short supply; language is again a problem. There are also finite limits on the absorptive capability of the U.S. educational institutions in terms of teachers and facilities.

(5) In certain specialty areas, the training establishments of the U.S. military departments are already taxed to capacity; funds

and spaces are requirements for expansion; so also is relaxation
of security policies with respect to the nationals of a number
of countries.

(6) Patterns of cooperation by U.S. universities with the policy
desires of the Government are far from uniform.

(7) Currently, there are no funds available for educational development of many low income countries.

Encouraging Signs

There has been evidence, in recent months, of increased U.S. awareness of the import of the broader aspects of training. Constructive
moves include the following:

(1) An exploratory project, *High Level Human Resources for
Economic Development*, was initiated by the President, to survey
the need of less developed countries in administrative, managerial and technical categories; and to determine the advisability and practicability of a special U.S. assistance program.
Work has proceeded under supervision of an inter-agency
Task Group (Secretary of Labor, Deputy Undersecretary of
State, Directors of ICA and USIA). While the Task Group
is unlikely to proceed with the surveys-in-depth originally
contemplated, it has stimulated a new order of interest in
manpower planning on the part of recipient countries, U.S.
missions abroad, and Washington agencies.

(2) The Department of State has underway a detailed survey
of international education and training activities conducted
by agencies of the U.S. Government. Aside from the accu-
mulation of important statistical information, the work will
provide the basis for establishing an informational clearing
house and a more effective coordinating mechanism.

(3) On 4–5 April, the Department of State convened the first of
a series of periodic conferences to bring together the government agencies, the universities and the major private foundations with operative programs for education of foreign

nationals. Properly prepared and peopled, such conferences could be of great value. It is worth noting that the university presidents were vocal about the need for clearer national policies and guidelines.

(4) The Deputy Secretary of Defense issued recently a directive to the military departments underscoring the contribution of training of foreign military personnel to the achievement of international security objectives; and directing, as feasible, a 5–15% program increase in training (or orientation) for senior officers.

(5) The proposed FY-60 Military Assistance Training Program and the Technical Assistance Program reflect substantial increases over previous years. The latter includes a first entry into the undergraduate study field. Meanwhile, the geographic emphasis of the International Educational Exchange Service shifts away from Europe.

While commending these initiatives, the Committee has noted that follow-up has lacked vigor; and that even optimum execution would produce results far short of the minimum essential advance.

III—New Horizons

Policy formulation is not a pre-condition to a more comprehensive and responsive program to improve human knowledge, skills and attitudes in the less developed areas. The importance and compelling need therefore is amply underscored in official statements of basic United States security policy. The requirement is widespread recognition, in sectors public and private, of the essentially of properly trained and motivated manpower to the hoped-for evolution of the middle third of the world. This recognition can be stimulated. Education is, after all, among the most cherished elements of the American tradition; and expanded programs provide an opportunity for new initiatives in the conduct of our foreign policy.

The Committee appreciates the substantial nature and diversity of the educational, training and cultural programs—binational and international, public and private—now underway outside the purview of the Mutual Security Program and the International Educational Exchange Service; for example, upwards of 100 organizations have programs for Pakistani. Not having examined these programs, no comment is made thereon. In most cases, the United States can exercise only minimal control over the direction of these other activities; she has, however, the continuing information and influence to insure against duplication.

A look at the vastness of the requirements and at the current activities of the training and educational activities of the MAP, ICA and IEES have focused attention on four general areas. A vigorous approach to all four will provide the basis for the program our security interests demand. The areas, to be discussed in some detail, are:

(1) The formal training of leadership cadres, in all key sectors of national life.
(2) The support of educational systems in low-income countries, both allied and neutral.
(3) The exploitation of MAP supported military establishments in furtherance of political stability, economic growth and social change.
(4) The role of Americans in developing the professional and ethical code of foreign leaders.

IV—Leadership Programs

This, clearly, is the key challenge. All reports emanating from abroad conclude that a major, if not the principal, impediment to progress in the Afro-Asian countries is the severe shortage of individuals capable of filling responsible positions responsibly. Were this not reason enough to expand and improve our leadership programs, there is another—the traditional activities and growing capabilities of the Soviet Union for the development and control of elite groups.[1] We may elect to stand aloof from competition with her in the supply of military and economic aid. In the leadership area, we cannot!

---

1. To be expanded.

Non-Military Sector

Ways and means of achieving better performance in the top level managerial field have been well explored in various U.S. agency studies.[2] These suggest certain concurrent planning and implementation actions addressed directly to the shortfalls tabulated previously. It is to be noted that the efficacy of these actions will be largely a function of the initiative and competence of our Country Teams.

Organizational Aspects

Development of Country Plans

There is a requirement to stimulate and, where national sensitivities permit, to offer technical and other assistance for the establishment of machinery and procedures for systematic surveys and analyses of the manpower situation. None of the less developed nations has yet evolved anything approaching a human resources annex in support of national developmental plans. They are not, therefore, capable of measuring the gap over and above the actual and predictable outputs of indigenous institutions and the several operative overseas programs, or of sharply identifying priority of needs in public administration, in industry, business and labor, or in education.

This is patently a long term project, to be attacked incrementally. Other actions should not depend thereon.

Shift in Emphasis of U.S. Programs

Valid suggestions encompass two main categories: the immediate and the longer range.

The first envisages expansion of IEES "leader grant" programs; ICA attention to the private entrepreneurial sector and to the decision-makers in other than the public economic sector; and greater participation by U.S. professional associations, major foundations, and private institutions.

---

2. Among the most noteworthy are the several papers produced by the staff of the Presidential Task Group on High Level Human Resources for Economic Development, mentioned earlier; and a thoughtful study by Mr. James Howe of ICA.

The longer range problem dictates substantial entry into the field of undergraduate and graduate education in the U.S. to groom the future leadership, and in addition, the concept of "junior year abroad" for students studying in their home countries. It also involves, on a major scale, the collaboration of American universities, industry, and professional associations in conducting special "work-shops," on-the-job training and specialized projects, for national or multi-national groups, in all pertinent fields.

The longer range program holds the most promise. For one thing, there will be fewer conflicts with the immediate operating needs of the governments. More important, the collegian or junior executive is in his formative years. He may ultimately embrace an alien philosophy but only if the suasion is of the highest caliber; the lasting influence of undergraduate associations and intellectual intake is not to be underestimated.

Implementing Steps

The foregoing steps will require some additional funds, for they are additive to the essential activities now underway. They also imply some changes in legislation to remove restrictions on utilization of available local currency and, perhaps, to countenance the new directions (as, for example, wholesale departure from the general one year limit on training duration). It also involves expansion of staff and closer coordination among participating U.S. agencies and institutions.

These concrete steps are manageable for they follow established patterns. But there are others—less tangible infinitely more difficult.

Substantive Aspects

Selection of Personnel

It is evident that the success of the entire effort hinges on wisdom and foresight in the choice of trainees. And the burden thereof falls squarely on the U.S. field organizations. Effective performance pre-supposes that the Country team:

(1) Has adequate biographic registers, personal contacts and reliable informational sources to prepare unilateral lists of

promising candidates in all sectors; and priorities within lists.

(2) Has sufficient rapport and stature vis-à-vis the cooperating government to influence the latter's priorities, selection processes and choices; and to be assured that the trainee is scheduled for employment in posts commensurate with anticipated training.

(3) Is as attentive to the training of leadership and managerial cadres among the non-communist opposition as to the representatives of the ruling party; and astute enough to devise plans which will provide for such training under other than direct U.S. governmental sponsorship and with minimum impact on official relationships.

(4) Has full data on all U.S. programs, official and private, affecting the country; is effective in the coordination thereof; is in a position to exploit fully the potential of ICA university contracts in the leadership field; and capable of influencing the direction of unofficial programs to cover priority gaps.

(5) Is fully aware of activities in adjacent countries and how these activities might be utilized for the good of the country to which accredited.

Training Framework

It is not enough that the training or orientation course itself be carefully designed and competently conducted. The preparation of the trainee and his handling as an individual are of equal import. There must be facilities for, and help in, refresher instruction in English and other Western languages, where indicated or feasible; in this connection, it is essential that the selection base not be limited to those possessing a knowledge of English. There is the matter of cushioning transition from native habitat to the American scene and educational methodology and the consequent requirement for painstaking orientation prior to and after the overseas voyage; and the inverse to help adapt the individual for the return home and subsequent communication to his compatriots.[3] Beyond this—as discussed more fully in another section—is the matter of the comportment of the Americans with whom he is professionally and socially in contact: his acceptance as an equal; the understanding afforded his views; the intellectual and ethical challenges presented. The field, the Washington staff, and all others concerned share responsibility for the quality of the resultant impact.

The Follow-Up

The importance of continuing contact with the key decision-maker, actual or potential, subsequent to his training is self-evident. Sober reflection, after the individual's return and in light of new responsibilities, may produce valuable ideas on how training may be altered for improved applicability. Up-to-date knowledge of the individual's professional progress, evolving philosophy and attitudes provides the basis for evaluation of impact; tightens the bonds of association; determines the need for or desirability of further training; and generally promotes the U.S. national interest. The follow-up activities involve arduous tasks for the field. But there is no other means of determining program results or of exploiting the success achieved.

It may be asked if the Country Teams are now equipped and oriented to handle the responsibilities thus enumerated. Our own reservations on this score have given impetus to the companion annex on the U.S. personnel implications of the Mutual Security Program.

Military sector

Rationale

For reasons both military and political, there are pressing requirements for new foci in leadership programs for the Officer Corps

---

3. ICA has recently initiated a week long Communications Seminar for selected trainees following completion of their course of instruction. The emphasis is on professional conduct at home and the communication of ideas.

of the MAP supported forces—and, gain, principally of the less developed areas.

In the first instance, effective control and maneuver of armies (and to a lesser extent the naval and air arms) of growing modernity poses for the senior officers of the several military establishments, professional equipment requirements not dissimilar to the needs of the United States Services: an adequate mastery of military concepts and doctrine; and competence in tactics, logistics and management.

It is not enough, however, to restrict leadership inputs to U.S. norms. Except in specifically defined circumstances, our Armed Forces have no operative responsibilities within national frontiers; conforming generally to the precepts of Western democracies, they are not an integral part of the mechanism for maintenance of law and order. The prevailing concept is expeditionary—an instrument of latent power, unentangled domestically, ready for projection abroad should the exigency arise. Not so for the great bulk of the forces of the new nations. Their role has additional dimensions and their missions are actual as opposed to contingent. They are a key element in the maintenance of internal security and are largely determinant of whether stability or instability characterizes the routine of government. The Officer Corps is perforce deeply involved in domestic affairs. Those who lead, or are destined to lead, must therefore acquire qualifications and attributes beyond the criteria which identify the successful commander in combat.

Finally, the ranks of the Officer Corps in most less developed countries are a rich source of potential leaders of the national civil service, the professional class, and other non-military sectors. Here one finds a high degree of discipline, dedication and political moderation. Moreover, one must reckon with the possibility—indeed probability—that the Officer Cops, as a unit, may accede to the reins of government as the only alternative to domestic chaos and leftist takeover. Both considerations point to a program for selection and preparation of promising officers for eventual occupation of high level managerial posts in the civil sector, public and private.

Guidelines

It is recognized that practical limitations confront, over the short term, major augmentation of top level military leader programs— limitations which are identical with those described under the non-military sector. Notwithstanding, there is substantial scope for upgrading the military assistance training programs of the U.S. service departments in conformity with the foregoing.

Higher Level Military Education

Such programs merit first priority. Three avenues are open: development of regional facilities coupled with more extensive bi-national exchanges within regions; augmented local institutions; and accommodation of a larger senior officer load in the U.S.

(1) The long touted prospect for a Pacific Defense College should be brought to fruition and similar institutes planned for the Middle East, Latin America and Africa. Desirably, these should be school centers, providing not only strategy studies, but specialized courses for those charged with anti-subversion planning, for logisticians, civil affairs chiefs, and key management personnel. The advantages of a regional approach are self-evident.

(2) The U.S. might well encourage and support, in every country with substantial military forces, the organization of an institute on the concept of our own National War College; on the conversion of existing colleges to the all-service, military-civilian approach. MAAG personnel should be as active therein as the climate will permit—to insure, among other things, that the curricula grapples with concrete national problems.

(3) There are valid reasons for excluding foreign officers from the U.S. War Colleges and the Armed Forces Staff College. But, elsewhere—and with considerably less reason—the doors of our major school centers are not fully ajar (it is noted, for example, that only 123 foreign nationals are programmed through the Army Command and General Staff School in

FY-60). Although considerable effort will be involved, all U.S. Services—and particularly the Army—can develop, conduct and administer additional, specially tailored instruction in doctrine, tactics, logistics and management. The school locales need not be limited to military facilities; the growing competence of American universities in military science is exploitable.

Civilian Schooling, Undergraduate and Graduate
This envisages team play as among MAP, ICA and IEES at the country level. ICA and IEES are in a position to finance the education, in the U.S. or third countries, of high caliber career officers in military-applicable fields such as psychology, political science, law, engineering and business administration. MAP can assist ICA in the identification of officers who should be trained for key responsibilities in the civil sector. IEES can assist in the establishment of middle level courses in local educational facilities for officer instruction in administration, finance, military justice and management.[4]

Orientation and Observer Visits
The upper limits of the modest increase in Stateside trips for leaders prescribed (with qualifications) by the Department of Defense should be attained and exceeded. Strains on the military departments would be eased by shifting emphasis from the extreme top level of the military hierarchy to the potential successors a few years hence: the representational burden would be less, the communication problem more surmountable, and the benefits more lasting. Our officials have probably been overconcerned about representation, insufficiently attentive to the substantive impact sought. Where language capability exists, senior foreign officer itineraries should encompass (or even built around) participation in scheduled University or Association seminars and conferences, judged to be within the visitor's scope of interest by reason of functional

4. This thought, and certain others, reflect ideas advanced by the "Study on MAP in the Underdeveloped Areas" prepared for the Committee by the Foreign Policy Research Institute of the University of Pennsylvania, by Dr. George Liska; and by Dr. Buy Pauker.

or geographic coverage; dividends would accrue from his chance to contribute and by his viewing of civilian-military collaborations as practiced in this country. MAP should also support regional conferences to improve personal contacts and promote exchange of ideas and techniques among the military elite of adjacent countries. One possible result, of great value, might be the emergence of more uniform and viable concepts of civil-military relationships.

The Neutral Countries
The stakes for which we contend justify attention to every possibility to improve the competence and influence the orientation of the office corps of these nations. The attach personnel should be so instructed; and the special efforts involved in securing Presidential determinations for training in the U.S. or third countries accepted.

The Advisory Role
The key influence in the development of military leaders of superior motivation and integrity may well be that exerted by the MAAG personnel. It is mentioned here because it is integral to this discussion. However, the cardinal importance of this function dictates separate treatment in subsequent pages.

Akin thereto, applicable to the military sector, and incorporated by reference, are what have been called the "Substantive Aspects": the responsibilities of U.S. personnel in the selection of trainees, in the establishment of the training environment, and in the follow-up and evaluation phases.

A collateral requirement, common to all training in the U.S. is expansion of English language instructional facilities in the cooperating countries. The U.S. Military Departments, the USIS, and the USOMs have all made some inroads on this problem in various ways.[5] But the demand, even at present level of activity, is far in excess of available capacity. Here, then, is a principal bottleneck.

---

5. Electronic Teaching Laboratories; English courses in local educational systems; bi-national centers; text books; and refresher training facilities in this country, utilized by trainees upon arrival.

A coordinated effort, built around the relatively large USIS operators in most countries, is indicated.

Special Problems of Africa

It is appropriate, at this juncture, to point up the leadership implications of the African continent, and more especially those portions still in colonial status or newly emerged therefrom. The sovereign state of Ghana, for example, mans only a third of the essential posts in her embryonic civil service; for another—and the critical—third, she is quite dependent on alien employees without assurance of tenure; and the remainder are unfilled. In the non-British colonies, the situation is worse. The problem is staggering. On the other hand, Africa is the one area of the world where we have the leisure for forward planning, where we can lay the groundwork for the sort of comprehensive attack outlined by the Presidential Task Group, where we can begin to identify and groom the future national leaders. The overall approach should be multi-lateral, combining Western European efforts and our own, with broad African representation. We should, however, have a highly selective unilateral program. For any long term African project, looking to the development of high-level managerial talent, to be successful, an adequate planning-operational task force must be fielded, peopled largely by juniors and with their futures guaranteed so the continuity may obtain. Its members should embrace political, economic, military, sociological, anthropological and other competence so the approach will be comprehensive and balanced from the outset.

V—Development of Indigenous Educational Systems

The Situation

Their importance notwithstanding, programs for the production of leaders, professionals and skilled technicians—the emphasis of the US. training effort—are designed only to provide an adequate superstructure. A parallel, even more pressing, need is the development of the base; for if progress is sensitive to the quality of leadership, it is also dependent upon effective response of those who follow to the leader's bidding. In the less developed areas, an adequate response of not forthcoming; nor can it be forthcoming so long as ignorance, illiteracy and lack of basic skills are characteristics of the great bulk of the citizenry. Education of the human beings which constitute the major resource of the poorer countries is a fundamental requirement.

The nations of Latin America, Asia and Africa are conscious of the weaknesses—in breadth, depth, diversity and quality—of their educational systems; of the urgency of remedial action, and of the magnitude of the gap, in capital and human terms. They are equally conscious that the responsibility is theirs and theirs alone; it could not be otherwise, for educational institutions are so linked to the national character and fabric that no sovereign state can readily accept collaboration in the design or direction thereof. On the other hand, significant expansion of facilities involves major outlays of capital which is just not available in most countries.

Financial assistance to indigenous educational institutions has not been a feature of U.S. aid programs, although minor amounts have been expended on schools directly linked with economic development. Other demands coupled with legal restrictions have precluded use of any significant amounts of U.S. foreign currency holdings for the support of cooperating country school systems.[6] Indeed, there have been complaints that U.S. aid programs have operated to the detriment of supported country investment in national schools: it is said, in Latin America, that the pattern of development aid has required such large scale use of local currency resources, as matching contributions to complete, and thereafter maintain, major construction works that the development of public infrastructure, and notably schools, has fallen well behind needs.

A Program Basis

There is a rising clamor, within and without the U.S. government for a strong program of aid to the educational institutions of the low

---

6. Technical assistance is, of course, available for provision of instructors, U.S. university contracts, etc.

income countries. It is convincingly argued that only by broadening and improving the now narrow educational bases can there begin to be a solution to the long term trained manpower requirements generated by national economic development plans. Adequate systems of educational institutions are equally essential for political stability and social adjustment. They provide the best—perhaps the only effective—medium for acquainting and inculcating youth with national values and the ingredients of national esprit; and with traditions, culture, ideals and aspirations. They provide the forum for development of codes of public morality and personal ethics, for defining responsibility to one's fellow man. They provide ever expanding reservoirs of raw material for tomorrow's leadership; and the means of identifying this potential. Given wise guidance and competent administration, a vigorous and growing educational complex is the principal counter to Communist subversion. Beyond this, the United States would stand to gain additional benefits from an educational support program of some magnitude. It will be of enormous value to American prestige and goodwill to be identified with visible symbols of friendship and progress like schools, colleges, libraries and laboratories. There is no more meaningful way of breaking down the myth of imperialist exploitation, of indicating our interest in individual opportunity and social democracy.

Financing

A price tag attaches to any such concept—one must think in terms of several hundred million dollars over the next few years. However, it need not be primarily new money. The scheduled accumulations of soft currency in repayment of development loans promise a major source of financing. Congress has not indicated how such moneys will be employed; substantial portions could be earmarked for educational purposes. Moreover, legislative authorization could provide for such use of portions of foreign currencies generated by future PL-480 activities. Thus dollars would be required only for those countries where the U.S. did not own substantial quantities of local currency; and for teachers and equipment which could not be funded otherwise.

Organizational Arrangements

There are numerous possibilities for administering an educational development program. A multi-lateral approach, through an independent mechanism or International Development Agency affiliate, has distinct psychological and economic advantages and might be more palatable to certain countries; it would, however, be more ponderous and slow, less exploitable from the vantage of U.S. interest. A new Human Resources or Cultural Cooperation Agency, co-equal to ICA; a Semi-public Foundation, linking the government and the universities; a government Fund with relations to State and ICA paralleling those of the Export-Import Bank; and a broadened ICA charter—all have advantages and disadvantages. The key to any organizational choice is that educational assistance must be closely and continuously integrated with the total country development plans. This tends to suggest that ICA should have the responsibility.

Management

More important to the effectiveness of the envisaged program than Washington organizational arrangements is the work of the *Country Team*. The latter must be competent in garnering adequate information to be able to analyze the national educational problems; in stimulating country development of comprehensive and balanced plans for expansion of facilities, for production of teachers and for determination of student population; in encouraging devotion of maximum country resources to education; and of insuring that request for assistance relate to priority needs and are consistent with overall plans. Equally, the Country Team has the responsibility of coordinating educational activities of private U.S. agencies and of influencing them, as appropriate, to direct emphasis to better support the key requirements.

This stress on *priorities*, as the directrix of aid, is advised. The educational problem is of such vast proportions that U.S. input must be viewed as primarily catalytic. Our aim is to stimulate the greatest feasible local effort, deploying our limited resources to cover the critical needs which cannot be met through any other means. It will require sound judgment to determine the proper division of investment and energy between the education of personnel needed today and those required in the future. The bottlenecks may range from teachers colleges to equipment for vocational training centers to elementary textbooks. It may be that the greatest single contribution will be in the provision of training aids, adapted to the local scene. In any case, while recognizing that there are minimum thresholds of comfort and cheer for satisfactory student morale, our interest should be in the quality of instructional content rather than of physical plant.

In the field of general education, as in the development of national leadership, the military establishments can play a significant role. To this area, we now turn.

VI—New Roles for the Military

In the past year, a number of informed and thoughtful observers have pointed out that the MAP supported military establishments throughout the less developed areas have a political and socio-economic potential which, if properly exploited, may far outweigh their contribution to the deterrence of direct military aggression. Part of the reasoning rests on the example of history, of which the role of the military under Kemal Ataturk is representative; part on the record of recent months which has witnessed military accession to dominant position in the national affairs of several Asian states; and part of the growing realization that armies are often the only cohesive and reliable non-communist instrument available to the fledgling nations.

The thesis can be defended that the armies—and their relatively small air and naval counterparts—are the principal cold war weapon from the shores of the East Mediterranean to the 38th parallel. By the way of substantiation, one can point to command structures which provide for the rapid and effective dissemination of orders, information and propaganda to the lowest echelons; to the patterns of unit deployments which cover the country from the capital to the most remote frontiers; to the identification of officer and soldier with the village in which he was spawned; and to the intangibles of the military mystique—of variable strength, it is true—built of pride in the tradition of arms, in contributions to the winning of national independence, in sense of duty to the State.

It is not enough to charge armed forces with responsibility for the military aspects of deterrence; they represent too great an investment in manpower and money to be restricted to such a limited mission. The real measure of their worthiness is found in the effectiveness of their contribution to the furtherance of national objectives, short of conflict. And the opportunities therefore are greatest in the less developed societies where the military occupy a pivotal position between government and populace. As one writer has phrased it, ". . . properly employed, the army can become an internal motor for economic growth and socio-political transformation."

Education and Vocational Training

Aside from constituting a principal reservoir for leadership material, one of the military's major contributions to national growth is in the spread of education and skills. Literacy and a level of formal schooling are among the basic criteria of a fully effective soldier; a military establishment adequate to its actual and contingent tasks must include a wide variety of technical and managerial competence. Both are relevant to economic development and social evolution. Given the narrowness of the national educational system, and the obstacles to expansion in the civilian sector, it is logical that training facilities and input, which are required, in any case, to meet military needs, should be exploited for the overall advantage of the country. The returns are proportionately greater when the armed forces are essentially peopled with conscripts as opposed to careerists.

The Three Rs
Practical literacy training for every soldier is a manageable goal, as the programs of the Turkish Armed Forces are demonstrating.

It enhances the individual's usefulness in service; it qualifies him for further education; and it equips him to disseminate his knowledge to his home community. As one source has suggested, the ripple effect of military instruction in the official language may be the best method of assuring that language's pre-eminence over local dialects.

Secondary Schooling

There is scope and need for the institution of off-duty courses akin to those which have long been a feature of the U.S. armed forces. The military organization facilitates identification of men of requisite capability and the exigencies of service provide a captive student population.

Vocational Training Centers

This area holds great promise both in reducing the burden on the U.S. of training low level personnel in U.S. facilities, and in meeting the demands of the civil economy. It is the essence of the "dual purpose" concept which has been elaborated in a separate Committee monograph. To the extent conflicts with the primary military mission are avoided and the civilian requirements are not exceeded, there is every justification for programming a student input which exceeds the military needs for artisans, administrative personnel and other commerce-applicable skills.

English Language Instruction

Facilities are not available in most MAP supported countries for providing English instruction for the minor numbers scheduled to be trained in the U.S. There are, however, cogent reasons for expanding knowledge of the English tongue: to broaden the selection vase for overseas training; to help the military in subsequent civilian pursuits involving foreign business contacts; to promote closer orientation and communication between the United States and the recipient country.

One cannot generalize the relative importance of these avenues, the extent to which they should be followed, or the methods. This can only be determined by specific country analysis. In some countries, encouragement and perhaps minor technical assistance to recipient governments may suffice. In others, direct military assistance may be most appropriate while, elsewhere, the answer may lie in ICA programs under MAAG supervision. What is universally needed is a coordinated survey, planning and execution at the Country Team level.

Strengthening of Internal Security

The maintenance of internal security constitutes a major responsibility of these armed forces, whether assigned directly or not. Superior performance will provide the environment of confidence so necessary to national growth. But the dimensions of security are as much political and social as orthodox military and, in the former respect, understanding and positive action have been generally wanting.

Indoctrination

There must be comprehension of the complex nature of the subversive forces at plan and of the variegated methods of communist attack. Similarly, there must be full knowledge of the means of counterattack available to the nation and of the place of the military therein. Most of all, there must be invoked the motivation to combat these influences, whenever and wherever they surface. Much of this is dependent on wise and inspiring leadership but a well planned and conducted program of Troop Information is an essential corollary. It should be a permanent feature of military life, worked and re-worked to insure it deals with vital national problems, and in terms meaningful to the average soldier. Its importance can hardly be exaggerated for it fills a void which has no parallel in the radio-periodical replete West.

Action

If the military is properly led, indoctrinated and motivated, the activities open to it are numerous. In certain instances, a key requirement may be direct military action against armed dissidents;

consequently, appropriate elements of the army should be equipped and trained for unorthodox warfare. The main emphasis, however, will be in non-violent fields. An informed soldiery, widely based, is in an ideal position to transmit to the populace the thrust of its own indoctrination. By the example of its own discipline, confidence and deportment, the army provides assurance of physical protection and the identity of interest between protector and protected. Where direct military assistance to community projects is feasible—on the model of noteworthy "civic actions" in the Philippines, Vietnam and Laos—the army can demonstrably advance economic and social objectives.

Promotion of National Unity

Here is the ultimate test of the armed forces. Their role, in the countries under discussion, is unique. They are at once the guardians of the government and the guarantors that the government keeps faith with the aspirations of the nation. It is in their power to insure that the conduct of government is responsive to the people and that the people are responsive to the obligations of citizenship. In the discharge of these responsibilities, they must be prepared to assume the reins of government themselves. In either capacity—pillar or ruling faction—the Officer Corps, at least, must possess knowledge and aptitudes far beyond the military sphere.

Successful discharge of this role depends on something more, however. It becomes the rallying point for energies and allegiance only to the extent that it personifies the spirit of the nation. Thus, to power and organization must be added adaptation to and visible reflection of national symbols, culture and values; and unwavering integrity. Stimulation, through military assistance, of these qualities is perhaps more important than successive increments of combat effectiveness.

VII—Development of Values

Up to this point, we have concentrated on defining the quantitative measurements of future programs in the human resources field.

We have done this only to establish a framework within which expanded activities may be planned—not from any mistaken belief that the exposure of increased numbers of individuals to formal instruction will, per se, lead to accelerated national progress along paths desired by the United States. As manifested by earlier references, we are acutely conscious that the indispensable complements to learning are viable concepts to guide the application of that learning; that a nation cannot progress without ethical codes to regulate the conduct of its citizens and institutions. We recognize that the test of leadership is less its competence in the organization of men than its fashioning and exemplification of the principles which inspire and drive the organization.

The special pertinency of these matters to the Afro-Asian area is evident. There the political and social revolution has uprooted most of the symbols, beliefs and concepts to which men previously clung. The gap must and will be filled. The U.S. has a vital interest in the nature of the new symbols and concepts for they are critical to the attainment of our foreign policy objectives.

It is one thing to subscribe to the fundamental importance or proper standards; it is quite another to materially influence their formulation and their acceptance. This component of our programs for the training of foreign nationals has been indifferently pursued and has met with scant success. The reasons are readily identifiable. While we have embraced "the struggle for the minds of men" as a slogan, we have been inept at translating it into personalized terms and meaningful courses of political action. We have been ineffective in codifying and communicating the principles by which we live; and we have entertained the misconception that our approval or our widely heralded social traits signified absorption of the political and moral precepts we are incapable of articulating. We are essentially non-political and empathy is not our forte. Most of all, we have invoked the myth of non-interference to cloak timidity, lack of assurance, sometimes want of moral courage when confronting issues which, admittedly, run close to national nerve centers and traditions. Yet nothing covert or insidious is involved. The tasks call for sophisticated handling but they are above board: to inculcate standards consistent with, and designed to support, the aspirations of the newer nations of the East. Alternate, incompatible standards are already being proffered.

There is no programming guidance which spells out the chapter and verse of this area of activity; nor, in fact, can there ever be set rules to govern the development of motivation, integrity and moral principles. A few points are, of course, clear. The complexity and delicacy of the problem dictates a highly selective approach; our aim is to build the current and future leadership that it may coalesce and build the nation. The intangible inputs to leadership can only be supplied by individuals, and particularly the membership of the Country Team, who have direct contact with the foreign elites.

As we see it, the categories of contact are two. The first, transitory as to time but not impact, involves the American associates to form part of the environment of the leader's training in this country. The second, and more significant, is the advisor-advised relationship.

U.S. Training Environment

We have already alluded to the requirement for raising our sights with respect to the objectives of leadership training in the United States. Extra-curricular activities should be as carefully planned as the formal course of instruction, and the keynote should be something more than traditional American hospitality. Here is the opportunity for indoctrination in the dynamics of our society and for give-and-take discussions on the elements thereof adaptable and transferable to the trainee's native land. There should be conscious efforts to demonstrate the identity among Constitution, government and governed; our theorems of public service; the responsibilities of the citizen to State and community; the role and importance of our national symbols; and the other major factors which contribute to balance, stability, confidence and progress within the American society. Conversely, attention should focus on the pressing deficiencies and needs in the trainee's own society and understanding but forthright comment on what remedial actions are feasible.

Exchanges of this nature cannot be haphazard; their efficacy depends on thorough knowledge of the individual's background and passable skill in political dialectics. It will require real work and real imagination; and adequate arrangements with, and full support by the military installations, universities, commercial establishments where the basic instruction takes place. Most important is the selection of the personnel to whom the indoctrination, conditioning and grooming activities are entrusted; their interest, comprehension, knowledge of the trainee's country and preferably its language, tact, ability to reduce arguments to meaningful terms, and the example they set, are the final determinants of success or failure. Here is where the real costs of this training lie. The dollar expenditure in a year's course at the Army's Ft. Leavenworth or the Harvard Business School for eight Indonesian General Staff Colonels is no more than that required for pilot training of an Indonesian lieutenant. But the input of effort, imagination and motivation demanded of the hand picked Americans acting as these colonels' counselors cannot be priced.

It should be noted in passing that the Defense Department has an infinitely better mechanism—should it be willing to employ it—for the handling of these activities than do State or ICA.

Role of the Advisor

In the last analysis, inculcation of the values which distinguish responsive and responsible leadership rests with the members of the Country Team. It is only at this level that effective communication between nations can take place; that compatibility of United States and recipient country aims and objectives can be ascertained; and that progress towards mutual objectives can be measured and assured.

The starting point, as this paper has repeatedly underscored, is knowledge: knowledge of the attitudes, aspirations and pulse of a selective cross-section of the populace, and of their national institutions; knowledge of the background, views and factors which motivate the leadership elite; knowledge of the extent to which community of interest among government, armed forces and people is lacking, and why; and knowledge of the temper of the opposition and the nature of the weaknesses it exploits. There must, of course, be knowledge of the basic characteristics of local traditions, culture and religion; of the well springs of national pride and superstitions; and of prevailing social customs and practices. Extensive personal contacts with all strata of society can alone provide such knowledge. This is the first, and key, collective responsibility of the Country Team; the routine of reports, inspections and administration must be subordinated thereto.

Through understanding of the local scene and the identification of the major vulnerabilities inherent therein are essential bases for the reorientation and improvement of the national leadership. The others, and all-important, are the careful choice of the instrument—the relationship between the U.S. representative and the native leaders with whom he is associated—and the equally careful determination of the media to be utilized. We stress the necessity of meticulous attention to the selection process. As one uniquely successful military advisor has phrased it, we are dealing with "one of mankind's most sophisticated activities" and consummate wisdom and skill are required.

An honest answer to the question, "how can an advisor strengthen the national leadership, and through that leadership the stability and growth of the nation must be that the potential is limited only by the individual's ingenuity and dedication, on the one hand, and the effectiveness of this rapport with key indigenous figures on the other. However, one can establish certain directional signs. Since we have pondered the military more deeply, models can be constructed in that area.[7] But the approach to the non-military leadership problem is generally similar.

Force of Example

It is basic that the advisor demonstrate, in his own conduct, the very ideals and traits he seeks to inculcate in others. Integrity and

---

7. Much of what follows has been taken from a Confidential memorandum prepared by Colonel E. G. Lansdale, Office of Special Operations, Department of Defense.

devotion to duty must be respected in his every action. While conforming to local customs, he must meticulously observe the same rules and spirit of military courtesy, vis-à-vis the local forces, as practiced in his own service. He must display, on all inspections and visits, the same concern for the health, welfare and comfort of the troops and for objective standards of military justice as accords with the best traditions of the U.S. forces. These things rub off. There is evidence that the example of MAAG officers has often resulted in the adoption of practices which have strengthened local military esprit and cohesion.

The corollary to example is suggestion in matters which are vital to the morale and vigor of a military establishment. Practices which have a debilitating effect thereon, which reflect on the integrity of leaders, merit the attention of advisors. These may include the diversion of portions of troop pay and rations; command acceptance of unsatisfactory living conditions; partiality in bestowal of promotions and other rewards; inequities in the system of military justice; in short, any action which reflects abuse of prerogative or disregard for the paternalistic responsibilities of the Commander. The advisor must know the facts; comprehend the background thereof; be forthright in discussions; and, above all, have effective solutions. In certain areas, the answer may be straightforward. No special problems exist in encouraging counterparts to correct omissions as, for example, in frequency and thoroughness of inspections; or display greater interest and energy in troop welfare programs; greater energy in welfare activities. More imagination is required where reversal of precedent is involved. Convincing the Commander that the establishment of troop messes is, on its own merits, an excellent course of action may be the optimum—and only—answer to "squeeze" of subsistence allowances. Suggestion that the leader conduct a troop information program on the fundamentals of military justice may focus his attention of deficiencies which had previously gone unnoticed.

Development of Symbols

The traditions which sustain and uplift military forces are generally lacking in the newly emerged nations. They can, however, be found in the cultural heritage, refurbished and made meaningful. The U.S. Army helped build Jos Rizal into the Philippine national hero; and did the same with respect to the legendary figures who today furnish inspiration for the armed forces of Vietnam. The U.S. MAAGs have the research facilities, the contacts and the troop information know-how to encourage and assist the Ministers of Defense in the development of symbols which reflect the highest ideals of the nation.

Formulation of a Military Creed

We have pointed out the unique responsibilities of the military forces—one might almost say armies—in the development of political stability and national unity. How well these responsibilities will be discharged depends upon the evolution of proper standards of service to guide the leaders; and upon the latter's effectiveness in securing acceptance thereof by all ranks. To the extent that the advisor is attuned to the local environment, perceptive of the significant undercurrents, able to communicate his understanding and motives, and discreet in his approach, he can exercise appreciable influence on the formulation and expression of enduring principles. The latter include the relationship of the military instrument to the State and to the civil power; professional and personal codes for military men; the deeper meaning behind the observance of the forms of military courtesy; and the constraints on the military in the emergency discharge of the functions of government. His influence in the dissemination of these creeds and concepts may be no less important. Forethought and imagination can assist in effective design and direction of the troop information and education programs to be conducted by commanders for the troops.

Increased Unity of Army and Populace

The achievement of internal security involves more than adequate physical protection. The populace must be confident of the motives of the protectors; assured that the price of protection is not the deprivation of individual rights and privileges, that the military is indeed the servant of the State. The advisor must be able to suggest ways and means of promoting mutuality of objective and interest between the civil community and the military. Joint consultative committees are an excellent mechanism for the quick resolution of points of friction in Local community relations. If there are unit farms there should be no occasion for the commandeering of provisions. Military equipment and labor, temporarily idle, can expedite completion of village communal projects. Army medical facilities have the capacity to handle emergency cases, to help control the spread of disease or to eliminate critical sanitation problems.

The membership of the Country Team must be no less imaginative and persuasive in the non-military leadership sectors, where the search continues for meaningful forms and concepts of government, tuned to domestic and external realities. The increasing tendency, throughout Afro-Asia, to relinquish national responsibility to the military instrument is evidence of the non-viability of the Western forms and concepts which were originally embraced, deficiencies in local political leadership, or both. While the military deserves our full support in their discharge of their trusteeship responsibilities, it is in our best interest that the reins of government be returned to the civil authority as soon as one adequate to its tasks can be created. It is the duty of American field representatives to ascertain what has gone wrong and to proffer guidance and advice in the development of governmental and institutional structures and concepts of service, which will restore the confidence of the populace. Only thus can an enduring relationship be established among the governments, the military and the people themselves. The record is witness to the tremendous influence exerted by a few dedicated Americans over the policies and points of view of key decision-makers; the value of their efforts, both to the country concerned and the United States, has been inestimable. It is regrettable, however, that these initiatives have been so limited in number and that they have sprung from the individual rather than governmental direction and impetus. Yet this is the real test of our ability to develop national leaders of integrity, objectivity and devotion to standards compatible with our own; and, through these leaders, to insure the kind of stability and growth that constitutes the basis of our aid. Our selection, preparation and guidance of our field representatives must henceforth reflect this basic fact.

VIII—Requirements and Recommendations

The foregoing discussion constitutes the arguments for and describes the broad objectives of efforts commensurate with the importance of the human side of development to the total mutual security program. Full attainment of these objectives may well be infeasible. Long term and complex undertakings are involved. Progress will be slow and not susceptible to precise measurement. The most difficult obstacles involve intangibles: it will be easier to surmount fiscal and legislative problems than to condition and motivate American trainees for a series of responsibilities without precedent. We are convinced, however, that we cannot set our sights on any lower targets. For, we repeat, the achievement of political stability and economic growth throughout the less developed areas depends upon the competence of the national leadership, today and henceforward.

Our proposals have dealt mainly with new emphasis, with the strengthening of the training framework and with qualitative improvements as to substance. These requirements do not translate into concrete recommendations. What follows, therefore, is a mixture of the general and specific.

Re-Enunciation of Policy

The first requirement is an attitudinal shift: widespread recognition and acceptance of the essentially of greater efforts in the development of human resources; and the gearing for such cohorts. While it must permeate both government and private sectors, the initiative lies with the Executive Branch. Existing policy must be reviewed and updated: and there must be teeth. The sympathy and support of the Congress must be secured. Similarly, mechanisms must be found for eliciting the understanding of and greater cooperation from the American educational apparatus, the private foundations and the industrial and business world.

We *recommend* that the National Security Council be seized with this matter and that it:

(1) enunciate the need for greater efforts to identify, train and groom the foreign leadership cadres in all key sectors and provide the authorization for the MAP, ICA and IES actions to meet this need;

(2) underscore the policy of the United States to provide substantial assistance for the development of national educational systems;

(3) provide guidelines for closer relationships with and support from the private sector;

(4) stress the importance of the advisory function of American representatives in contact with foreign nationals;

(5) issue the requisite instructions to give force to the above and charge the OCB with the responsibility for follow-up and evaluation.

Organization and Management

The conduct of leadership programs of the nature and size we have envisaged will require a considerably strengthened U.S. organizational framework and an increased capability to manage and coordinate the activities at the country level, in Washington and at the locales where training or orientation takes place.

Country Teams must assume a new order of responsibility as regards selection and programming of trainees, both with and independent of the local government. It has heavy coordination tasks in several arena. It needs comprehensive and up-to-date biographic registers and other data. All Teams will require a full time individual as central control point; most will need some personnel augmentation.

Department of Defense's present training management arrangements are inadequate; however, that organization has the capability to effect the necessary readjustments. Within ISA, the training element must be reinforced and moved from its present backwater to the status of a major division under the Director of the Military

Assistance Program elsewhere proposed. The several Departments will need to create separate mechanisms for planning and monitoring the training and orientation visits of an expanded group of military leaders.

The training staffs of the *International Cooperation Administration* will likewise need to be augmented. These are already overtaxed in handling current programs. *Department of State's* responsibilities will likewise increase. Aside from expanded and more carefully tailored International Educational Exchange Service activities, it has a primary interest in the totality of programs designed to build the national leadership of foreign countries. It must therefore assume an active coordinating role not only with respect to the activities of MAP and ICA in this field, but also as regards those of the international agencies and private foundations and institutions.

These requirements are clear; their measure and the extent to which they are met will be proportional to the vigor of the new national approach. Recommendations in the premises would be redundant.

Legislative Action

Part of the "gearing up" involves both revisions of existing law, and further enactments.

The underlying objectives of leadership programs apply with full force to all nations of the Free World. This aspect of military assistance is of such importance to the United States that it should proceed even where the country concerned is not eligible under the provisions of Section 142(a) of the Mutual Security Act; likewise, it should not require the special Presidential determinations prescribed by Sections 105 and 141 of the same legislation.

> Accordingly, we *recommend* that the Executive Branch seek Congressional action to divorce training assistance from Section 142(a), if not earlier repealed, as well as Sections 105 and 141 of the Mutual Security Act of 1954.

The bulk of the expenditures involved in the massive support of indigenous educational institutions would be in the currency of the recipient country. U.S. holdings of such currencies will increase markedly over the next two decades as a result of Development Loan Fund operations and expanded PL-480 activities; and will far exceed predictable needs for support of U.S. missions.

We *recommend* that the Executive Branch seek Congressional action to:

(1) Specify support of local educational systems in the less developed countries as a principal purpose in the utilization of the foreign currencies accruing from development loan repayments.
(2) Modify or extend other pertinent legislation to provide greater authorization for use of U.S. own foreign currencies for training and educational purposes.

Congress does not now get a full picture of the training and educational activities programmed annually in the non-military sector. The International Education Exchange Service programs are presented as an element of the overall Department of State operations. Moreover, the IEES must compete for funds within the context of what is essentially an administrative budget. We believe that the prospect of securing the additional resources required for expanded leadership programs, and coordination as well, would be enhanced by combining IEES and ICA proposals for the purposes of Congressional presentation. Such action would further emphasize the new accent on human resources development.

> We *recommend* that title III of the Mutual Security Act be broadened to include all non-military U.S. programs for training and education.

Basic Planning

As underscored in this paper, the nerve center of an expanded program is the Country Team. The needs, problems and exploitable opportunities vary widely from nation to nation; and they can only be ascertained on the ground.

The Washington agencies must activate new efforts by the revision of instructions, guidance, authorities and latitude. Detailed planning and preparations are the tasks of the field.

It would be presumptuous to suggest the content of the planning directives to the Country Team. It would appear, however, that four separate areas should be covered and that there should be parallel instructions through State, ICA and DOD channels:

As to High-Level Manpower Development:

(1) Collaboration with, and offer of technical and other assistance to, the host government in establishment of machinery and procedures to survey and analyze priority needs.

(2) Cooperation with host country in developing a training plan to meet critical known needs for decision-making, managerial and professional personnel: and active participation in the selection process.

(3) Development of unilateral U.S. plans, as necessary, to insure balanced coverage particularly with respect to the private sector and the non-communist opposition.

(4) Determination of ways and means for fuller exploitation of ICA University Contract program, operating in the host country, for support of leadership activities through scholarship competitions, grants for faculty development and student overseas study.

(5) Attention to long range, as well as short term, leadership requirements.

As to Support of Indigenous Educational Systems:

(1) Encouragement to host country in latter's development of sound long range plans for expansion of educational systems; and in devotion of maximum resources thereto.

(2) Willingness of U.S. to consider requests for Financial assistance where such is justified in meeting priority needs.

(3) Independent survey to determine priority needs and optimum nature of U.S. support.

As to Exploiting Potential of Military Structure:

(1) Field investigation of feasibility of promoting education through the local military establishments and primarily in the fields of universal practical literacy training; of vocational training centers with capacity beyond military requirements; and of night or off-duty schools at the secondary level. As a corollary, development of country team plans for coordinated exploitation of these possibilities.

(2) MAAG cooperation in the identification of promising military personnel For IEES or ICA grants and scholarships to prepare them for responsible posts in the non-military sector.

(3) Support for development of higher level military schools in host country with curricula to include national political and economic matters; and for senior officer attendance at civilian graduate schools.

(4) MAAG encouragement to host Ministry of Defense in development of improved troop indoctrination programs; and provision of technical assistance in the preparation and conduct thereof.

As to the Advisory Role:

(1) Enunciation of principle that a primary function of the members of the Country Team is to improve the competence and sense of responsibility of their foreign opposites; and that effectiveness in the discharge of this role shall constitute a fundamental basis of future performance evaluations.

(2) Re-emphasis of the essentiality of comprehensive knowledge of the local traditions, attitudes, culture, customs and significant undercurrents; of the identification of the major vulnerabilities in the local structure; and of extensive personal

contacts in all strata of society as the underpinning of substantive advisory efforts to develop leadership adequate to its tasks and responsive to the aspirations of the populace.

(3) Forceful suppression of the American tendency to do the task himself and the substitution of the tolerance and forbearance of the true teacher.

(4) The overriding importance of demonstrating the highest standards of integrity and ethics in professional and personal conduct; of exhibiting moral courage to point out deficiencies in the attitudes and performance of local officials; and of devising and proposing remedies in keeping with native mores.

Subsidiary Planning

Of the numerous supporting actions to be undertaken at the Washington level, those designed to improve the handling of the trainee are the most vital. They include:

(1) Development by the Office, Secretary of Defense and the Military Department of definitive guidance to the training establishments for the meticulous programming of off-duty activities for earmarked leaders; such guidance should provide information of techniques demonstrated to have been successful.

(2) The most careful selection and preparation of interpreter-escorts, official or private, for high level personnel who lack knowledge of the English language.

(3) Efforts to secure greater cooperation from the universities and business sector with respect to the desired extracurricular inputs; to this end. the collaboration initiated by the recent State Department Annapolis conference should be intensified and extended to the working level.

(4) Development of methods to elicit greater attention on the part of private institutions operative in the foreign field to the development of indigenous managerial competence and Leadership ability.

(5) Development of facilities and procedures to insure that the content of training and education, pursued either in major institutions or under special tutorial arrangements, are adapted and tailored to the specific requirements of the individual's background and probable future utilization.

(6) Organization of a permanent interdepartmental task force, peopled with young careerists, to tackle the problem of identifying and grooming a highly selective group of political national leaders for those portions of Africa still in colonial status, or newly emerged there from; the principal criteria of such a group to be continuity and breadth of collective competence.

The Ultimate Requirement

The basic determinant of our performance will necessarily be the quality of the American personnel who provide the training and counsel. Improvement of that quality must engage our major efforts, now and over the long term. There is much that can be done to orient our representatives more fully.

The Executive Branch agencies need to maintain continuing contact with the research institutions evaluating the performance of our representatives abroad and reflect the constructive suggestions emanating therefrom in selection and preparation processes. But our basic deficiencies in linguistics, in political awareness, empathy and cross-cultural comprehension can only be restricted through a measurable reorientation of the American educational system. Contribution to the development of guidelines for such reorientation is an important responsibility of State, Defense and Health, Education and Welfare in close collaboration.